S 1.1: 969-76/V.3

Foreign Relations of the
United States, 1969–1976

Volume III

Foreign Economic Policy, 1969–1972; International Monetary Policy, 1969–1972

<table>
<tr><td>Editor</td><td>Bruce F. Duncombe</td></tr>
<tr><td>General Editor</td><td>David S. Patterson</td></tr>
</table>

United States Government Printing Office
Washington
2001

0872-B

DEPARTMENT OF STATE PUBLICATION 10865

Office of the Historian

Bureau of Public Affairs

For sale by the Superintendent of Documents, U.S. Government Printing Office
Internet: bookstore.gpo.gov   Phone: (202) 512-1800   Fax: (202) 512-2250
Mail: Stop SSOP, Washington, DC 20402-0001

ISBN 0-16-050884-3

Preface

The *Foreign Relations of the United States* series presents the official documentary historical record of major foreign policy decisions and significant diplomatic activity of the United States Government. The Historian of the Department of State is charged with the responsibility for the preparation of the *Foreign Relations* series. The staff of the Office of the Historian, Bureau of Public Affairs, plans, researches, compiles, and edits the volumes in the series. Official regulations codifying specific standards for the selection and editing of documents for the series were first promulgated by Secretary of State Frank B. Kellogg on March 26, 1925. These regulations, with minor modifications, guided the series through 1991.

A new statutory charter for the preparation of the series was established by Public Law 102–138, the Foreign Relations Authorization Act, Fiscal Years 1992 and 1993, which was signed by President George Bush on October 28, 1991. Section 198 of P.L. 102–138 added a new Title IV to the Department of State's Basic Authorities Act of 1956 (22 USC 4351, *et seq.*).

The statute requires that the *Foreign Relations* series be a thorough, accurate, and reliable record of major United States foreign policy decisions and significant United States diplomatic activity. The volumes of the series should include all records needed to provide comprehensive documentation of major foreign policy decisions and actions of the United States Government. The statute also confirms the editing principles established by Secretary Kellogg: the *Foreign Relations* series is guided by the principles of historical objectivity and accuracy; records should not be altered or deletions made without indicating in the published text that a deletion has been made; the published record should omit no facts that were of major importance in reaching a decision; and nothing should be omitted for the purposes of concealing a defect in policy. The statute also requires that the *Foreign Relations* series be published not more than 30 years after the events recorded.

Structure and Scope of the Foreign Relations Series

This volume is part of a subseries of volumes of the *Foreign Relations* series that documents the most important issues in the foreign policy of the administration of Richard M. Nixon. The subseries will present a documentary record of major foreign policy decisions and actions of President Nixon's administration. This volume documents U.S. general foreign economic policies and U.S. international monetary policy during President Nixon's first administration from 1969 through 1972. Volume IV, to be published in 2002, will include documentation on U.S. policies on foreign assistance and international development, trade, expropriation of U.S. properties abroad, and commodities and strategic materials for the first Nixon administration.

Focus of Research and Principles of Selection for Foreign Relations, 1969–1976, Volume III

The editor of the volume sought to present documentation illuminating responsibility for major foreign policy decisions in the U.S. Government, with emphasis on the President and his advisers. The documents include memoranda and records of discussions that set forth policy issues and options and show decisions or actions taken. The emphasis is on the development of U.S. policy and on major aspects and repercussions of its execution rather than on the details of policy execution.

Compared with their ongoing preoccupation with international political and strategic policy, President Nixon and his Assistant for National Security Affairs, Henry Kissinger, did not express much interest in foreign economic matters. They nonetheless understood that domestic and foreign economic developments could have profound effects on their political programs and goals. In particular, the Nixon administration inherited a serious U.S. balance-of-payments deficit, which threatened to destabilize the international economic system. During the first term, 1969–1972, Nixon administration officials undertook an intensive re-evaluation of U.S. monetary and trade policies. From this reappraisal came several foreign economic initiatives, many of which were formulated in the Department of the Treasury, to try to stop the flow of U.S. capital abroad.

The first part of this volume documents the various foreign economic options that Nixon administration officials considered in trying to alleviate the balance-of-payments problem. Some of the following proposals were stillborn, but others became Nixon administration initiatives: reduction in non-military U.S. personnel stationed overseas; efforts to get Japan and especially West Germany to offset the costs of the U.S. military presence abroad with the purchase of more U.S. military equipment; reduction in the Interest Equalization Tax; revaluation of exchange rates of countries with trade surpluses; opposition to foreign governments' preferential trade policies; reductions in foreign aid; and reform of the international monetary system.

The second part of this volume treats the administration's interest in reform of the international monetary system. President Nixon and his economic advisers increasingly believed that the creation of a new economic system could alleviate major U.S. fiscal problems, such as tariff inequities and declining gold reserves. One proposal called for major European nations' acceptance of the International Monetary Fund's plan of Special Drawing Rights (SDRs). Another called for flexible exchange rates. Nixon administration officials hoped to persuade individual countries, especially in Europe, to devalue or revalue their currencies, abolish fund controls, and agree on common trading rules, all of which would avert a large-scale financial crisis and promote international trade. Ultimately, the collapse of the British pound and European disagreements over currency revaluation prompted President Nixon to announce his New Economic Policy in August 1971, which ended the convertibility of dollars to gold and imposed a 10 percent surcharge on imports, as well as imposing domestic wage and price controls for 90 days.

Editorial Methodology

The documents are presented chronologically according to Washington time or, in the case of conferences, in the order of individual meetings. Memoranda of conversation are placed according to the time and date of the conversation, rather than the date the memorandum was drafted.

Editorial treatment of the documents published in the *Foreign Relations* series follows Office style guidelines, supplemented by guidance from the General Editor and the chief technical editor. The source text is reproduced as exactly as possible, including marginalia or other notations, which are described in the footnotes. Texts are transcribed and printed according to accepted conventions for the publication of historical documents within the limitations of modern typography. A heading has been supplied by the editors for each document included in the volume. Spelling, capitalization, and punctuation are retained as found in the source text, except that obvious typographical errors are silently corrected. Other mistakes and omissions in the source text are corrected by bracketed insertions: a correction is set in italic type; an addition in roman type. Words or phrases underlined in the source text are printed in italics. Abbreviations and contractions are preserved as found in the source text, and a list of abbreviations is included in the front matter of each volume.

Bracketed insertions are also used to indicate omitted text that deals with an unrelated subject (in roman type) or that remains classified after declassification review (in italic type). The amount of material not declassified has been noted by indicating the number of lines or pages of source text that were omitted. Entire documents withheld for declassification purposes have been accounted for and are listed with headings, source notes, and number of pages not declassified in their chronological place. All brackets that appear in the source text are so identified by footnotes.

The first footnote to each document indicates the source of the document, original classification, distribution, and drafting information. This note also provides the background of important documents and policies and indicates whether the President or his major policy advisers read the document.

Editorial notes and additional annotation summarize pertinent material not printed in the volume, indicate the location of additional documentary sources, provide references to important related documents printed in other volumes, describe key events, and provide summaries of and citations to public statements that supplement and elucidate the printed documents. Information derived from memoirs and other first-hand accounts has been used when appropriate to supplement or explicate the official record.

The numbers in the index refer to document numbers rather than to page numbers.

Advisory Committee on Historical Diplomatic Documentation

The Advisory Committee on Historical Diplomatic Documentation, established under the Foreign Relations statute, reviews records, advises, and makes recommendations concerning the *Foreign Relations* series. The Advisory Committee monitors the overall compilation and editorial process of the series and advises on all aspects of the preparation and declassification of the series. The Advisory Committee does not attempt to review the contents of individual volumes in the series, but it makes recommendations on problems that come to its attention.

The Advisory Committee has not reviewed this volume.

Presidential Recordings and Materials Preservation Act Review

Under the terms of the Presidential Recordings and Materials Preservation Act (PRMPA) of 1974 (44 USC 2111 note), the National Archives and Records Administration (NARA) has custody of the Nixon Presidential historical materials. The requirements of the PRMPA and implementing regulations govern access to the Nixon Presidential historical materials. The PRMPA and implementing public access regulations require NARA to review for additional restrictions in order to ensure the protection of the privacy rights of former Nixon White House officials, since these officials were not given the opportunity to separate their personal materials from public papers. Thus, the PRMPA and implementing public access regulations require NARA formally to notify the Nixon estate and former Nixon White House staff members that the agency is scheduling for public release Nixon White House historical materials. The Nixon estate and former White House staff members have 30 days to contest the release of Nixon historical materials in which they were a participant or are mentioned. Further, the PRMPA and implementing regulations require NARA to segregate and return to the creator of files private and personal materials. All *Foreign Relations* volumes that include materials from NARA's Nixon Presidential Materials Staff are processed and released in accordance with the PRMPA.

Declassification Review

The Information Response Branch of the Office of IRM Programs and Services, Bureau of Administration, Department of State, conducted the declassification review for the State Department of the documents published in this volume. The review was conducted in accordance with the standards set forth in Executive Order 12958 on Classified National Security Information and applicable laws.

The principle guiding declassification review is to release all information, subject only to the current requirements of national security as embodied in law and regulation. Declassification decisions entailed concurrence of the appropriate geographic and functional bureaus in the Department of State, other concerned agencies of the U.S. Government, and the appropriate foreign governments regarding specific documents of those governments.

The final declassification review of this volume, which began in 1999 and was completed in 2001, resulted in the decision to withhold about .03 percent of the documentation proposed for publication; no documents were withheld in full. The editor is confident, on the basis of the research conducted in preparing this volume and as a result of the declassification review process described above, that the documentation and editorial notes presented here provide an accurate account of U.S. general foreign economic policies and U.S. monetary policy from 1969 to 1972.

Acknowledgments

The editor wishes to acknowledge the assistance of officials at the Nixon Presidential Materials Project of the National Archives and Records Administration (Archives II), at College Park, Maryland.

Bruce F. Duncombe collected documentation for this volume and selected and edited it, under the supervision of David S. Patterson, General Editor of the *Foreign Relations* series. Matthew L. Conaty provided research support in the final preparation of the volume. Rita M. Baker and Vicki E. Futscher did the copy and technical editing, and Susan C. Weetman coordinated the final declassification review. Do Mi Stauber prepared the index.

Marc J. Susser
The Historian
Bureau of Public Affairs

September 2001

Contents

Sources

Sources for the Foreign Relations Series

The *Foreign Relations* statute requires that the published record in the *Foreign Relations* series include all records needed to provide comprehensive documentation on major U.S. foreign policy decisions and significant U.S. diplomatic activity. It further requires that government agencies, departments, and other entities of the U.S. Government engaged in foreign policy formulation, execution, or support cooperate with the Department of State Historian by providing full and complete access to records pertinent to foreign policy decisions and actions and by providing copies of selected records. Many of the sources consulted in the preparation of this volume have been declassified and are available for review at the National Archives and Records Administration.

The editors of the *Foreign Relations* series have complete access to all the retired records and papers of the Department of State: the central files of the Department; the special decentralized files ("lot files") of the Department at the bureau, office, and division levels; the files of the Department's Executive Secretariat, which contain the records of international conferences and high-level official visits, correspondence with foreign leaders by the President and Secretary of State, and memoranda of conversations between the President and Secretary of State and foreign officials; and the files of overseas diplomatic posts. All the Department's indexed central files through July 1973 have been permanently transferred to the National Archives and Records Administration at College Park, Maryland (Archives II). Many of the Department's decentralized office (or lot) files covering the 1969–1976 period, which the National Archives deems worthy of permanent retention, have been transferred or are in the process of being transferred from the Department's custody to Archives II.

The editors of the *Foreign Relations* series also have full access to the papers of President Nixon and other White House foreign policy records, including tape recordings of conversations with key U.S. and foreign officials. Presidential papers maintained and preserved at the Presidential libraries and the Nixon Presidential Materials Project at Archives II include some of the most significant foreign affairs-related documentation from the Department of State and other Federal agencies including the National Security Council, the Central Intelligence Agency, the Department of Defense, and the Joint Chiefs of Staff.

Access to the Nixon White House tape recordings is governed by the terms of the Presidential Recordings and Materials Preservation Act (P.L. 93-526; 88 Stat. 1695) and an access agreement with the Office of Presidential Libraries of the National Archives and Records Administration and the Nixon estate. In February 1971 President Nixon initiated a voice activated taping system in the Oval Office of the White House and, subsequently, in the President's Office in the Executive Office Building, Camp David, the Cabinet Room, and White House and Camp David telephones. The audiotapes include conversations of President Nixon with his Assistant for National Security Affairs Henry Kissinger, other White House aides, Secretary of State Rogers, other Cabinet officers, members of Congress, and key foreign officials. The clarity of the voices on the tape recordings is often very poor, but the editors make every effort to try to verify the accuracy of the conversations. Readers are urged to consult the recordings for a full appreciation of those aspects of the discussions that cannot be fully captured in a transcription, such as the speakers' inflections and emphases that may convey nuances of meaning, as well as the larger context of the discussion.

Research for this volume was completed through special access to restricted documents at the Nixon Presidential Materials Project. While all the material printed in this volume has been declassified, some of it is extracted from still-classified documents. The Nixon Presidential Materials Staff is processing and declassifying many of the documents used in this volume, but they may not be available in their entirety at the time of publication.

Sources for Foreign Relations, 1969–1976, Volume III

In preparing this volume, the editor made extensive use of Presidential papers and other White House records at the Nixon Presidential Materials Project. The bulk of the foreign policy records at the Nixon Project are in the National Security Council Files. Within the National Security Council Files, the Agency, Country, and Subject Files proved to be of particular value. The editor also made use of the White House tapes recordings, especially for the high-level conversations concerning the formulation and implementation of the New Economic Policy. The editor selected for publication short extracts of three audiotapes of President Nixon's discussions dealing with international monetary policy and identified other relevant conversations in footnotes and editorial notes.

The records of the Department of State were another important source. The Department's central files contain the cable traffic recording U.S. economic relations with Japan and major West European countries;

memoranda of diplomatic conversations; and memoranda proposing action or providing information. Many important documents are found only in the Department's lot files. The conference files maintained by the Executive Secretariat contain briefing materials as well as records of conversations. Documentation on initiatives that were not approved is often found only in desk or bureau files.

Department of State historians also have access to records of the Department of the Treasury at the Washington National Records Center, particularly the records of the Secretaries of the Treasury, as well as Treasury Under Secretaries and Assistant Secretaries.

Almost all of this documentation has been made available for use in the *Foreign Relations* series thanks to the consent of the agencies mentioned, the assistance of their staffs, and especially the cooperation and support of the National Archives and Records Administration. In addition, John H. Taylor, Executive Director of the Richard Nixon Library and Birthplace Foundation, facilitated access to relevant tape recordings of the Nixon White House.

The following list identifies the particular files and collections used in the preparation of this volume. The declassification and transfer to the National Archives of the Department of State records is in process, and many of these records are already available for public review at the National Archives. The declassification review of other records is going forward in accordance with the provisions of Executive Orders 12958 and 13142, under which all records over 25 years old, except file series exemptions requested by agencies and approved by the President, should be reviewed for declassification by 2003.

Unpublished Sources

Department of State

Central Files. See National Archives and Records Administration below.

Lot Files. These files may be transferred to the National Archives and Records Administration at College Park, Maryland, Record Group 59.

S/S Files: Lot 73 D 153
Daily and afternoon summaries of incoming and outgoing cables concerning crisis information and foreign policy, 1969–1971

S/S Files: Lot 82 D 126
National Security Council, Council on International Economic Policy, and Under Secretaries Committee Miscellaneous Files, 1969–1977

Memoranda of Interviews. Conducted by the Staff of the Office of the Historian.
C. Fred Bergsten, August 25, 1997
Richard N. Cooper, November 14, 1997
Viron P. Vaky, January 20, 1998
Helmut Sonnenfeldt, January 22, 1998

National Archives and Records Administration, College Park, Maryland

Record Group 59, General Records of the Department of State

Subject-Numeric Indexed Central Files

E 1: General economic policy, plans
E 1 US: General U.S. economic policy and plans
FN 10: Foreign exchange
FN 10 FR, Foreign exchange, France
FN 10 IMF: Foreign exchange, IMF
FN 10 EEC: Foreign exchange, EEC
FN 10–1: Exchange rates
FN 12 GER W: Balance of payments, West Germany
FN 12 US: Balance of payments, U.S.
FN 13: Capital movements
FN 16 GATT: Revenue, taxation, GATT
FN 16 US: U.S. revenue and taxation
FN 17: Money, currency
FN 17 UK: Monetary policy, United Kingdom
FN 17 US: Money, currency, U.S.
FN 17–1: Monetary policy and reform
FN 19: Gold
POL UK–US: General policy between the U.K. and the U.S.
POL 7 US/VOLCKER: Visits, Meetings of Paul A. Volcker

Lot Files

E/CBA/REP Files: Lot 70 D 467, *Current Economic Developments*
   Master set of the Department of State classified internal publication *Current Economic Developments* for 1945–1969, maintained in the Bureau of Economic Affairs

S/S Files: Lot 71 D 175
   National Security Council and Senior Review Group meetings, 1969–1970

S/S Files: Lot 72 D 220
   Briefing books, fact books, President's and Secretary's visits and conference books, Secretary's and Under Secretary's appearances before Congressional committees, 1969–1971

S/S Files: Lot 73 D 288
   Cabinet, National Security Council, National Security Council Under Secretaries, and Senior Review Group miscellaneous memoranda, 1969–1972

S/S Files: Lot 74 D 164
   President's evening reading items and Secretary–President luncheon meetings, 1964–1969, and Kissinger–Irwin meetings, 1970–1972

S/S Files: Lot 80 D 212
   National Security Study Memoranda (NSSMs) and related papers, 1969–1976

S/S Files: Lot 81 D 309, NSC–U/SM
   National Security Council Under Secretaries Committee study memoranda, 1969–1976

S/S Files: Lot 83 D 276
   National Security Council Under Secretaries Committee memoranda, 1969–1977

S/S Files: Lot 83 D 305
National Security Decision Memoranda (NSDMs), 1969–1976

Nixon Presidential Materials Project

National Security Council Files
Agency Files
Back Channel Files
Country Files
Name Files
Presidential/HAK Memcons
President's Trip Files
Subject Files
VIP Visits

Transitional Task Force Reports

White House Central Files
President's Daily Diary
President's Office Files
Federal Government Organizations

White House Special Files
Haldeman's Notes

White House Tapes

National Security Council

Records of the National Security Council

Washington National Records Center, Suitland, Maryland

Record Group 56, Records of the Department of the Treasury

Office of the Secretary of the Treasury: FRC 74 A 4
Secretary Connally's Correspondence, 1971–1972

Office of the Secretary of the Treasury: FRC 80 A 1
Records of Secretary Shultz, 1972–1974

Office of the Secretary of the Treasury: FRC 74 A 7
Memoranda and Correspondence, 1966–1970

Office of the Secretary of the Treasury: FRC 74 A 17
Secretary's Memoranda, 1971

Office of the Under Secretary of the Treasury: FRC 79 A 14
Files of Frederick L. Deming and Paul A. Volcker, 1963–1969

Office of the Under Secretary of the Treasury: FRC 79 A 15
Files of Under Secretary Volcker, 1969–1974

Office of International Monetary Affairs: FRC 77 A 68
Records of the Office of International Monetary Affairs, 1970–1975

Office of the Assistant Secretary for International Affairs: FRC 83 A 26
Files of the Deputy to the Assistant Secretary, and Secretary of the International
Monetary Group, 1947–1977

Office of the Assistant Secretary for International Affairs: FRC 75 A 101
  Records of the Deming Group, Advisory Committee on International Monetary
  Affairs (Dillon Committee), and Cabinet Committee on the Balance of Payments,
  1963–1970

Office of the Assistant Secretary for International Affairs: FRC 76 A 108
  Records pertaining to the balance of payments, 1966–1971

Office of the Assistant Secretary for International Affairs Central Files: FRC 86 A 24
  Assistant Secretary of the Treasury Central Files and World Files, 1959–1979

Office of the Assistant Secretary of the Treasury for International Affairs: FRC 86 A 30
  Assistant Secretary of the Treasury Central Files and Volcker Group Files, 1969–1974

Record Group 286, Records of the Agency for International Development

AID Administrator Files: FRC 75 A 13
  Executive Secretariat files, 1968–1973

Selected Published Sources

De Vries, Margaret G., *The International Monetary Fund 1966–1971: The System Under Stress*, Volume I: *Narrative (Washington, D.C.: The International Monetary Fund, 1976)*
———, *The International Monetary Fund 1972–1978: Cooperation on Trial, Volume I: Narrative and Analysis* (Washington, D.C.: The International Monetary Fund, 1985)
The Economic Report of the President, 1970, 1972, 1973, 1974 (Washington, D.C.: Government Printing Office, 1971, 1973, 1974, 1975).
Haldeman, H.R., *The Haldeman Diaries: Inside the White House* (New York: G.P. Putnam Sons, 1994)
———, *The Haldeman Diaries: Inside the Nixon White House, the Complete Multimedia Edition* (Santa Monica, CA: Sony Electronic Publishing, 1994)
Kissinger, Henry, *White House Years* (Boston: Little, Brown and Company, 1979)
———, *Years of Upheaval* (Boston, Little, Brown and Company, 1982)
NATO Final Communiqués 1949–1974 (Brussels, NATO Information Service, 1975)
Nixon, Richard M., *RN, The Memoirs of Richard Nixon* (New York: Grosset & Dunlap, 1978)
Peterson, Peter G., *The United States in a Changing World Economy*, 2 Volumes (Washington, D.C.: Government Printing Office, 1972).
Safire, William, *Before the Fall: An Inside View of the Pre Watergate White House* (Garden City, NY: Doubleday, 1975)
Schultz, George P. and Kenneth W. Dam, *Economic Policy Beyond the Headlines* (New York: W.W. Norton, 1977)
Solomon, Robert, *The International Monetary System, 1945–1976: An Insider's View* (New York: Harper and Row, 1976)
U.S. Department of State, Department of State *Bulletin*, 1969–1972.
U.S. Foreign Policy for the 1970's: A New Strategy for Peace, A Report to the Congress by Richard Nixon, February 18, 1970
U.S. Foreign Policy for the 1970's: Building For Peace, A Report to the Congress by Richard Nixon, February 25, 1971.
U.S. Foreign Policy for the 1970's: The Emerging Structure of Peace: A Report to the Congress by Richard Nixon, February 9, 1972.
U.S. Foreign Policy for the 1970's: Shaping a Durable Peace, A Report to the Congress by Richard Nixon, May 3, 1973.

U.S. National Archives and Records Administration, *Public Papers of the Presidents of the United States: Richard Nixon, 1969, 1970, 1971, 1972* (Washington, D.C.: Government Printing Office, 1970, 1971, 1972, 1973)

United States Foreign Policy, 1969–1970, 1971, 1972: A Report of the Secretary of State (Washington, D.C.: Government Printing Office, 1971, 1972, 1973)

Volcker, Paul A. and Toyoo Gyohten, *Changing Fortunes: The World's Money and the Threat to American Leadership* (New York: Times Books, 1992)

Abbreviations

ADB, Asian Development Bank
AF, Bureau of African Affairs, Department of State
AFDB, African Development Bank
AID, Agency for International Development
ARA, Bureau of Inter-American Affairs, Department of State
ASP, American Selling Price

BIS, Bank for International Settlements
BOB, Bureau of the Budget
BOP, balance of payments

C, Counselor, Department of State
C-20, Committee of 20 (forum to develop proposals on international monetary reform)
CAP, Common Agricultural Policy
CEA, Council of Economic Advisers
CECLA, Special Committee for Latin American Coordination
CESC, Conference on European Security and Cooperation
CIA, Central Intelligence Agency
CIEP, Council on International Economic Policy
CIEPDM, CIEP Decision Memorandum
CIEPSM, CIEP Study Memorandum
COCOM, Coordinating Committee on Export Controls
CY, calendar year

D, Deputy Under Secretary of State for Economic Affairs
DAC, Development Assistance Committee
DCI, Director of Central Intelligence
DISC, Domestic International Sales Corporation
DOC, Department of Commerce
DOD, Department of Defense

E, Bureau of Economic Affairs, Department of State
EA, Bureau of East Asian and Pacific Affairs, Department of State
EC, European Community
ECONCOM, U.S.-Japan Economic Committee
EDIP, European Defense Improvement Program
EEC, European Economic Community
EFTA, Free Trade Association
EUR, Bureau of European and Canadian Affairs, Department of State

FDIP, Foreign Direct Investment Program
FMS, Foreign Military Sales
FOB, freight on board

FonOff, Foreign Office
FRB, Federal Reserve Board
FRC, Federal Records Center
FRG, Federal Republic of Germany
FSO, Fund for Special Operations
FY, fiscal year

G-10, Group of Ten (United States, Canada, Japan, UK, France, Netherlands, Belgium, the FRG, Italy, Sweden, plus Switzerland as an observer)
GAB, General Agreement to Borrow
GATT, General Agreement on Tariffs and Trade
GNP, Gross National Product
GOJ, Government of Japan
GSA, General Services Administration

H, Bureau of Legislative Affairs, Department of State
HFAC, House Foreign Affairs Committee

IA-ECOSOC, Inter-American Economic and Social Council
IADB, Inter-American Development Bank
IBRD, International Bank for Reconstruction and Development (World Bank)
IDA, International Development Association
IDB, Inter-American Development Bank
IET, Interest Equalization Tax
IFI, International Financial Institution
IMF, International Monetary Fund
IO, Bureau of International Organization Affairs, Department of State
IPC, International Petroleum Company

J, Under Secretary of State for Political Affairs
JCS, Joint Chiefs of Staff

L, Office of the Legal Adviser, Department of State
LDC, less-developed country
LDX, term for classified fax used to pass messages between Washington agencies
LOS, Law of the Sea

MAP, Military Assistance Program
MBFR, Mutual and Balanced Force Reduction
MITI, Ministry of International Trade and Industry (Japan)
MOFA, Ministry of Foreign Affairs (Japan)

NAC, National Advisory Council on International Monetary and Financial Policies
NEA, Bureau of Near Eastern and South Asian Affairs, Department of State
NSC, National Security Council
NSDM, National Security Decision Memorandum
NSSM, National Security Study Memorandum
NTB, Non-Tariff Barrier

OAS, Organization of American States
OASIA, Office of the Assistant Secretary of the Treasury for International Affairs
OECD, Organization for Economic Cooperation and Development
OEP, Office of Emergency Preparedness
OFID, Office of Industrial Nations, Department of the Treasury
OIN, Office of Industrial Nations, Department of the Treasury
OMB, Office of Management and Budget
OPEC, Organization of Petroleum Exporting Countries
OPIC, Overseas Private Investment Corporation
OPRED, Operation Reduction

PAHO, Pan American Health Organization
PADM, Policy Analysis Decision Memorandum
PARA, Policy Analysis and Resource Allocation.
PASM, Policy Analysis Study Memorandum
PL, Public Law

REDCOSTE, Reduction of Costs in Europe
RG, NSC Review Group
RG, Record Group

SACEUR, Supreme Allied Commander, Europe
SCCN, Special Committee for Consultation and Negotiation)
SDP, Social Democratic Party (Germany)
SDR, Special Drawing Rights
SFRC, Senate Foreign Relations Committee
SOFA, Status of Forces Agreement
SRG, NSC Senior Review Group
SPCC, Southern Peru Copper Company
S/S, Executive Secretariat, Department of State
STR, Special Trade Representative or Special Representative for Trade
    Negotiations

TFID, Task Force on International Development

U, Under Secretary of State
UN, United Nations
UNCTAD, United Nations Conference on Trade and Development
UNGA, United Nations General Assembly
UR, Uruguay Round of Trade under GATT auspices
USC, NSC Under Secretaries Committee
USDA, United States Department of Agriculture
USIA, United States Information Agency
USEC, United States Mission to the European Economic Communities in Brussels
USOECD, United States Mission to the Organization for Economic
    Cooperation and Development
USUN, United States Mission to the United Nations in New York

VFCR, Voluntary Foreign Credit Program

Persons

Agnew, Spiro T., Vice President of the United States, January 1969–October 1973

Aichi, Kiichi, Japanese Foreign Minister until July 1971

Allen, Richard, Deputy Director, Council on International Economic Policy, from 1971

Annenberg, Walter H., Ambassador to the United Kingdom, April 1969–October 1974

Armstrong, Willis C, Assistant Secretary of State for Economic Affairs, February 1972–April 1974

Atherton, Alfred L., Jr., Deputy Assistant Secretary of State for Near Eastern and South Asian Affairs from March 1970

Barre, Raymond, Vice President for Financial Affairs, Commission of the European Communities

Bennett, Jack F., Deputy Under Secretary of the Treasury for International Monetary Affairs until July 1974; thereafter Under Secretary for Monetary Affairs

Bergsten, C. Fred, Member, National Security Council Staff, 1969–1971

Berlin, Lawrence H., Deputy Associate Assistant Administrator for Development Finance, Agency for International Development

Boeker, Paul, Director, Office of Financial Development, Bureau of Economic Affairs, Department of State, May 1970–July 1971; thereafter economic-commercial officer at the Embassy in Bonn

Brandt, Willy, West German Foreign Minister, December 1966–October 1969; thereafter Chancellor

Brown, Winthrop G., Deputy Assistant Secretary of State for East Asian and Pacific Affairs until April 1972

Brunthaver, Carroll G., Assistant Secretary of Agriculture for International Affairs and Commodity Programs, 1969–1973; thereafter President, Commodity Credit Corporation

Burns, Arthur F., Counselor to the President, January 1969–January 1970; thereafter Chairman of the Federal Reserve Board

Butz, Earl L., Secretary of Agriculture from December 1971

Carli, Guido, Governor for Italy, International Bank for Reconstruction and Development

Cohen, Edwin S., Assistant Secretary of the Treasury for Tax Policy, 1971; Under Secretary of the Treasury from 1972

Colman, John C., Deputy Assistant Secretary of the Treasury for International Affairs

Colombo, Emilo, Italian Treasury Minister to 1970; Premier, August 1970–January 1972

Connally, John B., Jr., Secretary of the Treasury, February 1971–May 1972

Cooper, Richard N., Member, National Security Council Staff, 1969–1970

XXIII

Daane, Dewey, Member, Board of Governors, Federal Reserve Board
Dahrendorf, Ralf G., Commissioner of the European Community in charge of external relations, May 1970–September 1974
Dale, William B., U.S. Executive Director, International Monetary Fund
Dam, Kenneth W., Deputy Director, Office of Management and Budget
Davis, Jeanne W., Director, NSC Staff Secretariat, 1970–1971
De Gaulle, Charles, President of France until April 1969
Debré, Michel, French Foreign Minister until June 1969

Eberle, William D., Special Representative for Trade Negotiations, 1971–1975; also Member, Council on International Economic Policy, from 1971
Ehrlichman, John D., Counsel to the President, January–November 1969; Assistant to the President for Domestic Affairs, November 1969–May 1973
Eliot, Theodore L., Jr., Special Assistant to the Secretary of State and Executive Secretary of the Department of State, August 1969–September 1973; thereafter Ambassador to Afghanistan
Emminger, Otmar, Director, Bundesbank
Enders, Thomas O., Deputy Assistant Secretary of State for International Monetary Affairs, Bureau of Economic Affairs, until August 1969; Deputy Chief of Mission in Belgrade, August 1969–December 1970; Deputy Chief of Mission in Phnom Penh from January 1971

Flanigan, Peter M., Assistant to the President, 1969–1972; thereafter Executive Director, Council for International Economic Policy
Freeman, John, British Ambassador to the United States, March 1969–January 1971
Fukuda, Takeo, Japanese Foreign Minister, July 1971–July 1972

Gilbert, Carl J., Special Representative for Trade Negotiations, 1969–1971
Giscard d'Estaing, French Finance Minister, 1962–1966; President of France from June 1969
Greenwald, Joseph A., Deputy Assistant Secretary of State for Economic Affairs, February–July 1969; Representative to the Organization for Economic Cooperation and Development in Paris, July 1969–October 1972; thereafter Representative to the European Communities in Brussels

Haig, General Alexander M., Jr., Senior Military Assistant to the Assistant to the President for National Security Affairs, January 1969–June 1970; Deputy Assistant to the President for National Security Affairs, June 1970–January 1973; thereafter Army Vice Chief of Staff
Haldeman, H. R., Assistant to the President, January 1969–April 1973
Hardin, Clifford M., Secretary of Agriculture, January 1969–December 1971
Harlow, Bryce N., Assistant to the President, January 1969–January 1970; thereafter Counselor to the President
Hartman, Arthur A., Special Assistant to the Under Secretary of State and Staff Director for the NSC Under Secretaries Committee
Heath, Edward, British Prime Minister, June 1970–March 1974
Helms, Richard M., Director of Central Intelligence until February 1973

Hillenbrand, Martin J., Assistant Secretary of State for European Affairs, February 1969–April 1972; Ambassador to the Federal Republic of Germany, June 1972–October 1976
Hinton, Deane, Assistant Director, Council on International Economic Policy, 1971–1973; thereafter Deputy Director
Hirschtritt, Ralph, Director, Office of Balance of Payments Policy, Options and Strategy, Department of the Treasury; Deputy to the Assistant Secretary of the Treasury for International Financial and Economic Affairs
Hodgson, James D., Secretary of Labor, July 1970–February 1973
Holdridge, John, Member, National Security Council Staff, 1970–1972
Hormats, Robert, Member, National Security Council Staff, 1970–1972
Houthakker, Hendrick, Member, Council of Economic Advisers, January 1969–June 1971

Ingersoll, Robert S., Ambassador to Japan, April 1972–November 1973
Irwin, John N., II, Under Secretary of State, September 1970–July 1972; Deputy Secretary of State, July 1972–February 1973

Jenkins, Roy, British Chancellor of the Exchequer, November 1967–June 1970
Johnson, Lyndon B., President of the United States until January 20, 1969
Johnson, U. Alexis, Ambassador to Japan until January 1969; Under Secretary of State for Political Affairs, February 1969–February 1973
Johnston, Ernest, Member, National Security Council Staff
Jurich, Anthony J., Special Assistant to the Secretary of the Treasury for National Security Affairs

Katz, Abraham, Director, Office of Regional and Political Affairs, Bureau of European Affairs, Department of State, until January 1974
Katz, Julius L., Deputy Assistant Secretary of State for International Resources and Food Policy, Bureau of Economic Affairs, until July 1974
Kearns, Henry, President and Chairman, Export-Import Bank, 1969–1973
Kennedy, David M., Secretary of the Treasury, January 1969–January 1971; Ambassador at Large for Foreign Economic Development, February 1971–March 1973; also Representative to the North Atlantic Treaty Organization, March 1972–February 1973
Kiesinger, Kurt Georg, West German Chancellor until October 1969
Kissinger, Henry A., Assistant to the President for National Security Affairs, January 1969–November 1975; also Secretary of State from September 1973

Laird, Melvin R., Secretary of Defense, January 1969–January 1973
Larre, René, Director of the Treasury, French Economics Ministry, 1967–1971
Lucet, Charles, French Ambassador to the United States until April 1972

MacLaury, Bruce K., Deputy Under Secretary of the Treasury for Monetary Affairs, 1969–1971
Malfatti, Franco Mario, President of the Commission of the European Communities, 1971
Mansholt, Sicco, President of the European Commission, 1972

Martin, William McChesney, Jr., Chairman of the Federal Reserve Board until January 1970

Mayo, Robert P., Director, Bureau of the Budget, January 1969–July 1970; Counselor to the President, July 1970–1972; thereafter Director, Bureau of the Budget

McCracken, Paul W., Chairman, Council of Economic Advisers, January 1969–November 1971

McGinnis, John J., Deputy Special Assistant to the Secretary of the Treasury for National Security Affairs

Meyer, Armin H., Ambassador to Japan, July 1969–March 1972

Mizuta, Mikio, Japanese Finance Minister from July 1971

Moorer, Admiral Thomas H., Chief of Naval Operations until July 1970; thereafter Chairman of the Joint Chiefs of Staff

Morse, Jeremy, Chairman, C-20 Deputies Committee

Moynihan, Daniel Patrick, Counselor to the President, January 1969–December 1970

Nixon, Richard M., President of the United States, January 20, 1969–August 9, 1974

Ohira, Masayoshi, Japanese Foreign Minister from July 1972

Palmby, Clarence, Assistant Secretary of Agriculture

Pauls, Rolf, West German Ambassador to the United States, 1969–March 1973

Pearce, William R., Deputy Special Representative for Trade Negotiations

Pedersen, Richard F., Counselor of the Department of State, January 1969–July 1973

Peterson, Peter G., Assistant to the President for International Economic Affairs, and Executive Director of the Council for International Economic Policy, 1971–January 1972; Secretary of Commerce, January 1972–January 1973

Petty, John R., Assistant Secretary of the Treasury for International Affairs, May 1968–February 1972

Pompidou, Georges, President of France from June 1969

Read, Benjamin H., Special Assistant to the Secretary of State and Executive Secretary of the Department of State, until February 1969

Reuss, Henry S., Democratic Congressman from Wisconsin; Chairman, Joint Economic Subcommittee on International Exchange and Payments

Rey, Jean, President of the Commission of the European Communities, July 1967–July 1970

Richardson, Elliot L., Under Secretary of State, January 1969–June 1970; Secretary of Health, Education and Welfare, June 1970–January 1973; Secretary of Defense, January–May 1973; Attorney General, May–October 1973

Ritchie, A. Edgar, Canadian Ambassador to the United States until January 1970

Rodman, Peter W., Member, National Security Council Staff, 1970–1972

Rogers, William P., Secretary of State, January 21, 1969–September 3, 1973

Rush, Kenneth, Ambassador to the Federal Republic of Germany, July 1969–February 1972; Deputy Secretary of Defense, February 1972–January 1973; Deputy Secretary of State, February 1973–May 1974

Samuels, Nathaniel, Deputy Under Secretary of State for Economic Affairs, April 1969–April 1972

Sato, Eisaku, Japanese Prime Minister until July 1972

Schaetzel, J. Robert, Ambassador to the European Communities until October 1972

Schaffner, Philip P., Director, Office of Balance of Payments Programs, Operations and Statistics, Department of the Treasury

Schiller, Karl, West German Economics Minister until July 1972

Schmidt, Helmut, West German Defense Minister until July 1972; Minister of Economic Affairs and Finance, July–December 1972; Minister of Finance from December 1972

Schoellhorn, Johann, West German State Secretary, Ministry of Economics

Schumann, Maurice, French Foreign Minister, June 1969–April 1973

Schweitzer, Pierre Paul, Managing Director, International Monetary Fund

Scott, Harold B., Assistant Secretary of Commerce for Domestic and International Business

Sharp, Mitchell, Canadian Secretary of State for External Affairs until August 1974

Shimoda, Takeso, Japanese Ambassador to the United States until December 1970

Shultz, George P., Secretary of Labor, January 1969–June 1970; Director, Office of Management and Budget, June 1970–May 1972; Secretary of the Treasury, and also Assistant to the President, May 1972–May 1974; also head of the Council on Economic Policy from December 1972

Siciliano, Rocco C., Under Secretary of Commerce, 1969–1971

Solomon, Ezra, Member, Council of Economic Advisers, 1971–1973

Sonnenfeldt, Helmut, Member, National Security Council Staff, January 1969–January 1974

Springsteen, George S., Jr., Deputy Assistant Secretary of State for European Affairs until June 1972; Acting Assistant Secretary, June 1972–August 1973; thereafter Deputy Assistant Secretary for European Affairs

Stans, Maurice, Secretary of Commerce, January 1969–January 1972

Stein, Herbert, Member, Council of Economic Advisers, January 1969–November 1971; Chairman, January 1972–July 1974

Strauss, Franz Josef, West German Finance Minister until October 1969

Tanaka, Kakuei, Japanese Prime Minister, July 1972–December 1974

Train, Russell, Under Secretary of Interior, 1969–1970; thereafter Director, Council on Environmental Quality

Trezise, Philip H., Representative to the Organization for Economic Cooperation and Development, Paris, until July 1969; Assistant Secretary of State for Economic Affairs, July 1969–November 1971

Trudeau, Pierre-Elliott, Canadian Prime Minister

Ushiba, Nobuhiko, Japanese Ambassador to the United States from February 1971

Van Lennep, Emile, Treasurer General (Permanent Under Secretary, Ministry of Finance) of the Netherlands and Chairman of OECD WP-3

Volcker, Paul A., Under Secretary of the Treasury for Monetary Affairs, January 1969–June 1974

Walker, Charls E., Under Secretary of the Treasury, January 1969–January 1972; Deputy Secretary of the Treasury, January–December 1972

Wardhana, Mohammad Ali, Indonesian Finance Minister; also Chairman, C-20, from September 1972

Webster, Donald A., Senior Staff Member, Council on International Economic Policy

Weinberger, Caspar W., Deputy Director, Office of Management and Budget, July 1970–May 1972; Director, May 1972–January 1973

Weintraub, Sidney, Deputy Assistant Secretary of State for International Monetary Affairs, Bureau of Economic Affairs, October 1969–May 1970; thereafter Deputy Assistant Secretary of State for International Finance and Development

Wheeler, General Earle G., Chairman of the Joint Chiefs of Staff until July 1970

Whitaker, John C., Secretary to the Cabinet, 1969–1970

Willis, George H., Deputy to the Assistant Secretary of the Treasury for International Monetary Affairs, 1969–1973

Wilson, Harold, British Prime Minister until June 1970

Zijlstra, Jelle, President, Netherlands Bank; President, Bank for International Settlements

Foreign Economic Policy, 1969–1972

1. Summary of the Report of the Task Force on U.S. Balance of Payments Policies[1]

New York, undated.

The present U.S. balance-of-payments position is very precarious. Serious deterioration in the nation's trade accounts is being temporarily camouflaged by a combination of window-dressing special transactions and an abnormal inflow of foreign capital.

Existing balance-of-payments controls should be rapidly eliminated because they are wasteful and inefficient, undermine our free enterprise system, and thus reduce the rate of growth in the economy. Their dismantling is further indicated because whatever short-run payments relief they may have afforded in the past, they are now beginning to have a delayed adverse effect. Diplomatic efforts aimed at inducing other countries to hold more dollars than they normally would also should be terminated.

Given the present underlying weakness of our payments position, severe foreign-exchange pressures against the dollar could develop quickly. A series of protective actions is therefore necessary, involving the pursuit of disinflationary economic policies domestically and simultaneous reform of existing international monetary arrangements.

With respect to reform, confidential negotiations with the key industrial countries through the Group of Ten should begin immediately, with the main American objective being to secure quickly a significant realignment of parities of some currencies. To provide continuing flexibility in the international monetary mechanism, this one-time realignment should be accompanied by:

(1) The establishment of wider permissible trading bands for currencies under IMF rules (with fluctuations on either side of par to range up to 2 percent or 3 percent, instead of the present 1 percent maximum).

---

[1] Source: National Archives, Nixon Presidential Materials, Transitional Task Force Reports 1968–1969, Task Force Summaries (Arthur F. Burns, 1/18/69). No classification marking. Forwarded to the President-elect under cover of a January 18 letter from Arthur F. Burns in his capacity as Chairman of the Program Coordination Committee. Burns' letter is on the stationery of the Office of the President-elect and bears a New York address. The undated, 33-page Report of the Task Force on U.S. Balance of Payments Policies, chaired by Gottfried Haberler, is ibid., Task Force on U.S. Balance of Payments Policies.

(2) The provision for automatic adjustments in parities by small amounts in instances where a currency remained at the upper or lower end of its band for some specified time period.

Discussion aimed at providing wider bands and self-adjusting pegs should proceed even if significant one-time realignment of Group-of-Ten currencies cannot be successfully negotiated.

Such reform in itself would not solve the problem of outstanding dollar balances, and consequently the present de facto inconvertibility of the dollar into gold would continue. Nevertheless, a general increase in the price of gold should not be undertaken because its benefits would be distributed very unevenly and inequitably and because it would tend to fuel international inflationary tendencies.

Continuation of de facto inconvertibility of the dollar into gold need not be a crucial problem so long as visible progress is being made by the United States in pursuing domestic policies that promise reduction of new infusions of dollars into the international economy and so long as flexibility is imparted to the international monetary mechanism. Foreigners recognize that any large-scale attempt to convert dollars into gold would disrupt international trade and payments and would lead to an immediate American embargo on gold exports. If for any reason this premise proves false and a "gold rush" develops, the United States should suspend gold convertibility before our gold stock declines very much below its present level. Such suspension would not necessarily lead to a radical depreciation of the dollar on international exchanges. Instead, it is likely that many countries would continue the policy of pegging their currencies at the existing parities to the dollar. In a period of transition during which convertibility was suspended, negotiations aimed at introducing new flexibility into the international monetary mechanism could proceed.

2.   Editorial Note

The Nixon administration inherited a macroeconomic international economic environment characterized by declining U.S. merchandise trade and current account surpluses. The trade surplus declined from $6.8 billion in 1964 to $0.6 billion in 1968 and the current account balance had declined from a $5.8 billion surplus to, for the first time since 1959, a $0.5 billion deficit in 1968. The trade surplus remained constant at $0.6 billion in 1969 while the current account deficit mounted to just over $1.0 billion.

With postwar recovery, international capital flows had become an increasingly important part of international transactions in the 1960s. Many of these capital flows were associated with international direct investment on the part of the multinational corporations, and this issue came to a head in the 1970s under the rubric of economic nationalism in developing countries and the quest in UNCTAD and elsewhere for codes of conduct for multinational corporations. Other capital flows were associated with the increasing predilection of companies, financial institutions, and central governments to have portfolio and currency positions in other than their national currencies, in part related to the rise of the Euro-dollar market and the role of the U.S. dollar as a reserve currency. The U.S. balance on current account and long-term capital was in deficit most years from 1960, and increased from a $1.4 billion deficit in 1968 to a $3.0 billion deficit in 1969. The net liquidity balance-of-payments deficit increased from $1.6 billion in 1968 to $6.1 billion in 1969. However, the official reserves transactions balance of payments recorded a $1.6 billion surplus in 1968 and that surplus increased to $2.7 billion in 1969. U.S. monetary gold reserves had declined from $17.8 billion at the end of 1960 to $10.8 billion at the end of 1968, but then increased to $11.9 billion by the end of 1969. (*The Economic Report of the President, 1973*)

The perception of an increasingly precarious U.S. balance-of-payments position led the Johnson administration to take a number of measures to encourage exports, stem imports, and restrict international capital flows. Regarding these measures, see *Foreign Relations, 1964–1968,* volume VIII. The new administration in 1969 was faced with the question of whether or not to intensify these measures, roll them back, or adopt a new approach. The aforementioned measures, which were microeconomic in nature, were directed at single items that go into the balance of payments rather than the overall bottom line; as such they tended to be resisted by those who agreed the balance of payments needed correction but who favored a more free market-oriented, macroeconomic approach.

As to how to approach the balance of payments, one view was set out by C. Fred Bergsten in a March 26, 1969 (mistakenly dated April 26, 1969), memorandum to Kissinger commenting on Secretary Rogers' Briefing Book for his March 27 testimony before the Senate Foreign Relations Committee:

"There is no U.S. policy to 'eliminate our balance of payments deficit'. The Johnson Administration sought 'a sustainable balance' in our position. This Administration has not yet stated its objective. There is a highly significant difference between the two, and the Secretary of State should definitely not say that 'we are taking every feasible step to eliminate our deficit'. *This is a very important point."* (National Archives, Nixon Presidential Materials, NSC Files, Agency Files, State, Vol. II, Box 279)

In many quarters foreign assistance was viewed as an important source of the problem and there were many members of Congress in 1969 who favored sharp cut-backs in economic and/or security and/or military assistance.

U.S. military expenditures abroad (aside from issues related to Vietnam) were seen by some as an important factor in the balance-of-payments equation. Senator Mike Mansfield would again sponsor legislation to reduce U.S. forces in Europe for balance-of-payments reasons. The Johnson administration had already adopted a policy for the Reduction of Costs in Europe (REDCOSTE) and had negotiated an offset agreement with the Federal Republic of Germany to compensate for the balance-of-payments cost of maintaining a U.S. military presence in Germany. President Nixon soon ordered a 10 percent reduction in official, non-military personnel abroad, Operation Reduction or OPRED, for much the same reasons.

The Nixon administration from the outset was faced with next steps in the REDCOSTE program and negotiation of a new offset agreement with the FRG. With time, and the refinement of the Nixon doctrine, military burden-sharing with Europe and Japan became an important aspect of the foreign policy dialogue. In Europe this was part of NATO strategy and policy, but the underlying balance-of-payments problem was central to the debate. An early input on this issue was given by Robert E. Osgood in a March 26, 1969, memorandum to Henry Kissinger on the "Briefs for Secretary of State" before the Senate Foreign Relations Committee on March 27:

"In late 1968 the Secretary of Defense put forward a series of proposals, known as REDCOSTE, which would 'streamline' administrative and logistics and support elements. . . .
"Congressional pressures for reduction of U.S. forces in Europe have been based on the general objection that the U.S. is overcommitted and carrying an inequitable proportion of the collective defense burden in Europe. They have focused on the balance-of-payments difficulties that result from maintaining American forces in Europe. These pressures were manifested in Senator Mansfield's Resolutions of 1966 and 1967, calling for 'substantial' reductions and by the Symington Amendment, which would have denied Executive funds for more than 50,000 troops in Europe beyond December 31, 1968 (vice 405,000 in 1955, down to 320,000 in early 1969). The Soviet invasion of Czechoslovakia has blunted pressures for withdrawal, but they could well revive if projected European defense contributions are not forthcoming and the offset problem is not resolved." (National Archives, Nixon Presidential Materials, NSC Files, Agency Files, State, Vol. II, Box 279)

Regarding the Nixon administration's handling of REDCOSTE and the German offset problem in its first months, see Documents 18 and 22.

The U.S. balance-of-payments deficit and the increased foreign holding of dollar-denominated assets was a major source of new international liquidity in the 1960s, but was increasingly seen as a source of instability in the international monetary system as foreign holdings of dollars soon exceeded U.S. official reserve assets, calling the convertibility of dollars to gold into question. To help deal with this problem the Johnson administration had already set the groundwork for the creation of a new international reserve asset, the Special Drawing Rights (SDR) in the International Monetary Fund. Activation of the SDRs was one of the first tasks of the Nixon administration, and was one aspect of the new administration's effort to reform the international monetary system. The concluding paragraphs of the Summary of the Report of the Task Force on the Balance of Payments (Document 1) pointed to greater exchange rate flexibility as central to solving the balance-of-payments problem and recognized that the already de facto inconvertibility of the dollar to gold might have to be replaced with de jure inconvertibility, presaging fundamental reform of the international monetary system.

3.   **Action Memorandum From Richard Cooper and C. Fred Bergsten of the National Security Council Staff to the President's Assistant for National Security Affairs (Kissinger)**[1]

Washington, January 28, 1969.

SUBJECT

Proposed Precipitate Action on the Balance of Payments

The President met last Friday with his new Cabinet Committee on Economic Policy.[2] It comprises his domestic economic advisers: Secretary Kennedy, Secretary Stans, Budget Director Mayo, CEA Chairman McCracken, etc. They discussed the removal of present controls over the export of funds by American banks and businesses. The

---

[1] Source: National Archives, Nixon Presidential Materials, NSC Files, Subject Files, Box 309, Balance of Payments. Confidential; Urgent.

[2] The meeting on Friday, January 24, was held in the Cabinet Room 4:03–5:40 p.m. (Ibid., White House Central Files, President's Daily Diary) The Diary lists the following attendees: Kennedy, Hardin, Stans, Shultz, Burns, McCracken, Mayo, Stein, Houthakker, and Safire. See Document 9 regarding economic committees during the Nixon administration.

sentiment was very strong for immediate removal of these controls, with little consideration of the consequences of so doing or of the actions to be taken in response to those consequences. It now appears possible that Secretary Stans will announce a change in his part of the program as early as tomorrow (Wednesday).[3]

This question has a high foreign policy content. No action should be taken before a thorough review of both the effects on the balance of payments and foreign, especially European, reaction to removal of the controls. Removal of the controls might well result in a substantial increase in the payments deficit, or at least widespread expectations thereof, confronting the Administration with an international monetary crisis. It would evoke a strong negative reaction from high officials in Germany, France, the Netherlands, Switzerland, and possibly other countries—a reaction that would, among many other things, undercut our efforts to work out more satisfactory arrangements for sharing the financial burden of NATO.

The NSC is the natural place to consider the foreign policy implications of our balance of payments program and a meeting is scheduled for February 26 on international monetary arrangements.[4] You should urge the President to avoid making any decision or public commitments on this question until after the NSC review and to instruct his Cabinet Members (especially Secretary Stans) not to do so either. Attached is a draft memorandum to him on the subject.[5]

---

[3] Next to this sentence in the left margin someone wrote "not done."

[4] The meeting was canceled. See Document 16 and footnote 4 thereto.

[5] Not found, but see footnote 1, Document 4.

---

4. Memorandum From the President's Assistant for National Security Affairs (Kissinger) to President Nixon[1]

Washington, January 28, 1969.

SUBJECT

Foreign Policy and U.S. Controls on Foreign Investment

I understand that you have discussed with your domestic economic advisers the removal of our present controls on American investment

---

[1] Source: National Archives, Nixon Presidential Materials, NSC Files, Subject Files, Box 309, BOP. Confidential. A handwritten note on the memorandum reads: "Copy given to Bergsten on 2/4/69." Presumably this memorandum was attached to Document 3.

abroad. I heartily agree with the desirability of removing the controls. However, such a move has vitally important foreign policy implications, especially with respect to our relations with Europe.

Removal of the controls must be planned carefully and, to avoid risking an international monetary crisis, probably must be coupled with new and positive U.S. policy initiatives. I therefore urge you to defer any final decision on this matter until you can review the foreign policy aspects with the NSC, and to instruct your Cabinet officers likewise to defer any decision.[2] An NSC meeting on international financial matters is now scheduled for late February.[3]

---

[2] Next to this sentence the President wrote "I agree."

[3] Next to this sentence the President wrote: "I believe Kennedy, et al think we should act sooner—check with McCracken (who is the W.H. man in charge of this area) and set an earlier date for N.S.C. meeting if his check with the principals involved believe it is advisable." McCracken sent more or less weekly reports to President Nixon on balance-of-payments related matters, even after the President said he no longer needed to see them in early 1970; see Document 38. The NSC meeting was canceled; see Document 16 and footnote 4 thereto.

---

5.   Memorandum From the Assistant Secretary of the Treasury for International Affairs (Petty) to Secretary of the Treasury Kennedy[1]

Washington, January 28, 1969.

SUBJECT

Timing the Reduction or Removal of Balance of Payments Controls

Weighed against the obvious domestic political advantages of the abrupt removal of controls[2] are: (1) the adverse foreign reaction it will

---

[1] Source: Washington National Records Center, Department of the Treasury, Office of the Assistant Secretary for International Affairs: FRC 56 76 108, Studies and Reports, Volume 7, 2/68–11/69. Confidential; Limdis. Drafted by Petty on January 28. Copies were sent to Under Secretaries Walker and Volcker. A handwritten notation reads: "(Note: *very* limited distribution) per [T. Page] Nelson (Jan 31)."

[2] In a January 28 memorandum to Secretary Rogers entitled "Abolition of Interest Equalization Tax and Balance of Payments Controls on Direct Investment," Greenwald informed Rogers that at a meeting of the Economic Cabinet, most of the group, including the President, wanted to terminate the controls immediately but that final action had been put off for several days at the request of the Council of Economic Advisers. (National Archives, RG 59, Central Files 1967–69, FN 16 US) Presumably Greenwald was referring to the January 24 meeting (see footnote 3, Document 3), which the full Council of Economic Advisers attended.

create and the fallout of this reaction on (a) the SDR ratification and implementation, (b) monetary reform, (c) options available in crises, and (d) speculation for an increase in the official gold price.

A quick removal of controls, as viewed abroad, would *not* be justified by the U.S. balance of payments statistics, the underlying trend of our position or the state of our domestic economy.[3] It would signal that the new Administration

—has lower*ed* the priority of achieving equilibrium,
—has been seduced by the "window dressing" of the 1968 results,
—believes more of the burden of responsibility should shift abroad.

None of this would heighten their interest in pushing rapidly forward on the SDRs. In fact, a quick removal of controls could seriously jeopardize our efforts in all monetary areas. It would be regarded as leading to a substantial liquidity deficit in 1969, and possibly result in renewed gold losses to central banks.

Commerce will be announcing tomorrow a trade deficit for December—and this will not reassure anybody.

U.S. leadership in monetary reform is necessary if progress is to be made. Speaking from a position of strength is vital to our capacity to direct the course of events. As a review of the monetary system is high on the priority of this Administration, we must be careful not to inhibit our conduct of this review by appearing to belittle the responsibility of the deficit country in the balance of payments adjustment process.

The high priority we are giving to contingency planning[4] is a testament to the tenuous state of the international financial system. If a crisis such as that at Bonn,[5] or worse, occurs in the next few weeks, having done away with our controls would dangerously limit our options and undermine our capacity to control events in such an atmosphere!

We are in the process of preparing proposals to liberalize our controls and these alternatives—together with their costs and benefits—should be available shortly.

---

[3] A January 28 covering memorandum from Petty to Kennedy referred to a January 27 memorandum from Petty to Kennedy (attached) that put the balance-of-payments cost at least $2,100 million if the direct investment program were abandoned for 1969. (Washington National Records Center, Department of the Treasury, Office of the Assistant Secretary for International Affairs: FRC 56 76 108, Studies and Reports, Volume 7, 2/68–11/69)

[4] Reference is to contingency planning for an international monetary crisis; see Documents 110 ff.

[5] Reference is to a significant increase in holdings of dollars by the Federal Republic of Germany.

6. Volcker Group Paper[1]

VG/LIM/69–50   Washington, February 6, 1969.

ALTERNATIVES FOR A SOMEWHAT RELAXED AND REVISED 1969 BALANCE-OF-PAYMENTS PROGRAM

Question: What steps toward relaxation of the control programs might be taken and what might this cost?

I. Balance of Payments: Position and Outlook

1969 balance-of-payments projections present a bleak picture. The anticipated gain in the trade balance and the current account in general is more than offset by an anticipated reduction in foreign private capital inflow.

The trade projection assumes continuation of the 10% surtax and of current monetary policy; a GNP growth (current dollars) of 7.1% as compared with 9% last year; and less pressure on productive capacity.

The projected growth of total imports from 1968 to 1969 is only 5.2% (at mid-point of range). But, *excluding* autos and parts imports from Canada, exceptional food imports in 1968, and strike-induced imports in 1968, the growth is projected at about 8%.

The export projection assumes an 8% increase in industrial production in other advanced countries, compared with an 8.8% increase last year. The projected growth of total exports from 1968 to 1969 is 9.3% (at mid-point of range). But, *excluding* autos and parts exports to Canada, commercial aircraft, and agricultural products, it is 11.9%.

The capital projections assume no change in the IET, or in the Commerce and Federal Reserve programs beyond the changes already announced.

Finally, no substantial change in expenditures in connection with the Vietnam conflict is assumed.

1969 Projected Over-All Balance of Payments

The major items projected for 1969 by an interagency working group are shown in the following table. Most of the 1968 figures are still *estimates.*

---

[1] Source: Washington National Records Center, Department of the Treasury, Volcker Group Masters: FRC 56 86 30, VG/LIM/31–VG/LIM/50. Confidential; Limited Distribution. Circulated to members of the Volcker Group on March 18 under cover of a routing memorandum from Willis that indicated the paper was discussed at a February 28 meeting.

		1968 (est.)	*(bils. of $'s)* *1969* (proj.)	*Improve. or* Deterioration (-)
	Exports	33.4	35.7–37.3	
	Imports	33.3	34.5–35.5	
(a)	Trade balance (at mid-point of 1969 range)	0.1	1.5	1.4
(b)	Services bal. (incl. private remittances and govt. pensions)	0.8	1.1	0.3
	of which			
	(Direct investment income, fees & royalties)	(6.3)	(7.0)	
(c)	Current account bal. (a) + (b)	0.9	2.6	1.7
(d)	Direct investment (before deduction for funds borrowed abroad)	-3.3	-3.6	-0.3
	(use of funds bor. abroad)	(2.2)	(1.5)	(-0.7)
	(Net)	(-1.1)	(-2.1)	(-1.0)
(e)	Bank claims	0.3	—	-0.3
(f)	Other private U.S. capital	-1.7	-1.2	0.5
(g)	U.S. Gov't. capital (incl. economic grants)	-4.3	-4.2	0.1
(h)	Foreign private capital inflow:			
	Direct investment in U.S.	0.4	0.2	-0.2
	Loans to finance U.S. direct invest. abroad	3.1	1.3	-1.8
	Stock purchases (excl. $210 mil. Shell pur. in U.S. sub)	1.7	1.0	-0.7
(i)	Errors and omissions*	0.1	—	-0.1
	Subtotal	-2.8	-3.9	-1.1

---

*During 1960–67, the U.S. had consistent *deficits* in "errors and omissions," averaging -$600 mil. (-$210 mil. to -$997 mil.). The small estimated *surplus* in this item for 1968 could turn out to be merely a temporary favorable shift, possibly associated with unusually large capital receipts last year.

		1968 (est.)	1969 (proj.)	Improve. or Deterioration (-)
(j)	Receipts from Foreign Gov'ts: (or internat'l. instit., other than IMF)	2.9	not est. for last two items.	
	Military advance payments (- means run-off).		(-0.1)	(-) (0.1)
	Purchases of U.S. agency bonds by internat'l. instit.	(0.1)	(-)	(-0.1)
	Debt prepayments	(0.3)	(-)	(-0.3)
	German pur. of special Treasury issues, incl. $125 mil. by German commercial banks in 1968	(0.6)	(0.5)	(-0.1)
	Other Gov't. purchases of special Treas. issues	(1.4)	(not est.)	
	Purchase of medium-term U.S. bank CD's	(0.6)	(not est.)	
	"Liquidity" Balance	0.1	-$3.9 less total receipts obtained under (j)	

Some of the above projections such as foreign stock purchases here this year are obviously not much more than "guesstimates." But the projections clearly indicate that given the assumptions, a major adverse swing in our balance of payments this year is very likely.

With regard to foreign government investment in special Treasury issues and medium-term U.S. bank CD's, it should be noted that $911 million of the former mature in 1969 ($800 million held by Canada and $111 million held by Switzerland). About $2.4 billion of long-term bank CD's held by various foreign governments mature in 1969. *Even if all these were rolled-over in the same amount, as assumed in the above projections, there would be a deterioration* of that amount in the 1969 position relative to 1968 when such foreign government investments showed a *net increase.*

While no formal projection of the U.S. balance of payments beyond 1969 has been made, the probability of a continued deficit of a worrisome size is high.

II. Alternatives in Revising the Balance-of-Payments Program

Steps to move away from the restrictive aspect of the present program may need to be commenced promptly. This might involve a relaxation—beginning soon—which would entail some risks and the likelihood of an increased capital outflow. It might also involve the need, for balance-of-payments protection, of a continued tight money policy, even if there is some easing in domestic inflationary pressures. A relaxation of controls would be a clear step in the direction of removing them, without throwing caution to the winds.

A. The Direct Investment Program

A revised program involving a relaxation of direct investment controls has three basic alternatives: (1) modification and relaxation of the existing program; (2) shifting to a voluntary program; (3) abandonment of the investment controls.

Options available in each of these general alternatives are discussed below. (It should be noted that an FDIP report to be filed by direct investors by February 28 will give the first complete projection of 1969 direct investment plans, including projected capital outflow, use of foreign borrowing, earnings, and dividends to U.S. parents. Results from this report will not be available until sometime in March.)

1. *Modifying and Relaxing the Existing Program*

There are four primary areas in which this may be done:

(a) *Increase the level of minimum authorized investment.*

This is presently proposed as $300,000 for 1969, compared with $200,000 in effect in 1968. We would estimate that the balance-of-payments cost of increasing the level to $500,000 would amount to approximately $60 million and would relieve some of the burden of the Foreign Direct Investment Program for approximately 200 companies. Should the level be increased to $1 million, the additional balance-of-payments cost (over the $300,000 level) would amount to $160–200 million, with about 350 companies benefiting.

(b) *Increase the elective earnings allowable* from its present proposed 20 percent level to 30 percent. (The 20% proposal differs in several respects from the automatic exemption for a certain minimum level of direct investment described in (a) above. It is an optional method of determining a company's allowable direct investment in all cases where the minimum exempt amount is exceeded; hence, it is an alternative to the base-period investment method. This optional method would allow a firm to make direct investment in 1969 not less than 20% of its direct investment earnings in 1968. Data on the latter for the fourth quarter, 1968 are not due from direct investors until February 14 and some time will be required for processing, so that the figures below must be regarded as preliminary *estimates*.)

The net additional cost of a 30% earnings allowable would be an estimated $220 million, and approximately 85 companies would benefit. Raising the percentage to 40% would cost $530 million over the announced 1969 program cost and 160 companies would benefit. Increasing the percentage to 50% would involve additional payments costs of approximately $1 billion over the announced 1969 Program level, with over 230 companies benefiting.

(c) *Exemption from the program* of transactions with affiliated foreign nationals solely involved in a selling capacity. We do not have trading company data, but crude estimates based on available information suggest balance-of-payments costs on the order of $100 million. Companies with which this idea was floated expressed no interest in it, presumably because they feel the pressure of the present ceilings much more with respect to investment in their production affiliates than in their trading affiliates abroad. Also, they believed accounting and definitional problems would be unsurmountable.

(d) There has been a great deal of discussion about the possibility of collapsing Schedules A, B and C into a single schedule. This would do a great deal to simplify the regulations, reporting requirements, and administration of the program, and would be widely acclaimed by the business world. Data for estimating the payments cost of such a move will not be available until March. However, we would guess that the cost would be substantial—say, $1 billion—for the following reason. Many companies find their present quotas partially *unusable* because these are locked into area schedules where the companies have no specific investment plans.

The attached tables summarize the effects of the above proposals and provide a rough projection of the direct investment situation.[2]

We have not attempted to assess the incidental balance-of-payments costs, or benefits, that might attend a liberalization of the direct investment program—for example, the effects on foreign government and exchange market confidence in the dollar, and on U.S. exports and imports. These effects could, of course, be substantial.

2. *Voluntary Program*

Shifting to a voluntary program would depend upon the cooperation of a few hundred companies.

Information gathered this past year greatly increases the capacity to choose those companies which would most appropriately be included in a voluntary program. But a 1969 projection of direct investment by U.S. companies and a sources-and-uses-of-funds forecast with respect to their foreign affiliates would be needed to conceive a voluntary program adequately. This material will be gathered, hopefully, by the end of April; and a proposal could be in shape for announcement some weeks later.

---

[2] None of the attached tables is printed.

Among the basic questions which would have to be covered are:

In case borrowing costs in the U.S. decline relative to Europe, would companies be willing to maintain their existing outstanding indebtedness in Europe rather than refinance it in the U.S.? Would they be willing to do a large portion of new borrowing in Europe, rather than in the U.S. for direct investment purposes? Would they insist on counting exports as an offset to their direct investment outflows?

3. *Abandonment of Direct Investment Controls*

Abandoning controls would cost $2 billion or more—compared to what it was in 1968—depending upon the extent to which companies would refinance in the U.S. foreign debt created in prior years and where they would raise funds for new direct investment.

B. *The Federal Reserve Program*

The announced 1969 program left the bank program ceiling at essentially 103 percent and made no significant changes in the Program. The Fed resisted the general preference to exempt medium-term export credits, as did the OFDI, which would be greatly affected by such an exemption. It was felt that no major change should be made before the new Administration had had an opportunity to review the over-all U.S. balance-of-payments program.

It was announced last December that the Fed would review the Program early in 1969, and Governor Brimmer is now in the process of discussing with banks and other financial institutions their experience under the Program. The main considerations of the Program review are the reduction of inequities among financial institutions covered by the Program, and the methods that might be used to resolve any conflict between the need to stem potential dollar outflows and the need to assure that funds necessary to finance U.S. exports are available. In order to stimulate consideration by the banks of various alternatives, he has mentioned the following as examples:

(a) extending the IET to cover foreign credits and investments now covered only by the VFCR, including short-term bank loans;
(b) establish a special reserve requirement against credits to foreigners;
(c) create an auction system related to the total amount of bank lending to foreigners;
(d) make changes within the present program to minimize inequities, especially for the smaller banks;
(e) making special provisions to facilitate exports.

Suggestions (d) and (e) would overlap to the extent that higher ceilings approved for small banks would be concentrated on export credits.

The meetings of Governor Brimmer with institutions covered by the VFCR extend to March 11, and recommendations will then be made by the

Governor to the Board. The range of possibilities for some relaxation and simplification is quite large, and judgments of the balance of payments cost will vary depending on the extent to which additional extensions of credit are expected to stimulate exports that otherwise would not occur. Pending completion of the review by the Board no recommendations are made here.

C. Interest Equalization Tax

The IET rate is presently 18.75 percent on purchase of long-term debt (28-1/2 years or more) and equity securities. This is roughly equivalent to an annual cost of 1-1/4 percent.

The IET has operated as nearly an absolute barrier for American lending to foreign borrowers. Virtually no IET collections have been associated with loans to foreigners or purchases of foreign bonds.

Collection data show that well over half the IET payments in over four years were associated with American purchases of South African gold mining shares. Most of the balance came from purchases of outstanding issues of Canadian mining stocks and a few "special situation" issues. U.S. speculators in foreign mining shares have generally been able to resell "tax-paid" shares in the U.S. market at prices equal to or exceeding what they paid the foreign issuer *plus* IET.

We cannot predict with any precision what rate constitutes the threshold for substantial outflows based upon interest differentials alone. But an example of the potential for such outflows is the large volume of attractive convertible bonds issued abroad by U.S. companies in recent years to finance direct investment. A substantial reduction of the IET would seem very likely to encourage U.S. private purchases of these issues and thus defeat the purpose of the Foreign Direct Investment Program—that is, the encouragement of use of foreign capital for financing U.S. direct investment.

A reduction to one percent per year would *not* entail a substantial increase in capital outflow under the existing structure of interest rates here and abroad. A reduction to three fourths of 1 percent would be more risky because a sizeable pent-up U.S. demand for foreign issues probably exists, and a sizeable reduction of the IET could trigger it off, not only because of the reduced tax per se but also because of the psychological impact of a substantial liberalization step.

Also, interest differentials between here and Europe could shift by mid-summer sufficiently to make a three fourths percent rate quite costly and even a one percent rate costly.

The attached tables show IET collections and interest rate differentials. (The collections data suggest that from $850 million to $1 billion of foreign stock was purchased by U.S. investors during the period October, 1964, through October, 1968.)

The IET has related effects which must be borne in mind in evaluating changes in the rate:

—it facilitates the pursuit of an autonomous domestic monetary policy;
   —it stimulates development of the European capital market;
   —it facilitates operation of the Federal Reserve Program by relieving the pressure on U.S. banks of foreign demands for credit;
   —it restrains capital outflow to developed countries through channels not covered by other programs.

Since the need for these related effects may continue well beyond the expiration of the IET in July, 1969, continuation of the IET, at least on a standby basis, should be seriously considered.

---

7.   Memorandum of Conversation[1]

Paris, March 2, 1969, 12:41–1:49 p.m.

PRESENT

The President, General De Gaulle, Mr. Andronikov, Major General Walters

[Here follow brief opening remarks.]

The President said that he would like to have an understanding with General De Gaulle that if either of them wished to communicate directly with the other they could do so by private letters and such relations need not necessarily pass through the usual diplomatic channels. For any private matters below the Chief of State level, General De Gaulle could have his people communicate with Dr. Kissinger.

General De Gaulle asked whether Dr. Kissinger himself would bring the letters.

---

[1]   Source: National Archives, Nixon Presidential Materials, NSC Files, Presidential/HAK Memcons, Box 1023, De Gaulle 2/28–3/2/69. Secret. The meeting was held at the Elysée Palace; the time is taken from the Daily Diary. (Ibid., White House Central Files, President's Daily Diary) The two Presidents also met on February 28. Their discussion touched on economic issues, and President Nixon told de Gaulle that he thought "it was clear that both the USSR and the US would like to reduce the financial burden [of defense expenditures] on themselves. He wished to make clear that on this matter he would not make the decision in this matter on a financial basis, the US had to be able to afford whatever security required." (Ibid., NSC Files, Presidential/HAK Memcons, Box 1023, De Gaulle 2/28–3/2/69) The two also met on March 1; a record of that meeting is ibid. President Nixon traveled to Belgium, the United Kingdom, the Federal Republic of Germany, Italy, and France February 23–March 2.

The President said that this would not necessarily be so, but he might find the need at some time to send Dr. Kissinger over. He said that sometimes it was useful to avoid communications that were too formal in nature.

General De Gaulle agreed and said he would bear this in mind.

The President said that, insofar as discussions on monetary matters were concerned, he felt that the suggestion that these could be handled privately and discreetly through a special representative was a good one, and we would be prepared to talk with whoever the General might designate to represent France on such matters.

General De Gaulle said that after the President returned to Washington he would let him know who the French would appoint. This person, of course, would have an unofficial mission and would not be charged with settling matters but rather to take contact with his American counterpart.[2]

The President agreed to this.

General De Gaulle then asked whether the President had made similar arrangements with the British and the Germans.

The President said that this had not been done. We would talk with them in a more formal way. Both the British and the German Finance Ministers would be coming to the US, but he wondered whether the General felt it might be better to handle these matters with them in the same way as the French.

General De Gaulle said that he did not see any reason to do this.

The President then said that it was better if the conversations were conducted somewhat discreetly as formal discussions gave rise to speculation on the price of gold and so forth. The discussions would be initially exploratory.

---

[2] No record of an appointment of a special representative has been found, although continuing expressions of French interest periodically surfaced. On February 5 Houthakker wrote in a memorandum of a February 4 dinner conversation with the Financial Counselor of the French Embassy, George Plescoff, of the latter's "pitch" for bilateral U.S.-French conversations "on the entire range of international monetary problems." (VG/LIM/69–12; Washington National Records Center, Department of the Treasury, Volcker Group Masters: FRC 56 86 30, VG/LIM/1–VG/LIM/30) During Plescoff's introductory call on Treasury Under Secretary Volcker on February 19, Plescoff said he had not sought to have regular official contact with Treasury in recent years due to policy differences but that he now wished to develop a close and regular working relationship. Volcker thought conveying this message was the main purpose of his call. (Ibid., Files of Under Secretary Volcker: FRC 56 79 15, France) During his March 18 introductory, courtesy call on Treasury Secretary Kennedy, French Ambassador Charles Lucet said that "France hoped the United States would eventually take the initiative to arrange some quiet, unpublicized talks on the problem of international monetary reform." (Ibid.) In an April 19 memorandum to Secretary Rogers, reporting on his April 9 conversation with French Foreign Minister Debré during the April 10–11 NATO Ministerial meeting in Washington, Kissinger reported: "Debré raised the possibility of very confidential US-French conversations, recalling that this idea had been broached previously at the time of the President's visit to Paris." (Ibid.)

General De Gaulle then repeated that he would notify the President, after his return to Washington, who the French representative would be and reiterated that this man would be an unofficial representative.

The President said he felt that one could not make much progress when one was working in a goldfish bowl. On other matters of consultation, our Secretary of Commerce, Mr. Stans, would soon be coming to Europe. His discussions would be strictly on matters of trade and in a broad sense. He would not get into matters such as the Common Market and who should belong to it. Rather he would discuss such matters as trade and restrictive practices which we or others might have. His policy would be not to have our Government play as active a role as in the past in attempting to determine the shape and form of Europe. We had ideas which we would submit, but we felt that this was essentially a matter for Europeans.

General De Gaulle said that there was GATT and it was normal for our Ministers to speak of this agreement and its application.

[Omitted here is a lengthy discussion of Vietnam.]

---

8. Memorandum of Conversation[1]

Washington, March 11, 1969, 10 a.m.

SUBJECT

> Secretary Kennedy's Meeting on Proposed 1969 Revised Balance of Payments Program

PARTICIPANTS

> Treasury:
> Secretary Kennedy
> Under Secretary Volcker
> Assistant Secretary Petty
>
> State:
> Secretary Rogers
> Acting Assistant Secretary Greenwald
> Deputy Assistant Secretary Enders

---

[1] Source: Washington National Records Center, Department of the Treasury, Office of the Assistant Secretary for International Affairs: FRC 56 76 108, Studies and Reports, Volume 7, 2/68–11/69. Confidential. Drafted by Petty on March 13 and approved by Volcker. The meeting was held in Room 4426 of the Treasury Department.

Commerce:
Secretary Stans
Mr. Cadle, Acting Director, OFDI

Federal Reserve:
Chairman Martin

CEA:
Chairman McCracken
Mr. Houthakker

BOB:
Director Mayo

White House:
Counsellor to the President Burns

Under Secretary Volcker introduced the discussion by giving a brief report on the foreign exchange markets which indicated that the pressure on the French franc and the pound sterling was modest and the atmosphere of last Thursday[2] no longer prevailed. Mr. Volcker referred to the proposed Memorandum to the President[3] and indicated that the proposed relaxation could cost in balance of payments terms an amount in the neighborhood of $1 billion, depending upon various developments. He reported that the staffs of the various agencies expressed considerable caution at the idea of moving ahead now to relax controls to the degree indicated. The primary concern was about the probable negative reaction abroad to such a relaxation. Foreigners would grumble that this relaxation will finance takeovers by American companies; it would make more difficult the activation of Special Drawing Rights, and it could impede the talks on monetary reform. Finally, Mr. Volcker reported that the IMF Managing Director Schweitzer suggested caution about the idea of relaxing controls and said that the cost could be reduced by not including the Federal Reserve Program in the relaxation.

Mr. Volcker closed with the question: Should the Federal Reserve be part of the relaxation? And what should be the timing of the announcement?

---

[2] March 6.

[3] Reference is to a draft memorandum to the President on "Relaxation of Balance-of-Payments Controls," which was circulated by Kennedy to the Secretaries of State and Commerce, the Budget Director, and the Chairmen of the Federal Reserve System and the Council of Economic Advisers on March 7, under cover of a memorandum inviting them to the March 11 meeting to discuss the draft. (Washington National Records Center, Department of the Treasury, Secretary's Memos/Correspondence, 1966–1970: FRC 56 74 7, Memo to the Secretary, March–April, 1969) An earlier version of the draft memorandum to the President, dated March 3 with the subject line, "Reversing the Trend Toward Restrictions by Beginning the Relaxation of Controls," is ibid., Deputy to the Assistant Secretary for International Affairs: FRC 56 83 26, Current Problems and Contingency Planning 11/68–4/69. See Document 15 for the memorandum that was sent to the President on April 1.

Secretary Kennedy pointed out the difficulty of the choice in view of the bad balance of payments numbers which are projected. "If we do nothing now," he said, "we get locked into the ways of the past; on the other hand, we do not want to touch off an adverse market reaction with possible side effects that are unpredictable."

Secretary Stans indicated that he was leaving for Europe on April 11, and he would not want to have the relaxation announced a week before he would go—as he would have to spend most of his time explaining the action. Second, he underscored the importance of an early announcement by pointing out that presently, regulations do not exist for the foreign direct investment program for 1969; and, to be fair to the corporations, they must come out shortly. Finally, he indicated that most of the advantages to the Administration would be attained through the OFDI relaxation, and therefore it is possible that it could be done separately.

Secretary Rogers indicated that President Nixon during his trip agreed to undertake consultations with the Europeans, and he indicated that it would be appropriate to do that on this matter. Mr. Volcker said that the Europeans would be likely to say: "No." Secretary Rogers indicated that this is what consultation is all about. Secretary Kennedy commented that, in view of this, Mr. Volcker should propose to consult in Europe on this matter.

Counsellor Burns doubted that the balance of payments deficit as projected would be increased to the extent indicated. He added that consultations may occasion long delays in the announcement if they are undertaken thoroughly. The Europeans are concerned about the trade policies of the United States, and they do not understand the details of the OFDI. What they are anxious to avoid is a unilateral action in the trade area.

Chairman McCracken commented that there are different dimensions to foreign concern about the U.S. balance of payments. One concern is they would argue that we are taking the wraps off of our companies, permitting them to buy out European corporations. And the second concern is that we get on top of our inflationary problem. He supported the relaxation and pointed out it carried a greater obligation to control inflation at home.

Counsellor Burns said the fact the domestic economy was going too fast and the fact that the relaxation carried a greater obligation to control inflation provided all the more reason to pursue the course of relaxation of controls now. If we can announce our expenditure policy for fiscal 1970, the President's proposed balance of payments statement would be greatly strengthened.

Secretary Rogers doubted if more pressure to control inflation were needed—there is no lack of consciousness or determination in this regard. Secretary Kennedy added that we are not getting the budgetary cuts he would like to see.

Mr. Houthakker suggested that the relaxation could be presented as primarily a technical adjustment. Counsellor Burns said the matter was broader than that, and the announcement should be too: we should add the continued deferment of withholding tax on interest paid on foreign deposits. We must decide now whether we do or do not have a philosophy as a government; we must declare we are moving away from creeping restrictionism. The Europeans are as afraid as we are of the trend toward restrictionism.

While Secretary Stans did not feel there is any need for a ballyhoo statement because American interests would understand the significance of the move, Counsellor Burns felt that the President needed to state his principles now.

Mr. Petty inquired if an announcement of this sort was really of the nature that would require consultations; it is nowhere near the league of NPTs or ABMs. Secretary Rogers replied that the statements on the President's trip did not imply any limits to consultation.

Director Mayo indicated that any announcement would be strongly reinforced with an announcement on expenditure cuts and an extension of the tax surcharge.

Chairman Martin summarized his views and said that it would be appropriate to undertake consultations on this subject, but he emphasized that these consultations should be at the political level and not with the central banks or even with the G-10 Deputies. Mr. Volcker should make it clear that the United States is choosing general restraint over selective controls and we would take whatever steps necessary to control inflation.

Secretary Kennedy summarized: Mr. Volcker would go and make the necessary consultations, he would present this action in a positive manner and indicate that this Administration would seek an extension of the Interest Equalization Tax, an extension of the surtax, and include appropriate expenditure controls, as well.[4]

John Petty

---

[4] C. Fred Bergsten reported on this March 11 meeting to Kissinger in a March 12 information memorandum. He informed Kissinger that Burns and Stans had resisted Rogers' insistence on consultations and had been overruled by Kennedy. Bergsten wrote: "any decision to relax the present controls has been postponed. . . . Treasury Under Secretary Volcker will thus raise the issue in his upcoming European trip. He will inform them that we plan to reduce our reliance on controls but will seek their views on timing and complementary steps. This approach will stand in marked contrast to that of the previous Administration, which *enacted* the entire control program—a much more drastic step than the marginal *relaxation* now envisaged—and then sent teams to Europe and the Far East to inform them of the action. In fact, it could be argued that it is stretching the President's commitment quite far to consult on an issue of this magnitude. However, I supported Rogers on the grounds that any unilateral action should be avoided so shortly after the trip." (National Archives, Nixon Presidential Materials, NSC Files, Subject Files, Box 309, BOP) Under Secretary Volcker traveled to Bern, Bonn, Brussels, The Hague, Rome, and Stockholm March 21–26.

9.   **Editorial Note**

On March 14, 1969, Cabinet Secretary John C. Whitaker sent a memorandum to all members of the Cabinet asking their opinions on Cabinet Committees established by Executive orders of previous Presidents. Whitaker noted that President Nixon thought there were too many such committees, which duplicated those established by the Nixon administration or no longer served a useful purpose. On the foreign economic policy front Commerce Secretary Stans was given responsibility for making recommendations on the Export Expansion Advisory Committee, which provided guidance to the Export-Import Bank on allocations to promote export expansion, and Treasury Secretary Kennedy was to make recommendations on the National Advisory Council on International Monetary and Financial Policy (NAC), whose functions were to coordinate the activities of the U.S. representatives to International Financial Organizations and the Export-Import Bank. (National Archives, RG 59, S/S Files: Lot 73 D 288, Box 839, NSC/MTS) On April 14 Secretary of State Rogers wrote to Secretaries Stans and Kennedy supporting their committees as presently constituted. (Ibid.) Both committees continued to meet during the Nixon administration.

On June 2 Whitaker sent a memorandum to all members of the Cabinet transmitting a revised list of Cabinet committees and subcommittees, including the following committees that dealt with foreign economic policy:

The Cabinet Committee on Economic Policy, whose members were Vice President Agnew, White House Counselor Burns, Treasury Secretary Kennedy, Agriculture Secretary Hardin, Budget Director Mayo, Labor Secretary Shultz, Commerce Secretary Stans, and Council of Economic Advisers Chairman McCracken, who was responsible for staff support;
The Economic "Troika," which comprised Treasury Secretary Kennedy, Budget Director Mayo, and Chairman McCracken;
The Economic "Quadriad," made up of the Troika plus Federal Reserve Chairman Martin; and
The Committee for Comprehensive Review of Oil Import Controls chaired by Labor Secretary Shultz. Other members were Interior Secretary Hickel, Treasury Secretary Kennedy, Defense Secretary Laird, Secretary of State Rogers, Commerce Secretary Stans, Office of Emergency Preparedness Director Lincoln, and Phillip Areeda who provided staff support. (Ibid.)

The Cabinet Committee on the Balance of Payments, which had played an active role in balance-of-payments policy during the Kennedy and Johnson administrations, was not mentioned in either of

Whitaker's memoranda. Deputy Assistant Secretary of the Treasury for International Affairs John C. Colman commented in an April 17 memorandum to Under Secretary Volcker that the committee might be beyond the scope of Whitaker's inquiry because it had been initiated by a June 7, 1962, memorandum from President Kennedy to Treasury Secretary Dillon, not by Executive order. Colman noted that as the balance-of-payments problems became more pressing and the various programs of restraints and incentives became more detailed, the Deming Group, now the Volcker Group (see footnote 1, Document 109) increasingly shaped policy rather than the "unwieldy" Cabinet Committee. The conclusion of Colman's argument was that balance-of-payments issues should be taken up in the Cabinet Committee on Economic Policy and the Volcker Group. (Washington National Records Center, Department of the Treasury, Office of the Assistant Secretary for International Affairs: FRC 56 75 101, Cabinet Committee on the Balance of Payments, US/3/106–113, Establishment and Representation) Regarding the establishment of the Cabinet Committee on the Balance of Payments, see *Foreign Relations*, 1961–1963, volume IX, Document 10.

No formal record of the Cabinet Committee on the Balance of Payments' demise has been found, nor any record that it met during the Nixon administration.

---

10.   **Paper Prepared in the Department of the Treasury**[1]

Washington, March 17, 1969.

TALKING PAPER ON REVISED BALANCE OF
PAYMENTS PROGRAM

The Nixon Administration views with great concern the growing trend toward restrictionism around the world. Restraints on capital flows are now being reinforced by restraints on the trade account and the pressure in this area is mounting. We have not succeeded if a system

---

[1] Source: Washington National Records Center, Department of the Treasury, Office of the Assistant Secretary for International Affairs: FRC 56 76 108, Studies and Reports, Volume 7, 2/68–11/69. Confidential. The paper, which bears no indication of a drafter, may have been prepared for the President's meeting with the Economic Quadriad on March 18 (see Document 12) or for Volcker's European consultations (see footnote 4, Document 8).

of reasonable international equilibrium can only be obtained through excessive demand restraints coupled with selective restrictions. We believe that the process by which international payments between nations are adjusted must be improved in order that equilibrium relationships can be maintained without selective controls.

1. The selective controls on *Direct Investment* of the Johnson Administration were put together hurriedly; of necessity, inequities arose in the base periods selected. We have now had the benefit of statistical runs for 1968, and we consider it desirable and proper to make adjustments in the direct investment program which will have the effect of:

a. Substantially reducing the administrative burden, both to the Government and to the smaller corporations;

b. Providing some relief for those companies which were caught with an inequitable base period;

c. Relaxing somewhat on the restrictions on the amount of earnings retained abroad—which should help the situation on foreign borrowings:

("Help the situation": *for us means* that those companies which have had to repatriate more than 80–100 percent of earnings because of the formula will only have to repatriate 70 percent; this allowance should also help them repay foreign debt from the proceeds of their operations abroad; *the Europeans* if they interpret the statement favorably might see it as a slight easing of demand upon their banking resources which would help the debt "overhang" problem of our companies and also help to ease rates; others could interpret a relaxation as providing all the more money for takeovers.)

2. *The Interest Equalization Tax,* as you know, was created to remove the interest incentive which the lower money rates in New York usually allowed over comparable rates in European markets.

It seems to us that under present circumstances and with the tight money conditions in the U.S. that an adjustment in the IET rate is warranted. Congress gave us flexible authority to vary the rate with money conditions and since this is a unique delegation of authority we must use it when conditions warrant; otherwise, when *we go to extend* this legislation next year, Congress may withdraw that power.

3. *The Federal Reserve Program* has hit pretty hard the small and medium-sized banks who were left without a base period, and we may announce some modification or changes designed primarily to make the regional banks be more active in promoting exports.

Any attempt to put a balance of payments price tag on these intended steps would be misleading because the numbers involved in adjusting the targets in these complicated programs are difficult to translate into year-end balance of payments results. Basically, we have had the approach of not making the changes so small that they are unnoticeable; nor so large that they demonstrate a lack of caution.

Conclusion

Increasingly, our main thrust in balance of payments adjustment will be upon general measures rather than selective controls. There is no doubt about the determination of this Administration to recreate a proper balance in our economy. We will employ monetary and fiscal policy to the extent necessary and for as long as necessary to achieve this type of economic order. While we will be reversing the trend toward restrictionism by our intended modest relaxation we know full well that until general restraints have done their task, selective controls cannot be abandoned.

---

11. Memorandum From the Assistant Secretary of the Treasury for International Affairs (Petty) to Secretary of the Treasury Kennedy[1]

Washington, March 17, 1969.

SUBJECT

Interest Equalization Tax

The Problem

The IET expires on July 31 of this year. In view of the necessity for Congressional consultations and the likely extensive drafting time, we must plan now for the extension.

Congress has never been favorably disposed toward the IET but rather has supported it because of its necessity. The tax was proposed in 1963 and the Act only passed a year later. The Act has been renewed twice, in 1965 for 18 months and in 1967 for two years. In the most recent extension, the maximum rate of tax was increased (from one per-

---

[1] Source: Washington National Records Center, Department of the Treasury, Secretary's Memos/Correspondence, 1966–1970: FRC 56 74 7, Memo to the Secretary, March–April, 1969. Limited Official Use. Drafted by J. C. Colman on March 17. Sent through Volcker. A stamped notation indicates that Volcker initialed the memorandum. It is attached to Volcker's March 18 handwritten transmittal note to Kennedy: "My only added thought here is that the 'soundings' should be coordinated with proposed announcement on controls. This extension should be proposed, in general terms, at time of relaxation." Kennedy's handwritten reply on Volcker's note reads: "I agree. After the extension is proposed begin checking in Congress to determine whether any changes should be made."

cent to 1-1/2 percent per annum) and the President was given discretionary authority to vary the rate of tax.

Our problems with the balance of payments are still with us and undoubtedly will continue to be after July 31. Therefore, we will need the IET, at very least on a standby basis, as a means to restrain capital outflows from the United States. The IET has been very useful in effecting such restraint on portfolio outflows and bank lending to foreign borrowers and has supplemented both the Federal Reserve and Commerce Department programs. These are reasons enough to continue the tax.

The IET also will provide a very flexible policy instrument in the future when it may be appropriate to relax our monetary policy at least for domestic purposes. We would not want to be constrained from taking this action in fear of substantial capital outflows. Accordingly, extension of the IET will preserve our ability to carry out a relatively autonomous monetary policy.

In the prospective phasing out of our capital controls, there is the possibility that we may face large capital outflows by U.S. residents. There is undoubtedly substantial latent demand to purchase foreign securities or Euro-dollar convertible debentures issued by American corporations in recent years as well as to lend to major foreign borrowers. Therefore, to permit better phasing out of our capital controls and to mitigate these incipient outflows, we should retain a flexible IET.

Possible Legislation

The IET Act now on the books is a workable and effective instrument. There are a number of technical points, both substantive and non-substantive, which could be clarified in renewal legislation. However, if such amendments were to jeopardize the prospect of renewal, it would be entirely feasible to continue the IET without amendment.

Renewal is strongly recommended for the reasons cited above. If Congressional soundings indicate any substantial opposition or complications from an attempt to introduce amendatory legislation, then we should seek renewal without amendment.

The tax rate may now be varied from zero to 22.5 percent of the value of the security or loan subject to tax (equivalent to a maximum interest rate of 1-1/2 percent per annum). The President has the right to vary the rate by Executive Order. The maximum rate has proved to be effective in restraining almost all outflows for debt securities and loans and most equity securities other than speculative mining stocks. Accordingly, there is no reason to seek a higher statutory maximum rate or any change in the discretionary authority to alter the rate.

The IET rate now must move together for the tax on acquisition of both stocks and debt instruments. In the past, Treasury has always rationalized the IET rate in relation to debt issues. There is very little economic basis for holding that the IET rate should move together on both debt and equity issues. It thus might be preferable to consider having the tax move separately, at the discretion of the President, and possibly to set a higher maximum rate of tax for the purchase of equity securities. However, such a proposal would draw the opposition of the investment community as it has in the past, present substantial drafting and administrative problems and likely complicate renewal legislation. Accordingly, it appears favorable *not* to introduce any amendment in this area.

An amendment should be considered to give the President discretionary authority to exempt new issues from the application of the tax while retaining the tax on outstanding securities. We have such a precedent established in the present exemption of new Canadian offerings from the tax while the IET barrier still applies for outstanding Canadian securities. The introduction of such discretionary authority on a global basis among the developed countries wherein the IET applies, would give a new degree of flexibility for phasing out our capital controls. In particular, this would give more latitude to permit a limited amount of capital outflows for new financings in the U.S. markets without incurring substantial risk of large portfolio capital outflows to purchase outstanding foreign securities (particularly equities).

There are several other housekeeping and technical improvements that we could make in this legislation. For the most part, the matters are non-substantive, but they would close loopholes and improve administration. There are a number of substantive matters which should be handled by legislation (e.g., the IET status of leases, oil and gas interests and other hybrid ownership interests such as commodity futures; the treatment of captive foreign sales finance companies; and the treatment of foreign stock or debt obligations acquired out of foreign sourced borrowings). Among the substantive matters, it appears that amendments relating to the treatment of leases and captive foreign sales finance companies are the most important. In these two areas we find the greatest number of taxpayer questions and possible inequities in interpretations of the present statute.

The current law is awkward in delineating conditions to grant partial exemption of individual countries from the application of the IET. At present, countries can be exempted only by classification as "less developed" or through the finding by the President that exemption in whole or in part is required in the interest of international monetary stability. Over the years we have had numerous requests (e.g., Bahamas, Iran, Ireland, Spain) for partial or total exemption from the IET. In most cases the requests have been founded more on political grounds than on any economic hardship. Any amendment to give the President greater discretion in granting partial exemption from the IET to particular countries would undoubtedly severely complicate renewal legislation and bring a host of foreign governmental requests for exemption. Accordingly, it is recommended that *no* amendment of this sort be considered.

Recommendations:[2]

1. That you authorize Messrs. Cohen and Petty to begin immediately soundings on the Hill of a proposal to renew the IET legislation for two years from its expiration on July 31, 1969. Such soundings would especially involve the schedule for public and executive hearings and the relation of such hearings to the schedule for tax reform hearings.

2. That the soundings include discussion of an amendment to give the President authority to exempt new issues while maintaining the tax on outstanding issues from countries to which the tax now applies.

3. That the soundings include discussion of technical amendments, including substantive changes relating to the treatment of leases and captive foreign sales finance companies.

---

[2] There is no indication of Kennedy's approval or disapproval of the recommendations.

12.   Memorandum From the President's Assistant for National Security Affairs (Kissinger) to President Nixon[1]

Washington, March 17, 1969.

SUBJECT

Reductions of Controls on U.S. Capital Outflows: Foreign Implications and a Note of Caution

Issue

I understand that you will discuss the reductions of our present capital controls with your economic Quadriad tomorrow afternoon.[2] There are major foreign policy implications of our moving in this direction. As a result of the considerations outlined below I recommend that you not commit the Administration irrevocably to the abolition or large scale reduction of the controls until an alternative solution to our international monetary problems is in sight. I have no objection to the limited reduction which is proposed for the near future although I agree fully with Secretary Rogers that it should not be undertaken until after full consultation with our European allies.[3]

Foreign Policy Aspects

Eliminating restraints on private investment abroad has three foreign policy aspects. The first is that the initial effect of easier monetary conditions in the U.S. in the absence of controls would be an enlarged payments deficit, to which most of the countries of continental Europe would object strongly. Foreign disapproval would be expressed relatively quickly, even before the emergence of a large deficit, since foreign officials can look ahead. The move would be interpreted as a disavowal of our earnest intentions to maintain a strong payments position.

---

[1] Source: National Archives, Nixon Presidential Materials, NSC Files, Subject Files, Box 309, BOP. Confidential. Drafted by Bergsten who, in his March 17 cover note to Kissinger, wrote: "Pursuant to your instruction, attached is a memo to the President informing him of the major foreign policy implications of the proposed line of action and advising him to adopt a 'go slow approach' in implementing it." There is no indication that the President saw the memorandum; an undated cover note to Colonel Haig reads: "I don't think you want this to go to the President now—it was being provided for his meeting with the Quadriad on 3/18. If the information is still valid for the President, perhaps the reference to the Quadriad meeting should be deleted." Haig wrote on the note "OBE—File."

[2] The President met with McCracken, Kennedy, Martin, Mayo, and Burns in the Cabinet Room from 4:18 to 6:06 p.m. on March 18. (Ibid., White House Central Files, President's Daily Diary)

[3] See footnote 4, Document 8.

Such officials, incidentally, do not share U.S. antipathy to controls over capital movements. Nor does the foreign business community. Except for Germany, all the European countries maintain some form of restraints on international capital movements. Even Switzerland, the citadel of free enterprise, controls the access of foreigners to the Swiss capital market.

The main effect of this reaction would be a setback to our efforts to improve the monetary system through cooperative steps with the Europeans. Thinking that the U.S. no longer cares about its payments position, their propensity to cooperate even in the activation of Special Drawing Rights, let alone more far-reaching reforms such as adoption (or even serious study) of greater exchange rate flexibility, will be sharply reduced. In short, we may be circumscribing our option of a cooperative solution—forcing us inevitably toward the kind of unilateral action described below. (The counter-argument is that a cooperative approach will not work anyway and that unilateral U.S. moves are inevitable. I do not share this pessimism.)

Second, many—probably most—Europeans welcome U.S. controls on direct investment (i.e., investment involving U.S. management control) as providing some slowdown to the takeover of European industry by American firms. This potentially explosive anxiety is by no means confined to government officials. To be sure, Europeans are ambivalent about American investment. Except for those firms feeling the direct competition, they generally welcome the infusion of technology and even new management techniques. But, because of the central position of the U.S. dollar in the international monetary system, we are open to charges of dollar imperialism if American capital is permitted to move to Europe without restraint—at least as long as our balance of payments is in sizable deficit. Some kind of restraint on direct investment—even the pre-1968 voluntary restraints were helpful in this regard—provides the necessary ambiguity on our side, combined with their own ambivalence, to diffuse the issue.

Finally, and most important, the alternative policies which we might be forced to adopt in lieu of capital controls could be much more damaging to U.S. foreign policy. Troop withdrawals, additional pressure on Germany and others for "better" offset arrangements, and further restrictions on the aid program are only the most obvious possibilities—and ones which we should reject for obvious foreign policy reasons. Unilateral U.S. suspension of gold convertibility—essentially adoption of a floating exchange rate of the dollar—would represent a massive display of U.S. power and rupture all our efforts to forge a new partnership with Europe on the basis of greater equality. An increase in the official price of gold—which would represent only a temporary solution anyway—would also be a unilateral act rejected by most official Europeans and would betray $15 billion worth of dollar holders from Germany to Thailand. Adoption of trade controls, such as export subsidies and import surcharges, would be no economic improvement over capital controls and would be much more damaging to our foreign policy, because of the network of international rules which govern trade and which would be broken in the process.

As I understand it, the present proposal of the Secretary of Treasury is for some relaxation in all three of the present control programs but mainly affecting direct investment. The estimated gross cost to the balance of payments is about $400 million. The relaxation would come against an agreed projection of significant deterioration—at least $1 billion and possibly more—in our payments position in 1969. This first step will raise the problems outlined above to only a minor extent, but I recommend that you not commit yourself irrevocably to the abolition of investment restraints until a clear alternative is in sight.

---

13.   Memorandum From C. Fred Bergsten of the National Security Council Staff to the President's Assistant for National Security Affairs (Kissinger)[1]

Washington, March 24, 1969.

SUBJECT

German Offset Problem

Problem

The German offset problem arises because of the effects on the U.S. balance of payments of our military expenditures in Germany, which are approaching $1 billion per year. The Administration must negotiate a "good agreement" or risk: (a) heightened Congressional pressure for troop withdrawals, and (b) an increased balance of payments deficit

---

[1] Source: National Archives, Nixon Presidential Materials, NSC Files, Country Files–Europe, Box 681, Germany, Volume I, through 4/69. Secret. An attached memorandum from Kissinger to the President, undated, entitled "Preliminary U.S. Position on German Offset Problem," refers to an "attached" memorandum from Secretaries Rogers and Kennedy and Under Secretary Packard (not found) proposing "that you authorize Under Secretary Volcker to take a 'hard' line on the offset question during a visit to Bonn next week for exploratory talks on a wide range of monetary issues." No record has been found that the memorandum went to the President or that he acted on its recommendations.

which under the present international monetary system can cause us serious economic and foreign policy problems. Treasury, with Defense and State not far behind, wants to meet these problems by requiring Germany to spend in the U.S. roughly equivalent amounts of money, linked as closely as possible to military items (purchases of U.S. military equipment, training of German military personnel in the U.S., support costs for U.S. military expenditures in Germany, etc.).

The real issue is what constitutes a "good agreement" and to what end we should use the leverage with the Germans provided by our military position. The German Cabinet has decided to offer a package, for two years, which will offset about 75 percent (about $700 million annually) of our expenditures. It would include $350 million of military procurement, about $70 million of non-military procurement, and about $300 million of loans of various types. It is probable that most of the non-military procurement and some of the loans would occur independent of the offset arrangement, i.e. the U.S. would get no *additional* balance of payments benefits from them. Some of the military procurement would occur anyway too, but military purchases are conventionally accepted as true offsets and hence meet our domestic political problem.

Background

The previous Administration adopted a progressively tougher line with Germany on the offset. U.S. troop levels in the FRG were linked explicitly to German commitments to fully offset the resultant costs to our balance of payments. Accepted methods for achieving the offset evolved:

—From military purchases which Germany would have made anyway, and which thus provided no additional real help for our balance of payments.
—Through purchases of U.S. Treasury bonds which caused the Germans some pain, though not much because of the huge payments surpluses they were running, and which helped our balance of payments statistically but were criticized by many as only "postponing the problem".
—To commencement of efforts to get Germany to pick up a large part (perhaps $400 million annually) of our own expenditures in the FRG, which would clearly help our balance of payments but are seen by the Germans as politically indefensible support costs reminiscent of the occupation.

In addition, in 1967 Germany fully committed itself not to buy gold from the United States. This has no impact on our balance of payments statistics, but is by far the most important part of the "offset" package. It means that Germany, despite its huge and persistent payments surpluses, will put no pressure on U.S. reserves and thus reduces sharply the constraints generated by our payments deficits. There is no evidence of serious German unhappiness with this part of the package.

Our offset talks with Germany have proceeded largely independent of our over-all international monetary policy. In the latter context, we have pressured the Germans to eliminate their surpluses—most recently at the crisis conference in November when we took the unprecedented step of explicitly urging them to upvalue their currency.[2] We have given no indication to Bonn that cooperation on over-all monetary policy would affect our position on the offset.

Alternatives:

1. The U.S. could continue to link troop levels to offset expenditures in the U.S.:

(a) Achieved only through "real" devices such as additional military purchases and payment of support costs; or
(b) Achieved in large part through loans, i.e., accept the present German offer, or seek to harden it only marginally.

Pros

—Especially if via (a), would undercut Congressional efforts to use balance of payments arguments to force troop withdrawals.
—Would provide significant help for our balance of payments which is, of course, a continuing problem.

Cons (each much more serious if via (a))

—Could further erode German confidence in our security commitment.
—Could lead to eventual troop withdrawals since FRG unlikely to meet U.S. demands indefinitely.
—Could cause FRG at some point to renege on gold commitment, which could seriously jeopardize U.S. financial position and hence produce, inter alia, massive domestic pressure here for troop withdrawals if Germany actually began to buy U.S. gold.

2. The U.S. could drop completely the link between troop levels and balance of payments effects.

Pros

—Major payoff in relations with Germany (and perhaps some with rest of NATO).
—Major restoration of credibility of U.S. security commitment (included in Soviet perception).

Cons

—Would invite massive Congressional pressure for troop withdrawals.

---

[2] Reference is to the G-10 meeting in Bonn in November 1968; see *Foreign Relations, 1964–1968,* vol. VIII, Documents 214–220.

—Would completely ignore our international monetary problems.

—As a result, and especially if we move toward elimination of our present capital controls, would generate widespread views that U.S. no longer cared about its balance of payments and hence could touch off a major financial crisis.

—Would simply give away a major U.S. negotiating lever.

3. The U.S. could substitute for the explicit link between troop levels and German offset expenditures a request for sharply accelerated over-all German cooperation on international monetary matters, particularly agreement to:

(a) *Press actively* for early and sizeable activation of SDRs.
(b) Initiate meaningful studies of ways to improve the adjustment process including greater flexibility of exchange rates.
(c) Continuation of the gold commitment; and
(d) Possibly upvaluation of the DM after the elections in October.

Pros

—Would increase credibility of our security commitment.

—Should improve our over-all relations with FRG.

—Could produce a major breakthrough in improving the international monetary system.

—Would use our leverage with FRG in most profitable way.

—Would avoid any budgetary requirements of the Germans.

Cons

—Requires educational effort with Congress to avoid renewed pressure for troop pullbacks.

—Risks inadequate German performance on over-all monetary policy and hence possibility of future serious bilateral problems.

Recommendation:

That we:

(a) Accept the German package *for one year only;*
(b) Indicate to them that for the future we will drop our insistence on military offsets per se if they provide satisfactory cooperation on over-all international monetary matters.

Germany is unlikely to accept "real" offsets to our military expenditures unless we commit ourselves to a fixed level of forces in Germany for several years and/or the President makes it his top priority requirement. If he were to do so, the credibility of our security commitment and political relations with Germany would suffer enormously.

Further loans would neither allay our domestic pressures for the longer run nor really get us very much help on the monetary front.

Complete abandonment of the issue gives away a major U.S. bargaining lever and risks major financial difficulty. We should thus change our offset policy to (a) reduce the political and security problems caused by demands for support costs and (b) to pursue positively our major international monetary objectives. These objectives are (a) assurance of sufficient international liquidity via Special Drawing Rights; (b) improvements in the adjustment process, probably including greater flexibility of exchange rates; and (c) restoration of stability in the exchange markets which will require an upvaluation of the DM. Active cooperation by Germany on each of these issues—on upvaluation after their election in October—is a necessary component of a satisfactory approach. It will be difficult to move the bureaucracy quickly in this direction but the potential gains in both political and economic terms are well worth it.

Because it will take up to a year to monitor German performance and to educate the American public on this approach, we should inform Germany at once of these changes in our position for the future, but accept their package for this year as a transitional device. (If they want to soften their package as a result, we should be willing to consider so doing.)

14. Telegram From the Embassy in Italy to the Department of State[1]

Rome, March 26, 1969, 2010Z.

1803. Pass Treasury for Secretary Kennedy and Petty from Volcker. Subject: Summary of European reaction to relaxation of capital controls.

I have now completed consultations with all countries visited re proposed relaxation of capital controls. At my instruction, McGrew also consulted Larre of French Treasury in Paris.[2] This will summarize reactions and my conclusions:

1. Major countries (Germany, France, Italy) expressed least concern, all noting desirability in principle of relying on less controls and recognizing value of clear signal to that effect. Italian Treasury Minister Colombo and Blessing nonetheless specifically noted adverse impact on balance of payments would make SDR activation more difficult and weaken U.S. bargaining position in other respects.

2. Swedes expressed their concern most forcibly and openly, against background of full support for basic U.S. position re SDRs and other matters.

3. Dutch, Belgians and Swiss in varying degrees counseled caution and delay pending clear signs of balance of payments improvement, particularly in trade accounts. Impression left was that we will be reminded of "premature" easing during future bargaining on monetary reform if overall balance of payments fails to improve.

4. These reactions were received in context of my presentation that strongly emphasized: (1) value of "concrete" move to signify long-term objective to minimize reliance on controls, (2) "limited" and "prudent" nature of move, (3) decision to retain basic control apparatus for time being and to request renewal of IET authority, and (4) possible value of affirming in this way commitment to liberal trade and payments at a time when protectionist pressures are rising world wide.

5. My conclusion is that we should go ahead on agreed basis against background of strongest possible stance re monetary and fiscal restraint. Announcement should be related to surtax announcement and presidential endorsement of spending restraint. Timing and nature of future moves should be left vague. It seems to me essential that President request renewal of IET authority to avoid any impression of "recklessness" or implication that controls will be entirely dismantled at an early date. Statement should clearly recognize that U.S. accepts, as corollary of relaxation of controls, additional burden on monetary and fiscal policies as basic tools for dealing with balance of payments.

6. Alternative approach would be to forego inclusion of Federal Reserve program in package at this time. This would certainly ease European concerns over possible balance of payments impact. However, I do not feel this compromise approach essential in light of reactions received. European attitudes do confirm, however, that proposed actions, while useful, do carry some risk of weakening our bargaining position.

Ackley

15.   Memorandum From Secretary of the Treasury Kennedy to
       President Nixon[1]

Washington, April 1, 1969.

SUBJECT

Relaxation of Balance-of-Payments Controls

It is important that this Administration signal at an early date and in a concrete way its intention to reverse the trend toward controls and restrictions on international payments. To that end, we propose a limited but significant relaxation of the present controls on capital movements.

This recommendation is being made following a series of consultations just undertaken in Western Europe by my Under Secretary for Monetary Affairs, Paul Volcker. The reactions he received ranged from unenthusiastic to cautionary.[2] It was particularly pointed out that these proposed steps will not make things any easier on an early and sizeable activation of the Special Drawing Rights. This reaction was anticipated, and emphasizes the necessity in European eyes for accompanying relaxation of controls with evidence of restrictive monetary and fiscal policies. European reservations are not, however, a compelling reason for delay.

I am joined in this recommendation by Secretary Rogers, Secretary Stans, Chairman Martin, Chairman McCracken, and Director Mayo.

In making this recommendation, we are running a risk in terms both of weakening our balance-of-payments position this year and of adverse reactions abroad. In particular, we are proposing this relaxation in face of staff projections of a substantial balance-of-payments deficit in 1969 on the liquidity basis and the absence of evidence that the deterioration in our trade accounts has yet been reversed. In fact, a February trade deficit has just been announced.

The more widely used definition of our balance of payments, the so-called liquidity measure, showed a small surplus of $158 million in 1968. However, this surplus was achieved only by virtue of an unprecedented inflow of private capital stimulated by controls, tight money, and the attraction of our stock market. In addition, there was an element of "statistical window-dressing" (mainly foreign governments' buying

---

[1] Source: Washington National Records Center, Department of the Treasury, Office of the Assistant Secretary for International Affairs: FRC 56 76 108, Studies and Reports, Volume 7, 2/68–11/69. Confidential. An earlier draft of the memorandum had been discussed at a meeting on March 11; see Document 8.

[2] See Document 14.

medium-term securities at our behest rather than investing in short-term Treasury bills and time deposits). The less familiar official settlements measure (not ordinarily affected by our "window-dressing") showed a substantial surplus of $1,600 million.

The first quarter of 1969 will show a very large deficit on the familiar liquidity basis. The official settlements measure, on the other hand, will show a surplus—still reflecting our tight monetary policy.

Attachment A[3] tells the story for 1968, and shows the 1969 forecast of a further deficit of around $3 billion on the liquidity measure. The official settlements outcome is more difficult to forecast but it is not likely to be so bad. While balance-of-payments forecasts have particularly wide margins of error, there is good reason to believe that deterioration in the capital accounts will more than offset an anticipated gradual increase in the trade surplus later this year.

These projections make no allowance for the relaxations we are proposing. Potentially, these relaxations could add almost $1 billion to the deficit. However, we would expect the net cost to be considerably less—perhaps no more than $500 to $600 million—if money remains tight in the U.S.

Aggravation of the already difficult balance-of-payments problem carries important economic and political risks. The result could be to intensify pressures for maintenance of restrictive monetary policies to protect the balance of payments, even if that would be less appropriate than at present in terms of the domestic economy.

A further danger is psychological. Some financial officials abroad view the action as premature, and may reduce their willingness to cooperate with the U.S. in other areas. In particular, it will make more difficult our objective of obtaining an early activation, in appropriate size, of SDR's. Moreover, we must guard against any lessening of the sense of urgency in the U.S. about dealing with the balance-of-payments problem, including efforts to economize on net government spending abroad.

On balance, we think these risks are acceptable. The main advantage is to indicate, early in your Administration, a firm intent to reject "creeping restrictionism" as an answer to our problems; also to demonstrate that the philosophy of achieving solutions consistent with market forces should carry over into the trade area.

The potential losses entailed, while significant, may not themselves be the critical margin in the viability of the present monetary

---

[3] Not printed. Attachment A gives the balance-of-payments result for 1968 and the projection for 1969. The projection for the liquidity deficit in 1969 was $3 billion compared to an actual deficit of $1.1 billion in 1968.

system. Properly presented, the moves proposed should suggest confidence and prudence, rather than a willingness to throw caution to the winds.

To maximize the benefits with minimal risk, it is essential that this relaxation be accompanied by an expression of your broad balance-of-payments strategy and objectives. Therefore, we propose an announcement along the lines of Attachment B.[4]

This announcement would express your determination to create over time a viable balance-of-payments picture *without* a mass of controls, reversing the restrictionist trend of the past. But it would also highlight the actions you are taking to strengthen our economy and the dollar, to develop an effective export program, and to work toward monetary reforms.

The question of whether this action now implies that a second installment, and maybe a third installment, is due at a predictable time in the future is one upon which we believe judgment should be reserved. Developments in our domestic economy later on this year, for example, may raise a serious risk of a substantial capital outflow if our Interest Equalization Tax is down too low. We would contemplate that the Interest Equalization Tax could be utilized in a flexible manner in the future. However, any relaxation in the Commerce or Federal Reserve programs should be considered as a decision that would be very difficult to reverse in the future.

A. The Direct Investment Program

A modest relaxation of the mandatory Direct Investment Program can be undertaken and we concur in the proposal of Secretary Stans which would involve raising the ceiling $400 million to $3.35 billion.

Two key features are part of this proposal:

(a) Raise the minimum investment allowable for each company from $300,000 to $1 million

—recommended by industry
—substantially eases administrative burden
—substantially reduces number of companies involved in detailed reporting by about 60%
—helps LDCs as well as other areas.

(b) Raise the alternative earnings base from 20 to 30 percent (giving the companies a more meaningful option in selecting a reference base)

---

[4] Not found. Attached is the actual statement as released on April 4; see footnote 5, Document 16. An attached April 10 memorandum to the files by Philip P. Schaffner, Director of the Office of Balance of Payments Programs, Operations and Statistics, indicates that the April 4 text was drafted in the White House "using Treasury's draft."

—strongly recommended by industry
—introduces more "equity" in the arbitrary base period
—assists foreign debt servicing through retained foreign earnings.

It is important to note that OFDI's chance of not exceeding the $3.35 billion ceiling rests on the companies' carrying forward about $2 billion of unused investment quotas from 1969 to 1970. There is a good chance of this happening only if present tight U.S. monetary policy is continued.

Some thought has been given to raising the ceiling $600 million, rather than $400 million. This would be done by raising the alternative base percentage from 20 to 35 percent. However, this would only benefit about 25 additional companies, and $200 million seems to be too expensive for such a small return.

Beyond this immediate announcement, we are studying additional ways to simplify the Commerce program.

B. The Federal Reserve Program

Chairman Martin advises that the Board of Governors recommends that the Federal Reserve guidelines for restraints on credits to foreigners be modified to reduce the inequities in the position of many of the smaller banks and to give some additional room for export financing. First, the Board would increase the ceiling for bank lending to foreigners by about $400 million. The room for expanding such lending would actually be about double that amount since banks are presently about a half billion dollars below the aggregate ceilings. Virtually all of the increase would be available to the small banks. Second, the Board would also lift the limit on loans by non-bank financial institutions, such as insurance companies, by about $40 million. Banks and non-bank financial institutions would be asked to continue to give top priority to credits to finance U.S. exports.

The Board believes the proposed increase in lending limits takes account of the Commerce direct investment controls, to which the credit restraints are closely related, and would, in fact, lead to no more than a modest outflow of bank credits this year, under prevailing monetary conditions.

C. The Interest Equalization Tax

Reduction of the IET rate by 1/2 percent from its present 1-1/4 percent to 3/4 percent could be undertaken now without risk of a substantial outflow. A smaller reduction would carry the risk of being termed "tokenism." A larger cut would run counter to the philosophy of gradualism, which must be employed in phasing out these controls, and would sharply increase the risk of an accelerated outflow of United

States funds to acquire issues previously placed abroad by American corporations. If this occurred, the IET rate would need to be raised again quickly, and this would reflect on our judgment in reducing the rate too far in the first instance.

The IET expires in July and responsible business groups concur that the legislation should be extended. It is important that we have this tax authority available (with the option of increasing the rate) for the time when our domestic situation might call for an easing of monetary policy. The IET also serves to reinforce both the Commerce and the Federal Reserve programs.

Recommendations:[5]

(1) That you approve the $400 million ceiling increase in the Direct Investment Program.

(2) That you approve lowering the IET 1/2 percent, down to 3/4 percent.

(3) That we seek an extension of the IET, past its July expiry. Particulars of the extension can be considered in the near future.

(4) This announcement should be made on Friday, April 4. It would be desirable for market reasons, if the announcement could occur *after* the Stock Exchange closes at 2 p.m.

(5) That the announcement of the relaxation be part of a balance-of-payments strategy message.

(6) That the message take the *form* and *strategy* of Attachment B (draft message).

David M. Kennedy

---

[5] There is no indication of President Nixon's approval or disapproval of the recommendations. See also Document 16.

16.   **Action Memorandum From C. Fred Bergsten of the National Security Council Staff to the President's Assistant for National Security Affairs (Kissinger)**[1]

Washington, April 1, 1969.

SUBJECT

- Relaxation of Balance of Payments Controls

The attached memorandum from Secretary Kennedy recommends that the President announce shortly the modest relaxation of all three aspects of our controls over private capital outflows already decided.[2] The recommendation is agreed to by Secretaries Rogers and Stans, Chairman Martin, Paul McCracken, and Bob Mayo.

I recommend that you support the recommendation, although it carries significant foreign policy (and domestic economic) risks as outlined in the memo itself and conveyed to you in my earlier memos. There are, however, two specific problems of concern to us, one relating specifically to our new emphasis on consultations and one relating to the decision-making process.

This recommendation was delayed for two weeks to permit Treasury Under Secretary Volcker to consult with the Europeans on it.[3] None of the Europeans oppose the move outright, but virtually all of them were highly cautionary. They indicated that any resultant increase in the U.S. payments deficit would weaken our over-all bargaining position, particularly with regard to early and sizeable activation of Special Drawing Rights. The major implication of this conclusion is that our preferred multilateral approach to monetary reform is now less likely to succeed, and we may be forced to take unilateral steps which could be seriously disruptive to the entire Atlantic Alliance.

Since we do not plan to reduce the pressure on the Europeans to move ahead on SDRs—and on much more "radical" reforms—the question of our sincerity in undertaking consultations will arise at some point in the near future. We gave them a chance to record their views and they did so. Our future action may well imply that we have ignored those views. I flag this as an early case of the obvious problem that the new emphasis on consultation will create.

---

[1] Source: National Archives, Nixon Presidential Materials, NSC Files, Subject Files, Box 309, BOP. Confidential.

[2] See Document 15.

[3] See Document 14.

On decision making, this is a prototype case of unsatisfactory ad hoccery. The President is being asked to enunciate his over-all international monetary policy without ever considering that policy. He has been given no choices, nor even a paper on the over-all subject. In retrospect, the decision to lift the subject from the NSC agenda was a mistake[4]—since the Secretary of Treasury has not exercised the responsibility which he sought and received.

This factor does not lead me to recommend your opposing the proposed action, since the President has made known his strong desire to begin relaxing the controls as soon as possible. But I suggest that you remind the President that he is being asked to do something without consideration of its context and without systematic exploration of its full implications, and recommend that he instruct the Secretary of Treasury to present an options paper for his consideration in the near future.

Recommendation:

That you sign the attached memorandum to the President, recommending that he:

(1) Approve the proposed relaxation of controls.
(2) Do so between 2 P.M. Thursday and 11 A.M. Saturday for market reasons.[5]
(3) Instruct Secretary Kennedy to prepare an options paper on our international monetary policy with a meeting to take place on it at an early date.[6]

---

[4] The meeting had been scheduled for February 26. See footnote 4, Document 3.

[5] April 3–5. The President released a balance-of-payments statement at Key Biscayne, Florida on April 4. See *Public Papers of the Presidents of the United States: Richard Nixon, 1969*, pp. 265–267.

[6] Possibly a reference to the Treasury Department's Basic Options paper prepared for the meeting with the President on June 26; see Document 130. On April 11 Kissinger sent the President a memorandum entitled "Relaxation of Balance of Payments Controls," repeating his support for the President's limited action despite certain foreign policy risks. Kissinger noted, however, that because of Secretary Kennedy's reluctance to have the matter referred to the NSC the President had, in effect, been asked to make his balance-of-payments strategy statement without an opportunity to address the subject systematically and in context. Kissinger recommended the President ask Secretary Kennedy to prepare a memorandum outlining options in the balance-of-payments and international financial area and attached a memorandum for the President's signature so instructing Secretary Kennedy. The President initialed the memorandum for Secretary Kennedy on April 15 requesting a paper on "what my choices are" with respect to international monetary policy, "a paper which will permit me systematically to look at the available options." (National Archives, Nixon Presidential Materials, NSC Files, Subject Files, Box 309, BOP)

17.   Memorandum From the Director of the Office of Industrial
        Nations, Department of the Treasury (Widman) to Secretary
        of the Treasury Kennedy[1]

Washington, April 3, 1969.

SUBJECT

Briefing for your Meeting with Minister Fukuda in Sydney

Date and Time: Thursday, April 11, 1969, about noon

Persons Expected to Attend:

Japan: Takeo Fukuda, Minister of Finance
        Yusuke Kashiwagi, Vice Minister of
        Finance for International Affairs

United States: Secretary Kennedy
        Assistant Secretary Petty
        Ralph Hirschtritt

I. Background

Your meeting with Minister Fukuda should take place against the
background of increasing dissatisfaction with the current status of the
U.S.-Japanese partnership arrangement. Japan is demanding the
reversion of Okinawa and we in Treasury at least are becoming
increasingly concerned with the trade and financial relationships. We
had a bilateral balance of payments deficit with Japan last year of
more than a billion dollars—including $1.1 billion on trade. The best
forecasts that our people can produce show this trade deficit likely to
rise to a range of $3 to $3-1/2 billion within five years. Our gross military expenditures in Japan are approaching $600 million and the
Japanese spent less than $100 million here. I do not think the
American people will tolerate the development of a trade deficit such
as now appears to be in the cards nor do I see how the U.S. can
approach balance of payments equilibrium with such a deficit with
Japan.

The NSC mechanism is currently considering U.S. policy toward
Japan. We in Treasury have not been satisfied with the paper which is

---

[1] Source: Washington National Records Center, Department of the Treasury,
Secretary's Memos/Correspondence: FRC 56 74 7, Memoranda to the Secretary,
March–April, 1969. Secret. Sent through Petty and Volcker. Copies were sent to Volcker,
Colman, Jurich, Hirschtritt, and Cross.

before the Review Group.[2] There are attached at Tab A: (a) a talking paper prepared for Treasury spokesmen at the Review Group[3] and (b) a copy of a Treasury comment for dissent attached to the document.

Your conversation should also be against the background of the strong position taken by Secretary Fowler in meetings with Japanese Minister Mizuta last year. (See Tab B)[4] We insisted on balance of payments cooperation arrangements in 1968 which were negotiated by Mr. Petty under the direction of a Treasury–State–Defense steering group. These negotiations produced a package with a nominal value approaching $500 million although much of it was little more than window dressing. (See Tab B also.)

Minister Fukuda will probably not initiate any discussions on this subject but he will be alert to clues as to your attitude toward offset agreements.

Japan's great economic and financial strength is new and the Japanese themselves are not yet accustomed to it. They consistently underestimate their strength. They may even express some worries about their balance of payments position this year, arguing that the expected slowdown in the U.S. will cause a very drastic reduction in their exports. The thinking of Japanese leaders still tends to be very parochial and self-centered. Their concern is with appeasing their political opposition in Japan and neither the government itself nor the Japanese Diet has an adequate appreciation for the influence of economic developments in Japan on the rest of the world. They want to be treated by the U.S. as an equal partner but also to continue to receive the special benefits that a guardian might bestow upon his ward. Anything which appears on the horizon as a possible threat to the Japanese commercial or financial position is likely to bring a highly emotional reaction. Consequently, it is difficult to get the Japanese to assume responsibilities and costs commensurate with their current and prospective economic strength.

II. What Minister Fukuda will Want

We might expect Minister Fukuda to ask the following:

a. Early Congressional action on ADB special funds—Tab C[5]

b. A comprehensive report on U.S. discussions with other industrial countries on the various issues involved in improving the international monetary system—SDR's, greater flexibility in exchange rates,

---

[2] Reference is to NSSM 5; see Document 20.

[3] Not printed.

[4] Not printed. See *Foreign Relations, 1964–1968,* vol. VIII, Document 179.

[5] Tabs C–J are not printed.

realignment of rates, and treatment of South African gold. For political reasons Fukuda must be able to say that Japan is intimately involved in all of these discussions—Tab D

c. U.S. support for an increase in Japan's IMF quota—Tab E

d. A reassurance that the U.S. will not increase the price of gold.

e. A substantial purchase of gold from the U.S. in the near future—Tab F

f. Assurances that the U.S. will see to it that Japan gets the right to purchase new gold production for monetary reserves if European central banks are allowed to do so—Tab F

g. A continuation of Japan's IET exemption—Tab G

h. That the U.S. forego restrictions on trade, the imposition of any border tax and make no arrangements to restrain exports of textiles to the U.S.—Tab H

Recommended positions on these questions may be found at the tabs indicated.

III. Areas in which you might wish to take an Initiative

a. Japanese ratification of SDR and support for early activation in a substantial amount—Tab I

b. Japanese leadership in support of the ADB—Tab C

c. Balance of payments cooperation (actions to offset U.S. military expenditures in Japan)—Tab J

d. Increased Japanese efforts toward trade liberalization—Tab H[6]

IV. General Comments

You probably will also wish to chat with Minister Fukuda about the forthcoming meeting of the U.S.-Japan Cabinet Committee on Trade and Economic Affairs. We do not as yet have any information on a specific date although the meeting is expected to take place in Japan in July.

Many of the foregoing issues can only be touched upon in your meeting with Minister Fukuda. Mr. Petty hopes to arrange a meeting with Vice Minister Kashiwagi which could go into more detail and cover points omitted.

---

[6] Under Secretary Volcker added point d by hand.

Tab A[7]

Washington, March 24, 1969.

TREASURY COMMENT

NSSM ON JAPAN

The Treasury believes that this paper does not give adequate attention to the relative sharing of costs and benefits of the U.S.-Japanese partnership and incorrectly assesses the trends as "increasingly valuable" to the United States. It is the Treasury view that Japan is not carrying an equitable share of the financial burden of the partnership, either budgetary or balance of payments. Furthermore, the inequity appears to be growing rather than diminishing. Unless we are able to reverse this trend and demonstrate that Japan is moving promptly and steadily to assume a greater share of these financial responsibilities, we must expect Congressional and public pressures for trade restrictions and the growth of anti-Japanese sentiment within the United States. The ability to reach an accommodation with Japan on the burden sharing question may be crucial to the continuation of the present partnership.

The scheduled meeting between President Nixon and Prime Minister Sato provides an opportunity for substantial progress in bringing about an equitable sharing of costs and benefits.[8] We believe that the United States should not underestimate what Japan is willing to pay for the reversion of Okinawa. We believe, furthermore, that U.S. balance of payments and trade goals should be given a high priority in the quid pro quos we should seek for concessions on Okinawa.

The Treasury feels that NSSM-5 does not focus sharply enough on the question of priorities among U.S. goals and that to the extent that it does touch on this question insufficient weight is given to the need for large-scale contributions by Japan toward equilibrium in the U.S. balance of payments. Loss of world confidence in the dollar would be a disastrous blow to the security of the free world as well as to the world's economic health and progress and the prestige of the United States. Preservation of confidence in the dollar requiring the elimination of our balance of payments deficit should be considered in that context, along with the level of forces in Japan or nuclear storage rights in Okinawa or Japanese aid for other countries in Asia.

---

[7] Confidential.

[8] In the opening days of the Nixon administration, arrangements were agreed in principle for Prime Minister Sato to pay a State visit to Washington in November at dates to be agreed on.

Throughout the paper there is a tendency to assume that the balance of payments problems will be solved "in a global context" making it unnecessary to look to bilateral actions by Japan as a major contribution to this problem. While the Treasury agrees that a multilateral agreement of some type may be necessary before the U.S. restores a sustainable payments equilibrium, we remain convinced that Japan, along with Germany and other major surplus countries, must bear a very substantial part of the required payments adjustment and that bilateral actions, particularly involving the military accounts, will be necessary.

For two years the U.S. has had overall bilateral payments deficits with Japan of almost $1 billion annually. With no other country have we had deficits which even approach this magnitude. The major deficit elements are our military expenditures, now approaching $600 million annually, and a trade deficit which reached $1.1 billion in 1968. Our latest projections indicate that unless special action is taken, our trade deficit with Japan may climb to $3 billion or more in five years. We cannot tolerate such a development—either politically or in terms of maintaining dollar confidence. We cannot rely on the "hope" (as this document recommends) that the Japanese will assume their fair share of the costs, but should make clear to them at the highest level that a major redistribution is necessary if the partnership is to remain viable. We should, furthermore, assign high priority to this objective in our negotiations with Japan on specific issues.

---

18. Editorial Note

The National Security Council, in its meeting on April 8, 1969, discussed the North Atlantic Treaty Organization and possible negotiations on the German offset problem. The State Department's position for the NSC meeting was set forth in an April 7 memorandum from Assistant Secretary of State for European Affairs Hillenbrand to Secretary Rogers. (National Archives, RG 59, S/S Files: Lot 71 D 175, April 8 NSC Mtg) National Security Decision Memorandum (NSDM) 12, dated April 14, recorded the President's decisions at the NSC meeting on REDCOSTE and the German offset. Concerning the German offset negotiations, NSDM 12 reads:

"We should proceed with offset negotiations, for this year, taking fully into account their possible impact on the political situation in the

Federal Republic of Germany. The subject of support costs should not be raised and we should not seek any substantial increase in the currently anticipated level of German military procurement and should not press the issue to the point of risking a possible row with the FRG. At the same time, we should seek to improve the value to us of other measures to be included in the package. We should indicate to the Germans our willingness to explore a broadening of the discussion in future years to include discussions of monetary cooperation in general.

"As this year's negotiations proceed, the President will wish to re-examine the package being negotiated to determine if we should move the offset negotiations into a broader monetary context in the present round." (Ibid., S/S Files: Lot 83 D 305, NSDM 12)

---

19. Information Memorandum From C. Fred Bergsten of the National Security Council Staff to the President's Assistant for National Security Affairs (Kissinger)[1]

Washington, April 14, 1969.

SUBJECT

The President's Expression of Foreign Policy Views at Cabinet Committee on Economic Policy

The President expressed a number of interesting foreign policy views at the April 10 meeting with his economic advisers.[2] Foreign economic policy topics dominated the overall discussion.

1. The President linked NATO and soybeans. He said that his support for NATO would be seriously jeopardized if the Europeans took restrictive action against U.S. exports because mid-western Congressmen, whom he can now control on security matters, would shift their views if European trade restrictions hurt them directly.

2. The President also said that the EEC "could forget U.S. political support" if it turned inward economically.

---

[1] Source: National Archives, Nixon Presidential Materials, NSC Files, Agency Files, Box 215, Council of Economic Advisers. Confidential.

[2] The Cabinet Committee on Economic Policy met in the Cabinet Room 4:19–6:02 p.m. Attendees were Agnew, Walker, Hardin, Stans, Shultz, Mayo, McCracken, Burns, Safire, Samuels, Moynihan, and Bergsten. (Ibid., White House Central Files, President's Daily Diary)

3. The President is prepared to take a hard look at the possibility of a major U.S. initiative regarding U.S.-European agricultural trade. He noted that we could do the Europeans "no greater favor" than to convey our farm policy experience to them in time to head off similar mistakes there. A task force chaired by CEA, of which I am a member, is developing proposals.

4. The President again expressed his great interest in East-West trade, essentially for political reasons. He specifically wants to look at the possibility of agricultural deals with Eastern Europe "in two or three months." The President instructed the CEA to prepare a study on the quantity of U.S. exports which might be involved in a trade liberalization package and to include Eastern Europe in their study of U.S. agricultural trade. I will coordinate these with our NSSM 35 exercise.[3]

5. The President suggested that Secretary Hardin might include one or two Eastern European countries on his forthcoming trip.

6. The President indicated that foreign economic policy should be discussed in the NSC for political considerations and the Cabinet Committee on Economic Policy for economic considerations. However he expressed the primacy of the political aspects of most foreign economic problems (reminding Treasury of his approach to the German offset!) and, on East-West trade, referred to "kicking the subject up to the NSC". (Paul McCracken had apparently raised this jurisdictional issue with the President.)

The course of the discussion fully justified my attendance at the meeting and I thanked McCracken for acceding to your request that I be able to attend.[4]

---

[3] NSSM 35, dated March 28, 1969, called for a study of "US Trade Policy Toward Communist Countries." (Ibid., RG 59, S/S Files: Lot 80 D 212, NSSM 35)

[4] Neither the Department of State nor the NSC were members of the Cabinet Committee on Economic Policy.

20.   **Editorial Note**

In National Security Study Memorandum (NSSM) 5, dated January 21, 1969, Henry Kissinger informed the Secretaries of State, Defense, and Treasury, the Director of Central Intelligence, and the Chairman of the Joint Chiefs of Staff that the President had directed the NSC Interdepartmental Group for East Asia to prepare a study of alternative U.S. policies with regard to the full range of U.S.-Japanese issues. A Treasury representative was specifically designated to sit on the NSC Group for this study. (National Archives, RG 59, S/S Files: Lot 80 D 212, NSSM 5)

In response to NSSM 5, an undated paper prepared by the Interdepartmental Review Group for East Asia was transmitted under cover of an April 28 memorandum from Jeanne W. Davis of the NSC Secretariat to the Office of the Vice President, the Office of the Secretary of State, the Office of the Secretary of Defense, and the Office of the Director of Emergency Preparedness, with copies to the Under Secretary of State, the Chairman of the Joint Chiefs of Staff, and the Director of Central Intelligence. Davis' memorandum noted that revisions had been made pursuant to a discussion in the Review Group on April 25. Part V (pages 35–43) of the paper covered U.S.-Japan economic issues and identified key policy matters for the United States as "(1) trade, and (2) US balance of payments considerations, particularly the implication of US military expenditures in Japan." The NSSM 5 response paper and an "agreed summary paper" that Davis circulated to the same addressees on April 29 were intended for discussion at an April 30 NSC meeting. (Ibid.) The summary paper noted that the NSC meeting would "concentrate on Okinawa and other security issues" but it was recognized that trade, balance of payments, and aid policy issues were "an integral part of Japan policy and that they should be considered, particularly in developing a negotiating position on Okinawa." (Ibid.) See Document 17 for the Department of the Treasury's dissent from the economic approach being taken by the NSC Interdepartmental Group. That dissent was repeated in an April 25 memorandum from John C. Colman, Acting Assistant Secretary of the Treasury for International Affairs, and Anthony J. Jurich, Special Assistant to the Secretary of the Treasury, to the NSC Review Group on NSSM 5. (Attached to memorandum from Petty to Kennedy, May 5; Washington National Records Center, Department of the Treasury, Secretary's Memos/Correspondence: FRC 56 74 7, Memos to the Secretary, May–June 1969)

The National Security Council took up the NSSM 5 response paper during a 10:30 a.m.–12:11 p.m. meeting in the Cabinet Room on April 30. (National Archives, Nixon Presidential Materials, White House Central

Files, President's Daily Diary) Pursuant to the NSC meeting, on May 28 Kissinger sent National Security Decision Memorandum (NSDM) 13 to the Secretaries of State, Defense, and the Treasury and the Director of Central Intelligence setting out the President's decisions on U.S. policy toward Japan. NSDM 13 dealt primarily with defense/security/ Okinawa matters, but the first decision related to economic issues: "We shall basically pursue our current relationship with Japan as our major partner in Asia, seeking ways to improve this relationship from the viewpoint of U.S. national interests and to seek an increasingly larger Japanese role in Asia." (Ibid., RG 59, S/S Files: Lot 83 D 305, NSDM 13)

---

21. Memorandum From Secretary of the Treasury Kennedy to President Nixon[1]

Washington, May 13, 1969.

SUBJECT

The First Quarter Balance of Payments Results and Announcement

Later this week (probably on Thursday),[2] the regular announcement will be made of the balance of payments results for the first quarter. This will not be happy reading.

The measure most widely used by the press—the so-called "liquidity" balance—will be in deficit, seasonally adjusted, by $1.8 billion, or an annual rate of $7.2 billion. While the informed public and foreign officials are already aware that we had a sizeable deficit on this basis, the actual near-record figure will nonetheless be startling. It can only add to the already uncertain atmosphere in international financial markets.

Actually, the immediate situation is not nearly so bad as the "liquidity deficit" makes it look; moreover, the alternate measure of results ("official settlements") shows a very substantial surplus of $1.1 billion for the first quarter. This surplus reflects the strong performance of the

---

[1] Source: Washington National Records Center, Department of the Treasury, Deputy to the Assistant Secretary for International Affairs: FRC 56 83 26, Contingency Planning 1969. Confidential. A May 14 cover note from Petty's office to Willis indicates that distribution in the Treasury Department was limited to the Secretary, Under Secretaries Walker and Volcker, Petty, and Willis. There is no indication that this memorandum was forwarded to the President's attention, but the President was subsequently informed of the balance-of-payments results by McCracken; see Document 129.

[2] May 15.

dollar in the exchange markets and the fact that official dollar holdings of many European central banks got uncomfortably low—even before the recent exchange crisis.

Nevertheless, the liquidity deficit will make the headlines. The heavy dependence of the official settlements surplus upon short-term capital inflows related to the tight money conditions in the United States renders this performance more suspect.

Only technicians will fully unravel the confusions inherent in the different measures of our balance of payments. However, all sophisticated observers will recognize that the structure of our balance of payments is in poor shape. The major culprit is the long period of domestic inflation and excess demand, which has dwindled away our historic large trade surplus—averaging $4 to $6 billion in the first half of the 1960's—to a small deficit. Consequently, earnings on the trade account are simply not available to pay for the balance of payments costs of our aid and military commitments overseas, or for private foreign investment.

For the time being, the adverse impact of the shrinking trade balance has been largely offset by extraordinary capital inflows—long and short term. But we must recognize that certain capital inflows are quite subject to reflow. In looking ahead, we should be under no illusions about our ability to achieve and maintain a sustainable payments position without a sizeable positive trade balance.

Special Factors in the First Quarter

Two important factors contributed to the deterioration in the first quarter.

—U.S. corporations apparently placed an exceptionally large volume of funds abroad, either directly or through their foreign subsidiaries. This reversed the artificial pull-back of funds to the United States last December, when companies made sure they got under their direct investment quotas.

—In addition, the first quarter was almost free of so-called "special" official transactions, which also contributed heavily to the statistical liquidity surplus recorded in the fourth quarter of 1968. As a matter of policy, we have not pressed foreign countries to alter the form of their dollar holdings simply to "dress up" our statistics.

For these reasons, it is logical to average the last two quarters to arrive at a fairer estimate of the trend in the payments, as shown in the table attached.[3] While the six-month average shows a sizeable deficit on the liquidity basis, it does not show a basic deterioration. Moreover, the official

---

[3] Not printed. This short table gave balance-of-payments results for 6-month periods ending in March 1969, September 1969, March 1968, and September 1968.

settlements basis shows an improving trend—a fact that deserves more emphasis, even though we cannot forget it is highly subject to variation.

Outlook

A new Government staff review of the balance of payments outlook for this year points to a near-record deficit of about $4 billion on the liquidity basis, before allowing for any "Special Transactions". Estimates on the official settlements basis might show approximate balance for the year as a whole but it could also give way to a sizeable deficit.

While these projections point up the structural weaknesses in our balance of payments, our position could well be sustainable for some time, provided:

(1) Tight money in the United States retains the short-term capital inflow, and
(2) Progress in curbing inflation offers a firm prospect of future improvement in our trade balance. But neither the financial community nor foreign officials are likely to maintain optimism for long, unless progress is visible on the "fundamentals."

Meanwhile, we must live with the fact that the weakness in our balance of payments compromises our negotiating posture in the economic and the financial field generally. It does not provide a firm base for leadership in pushing for international monetary reform; in this sense, our payments performance is our own worst enemy.

Implications

The potentially unsettling consequences on the international exchange markets of our own balance of payments performance is further complicated by the release this week of poor trade figures by both the U.K. and France. The other side of the coin is the very strong performance by Germany, Japan, and Italy. (It is not entirely a coincidence that these countries carry relatively light defense burdens.) The refusal of the Germans to revalue in the face of the strongest kinds of market pressures—and the refusal of the Italians or Japanese to even consider revaluation—only points up the difficulty of redressing these basic imbalances in an orderly way.

Three implications seem to me perfectly clear:

(1) Progress on the side of controlling inflation and eliminating excess demand is as essential to maintain the strength of the dollar abroad as it is domestically. We *cannot* expect dramatic or quick results in terms of the trade balance, but signs of progress are essential to maintain confidence that we have the will and the ability to achieve eventual equilibrium.
(2) We must continue to work toward some *revaluation* of exchange rates by chronic surplus countries (at least by Germany). This would be

a necessary prelude to more thoroughgoing monetary reform. It would also be "preventive therapy" against the possibility of one-way *devaluation* by the French and British that would simply leave us and the monetary system worse off.

(3) At this stage, we are in no position to seek further important relaxation of our balance of payments measures, including defense offsets, investment controls, and aid tying.

Meanwhile, we will continue to work with other leading countries on "evolutionary" reforms—pushing the Special Drawing Rights in the IMF, actively exploring the feasibility of agreed changes toward more flexibility in exchange rates, and (subsequently and for the more distant future) considering the possibility of consolidating all reserve assets in the IMF.

However, we must also recognize that the events of recent weeks and our own balance of payments difficulties point out the political and economic roadblocks to orderly agreed change. We can anticipate the probability of further currency crises. Conceivably, such a crisis could be turned to a constructive purpose, and help accelerate the process of desired change. But a crisis atmosphere could also defeat the process of orderly change and cooperation by giving rise to uncoordinated, independent actions detrimental to our basic objectives in this area.

I am reviewing again our main alternatives in this difficult situation and will report to you shortly.

David M. Kennedy[4]

---

[4] Printed from a copy that indicates Kennedy signed the original.

22.   **Memorandum From the Chairman of the National Security Council Under Secretaries Committee (Richardson) to President Nixon**[1]

Washington, May 26, 1969.

SUBJECT

Report of the Under Secretaries Committee on REDCOSTE

The Under Secretaries Committee has completed its examination of the REDCOSTE proposals, which you directed (NSDM-12)[2] be examined by it, taking into account our desire not to undercut our efforts to get our Allies to increase their defense efforts and our desire not to reduce our combat capability.

The Committee concentrated on those items on which no agreement to proceed had been reached previously, as well as those items where agreement in principle existed but proceeding was dependent upon discussion with host countries (i.e., Turkey and Spain).

In addition, the Committee reaffirmed those REDCOSTE proposals previously agreed and approved the proposed implementing schedule.

On those proposals upon which inter-agency agreement was pending, the Committee agreed that we should proceed with some degree or form of implementation of all but one of the proposals examined. However, implementation of several of the proposals is conditional and subject to responses and reactions of our European Allies.

On the basis of our tentative conclusions, it is anticipated that those REDCOSTE proposals previously agreed, together with those recommended herein for approval, should permit a possible reduction of about 27,400 military, 1,800 US civilians, and 7,100 Foreign National personnel. It is expected that there will be annual budget savings (after FY 1972) of about $355 million and a saving of $128 million in the balance of payments.

However, these figures are dependent upon Allied agreement to take over certain tactical missions, (Hawk and Nike Battalions in

---

[1] Source: National Archives, RG 59, S/S Files: Lot 83 D 305, NSDM 12. Secret. Drafted by Colonel G. D. Overbey (EUR/RPM) on May 21 and concurred in by U. Alexis Johnson, Brigadier General Hampton (OSD/ISA), Major General Orwat (JCS), Springsteen (EUR), and Hartman (U). An earlier draft, prepared by the Interagency Working Group chaired by Under Secretary Johnson, was sent on May 14 by Staff Director Arthur A. Hartman to the Deputy Secretary of Defense, Kissinger, the Director of Central Intelligence, and the Chairman of the Joint Chiefs of Staff informing them it would be discussed at the Under Secretaries Committee meeting on Thursday, May 15. (Ibid.) On June 5 Kissinger sent Richardson a memorandum stating "the President has reviewed your memorandum and approves the recommendations." (Ibid., Lot 83 D 276, NSC–U/DM 9) A handwritten note at the top of the memorandum printed here indicates that the President approved.

[2] See Document 18.

Germany and Sergeant Missiles in Italy) as well as Turkish assumption of certain facilities. If agreement is not obtained, the above figures will be reduced by about one-third.

Therefore, if fully implemented, we could achieve about 80% of the estimated 45,000 personnel reductions (32,000 military) and $429 million and $158 million savings in budget and balance of payments which the Secretary of Defense originally hoped to achieve. To have fully realized these projected savings would have meant a highly visible reduction of our forces in Europe, withdrawal of some NATO committed units (beyond those being offered to our Allies), and some degradation of combat capability, which might have been taken as a signal by our Allies of a lessened US interest in NATO.

With regard to the effect on the combat capability of US forces, it is our view that the cumulative impact of the REDCOSTE adjustments which the Committee agreed to make will not be significant. It is, of course, obvious that any reduction of this magnitude will have some impact upon military operations. However, the reductions have been effected essentially in the non-combat areas and every attempt will be made to minimize the impact upon combat capability. In this regard, General Goodpaster has been briefed, for his cognizance when he becomes SACEUR, on our conclusions and the magnitude and nature of the REDCOSTE proposals as well as the manner in which we propose to handle implementation with our NATO Allies.

In our scenario at Tab A[3] it will be noted that we intend to handle each measure as an individual and independent action. Consistent with this approach, we have agreed that the Government will not make an announcement, as has been the practice in the past, concerning the totality of the reduction to be made. In consonance with the guidance in NSDM-12 that the proposals not be handled as a package, we do not intend to make public nor inform our Allies about the total personnel to be eliminated or the total savings anticipated. However, we would tell NATO, at the Military Committee level, and the respective host countries concerned, about certain significant measures. Our approach would be in terms of the kinds of things we are doing to streamline and tighten up our military establishment in Europe, rather than in terms of the quantitative savings or reductions we expect to achieve.

Following are the REDCOSTE proposals examined by the Committee and its conclusions. (The summary sheets at Tab B,[4] describe the individual proposals and discuss the factors considered and anticipated savings and personnel reductions):

---

[3] Entitled "Scenario for Implementation"; not printed.

[4] Not printed.

1. *Proposal:* Reductions in US personnel and facilities in Spain.

Conclusion: Implementation should be contingent upon and be in context of the outcome of base negotiations with Spain.

2. *Proposal:* 60% reduction of US military personnel and dependents and facilities in Turkey.

Conclusion: We should continue to negotiate takeover of the facilities with the Turks, awaiting Turkish reactions before proceeding with implementation of the planned reductions or considering other options. (Other unilateral reduction proposals not related to or contingent upon the on-going negotiations could proceed.)

3. *Proposal:* Reduce US element of NATO staffs (19 headquarters) by 15%.

Conclusion: Any reduction in the manning of NATO staffs should be the result of normal personnel surveys and reviews rather than a unilateral decision to reduce the US element by 15%; this should be handled within the context of our efforts to share the defense burden with our Allies. However, the question of the level of US participation should be considered again in the context of Presidential decisions about the future level of US forces in Europe and attitude, in the long-term, toward NATO.

4. *Proposal:* Reduce Aviano Air Base, Italy, and relocate tactical unit in Italy.

Conclusion: Aviano should be retained in a fully operational status and the Quick Reaction Alert detachment not be relocated as proposed.

5. *Proposal:* Offer of 8 Air Defense Battalions (Hawk and Nike) to the Federal Republic of Germany; if they refuse offer, two Hawk Battalions would be withdrawn.

Conclusion: We should propose to the Federal Republic of Germany that they take over the 8 Air Defense Missile Battalions (4 Hawk and 4 Nike); the decision on whether to withdraw 2 Hawk Battalions if the Germans refuse to take them over would await German reaction and be re-examined again this summer in the context of the US response to the NATO Defense Planning Questionnaire (DPQ) for 1970 force commitments.

6. *Proposal:* Reduce activities at Athens International Airport and place facilities on stand-by basis.

Conclusion: The facility and support contingent at Athens should be retained in an operational status; an initial reduction should be made to a 1,100 personnel level; and a Department of Defense study should be made to ascertain whether further reductions should be undertaken while retaining the facility in an operative status.

7. *Proposal:* Reduce and relocate USAFE Headquarters, Germany; reduce two air bases.

Conclusion: (a) USAFE should be retained at Wiesbaden but reduced by 1,250 personnel; (b) the United States Air Force should attempt further Air Force reductions in the Wiesbaden area and elsewhere in Europe at once; (c) the question of retention at Wiesbaden should be considered again by the Department of Defense within the context of Presidential decisions to be made later this year concerning our long-term attitude toward NATO and the future level of our military presence in Europe; and (d) the matter of increase and acquisition of other air bases in Germany, previously included in this REDCOSTE proposal, should be examined in the context of the overall US European air base posture.

8. *Proposal:* Reduce SETAF (Southern European Task Force), withdrawing Army Sergeant Missile Unit from Italy; reduce Camp Darby Army Depot complex.

Conclusion: (a) *SETAF/Sergeant Missile Unit:* We should request the Italians to take over the Sergeant Missile Battalion; however, the decision on whether to withdraw the unit would be made in the light of the Italian reaction. In any event, substantial reductions, about 1,300 US and 600 Foreign National personnel, should be made by the Department of Defense by streamlining and consolidating SETAF Headquarters and support functions while continuing the essential peacetime functions. (b) *Camp Darby Army Depot Complex:* The Camp Darby Army Depot complex should remain operative and its essential functions continued, but it should be reduced by about 400 US and 900 Foreign National personnel to a level of about 800 personnel, by streamlining and consolidation, including modification, of support functions.

A scenario for implementation of REDCOSTE, covering proposals previously agreed and the foregoing proposals examined by the Committee, is at Tab A.

Individual summary sheets, describing in detail the REDCOSTE proposals which were considered on a case-by-case basis, issues involved and recommendations, are at Tab B.

ELR

23.   Editorial Note

Beginning in late April 1969 exchanges of visits and messages between Washington and Tokyo set the stage for the Okinawa reversion negotiations and Japanese Prime Minister Sato's November 19–21 visit to Washington. U.S. policymakers were determined to keep economic issues on the agenda, but no formal linkage to the Okinawa negotiation and its related nuclear issues was stated.

On April 26 the Embassy in Tokyo transmitted the text of a paper that Fumihiko Togo, Director of the America Bureau in the Foreign Ministry, would use in Washington during his consultations scheduled to begin April 28. On the economic issues Togo's paper stated: "The current duty of the Japanese government is to . . . aim at a rational approach to bilateral economic issues . . . and in keeping with the increase in Japan's national strength, to fulfill international obligations commensurate with Japan's status as the leading Asian developed country. . . . [Japan's] role should be to progressively assume international political responsibilities, and to contribute actively in the field of economic development." (Telegram 3311 from Tokyo; National Archives, Nixon Presidential Materials, NSC Files, Country Files–Far East, Box 533, Japan, Volume)

Regarding Foreign Minister Kiichi Aichi's visit to Washington in early June, the Embassy in Tokyo on May 22 reported that Aichi would be prepared to discuss economic aid and bilateral economic problems in the context of Togo's paper, which had no formal status but was an authoritative reflection of Prime Minister Sato's views. The Embassy further noted that Aichi and others were of the view that Secretary Stans (who had visited Japan in May) had seemed more interested in liberalization of capital and trade than in the textile problem. Aichi, Togo, and others agreed Japan should move ahead faster on liberalization but would have great difficulty in appearing to move away from liberalization with regard to textiles. Chargé Osborn reported that he told the Japanese officials that "Secretary Stans had not given us in the Embassy any impression of being anything but extremely earnest on textiles and quite serious in warning that alternative might be unilateral restrictive action." (Telegram 4060 from Tokyo; ibid.)

Further to Aichi's forthcoming visit, the Embassy on May 30 sent a cable reporting Aichi's plans to adhere to the approach in Togo's paper, but also indicating that Aichi would say "that Japan intends to assume greater share of own defense burden and to increase economic assistance to other Asian countries." Aichi reportedly would give Secretary Rogers separate papers outlining Japanese intentions on these two issues. The thrust of the economic paper was said to express "Japanese willingness to increase its overseas aid programs over the next ten years in proportion to the rate of increase in Japan's national income . . . [and] to operate through both multilateral (Asian Development Bank, Mekong Development Plan, ASEAN, Consortia, etc.) agencies and bilateral means to assist key countries in Asia (Korea, Taiwan, Cambodia, Laos, Viet-Nam, Indonesia and Thailand)." (Telegram 4325 from Tokyo; ibid.)

At the conclusion of his meeting with Foreign Minister Aichi on June 2, President Nixon noted they had been discussing Okinawa and trade and investment problems in a preliminary way and "asked Aichi to inform Sato that it would be in our interest to try to resolve these when he came to Washington." The President added that agreement would require additional, preliminary, hard work and that he looked to continuing discussions in Tokyo with U.S. Ambassador to Japan Armin Meyer, in whom the President had earlier told Aichi he had "every confidence;" with Secretary Rogers, who was to travel to Tokyo at the end of July; and with Japanese Ambassador Shimoda in Washington. A copy of the memorandum of conversation is ibid.

Secretaries Rogers and Stans traveled to Tokyo for the seventh meeting of the Joint Japan-U.S. Committee on Trade and Economic Affairs July 29–31. Secretary Rogers had separate meetings with Prime Minister Sato and Foreign Minister Aichi concerning Okinawa. He carried with him a July 22 letter from Nixon to Prime Minister Sato that read in part: "We consider the meetings of Cabinet representatives of our two governments to be a valuable means of reviewing the broad range of our economic activities and seeking ways in which to overcome obstacles to expansion of our large and growing trade and economic relations. . . . I look forward to seeing you in Washington later this year when we can review problem areas between us and decide how we can achieve further progress toward our common goals." (Ibid., RG 59, S/S Files: Lot 72 D 320, Japan: Nixon to Sato)

During the economic meetings the Japanese side declared its intention to expand substantially economic assistance, particularly for Asia, and to liberalize a considerable part of its remaining import quota restrictions by the end of 1971. The two sides exchanged views on the textile problem and Japan agreed to continue the discussion in September, without committing to any particular course of action. (Ibid., E/CBA/REP Files: Lot 70 D 467, *Current Economic Developments*, No. 837, August 5, 1969, pages 8–14)

On textiles President Nixon had approved, pursuant to a July 21 Decision Memorandum from Arthur Burns, a policy of attempting to limit growth of textile imports by negotiating comprehensive bilateral agreements with Japan, Korea, Taiwan, and Hong Kong (in order to avoid having to enlist European cooperation). (Ibid., Nixon Presidential Materials, NSC Files, Subject Files, Box 399, Textiles, Volume I) By contrast, in his cable to the Embassy in Tokyo reporting on his August 8 luncheon meeting with Japanese Ambassador Shimoda upon the latter's return from the July economic conference, Under Secretary U. Alexis Johnson reported that Shimoda said it would be easier for Japan to do something on textiles within the GATT framework than bilaterally. Responding to Shimoda's question about a connection between economic issues and Okinawa, Johnson said "that while matters were, of course, separate and we would continue to deal with them separately there was no getting around fact that Japan's 'image' here, and especially in the Congress, was much affected by Japan's posture on economic matters and, accordingly, this influenced attitudes in Congress on Okinawa." (Telegram 133630 to Tokyo, August 9; ibid., Country Files–Far East, Box 533, Japan, Volume I)

In drafting the joint communiqué for the November 19–21 meetings between President Nixon and Prime Minister Sato in Washington, the Japanese side sought to have it deal only with Okinawa while the U.S. side thought other items on the agenda, including trade, foreign assistance, and textiles, should be included. An exchange of cables between the Department of State and the Embassy in Tokyo regarding the communiqué language is ibid., Box 534, Japan, Volume II, 10/69–6/70. The joint statement issued on November 21 has Okinawa as its primary focus, but also dealt with other matters, including trade liberalization and foreign assistance. For text, see *Public Papers of the Presidents of the United States: Richard M. Nixon, 1969*, pages 953–957. The communiqué did not mention textiles, however, despite Japan's agreement to hold secret bilateral talks as a precursor to efforts to negotiate a multilateral agreement. Prime Minister Sato had "stressed it would put his government in a very difficult position if it became public knowledge that bilateral talks had been going on between U.S. and Japan before multilateral talks got underway." (Telegram 9407 from Tokyo, November 12; National Archives, Nixon Presidential Materials, NSC Files, Country Files–Far East, Box 534, Japan, Volume II 10/69–6/70)

24.   Editorial Note

In the Spring of 1969 the NSC Under Secretaries Committee, pursuant to NSDM 12, coordinated and monitored the Nixon administration's preparations for negotiations with Germany on the offset question. Meetings of U.S. and German experts were held in Washington on May 13 and 14 and in Bonn on May 20 and 21. Concerning the earlier meetings, Helmut Sonnenfeldt sent Henry Kissinger a May 20 memorandum reporting on his luncheon meeting with German Ambassador Pauls that day. According to Sonnenfeldt, Pauls said "the Germans had been baffled" by some U.S. positions which seemed to be related to German performance on currency matters and a possible link between Mark revaluation and an offset settlement. (National Archives, Nixon Presidential Materials, NSC Files, Country Files–Europe, Box 681, Germany, Volume II, 4–6/69) In a May 22 memorandum, Kissinger asked Bergsten and Sonnenfeldt to look further into matter, saying "one thing we *must* avoid is any arm-twisting of the Germans." (Ibid.)

In preparation for the next round of negotiations in Bonn on June 2 and 3, on May 23 Assistant Secretary of State for European Affairs Hillenbrand sent Deputy Under Secretary Samuels, chairman of the U.S. offset negotiating team, a memorandum for a May 26 meeting of the Under Secretaries Committee on the offset negotiations. Hillenbrand said the principal issue for the meeting was approval of a memorandum to the President and he attached a State draft and a Treasury counter-draft that "unfortunately differs in tone and negotiating content." The State draft was silent on monetary linkage, but the Treasury draft said: "We see no advantage in explicitly bargaining with the Germans on Special Drawing Rights or other monetary cooperation questions in connection with the offset agreement. We do believe the discussions during the course of the offset would show the need for discussing broader monetary questions. Further, it is our opinion that a firm negotiation could be an inducement toward discussing these broader and longer range questions." (Ibid., RG 59, S/S Files: Lot 83 D 305, NSDM 12)

A May 29 memorandum from Elliot Richardson to President Nixon summarized the negotiations thus far and presented the Under Secretaries' recommendations for the upcoming talks. Regarding the question of linkage, the last paragraph of Richardson's memorandum reads:

"We have not raised with the Germans the question of using the offset issue as part of the bargain on broad monetary compensation. There are no indications of fruitful possibilities along that line at the moment. However, we will remain alert to this possibility, if it at any time seems promising, in the course of the agreement period. Also in accordance with the NSDM 12, we would in our discussions avoid any commitment on U.S. force levels." (Ibid., Nixon Presidential Materials, NSC Files, Country Files–Europe, Box 681, Germany, Volume II 4–6/69)

Attached to Richardson's memorandum is an undated memorandum to the President, signed but probably not sent, in which Kissinger argued somewhat differently: "On the merits, the Germans should make every concession we ask. After their failure to revalue or take any alternative measures, they should do everything possible to offset their huge balance of payment surplus." Crossed out language in the conclusion reads:

"The merits are all on our side. And I told the Germans that you would take into account on the offset their overall monetary performance, which has been completely unforthcoming on revaluation or any alternatives. The Under Secretaries' Committee does not think that including the broader monetary issues in the offset talks would be fruitful at this time. There are major international monetary decisions to be made in the next few months, however, and the offset is one of our few levers with Germany. I therefore think we should leave the door open for awhile."

At the June 2–3 discussions in Bonn, the U.S. side presented its positions, and the Germans made several comments. The status of the negotiations in June and July was summarized in a July 7 memorandum from Richardson to President Nixon (ibid., RG 59, S/S Files: Lot 83 D 305, NSDM 12) and a July 7 memorandum from Bergsten to Kissinger. (National Archives, Nixon Presidential Materials, NSC Files, Country Files–Europe, Box 682, Germany, Volume III 7–11/69) A 2-year agreement for $1.52 billion by categories of FRG expenditures was finally signed on July 9. The joint statement summarizing the terms is in Department of State *Bulletin*, August 4, 1969, page 92. Bergsten's evaluation of the agreement is in a July 9 memorandum to Kissinger. (National Archives, Nixon Presidential Materials, NSC Files, Country Files–Europe, Box 682, Germany, Volume III 7–11/69)

25.   Memorandum From the President's Assistant for National Security Affairs (Kissinger) to the Under Secretary of State (Richardson)[1]

Washington, July 21, 1969.

The President has ordered a ten per cent reduction in all American overseas civilians directly hired by the U.S. Government and certain American military personnel overseas. Each agency with personnel overseas will be required to meet the ten per cent quota, and reductions will be made on a country-by-country basis, insofar as praticable. The reduction should take account of national security priorities and special local problems, without prejudice to the objective of ten per cent for each agency. Attention should be given to the political problems raised by cuts in U.S. personnel in Thailand. Civilian personnel in South Vietnam will be cut by more than ten per cent.[2]

The President has directed the Under Secretaries Committee to report by September 30 its plans to carry out this directive, and actions already undertaken. Monitoring will thereafter be the responsibility of the Bureau of the Budget, which should make quarterly reports to the Under Secretaries Committee.

It is anticipated that the reductions will approximate 14,900 military and 5,100 civilian personnel.

The reductions will be based on the actual strengths as of June 30, 1969, as determined by the Bureau of the Budget for the Under Secretaries Committee, minus outstanding BALPA cuts and other programs of reductions which have been approved.

The reductions do not apply to U.S. military forces committed to NATO or in Berlin or essential to their support, to forces stationed in Korea or in Vietnam, or to units stationed elsewhere in Southeast Asia that are directly engaged in related military operations. The exception in these areas does not, however, apply to direct-hire or contract U.S. civilian personnel working with our military commands there.

Peace Corps Volunteers, but not administrative personnel, are also exempted.

---

[1]   Source: National Archives, RG 59, S/S Files: Lot 73 D 288, Box 838, NSC/USC Memos. Secret.

[2]   This memorandum launched Operation Reduction, OPRED, a military and civilian counterpart to the balance-of-payments/budgetary REDCOSTE exercise already underway in Europe. For a statement regarding the OPRED objectives and the Department of State's November 24 announcement of post closings to comply with the July 21 directive, see Department of State *Bulletin*, December 22, 1969, p. 591.

The reductions should commence as soon as possible, and must be completed during FY 1970.

The Committee should also consider means of reducing the number of foreign personnel hired locally by U.S. agencies abroad. Special study should be given to means of reducing U.S. contract personnel whose contracts are not directly with the U.S. Government.

Defense and CIA will together prepare plans for the reduction in Intelligence Community personnel, submitting these plans for review by the Under Secretaries Committee working group. Recommendations will be made in consonance with the priorities for intelligence coverage established by the United States Intelligence Board, and the objective of a reduction of ten per cent in overseas personnel will be accomplished in such a way as to cause the least possible loss of access to intelligence needed for national security purposes.

Henry A. Kissinger

---

26.   Paper Prepared by Consultants[1]

Washington, undated.

VIII. FOREIGN ECONOMIC TRENDS

The Separation Between Foreign Economic and Political Policy

Broadly speaking, the United States during the last two decades has preserved a rather sharp distinction between foreign economic policy and the main lines of foreign policy. This distinction arose partly because of an internal division of labor between economic and political issues within the U.S. Government—and within other governments—

---

[1] Source: National Archives, Nixon Presidential Materials, NSC Files, Subject Files, Box 397, A Strategic Overview. Secret. Printed here is section VIII, pp. 66–71, of the 78-page, undated paper entitled "The United States Position in the World: An Overview," forwarded to Kissinger under cover of a memorandum from Robert Osgood on August 20. Osgood noted that the paper was his synthesis of three "sets of books" prepared by the Department of Defense, CIA, and the Department of State in response to NSSM 9 and other NSSMs and analyses, and he credited Richard N. Cooper with preparation of section VIII of the study. There is no indication of how the study was distributed or used. A copy of NSSM 9, "Review of the International Situation," issued on January 23, is ibid., RG 59, S/S Files: Lot 80 D 212.

but partly also because of an underlying assumption that the most felicitous economic environment for the achievement of broad U.S. foreign policy objectives is a thriving, open, and non-discriminatory world economy. Trade is so essential to most countries of the world that successful trade performance becomes a precondition for peaceful and cooperative actions in other areas. Thus, given general guidance for the achievement of a liberal trading environment, it was felt that foreign economic policy should be left alone, free from interference by shorter-term political considerations.

There have, of course, been exceptions to this separation between economics and politics in foreign affairs. In the realm of East-West trade the United States has maintained tight and discriminatory controls for political reasons. The United States lent strong support to the formation of the European Economic Community, a discriminatory trading bloc, on grounds that were fundamentally political. Foreign aid has always been treated more as an arm of general foreign policy toward the Third World than as an aspect of foreign economic policy. But by and large, international trade negotiations and international monetary discussions have proceeded in their own way and at their own pace, aimed at the broadly political objective of freedom of trade and other economic transactions on a multilateral and non-discriminatory basis.

It may be more difficult to preserve this semi-separation between economic and political relations with other countries in the next decade than it has been in the past two decades. Two developments, in particular, introduce new complications: (1) the increasingly complex interaction between foreign trade, international investment, and domestic economic policy, and (2) the growing movement toward preferential trading arrangements. A slightly countervailing tendency is the increasing multilateralization of foreign aid, whereby bilateral political considerations tend to be removed from the donor-recipient relationship.

Trade and Investment

Economic relations among industrial countries have broadened considerably, providing today many more points of contact than the mere exchange of merchandise and occasional travelers. Liquid funds move in large volume between major financial centers. Bond markets are tied more closely together. There has been a vast increase in private American investment abroad, involving managerial control. As a result, a growing amount of international trade is intra-firm trade. All of these developments have profound implications for such traditional national economic policies as monetary policy, tax policy, and business regulation.

Pressure on national monetary policy has already become acute and has evoked such economically "disintegrative" reactions as the interest equalization tax and other restraints on capital outflows from the United States, a German tax on foreign holdings of German bonds, prohibition of foreign mutual funds in Italy, and a host of similar devices in most other industrial countries—all designed to preserve some insulation between domestic and foreign monetary conditions. Pressure on national business regulations is still moderate, but it has given rise to international attention and to foreign concern over the "extra-territorial" extension of U.S. laws and regulations, mainly to U.S.-owned firms abroad. With high international mobility giving rise to easy escape from national regulations and restrictions, the problem will grow more serious.

The increasing attention being given to "non-tariff barriers" to trade also reflects the more numerous points of contact between domestic and foreign economic policies. With tariffs and other explicit barriers to trade sharply reduced among industrial countries, the temptation will be strong to use more subtle techniques for protective purposes. And measures motivated by health, safety, or revenue considerations rather than by protectionism will nevertheless appear as irritating, and hence suspect, obstacles to actual and prospective foreign exporters.

All these developments will compel a searching re-examination, jointly with major countries, of heretofore strictly domestic policy, and this re-examination will create corresponding tension within countries between those segments of the population with a primarily domestic orientation and those whose orientations are increasingly transitional.

Preference Areas

The late 1950s and early 1960s were marked by the successful formation of a number of trade preference areas, notably the European Economic Community, but also the European Free Trading Association, the Central American Common Market, and the Latin America Free Trade Area. Countries that for economic or political reasons do not want full association have frequently pressed for partial affiliation to these various trading blocs. Such affiliation is most advanced in the case of the European Economic Community, where to various degrees Greece, Turkey, the French African countries, Nigeria, and East Africa have achieved some sort of special trading status.

These arrangements point to a substantial erosion of the U.S. objective of an open, non-discriminatory world trading economy. In combination with the factors noted above, they have led to increased pleas for direct U.S. involvement in special trading arrangements, to which the U.S. yielded in the case of the Canadian automotive pact. As these developments progress, foreign political and foreign economic policies will merge, since bilateral trade pacts not only confer favors, but also presuppose political harmony and mutual goodwill—or tutelage—for their effective operation. The United States may expect to be put under increasing pressure to acquiesce in such discriminatory trade arrangements and even to participate in them, especially to grant preferential access to Latin American products coming into the U.S. market.

For political reasons, the United States has encouraged Britain to join the European Economic Community. British membership would inevitably involve several smaller European countries as well and would create a large and formidable trading area entailing some economic costs to the United States. Consequently, British membership would give rise to internal and international frictions with considerable influence on American foreign policy.

In response to pressure from the less developed countries for special trading arrangements, the U.S. has become involved in discussions of a system of world-wide tariff preferences granted by all developed countries to all less developed countries. Certain leaders in the less developed world have laid high hopes on such a scheme. They greatly exaggerate the economic benefits it would bring to their countries, but they consider preferential trading privileges symbolic of the true intentions of the wealthy nations toward the poor ones.

The pressure for preferences reflects a very real problem that will become increasingly acute in the next decade—the need for foreign markets for the rapidly growing output of light manufacturers in the less developed countries. As the LDC's develop efficiently, the output of some products will exceed the home demand for them, giving rise to exportable surpluses; and in any case the LDC's will need to earn foreign exchange to keep their economies both operating and growing. The manufactured products they can export competitively are of the "low-wage" type and hence are politically sensitive in virtually all developed countries. Yet successful economic development in the Third World requires a changing structure of world trade and output which the developed countries can ignore only by closing their markets to the very products that the LDC's, in the course of development, are able to produce efficiently. Assurance of foreign markets is a corollary of U.S. encouragement to development efforts, and in the absence of such markets many otherwise promising development prospects will fail.

International Monetary System

There are likely to be important changes in the international monetary system over the next decade. The reasons lie in the structure of the present system rather than in the purposes and actions of particular governments. Two principal deficiencies in the present system have become evident in recent years. Our method for generating international liquidity, necessary to provide the monetary base for growing foreign trade, is inadequate; and our methods for controlling imbalances in international payments are defective. The U.S. balance of payments deficit, a persistent problem for the United States that will continue for at least several years into the future, reflects these more general deficiencies.

The traditional form for international liquidity has been gold. Gold was accorded a central although unprominent role in the present payments system, laid down by American and British planners a quarter of a century ago. There is clearly not enough new gold at its present price to serve both the growing monetary needs of the world economy and the enlarged private demands for industrial and artistic uses.

The latent shortage of gold would have become evident years ago had not the U.S. dollar served as a kind of surrogate gold in providing international liquidity to nations around the world. (Indeed, one of the problems in framing a sensible policy for the U.S. balance of payments is that U.S. deficits have supplied needed liquidity to the rest of the world.) But this expanded role of the U.S. dollar has left other countries, especially in Europe, uneasy about the capacity implicit in present arrangements for the United States to pursue its international political and economic objectives without regard to the wishes of its allies, while they are nonetheless expected to finance these objectives by accepting and holding dollars in unlimited amounts. Most other advanced nations share broad U.S. objectives, but the very sharp increase in U.S. direct investment in Europe in the early 1960's and the subsequent escalation of our military expenditures in Vietnam brought home the possibility that they might be called upon to finance very large expenditures, public or private, on which they were not consulted and to which they might even object. For this reason, there is a general unwillingness among major countries to acknowledge the reserve currency role of the dollar as a continuing and permanent feature of the payments system.

A solution to the international liquidity problem is near at hand, following five years of negotiation among major countries, in the creation of Special Drawing Rights (SDR's). These will offer a new, man-made form of surrogate gold unrelated to any particular national currency. Creation of SDR's will represent a far reaching step in international monetary cooperation, and with continuing goodwill it will solve the problem of a shortage of monetary gold.

The second deficiency in the payments system concerns the correction of imbalances in international payments. Countries pursue separate policies and they are subject to separate pressures and disturbances. They have divergent rates of growth, and the impact of economic growth on the balance of payments varies from country to country. Their choices between inflation and unemployment and with respect to foreign policy will differ. For all these reasons, countries are bound from time to time to experience imbalances in their international payments. The Vietnam war provides a recent dramatic example, where for reasons of national security, overseas expenditures for the United States were increased sharply.

Under the present rules, laid down twenty-five years ago, temporary imbalances in payments are to be financed out of international reserves and by borrowing directly and indirectly from creditor nations. Where an imbalance persists, it is to be corrected by a change in the value of the country's currency with respect to other currencies; that is, a change in its exchange rate. This mode of adjustment has been difficult to apply in practice, however, and has become increasingly disruptive of international financial order. Countries in payments surplus are not under the same kinds of pressure as countries in deficit to adjust their exchange rate in response to a persistent imbalance. Considerations of international prestige dictate postponement of exchange rate changes, for a change in the value of the currency is (sometimes wrongly) taken as an acknowledgment of poor economic policies. Finally, public anticipation of changes in exchange rates give rise to large and disruptive movements of speculative funds, out of currencies expected to be devalued, into currencies expected to be revalued. With the growing international mobility of capital, these speculative movements have grown dramatically in size.

The currency crises during 1967–1969 reflect this deficiency in the present payment system. In late 1967 large movements of funds preceded devaluation of the British pound—indeed partly forced it as Britain exhausted its reserves—and large amounts of funds have been moved out of France and into Germany during the subsequent period, all in anticipation of changes in exchange rates.

The absence of an effective adjustment process will induce countries in periods of financial strain either (a) to deflate their domestic economies beyond what is desirable on domestic grounds or, more likely, (b) to impose tight controls on their economic transactions with the rest of the world, thereby violating the basic open and non-discriminatory world trading economy which the United States has strived to achieve. Such controls have been used with increasing frequency, after a long period of gradual relaxation of the restraints on international transactions imposed during and immediately following the Second World War. If these violations are not to become increasingly severe and more widespread, the balance-of-payments adjustment process must be markedly improved in the coming years; for example, by improving the methods by which exchange rate changes can be utilized as part of the process.

The weakness of the structure of the U.S. balance of payments has been masked during the past year by large inflows of short-term funds attracted by high interest rates in the American economy. A change in domestic economic conditions should lead to substantial improvements in the trade balance but probably not enough to correct the basic imbalance. This is an additional reason for the United States to be interested in more general improvements in the process of balance-of-payment adjustments.

27.   Memorandum From the President's Assistant for National Security Affairs (Kissinger) to President Nixon[1]

Washington, September 15, 1969.

SUBJECT

Payments Effects of U.S. Government Transactions, FY 1968–70

Attached at Tab A is Bob Mayo's report on the balance-of-payments effects of recent and current U.S. Government international transactions. Comments by Arthur Burns and Paul McCracken are at Tabs B and C.[2]

The key elements of the reports are:

1. The payments effects of all government transactions leveled off during the past two years at about $2 billion net deficit.

2. This figure, however, includes window-dressing receipts of about $1.5 billion.

3. The deficit on *regular* transactions has thus been about $3.5 billion, although it has shown steady improvement and is expected to diminish by 12% to about $3 billion in FY 1970.

---

[1] Source: National Archives, Nixon Presidential Materials, NSC Files, Subject Files, Box 309, Balance of Payments. No classification marking. Bergsten sent this memorandum to Kissinger under cover of an August 26 memorandum indicating it had been revised (from an August 13 version) pursuant to Kissinger's instructions and comments from McCracken and Burns. Bergsten recommended Kissinger sign the memorandum to the President. (Ibid.)

[2] None of the attachments is printed. Mayo's memorandum is dated August 8, Burns' is dated August 11, and McCracken's is dated August 15.

4. Because this Administration has decided to eschew window-dressing statistical gimmickery, however, the total net payments effect of government transactions will deteriorate this year.

5. The Defense Department accounts for over two-thirds of the gross payments—almost $5 billion annually—and is responsible for the total net deficit on regular transactions plus offsetting the effect of the special transactions.

6. Non-defense agency transactions now produce a slight favorable balance on their regular transactions, which should grow somewhat in 1970. Much of the inflow is return on previous loans.

7. AID, which is often labeled as a major source of the U.S. payments deficit, has steadily reduced its foreign payments to the relatively small figure of $145 million in 1970. This is a good bit less than half its receipts and less than the combined payments of Interior, NASA and the Panama Canal. The AID receipts are mainly repayments on past loans.

Analytically, this report is useful but cannot be simply compared with our overall payments position—as many people do to conclude that "the deficit is caused by the government spending." This is because there are large offsetting feedbacks to the government expenditures which show up in the private accounts.

For example, Korea and Thailand would not buy as many U.S. exports if they earned no dollars from DoD programs. Even Japan and major countries in Europe adopt easier economic policies because of our military expenditures there, of which some share comes back to us. This is not to say that government expenditures are not a major factor in our payments deficit—but simply to flag the error in simplistic comparisons.

Paul McCracken comments that we should carefully consider the domestic economic effects of the policies, which we inherited from the previous Administration, to minimize foreign expenditures for government programs. He is referring to such practices as the 50 percent preference extended by DoD to domestic suppliers and AID's tying policies, which create some balance of payments savings but are quite costly in budgetary terms. (Reductions in the *level* of our overseas programs, as per your recent directive on personnel and the Vietnam troop withdrawals, of course help our balance of payments. McCracken is here referring to the foreign exchange costs of a *fixed* level of government programs.)

Arthur Burns, on the other hand, suggests that you ask the Treasury Department to make recommendations on steps to reduce further the balance of payments costs of overseas government expenditures. Any such steps would probably carry the increased budgetary costs mentioned by McCracken and have small payments effects, unless they represented major program changes.[3]

An interagency committee, chaired by Treasury, is in fact already reviewing present policy and will be making recommendations soon on possible changes. I therefore think that you do not need to take any action now. One change—the elimination of the "additionality" requirements under our AID programs—has of course already been made.

---

[3] In the margin next to this paragraph the President wrote "no" and someone added the date 9–24–69. In his September 25 covering memorandum to Kissinger (see footnote 1 above) Bergsten interpreted the President's "no" as pertaining to Burns' suggestion, in the first sentence of the paragraph, rather than to the analytical point in the second sentence, which he said would put the President in error. Bergsten wrote: "I am sure that Burns did not feel very strongly about his suggestion, which was made August 11, and I see no reasons to pursue the matter any further, since no action is called for under either interpretation. Inaction is particularly appropriate because of the uncertainty over the 'no' meaning and in view of Burns' sensitivity over his memos going to the President through you." On September 29 Kissinger approved Bergsten's recommendation to take no action on the "no" written in the margin.

---

28. Memorandum From Secretary of the Treasury Kennedy to the President's Assistant for National Security Affairs (Kissinger)[1]

Washington, October 10, 1969.

SUBJECT

Taxation of U.S. Firms Doing Business in Berlin

This is in reply to your memorandum of September 15, 1969, asking for views and suggestions on the German request that the United States forego its share of tax on income derived from U.S. corporate investment in Berlin to the extent that such income is accorded preferential tax treatment under German law.[2] The Germans raised this issue in NATO in 1968, and have raised it through our Embassy in Bonn on several other occasions. In essence, they seek a "tax-sparing" concession under which the United States would give a foreign tax credit for an

---

[1] Source: National Archives, Nixon Presidential Materials, NSC Files, Country Files–Europe, Box 682, Germany, Volume III, 7–11/69. Confidential.

[2] The memorandum was not found.

amount of German tax which has not in fact been paid—for a tax which has been spared by virtue of the German tax subsidy. Treasury's policy in the past has been to oppose any tax-sparing provision with respect to Berlin.

Such a provision would require legislation, or a treaty amendment approved by a two-thirds quorum vote of the Senate, and there is reason to believe that we would have great difficulty in selling this idea on the Hill, particularly in view of the fact that the Senate has previously refused to go along with tax-sparing proposals, or even with the extension of the investment tax credit—a more modest incentive than tax-sparing—to stimulate U.S. investment abroad in the context of our tax treaties with less-developed countries.

There are several factors which we feel militate against the German request. First, we believe the Federal Republic of Germany is in a sufficiently strong economic position to enable it to subsidize the Berlin economy in ways which would not, in order to be completely effective, require the United States to give up the tax normally due. The United States is being asked to make a questionable departure from established practice and policy which is not necessary to achieve the German objectives for the Berlin economy. In any case, given the U.S. balance of payments position vis-à-vis Germany, any special provision to encourage the outflow of U.S. capital to that country seems unwarranted. Second, the incentive effect of the lower corporate tax in Berlin is not necessarily nullified by our system of taxation, since under current law the U.S. tax is only applicable (except in certain abuse situations) to repatriated profits from U.S. subsidiaries in Berlin. Therefore, if profits are retained abroad, the Berlin corporate tax incentive remains viable. Third, where there are U.S. corporations doing business in Berlin with excess foreign tax credits generated through their other German operations (or, in the case of U.S. taxpayers using the "overall" foreign tax credit limitation, their worldwide operations) such excess credits can be applied to reduce the U.S. tax on income from investments in Berlin.

There are other considerations which reinforce the above arguments, including how we could justify this exception to countries such as Jamaica and Ireland that have already requested similar treatment. Our balance of payments program has generally distinguished between industrialized countries and LDC's, with the latter receiving special consideration; if we willingly discriminate in favor of a strong industrialized country, we can certainly expect complaints from other countries and, based on past experience, perhaps from such international organizations as the OECD.

David M. Kennedy

29.   Letter From the Chairman of the Board of Governors of the
        Federal Reserve System (Martin) to Secretary of the Treasury
        Kennedy[1]

Washington, October 21, 1969.

Dear Dave:

I regret that I shall have to miss tomorrow's meeting on the 1970
balance of payments measures.[2]

Enclosed with this letter is a statement on the balance of payments
problem, which provides strong reasons for minimizing any relaxation
in the programs and for pressing toward equilibrium in the U.S. balance
of payments.

I am sending copies of this letter and the enclosed statement to the
other participants in tomorrow's meeting.

Sincerely,

Bill

Enclosure

1. For almost two years foreign monetary authorities as a group
have experienced a drain on their dollar holdings. Despite the worsening in the structure of the U.S. balance of payments, the inflow of short-
term funds through U.S. banks has kept the dollar strong in exchange
markets by making the holding of dollars attractive to private individuals, business and financial institutions abroad.

---

[1] Source: Washington National Records Center, Department of the Treasury, Office of
the Assistant Secretary for International Affairs: FRC 56 76 108, BOP Improvement
Measures, Volume 4, 66–69. No classification marking. A handwritten notation on the letter reads: "Copy for Mr. Volcker 10/21 6:45 pm copies to Messrs. Petty and Schaffner."

[2] The meeting has not been identified, but on October 29 Paul H. Boeker sent a memorandum to Assistant Secretary of State for Economic Affairs Trezise informing him that
"interested USG agencies are having second thoughts about the Fed's proposed revisions
in the VFCR Program announced at last week's meeting of the Cabinet Committee on
Economic Policy." Boeker explained that the Fed had consistently opposed increased
export credit extension because of its adverse short-term balance-of-payments impact but
that "all member agencies of the Cabinet Committee on Export Expansion except the Fed
expressed support for the exemption of all export credit from VFCR guidelines." Boeker
recommended Trezise contact Governor Brimmer to support further interagency study of
the practical consequences of the proposed revision of the VFCR program (before any
announcement of new guidelines was made). Trezise's handwritten note on Boeker's
memorandum reads: "Call to Brimmer not necessary now. PHT." (National Archives, RG
59, Central Files 1967–69, FN 6 XMB)

a. In 1968 the deficit on the liquidity basis improved substantially as a result of the January 1 balance of payments program, and the surge of foreign purchases in the U.S. stock market, despite a fall-off in the trade surplus. But the official settlements position improved even more, as a result of the Eurodollar inflow.

b. In the first half of 1969, the liquidity balance deteriorated sharply for a variety of reasons: a further fall in the trade surplus, a drop-off in stock purchases by foreigners, an increase in direct investment outflows, and the attraction of American funds to the Eurodollar market. But the official settlements balance was in sizable surplus, again because of the Eurodollar inflow.

c. The U.S. payments position has thus been protected in the past two years by short-term borrowing—in an amount exceeding $10 billion.

2. This protection has come to an end. A mere cessation of the Eurodollar inflow is enough to throw the official settlements balance into deficit (as has happened in the past two months). If, as seems likely, U.S. banks begin to repay Eurodollar borrowings, the official settlements deficit will probably exceed the liquidity deficit.

3. Thus foreign monetary authorities will very likely be accumulating large amounts of dollars next year and beyond.

a. No doubt, there is some appetite abroad for additional dollars at the moment. Some countries—notably the United Kingdom and France—have debts to repay. Others would be pleased to rebuild their dollar holdings, which have been depleted in the past two years.

b. But the appetite is limited. A large official settlements deficit is very likely to lead, rather soon, to a large drawdown of U.S. reserves (gold, our IMF position, SDR's).

c. The attitudes of foreign monetary authorities toward the accumulation of dollars, in counterpart of our large official settlements deficit, will no doubt be influenced by whether they regard the large deficit as temporary or permanent. Some reversal of the surplus of 1968–69 will be regarded as normal.

d. But if the U.S. authorities are seen to be dismantling the programs to restrain capital outflows in the face of a large deficit, foreign monetary authorities are likely to be disturbed and to conclude that the United States deficit is here to stay. This in turn is likely to lead them to ask for conversion of greater amounts of dollar accruals into gold, Fund positions, or SDR's.

e. Beyond this, many officials abroad, particularly in the Group of Ten countries, might well regard a significant relaxation of balance of payments restraint programs in the face of a large deficit as somewhat of a breach of faith. They were willing to go along with SDR activation on the grounds that it would *help* the balance of payments adjustment process. Thus they overlooked the unsatisfactory U.S. payments position in agreeing to SDR activation. A significant relaxation of restraint programs now would embarrass those European officials who were so cooperative regarding SDR activation in substantial amounts. It would also very likely jeopardize future negotiations regarding SDR's.

4. Beyond these considerations, there is the basic question of where the United States is heading with its balance of payments policy.

a. The initiative of Secretary Kennedy regarding a study of limited exchange rate flexibility is unlikely to lead to sizable revaluations of other currencies against the dollar, over and above the present upward move of the DM.

b. Apart from stopping inflation in the United States and bringing about a gradual improvement in the trade balance, there is little else the United States can point to as a policy to improve the payments position.

c. In these circumstances, a sizable *relaxation* of capital restraint programs can only be seen by close observers as leading to some sort of crisis—presumably a suspension of convertibility of the dollar into gold.

d. While this possibility has been in the minds of many officials abroad, it has been regarded as a last resort in circumstances of unavoidable crisis. In such circumstances, suspension would be understood and accepted in relatively good grace abroad.

e. But if avoidable U.S. actions themselves precipitate the process that leads to suspension, the financial and political repercussions abroad are likely to be grave.

5. All these considerations point to the desirability not only of minimizing the extent to which the Commerce and Federal Reserve programs are relaxed for 1970 but also of continuing to press toward equilibrium in the U.S. balance of payments.

---

30.   **Editorial Note**

Japanese Prime Minister Sato made a State visit to Washington November 19–21, 1969. Six memoranda of his conversations with President Nixon are in the National Archives, Nixon Presidential Materials, NSC Files, VIP Visits, Box 924, Sato 11/19–21/69. During two of those conversations, on November 20 in the Oval Office from 10:18

a.m. to 12:30 p.m., and again on November 21 from 10:21 to 11:10 a.m., the President and the Prime Minister discussed an accommodation on textiles. The Prime Minister said he was bound by a unanimous resolution in the Diet against a bilateral agreement with the United States on textiles. The President suggested that before the United States "at an appropriate time" took the issue to GATT he and the Prime Minister attempt to work out a common position in order to avoid a confrontation in Geneva. Documentation on the bilateral textile negotiations is scheduled for publication in a forthcoming *Foreign Relations* volume covering Japan.

At the November 20 meeting the President and Prime Minister also discussed trade and capital liberalization and Japan's economic role in Asia. Regarding liberalization, the President said that if Sato could make a good statement on liberalization it would help him hold protectionism at bay domestically: "if Japan, which currently enjoyed such a favorable balance of trade, did not relax its restrictions people here would question why we should." The Prime Minister "agreed completely" with the President that apart from textiles they should broadly move toward freer trade.

The President noted that "Japan was now at a point where it could play a greater role . . . not just in Asia but on the world scene . . . that Japan should move to a 'higher posture' in the area of trade, investment, political development of Asia and, to the extent we can agree between us even in security . . . the world would be healthier if Japan could be added 'as a fifth finger' to the four existing areas of great power, the United States, Western Europe, the Soviet Union and China." Prime Minister Sato replied that he hoped the Japanese people understood how much they were indebted to the United States for its assistance and cooperation after World War II, and how it had been "quite a shock to Japan" to learn that the Allied Powers had been preparing postwar Japan policy during the height of the war. In that context, and without making any firm commitments, he and the President exchanged views on how Japan might cooperate in Asian development during the post-Vietnam period.

31.   **Action Memorandum From the President's Assistant for National Security Affairs (Kissinger) to President Nixon**[1]

Washington, November 28, 1969.

SUBJECT

   Balance of Payments Program for 1970

At Tab A are recommendations from Secretary Kennedy for next year's balance of payments control programs on foreign investment by U.S. companies and banks.[2] An early announcement is needed to permit the companies and banks to develop their own plans in light of the new program. I have checked this memorandum with Arthur Burns.[3]

Level of Restraint

Secretary Kennedy, with the concurrence or acquiescence of all relevant parties, recommends a modest liberalization of the present controls on foreign investment by U.S. firms:

1. An increase in the level of foreign investment for each firm exempted from the controls, from $1 million to $3 million.
2. Exemption from control of an additional $2 million per firm for investment in LDCs.

These steps represent a compromise between the preferences of some for more liberalization and the preferences of others for less. They would:

—Be a next move toward implementing your April 4 call for "ultimate dismantling of the network of direct controls."[4]
—Eliminate about 350 companies from coverage by the Commerce program, which would be popular politically.
—Risk an increase in capital outflows of up to $600 million. (The net effect on our balance of payments would be decidedly smaller because any additional capital outflows would generate additional U.S. exports.)

---

[1] Source: National Archives, Nixon Presidential Materials, NSC Files, Subject Files, Box 309, Balance of Payments. Confidential. Attached to Document 32.

[2] Secretary Kennedy's November 19 memorandum and its attachments, including an undated memorandum from Secretary Stans, are not printed. An earlier version of Secretary Kennedy's memorandum, dated November 5, did not go forward to the President. (National Archives, Nixon Presidential Materials, NSC Files, Subject Files, Box 309, Balance of Payments)

[3] An earlier version of this memorandum was forwarded to Kissinger under cover of a November 20 memorandum from Bergsten, in which Bergsten noted that he had discussed the memorandum to the President "at length" with Burns and had "cleared" it with him. (Ibid.)

[4] See footnote 5, Document 16.

—Risk foreign policy problems, if our balance of payments turns sour enough next year to require us to take tough unilateral actions—such as suspension of the gold convertibility of the dollar—since we might be blamed for creating the problem ourselves by relaxing our defensive measures.

Five other options were considered:

1. Tightening of the controls. (This would signal a new policy direction for the Administration, contrary to our basic philosophy of freer trade and payments.)
2. No change from 1969. [This would disappoint some businessmen but would reduce the risks cited above. It was initially preferred by the Budget Bureau and the Federal Reserve. It is strongly opposed by CEA (Tab B).][5]
3. Liberalization on investment in LDCs only. (This is strongly supported by Arthur Burns, who would increase the level of investment exempt from control to $5 million *for LDCs only.*)
4. Slightly greater liberalization than finally proposed by Secretary Kennedy, by eliminating the present program's preferential treatment from LDCs in addition to the two steps proposed by Secretary Kennedy. (Its gross payments effect of up to $900 million would run greater real and psychological risks but would be better received by some businessmen. It is preferred by Secretary Stans.)
5. A large reduction or complete elimination of the controls. (This was deemed by all as too risky in view of next year's unfavorable balance of payments outlook.)

Treatment of LDCs, including Latin America

In your speech on Latin America, you said that, "We are examining ways to modify our direct investment controls in order to help meet the investment requirements of developing nations in Latin America and elsewhere."[6]

Secretary Kennedy's proposal would redeem that pledge by the increase in the overall restraint level and the preferential "minimum allowance" for investment in LDCs. Arthur Burns' proposal would do so to an even greater extent, by providing a greater degree of LDC preference and less cumbersome rules to implement it.

Tightening of the controls or the "no change" option would clearly not redeem your pledge. Neither would Commerce's proposal, which

---

[5] Brackets in the source text. Tab B, McCracken's November 11 memorandum for the President, is not printed. He noted that "maintaining the momentum towards our goal of a more free and open economy . . . should be a primary objective of economic policy . . . [but] the outlook for our balance of payments is not rosy enough to permit complete abandonment of these programs, but neither is it so bad that we cannot do anything at all." McCracken's recommendation was to "urge . . . that a further modest step be taken soon."

[6] For text of the October 31 address, see *Public Papers of the Presidents of the United States: Richard M. Nixon, 1969,* pp. 893–901.

would eliminate the favored treatment for LDCs under the present program.

Recommendation:

That you approve the proposal of Secretary Kennedy, agreed or acquiesced in by Arthur Burns, Secretary Stans, and all other relevant parties, for modest liberalization in 1970 of our controls on capital outflows by U.S. corporations and banks.

Approve[7]

Prefer liberalization for investment in LDCs only, as preferred by Arthur Burns. (I would find this fully acceptable.)

Prefer no liberalization, as initially proposed by the Federal Reserve and the Budget Bureau.

Prefer slightly greater liberalization as initially proposed by Commerce.

---

[7] The President initialed his approval of the first and second options.

---

32.   Memorandum From the President's Assistant (Flanigan) to the Staff Secretary of the National Security Council[1]

Washington, December 3, 1969.

RE

Log 2310

Our balance of payments has been in deficit for a decade. During the recent election campaign the President strongly criticized the Democratic administration for not having taken steps to cure this serious problem. Since we have been in office we have already had a modest relaxation of foreign investment control. In the first year of this Administration the balance of payments deficit has risen dramatically to a $10 billion deficit on a liquidity basis, two and one-half times the previous peak figure. The outlook for 1970 is not encouraging.

Our apparent unwillingness to take strong action in this area as opposed to the strong action taken in other areas, such as monetary and

---

[1] Source: National Archives, Nixon Presidential Materials, NSC Files, Subject Files, Box 309, Balance of Payments. Confidential. Document 31 and its tabs are attached.

fiscal policy, raises questions in the US and abroad as to the seriousness with which we regard this problem.

Based on the above, I strongly recommend liberalization for investment in LDCs only (set forth as No. 3 on page 2 of Dr. Kissinger's memo).[2]

---

[2] An attached December 12 handwritten note from John Brown to Haig notes that this memorandum was received after the President had taken an action on the recommendations in Kissinger's memorandum (Document 31), but that since the President had approved two different courses of action, "this issue may still be alive. Flanigan wants you to know that he feels strongly on his recommendations."

---

33. Action Memorandum From C. Fred Bergsten of the National Security Council Staff to the President's Assistant for National Security Affairs (Kissinger)[1]

Washington, December 9, 1969.

SUBJECT

Urgent Need for Presidential Decision on Balance of Payments Program for 1970

Issue

The President approved two contradictory options for the 1970 investment control program (Tab A).[2] The issue is now quite urgent because the hundreds of companies covered by the program are already making their plans for next year; Commerce and Treasury are both agitating daily for a decision. I urge you to take up the matter orally with the President as soon as possible to reconcile the inconsistencies.

Option 1 (your recommendation in Tab A)

1. Increase level of foreign investment exempted from control for each firm from $1 million to $3 million.

2. Exempt from control up to *an additional* $2 million per firm for investment *in LDCs*, on a case-by-case basis. (This would meet the

---

[1] Source: National Archives, Nixon Presidential Materials, NSC Files, Subject Files, Box 309, Balance of Payments. No classification marking.

[2] See Document 31 and footnote 7 thereto.

President's pledge to modify the controls to facilitate private investment in the LDCs, which he made in the Latin America speech.)

3. Recommended by Secretary Kennedy, with the concurrence or acquiescence of all relevant parties. The Secretary worked this out as a compromise between Secretary Stans' desire for greater liberalization and Arthur Burns' desire for no liberalization at this time.

Option 2 (cited as "fully acceptable" to you in Tab A).

1. Increase level of foreign investment exempted from control from $1 million to $5 million for investment *in LDCs only,* as a general rule (not case-by-case).

2. Pros:

—Would redeem President's pledge to promote investment in LDCs more than Option 1.
—Would hurt U.S. balance of payments less.

3. Con: less popular with U.S. business community, which expects liberalization of investment to all areas.

4. Strongly supported by Arthur Burns and Peter Flanigan. (Tab B)[3]

Evaluation

Either approach is fully acceptable from a foreign policy standpoint. Option 2 is more clearly directed toward the LDCs. It also runs less risk of later problems with the Europeans, if our balance of payments turns sour and requires drastic U.S. actions, because it will hurt our balance of payments less; we would then be less susceptible to charges of having induced a crisis ourselves.

The main virtue of Option 1 is bureaucratic: Secretary Kennedy worked it out in a series of lengthy sessions with Stans and Burns. You favored it in your earlier memo. And Stans will be even more unhappy if Option 2 is chosen.

Recommendation:

That you recommend to the President that he choose Option 2—the Burns proposal, strongly supported by Flanigan, that we liberalize for investment in LDCs only.[4]

---

[3] Not printed. On December 4 Flanigan sent Kissinger a memorandum noting the President's conflicting decisions, recalling his December 3 memorandum to the Staff Secretary (Document 32), and strongly urging that when Kissinger asked the President for clarification he guide him toward the Burns proposal.

[4] At the top of the first page of this memorandum, Kissinger wrote: "OK—Let's take Burns option." The date of December 11 is stamped below Kissinger's note. Another note by Haig indicates he routed the memorandum back to Bergsten for action.

34. Memorandum From Secretary of the Treasury Kennedy to President Nixon[1]

Washington, December 15, 1969.

SUBJECT

Conversations with European Officials

In connection with my participation in the NATO Ministerial meeting in Brussels, I visited the Netherlands, the United Kingdom, Germany and France between December 2 and 10, calling on the following officials:[2]

In Brussels—President Rey and Vice President Barre of the Commission of the European Communities and Minister Snoy and Governor Ansiaux of Belgium;
In The Hague—Minister Witteveen and Governor Zijlstra;
In London—Prime Minster Wilson and Chancellor Jenkins;
In Germany—Minister Schiller and Bundesbank President Blessing (I was a luncheon guest of Finance Minister Moeller);
In Paris—Minister Giscard d'Estaing and Governor Wormser.

In order to be in Washington for the conference on the tax bill, I had to cancel my plan to visit Minister Colombo and Governor Carli in Rome. However, Under Secretary Volcker is keeping those appointments.

On each call, I stressed the Administration's determination to control inflation in the United States and outlined the policies being employed and our current expectations.

I found great concern over the effect which our tight money and high interest rates were having on European economies. Yet, Giscard d'Estaing told me privately that the Common Market Finance Ministers were afraid that we would not or could not control our inflation and would continue to experience such serious balance of payments deficits as to imperil world confidence in the dollar and threaten the international monetary system.

The hope was expressed that we could achieve more restraint through the budget and the reports which I had to give them on the tax

---

[1] Source: National Archives, Nixon Presidential Materials, NSC Files, Agency Files, Box 289, Treasury, Volume I. Confidential. Attached to a December 19 memorandum from Kissinger to the President that summarizes Kennedy's report on his European trip. Stamped on Kissinger's memorandum is "The President has seen" with a December 22 date. In a December 18 memorandum to Kissinger, Bergsten recommended that he sign the memorandum for the President and noted that "continued U.S.-French differences on international monetary policy and the threat posed by EC preferential trade arrangements to our support of the Common Market" would be of particular interest to Kissinger. (Ibid.)

[2] Memoranda of these conversations are in the Washington National Records Center, Department of the Treasury, Secretary's Memos: FRC 56 74 17, Memcons 1969.

bill were very discouraging. Schiller suggested an "interest rate disarmament" conference among a few major countries with the objective of lowering interest rates about 2 percentage points without precipitating disruptive international capital flows. I asked him to give us a little more time to break the back of inflation, but we may want to do this in the spring.

I found Schiller ready to move ahead on the studies of limited exchange rate flexibility as a means of strengthening the international monetary system. He feels that the achievement of common economic policies and uniform price movements within the Common Market is at least a decade away and agrees that in the meantime we must be able to use exchange rate changes as a means of adjustment within the Common Market as well as with other countries. Witteveen and Zijlstra also agree that a common central bank for the EC is a final step which is many years away. Rey and Barre, on the other hand, want to eliminate the possibility of exchange rate change by individual Common Market countries as soon as possible and hope to get agreement within the next year that any such changes would require unanimous consent. If we are to avoid recurrent financial crises, I believe we must make it easier, not harder, for countries to appreciate their currencies against the dollar and I am convinced that it will be necessary to preserve this option for individual Common Market countries for many years to come.

I told my hosts that in striving to improve our balance of payments we were concentrating on fundamentals—first and foremost on the control of inflation. But I also referred to our efforts to negotiate the reduction of barriers against U.S. exports, our desire to remove the disadvantage to our trade resulting from the employment of the value added tax system in Europe, and our concern over the prospective proliferation of preferential trading arrangements between the Common Market and its neighboring countries in Europe which are not prospective members. Rey made it quite clear that the Communities expect to conclude a network of such arrangements (Spain, Israel, Switzerland, Sweden, etc.). Our trade will be adversely affected and our support of the Common Market may be called into question politically at home.

While I was in Europe, the free market price of gold dropped to $35.00 and many of the Europeans were anxious to find a way to ensure that it did not drop significantly below that level. It seems apparent that if it did—at least by any substantial amount and for any significant period of time—a number of European central banks would step in to support the market, either through the Bank for International Settlements or directly. I left Under Secretary Volcker in Europe to negotiate with the South Africans on this issue, and I am hopeful that we can reach an agreement which will keep the price from falling further and thus make this issue moot.[3] The French pointedly reminded me, however, that they have never adhered to the Washington agreement of last year and consider themselves free to buy or sell on the free market at any time.

My conversations touched briefly on a few other points. There was support for the view that the question of a possible link between Special Drawing Rights and aid to less developed countries ought not to be considered until the world has had experience with the SDR and it has been accepted. Initiating studies of this question now would be most inadvisable.

Finally, Giscard d'Estaing suggested that we might consider jointly how our two countries could deal with the enforcement problems presented by the Swiss banking secrecy laws. I plan to follow through on this suggestion.

It is evident that we and the French still have some troublesome differences of approach to the problems of the monetary system. Giscard showed a personal interest in discussing these differences and I plan to invite him to the U.S. for a further exchange.

Giscard, as well as Ambassador Shriver, indicated that Pompidou will want to discuss with you financial and economic matters.[4] We will prepare a briefing paper for this visit. They also indicated that Pompidou is planning to go to Chicago and suggested that, if possible, I should plan to make a trip to Chicago.

My conversations on this trip have left me more firmly convinced than ever that the major countries of the world have become so interdependent economically and financially that not even the large European countries can achieve their economic objectives in the absence of U.S. price stability. Our responsibility to stop inflation and use our leadership wisely is not limited to the citizens of our own country but is a responsibility to the world.

David M. Kennedy

---

[3] See Document 145.

[4] President Pompidou was scheduled to visit the United States February–March 1970; see Document 36.

35.   **Memorandum From the Assistant Secretary of the Treasury for International Affairs (Petty) to Secretary of the Treasury Kennedy**[1]

Washington, February 11, 1970.

What Should Be our Policy Toward Aid Tying?

1. U.S. foreign economic assistance was "tied" to U.S. procurement beginning in 1959, originally as a method of offsetting lagging Congressional support of the program. Presentationally, it was argued that tying almost totally eliminated the balance of payments costs of foreign aid: by providing real resources rather than financial resources. In addition we benefited our exporters while accomplishing the development task and the procedure made our aid funds only marginally less efficient—but this was a cost deemed necessary to assure sustained adequate levels of aid appropriations.

2. Both inside and outside the Executive branch question arose on the validity of the claim that tying aid virtually removed the balance of payments costs of the program. This generated pressures to ensure "additionality," i.e. that aid financed exports were additional to goods that aid recipient countries would have purchased from the U.S. commercially in any event. The techniques to bring about "additionality" varied from country to country but they rapidly led to resentment and the development of political problems with developing countries.

3. President Nixon's decision last June to eliminate the "additionality" requirements under our foreign aid program was prompted by a desire to eliminate this political lightning rod from attracting anti-U.S. sentiment in the aid countries. This had the effect of reducing the effectiveness of aid tying. Since that time the tying rules have been further relaxed in the case of Latin America. Henceforth U.S. aid dollars lent to finance imports may be used to procure commodities in either the United States or in Latin American countries. The latter is being given a further advantage of qualifying for such procurement even when the imported component of the item being sold amounts to fifty percent (for U.S. suppliers, only ten percent imported component is normally allowed). The President also decided that tying restrictions be lifted completely for U.S. aid dollars going to Latin America to finance local costs. He decided a similar liberalization on tying of local cost financing

---

[1] Source: Washington National Records Center, Department of the Treasury, Office of the Assistant Secretary for International Affairs: FRC 56 76 108, US/3/501, Tied Aid Procurement, Volume 2 1966–70. Limited Official Use. Sent through Volcker.

by the Inter-American Development Bank's Fund for Special Operations.

4. What does all this add up to?

—With the end of additionality the effectiveness of tying is questionable.

—Removal of the Special Letter of Credit in connection with local cost financing in Latin America by AID and the FSO has the effect of untying for "world-wide" procurement since recipient countries will now be receiving U.S. dollars unrestricted as to subsequent use.

—While the measure is now a regional preference for Latin America, experience with the elimination of "additionality" and evidence of already mounting pressures for partial or full untying elsewhere in the less developed world suggest that restricting the new policy to Latin America alone is not likely to be sustainable.

—There would be a further balance of payments cost to untying in Asia and Africa. Aid constitutes a higher percentage of imports in such countries as India and Pakistan and our share of commercial trade is lower than in Latin America.

5. Determining the "true" balance of payments effects of aid tying has been and continues to be a statistical playground. Past estimates within the Executive Branch of the "cost" of a given tying (or untying) measure have varied widely, with State/AID generally on the low or "de minimis" side, Commerce generally on the high side and Treasury generally in a tentative middle posture. As evidence of this, in calculations last year of the "benefits" from the additionality program, State/AID estimated $35 million world-wide, Commerce estimated upwards of $350 million and Treasury estimated something in excess of $125 million. For Latin America hemispheric untying, Treasury estimated $200 million balance of payments costs. The NSC used a $50 million estimate. From there on, the costs were "nibbled" away by arguments about de minimis effects.

6. Perhaps a better way of looking at the costs of untying is in the context of what we are doing relative to other aid giving countries. If, for example, other donor countries untied their aid simultaneously with the untying of U.S. aid, we would presumably pick up some additional procurement under their programs. However, other programs in the aggregate amount to less than the U.S. program. Nevertheless, their aggregate share of exports to the LDCs greatly exceeds that of the U.S. Consequently, what the U.S. balance of payments would gain from untying by other donors would fall far short of what would be lost through the untying of the U.S. program. Specifically, with the U.S. providing roughly 50 percent of total aid to LDCs and providing only 25 percent of total exports to LDCs, with complete worldwide untying we would stand to incur a balance of payments loss in the aggregate, of at least one half of the total amount of our aid program.

7. It is clear to me that the tying of aid is on the way out, and I think it is desirable that this is the case. This is a form of selective control that is not in keeping with our philosophy, and it is certainly not the most efficient form of economic assistance. However, many countries tie, and it is in keeping with our leadership role that if we go to untying beyond Latin America that we do it in a "burden sharing" manner in which all other donor countries also untie. However, further unilateral untying by the United States would jeopardize our negotiating position in getting other donors to join us. Consequently, I would recommend that the National Advisory Council recommend to the President an initiative to be taken by the United States at the OECD Ministerial Meeting in May whereby the United States would propose that we negotiate—probably through DAC, the Development Assistance Committee—the multilateral untying of bilateral assistance by donor countries. The NAC would also consider how far a multilateral proposal would go toward complete aid untying. Many countries are as attached to aid tying as we have been. They will not quickly accede to this suggestion; but by making this gesture, the U.S. would get the immediate political benefits with the LDCs; and we will move the developed countries along toward this desirable objective. It would permit us in the meantime to discontinue further unilateral untying—so that the time framework would be more in pace with our removal of selective controls over direct investment and banks. Right now we run the danger of removing most government balance of payments controls and still being left with the Commerce and Fed controls.

Recommendation: That we be authorized to commence with an NAC Alternates Meeting whereby a specific proposal to the President is developed to negotiate multi-laterally the untying of bi-lateral (and conceivably multi-lateral) aid, which would be submitted to an NAC Principals' Meeting as soon as possible. This timing would provide adequate preparation for the May ministerial conference.

Approve[2]

Disapprove

Other

---

[2] Secretary Kennedy initialed this option on February 20.

36.   Memorandum of Conversation[1]

Washington, February 26, 1970, 10:30 a.m.

[Omitted here is a discussion of unrelated matters.]

Economic Situation

President Nixon said that he did not wish to impose on the President's time but he would like to say a few words about the international monetary situation. He was not an expert in this field as President Pompidou was. As he had told him the previous evening,[2] he would hope that there would be close communication between our finance ministers and central bankers on a confidential basis to work out a more stable situation than the one we presently have. On his part he could assure President Pompidou that through an austerity budget we were doing everything we could to cool the U.S. economy so that our inflation would not be a factor of instability which it is at present.

President Pompidou said that he and Secretary Kennedy had talked about this.[3]

President Nixon said that he had great respect for Mr. Volcker, the Under Secretary, but the man with the most influence in this matter would be Mr. Burns who thinks in more imaginative terms regarding the need for new approaches. He did not know what these approaches should be but Burns had new ideas.

President Pompidou said that if Burns were in Paris in the next few months he would like to see him alone. He had not wished the previous day to speak before all of the Treasury people.

President Nixon said that one must know Burns to appreciate him. He talks slowly but thinks fast. President Pompidou could talk frankly to him as Burns was most discreet. President Pompidou knew that a

---

[1] Source: National Archives, Nixon Presidential Materials, NSC Files, Presidential/HAK Memcons, Box 1023, President/Pompidou February 24 and 26, 1970. Top Secret; Sensitive; Nodis. Presidents Nixon and Pompidou met in the Oval Office from 10:40 a.m. to 12:37 p.m. (Ibid., White House Central Files, President's Daily Diary) President Pompidou visited the United States February 23–March 3. He met with President Nixon in the Oval Office on February 24 and 26; a memorandum of the February 24 conversation is ibid., NSC Files, Presidential/HAK Memcons, Box 1023, President/Pompidou February 24 and 26, 1970. Following his Washington program President Pompidou traveled to Cape Kennedy, San Francisco, Chicago, and New York.

[2] President Nixon gave a dinner at the White House in honor of President Pompidou on February 24, and in turn attended a dinner hosted by the French on February 25. (Ibid., White House Central Files, President's Daily Diary)

[3] President Pompidou met with Secretary Kennedy at Blair House at 10 a.m. on February 25; see Document 37.

bureaucracy does not engender new ideas. They generally defend the status quo and try and patch it up. Burns as a top economic and financial expert thinks in innovative terms now although in a few years he will be part of the bureaucracy and therefore we should take advantage of this opportunity.

Europe

President Pompidou said he would like to ask the President to say a few words about Europe. He wanted to know what importance he should give to the statements by Ambassador Schaetzel concerning the fears and even opposition to the European Common Market by the United States.[4]

President Nixon replied, "None." In his view it was very important for the European Common Market to develop in its own way. It will be increasingly competitive with the U.S. as the U.K. comes in and it may become a rather serious problem for us in an economic sense. But the President said he took the long view that a strong productive European Community including the United Kingdom is in the interest of world peace and stability. The U.S. would have to pay some costs for achieving this bigger goal and the President did not agree with those who rejected this point.

President Pompidou said he had spoken about this to the Congressional leaders he had received the previous day.[4] It was certain that as the European Community developed it may cause economic rivalry. The French would do all they could to insure that it would be open and as liberal as possible so that economic tensions would not become awkward. One should not be too impressed by political figures in France and in the U.S. who are sensitive to the worries of their constituents. Many protested against the French agricultural system which did have many faults, but he could say that the sales of U.S. agricultural surpluses to Europe had doubled since 1958.

President Nixon said that as President Pompidou had said at dinner, if we could only get agricultural subsidies off our books we would be able to give all sorts of assistance to the underdeveloped countries, and added, "some day we must bite that bullet."

[Omitted here is discussion of Vietnam, military matters, and miscellaneous subjects (scientific and technical cooperation).]

---

[4] Not further identified.

37. Memorandum From Secretary of the Treasury Kennedy to President Nixon[1]

Washington, March 2, 1970.

SUBJECT

Meeting with President Pompidou

I believe that my meeting with President Pompidou served a most useful purpose.[2] President Pompidou questioned me closely on the possibility of a recession in the United States and on the probable course of interest rates. However, his basic concern for the longer run appeared to be that the United States might not persevere in its effort to control inflation and the balance of payments. Dr. Burns and I tried—successfully I think—to reassure him on this point.[3]

President Pompidou emphasized the fact that the U.S. dollar is the pivot or the reference point on which the international monetary system rests. He feels that the system can only function well if the dollar maintains a stable value. Failure of the United States to preserve price stability forces all other countries either to accept inflation in their own countries or to revalue their currencies—an action which, he said, was politically extremely difficult.

Dr. Burns and I assured the President that we were very conscious of this responsibility to the world and were determined to bring inflation under control. Restoration of general price stability was a primary objective of our policy. Given the extent of pent-up demand for investment, we did not feel that there was a great danger of recession.

President Pompidou also said that a perpetual U.S. balance of payments deficit would lead to a dollar crisis which would become a general world economic crisis.

My answer was that we were attacking the fundamentals of the payments problem through our attack on inflation. I had Under Secretary Volcker describe the other elements in our balance of payments program.

---

[1] Source: Washington National Records Center, Department of the Treasury, Files of Under Secretary Volcker: FRC 56 79 15, France. Confidential. Drafted by F. Lisle Widman on February 27 and revised by Volcker. The memorandum was forwarded to the President under cover of a March 5 memorandum from Kissinger. (National Archives, Nixon Presidential Materials, NSC Files, Agency Files, Box 289, Treasury Volume I)

[2] The February 26 memorandum of the February 25 conversation, also drafted by Widman, is ibid.

[3] Burns is not listed as a participant in the memorandum of conversation, but a February 18 briefing memorandum from Assistant Secretary of State Hillenbrand to Secretary Rogers indicates that Burns, Budget Director Mayo, and Herbert Stein were to join the group at Blair House at 10:30 a.m. (National Archives and Records Administration, RG 59, S/S Files: Lot 71 D 175, Box 130, NSC Meeting February 23, 1970–France)

President Pompidou feels that international payments problems should be dealt with—not by setting up a mechanism for greater flexibility of exchange rates—but by stopping inflation and thus obviating the need for exchange rate changes. He noted the trend in the Common Market toward freezing of rates.

I assured President Pompidou that we did not look upon increased flexibility of exchange rates as a means of escaping the responsibility of achieving and preserving general price stability in the United States. We did feel, however, that the possibility of employing techniques for limited exchange rate flexibility to strengthen the monetary system ought to be carefully examined.

I stressed the importance of continuing consultations and close cooperation in the financial sphere among the major countries and mentioned specifically the forthcoming visit of French Minister of Finance Giscard d'Estaing, who has accepted my invitation for a meeting at Camp David in early May.

David M. Kennedy[4]

---

[4] Printed from a copy that indicates Kennedy signed the original.

---

38. Editorial Note

On March 2, 1970, President Nixon sent a memorandum to Haldeman, Ehrlichman, and Kissinger, "for discussion with the group and implementation," reflecting on his and their use of time during the first year of the administration. The President concluded that "the greatest weakness was in spreading my time too thin—not emphasizing priorities enough." He wanted new rules that applied to his time to apply to Ehrlichman's and Kissinger's time as well, and lower priority issues to be handled by the Executive agencies and White House staff.

The foreign policy issues the President wanted brought to his attention were East-West relations, policy toward the Soviet Union, policy toward Communist China, policy toward Eastern Europe to the extent it affected East-West relations at the highest level, and policy toward Western Europe where NATO and the major countries (Britain, Germany, and France) were involved. At the "next level out" was policy toward the Middle East, followed by policy toward Vietnam and anything related to Vietnam, Laos, and Cambodia. For the rest of Asia and most of Africa and Latin America, the President did not want matters submitted to him unless they required a decision that could only be handled at the Presidential level.

The President turned to specific economic matters under the domestic affairs rubric, where he would take personal responsibility where the decisions affected recession or inflation. In his memorandum the President wrote:

"I do not want to be bothered with international monetary matters. This, incidentally, Kissinger should note also, and I will not need to see the reports on international monetary matters in the future. Problems should be farmed out, I would hope to Arthur Burns if he is willing to assume it on a confidential basis, and if not Burns to Houthakker who is very capable in this field. I have no confidence in the Treasury people since they will be acting in a routine way. International monetary matters, incidentally, are a case in point in making the difficult decision as to priorities. I feel we need a new international monetary system and I have so indicated in several meetings. Very little progress has been made in this direction because of the opposition of Treasury. I shall expect someone from the White House staff who will be designated who will keep the pressure on in this area. The man, however, who could really be the lead man is Arthur Burns because he feels exactly as I do and it might be that he could exert some influence on the others. . . . Where an item like foreign aid is concerned I do not want to be bothered unless it directly affects East-West relations. . . . A lot of miscellaneous items are not covered in this memorandum but I think you will be able to apply the rules . . . trade policy is a case in point. This is something where it just isn't going to make a lot of difference whether we move one way or another on the glass tariff. Oil import is also a case in point. While it has some political consequences it is not something I should become deeply involved in." (National Archives, Nixon Presidential Materials, NSC Files, Subject Files, Box 341, HAK/RN Memos 69–70)

39.   **Paper Prepared in the Department of the Treasury**[1]

Washington, undated.

SUGGESTED REVISION

U.S. BALANCE OF PAYMENTS OBJECTIVES

The United States seeks over time a pattern of international trade and payments which will serve the basic objective of expanding the multilateral system under which national economies achieve greater efficiency in an atmosphere of fewer and fewer restrictions on the exchange of goods, capital and services. When and if the United States payments position is strong, this type of multilateral system allows our basic foreign policy of peace through partnership to be pursued with less strain on the dollar and the international monetary system.

We require the composition of our international transactions to be such as will preserve world confidence in the U.S. dollar as (a) a vehicle for international transactions; (b) a preferred form in which to hold national reserves and a satisfactory standard for an international payments system conducive to sound economic growth throughout the world. We require a record in our international trade and payments which leaves us free to pursue full employment, a satisfactory rate of economic growth, reasonable price stability and an equitable distribution of income at home, without causing excessive strain on our net liquidity position.

The balance in our goods and services transactions should show a substantial surplus.[2] A surplus on merchandise trade and services will in itself be an important factor in preserving confidence in the dollar. To contribute to confidence, however, this surplus would probably need to compare favorably, as a proportion of GNP, with that of other major industrial nations. We can expect income from direct investment to continue to rise, but we must also anticipate that the increase will tend to be offset by rising net tourist outflows and such other invisibles.

---

[1] Source: Washington National Records Center, Department of the Treasury, Office of the Assistant Secretary for International Affairs: FRC 56 76 108, Commentaries and Reports, Volume 2 1966–71. Confidential. Attached to an April 3 memorandum from George H. Willis to Assistant Secretary of the Treasury Petty, which indicated that the paper originated with Widman. The text printed here is Willis' suggested revision of that paper.

[2] According to Willis' memorandum to Petty, Widman and Willis seemed to be favoring a balance of trade surplus of about 1/2 of 1 percent of GNP or a trade surplus of $5 billion in a trillion dollar GNP, and a goods and services surplus, excluding government grant transfers, of $6.5 to $7 billion.

Only by such a surplus can we afford our military and political postures abroad and supply real capital to less developed countries and to other nations requiring foreign capital for the development of their resources. Should we fail to restore and then maintain such a surplus, we would progressively erode the dollar's role—itself the fulcrum to the monetary system. With a reduction of world confidence in the dollar, public and Congressional support for a liberal trading and investment policy would further diminish, along with support for our military commitments overseas.

---

40.   Memorandum From the Deputy Assistant Secretary of State for European Affairs (Springsteen) to the Deputy Under Secretary of State for Economic Affairs (Samuels)[1]

Washington, May 7, 1970.

SUBJECT

Review Group Meeting May 7 on NSSM 79 and 91[2]

The NSSM 79 exercise has pointed up differences among Government agencies concerning the future development of the European Communities. The agencies dissenting from the Department's view would not agree to state the differences in the framework of a single paper and submitted separate written statements.[3] It is possible to summarize the issues and differences as follows:

---

[1] Source: National Archives, RG 59, S/S Files: Lot 80 D 212, NSSM 79. Confidential. Drafted by A. Katz (EUR/RPE) and cleared by Camps (S/PC), Gold (E), and Higginson (E/OT). Also addressed to Pedersen (C) and Cargo (S/PC).

[2] The Review Group meeting was held on May 13. NSSM 79, dated October 13, 1969, is entitled "UK Accession to the European Community." NSSM 91, dated March 27, 1970, expanded the scope of NSSM 79 to cover preferential trading arrangements of the European Community with countries not applying for full membership. (National Archives, RG 59, S/S Files: Lot 80 D 212)

[3] On April 23 Hillenbrand, in his capacity as Chairman of the NSC Ad Hoc Group (established pursuant to NSSM 79), sent Kissinger, in his capacity as Chairman of the NSC Review Group, a memorandum entitled "Enlargement of the European Community, NSSM's 79 and 91." Hillenbrand noted that it had not been possible to reach agreement in the Ad Hoc Group on either substance or presentation and he attached a State Department paper, a joint Treasury–Commerce–Agriculture paper, and an STR paper. (Ibid.)

Appraisal—On the transitional tariff effects, the Department's study shows practically no adverse effects to our industrial exports if the Community is enlarged to ten, and moderate (up to $300 million maximum damage) if complete free trade arrangements are extended to all the EFTA neutrals.

The Department's study estimates damage to our agricultural trade of $100 million if CAP prices remain unchanged.

The dissenting agencies do not quarrel directly with these studies, although they play up the imprecision of any quantitative projections. Agriculture's estimates of damage to the world grain market are more moderate than the Department's and about the same for damage to U.S. exports. USDA does, however, express concern that U.S. soybean sales may somehow be threatened. The Department sees no reason why enlargement should in any way reinforce or renew the threat to soybeans which has been successfully warded off. Our GATT rights for soybeans in both the EC and the UK are strong and uncontested. USDA also anticipates sharp losses (unquantified and unexplained) for US exports of tobacco, lard, and canned fruits. The Department's studies do not bear out this concern. Both the Department and USDA agree that other suppliers of beef products, dairy products and sugar would be hurt. The U.S. has quotas on these commodities, but we may be under some pressure to enlarge or alter them.

All agencies agree that the longer term dynamic effects will be more important. The Department's study points out that the income growth will lead to increased European imports, but that the enhanced competitive position of Europe, and some of its common policies may have an adverse effect on U.S. economic interests. The Department's conclusions are that the Common Market has been a boon to our industrial exports and investments. British accession, the Department feels, will reinforce the basically liberal outlook of the Commission, the FRG, The Netherlands and others.

The dissenting agencies are more pessimistic concerning the future. They see our competitive position eroding and they believe that enlargement and further deepening of the Community will result in a number of autarkic measures aimed at the U.S. in both trade and investment. In particular they express concern that preferential industrial and procurement policies would adversely affect nearly $4 billion of high technology items or over 35 percent of total U.S. exports to Europe.

The Department sees no basis in fact or discernible trends to warrant such a pessimistic conclusion.

Strategy and Recommendations

While no one suggests questioning the basic policy of support for the Community and its enlargement, the differences in appraisal are reflected in different overall strategies and recommendations.

All agencies appear to agree on both continuing support for European unity and enlargement of the Community, as well as on the need to influence developments in the Community in such a way as to maximize our economic benefits and minimize our losses.

All agree that we should, in connection with the negotiations, exercise fully our GATT rights augmented by bilateral and multilateral diplomacy. All would agree that we should continue to follow internal developments in the Community and influence them in our best interest.

The dissenting agencies, however, adopt a harder and more interventionist tone. They would invoke the U.S. troop presence in Europe and other elements of leverage. They would make the participants in the enlargement negotiations see that the ability of any U.S. administration to maintain its military relationship with Europe could be jeopardized if there was serious damage to our economic interests. They would want us "promptly and firmly" to demonstrate by our statements and our actions an intent to protect our basic economic and financial interests. We would "make clear without delay" or "stress at the outset" a number of U.S. desiderata and "that we are prepared to use such leverage as is available to us as a world power."

It is clear from the discussions in the ad hoc group and the drafting group that what these words are meant to convey is a major and clearcut effort to put the Europeans on notice. The Department does not believe that such a diplomatic campaign is required by the facts. We believe it would be interpreted in Europe as a clear reversal of the President's position on European unity and on nonintervention in the process of unification. It would be read as a signal that henceforth we will put our economic and commercial interests above our political objectives. The agencies, at least on the working level, wish the U.S. to give such a signal, and in the paper submitted by Treasury, Commerce and Agriculture, have come close to saying so explicitly.

In addition, the agencies would pose specific conditions to enlargement—the toughest being in agriculture where they would insist that there be a reduction in agricultural protection. USDA would have us stress that a midpoint between present EC and UK grain prices "would be acceptable."

The Department agrees with the other agencies that we should use what leverage we can to effect a lowering of CAP grain prices. The problem is that this is likely to be the most intractable aspect of the negotiations. We believe we may be able to influence or reinforce a trend in the EC towards more sensible prices, but we are unlikely to get very much in the course of the enlargement negotiation and for the U.S. to pose hard conditions may well jeopardize the negotiations. There is no disagreement and no apparent problem on maintaining UK and EC zero bindings for soybeans.

The agencies would also make clear *in connection with the accession negotiation* our opposition to what are only distant dangers in connection with the *ongoing development of the Community.* Specifically, they mention nontariff barriers such as a "buy European" policy. STR wants us to make clear we would expect compensation for trade and investment barriers not the inevitable result of a customs union.

The Department feels it would be diplomatically inappropriate to intervene in the negotiations by "making clear" in connection with the enlargement negotiation a number of positions which relate to the internal work of the EC and which will not arise as part of the enlargement negotiation. To do so would only be interpreted as a major diplomatic campaign reversing U.S. policy on the Community. We have other ways of defending our interests on the Community's internal development and have a pretty good record so far.

Furthermore, the points the agencies would have us make would be interpreted as challenging the right of the EC to develop an *economic union* as opposed to a mere *customs union.* If we want the European countries to become more united economically and politically, we cannot object to their adopting a collective procurement policy or a common investment policy. We *can* try to influence the *content* of such policies in a liberal outward looking direction. But it would be contrary to our policy of encouragement of unity if we were to seek to block the development of common policies.

The dissenting agencies would also have the U.S. actively seek to establish a continuing consultative mechanism through which we could be kept informed of the negotiations and register our concerns. The Department feels that we should be prepared to respond positively to a European initiative for a US-EC consultative mechanism, but we doubt that the French will permit the EC to set up such a mechanism at this time. Furthermore, to request such a mechanism *in connection with the negotiation* would be interpreted as intervention and resented by the parties. Such a request would also encourage other affected countries less interested in the success of the negotiations to seek to read themselves into negotiations. The Department believes that we can rely on normal diplomatic channels and informal high level visits, as well as existing international forums such as the OECD to keep ourselves informed and to make our views known.

Finally, the Department's strategy, besides trying to influence the accession negotiations and the continuing internal development of the Community, also contemplates engaging the Community in multilateral negotiations. Some of the agencies during our discussions expressed doubts about the feasibility or desirability of a major new round of trade negotiations in the near term. The dissenting agencies do not view such a negotiation "as an acceptable substitute" to getting what we want during the negotiation.

The Department clearly does not see a trade negotiation as a substitute for appropriate action to protect our interests during the accession negotiation. But in the last analysis only by lowering the Community's barriers through reciprocal action will we reduce the incidence of discrimination which is inherent and inevitable in a customs union. Perhaps more important, the Department's study points out that the Community will be engaged for the better part of the decade in the complex task of digesting the new members while moving towards an economic and monetary union. A major negotiation will be useful in maintaining the outward looking orientation of the Community and to cement the Alliance in the economic field. We are aware that this decision will be made only after the President's Commission on Trade and Investment makes its report. However, we should be gearing up now for such an effort by developing viable negotiating approaches on NTBs including preferential government procurement and agriculture.

EFTA neutrals and EC preferences

Only STR has included dissent on these issues although some of the other agencies are known to have strong views on the issues.

On the EFTA neutrals, STR wants us to make clear our policy from the outset. The Department feels that this situation is so fluid and delicate that we should adopt a low profile and a holding position until the issues between the EC and the EFTA neutrals are clarified, and we have suggested such a response to queries that holds open all our options. We do not want to adopt positions that tend to force the neutrals and the EC into agreeing on full membership of the neutrals, which might undermine the political development of the community. Furthermore, we must take into account the peculiar problems of Austria and Finland.

On EC preferential arrangements, STR has provided its recommendations. The Department's paper merely sets out the problems in all their complexity.[4] In general, we find STR's recommendations a bit too detailed and tactical for Review Group consideration at this stage.

Although the Department has not yet developed its position on the options, STR's recommendations as presently worded would give us too rigid a framework for diplomatic maneuver. We believe the NSC should only give general guidelines and leave it to the bureaucracy to work out the detailed positions in each case.

---

[4] Reference is to an undated memorandum on "EC Preferential Trade Arrangements" which Richardson gave Kissinger on February 26. The memorandum explained how the preferential trade agreements were contrary to GATT MFN obligations and U.S. trade interests. The memorandum is attached to the memorandum printed here.

41.   Memorandum From Secretary of the Treasury Kennedy[1]

Washington, June 30, 1970.

MEMORANDUM FOR

The Honorable Maurice Stans
The Honorable George Shultz
The Honorable Robert Mayo
The Honorable Paul W. McCracken
The Honorable Nathaniel Samuels
The Honorable Carl Gilbert

SUBJECT

Tax Adjustments at the Border

Chairman McCracken's memorandum of June 8 suggests that we proceed with the three points outlined by Ambassador Gilbert while setting aside the issue of the basic inequity of GATT rules.[2] I do not believe that approach would relieve either our economic or political difficulties. Of the three points proposed by Ambassador Gilbert, two are clearly of minimal importance and solutions would result in no substantial trade benefits for U.S. producers. The third faces us with the same basic issue of GATT inequity which Chairman McCracken suggests we set aside. Any substantive proposal on changes would require an amendment of GATT provisions concerning the amount of allowable adjustments.

---

[1] Source: Washington National Records Center, Department of the Treasury, Secretary's Memos/Correspondence: FRC 56 74 7, Council of Economic Advisers. Confidential. Forwarded to Kennedy under cover of a June 25 memorandum from Petty.

[2] McCracken's June 8 memorandum summarized the results of a June 5 meeting, where agreement was reached on how to proceed at the July GATT meeting. Gilbert outlined three points: "opposition to adjustments for taxes occultes; a requirement for confrontation and justification in the event of changes in a country's tax system involving border adjustments, and international control or surveillance of 'averaging.'" GATT rules allowed Contracting Parties to levy border taxes, sometimes known as border tax adjustments, imposing domestic, indirect taxes (i.e., excise, value added, and turnover taxes) on imports and rebating and/or excusing such taxes on their exports. A number of European nations and Japan, which relied heavily on indirect taxes (such as value added and turnover taxes), imposed significant border taxes, whereas the United States, which relied primarily on direct taxes (particularly income and property taxes), had only very limited scope for making border tax adjustments. In many circles this was viewed as discrimination against U.S. exports and subsidization of imports into the United States, contributing significantly to the U.S. balance-of-payments deficit. A number of papers regarding border taxes are in the Volcker Group records in the Washington National Records Center, Department of the Treasury, Volcker Group Masters: FRC 56 86 30. Border taxes were discussed in the GATT Working Party on Border Tax Adjustments. Documentation is in the National Archives, RG 59, Central Files 1970–72, FN 16 GATT.

The U.S. has talked about taxe occulte[3] and averaging primarily for tactical purposes—keeping the talks alive while we consider the basic issue. The problems of averaging and border adjustments for taxe occulte have largely passed us by as they do not inherently exist in the value added tax system. As Italy and Belgium will be adopting the TVA within 18 months, only Spain and Austria, among the developed nations, will be left with cascade tax systems[4]—the area of most abuse regarding averaging and taxe occulte. A modification of taxe occulte procedures would limit possible U.S. action while leaving Europeans free to obtain benefits equivalent to adjustment for taxe occulte by simple modifications of their TVA systems. It is clear that there is little economic or political advantage in pursuing a change regarding these points.

As for the third point, I agree that countries should not be allowed unilaterally to disrupt the international trading mechanism by changes in their border adjustments.

Border tax adjustments will continue to be a problem as EC tax harmonization proceeds. Eventually all of Western Europe will be using the TVA and making substantial changes in their border adjustments. These changes, condoned by the bias in the GATT rules, will have serious disruptive effects on both trade and international balance of payments adjustments. Failure to resist this undercutting of our economic strength will badly damage our ability to prevent other similar actions.

In order to argue that changes should be controlled, we must demonstrate that they have trade effects. But in most instances this is true only if direct taxes are, in part or in whole, passed forward to the consumer and/or indirect taxes are partially absorbed by the producer. Either position directly contradicts GATT rules and confronts us with the issue of amending them to correct the bias in favor of indirect tax systems. Unless the rules are amended, countries would argue that their actions are in conformity with GATT and they have no responsibility to offset any trade effects of changes in adjustments.

Thus advocacy by the U.S. of proposals covering the points raised by Ambassador Gilbert would seem to make sense only as part of a

---

[3] The taxe occulte is the "hidden" amount of tax that accrues in the value of a product, depending on the number of transactions that occur during a product's production and distribution. Unlike value added taxes where the rate of application is generally clear, when taxe occulte occurs the effective rate is difficult to gauge, giving rise to the question of what is the appropriate, "average" rate for border tax purposes. See *Border Tax Adjustments and Tax Structures in OECD Member Countries* (Paris: Organization for Economic Cooperation and Development, 1968), pp. 20–21 and 58–63.

[4] The cascade tax, or the turnover tax, was used in several European countries. Community members were expected to replace their cascade taxes with value added taxes.

package which includes a major change in how nations handle border adjustments for taxes.

Chairman McCracken's thesis that past changes in tax adjustments at the border are washed out by exchange rate changes disturbs me.[5] It seems to me wrong in implying an equilibrium that simply does not exist and cannot practicably be obtained.

We have all recognized the absolute necessity of attaining a stronger goods and services position. The present bias in the border tax adjustment rules complicates the achievement of this goal.

The plain fact is that exchange rate changes of the last 10 or 15 years have not and will not eliminate the problem of existing border tax adjustments: our trade balance and balance of payments structure have deteriorated in recent years. The fact that some exchange rate changes might have been different without the border adjustments, if true, provides no answer to the U.S. structural problem. Furthermore, numerous changes in border adjustments have occurred which were not offset even partially by exchange adjustments. Thus, Belgium and Italy have not modified their exchange rates since 1949, the Dutch since 1961, and most of Scandinavia since the immediate post World War II period. Changes in taxes and border adjustments have occurred regularly, with rates and product coverage generally increasing. It is only with respect to the 1960 and 1968 German revaluation and the 1961 Dutch revaluation that we can conceivably say that exchange rate change even went in the right direction in order to offset in part the trade effects of the border adjustment. But even in those cases, it cannot be definitively stated that the trade effects of cumulative border tax adjustments were effectively offset. It seems to me fruitless to argue that remaining disequilibria can simply be offset by further exchange rate changes that in practice are both unlikely in the degree necessary and deeply disturbing to the international monetary climate.

Carried to its logical conclusion, Chairman McCracken's argument implies that the U.S. need not worry about the level of existing U.S. and foreign tariffs, U.S. and foreign subsidies or most U.S. and foreign import barriers as changes in exchange rates have eliminated their economic impact on U.S. and foreign trade interests. If this were so, the trade message submitted by the President need not have called for tariff reducing authority nor provided for retaliatory authority against foreign subsidies in third country markets. Although exchange rate

---

[5] McCracken argued that if a country made a 10 percent border tax adjustment for, say, a value added tax, by rebating that amount on exports and levying that amount on imports, any trade impact of that adjustment would be offset by a corresponding 10 percent appreciation in that country's currency, which would render its exports 10 percent more expensive in foreign currencies and its imports 10 percent more expensive in domestic currency.

changes may conceivably eliminate balance of payments disequilibrium, in the sense of reserve losses and gains, we must always question whether the process of adjustment is desirable, the new equilibrium is appropriate for the world and for the U.S., and the resulting payment structure and resource allocation are truly efficient. A new equilibrium with the EC in a heavy trade surplus and the U.S. relying on capital inflows would be structurally unsatisfactory for the U.S. and for the entire world.

On a political level, I also do not believe that an argument that exchange adjustments have eliminated the impact of old border adjustments will be persuasive. Certainly these exchange adjustments do not eliminate our countervailing duty problems as the border adjustments continue to exist. In this regard I would point to recent statements by Congressman Mills that he intends to amend the countervailing duty law to require action against all rebates of taxes.

As I mentioned before, any effective mechanism for controlling changes in border adjustments must have as its basis the same arguments already put forward on the amount of adjustment for direct and indirect taxes. To achieve an effective control limiting a country's ability to make such adjustments or changes in them would require a basic amendment to the GATT rules. By limiting our substantive proposals to controlling changes in adjustments we do not reduce the need for achieving a structural change in GATT. We would, however, have thrown out one of our basic arguments, receiving nothing in exchange, and prejudicing our credibility on other U.S. initiatives.

David M. Kennedy[6]

---

[6] Printed from a copy that indicates Kennedy signed the original.

42.   Letter From Secretary of Agriculture Hardin to Secretary of State Rogers[1]

Washington, July 18, 1970.

Dear Mr. Secretary:

I refer to National Security Decision Memorandum (NSDM) 68, of July 3, 1970 which directs U.S. policy toward the European Community, and NSDM 45 of March 2, 1970 which directs U.S. policy toward the Spanish Trade Agreement with the European Community.[2] It is my understanding that NSDM 68 resolves the question which has held up implementation of NSDM 45.

NSDM 68 directs the Under Secretaries' Committee to coordinate the implementation of U.S. policy toward the European Community. There is a clear and compelling need for the Committee to move quickly. Action must be taken to restore confidence in the agricultural trading community that this Administration intends to defend U.S. agricultural interests. Accordingly, we propose that the Committee decide without further delay to:

1. Formally notify the parties to the Spanish/EC and Israeli/EC preferential trade agreements that we oppose implementation of these agreements, "in the context of opposition to all preferential arrangements illegal under the international trading rules of GATT" (NSDM 45), and that we intend to inscribe the matter on the agenda of the September Session of the GATT Council under the complaint procedures of Article XXIII:2. The two agreements were signed in Brussels on June 29, 1970. They will enter into force soon, possibly October 1, 1970. They are inconsistent with GATT provisions.

2. Formally notify the parties to the Tunisia/EC and Morocco/EC preferential agreements of our opposition to these agreements also. These agreements violate GATT provisions in the same way as the two agreements mentioned above. We should tell the parties at the same time that we intend to inscribe these agreements also on the September GATT Council agenda under the complaint procedures of Article XXIII:2. These two agreements were signed in Brussels on March 31, 1969. They have been in force since September 1, 1969.

3. Formally notify the EC and the applicant countries that we are able at this time to identify agriculture as a critical area for the United States in the accession negotiations and that within agriculture, grains

---

[1]   Source: National Archives, RG 59, S/S Files: Lot 81 D 309, NSC–U/SM 73A. Secret.

[2]   Neither printed. (Ibid., Lot 83 D 305)

and soybeans are particularly sensitive. Accordingly, the U.S. expects the present EC duty-free status of soybeans to be extended to the enlarged Community, and the grain prices for the enlarged Community to be reduced by $15 per ton from present EC levels.

It is clear that the European Community's Common Agricultural Policy is already seriously curbing agricultural exports from the United States and the rest of the world. U.S. exports to the EC subject to variable import levies have declined 47 percent since 1967. This decline is largely attributable to the Community's protective system. On grains, for example, the Community's high support prices, variable import levies and export subsidies have reduced Community net imports from 12 million tons to less than 4 million tons in the last three years. If this system is extended unchanged to an enlarged Community, further U.S. agricultural trade losses will be heavy as a result of curtailed market opportunities in Europe and subsidized European competition elsewhere. Losses will be in such critical commodities as grains, fruits, and tobacco.

We suggest that the Committee meet within the next week to take decisions on the matters set out above.[3] Prompt action in these cases is imperative. At an appropriate time, we will wish to make additional proposals to the Committee respecting the legality of the EC's variable levy system and other such matters.

Sincerely,

Cliff

---

[3] Under Secretary of State U. Alexis Johnson replied to Secretary Hardin's letter on July 25, informing Hardin that Deputy Under Secretary Samuels would chair the Under Secretaries Committee to carry out NSDM 68 and would hold a meeting of the Committee on August 12. (Ibid., NSDM 68) See Document 43.

43. Memorandum From the Deputy Under Secretary of State for Economic Affairs (Samuels) to the President's Assistant for National Security Affairs (Kissinger)[1]

Washington, August 20, 1970.

SUBJECT

USC Meeting on EC Enlargement

On August 12 the Under Secretaries Committee held its first meeting on the enlargement of the European Communities pursuant to the directives of NSDM 68.[2] As Chairman of the Committee for this meeting I would like to summarize for you the principal issues discussed:

1. *Consultative Mechanism.* I recounted to the Committee my recent talks with Commissioner Dahrendorf to establish a series of regular US–EC consultations. Dahrendorf and I tentatively agreed that these consultations should be held at least semi-annually and more frequently if necessary.[3] An agenda for each consultation would be agreed in advance and there would be maximum continuity and follow-up. The first consultation is tentatively scheduled for mid-October in Washington and we will confirm precise dates shortly. The Under Secretaries Committee agreed to this procedure. It was also noted that to ensure maximum continuity it would be desirable, insofar as possible, for the same people on both sides to participate in each of these meetings.

2. *Notification to Europeans of US Interests.* Discussion on this subject centered on two issues: the substance of our initial notification and the form of notification.

As to the substance, a draft "talking points" paper had been circulated prior to the meeting, and some preliminary comments were made on it at the meeting. Several agencies took the view that the language in NSDM 68 (Para 1) supersedes other statements by the President on

---

[1] Source: National Archives, RG 59, S/S Files: Lot 73 D 288, Box 837, USC/NSC. Confidential.

[2] See Document 42 and footnote 3 thereto. In preparation for the meeting, on August 7 Staff Director Arthur A. Hartman circulated to the Under Secretaries Committee several papers, including "Draft Talking Points To Be Used With Parties in EC Enlargement Negotiations." (National Archives, RG 59, S/S Files: Lot 81 D 309, NSC–U/SM 73A)

[3] In his August 5 Evening Report to the President, Secretary Rogers wrote that during the trade policy talks in Geneva, Deputy Under Secretary Samuels and EC Commissioner Dahrendorf had come to a verbal understanding on periodic talks on matters of mutual interest. Rogers thought the initial consultation would be in Washington between mid-October and mid-November, and Dahrendorf would head the EC delegation. He also pointed to a possible visit by Commission President Malfatti in early 1971 for an exchange of views with President Nixon. (Ibid., S/S Files: Lot 74 D 164)

European policy—notably the President's February message on foreign policy[4]—while State contended that all of the President's statements to date are consistent and may be drawn upon to express US policy. Specifically the view was expressed that the policy of favoring broadening and strengthening the community has now been watered down to favoring only "expansion" of the membership of the Community. An inter-agency working group was instructed to develop further the substance of the initial communication of US interests to the Community.

As to the form of notification to the Commission, there was agreement that it should take place at an early date, probably at the first US–EC consultation in October. Communication would also be made to national governments through our embassies. There was discussion of the pros and cons as to whether the communication should be oral or written, but it was decided to wait until the substance was agreed before deciding this point.

3. *Preferential Arrangements.* A position paper on EC preferential arrangements with Morocco, Tunisia, Spain, and Israel had been circulated prior to the meeting. The thrust of the paper was:

a. These four arrangements as presently constituted are inconsistent with the GATT.
b. We should identify, as soon as possible, potential damage to specific American exports and try to set up a bilateral meeting with the European Communities to look at possible measures to reduce the anticipated injury.
c. We would not wish to push formal GATT consideration of the preferential agreements while the bilateral talks are in progress.

Several agencies, notably the Department of Agriculture, took issue with this approach. They suggested instead that we promptly notify the EC and (presumably) the four Mediterranean countries that we object to the principle of these arrangements as contrary to the GATT and, unless they have proposals to redress the present situation, we intend to raise this issue at the September 29 GATT Council meeting to reiterate American opposition to the principle of these agreements and to invoke GATT Article 28. This action could lead to requests by us for compensation or failing to get satisfaction, for authority to retaliate.

An inter-agency working group was instructed to look into the details of such a course of action and report back to the Committee.

4. *Assessment of Specific Trade Interests.* For use throughout the course of the enlargement negotiations, a technical working group was instructed to begin as soon as possible to assemble the detailed tariff

---

[4] *U.S. Foreign Policy for the 1970's: A New Strategy for Peace, A Report to Congress,* February 19, 1970 (Washington: U.S. Government Printing Office, 1970). Also printed in *Public Papers of the Presidents of the United States: Richard M. Nixon, 1970,* pp. 116–190.

and other technical information necessary to assess the effect on US interests of specific proposals as they are put forward at Brussels.

By and large the first Under Secretaries Committee meeting elicited a lively exchange on the above issues. In view of the September 29 GATT meeting and the first US–EC consultation in mid-October, it will likely be necessary to hold another meeting of the Under Secretaries Committee in early September.

Conclusion. In summary, it is clear that there is a deep-seated and widespread hostility toward the Community in several agencies of the Executive Branch. Political considerations are brushed aside as largely irrelevant, and attention is focused on short-term economic considerations in a manner out of proportion to our long-term interests. It would be desirable for US policy toward the Community to be made unmistakably clear to the heads of all the Executive Agencies, with the directive that this be conveyed clearly to their staffs.

NS

44.   Editorial Note

The first in a series of bilateral consultations between the United States and the European Community was held October 15–16, 1970, in Washington. For a summary, see Document 47. In preparation for this consultation, the Under Secretaries Committee met on October 12 to discuss the issues. Prior to the meeting, on October 9 Staff Director Arthur Hartman distributed to the Committee an Objectives paper and copies of two papers cabled to USEC October 9 for delivery to the Commission setting forth U.S. positions. (National Archives, RG 59, S/S Files: Lot 81 D 309, NSC–U/SM 73B) On October 10 Hartman distributed to the Committee four additional position papers on EC enlargement, agriculture, preferential arrangements, and the GATT work program. (Ibid., NSC–U/SM 73C)

On October 9 Hartman also sent Under Secretary Irwin a briefing memorandum for an October 10 luncheon with Deputy Under Secretary Samuels and the October 12 Under Secretaries Committee meeting. Hartman wrote in his memorandum: "we can anticipate that the domestic agencies—Commerce, Treasury, Labor, and Interior—and to some extent the Office of the Special Trade Representative

(Ambassador Carl Gilbert) will want to take a hard line with the Europeans. In the previous Under Secretaries Committee meeting on this subject in August [see Document 43], State was subjected to a cross-fire of criticism from these agencies and received no offsetting support. This time we have alerted the NSC representative (Fred Bergsten) of the need to emphasize the President's support for EC enlargement and our basic policy of not interfering directly in negotiations between the British and the European Communities."

Hartman went on to say that Agriculture would likely be the most difficult issue in the consultation, and Assistant Secretary of Agriculture Palmby would suggest a reduction in the unified grain price. Hartman cautioned that "the important thing from our point of view is that such a request be made in the context of U.S.-EC relations, and not be linked in any way as a condition to our acceptance of U.K. membership in the Community." (National Archives, RG 59, S/S Files: Lot 83 D 305, NSDM 68)

While he was in Washington, EC Commissioner Ralf Dahrendorf met with Henry Kissinger at 6 p.m. on October 15. In his October 14 and 15 briefing memoranda for the meeting, Bergsten told Kissinger that "we are treading on the brink of a trade war" and that Dahrendorf was particularly concerned about the Mills bill, U.S. "unpredictability," and a perception that the United States was turning inward. (Ibid., Nixon Presidential Materials, NSC Files, Subject Files, Box 322, European Common Market, Volume I 1969–1970) According to the October 19 memorandum of the October 15 conversation, Kissinger assured Dahrendorf "that the Administration was in favor of free trade. Textiles were the lone exception, based on the President's campaign commitment to that industry. If the textile issue could be resolved through negotiations, Dr. Kissinger was confident that the threat of trade legislation could definitely be avoided." (Ibid.)

In an October 16 information memorandum to Kissinger summarizing the Dahrendorf visit, Bergsten noted that he agreed with Kissinger's assessment of the trade legislation "for this year," but cautioned that the problem was longer term and U.S. trading partners also needed to take free trade initiatives to help hold protectionism "at bay." Bergsten concluded that the Dahrendorf talks "went well from a procedural standpoint, and the consultative mechanism has been well launched." He cautioned, however, that "our major trade problems with the Community are not politically susceptible to resolution satisfactory to the United States, and I envisage increasing difficulty in overall U.S.-European relations as a result." (Ibid.)

45.   Editorial Note

Following negotiation of the 2-year offset agreement with Germany on July 9, 1969 (see Document 24), U.S. and German officials began to explore the prospect of German willingness to consider budgetary support to help defray foreign exchange costs of U.S. troops in Germany for the next offset beginning in July 1971. Deputy Under Secretary Samuels and Ambassador Pauls, for instance, discussed this possibility on January 29, 1970. (Evening Report from Secretary Rogers to the President, January 30; National Archives, RG 59, S/S Files: Lot 74 D 164) Moreover, the Under Secretaries' Committee recommended that during Chancellor Willi Brandt's visit to Washington in early April 1970, the President should discuss with him in general terms "the question of seeking new methods, including budget support, to reduce the financial burden resulting from the stationing of U.S. forces abroad." The Committee recognized that the issue was not an easy one for Brandt who might find it difficult to sell budgetary support for U.S. troops to the German people, particularly when the United States might not be prepared to offer the Germans the kind of troop support they would undoubtedly want in return The Under Secretaries' Committee attached to its recommendations its five-part study (with 11 appendices), "Foreign Exchange Offset and Budget Support for U.S. Forces in Germany and Other NATO Countries," which presented various options for the Nixon administration on these matters. (Memorandum from Richardson to Nixon, March 25; ibid., S/S Files: Lot 73 D 288, NSC–U/DM 30)

President Nixon decided, however, "to defer a judgment at this time on whether the U.S. should seek budget support from Germany in the next offset arrangement, beginning in July 1971." Although he wanted U.S. officials during the Brandt visit to indicate to their German counterparts in a general way "the desirability of improving the methods of easing the financial burden to the U.S. of maintaining our troops in Germany," he did not want them to raise the specific issue of budget support. If the Germans raised it, the U.S. officials could respond that they would certainly "consider it as one possible means of achieving improved methods for easing the U.S. financial problem." (Memorandum from Kissinger to the Secretaries of State, Defense, and the Treasury, April 8; ibid., Nixon Presidential Materials, NSC Files, Agency Files, Box 289, Treasury Volume I)

In June 1970 German Defense Minister Helmut Schmidt told Ambassador Kenneth Rush that the current offset agreement could not be continued in its present form after its expiration, and instead he had proposed to the NATO Defense Ministers a new type of multilateral

contribution to help the United States meet its European defense burdens. (Telegram 6764 from Bonn, June 12; ibid., Country Files–Europe,
Box 683, Germany, Volume V 4/10/70–7/31/70) Later in the year he
told Rush that any future financial burden-sharing contribution would
have to come out of the German defense budget, which could not be
increased, so he hoped any U.S. request for financial burden-sharing
would be small. He stressed that any German contribution would have
to be in a multilateral framework. (Telegram 11830 from Bonn, October
13; ibid., Box 684, Germany, Volume III 8/1/70–11/70)

**46.   Memorandum From Secretary of the Treasury Kennedy to
President Nixon**[1]

Washington, October 13, 1970.

It is with considerable concern that I view the interpretations being
placed upon your remarks concerning NATO made in your briefing
aboard the *Saratoga* and press conferences in Ireland.[2] Numerous classified cables and press reports suggest that we are dropping the broad
"burden sharing" concept. Since a satisfactory "burden sharing"
arrangement with our NATO Allies would help us and the Alliance
politically, militarily, and financially, I believe we should continue to
press for a satisfactory solution.

In my view the domestic political situation, particularly on the Hill,
concerning reductions in our NATO forces is serious. This political
problem is intimately tied to our critical budgetary and balance of payments condition. At the same time we must be careful that our relations
with our European Allies are not upset by any precipitous action either
by ourselves or by the Congress. With a proper "burden sharing" mix
all of these problems can be met or at least blunted for a sufficient period of time to enable us to adjust to new conditions.

There have been a number of discussions by myself personally and
my staff with counterparts from our NATO Allies. It must be recognized

---

[1]   Source: Washington National Records Center, Department of the Treasury,
Secretary's Memos/Correspondence, 1966–1970: FRC 56 74 7, Memo to the President
September–December 1970. Confidential. Copies were sent to Secretaries Laird and
Rogers.
[2]   See *Public Papers of the Presidents of the United States: Richard M. Nixon, 1970*, pp.
782–783 and 804–809.

that the current initiative in "burden sharing" being undertaken under the leadership of Germany is unprecedented.[3] In addition to whatever benefits may accrue to us it has increased the unity and thereby the strength of our Alliance. This in itself has made the preliminary efforts worthwhile.

The "burden sharing" mix mentioned above in my opinion is important to consider, for no one element of "burden sharing" will provide the complete solution to our political, military, or financial problems. We have looked at this problem carefully and believe that an appropriate mix would consist of some direct budgetary contribution on a multilateral basis to the U.S.; an offset agreement between the U.S. and the Federal Republic of Germany; a transfer of certain military functions from the U.S. to our NATO Allies; and an improvement and modernization of our Allies' national forces.

The U.S. should also consider for both tactical and substantive reasons a small reduction in our own forces committed to NATO. The Europeans have consistently stated that they are concerned that we do not make "substantial" reductions. A small reduction would be proof to our Allies that we are truly having problems and that their "burden sharing " effort was warranted as the reduction would have been much greater if they had not been forthcoming. Further, I detect a continuing tendency on the part of some of our Allies not to believe that we are having serious difficulties and that we therefore will not take any action. A small reduction would reinforce our verbal statements that they must do more for themselves in addition to helping our budgetary and political problems with the Congress.

In some of the internal cables recently sent on this subject and discussions which have been held within the Executive Branch a particular fallacy has developed. There are those who argue that we urge the Europeans to come up with additional funds with which they either improve their own forces or contribute to the U.S. In my opinion these cannot be equated. The Europeans have consistently made it quite clear that if they come up with additional funds, particularly in the short term, it will be because of the help they can provide the U.S. There is no indication that they plan significantly to increase their own defense budgets in order materially to improve their own national forces. Aside from difference of opinion as to the military need, if the European governments were to increase spending on their own forces, that would tend to be inflationary for them to the extent that they spent the money in their own country. This is an important reason why they are unlikely to do it.

---

[3] See Document 45.

Further, the argument being raised by some that we would be considered mercenaries has no validity. All we are asking in direct budgetary contributions is that the Europeans pay some share of the cost of local supplies and services. The U.S. forces would continue to be paid by us in their entirety.

We have an opportunity to improve the Alliance as well as helping to solve some of our problems. A well-planned negotiating effort with our Allies concerning "burden sharing" around the framework mentioned above will materially help. I must, however, say that the cables issued subsequent to your statements and discussed particularly with the Germans will make the task more difficult. An immediate clarification along the lines of the draft cable prepared by Mel Laird and discussed with you would immeasurably help to rectify the situation.[4] I therefore urge that we take this step and start a dialogue as requested by the EURO group minute as soon as possible.

David M. Kennedy[5]

---

[4] The draft cable was not found.

[5] Printed from a copy that indicates Kennedy signed the original.

---

47.   Information Memorandum From the President's Assistant for National Security Affairs (Kissinger) to President Nixon[1]

Washington, November 13, 1970.

SUBJECT

Initiation of Formal U.S. Consultations with the European Community

State has forwarded a summary of the recent consultations between the U.S. and the European Community (Tab A), the first in a series which will probably represent a new stage in our relations with the Community. We hope that the consultations will defuse, and perhaps

---

[1] Source: National Archives, Nixon Presidential Materials, NSC Files, Subject Files, Box 322, European Common Market, Volume I 1969–1970. Limited Official Use. Forwarded to Kissinger under cover of a November 6 memorandum from Bergsten who recommended it be sent forward to alert the President to the issues between the United States and the Community. Presumably after the memorandum came back from the President with his marginal notes, Kissinger wrote at the top: "Bergsten—keep this note in mind."

even help solve, the numerous contentious issues that will increasingly be arising between us.

This first meeting was carried out with unusual procedural smoothness. Substantively, there was less harmony. The discussions concentrated on four main topics:

a. *U.S. Trade Legislation.* Community representatives avoided threats, but made clear that they would probably have to react on the trade *and investment* fronts in response to shoe quotas and the excessive relaxation of the escape clause contained in the House trade bill. If the U.S. avoids enactment of protectionist legislation, however, the Community has offered to assist in a voluntary U.S.-Japanese textile agreement by not raising its own barriers to protect against diversion of Japanese sales to Europe.

b. *Community enlargement.* We made it clear that we continued to support enlargement, but that the Community would have to consider the effects on the economic interests of third countries, such as the U.S.

c. *Agriculture.* We explained our concern over the stiff agricultural protectionism of the Community. The Community said that a reduction of farm support prices (and hence increased imports) was out of the question, but that perhaps it could avoid exacerbating the problem through new price increases.[2]

d. *Community preferential arrangements.* The U.S. objected to the Community preferential arrangements with a whole range of Mediterranean countries as a violation of the Community's most-favored-nation commitment with injurious effects on our exports. The Community said that they are pursuing the agreements as the only instruments available to *the Community as a unit* to carry out a "European political responsibility" to the poor countries south of Europe.

This memo represents a reminder of an area of difficulties between our own domestic commercial interests and our European policy, which is now largely confined to the economic area but is likely to intensify and could easily spill over into the political arena.[3]

---

[2] The President partially encircled this paragraph and underscored "explained," next to which he wrote "We should *complain.*"

[3] The President wrote at the end of the memorandum: "K—it seems to me that we 'protest' and continue to get the short end of the stick in our dealings with the community. Agriculture is a prime example—The Congress is simply not going to tolerate this too passive attitude on the part of our representatives in such negotiations."

Tab A

Memorandum From Acting Secretary of State Irwin to President Nixon

Washington, October 29, 1970.

SUBJECT

US–EC Consultation October 15–16

Ralf Dahrendorf, Commissioner of the European Community (EC) in charge of Foreign Relations and Foreign Trade, and a delegation from the EC Commission met with an inter-agency delegation led by Deputy Under Secretary of State Nat Samuels on October 15 and 16 in the first of a series of consultations between the US and the EC pursuant to NSDM 68. The discussions centered largely on (1) US trade legislation, (2) EC enlargement, (3) EC agricultural policy, and (4) EC policy on preferential trading areas.

(1) US Trade Legislation

Dahrendorf expressed the fear that the Trade Bill could lead to an escalation of protective measures throughout the world that could seriously disrupt the international exchange of goods and capital. Although careful to avoid threats and explicitly saying that the Community does not intend to make threats, he said it would be unwise for us to think that the European Community would be unable to take common action in response to grave injury to the economic interests of its member states resulting from the Trade Bill. EC officials also made clear that American protectionist measures would strengthen the hand of those seeking to discriminate against European subsidiaries of American firms.

The Community would be directly and importantly affected by quotas on shoes, Dahrendorf said, and would most certainly react. But it is the modification of the escape clause, including the trigger mechanism in the Trade Bill, which is most troublesome because it has the potential to change the total complexion of world trade. The Community also objected to the Domestic International Sales Corporation as being an export subsidy in violation of GATT.

As a positive contribution to a solution of the textile impasse with Japan, the EC delegation indicated, subject to some qualification, it would not raise textile barriers against Japan if the US and Japan were able to arrive at a reasonable voluntary textile arrangement prior to enactment of US legislation.

(2) EC Enlargement

Nat Samuels assured the EC side that we continue to support the accession of the UK to the Common Market but we expect the parties to the negotiations to take fully into account the trading interests and GATT rights of the US and other third countries. The US side suggested the Community consider the effects of enlargement on third countries and made clear that we regard this bilateral consultative forum as appropriate for raising specific trade problems that might arise in the course of negotiations. Dahrendorf responded with an explanation of the problems and delicacy of dealing with third countries while the negotiations with the British and other applicants were proceeding but offered to consider specific suggestions that the US might make.

(3) Agriculture

Nat Samuels and Assistant Secretary of Agriculture Palmby set forth our concerns over the high level of agricultural protectionism in the Community and stressed the need to reduce grain support prices. This would have an important beneficial effect on our exports and reduce the adverse effects of extending the EC agricultural policy to the UK and other applicants. The EC delegation explained that the Commission is resisting political pressures for an increase in grain prices in the Community but insisted that a reduction in grain prices was politically out of the question. The most that could be hoped for was to continue to keep the grain price stable for several more years. At the current levels of inflation in Europe, stable prices would erode the real return to farmers and thus their stimulus to production, while bringing an improvement to the U.S. exporter in terms of real prices. It was agreed to hold subsequent policy-level discussions between the US and the EC on a variety of agricultural trade items, although the EC is unable to publicize explicitly its willingness to include discussions on grain prices lest this spark a political explosion.

(4) EC Preferential Arrangements

The US side made clear its objection in principle to the EC preferential trading arrangements in the Mediterranean which we believe violate the most-favored-nation principle of GATT. Dahrendorf defended these arrangements on political grounds and pointed out that these arrangements are for the time being the only instrument available to the Common Market to meet its responsibility to the Mediterranean littoral. He claimed the Common Market did not seek the arrangements for commercial advantage, and he insisted that they caused no commercial injury to the US or other third countries. The US side contested this by pointing out that the California–Arizona citrus industry has already complained of injury. It was agreed that without derogation from or compromising the question of principle, the US and the EC would jointly try to determine the damage to us resulting from these agreements.

John N. Irwin II

48. **Information Memorandum From C. Fred Bergsten of the National Security Council Staff to the President's Assistant for National Security Affairs (Kissinger)**[1]

Washington, December 3, 1970.

SUBJECT

The Absurdity of Possible Reductions in U.S. Forces Overseas for Balance of Payments Reasons

I was shocked to learn that Paul McCracken and Peter Flanigan had seriously raised with you the possibility of U.S. troop cuts abroad for balance of payments reasons.[2]

I take no stand on whether our overseas troop levels are correct. I do take the firmest possible stand that we should *never* reduce them for balance of payments reasons.

The last Administration had a major hangup over the balance of payments. It did everything from implementing mandatory capital controls, to proposing a tax on foreign travel by American citizens, to requiring the Defense Department to pay 50% higher prices to purchase U.S. commodities, to bringing down Erhard over the offset issue, to the additionality requirements on foreign aid. Even it, however, never reduced U.S. troops abroad for balance of payments reasons—though it considered the possibility repeatedly throughout its eight-year life.

The arithmetic demonstrates why. It is true that our foreign expenditures for military purposes are high. However, *drastic* reductions in our military capabilities would be required to produce *small* net gains for our balance of payments. When our deficit is running in the $3–$5 billion range, as it has for twelve years with temporary aberrations on either side of the range, the saving of a few hundred million dollars gets lost in the shuffle—and even a saving of that relatively small magnitude would require major shifts in troop deployments.

In view of the difficult decisions already made to maintain our troop levels in Europe, Vietnamize as rapidly as possible, and pull out of Korea at a pace which already causes major foreign policy problems, I do not see how we could seriously consider additional withdrawals for balance of payments reasons.

What would be the signal to the Soviets if we were to do so? It could only be that the U.S. had become so pitifully weak on the eco-

---

[1] Source: National Archives, Nixon Presidential Materials, NSC Files, Subject Files, Box 309, Balance of Payments. Secret. At the top of the memorandum, Haig wrote: *"Amen!"* when he rerouted it to Bergsten. Kissinger wrote: "I agree."

[2] Not further identified.

nomic and financial front that we could no longer make any pretense of maintaining our defense posture around the world.

It is bad enough to make overseas troop decisions on budgetary grounds, but this at least involves real resources and alternative uses of money. To do so for balance of payments reasons, in order to juggle the statistics marginally and enable us to tell the European *financial* officials "that we are doing something about our problem", would be criminal.

The underlying problem, as always, is the failure to properly perceive our balance of payments situation—and I deliberately do not say "balance of payments *problem*". An effort to clarify perceptions on this issue will be the first task of the new International Economic Policy Committee,[3] as worked out yesterday at George Shultz's meeting on the subject in which I participated. Hopefully, that exercise will dash any notions of troop cuts or other changes in serious policies for balance of payments purposes.

In addition, however, I urge you to stand firm against any such nonsense. I assume you will need little urging in this direction, but wanted to restate the case to you because of the absurdity of the proposal.

---

[3] Reference is to the Council on International Economic Policy (CIEP) established in January 1971; see Document 49.

---

49. Editorial Note

On January 18, 1971, President Nixon sent a memorandum to the Secretaries of State, Treasury, Agriculture, Commerce, and Labor; the Director of the Office of Management and Budget; the Chairman of the Council of Economic Advisers; the President's Assistant for National Security Affairs; the Executive Director of the Domestic Council; and the Special Trade Representative establishing a Council on International Economic Policy (CIEP). The President would chair the Council (in his absence the Secretary of State would chair the meetings), and the addressees of the memorandum were the Council's members. The President's memorandum was released to the public on January 19; see *Public Papers of the Presidents of the United States: Richard M. Nixon, 1971*, pages 40–41. The memorandum and additional documentation on the establishment of the Committee are scheduled for publication in a forthcoming *Foreign Relations* volume on the Organization and Management of Foreign Policy.

On February 1 Secretary of Defense Laird requested that the Department of Defense be represented on the CIEP, in part because of the balance-of-payments linkage with burden-sharing and offset negotiations. (Memorandum from Laird to Kissinger, February 1; National Archives, Nixon Presidential Materials, NSC Files, Agency Files, Box 226, DOD 12/1/70–2/23/71) In a February 19 memorandum to White House Staff Assistant John Campbell, Kissinger noted that Laird's request was reasonable but doubted the CIEP would have sufficient military or security business to warrant a permanent Defense Department member. Kissinger suggested getting Peterson's opinion before making a decision on Laird's request. (Ibid.) At least in part because of concerns about NSC control, Kissinger on July 17 sent a memorandum to Peterson, who had some sympathy with the idea, opposing Defense Department participation in the CIEP. (Ibid., Box 218, CIEP) On August 9, however, Peterson sent a memorandum to the CIEP members, including the Secretary of Defense, stating the President's decision that the Secretary of Defense should be a member of the Council and that the Department of Defense would participate fully in the Council's work. (Ibid.)

---

50.   Editorial Note

Under instructions from Henry Kissinger, in early 1971 the NSC Under Secretaries' Committee completed a six-section study entitled "Report on German Offset Negotiations," which it forwarded to the President under cover of a January 19, 1971, memorandum from Nathaniel Samuels, Acting Chairman of the Under Secretaries' Committee. In his memorandum Samuels made the following recommendations concerning the German offset negotiations:

"1. The Under Secretaries Committee recommends that you authorize the negotiation of a new two-year offset agreement with the Federal Republic of Germany covering the period July 1, 1971 through June 30, 1973.

"2. The Committee recommends that, as an initial negotiation position, we seek both maximum quantity ($850 million) and best quality of components in an agreement. Such an offset agreement, together with the recently agreed European Defense Improvement Program (EDIP) would then yield a total burden-sharing package of $1.0–1.1 billion annually.

"3. The Committee recommends that the U.S. negotiators be authorized if necessary in the course of the negotiations to reduce the quantity goal to achieve better quality. This could involve a fallback to about $700 million in terms of order of magnitude.

"4. It is recommended that, to the extent possible, offset negotiating efforts be directed principally to maximizing those offset components which best contribute to improving German and allied conventional defense capability, preferably through direct military procurement and, possibly, by German underwriting of certain Military Assistance Programs now financed by the United States and German assumption of certain costs now borne by the United States in Germany. These are high-quality components. Other components, such as civilian procurement, loans and sales of Eximbank paper, would be assigned lower negotiating priorities.

"5. Finally, the Under Secretaries Committee recommends your approval of the proposed negotiating scenario outlined in the enclosed report calling for a United States negotiating team to be headed by Deputy Under Secretary Samuels with negotiations concluded, if possible, by June 1." (National Archives, RG 59, S/S Files: Lot 73 D 288, NSC/USC Memos)

In a February 17 memorandum to the Chairman of the Under Secretaries' Committee, Kissinger reported the President's approval of these recommendations. (Ibid., Central Files 1970–73, FN 12 GER W)

The first round of negotiations was held in Bonn March 10–11. An undated Department of State paper summarizing these talks is ibid. The second round took place in Washington April 15–16. An undated Department of State paper summarizing these talks noted in part: "As at the first round of talks in Bonn, the atmosphere was very good. However, the German position had advanced very little and at the conclusion the two sides were still quite far apart." (Ibid.)

Following this impasse intensive behind-the-scenes maneuvering and consultations took place prior to the third round of negotiations in Bonn June 28–29. Telegraphic communications between the Embassy in Bonn and the Department of State on these efforts are ibid. A June 25 memorandum from Ernest Johnston of the National Security Council Staff to Kissinger advised that Kissinger recommend to the President that a State Department position to accept a possible further German compromise be rejected. Johnston pointed out the severe split among the State, Treasury, and Defense Departments on the U.S. position for the upcoming Bonn discussions, the shortness of time, and the uncertainty over whether the Germans were prepared to compromise further. He recommended that U.S. negotiators continue to press the Germans strongly but that no U.S. decision on what to accept be made until after the Bonn meetings.

(Ibid., Nixon Presidential Materials, NSC Files, Country Files–Europe, Box 685, Germany Volume IX 4–8/71)

Regarding the final U.S.-German negotiations leading to the initialing of an Agreed Minute on offset in Brussels on December 10, see Document 86. Additional documentation on the German offset negotiations during 1971 is scheduled for publication in a forthcoming *Foreign Relations* volume on Western European regional issues.

---

51.   Information Memorandum From the President's Assistant for National Security Affairs (Kissinger) to President Nixon[1]

Washington, February 9, 1971.

SUBJECT

Foreign Attitudes Toward U.S. Economic Policies

Secretary Rogers has sent you a memorandum summarizing the views of our principal ambassadors on European and Japanese attitudes toward the U.S. economic situation (Tab A).[2]

The Europeans are, of course, very sensitive to the health of the American economy since it greatly influences their own situation. Most of them express strong recognition of a need for a resumption of U.S. economic growth—even the French, who because of their monetary and nationalistic investment concerns, have not generally felt this way in the past. There is great worry, particularly in financial circles, about the other side of the balance—the possibility of a resumed U.S. inflation—but the greater stress by officials with broader concerns is clearly on the need for an up-turn in the American economy.

U.S. inflation or an immoderate resumption of U.S. growth are most worrisome for their international monetary implications, and their exacerbating European domestic inflation. Many worry, for example, that a

---

[1] Source: National Archives, Nixon Presidential Materials, NSC Files, Subject Files, Box 323, Foreign Aid, Volume I 7/70–1971. Confidential. At the top of the memorandum, the President wrote: "Be sure this gets to Peterson,"and Kissinger wrote: "Send comments to Shultz." The memorandum is attached to a January 28 memorandum from Bergsten recommending that Kissinger forward the report to the President. Bergsten wrote that "responses reflect the usual foreign schizophrenia toward the U.S. economy," especially the European perception of the threat of a continued U.S. slowdown.

[2] Dated January 22; not printed.

continued rapid lowering of U.S. interest rates will cause a massive flow of funds to Europe, weakening the international monetary system and their own efforts to restrain inflation. The Europeans are disturbed that our colossal monetary importance, combined with the inflexibility of international exchange rates, drags their interest rates behind ours and vitiates the effect of their monetary measures on their domestic economies or on their balance of payments.[3] (To avoid some of these consequences, and to avoid charges that we don't care about our balance of payments, we have already increased the Export-Import Bank's borrowing abroad and reduced the margin requirements which were to some extent pushing U.S. banks to disgorge their previous foreign borrowings.)

Consequently, the foreigners tend to favor U.S. use of fiscal measures rather than monetary measures as medicine for our current problems. They disagree on the domestic effectiveness of incomes policies, and are therefore ambivalent about how the United States should use such measures. However, they do seem to favor some use of strict Federal Government power to help slow wage and price increases. State did not quiz the ambassadors on U.S. trade policy, but most ambassadors made a strong point about foreign concern over the direction these policies have been taking. Part of their interest in resumed U.S. economic growth stems from the belief that U.S. protectionism has gathered force from our economic slowdown.

---

[3] The President drew a line in the left margin next to this paragraph and wrote: "Shultz—An early project for the Peterson Council should be examination of the need for a new Int'l Monetary system. This should be undertaken with the closest consultation with Treasury, C.E.A. and Burns." On March 10 Kissinger sent a memorandum to Shultz and Peterson containing the President's instruction. (National Archives, Nixon Presidential Materials, NSC Files, Agency Files, Box 218, CIEP)

---

52. Editorial note

John Connally replaced David Kennedy as Secretary of the Treasury on February 11, 1971, and Kennedy was sworn in as Ambassador at Large for Foreign Economic Policy Development. On December 29, 1971, President Nixon announced that he intended to appoint Kennedy as U.S. Permanent Representative to the North Atlantic Treaty Organization, which he did on March 17, 1972. Kennedy continued to serve as Ambassador at Large for Foreign Economic Policy Development and remained in that position until March 8, 1973.

On December 2, 1971, Kennedy, who was in London, sent a back channel message to Kissinger at the White House outlining his understanding of the parameters of his prospective appointment as Permanent Representative to NATO. To realize the President's objective of a strong representation in NATO, Kennedy recommended, among other things, that the President make a "clear and unequivocal" statement emphasizing particularly that Kennedy was being assigned to Brussels as "Ambassador at Large and as a member of the Cabinet to illustrate the importance the President attaches to NATO and our economic relations with Europe in general." Kennedy also requested that the Ambassadors to USEC and USOECD clear with him all important issues to "ensure the President's policies and programs were properly and consistently presented to the Europeans." (Attachment to letter from Kennedy to Connally, December 6; Washington National Records Center, Department of the Treasury, Records of Secretary Shultz: FRC 56 80 1, Miscellaneous)

Kissinger discussed Kennedy's message with the President during an Oval Office meeting at noon on December 2. He reported that Kennedy was prepared to accept the NATO appointment subject to some conditions, which Kissinger explained. As Kissinger concluded, the President said "those are all fine." He wanted "somebody who will be my man, who will play ball. Rogers probably wants him out of his hair at State anyway. Don't tell him about the understanding." (National Archives, Nixon Presidential Materials, White House Tapes, December 2, 1971, 11:35 a.m.–12:13 p.m., Oval Office, Conversation 628–2)

---

53.   Memorandum From the President's Assistant for International Economic Affairs (Peterson) to President Nixon[1]

Washington, February 22, 1971.

SUBJECT

First Steps

---

[1] Source: National Archives, Nixon Presidential Materials, NSC Files, Agency Files, Box 218, CIEP. Confidential. A stamped notation reads: "The President has seen." Attached to a March 1 memorandum from Peterson to Kissinger regarding the CIEP's role. Another copy is attached to a February 24 memorandum from Bergsten to Kissinger, which called Kissinger's attention to item IV on "rethinking" balance of payments and international financial policy, in which Peterson was reflecting Shultz' desire "to rid ourselves completely of the capital controls inherited by the Administration." Bergsten noted that this "could cause serious foreign policy problems and in fact the international monetary scene could become very troublesome before the year is out if our payments position remains in heavy deficit." (Ibid.)

I summarize below my first week's efforts. I ask for your approval for several initial actions in which Messrs. Ehrlichman, Kissinger, and Shultz concur:[2]

I. *Immediate Problems* (Tab A)[3]—That you give me two weeks for an effort to try to assure that your next decision on shoes and cheese is based on a complete analysis of the issues and the impact of this combination of measures upon our basic trade posture,

II. *A Positive Trade Strategy* (Tab B)—Preparation of a Positive Trade Strategy for 1971–72 designed to put the Administration on the offensive in its support of liberal trade policy; principally, with a comprehensive and constructive program for industrial adjustment to foreign competition. Such a program should help minimize the possibility of a Congressional initiative for restrictive legislation.

III. *A Tri-Partite Initiative* (Tab C)[4]—Planning for a major international initiative on a broad range of international economic problems focusing on the US–EC–Japan relationship.

IV. *Balance of Payments Strategy* (Tab D)[5]—A basic rethinking of our approach to balance of payments and international monetary problems.

---

[2] The President initialed his approval of each of the four recommended actions.

[3] None of the tabs is printed. They are sections of an undated and untitled 11-page paper attached to the copy of the memorandum cited in footnote 1 above.

[4] Section III of the paper was summarized in a January 25 memorandum from Bergsten to Kissinger: "The Bureau of Economic Affairs has recommended that the Secretary of State propose to the President that he call a summit conference of Western leaders on international economic problems for this autumn. I understand the Secretary is interested, and you may recall that he alluded to such a possibility at our meeting with the President on U.K. agricultural policy last Monday (January 18)." Bergsten considered the State Department idea "grandiose" and was skeptical the summit could be organized, but stopped short of "throwing cold water on State's idea" at that time. (National Archives, Nixon Presidential Materials, NSC Files, Agency Files, Box 216, CEA) No documentation on a formal State Department proposal for a summit was found.

[5] Section IV of the paper made a recommendation to "review our fundamental policies with those in the Administration having responsibility in this area, and some knowledgeable outsiders as well, in order better to fashion the fundamental approach we should take over the next few years."

54.   Memorandum From the Director of the Office of Management and Budget (Shultz) to the Members of the Council on International Economic Policy[1]

Washington, March 2, 1971.

SUBJECT

The Capital Control Programs

Each of these programs imposes costs on U.S. business and financial institutions and, through them, on the economy as a whole.

The programs were enacted and have been maintained despite these costs on the grounds that they achieve a result: an improved balance-of-payments position for the United States.

Some have argued that the costs are such as to suggest relaxation of the programs despite the presumed result. This point of view highlights the importance of the *costs.*

There are additional arguments against retaining the controls. The ability of these programs to achieve substantial and desirable *results* is questioned. If this argument is correct, then the balance of payments argument is irrelevant and, in view of the undoubted costs, the programs should be abandoned. Material presented in the attached memorandum leads me to that point of view.

George P. Shultz

Attachment

CAPITAL CONTROLS: QUESTIONABLE RESULTS AND UNDOUBTED COSTS

Controls on capital outflows from the United States were designed as temporary measures to deal with short-term problems in the U.S. balance of payments during the mid-1960s.

Three programs are now in effect:

1. *The Interest Equalization Tax,* designed to restrict the sale of foreign securities in the United States;
2. *The Voluntary Foreign Credit Restraints Program,* designed to restrict the availability to foreigners of banking services in the United States; and

---

[1] Source: National Archives, Nixon Presidential Materials, NSC Files, Agency Files, Box 218, CIEP. No classification marking. Sent through Peterson. The memorandum is the attachment to Document 55.

3. *Foreign Direct Investment Program,* designed to restrict U.S. financing of foreign direct investments by U.S. firms.

The President has pledged himself to "bring an end to self-defeating controls on investment at the earliest possible time."

This memorandum reviews the reasons why I believe it is timely to redeem the President's pledge.

Estimates of Effectiveness of Individual Programs

The balance of payments is not necessarily determined by trade and capital flows in the direct and predictable way which casual reasoning suggests.

As a result of the format in which the accounts are conventionally arranged, the flow of reserves happens to be the last item listed in the international financial accounts. The assumption that this residual account will be the one to absorb the impact whenever there is a change in some other account is unwarranted. It is equally plausible that one of the other accounts will respond.

For example, it is by no means clear that a reduction in the outflow of U.S.-owned capital will have any effect on the flow of reserves. A priori, any number of accounts could absorb the change. In particular, economic reasoning suggests that the closest substitute category (foreign capital flows) will take up the slack. To the extent that capital from one source is a close substitute for capital from another, the reduction in U.S. capital outflows should be offset by an equal reduction in foreign capital inflows. There is no reason to expect that capital controls would, in any significant sense, actually reduce the net outflow of reserves.

Compliance with the administrative regulations under the control program appears to have been satisfactory. However, the Office of Foreign Direct Investment believes that the longer the controls are in effect, and as costs of compliance to U.S. business rise, compliance problems will grow more serious. In any case, nominal compliance with regulations is not the major test of effectiveness of the programs. Effectiveness is best measured by:

—The degree to which balance of payments gains are offset by losses resulting from nonregulated transactions induced by the control;

—The relevance of the controls, given the role of the United States in the international monetary system.

I am aware of three direct attempts to estimate the balance-of-payments effects of specific parts of the U.S. capital control programs. These studies are summarized below:

The Interest Equalization Tax

In his study, Cooper[2] compared movements in controlled and uncontrolled capital flows before and after the inception of the IET. He found that net purchases of taxable securities fell by $500 million between the half year just preceding proposal of the tax and a year later. This effect was completely offset by increases in U.S. direct investment, long-term lending by banks, and short-term lending by banks and others. As it happened, the U.S. balance of payments hardly improved despite a $2.7 billion increase in the surplus on goods and services. Cooper therefore concluded that the IET "failed in its broader objective of improving the U.S. balance of payments."

The Voluntary Foreign Credit Restraint Program

Laffer[3] developed two empirical relationships relating capital flows to economic variables using monthly statistics prior to the inception of the VFCRP. Under test, these two relationships proved to be accurate predictors of both private U.S. short-term capital outflows and foreign private short-term capital inflows.

Based on data for the sixteen months following the inception of the VFCRP, the same relationships were then used to estimate the effects of the program on short-term capital flows.

The graph below displays the cumulative balance-of-payments effects reported by Laffer. According to the graph, outflows of U.S. private short-term capital were definitely retarded. These favorable balance-of-payments effects were, however, by early 1966, almost precisely offset by compensating unfavorable movements in private foreign short-term capital flows.

[Omitted here is the graph illustrating the conclusion.]

This led Laffer to conclude that:

. . . The net effects of the VFCRP on the U.S. balance of payments seem to be quite negligible. In fact, for a long time, the VFCRP appears to have cost the United States in terms of foreign exchange, and only after a year or more in operation were the net effects on the U.S. official settlements balance of payments non-negative. Therefore, the ostensible success of this program with respect to U.S. capital flows appears to have been negated by foreign capital flows.

---

[2] Richard N. Cooper: "The Interest Equalization Tax: An Experiment in the Separation of Capital Markets," paper # 78, Economic Growth Center, Yale University, 1967. [Footnote in the source text.]

[3] Arthur B. Laffer: "Short-Term Capital Movements and the Voluntary Foreign Credit Restraint Program," unpublished paper, University of Chicago, 1969. [Footnote in the source text.]

The Foreign Direct Investment Program

The CPR[4] Study came to the following conclusions:

The available statistics regarding the OFDI program . . . cast doubt on the extent to which the program actually restricts direct foreign investment today. The figures set forth show that U.S. firms have never invested the full amount permitted by OFDI quota. . . .

Of course, not all of these allowables can be utilized by individual firms. However, even after taking this wastage into account, it is clear that generous investment allowables are available in most cases to U.S. firms wishing to expand their investments abroad. . . .

These facts naturally raise questions as to why we need a direct investment control program, costing about $3 million per year to administer, plus much larger amounts in compliance costs incurred by the firms subject to OFDI controls.

The Cost of Capital Controls

Although there is no precise measure of the costs of maintaining capital controls, the type of costs and their significance in the aggregate are evident:

—The prestige costs to our country of unsuccessful attempts to manipulate our balance of payments via controls;

—The administrative costs to the Government in running the program, and to the private sector in complying with it;

—The economic costs resulting from the inefficient reallocation of resources by business and financial institutions as they respond to the program;

—The commercial costs of lost business for U.S. financial institutions as other countries develop their own financial intermediaries;

—The political costs to the Administration of continuing an unpopular program.

An Overall Assessment

1. From an economic point of view, there is no reason to expect the capital control programs to succeed. When Americans are inhibited from transmitting capital abroad, it is logical that foreigners will do the investing in their place. As a consequence, foreigners will reduce their U.S. investments. There is no reason to expect that net capital flows (or reserves) will change one way or the other as a result of these programs.

2. Detailed studies of the capital control programs have uncovered absolutely no evidence of any effect on the balance of payments.

3. The programs impose severe administrative costs on both government and business; they misallocate resources; and they penalize

---

[4] Center for Political Research: *Federal Control of Foreign Direct Investments,* research report, May 11, 1970. [Footnote in the source text.]

Americans for transacting freely with foreigners. Ironically, they have no demonstrable favorable effects.

4. The common and primary purpose of the capital control programs is to stem the net outflow of U.S. official reserve assets by obstructing American investments and loans to foreigners. All available evidence suggests that these programs cannot and have not accomplished or even worked towards this purpose.

---

55.   CIEP Study Memorandum No. 1[1]

Washington, March 8, 1971.

MEMORANDUM FOR

The Secretary of State
The Secretary of the Treasury
The Secretary of Agriculture
The Secretary of Commerce
The Secretary of Labor
The Director, Office of Management and Budget
The Chairman, Council of Economic Advisers
The Assistant to the President for National Security Affairs
The Executive Director of the Domestic Council
The Special Representative for Trade Negotiations

SUBJECT

Development of an International Economic Strategy for 1971–1972

The President has decided that:[2]

1. The Administration should develop a positive trade and legislative strategy for 1971–1972. This strategy should include a comprehensive and constructive program for industrial adjustment to foreign competition. Such a program should help minimize the possibility of a Congressional initiative for restrictive legislation.

2. In order to assure that the shoe case is considered in this larger context of Administration trade and legislative strategy, the President has directed that I prepare a complete analysis of the issues and the impact of the shoe case within two weeks.

---

[1] Source: National Archives, Nixon Presidential Materials, NSC Files, Agency Files, Box 218, CIEP. Confidential. Initialed by Haig.

[2] See Document 53.

3. We should begin intensive planning for a major international initiative on a broad range of international economic problems focusing on the US–EC–Japan relationship. While the main emphasis shall probably be on trade problems, it should also consider important related issues such as investment, aid, and monetary problems.

4. The Administration should initiate a basic review of its approach to the balance of payments and international monetary problems. One illustration of the many issues that arise in the context of our balance of payments programs is the capital control program. I attach a paper from Mr. Shultz on that particular subject.[3]

Action Requested:

1. I would appreciate your preliminary suggestions on subjects to be included in items (1) and (3) by March 15. The purpose of this initial outline of subject areas is to define the possible scope of the effort and to serve as a basis for discussion at the first meeting of the Council to be scheduled shortly.

2. I would appreciate receiving any additional comments you have on the shoe case by March 12, 1971.

3. Your comments by March 30 on the paper submitted by Mr. Shultz would be welcome.

Peter G. Peterson

---

[3] Document 54.

56.   Paper Prepared in the Department of State[1]

Washington, March 16, 1971.

INTERNATIONAL ECONOMIC STRATEGY FOR THE 1970'S

I. The Problem

The character of our economic relations with Western Europe and Japan have been strained. We are at odds on a variety of problems. Most important, at the moment, are textiles, agriculture and monetary issues. On the horizon are problems of reconciling various national policies which affect the economies of other countries, U.S. investment, and international trade in general. More specifically, some of the most immediate issues facing us are that:

—U.S. industry and labor are demanding import restrictions on a variety of products.

—The U.S. farm bloc is concerned over access to the European Common Market and over prospective losses when Britain enters.

—Despite the economic benefits to the United States of an enlarged European Community, specific sectors of U.S. industry may be adversely affected when the British become part of the Community.

—American labor is concerned about jobs presumably lost as the multinational corporation establishes production abroad.

—American industry wants greater access to the Japanese market for exports and investment.

—Foreigners are concerned about the resurgence of protectionist sentiment in the United States as illustrated by the Mills bill, voluntary textile, steel and meat restrictions and quotas for imports of dairy products.

—Europeans are concerned about our balance of payments deficit, particularly stemming from massive flows of short-term capital, and our attitude toward it.

—Foreigners are uneasy about the growing power of the U.S.-based multinational corporation.

Despite these problems the world economy has been growing rapidly and U.S. international trade and investment are thriving. The fact of our success, however, has produced sharp adjustment problems—domestically and internationally—that require urgent attention.

If these problems are not dealt with, the international institutions for economic cooperation, developed in the postwar period and which serve us well, could be threatened.

---

[1] Source: National Archives, RG 59, Central Files 1970–73, E 1. Confidential. Drafted by A. Reifman and J. Renner (E), A. Katz (EUR), and E. Preeg (S/PC) on March 16. Sent to Peterson under cover of a March 16 memorandum from Samuels who indicated it responded to Peterson's request in CIEPSM No. 1 (Document 55).

Even more important, there would be serious political fall-out if world economic cooperation deteriorated. We cannot expect the same cooperation on political and security issues from our major allies in an atmosphere of increasing acrimony over economic issues. Public support at home for our international security policies would be undermined. And, if the economic climate deteriorates sufficiently, the poor countries will have greater difficulty in standing on their own feet.

What we need is a framework among the industrialized countries—principally the U.S., the EC, and Japan—to deal with these existing concerns as well as the new developments we will be facing in the years ahead. The industrialized countries need to intensify their economic cooperation in all areas, including a better ordering of trade relationships directed toward more liberal access to markets, and a more smoothly functioning monetary relationship. Such a program can be undertaken only in cooperation with other countries. Acting alone, and on each problem separately, governments are under pressure to find narrow solutions to domestic problems at the expense of foreigners.

Such a program will require considerable preparation at home and careful consultation abroad. Until it can be developed, we need an interim program to deal with immediate pressures.

II. An Interim Program

An interim program might have four major components:

—International action on specific problems, particularly textiles and certain agricultural products;
—international consideration of the agenda and schedule for a broad economic initiative;
—domestic discussion of issues with Congress and the public;
—trade legislation.

A. Textiles and Various Agricultural Problems

Concerning textiles, we must first deal with the short run problems of imports from Japan and other Asian suppliers through 1973. We should also, however, take up GATT Director General Long's proposal that a multinational consideration of trade problems for all textiles be undertaken before the expiration of the current arrangement on cotton textiles. In the face of increased imports from low wage countries the textile industries in developed countries constitute a strong force against trade liberalization. If Long's proposal could be acted upon, the textile issue might be isolated.

In addition to an effort to settle the textile problem, we should press forward to resolve several highly politicized agricultural problems with the EC—citrus, tobacco, poultry, and lard—and should seek to avoid an increase in EC corn prices. We should recognize, however, that the probability of success is small. We have been trying to deal with trade problems one by one for years with no positive results. In this context governments find it difficult politically to stand up to particular interests.

B. International Consideration of a Broad Economic Initiative

The possible substance of a broad economic initiative is described in Part III of this memorandum. Such an undertaking will require a period of international consultation, as well as domestic soundings. The prospects for a major initiative can also mitigate domestic concerns and pressures, even though actual negotiations may not begin for some time.

We believe it is important, therefore, to initiate international consideration of a comprehensive economic program at the OECD Ministerial Meeting in June.

The organization is the right one in terms of membership. June is the time when the UK entry negotiations will be reaching a crunch and public interest and concern in this country are expected to be considerable.

No binding commitment to international negotiations can be expected before the basic decision on UK entry is made. However, such a commitment must be prepared by a careful process of international consultation and discussion in the media.

The OECD Ministerial Meeting would lay out the need for an international economic action program for the 1970's, and appoint a special group to prepare the guidelines for such a program. This group should consist of high-level government representatives of the U.S., the EC, the UK, Japan, and Canada. Such a group would begin serious work in the fall of 1971 and outline the content of such an action program.

C. Domestic Discussion

We also need to enter into low-key but extensive consultations with Congress and to make a major effort to raise the level of public consideration of the issues at home. We must show how much we have gained from an open, integrated world economy, what we risk by standing still, and what we lose by moving backward.

While there is no substitute for good policy, such policy cannot grow without public understanding and support. The forthcoming reports of the Williams Commission and the Boggs Congressional Subcommittee could be keystones of a public discussion program. But the enormous prestige and influence of the President will be required to coalesce support for a liberal policy.

D. Interim Trade Legislation

The basic question is whether there is any advantage to be gained by seeking interim trade legislation. Our efforts in 1970 to relax the escape clause led to results that would have been disastrous if the Mills Bill had passed. The relaxation of the escape clause in that Bill would have resulted in an enormous amount of new restrictions that would have set off a trade war. In any case, the Tariff Commission, by interpretation, has already relaxed the escape clause, and particularly adjustment assistance criteria. It would, of course, be highly desirable to eliminate ASP, but given the difficulties attendant upon seeking new legislation now, action could well be deferred until comprehensive new legislation is sought.

The lack of authority to provide tariff concessions for new escape clause actions which might be taken in the next year or so is troublesome, but, if necessary, we can live with it.

There is one measure which we are under an international obligation to present to Congress—the generalized preference scheme for developing countries. The precise timing and tactics of submission of this legislation must be carefully worked out.

If we should decide to seek interim legislation, the most likely elements would be:

1. Relaxing the adjustment assistance and escape clause provisions of the Trade Expansion Act.
2. Minor tariff reduction authority essentially to permit us to grant comprehension [*compensation*?] for our escape clause actions.
3. Repeal of ASP.

III. A New International Economic Initiative

A major international initiative should cover the whole gamut of economic issues of the 70's, although trade, agriculture, and monetary issues will likely be among the most predominant. The major areas for consideration are: agriculture, non-agricultural trade, foreign investment, international finance and assistance to the developing countries. These are briefly described below.

1. Agriculture

Governments of all countries use a wide range of domestic support programs and trade restrictions to help their farmers. The United States has suffered from agricultural policies of other countries, particularly the Common Market and Japan. We are an efficient agricultural producer. Thus, measures to put agricultural trade on a more liberal basis would be in our interest. We also would have to permit an increase in agricultural imports.

In preparing for negotiations which would likely have to deal with the whole range of domestic agricultural programs as well as agricultural trade policies, we should consider the desirability of pursuing the following topics:

a. Stand-still agreements to prevent further restrictions or changes in support programs pending comprehensive negotiations.
b. Internationally negotiated price support levels.
c. Internationally negotiated production controls.
d. Income support programs for families in lieu of conventional price–production–marketing programs.
e. Measures to stimulate demand for farm products. Surplus disposal policies, including food aid. Export subsidies.
f. Other trade barriers.

Since U.S. agricultural exports would expand more than our imports if more efficient agricultural policies were adopted, reciprocity would likely require U.S. concessions on industrial goods as well as agricultural goods.

2. Industrial Tariffs

We have two main reasons for wanting to bring about the reduction of industrial tariffs:

—The enlargement of the European Community in the short run will likely cause some deterioration in the competitive position of American exports. A lowering of the common external tariff of the European Community would ameliorate this problem,
—Foreign governments, especially Japan, and including Canada, have high barriers against products with a large technological component where the American comparative advantage is unusually great.

The Europeans can be expected to insist that some formula be adopted to bring the tariff structures of the major industrialized countries more in conformity with each other.

We will need to consider a formula that would result in both tariff reduction (to satisfy our demands) and tariff harmonization (to satisfy the Community's demands). We might also consider a virtual phasing out of tariffs in certain sectors or under certain conditions.

3. Quantitative Restrictions (Including Voluntary Restraints)

Japan is the major sinner as far as American exports are concerned. Liberalization of Canadian quotas would also benefit our exports.

Japan, in turn, can be expected to insist on a definite schedule for the elimination of discriminatory measures against Japan and the reduction of other quantitative restrictions, including our voluntary restraints.

4. Other Trade Restrictions

Foreign governments have a multitude of other trade restrictions. Their significance in potential trade terms varies greatly. We need to identify those which are the most significant and on which we could make headway. Government procurement policies form one such area. Japan, with a multiplicity of controls on imports, and Canada, with various practices to encourage investment at the expense of imports, would be our major targets. The Europeans also have a number of restrictions that should be included in the negotiations.

Foreign governments will press the U.S. on a number of our own restrictions—including the absence of an injury clause in our countervailing duty law and our failure to abide by the terms of the anti-dumping code—and we must carefully assess our overall interests in this area at an early date.

5. International Investment

The investment issue among developed countries is a composite of assertions with political and economic content. Possible problem areas include:

—European and Japanese fear of loss of control over the direction of domestic economies when decision-making for large enterprises is in the hands of foreigners.
—The sovereignty issue also arises when the U.S. seeks to assert extraterritorial control, such as in commercial dealings of firms under its control with Communist countries; and in connection with United States anti-trust proceedings as they relate to operations in foreign countries.
—Fear that multinational corporations limit competition.
—Fear that firms go where labor is cheap to the detriment of workers in high wage countries.
—Suspicion that intra-company *pricing* is based more on *tax* structures than on market considerations.

There have been persistent suggestions for formulation of a set of rules or a code dealing with foreign investment issues. There is, in fact, in existence the Capital Movements Code of the OECD, as well as various bilateral treaties, which provide for national treatment of foreign investments, with certain escapes. We doubt that an attempt at more precise formulation of a code at this time would improve the present position, and it might well worsen it.

No matter how we decide to deal with the broad issue, we should try to mitigate problems which are unnecessarily abrasive, such as sovereignty issues related to our trade control with Communist countries and specific taxation issues which need settlement among countries. We should also be alert to potential EC restrictions as a common industrial policy is developed.

We need a) to depoliticize the subject, b) to assure that no nation's major goals are seriously eroded by the international mobility of firms, c) to avoid conflicting jurisdictions over multinational firms, and d) to assure equitable treatment for the firms.

The U.S. may not need to press this subject since on most of these issues it is hard to see what we have to gain—but we must be prepared to respond if other countries put foreign investment on the agenda.

6. International Monetary Relations

Various issues in this field are being examined:

—The IMF is continuing (with all deliberate speed) its examination of limited exchange rate flexibility.
—The SDR system is in being, although there may be a problem about a year hence in connection with the appropriate amount to be created in the next basic period beginning in 1973 (and it is probably unwise for us to attempt to raise this issue now).
—The two-tier gold system, despite some increase in the price of commodity gold, is functioning well.

The major problem which now exists relates to the continuing U.S. deficit, stimulated most recently by interest rate disparities between the United States and various European countries, chiefly Germany, and the resulting large short-term capital flows.

In addition, there is substantial European concern stemming from recent articles by U.S. academics advocating a "passive" policy or U.S. "benign neglect" of its balance of payments, which Europeans take as meaning less cooperation with them and an attempt by the U.S. to force them to take the remedial action instead of trying to work out with them an acceptable joint solution.

We will need to achieve four things:

—Creation of an amount of SDR's in 1973 and after that will assure a continuation of the system.
—Stronger programs to control short-term capital flows, preferably through U.S. unilateral action but perhaps on a joint basis with other countries.
—A clear recognition of responsibilities by both surplus and deficit countries, including the relationship of more flexible exchange rates to the adjustment process.
—Better coordination of the domestic monetary policies of the major countries.

7. Aid

Development of constructive policies for relations between developed and less-developed countries requires agreement on priorities and actions among the developed countries. To some extent this has been accomplished:

—The developed nations have all agreed to seek a system of generalized preferences to help LDC exports.

—There is general agreement that aid flows through multilateral institutions should be augmented, but with some reservations.

—The United States has not endorsed a specific aid target; however, the President has proposed that the downward trend in U.S. aid appropriations be reversed.

—Insofar as it is beneficial to developing countries, a reciprocal untying of bilateral aid would be desirable. We are attempting to negotiate such an arrangement in the OECD, although France remains a holdout to agreement at this point.

Any initiative for the 1970's should give a prominent place to development issues; and this must build on the major areas of agreement, particularly in the trade field.

8. U.S. Legislation

Any program will require public and Congressional support. The question of when we ask for legislation and what type of legislation is desirable has to be carefully considered as we progress in our international and domestic consultations.

It is particularly important that we keep Congress fully involved in the international discussions. This could be achieved by having Congressional representation on our delegations to various international meetings. Whether we do this or not, frequent and close consultations with Congress is essential.

Clearly, we will need legislation at some stage in the game. The questions of *what* and *when* cannot be decided until we get a clearer view of what we want and what foreign governments are prepared to do.

In any case, legislation probably will be needed to provide authority to reduce tariffs and non-tariff barriers, to negotiate about domestic agricultural support programs, and to repeal ASP.

An imaginative new adjustment assistance program is essential if we are to embark on a major trade liberalization initiative, and such a program will also likely require legislation. We have already submitted suggestions to you on the possible form such an adjustment assistance program might take.

57.   **Memorandum From Secretary of the Treasury Connally to the President's Assistant for International Economic Affairs (Peterson)[1]**

Washington, March 29, 1971.

CIEP Study Memorandum #1[2] rightly focuses on some key issues before the Administration. We will be sending along some suggestions for the first three items shortly.

However, I believe the memorandum raises, by indirection, important organizational issues that need to be resolved. Specifically, paragraph 4, which calls for a basic review of our approach to balance of payments and international monetary problems, seems simply to ignore existing responsibilities of the Treasury and present coordinating machinery.

I have assumed that the deliberations and responsibilities of the Volcker Group were to be continued—this has been the channel for issues such as those posed in paragraph 4. Obviously, as appropriate, the results of the Volcker Group work could be reviewed at sessions of the Council on International Economic Policy. I do not know whether you contemplate some other procedure; if so, we had better clarify this now.

Although not raising the matter directly, your memorandum also brings to mind a second issue—that of the role and function of the National Advisory Council on International Monetary and Financial Policies in coordinating, under Congressional mandate, our international lending activity. We have assumed that the NAC, too, would maintain its responsibilities and that its functions would not be the subject of any jurisdictional grab by others. As you know, the day to day work in this area for the past twenty-five years has been conducted quietly and efficiently at the staff and Assistant Secretary level.

In view of the creation of the CIEP, it may be that matters referred by the NAC Alternates to the Principals in the past would, hereafter, go to the Council. I would be prepared to function on that basis.

John B. Connally[3]

---

[1] Source: Washington National Records Center, Department of the Treasury, Files of Under Secretary Volcker: FRC 56 79 15, CIEP Study Memoranda. Confidential. This memorandum and Document 58 are attached to a March 12 memorandum from Assistant Secretary Petty to Connally to the effect that the CIEP's effort to get jurisdiction over balance-of-payments and international monetary issues was paralleled by State's effort to be the focus for coordination of all foreign assistance agencies, which would impinge on Treasury's responsibilities for the international financial institutions.

[2] Document 55.

[3] Printed from a copy that indicates Connally signed the original.

58. Memorandum From Secretary of the Treasury Connally to President Nixon[1]

Washington, March 29, 1971.

I understand you should soon have on your desk for decision matters relating to the organization of the Administration for foreign economic policy, filling out the framework established by the Council for International Economic Policy. I believe it is important that this matter be cleared up promptly. It is even more important that the arrangements be effective, workable, and consistent with operating responsibilities.

Internationally, my major concern, as Secretary of the Treasury and your chief financial official, must be with international monetary and balance of payments policy. The Treasury Department, by the nature of its statutory responsibilities and role, necessarily carries the principal burden in this area—it is part and parcel of the daily job, and the Congress, the public, and foreign governments properly look to me as the spokesman. That responsibility carries with it a further responsibility to advise you on these matters.

Equally clearly, there is a need for coordination and consultation—most closely with the Federal Reserve, but also with State, the Council of Economic Advisers, and others. In practice, throughout your Administration, the principal channel for coordination of international monetary policy has been through the Under Secretary of the Treasury for Monetary Affairs—the so-called "Volcker Group," where all relevant agencies are represented. I have found considerable agreement that this channel has worked effectively, and I assume it will remain in place.

Essentially, I believe this Group could and should, under my immediate direction, formally function as a committee of the CIEP, recognizing that some sensitive matters in this area need to be treated in a more restricted forum than the full Council. Indeed, I am at a loss to see in what other way this area can be handled consistent with my present responsibilities and those of the Department, yet assuring the full Administration consultation and coordination you seek through CIEP.

I am also closely concerned with the foreign assistance area.[2]

---

[1] Source: Washington National Records Center, Department of the Treasury, Files of Under Secretary Volcker: FRC 56 79 15, CIEP Study Memoranda. Confidential. See footnote 1, Document 57.

[2] In a March 1 memorandum to Kissinger, Peterson addressed the Council's role on foreign assistance issues; see footnote 1, Document 53.

Your constructive reorganization of our bilateral programs will require some new arrangements. There are special problems in melding the thought of an over-all coordinator for aid, as urged by Rudy Peterson, and the concept of the CIEP. I have sent to George Shultz a more detailed memorandum,[3] outlining what seems to me a sensible solution, but also wanted you to have the essence of my thinking directly.

Essentially, the new bilateral aid agencies could be coordinated through a CIEP subcommittee, chaired either by State, or—to fit the concept of a divorce from short-term foreign policy—by Pete Peterson or one of his assistants. If one man needs to show the flag in Congress, the Secretary of State would seem to remain the logical choice. However, I would stop well short of any concept of a single coordinating "czar" in this area. Inevitably, that would cut across the CIEP arrangements and blur—possibly to the point of extinction—your basic idea of keeping separate the several distinct elements in the foreign assistance program.

We already have the National Advisory Council mechanism, with a Treasury Chairman, for the multilateral programs. Among other things, this provides the Congressionally sanctioned vehicle for the Treasury legislative effort in this area, which has been rather successful through the years. I believe the NAC should continue in practice as a parallel committee of the CIEP.

The big issues—how much money to allocate to the bilateral and multilateral programs, the basic policy guidelines—are certainly matters for the CIEP, itself.

John B. Connally[4]

---

[3] Not found.

[4] Printed from a copy that indicates Connally signed the original

59. Memorandum From the President's Assistant for International Economic Affairs (Peterson)[1]

Washington, March 30, 1971.

MEMORANDUM FOR

Paul A. Volcker
Hendrick S. Houthakker
C. Fred Bergsten
Arthur B. Laffer
Robert Solomon

As indicated in CIEP Study Memorandum No. 1 of March 8,[2] the President has directed a basic review of our policy approaches toward the balance of payments and international monetary problems within the framework of the Council on International Economic Policy. He wants this work to proceed on a high priority basis. I have also discussed with the respective heads of your operations the virtue of keeping the initial work group small and restricted, to those with real expertise in the field.

I am, therefore, creating an Ad Hoc Group on the subject, comprised of the addressees of this memorandum. The President has also indicated that we should bring in the best people from outside Government to participate in our efforts as they develop.[3] I am assuming, of course, the "Volcker Group" will continue to coordinate the implementation of U.S. international monetary and balance of payments policy. Everything I've heard is that this is one of the best interagency groups in the Government.

As I see it, we first need to lay out an agenda of the policy issues in this area which need to be discussed. I have discussed monetary problems with a number of people both inside and outside of Government during my six weeks here. I'm simply attaching a preliminary list of what some of those areas are that have come up in some of my discussions.

I would hope we could discuss these ideas, and others which you might suggest for our work agenda, at our first meeting on March 31 at 9:00 a.m. in my office.[4] I would also hope we could discuss some ideas on how to go about the work, and what outside inputs we might use.

---

[1] Source: Washington National Records Center, Department of the Treasury, Files of Under Secretary Volcker: FRC 56 79 15, CIEP Study Memoranda. No classification marking. Copies were sent to Burns, Connally, Kissinger, and McCracken.

[2] Document 55.

[3] This directive has not been further identified.

[4] No record of a meeting has been found.

Attachment

1. What should be the objective of U.S. balance of payments policy, both in the short term and over the long run? Do we need to adopt a balance of payments target at all? If so, how should such a target be formulated? Should our target relate to our overall balance (on what definition?) or to particular components of the U.S. balance of payments?

2. What policy measure should we adopt in pursuing any balance of payment target we might choose? For example, do we want to encourage foreign investments by U.S. firms? How should we finance deficits?

3. What should be our objectives for the future development of the international monetary system? What is our view about the future role of the dollar in the system? The role of SDRs? The role of gold? What changes do we want in the adjustment process, if any, especially toward increasing the flexibility of exchange rates? How do we go about achieving these objectives?

4. Do we want any new approaches to deal with the large movements of short-term capital which now seem to characterize the system?

5. What should be our policy toward monetary integration in the Common Market? Do we favor it or oppose it? How can we influence its substance and its timing so that it will fit into a satisfactory worldwide monetary framework?

I would hope we could discuss these ideas, and others which you might suggest for our work agenda, at our first meeting on March 31 at 9 AM.

60.   Memorandum From the Under Secretary of the Treasury for
Monetary Affairs (Volcker) to the President's Assistant for
International Economic Affairs (Peterson)[1]

Washington, April 1, 1971.

SUBJECT

Capital Controls Program

In CIEP Study Memorandum No. 1, you requested comments on a
paper by Mr. Shultz which recommended abandonment of the capital
control program.[2] Although the Treasury fully concurs in the view that
these controls should be removed as soon as the U.S. balance of payments position permits, we believe that it would be a serious mistake to
remove them at the present time.

The issue at present is not simply one of the statistical or even economic effectiveness of the controls.[3] It seems to me unavoidable that
removing the controls at this time would be interpreted abroad as
"malign neglect" of our responsibilities as a key currency country for
the stability of our currency and the monetary system and as an overt
affront to other countries dealing with what they consider to be highly
excessive dollar inflows. Beyond any effort on our part to explain the
"ineffectiveness" of the controls, action could not only trigger loss of
confidence in the dollar and a major international financial crisis, but, in
the eyes of much of the world, cast us in the role of initiating villain. As
you know, our official settlements deficit last year, excluding the SDR
allocation, was $10.7 billion. In the first three months of 1971, the rate is,
unfortunately, much higher. While we do not expect the deficit to continue at anything like this level, there is grave concern among foreign
monetary authorities at the present time.

It is important to note that the Congress accepts the need for retaining the controls at present without a murmur and, in fact, insisted upon
giving us more authority to apply controls over our objections.   The

---

[1] Source: Washington National Records Center, Department of the Treasury, Files of
Under Secretary Volcker: FRC 56 79 15, CIEP Study Memoranda. Confidential. A 17-page,
March 23 analytical memorandum from Wilson Schmidt to Volcker on the "Effect of
Capital Controls Program" is attached but not printed.

[2] Documents 55 and 54, respectively.

[3] On March 18 Federal Reserve Governor Brimmer sent Assistant Secretary Petty a
letter to which he attached the Federal Reserve's preliminary conclusions regarding
Shultz' paper. The preliminary conclusions were that the paper was "superficial," failed
"altogether to do justice to the analytical complexity of the questions raised by the [capi-
tal controls] program," and was "deliberately misleading." (Washington National
Records Center, Department of the Treasury, Files of Under Secretary Volcker: FRC 56 79
15, CIEP Meetings)

Interest Equalization Tax extension passed the House without dissent.[4] In the hearings, there was specific recognition of the inadvisability of eliminating the controls, and even directly affected financial houses did not ask for elimination at this time but, rather, accepted the need for continuance.

Finally, on the issues raised by Mr. Shultz, we simply do not find the evidence presented persuasive, although I suspect we can all agree there is very considerable "slippage" in controls of this type.

Paul A. Volcker

---

[4] The vote on HR 5432 was 393 to 5, with 34 members voting. See *Congressional Record*, March 10, 1971, pp. 5859–5866.

---

61.   CIEP Decision Memorandum No. 3[1]

Washington, April 8, 1971.

MEMORANDUM FOR

The Secretary of State
The Secretary of Treasury
The Secretary of Agriculture
The Secretary of Commerce
The Secretary of Labor
The Director, Office of Management and Budget
The Chairman, Council of Economic Advisers
The Assistant to the President for National Security Affairs
The Assistant to the President for Domestic Affairs
The Special Representative for Trade Negotiations

---

[1] Source: Department of State, S/S Files: Lot 82 D 126, Box 5197, CIEP Decision Memoranda. Confidential. Transmitted to the National Security Council under cover of an April 5 memorandum from Peterson to Kissinger and Shultz, which noted that the paper had been approved by the State Department. Another copy is attached to an April 6 memorandum from Bergsten to Kissinger recommending that Kissinger approve the organizational arrangements in time for the President to approve and announce it at the first CIEP meeting on April 8. Bergsten noted that the Decision Memorandum was the result of long negotiations between Peterson and the State Department, which had concurred even though the memorandum was different from what State had proposed. (National Archives, Nixon Presidential Materials, NSC Files, Agency Files, Box 218, CIEP)

The President chaired the first meeting of the CIEP on April 8 from 10:40 a.m. to 12:17 p.m. in the Cabinet Room. Rogers, Connally, Hardin, Stans, Hodgson, Shultz, McCracken, Kissinger, Gilbert, Kennedy, Siciliano, Hinton, Webster, Bergsten, and Peterson attended. Franco Mario Malfatti, President of the Commission of the European Communities, joined the meeting at noon. (Ibid., White House Central Files, President's Daily Diary)

SUBJECT

Structure of the Council on International Economic Policy

This memorandum supplements my memorandum of January 19, 1971, establishing the Council on International Economic Policy (CIEP).[2] In order that I shall be provided the most effective assistance in considering international economic issues, I hereby direct that the Council system operate as follows:

1. Membership

The membership of the CIEP is as set forth in my January 19 memorandum. I shall also invite other agencies to participate in the Council on an ad hoc basis when matters for which they are responsible are to be considered.

I have designated Ambassador Kennedy as a member of the Council.

2. Meetings

The Council shall meet regularly and I shall approve the agenda. I shall chair the Council, but should it be necessary to convene the Council in my absence, the Secretary of State will chair its meetings.

3. Review Group

A Review Group of the Council is hereby established. The Review Group shall:

—Review papers for submission to the Council. Such review will assure that issues are fully and objectively stated, that department and agency views are fairly and adequately set out, that all realistic alternatives are presented, and that the issues require Presidential decision. A paper prepared by the Operations Group, task groups, or one or more which requires Presidential action but which need not be considered by the Council will be forwarded by the Executive Director to members of the Council simultaneously with its submission to the President.
—Assign action, for implementation or study, to the Operations Group.

The membership of the Review Group shall consist of the Assistant to the President for International Economic Affairs who will serve as Chairman of the Group and designated representatives of members of the Council at the senior political appointee level.

4. Operations Group

The Operations Group will carry out those functions described in my January 19 memorandum. The Executive Director, in consultation with the Chairman of the Operations Group, will refer particular issues to the Operations Group.

[2] See Document 49.

5. Task Groups

The Executive Director may also appoint Task Groups to work on particular problems, as outlined in my January 19 memorandum. I shall expect that he will call upon the best expertise in and out of the Government for staff work on such Task Groups.

6. Interdepartmental Groups

Whenever issues under consideration by NSC Interdepartmental Groups include significant economic issues, the Assistant to the President for International Economic Affairs shall be represented. Economic matters within the purview of the CIEP, and previously treated by the NSC Interdepartmental Groups, shall henceforth become the responsibility of the CIEP, and may be assigned to interdepartmental groups established within the Operations Group framework, or to Task Groups.

7. Consolidation of Existing Committees

Following due consideration, I shall announce the consolidation within the Council structure, to the extent practical, of existing committees and groups presently dealing with responsibilities that I have now assigned to the Council.

Richard Nixon

---

62. Memorandum From the Deputy Under Secretary of State for Economic Affairs (Samuels) to the President's Assistant for International Economic Affairs (Peterson)[1]

Washington, April 8, 1971.

SUBJECT

Capital Control Programs

I would like to comment briefly on the Capital Control Programs, including Mr. Shultz' memorandum of March 2.[2]

---

[1] Source: National Archives, RG 59, Central Files 1970–73, FN 13. Confidential. Drafted by L.J. Kennon (E/IFD/OMA) on April 2 and cleared by Deputy Assistant Secretary Weintraub.

[2] Document 54.

Without commenting in detail on the analysis in the Shultz memorandum, I agree basically with the conclusion that we should dismantle the capital controls programs. This should, however, be done progressively and not in one step, for reasons stated in the next paragraph. The controls distort resource allocation and the most efficient development of U.S. and European capital markets, raise the cost of doing business abroad, and give rise to resentments under certain circumstances in foreign countries over the dominating role that U.S. companies play in absorbing capital availabilities in the European capital market. Further, these controls get in the way of attempts to reduce artificial barriers to the flows of capital and resources. Moreover, by now we may have exhausted any short-term balance of payments benefits from the controls, although this conclusion could be debated on a technical level ad infinitum.

In stating the above, however, I believe it important that this unwinding should take place in an orderly fashion and take account of the problems involved. For example, in winding down the FDIP, whether we do it through increasing allowables or collapsing schedules or by some other device, we must bear in mind there exists $10.5 billion of outstanding American borrowing abroad which could readily flow into U.S. hands and greatly exacerbate our dollar outflow problem unless the dismantling is handled carefully. Although much of the massive outflow this and last year is a result of the U.S. and European business cycles and interest rate differentials being out of phase with each other and is probably capable of being better stabilized as interest rates change, abandonment of the structure of controls under present circumstances would be viewed as an affirmation of the current widely-held belief abroad that the fundamental U.S. attitude toward the balance of payments is in fact one of "benign neglect." This would have unfortunate monetary effects, and beyond that would further encourage foreigners to seek ways of insulating themselves from the effects of U.S. economic and monetary policies. I reiterate, therefore, that we should progressively wind down the controls toward elimination, preferably at a substantially accelerated rate over that which has so far prevailed.

NS

63. Telegram From the Department of State to Certain Posts[1]

Washington, April 21, 1971, 1630Z.

67590. For Ambassador From Treasury Secretary Connally. Subject: U.S. Balance of Payments.

1. In light increasing attention being given abroad, publicly and privately, to U.S. balance of payments problem,[2] appropriate Embassy personnel need to be able to draw on the following background concerning the immediate and longer range aspects of this problem and with principal elements of U.S. policy.

2. During week ending April 2, there appeared to be some movement of funds into Deutschemarks and Swiss francs for short-period speculation, whereas earlier movements were primarily in response to differentially high short-term interest rates in Germany. Because of this sudden burst of speculation, Treasury made available the following statement in response to inquiries.

Begin Verbatim Text. "Current rumors and speculation apparently grow out of large recent flows of interest-sensitive short-term capital. This is a matter that can be and is being dealt with on its own terms. This essentially short-term problem will not bring any change in the basic policies of the United States, which are well known, with respect to gold and the foreign exchange markets. Nor, as they have made clear, is it a cause for changes in the exchange rates of other countries." *End Verbatim Text.*

3. During week ended April 9, exchange markets much calmer, and flows reduced. Interest differentials narrowed between Euro-dollar market and German money market as result of (1) U.S. Treasury borrowing of $1.5 billion from foreign branches of American banks, (2) large withdrawals of funds from Euro-dollar market through previous week's flows into Germany that reduced supply of dollars in Euro-dollar market, and (3) market realization that monetary authorities now taking steps to reduce differentials, as indicated by reductions in German and U.K. discount rates, and can take additional measures if desired. Nevertheless, markets remain highly sensitive and nervous.

---

[1] Source: National Archives, RG 59, Central Files 1970–73, FN 12 US. Confidential. Drafted by G.H. Willis and W.C. Cates (Treasury); cleared by Under Secretary Volcker, Deputy Assistant Secretary of State Weintraub (E), and Curran (S/S); and approved by Deputy Under Secretary of State Samuels. Sent to the Embassies in OECD capitals, the USEC Mission in Brussels, and the OECD Mission in Paris.

[2] In late March and early April a number of posts reported on foreign concerns about the U.S. balance of payments. Telegram 68708 to The Hague, April 22, noted that telegram 67590 should help answer a number of questions about the balance of payments and measures taken. (Ibid.)

4. U.S. Missions not expected to take initiative in discussions of this matter, but if questioned, should take the line indicated in Treasury statement as well as drawing on elaboration below.

5. Official view is that recent large accumulations of dollars in Europe are primarily due to short-term capital movements growing out of different cyclical circumstances in U.S. and Europe. These movements should be distinguished from the basic balance of payments positions on current and long-term capital account which are more persistent and much less volatile.

Basic Payments Positions

6. The United States basic deficit for 1970 is in the neighborhood of $2-1/2 to 3 billion. This is not satisfactory but is not significantly larger than average of past five years. U.S. current account surplus excluding government grants, at $2.3 billion in 1970, was higher than average of 1968–69 by over $1 billion, though smaller than 1961–65 average of $5.7 billion.

7. Basic balance of payments positions are not especially strong in Europe. A major part of offsetting surpluses to the U.S. basic deficit will probably be found, though data uncertain, in Canada and Japan. Continental European basic surpluses have been held down by U.S. restraints on long-term capital outflows. Large, current account surplus of Germany was nearly halved in 1970 as compared with 1969, and appears to be weakening somewhat further. Although current account surplus of EC as a whole remains large, this surplus now roughly balanced by aid and large long-term capital outflows, leaving basic balance in balance. Wage and price movements in Europe now suggest a more rapid pace of inflation relative to the U.S. and Canada and such movements also weigh against upward revaluations of European currencies. United States has exercised restraint on inflationary demand in 1969 and 1970 and unemployment has reached levels substantially higher than those experienced in Europe.

8. However, the U.S. basic balance remains unsatisfactory, reflecting serious deterioration in U.S. trade surplus from levels of early 1960's. This deterioration shows up primarily with Japan and Canada, although European agricultural policies present the threat of further deterioration. In addition a primary cause of current difficulties is our continuing large military defense burden including particularly in such surplus areas as Europe and Japan. Despite their surpluses many other developed countries, including both Japan and the EC, still have important restrictions against our imports.

9. USG is not following "passive" policy or policy of "benign neglect" as some Europeans assume on basis recent articles of some U.S.

academics. U.S. has taken actions to limit basic balance deficit including renewal of IET, and extension of Commerce and FRB programs covering corporate and bank capital flows. Administration hopes Congress will authorize DISC proposal to improve export performance and is working to make U.S. export credit facilities more competitive. Beyond that, negotiations must be pursued bilaterally and multilaterally to defend U.S. export interests, and to seek improvements in military burden-sharing arrangements. Our trade position is very different than it was in the early postwar period. The United States should not and will not seek solution by depressing the U.S. economy. In fact, such action would aggravate net capital outflow. It would also reduce U.S. imports, thus tending to depress the economies of some exporting countries.

10. Through its demand management policies, the United States has slowed down the U.S. economy markedly and we are now experiencing improved price performance that can only be helpful to balance of payments. The Administration has also taken steps to deal with inflationary pressures in construction and called attention to other specific points of inflationary pressure in the economy, with an eye to international as well as domestic implications of excessive price and wage advances. If further stimulus to the economy should be needed in the future, fiscal rather than monetary action would certainly be considered.

Short-Term Capital Flows

11. While short-term capital flows more transitory problem, large flows do represent serious problem for several European countries and for international monetary system. U.S. concern with this problem evidenced in President's report on "U.S. Foreign Policy in the 1970's" in which he listed objective of cooperation in monetary sphere "to handle large-scale shifts of liquid capital without exchange crises or losses in the ability of individual nations to pursue their monetary policies." President called for "an intensive examination to determine whether there is need to reinforce the present techniques and procedures of international monetary cooperation to enable us better to cope with such movements." This problem, though serious, is fundamentally different from the basic balance problem. It results from fact countries in different cyclical situations tend to different interest rate levels and monetary policies must have scope for domestic requirements. In 1970–71, this has meant substantial differential between U.S. interest rates which have been relatively low reflecting sluggishness of economy and our need for economic stimulus, and interest rates in certain European countries, which have been high reflecting continuing inflationary boom and desire for continued restraint in those countries. These divergencies in money market conditions are the major source of the massive U.S. official settlements deficit of 1970.

12. Even with available techniques for dealing with short-term capital flows, all nations must be prepared to ride out large swings in payments positions in such divergent cyclical situations. This is not something that can or should be dealt with by changes in exchange rate parities. If expansion of U.S. economy is accompanied by firming of U.S. money markets and there is an easing of monetary conditions in foreign financial centers, U.S. official settlements deficit should be substantially reduced. Questions of the appropriate policy mix as between fiscal and monetary policy are relevant for all advanced countries, not merely for the United States.

Summary

13. While we are concerned over both the basic balance and short-term capital flows, we are attacking problems in cooperation with others. Solution not seen in dramatic action in areas of international monetary system, and no emergency measures or special international meetings under consideration.

14. Recognizing there are no quick or easy answers to world balance of payments adjustment problem, USG intends to carry out its part of responsibility for improved structure. Orderly growth with price stability in U.S. is essential underpinning in such improvement. The extremes of slack and overheating offer no salvation for the balance of payments. A combination of orderly growth with better price stability than other leading industrial nations will be achieving in years ahead should move the U.S. along the desired path toward a stronger current and basic balance position.

Rogers

64.   **Memorandum From C. Fred Bergsten of the National Security Council Staff to the President's Special Assistant for National Security Affairs (Kissinger)**[1]

Washington, April 21, 1971.

SUBJECT

Your Lunch With Pete Peterson—April 22

There are no specific issues on which decisions are pending which you need to raise with Pete. You might, however, wish to stress to him your interest in early submission of our generalized tariff preferences legislation in view of the implications for Latin American policy. You might also wish to get his reading on the outlook for success of our latest textile gambit.

There is, however, a deeper and more philosophical point which will continuously pervade your relationship with Peterson: the relationship between foreign economic policy and overall foreign policy. It is roughly accurate to say that foreign economic policy has been the handmaiden of overall U.S. foreign policy throughout the post-war period; all of our great "economic" initiatives (IMF–IBRD, Marshall Plan, Kennedy Round, SDRs, etc) have been undertaken for essentially foreign policy reasons, and foreign policy considerations have dictated the U.S. position on virtually all issues of foreign economic policy.

There is now great and increasing pressure to change this relationship. In fact, it probably must be changed to some extent—to increase the "economic" content of foreign economic policy—for the same reasons that we are now seeking to share our global role in political and security matters. The creation of Peterson's job, of course, is an important indicator of this trend, and adds to the pressures for moving in such a direction.

However, some go so far as to say that foreign policy should now become the handmaiden of foreign economic policy;[2] that we should use

---

[1]   Source: National Archives, Nixon Presidential Materials, NSC Files, Country Files–Far East, Box 530, Japan Volume IV 1/71–6/71. No classification marking. The memorandum is Tab B to the "Additional Information" memorandum cited in footnote 2 below.

[2]   On April 22 Bergsten sent Kissinger a memorandum with "Additional Information" for his luncheon with Peterson that day. After commenting on NSSM 122 on Japan (Tab A), Bergsten wrote:

"Pete also wishes to raise with you major questions about the State Department. He already despairs at State's ability to carry out negotiations with sufficient toughness to get acceptable results and present a respectable image. He clearly views this as an institutional problem rather than simply one of present personalities, though he is fully aware that present personalities exacerbate the difficulty. He hopefully speaks of getting an Under Secretary who understands economic issues and could hold to a tough line on them.

our political and military muscle to pursue basically economic objectives. Pete himself believes that a trend in this direction is inevitable. There is certainly wide support for it in the Congress.

The obvious answer is that a new balance must be found between the economic and foreign policy components of foreign economic policy. This will often invade the heart of foreign policy, on such issues as German offset, general trade policy and therefore overall relations with key countries such as Japan and the Common Market; specific commodity problems such as meat, textiles, shoes, sugar, etc.; and East-West trade policy, on which the President has asked for a special CIEP meeting.

The important thing at this point is simply for Pete to know that you are aware of this problem, and the need to work it out with him on essentially a case-by-case basis. I see no general formula, or method for getting one, which can resolve the issue on a broader basis. You should make it clear, of course, that you are not prepared to see economic issues dominate foreign policy in areas where our political interests are sufficiently important.

"This line of Pete's thinking raises two problems for you. The first is the substantive problem I mentioned in my memorandum of yesterday (Tab B): his growing desire to use overall foreign policy to pursue economic objectives, which will cause you increasing problems in the future.

"The second is the problem of who does what in this field. I am more pessimistic than Pete about State. It is my view that their internal pressures will always cause them to soften in tough negotiations, whether on economic or other issues. I therefore suggested that Pete essentially forget about State and revitalize the Office of the Special Trade Representative by replacing Carl Gilbert with a tough negotiator who would be both effective and respected on the Hill. He could operate de facto as Pete's deputy and operating arm. I recommend that you promote this line when you discuss the matter with Pete today." (National Archives, Nixon Presidential Materials, NSC Files, Country Files–Far East, Box 530, Japan Volume IV 1/71–6/71)

65. Action Memorandum From the President's Assistant for International Economic Affairs (Peterson) to President Nixon[1]

Washington, June 2, 1971.

SUBJECT

OECD Ministerial Meeting

Secretary Rogers, who will head the U.S. Delegation to the June 7–8 OECD Ministerial Meeting, has submitted a memorandum outlining the proposed U.S. objectives and the issues to be discussed (Tab A).[2] The Ministerial Meeting will involve a high-level exchange of views on three agenda items:

1. Economic policies and prospects in the OECD area;
2. Perspectives for international trade;
3. Policies for cooperation with developing countries.

In addition, Australia will be welcomed as the 23rd full Member of the OECD.

Commerce, Agriculture, Labor, OMB, AID, Council of Economic Advisers, Ambassador Gilbert, and the Federal Reserve Board concur in the State proposals.

Secretary Connally (Tab B) is opposed to the idea of an OECD restricted trade group. Treasury believes it would constrain our freedom of action, and that we should not commit ourselves to "an initiative which . . . may be doomed to impotence or acrimony." If, nevertheless, you decide to support creation of the group, Treasury believes it "should not branch out into areas beyond trade policy."[3]

---

[1] Source: National Archives, Nixon Presidential Materials, NSC Files, Agency Files, Box 273, OECD. Confidential. A copy was sent to Kissinger. Attached to a June 5 memorandum from Huntsman to Peterson setting out marginal comments the President had written on Peterson's memorandum, but the source text bears no marginal comments.

[2] The 12-page "OECD: Objectives Paper," dated May 25, is not printed. A copy attached to a June 1 memorandum from Johnston to Kissinger is accompanied by a May 29 memorandum from Rogers to the President informing him that he planned to use it as the basis for U.S. participation at the June OECD Ministerial. (Ibid.)

[3] Tab B, a memorandum by Connally, is not printed. In a June 1 information memorandum to Kissinger, Johnston noted that the reasons for Treasury's opposition to the special trade group were not very clear, but he recommended that Kissinger support establishment in the OECD of a special group to study trade and related items. Haig approved for Kissinger. (Ibid.)

Apparently, Secretaries Rogers and Connally reviewed this with you on the plane to Austin, Texas,[4] but they have rather different impressions about what was agreed.

Secretary Connally has also suggested "that the Delegation focus attention on the degree to which defense expenditures are to be taken into account in the OECD's examination of our economic and balance of payments position."

On May 1, you authorized State to conduct consultations concerning the practicability of establishing an OECD restricted study group.[5] Subsequently, the OECD Secretary General advanced the proposal for such a group on his own responsibility. While final positions are unlikely to be taken by governments until the meeting, the extensive consultations carried out by State indicate wide interest and substantial support for the proposal which, under OECD rules, requires unanimity for adoption. The European Community, some members of which have reservations, could still block action, but the French statement that this matter could be worked out by "reasonable men" indicates the likely outcome.[6]

I do not believe it would be desirable at this late date to oppose formation of the group. To do so might be interpreted both as backing away from an idea we floated and as a stand against positive initiatives at a time when monetary relations are strained. The restricted group would permit us to talk quietly with the European Community, Japan, Canada, and the U.K. about how we will deal with economic problems, including agricultural trade, after Britain enters the Common Market. It is important that we get at this now that British entry seems assured. Finally, I anticipate that the working group would assist in the domestic process of developing a U.S. position for a possible multilateral negotiation, much as the NATO examination of allied defense strategy proceeded in tandem with examination of the same issues in the NSC.

On the other hand, I share John Connally's view that we should make clear we are not foreclosing our right to take other trade initiatives

---

[4] The President traveled to Austin on May 22 for the dedication of the Johnson Presidential Library. Rogers and Connally accompanied him, but did not return with the President later in the day. (Ibid., White House Central Files, President's Daily Diary)

[5] Not further identified. Telegram 79858 to Paris, May 7, informed the Embassy and the OECD Mission that the President had authorized "consultations concerning the practicality of establishing an OECD restricted study group to examine international economic problems and to recommend methods and programs for dealing with them. The President did not wish the United States to push to establish such a restricted group in the OECD unless there were co-sponsors and good prospects for success." (Ibid., Nixon Presidential Materials, NSC Files, Country Files–Europe, Box 678, France, Volume VII 4/71–12/71)

[6] Not further identified.

while the OECD study proceeds, and that the group's scope should be narrowed. I also believe it would be well to focus some attention on the defense burden at the OECD Ministerial. Therefore I recommend that you approve Option 3. Henry concurs.

I have reason to believe that Option 3 is acceptable to Secretary Rogers. Acting Secretary Irwin states that Secretary Rogers is so strongly opposed to Option 2 that he would like, if necessary, to discuss the matter with you by phone prior to your decision.

Options

Option 1: Approve State position, supported by all concerned, except Treasury, as submitted.[7]

Option 2: Agree with Secretary Connally that we should oppose creation of an OECD restricted Trade Study Group.

Option 3: Approve State proposal as modified in the attached draft telegram (Tab C).[8]

---

[7] The June 5 memorandum from Huntsman to Peterson (see footnote 1 above) indicates the President wrote "No" after Option 1.

[8] The President initialed his approval of this option. The June 5 memorandum from Huntsman to Peterson indicates the President also wrote: "I agree in principle with Connally all the way. Tactically we are boxed in. But I want the Connally line to influence all our decisions in this matter." Tab C is not printed, but see Document 66 for the revised text.

66.   **Typescript of Telegram From the President's Assistant for International Economic Affairs (Peterson) to Secretary of State Rogers in Lisbon[1]**

Washington, June 5, 1971.

Eyes Only for Secretary William P. Rogers From Peter G. Peterson. The President has approved the OECD objectives paper submitted by Secretary Rogers on May 29 with the following modifications:[2]

1. Under "Our Main Objectives" a new paragraph would be added:

We would seek bluntly and in a hard hitting manner[3] in Secretary Rogers' statement and in other ways to promote better awareness and understanding of the relationship of our military expenditures to our economic and balance of payments position. We would thereby endeavor to begin working toward bringing all of our OECD partners to focus attention on the degree to which defense expenditures made for the mutual benefit are to be taken into account in the OECD's examination of a member's economic and balance of payments position. (FYI: The President wants the line taken by Secretary Connally in Munich to be followed by all U.S. representatives.)[4]

2. The Section on perspectives on international trade would be clarified by deleting the existing subparagraph (pages 8–9) which contains a reference to "fiscal, monetary and investment matters"[5] and by inserting subparagraphs under "The US Views" along the following lines:

The purpose of the group should be to explore trade issues, including tariffs and tariff discrimination, non-tariff barriers, and agricultural policies in the light of the new conditions of the 70's. The group should seek to develop action program guidelines and to foster the political will to deal with trade problems of common concern,

---

[1] Source: National Archives, Nixon Presidential Materials, NSC Files, Agency Files, Box 218, CIEP. Confidential; Exdis; Immediate. Drafted by Hinton and initialed by Peterson, Kissinger, and Haig, who also wrote at the top, "LDX'ed to State." The telegram is a revision of Tab C to Document 65, pursuant to the President's instructions; see footnote 3 below. No telegraphic text of Peterson's message was found. The Secretary was in Lisbon attending the NATO Ministerial meeting.

[2] See footnote 2, Document 65.

[3] The expression "bluntly and in a hard hitting manner" was inserted according to the President's instruction as set out in the June 5 memorandum from Huntsman to Peterson; see footnote 1, Document 65.

[4] According to Huntsman's June 5 memorandum, the President was referring to Connally's May 28 speech at the American Bankers Conference in Munich. See Document 155.

[5] The deleted language reads: "The Group should develop guidelines for an action program covering a wide gamut of policy issues posed by the new conditions of the '70's, including tariffs and tariff discrimination, non-tariff barriers, and agricultural policies, as well as related fiscal, monetary and investment matters, bearing in mind the importance of this activity for non-OECD member countries."

bearing in mind the importance of this activity for non-OECD member countries.

Establishment of the Group would in no way limit the U.S. Government, or any other Government, from pursuing its trade interests and rights in other ways, either bilaterally or multilaterally, including proposing trade or other initiatives in whatever forum considered appropriate.

The U.S. would interpret "trade related matters" narrowly. In particular, the group would be expected to avoid duplication of the fiscal and monetary policy work of the IMF, the Group of Ten, EPC, and WP-3.[6]

3. The Assistant to the President for International Economic Affairs will review positions to be taken by the U.S. Representative on the Special Trade Group.

4. With respect to generalized preferences (page 11) it should be borne in mind that the reverse preference issue is currently being reconsidered within the CIEP.

---

[6] Telegram 9846 from USOECD, June 9, contained Secretary Rogers' report to the President on the June 7 OECD Ministerial meeting, which he had chaired. Rogers reported that the Group "was given a gratifyingly warm reception" despite U.S. statements that the United States would use it as a forum to seek reductions in agricultural protection and to deal with increased trade discrimination that would result from European Community enlargement. Rogers cited an American news agency's calling the agreement on the Special Group "a major diplomatic victory for the Nixon Administration." (National Archives, Nixon Presidential Materials, NSC Files, Country Files–Europe, Box 678, France Volume VIII 4/71–12/71)

---

67.   **Editorial Note**

On June 30, 1971, Peter Peterson sent CIEP Study Memorandum 7 to the Council's members, to which he attached a draft of his 133-page briefing on "The United States In a Changing World Economy." Peterson noted that, at the President's request, the essence of the draft had already been used in briefings with Congress and business and labor groups, but that the paper had not yet been reviewed by the CIEP and at that stage was "a rather personal document." Peterson indicated that it was slated for discussion during an intensive Review Group meeting at Camp David July 9–10 and asked the Council members for their views on further dissemination of the document. (Department of State, S/S Files: Lot 82 D 126, Box 5195, CIEP Study Memoranda)

Peterson had discussed his briefing with President Nixon on June 29, and under cover of a July 2 memorandum forwarded a copy of the report, as the President had requested, for his trip to San Clemente. (National Archives, Nixon Presidential Materials, NSC Files, Agency Files, Box 218, CIEP) On July 3 Haig sent Peterson a memorandum suggesting some revisions in his transmittal memorandum to the President, particularly on the issue of publishing the briefing. (Ibid.) Peterson resubmitted his memorandum on July 6. (Ibid.) The President flew to Kansas City and then continued on to San Clemente on July 6. Haig accompanied the President. (Ibid., White House Central Files, President's Daily Diary)

In a July 8 memorandum to Haig (for wire), Ernest Johnston of the NSC Staff called attention to a number of deficiencies in the briefing paper scheduled to be discussed at Camp David. Johnston concluded that "during the meeting I shall discreetly argue that publication of the document would cause severe foreign policy problems and, even worse, would contribute to Congressional pressure for a nationalistic international economic policy. OMB, CEA and State expect to take the same line. Should Peterson suggest delayed submission of preference legislation or a revision of our preference scheme, I will argue, on foreign policy grounds, for prompt submission and no back down in our current proposal." On the July 8 cover note from Kennedy to Haig, which suggests Johnston's memorandum was sent telegraphically to Haig at the Western White House, Kennedy wrote: "AMH Comments: 1. Hold firm. 2. Peterson is amenable to no publication—we want none. Per tel con with John Howard 7/9/71." (Ibid., NSC Files, Agency Files, Box 218, CIEP)

68.   Paper Prepared in the Department of State[1]

Washington, July 28, 1971.

US-FRG Offset Negotiations—Current Status

U.S. and German delegations met in Bonn June 28–29 for a third round of formal negotiations on a new offset agreement. Presentations during the formal sessions consisted mainly of reiterating previously stated positions. The only new idea advanced by the German side was the suggestion that the gap between the U.S. target and FRG offer be filled by a four-and-a-half-year Bundesbank loan of DM 2 billion ($572 million). The FRG offer, on a two-year basis, would consist of the following:

Military procurement	$929.5 million
Budget support	228.8 million
Bundesbank loan	572.0 million
Total	$1,730.3 million

As previously reported,[2] the FRG has proposed that a portion of the funds for military procurement and all of the funds for budget support be taken from money deposited in the Treasury under previous offset agreements. Thus, under the German proposal, only the following would be new money and constitute a balance-of-payments inflow for the United States:

Military procurement	$715.0 million
Bundesbank loan	572.0 million
Total	$1,287.0 million

We informed the German side that we were unable to accept the offer because it did not contain sufficient balance-of-payments benefit and because interest-bearing loans have not proven to be very satisfactory offset features in the past. We suggested that the Germans make an effort to improve their offer by increasing the budget support compo-

---

[1] Source: National Archives, Nixon Presidential Materials, NSC Files, Country Files–Europe, Box 685, Germany Volume IX 4–8/71. Confidential. Forwarded to Kissinger under cover of a July 29 memorandum from State Department Executive Secretary Theodore Eliot informing him the report was prepared by Nathaniel Samuels, chairman of the U.S. delegation to the offset negotiations. An attached July 31 memorandum from Sonnenfeldt apprised Kissinger of the current status of the offset negotiations in preparation for his August 3 meeting with Ambassador Pauls. Sonnenfeldt advised Kissinger to make it clear the Germans would have to improve their offer.

[2] Reference is to an undated status report by Samuels sent under cover of a June 24 memorandum from Eliot to Kissinger; both attached but not printed.

nent, using new money. The German negotiator replied that he was working under specific instructions from the FRG Cabinet and that he had little flexibility. He stated that he was authorized to make only "minor adjustments" in the German offer.[3]

At the conclusion of the formal sessions, the German chairman expressed concern that the two sides had not been able to reach agreement. He then informally outlined a "personal" proposal which he said had not been discussed with the Cabinet but which he believed the Cabinet might be persuaded to accept as an "alternate" German offer.

The following are the elements of this proposal:

Military Procurement—$929.5 million, of which $300 million would be taken from Treasury Accounts 1 and 2 and $629 million would be new German budget funds.
Budget Support—$314.6 million, of which $228.8 million would be taken from Treasury Accounts 1 and 2 and $85.8 million would be new German budget funds. Of the total, $228.8 million would be a lump-sum payment, $57.2 million would be utilized for rehabilitation of U.S. troop facilities in Germany during FY 1972 and FY 1973, and $28.6 million would be used to pay interest due the Bundesbank loan during FY 1972 and 1973.
Bundesbank Loan—$572 million for 4-1/2 years at 2-1/2% interest.

This proposal represents a slight improvement over the official offer. However, from the balance-of-payments point of view, the benefit to the U.S. would average only about $626 million per year (including the loan)—about half our estimated balance-of-payments costs in Germany. Therefore, State, Treasury and Defense prepared a counterproposal which was transmitted to the Germans on July 24.[4]

The counterproposal suggests a package comprised of the following on a two-year basis:

Military Procurement—$929.5 million, of which $14 million would be taken from Treasury Account 1.
Budget Support—$686.4 million, to be financed entirely from funds already on deposit in Treasury Accounts 1 and 2.
Bundesbank Loan—$572 million for 4-1/2 years at 2-1/2 interest.

Under the counterproposal, the total of military procurement would remain the same, but the amount of new money required would

---

[3] Telegram 7765 from Bonn, June 25, reported that Herbst, the chief German negotiator, told an Embassy official in Bonn that he would not go into the June 28 negotiations "with significantly more to put forward." He said that the Cabinet had approved only a "very slight margin" of negotiating room; his instructions were "extremely rigid." (National Archives, Nixon Presidential Materials, NSC Files, Country Files–Europe, Box 685, Germany Volume IX 4–8/71)

[4] A letter from Samuels to Herbst was transmitted in telegram 133748 to Bonn, July 23, and delivered by the Embassy on July 24. (Ibid., RG 59, Central Files 1970–73, FN 12 GER W 4/1/71)

be increased by DM 700 million ($200 million). The amount of budget support payments would be increased by the use of additional funds from Treasury deposits and Bundesbank credits would remain as proposed informally by Dr. Herbst. Treasury Accounts 1 and 2 would be almost entirely exhausted, so that in any subsequent offset agreement new money would be required and have a full balance-of-payments effect.

The counterproposal is substantially above either the formal offer or the personal Herbst proposal and there has been nothing in our negotiations thus far to suggest that the Germans might be prepared to improve their offer to this extent, if at all. However, we believe it is desirable to make this additional effort to bring about an improvement in their position.

The initial German reaction to our proposal has been very negative.[5] However, they are studying it further and we should have an official response soon. If our latest proposal is rejected, then a decision on our part to obtain this particular result would probably require intervention between the highest levels of both governments. Should we persevere, we would almost surely, at the least, pay a not inconsiderable price in terms of an irritated mutual relationship. It is our hope, however, that our proposal, even if not accepted in its present form, will provide a basis for a compromise within Presidentially approved guidelines.

We have just learned that the principal German negotiator, Dr. Herbst, has proposed to come to Washington for private talks next week. We have agreed that such discussions would be desirable and are in the process of making arrangements for meetings on August 3–4.[6]

---

[5] Reported in telegram 9070 from Bonn, July 24. (Ibid.) On July 21, as the U.S. proposal was being drafted, John J. McGinnis sent Secretary Connally a memorandum suggesting that the Germans would be unable to accept the proposal without a direct intervention by President Nixon with Chancellor Brandt. (Washington National Records Center, Department of the Treasury, Files of Under Secretary Volcker: FRC 56 79 17, German Offset) During his August 3 meeting with Kissinger, Ambassador Pauls said the German view was that all the concessions had been made by the German side and none by the United States. Pauls urged compromise since "the Germans could not swallow the latest U.S. proposal." (Memorandum for the record by Sonnenfeldt, August 4; National Archives, Nixon Presidential Materials, NSC Files, Country Files–Europe, Box 685, Germany Volume IX 4–8/71)

[6] On July 30 the Embassy in Bonn reported confirming these dates with Herbst. The Embassy also elaborated on the extreme negative reaction to the latest U.S. proposal. (Telegram 9349 from Bonn, July 30; ibid., RG 59, Central Files 1970–73, FN 12 GER W)

69.   **Editorial Note**

National Security Study Memorandum 122, dated April 15, 1971, had called for a new review of policy toward Japan, taking account of the 1969 NSSM 5 study and developments in the bilateral relationship since NSDM 13 was issued on May 28, 1969. Text of NSSM 122 is in the National Archives, RG 59, S/S Files: Lot 80 D 212, NSSM 122. Regarding NSSM 5 and NSDM 13, see Document 20.

A response to NSSM 122, dated August 2, was sent to the Chairman of the NSC Senior Review Group under cover of an August 2 memorandum from Winthrop Brown, who reported that it had been approved by the Interdepartmental Review Group for East Asia and the Pacific. Because of the interest in the study, particularly the economic aspects, throughout the government, he recommended that representatives from interested agencies be invited to attend the Senior Review Group meeting on the study. (National Archives, RG 59, S/S Files: Lot 80 D 212, NSSM 122)

A revision of the "Economic Options" section (pages 16–25) of the summary of the response to NSSM 122 was distributed to the Under Secretary of State, the Deputy Secretary of Defense, the JCS Chairman, the DCI, the Under Secretary of the Treasury, the Assistant to the President for International Economic Affairs, the OMB Director, and the CEA Chairman under cover of an August 5 memorandum from NSC Staff Secretary Davis. She also provided comment on the "Economic" section from the State Department and CEA. (Ibid.) The revision of the "Economic Options" section proposed, among other things:

"Option 1. *Take prompt, multilaterally-directed measures to eliminate or alleviate US trade and balance-of-payment problems, without directing actions at Japan in particular.*

"Option 2. *Increase pressure on Japan, in bilateral and multilateral forums, to stimulate its domestic economy (in order to achieve a better international balance) and to follow internationally-agreed rules of trade and investment.* (This is in addition to the measures in Option 1.)

"Option 3. *A CIEP-directed strategy for the negotiation, including the measures of Option 2 plus additional measures and a time schedule and targets.*"

The paper also listed several arguments for and against each of the three options but did not recommend approval or disapproval of any of them. A note at the end of the "Economic" section reads: "All of the above options assume a continuation of U.S. efforts to obtain satisfactory solutions to the textile and steel import problems."

In an August 5 memorandum to Under Secretary of State Irwin, Assistant Secretary Trezise and Deputy Assistant Secretary Brown summarized and analyzed among other things these three economic options and recommended that Irwin "set forth the case for Option 2, and urge an early Presidential decision in favor of this approach." They attached talking points for this presentation. (Ibid.)

The SRG met on August 6, August 27, and September 7 to take up policy toward Japan. At the August 6 meeting, "Kissinger made it clear from the outset that he wished to run the economic-trade section of the response [to NSSM 122] through the CIEP machinery, primarily to develop the kind of action plan envisaged by Treasury, Commerce, Labor and Agriculture in one of the options." Much of the discussion dealt with speculation about possibly loosening ties with Japan and the risks inherent in an independent Japan in Asia. At the close of the meeting, Kissinger said that the next SRG meeting would consider the paper being developed by the CIEP as well as one being written in the State Department on how the Asian situation might develop with an independent Japan. (Memorandum from Under Secretary of State for Political Affairs U. Alexis Johnson to Secretary Rogers, August 10; ibid.) The CIEP meeting took place on August 10; see Document 70.

The SRG meeting of September 7 focused directly on preparations for the bilateral ECONCOM meetings on September 9–10 in Washington (see Document 75). Papers for and resulting from these SRG meetings are in the National Security Council, Box 98 SRG Meetings, Japan 8/6/71, 8/27/71, and 9/7/71.

70.   **Information Memorandum From John Holdridge and Robert Hormats of the National Security Council Staff to the President's Deputy Assistant for National Security Affairs (Haig)**[1]

Washington, August 10, 1971.

SUBJECT

    CIEP Review Group Meeting on Japan

The CIEP Review Group meeting which we attended today brought out the following:

[1] Source: National Archives, Nixon Presidential Materials, NSC Files, Country Files–Far East, Box 536, Japan Volume V 7/71–9/71. Secret. Initialed by Haig. For background on this meeting, see Document 69.

—There is disagreement amongst the agencies as to precisely what reforms we wish Japan to undertake. Commerce would like Japan to allow in more American private investment; however, Treasury believes this would have a negative effect in the short run on our balance of payments. A number of agencies are pressing Japan to revalue the yen, although the amount of the revaluation acceptable to the agencies varies from Treasury's 20 to 25 percent (which Japan could not possibly accept) to State and DOD believing a 7 to 10 percent revaluation could be acceptable (which, if Japan liberalizes its import requirements and provides more foreign aid, seems to be a more logical position). Other suggested measures include a liberalization of imports and voluntary restraints by Japan on her exports. However, it is obvious that Japan will not do everything we seek and the agencies do not seem to be able to focus on which reforms we should press hardest for at the September Ministerial meeting.

—All agencies seem to agree that we have little effective leverage short of the threat of quota legislation or the Administration's imposing quotas under existing legislation (which Peterson and Commerce advocate).

—There is a great deal of concern with the U.S. balance of payments and trade situation in general, and with Japan in particular. Last year the U.S. balance of payments deficit was $3 billion and in 1971 the estimate is approximately $8.5 billion, while Japan is expected to realize a balance of payment surplus of approximately $7 billion in 1971. Approximately $2.5 billion of the U.S. deficit will be with Japan.

—There are basically two schools of thought as to how to handle the above problem: one advocates solving our balance of payments problems primarily through export incentives and border taxes on imports—which would not be directed specifically against Japan—but would affect trade with all our partners, along with requesting Japan to conform to accepted rules of international trade. The second school of thought says that since Japan is quite obviously the major problem, we should exert strong efforts to improve our trade and balance of payments with her and avoid invoking measures which would affect trade with the Europeans.

71.   Editorial Note

On August 21, 1971, Henry Kissinger met with Japanese Ambassador Ushiba in San Clemente. Ushiba was en route to Tokyo for consultations. In an August 19 briefing memorandum for this meeting, Holdridge and Hormats told Kissinger of Japanese concern about the 10 percent import surcharge and the suspension of gold convertibility the President had announced in his New Economic Policy address on August 15 (see Document 168). The memorandum noted that Ambassador Ushiba would want assurances that the President's economic measures, especially the surcharge, were not intended to discriminate against Japan. In an August 21 cover note on the memorandum, Colman informed Kissinger that Ushiba might mention that the administration was considering an exemption for Canada from the surcharge. (National Archives, Nixon Presidential Materials, NSC Files, Country Files–Far East, Box 536, Japan Volume V 7/71–9/71)

The memorandum of the August 21 conversation indicates that except for a discussion of textiles, economic issues hardly arose. On textiles Kissinger said he did not know where the textile negotiations, which bored him, stood. Ambassador Ushiba said he would be the point of contact for private communications with Prime Minister Sato. Later in the conversation Kissinger said he knew nothing about economics and thought economic leaders were usually "political idiots." (Ibid.)

---

72.   Memorandum From the President's Assistant for International Economic Affairs (Peterson) to the Under Secretary of the Treasury for Monetary Affairs (Volcker)[1]

Washington, August 25, 1971.

I've tried to reach you a couple of times but am on my way to San Clemente, so I'll give you the essence of the two things I wanted to cover with you:

---

[1] Source: Washington National Records Center, Department of the Treasury, Files of Under Secretary Volcker: FRC 56 79 15, PAV—Economic Stabilization Program. Eyes Only.

1. On Japan, there are some strong objections to the idea of bilateral balance goals on the part of OMB and George Shultz, on the grounds that it's bad policy that could haunt us later with other countries.

My response has been:

a. We start with overall balance of payments goals anyway on the multilateral scene for both countries;
b. We have done some detailed projecting that suggests balancing is a reasonable goal, so it's no doctrinaire commitment to zero balances. Besides, Japanese businessmen at the Hawaii Conference[2] have said it is feasible.

2. I would strongly urge you, Paul, to convene soon Paul McCracken and his key people (who impress me a great deal), Arthur Burns and his representatives, Ken Dam (in George Shultz's absence) to discuss where we are going on:

a. Negotiations in the near-term on exchange rate and what the scenario is not only on the target but what we do vis-à-vis the surcharge;
b. Very important, what kind of an overall system we want to emerge from all this in terms of such issues as:

(1) Reserve currency status;
(2) How parities are set (including various automatic and/or more presumptive approaches);
(3) Gold and its role, including possible price changes;
(4) Dollar overhang;
(5) More flexibility, etc.

Paul, some of these people have strong and interesting views on these subjects. I suspect that Treasury's and the U.S. Government's best interests are best served if you chair a collaborative effort to come up with a paper that outlines the issues and various approaches that might be considered more or less in the "spirit of Camp David",[3] rather than by inadvertence encourage these various departments to submit their own views to the President independently. In this way, I believe a paper can go forward in an orderly way from this group to John Connally and to the President.

I will be in California but I can pick up attendance at such meetings after I get back. In other words, please don't hold up anything on my account.

---

[2] Not further identified.

[3] The details of the New Economic Policy President Nixon announced on August 15 had been worked out in meetings of the President with his key economic advisers at Camp David August 13–15; see Document 168.

73.   **Editorial Note**

Pursuant to a request arising from the August 6, 1971, Senior Review Group meeting on Japan (see Document 69), State Department Executive Secretary Eliot, under cover of an August 16 memorandum, sent Kissinger an undated Addendum to NSSM 122, "The Possibility of a Looser Relationship With Japan and Its Consequences." (National Archives, RG 59, S/S Files: Lot 80 D 212, NSSM 122) The paper, which had not been reviewed by the East Asia Interdepartmental Review Group, dealt primarily with political-military-security issues and included the following language: "The purpose of a deliberate decision on our part to loosen ties with Japan would presumably be: a) to improve our chances of achieving a détente with China; b) to give us greater freedom of action to deal with Japan's commercial aggressiveness; c) to force Japan, once out of the hot house of association with the United States, to realize that its own interests require Japan to assume a major degree of responsibility for the welfare and progress of its neighbors; and d) to reduce our defense expenditures in the rest of Asia. . . . The postwar US/Japan relationship has been a unique arrangement. It has permitted Japan to conduct an unprecedented experiment in the development of national power and influence by economic growth without commensurate military power." The paper was distributed to members of the SRG under cover of an August 26 memorandum from NSC Staff Secretary Davis informing them it was an "additional paper" for consideration at the SRG meeting on August 27 in San Clemente. (Ibid., S/S Files: Lot 73 D 288, SRG Memos)

On August 24 Peterson sent members of the CIEP Review Group a 22-page paper, with three annexes, entitled "The Approach to Japan—Next Steps." (Ibid., S/S Files: Lot 80 D 212, NSSM 122) Also on August 24 Eliot, in response to an oral request from Holdridge, sent Kissinger a more concise summary of the NSSM 122 Response in reply to four questions Kissinger posed at the August 6 SRG meeting. (Ibid.) The questions were: "Where is Japan Going?; What Kind of Japan Do We Want?; How Do We Get It To Go There?; and What Are the Costs?" Eliot noted that the State Department paper commented in only a very general way on economic matters because the CIEP was preparing a more detailed paper on the economic aspects. Peterson's and Eliot's papers were circulated to members of the SRG under cover of an August 24 memorandum from Davis informing them they would be the basis for discussion in the SRG meeting in San Clemente on August 27. (Ibid.)

Peterson's paper considered a variety of issues, including those in the trade area and military procurement, and included the following language on yen revaluation:

"From the standpoint of achieving significant reduction in Japan's overall trade and payments surpluses—and corresponding if somewhat smaller improvement in the U.S. balances (both directly and through effects in third-country markets)—revaluation of the yen is our highest priority negotiating objective. In fact, it is contemplated that the surtax will remain until we get a satisfactory resolution of the exchange rate problem. We estimate, assuming general rate equilibrium, that a 15% *Japanese revaluation by itself* in terms of the dollar will improve our 1972 bilateral trade balance by about $1.5 billion or perhaps $2 billion. Thus, by itself, yen revaluation could be expected to help attain about 20% to 30% of our overall U.S. trade balance improvement target of about $6–$8 billion."

The paper listed some advantages to revaluation including "substantially strengthen[ing] the precedent for revaluations within the world monetary system, clearly of special interest to the U.S." The paper then continued:

"Revaluation would have certain disadvantages, however, relative to other less comprehensive objectives and measures:

"—It may lessen or counteract pressures on Japan for accelerated removal of restrictions on product (but not capital) imports, and of promotion techniques for exports, especially if a large revaluation is taken. Also, over the short run, a revaluation could have some perverse effects.

"—While a substantial yen revaluation could make a decisive difference in the impact of imports on some of our basic U.S. industries—such as steel and automobiles—it is unlikely to have a sufficient effect on a few specific U.S. industries such as textiles where Japan already appears to have a substantial cost advantage. Therefore, some, but fewer U.S. domestic political problems raised by Japanese import penetration in particular sectors will remain to be handled with supplementary measures, either quantitative restrictions (such as the President's commitment on textiles) or other voluntary and adjustment assistance measures."

74.   Memorandum From Secretary of State Rogers to President
        Nixon[1]

Washington, September 1, 1971.

SUBJECT

Eighth U.S.-Japan Joint Economic Committee Meeting

With the assistance of my colleagues on the Cabinet Committee,[2] as well as that of Peter Peterson and Henry Kissinger, we have been working at formulating the positions to be taken and the objectives to be sought in the meeting with the Japanese on September 9 and 10, which I will chair.[3]

In the light of this work I propose, with your approval, that the American delegation follow the guidelines set forth below. I am sending a copy of this memorandum to each member of the delegation, as well as to Mr. Peterson and Dr. Kissinger, for any comments they may desire to make. Additionally, I and my Cabinet Committee colleagues are meeting on September 2 with representatives of the non-governmental Advisory Council on Japan-U.S. Economic Relations.[4]

Very simply stated, our underlying objective is to preserve and strengthen our vitally important relationship with Japan. We should stress the importance which we attach to close cooperation with Japan and our recognition of her role as a responsible, cooperative world power. At the same time, we should attempt to persuade Japanese ministers to accept the fact that such a role requires early and effective measures to establish an appropriate balance in its external economic relationships, including those with the U.S.

If we are to achieve these objectives, and recognizing there may be special characteristics of the Japanese system, we must avoid appearing to single out Japan for discriminatory treatment on economic matters. As when dealing with other major countries, propos-

---

[1] Source: National Archives, Nixon Presidential Materials, NSC Files, Agency Files, Box 285, State Volume 13. Secret. Attached to a copy of a September 5 joint memorandum from Kissinger and Peterson to the President proposing NSDM 130 (Document 75). A handwritten note on the joint memorandum initialed by Kissinger and Peterson reads, "Sent forward 9/6/71."

[2] Probably a reference to the members of the Cabinet who would comprise the U.S. delegation to the Joint Economic Committee Meeting.

[3] Documentation on the process of formulating position papers is in the National Archives, Nixon Presidential Materials, NSC Files, Country Files–Far East, Box 536, Japan Volume V 7/71–9/71. On September 1 Kissinger sent a memorandum to Peterson and Irwin informing them that the State Department was responsible for all issues other than economic ones, and that the CIEP Working Group would prepare the negotiating paper on economic issues. (Ibid., RG 59, S/S Files: Lot 80 D 212, NSSM 122)

[4] Not further identified.

als from our side should be consistent with a broader equilibrium in the world economy.

We must also remember the oft-repeated Japanese plea to the United States, "Tell us what you want us to do, but don't publicly press us to do it."

The Japanese ministers should be made to understand that the U.S. will have to achieve a major turn-around in its balance of payments. Speaking plainly, this will require that countries which have run huge surpluses in their balance of payments with us will no longer be able to do so. Some countries which have had deficits with us will have to see those deficits increase. Given the large trading relationship between Japan and the United States, which we wish to see expanded, and the U.S. need for a satisfactory multilateral equilibrium, we will require a reasonably balanced trading relationship between the two countries. Our analysis strongly indicates that a global trade *surplus* of the dimension necessary for the U.S. equilibrium cannot be achieved with a *deficit* in our Japanese trade. It is our intention to review constantly progress in our over-all balance, and to appraise the consistency of developments in important bilateral accounts, to assure achievement of our goal. We hope Japan recognizes the validity of this analysis and aim, and will periodically review progress with us.

To this end, we should seek as priorities:[5]

1) A clear understanding by the Japanese ministers that the United States considers a major revaluation of the yen in relation to the dollar to be a condition precedent to a satisfactory economic relationship with the United States. We would not at this meeting indicate the level which we would consider satisfactory or negotiate bilaterally on this subject. If the Japanese proposed a figure in the neighborhood of 10%, we would need to indicate a larger order of magnitude is necessary. We would also indicate that we feel negotiations on this subject should be carried out in whatever multilateral forum is agreed upon by Europe, Japan and ourselves, referring to the September 15 meeting of the "Group of Ten."

---

[5] In an August 31 memorandum Under Secretary Johnson reported to Secretary Rogers on the August 27 SRG meeting on NSSM 122. Johnson noted that the discussion of economic issues was "brief and inconclusive." Peterson stressed the seriousness of the balance-of-payments situation and thought U.S. and Japanese balance-of-payments objectives were incompatible. Kissinger asked: "(a) How much revaluation of the yen did we want?, and (b) Had the President ever been given the opportunity to decide whether we wanted a monetary system based on fixed exchange rates or one based on floating rates? The President didn't just want to patch up an old system. If possible, he would like a good new one." Johnson reported that there was further, inconclusive discussion of the size of the yen revaluation and whether it should be pursued multilaterally or bilaterally. (National Archives, RG 59, S/S Files: Lot 80 D 212, NSSM 122)

2) We should seek elimination of Japanese quotas and other restrictions illegal under the GATT as well as non-tariff barriers and export subsidies, including tax incentives for exports.

We are particularly interested in the removal of quotas on certain farm products, computers, aircraft, and integrated circuits.

Additionally, we should seek:

3) Significant unilateral reductions of Japanese tariffs.

4) Japanese encouragement of imports, especially by general stimulation of the Japanese economy and investment in social infrastructure.

5) We should recognize as constructive the establishment unilaterally by the GOJ of a system to monitor Japanese exports to the United States of sensitive goods; e.g., automobiles, calculators, consumer electronics.

6) We should seek substantial, indeed dramatic, increase in the amount of Japanese economic aid, especially in Southeast Asia. Even more important than the amount would be softening of terms; e.g., less emphasis on export promotion and more on simple grant assistance.

7) We should seek increased Japanese military procurement in the United States as the Japanese defense budget rises.

8) Elimination of restrictions on capital investment inconsistent with our Treaty of Friendship, Commerce and Navigation and with the obligations which the Japanese have assumed in the OECD.

Fortunately, all of the above, except for the degree of revaluation which we seek, are included to a greater or lesser extent in the GOJ's eight-point program already approved[6] or in the package which the Foreign Office, the new Foreign Minister, and Sato are trying to get accepted.

At this meeting the Japanese will above all want to know our price for removal of the 10% surcharge. This is however, important to us in our negotiations relating to our total position with other countries, as well as Japan, and must in any case await a satisfactory overall exchange rate settlement. All we can say at this meeting is to promise its removal, as soon as our external position is assured.

We should stress, however, the very important steps which we are taking within the United States to correct the contribution of our own inflation to our trade imbalance.

On the side of our cooperation with Japan, we should offer cooperation with the Japanese in the following areas in which we have mutual interests.

---

[6] The Japanese positions were set out in telegram 8399 from Tokyo, August 26. (Ibid., Nixon Presidential Materials, NSC Files, Country Files–Far East, Box 536, Japan Volume V 7/71–9/71)

a) Joint effort to seek liberalization of the trade policies of the European Community.

b) Work within the OECD High Level Group to prepare the way for a major multilateral attack on trade barriers.

c) Development of international procedures for adjudicating investment disputes in developing countries.

d) A program to encourage private investors of both countries to establish joint ventures in less developed countries in an effort to obtain greater security for these investments.

e) Closer scientific collaboration in seeking solutions to common problems in the fields of transportation and ecology.

f) In the field of *nuclear energy* we should reaffirm the offer which we have made to ten countries—the EEC, UK, Canada, Australia, and Japan to discuss the possibility of selling them classified U.S. technology for use of the gaseous diffusion process for enrichment of uranium on a multilateral basis.

g) We should assure the Japanese that immediately upon the completion of the ECONCOM Meeting, the President will send the Agreement for Reversion of Okinawa to the Senate with a very strong recommendation for its early ratification.[7]

William P. Rogers

---

[7] There is no indication of Secretary Rogers' approval or disapproval.

75. National Security Decision Memorandum 130[1]

Washington, September 7, 1971.

TO

The Secretary of State

SUBJECT

U.S.-Japan Joint Economic Committee Meeting

The President has reviewed your memorandum of September 1, 1971 on this subject, as well as the CIEP paper of August 24, 1971.[2]

The President has directed that in the ECONCOM meetings, the U.S. Delegation be guided by the following principal points:[3]

1. Throughout the meetings, as proposed by the Secretary of State, we should endeavor to re-establish in the minds of the Japanese the significance and closeness of the U.S.-Japanese relationship through a series of forthcoming political and psychological measures. We should:

---

[1] Source: National Archives, RG 59, S/S Files: Lot 83 D 305, NSDM 130. Secret. Copies were sent to the Secretaries of Treasury, Defense, Agriculture, Commerce, Labor, Interior, and Transportation; Ambassador at Large Kennedy; the OMB Director; the Chairmen of the Council of Economic Advisers and the Council on Environmental Quality; the Special Trade Representative; the Assistant to the President for Domestic Affairs; the Director of Central Intelligence; and the Chairman of the Joint Chiefs of Staff. On September 9 Peterson sent a memorandum to Kissinger complaining that this Decision Memorandum should have been signed jointly by the two of them (or should have been a CIEP Decision Memorandum signed by Peterson), because the CIEP members looked to him as their spokesman. (Ibid., Nixon Presidential Materials, NSC Files, Agency Files, Box 218, CIEP) On a September 10 memorandum from Hormats regarding Peterson's complaint and another procedural issue, Kissinger wrote, "Life is too short for this sort of thing." (Ibid.)

[2] Rogers' memorandum is Document 74. The August 24 paper is not printed, but see Document 73. On September 3 Hormats sent Kissinger a memorandum regarding the "bureaucratic problem" Rogers' memorandum (which had "circumvented" Peterson) had created. Noting that Peterson was attempting to reconcile the CIEP paper with Rogers' memorandum, Hormats indicated that if agreement could be reached, he would recommend a joint memorandum from Kissinger and Peterson to the President summarizing the agreed objectives. (National Archives, Nixon Presidential Materials, NSC Files, Country Files–Far East, Box 536, Japan Volume V 7/71–9/71) Agreement on most issues was reached, and a draft joint Kissinger–Peterson memorandum to the President, September 5, became NSDM 130 after some revisions. (Attachment to memorandum from Hormats to Kissinger, September 4; ibid.) See also footnote 1, Document 74.

[3] The meetings were held in Washington September 9–10. See Department of State *Bulletin*, October 4, 1971, pp. 346–354, for the joint communiqué and statements by President Nixon, Secretary Rogers, and Foreign Minister Fukuda at the conclusion. The President's and Foreign Minister's remarks are also in *Public Papers of the Presidents of the United States: Richard M. Nixon, 1971*, pp. 945–947. Kissinger sent a September 10 memorandum to the President calling his attention to the "more salient aspects of the communiqué" and concluded: "On the whole discussions were amicable, but pointed up several unresolved economic issues, the most important being how much the yen will be revalued and how far Japan will move in the future to liberalize imports." (National Security Council, Box 98, 8/27/71 SRG Meeting—Japan)

—Assure the Japanese that shortly after the ECONCOM meeting the President will send the Agreement for Reversion of Okinawa to the Senate with a strong recommendation for its early ratification.

—Reaffirm our offer to explore with Japan and other countries the possibility of selling them U.S. technology for use in gaseous diffusion plants in third countries for enrichment of uranium.

—Indicate our desire for closer scientific collaboration in seeking solutions to common problems in the fields of transportation and ecology.

—Indicate our desire to cooperate to seek liberalization of the trade policies of the European Community.

—Indicate our desire to work within the OECD High Level Group to prepare the way for a major multilateral attack on trade barriers.

—Indicate our desire to develop international procedures for adjudicating investment disputes in developing countries.[4]

2. The U.S. new economic policy, with special emphasis on our balance of payments goals, should be clearly explained to the Japanese delegation. We should state strongly that it is our conviction that a reasonably balanced trade account between our two countries is necessary, and feasible by the end of 1973. It should be pointed out that, as we understand Japanese balance of payments and trade projections, they are incompatible with our objectives. It should be proposed that we work together to achieve mutually agreed compatible balance of payments goals.

3. The overriding U.S. objective is to obtain a revaluation of the currencies of our major trading partners, which will include a substantial revaluation of the yen. While negotiations on the exact amount of yen revaluation sought should be carried out multilaterally, Secretary Connally is authorized privately, if he wishes, to inform the Japanese Ministers that a revaluation in the range of 15 to 20 percent is necessary.

4. We should indicate that we would remove the 10 percent surcharge only when our external position is assured.

5. Beyond this, we wish to achieve our balance of payments goals primarily through trade liberalization, and we expect the Japanese to remove quotas and other import restrictions illegal under the GATT. We are particularly interested in prompt removal of quotas on agricultural items, computers, aircraft, and integrated circuits.

6. We should welcome the Japanese eight-point program, commend their efforts so far, and urge them to go further.

7. It should be made clear to the Japanese that we still seek a negotiated voluntary restraint agreement for textiles but will be prepared to

---

[4] Two additional points were included in the September 5 draft (see footnote 2 above). The first dealt with satellite television coverage of the Emperor's visit. The second concerned the election of a Japanese Chairman of the GATT in November, a proposal made in the August 24 CIEP paper.

solve the problem in other ways if an agreement is not forthcoming. Our continuing need for a voluntary restraint agreement for steel exports should also be made clear.

8. We should stress our desire for even closer economic cooperation in the future. To this end, we should propose periodic meetings with the Japanese,[5] starting with a special interagency mission to Japan by next January to assess with the Japanese specific progress toward agreed upon balance of payments goals, compatible economic policies and the eight-point program, to identify remaining or emerging trade problems, and work out constructive, timely solutions to common economic problems.

9. In discussing lower priority economic objectives, including increased Japanese defense procurement in the United States, increased aid on such terms, and investment liberalization, our delegates should make clear our wishes in low key, relating such secondary points to our overall balance of payments goals.

Henry A. Kissinger

---

[5] According to Hormats' September 4 memorandum to Kissinger, the State Department opposed this proposal "on the grounds that it is unnecessary and it would circumvent State's apparatus." Hormats noted that Peterson and the economic agencies saw this as their only remaining new initiative for the ECONCOM and recommended it be retained despite the State Department's objections.

---

76.   **Paper Prepared in the Department of the Treasury**[1]

Washington, September 10, 1971.

REQUIREMENTS FOR A SECURE U.S. BALANCE-OF-PAYMENTS POSITION

The purpose of this note is to set forth U.S. views regarding the requirements for a secure U.S. balance-of-payments position. We view such a position not simply as in the interests of the U.S. but as a pre-

---

[1] Source: Washington National Records Center, Department of the Treasury, Office of International Monetary Affairs: FRC 56 77 68, Briefing Book for the October 18–20 WP3/G-10 Deputies. Confidential. An earlier draft of this paper is presumably the August 28 paper discussed in the Volcker Group on August 31; see Document 173. In a September 8 letter to Volcker, OMB Assistant Director Dam cautioned against using the paper in G-10 discussions because focusing on quantitative goals before agreeing on the type of international monetary system the administration wanted might constrain long-term options. (Washington National Records Center, Department of the Treasury, Files of Under Secretary Volcker: FRC 56 79 15, PAV–Economic Stabilization Program)

requisite for a return to a smooth and orderly functioning international monetary system. Actions are needed which both compensate for the past erosion of the U.S. external position and offer the prospect of a strong position in the future. To achieve these results after years of deficit, the U.S. will require the reasonable prospect of some surplus in its basic external accounts for several years.

Achievement of a secure U.S. payments position presupposes an improved performance of the domestic economy. The President has taken such action. However, success plainly also requires the correction of certain elements which adversely affect U.S. international transactions. It is not proposed to deal here with the nature of the actions required but with the magnitude of the adjustment problem. For its part, the U.S., of course, remains determined to follow those domestic economic policies necessary to control inflation and make the economy more competitive. This paper is developed on that basis.

This paper does not deal with the future shape of the monetary system. No matter what the system, an improvement in the U.S. position along the lines described below will be necessary.

The Erosion of the U.S. Position

The deterioration of the U.S. external payments position is traced in the table on the following page.[2] The United States recorded persistent but not unmanageable balance-of-payments deficits throughout the 1960s. From 1960 through 1969, the net liquidity balance was in continuous deficit, averaging $3.1 billion per year. The official settlements balance was also in deficit during most of that period, averaging $1.1 billion per year. The deficit on current and long-term capital accounts (the basic balance) averaged $1.4 billion per year. A deterioration in the U.S.' basic position since 1964 is evident, with current and long-term capital accounts in deficit by $3 billion in 1970.

The situation turned sharply worse in 1970 and 1971. By the first half of 1971, the deficit on current and long-term capital accounts rose to an annual rate of $8.6 billion. While temporary factors presumably contributed, these data confirm an eroding trend.

With continuing payments deficits, the United States reserve position has been severely and persistently weakened. Gross reserves have fallen from a high of $26.2 billion in 1949 to the present level of $12.2 billion and now stand at about 27 percent of estimated 1971 imports, well below other countries' average level of reserve holdings relative to trade. Furthermore, liquid liabilities have risen sharply, from $21 billion

---

[2] The table is not printed.

in 1960 to more than $60 billion; liabilities to official holders amount to more than $44 billion.

The erosion of the merchandise trade position has been a primary element in the unsatisfactory U.S. balance of payments in the past several years and the major source, directly or indirectly, of the recent deterioration in the basic balance. The trade balance has deteriorated by more than $8 billion in the seven years 1964–1971 and is now in deficit. In 1964, the U.S. had a trade surplus of $6-3/4 billion, which amounted to 1.1 percent of GNP. In the entire first half of 1971, the trade deficit was running at a seasonally adjusted annual rate of $1.5 billion.

As in the case of the overall balance of payments, the deterioration in the trade position has accelerated recently. Before the President's new program was announced, trade deficits were forecast by U.S. Government experts of about $2 billion for 1971 and $3.5 billion for 1972. The forecast deterioration from 1970 to 1971 was $4 billion, partly attributable to special factors and partly to cyclical factors. Nevertheless, quite apart from the cyclical influences, the U.S. merchandise trade position is experiencing a continuing trend deterioration of more than $1 billion annually. This trend has also been observed by the OECD Secretariat and the IMF.

Over the years, the deterioration in the U.S. trade position is most pronounced in trade with Japan, Canada, and the European Community, although the recent sharp deterioration has been more widespread. The following table traces the deterioration in the trade balance between 1964, when the U.S. trade surplus reached its peak, and 1970, and more recently, by area:

Change in U.S. Trade Balance
($ millions)

	Between 1964 and 1970	Between 1970 and Second Quarter 1971 (Annual Rate)
Canada	-2240	-1650
Japan	-1440	-1570
EC	-700	-990
Other W. Europe	250	-830
Rest of World	-340	-340

The deterioration in the trade position has carried through into the balance on goods, services and private remittances. The contribution to an improved position from rising investment income receipts has been insufficient to overcome mounting outpayments resulting from the rapid growth of U.S. liabilities and high interest rate levels. The heavy burden of defense expenditures abroad has also served to offset potential improvements in the services accounts.

The long-term capital account was not a factor in the deterioration of the overall U.S. position until 1971, when uncertainty about exchange rates apparently had a large adverse effect. The net private long-term capital outflow declined from $4.5 billion in 1964, before comprehensive restraints on capital outflows came into effect, to $1.5 billion in 1970.

In 1964 the U.S. was a net supplier of long-term private capital to all areas of the world. Canada received $1.1 billion, Europe and Japan $2.2 billion and the rest of the world $1.2 billion. With capital restrictions, higher interest rates in the U.S., and a surge of investment in U.S. securities, this situation shifted sharply. From 1968 through 1970 the U.S. was a net *importer* of private long-term capital from the major industrial countries other than Canada, as follows:

Net Movements of Private Long-Term Capital
($ million)

	(average) 1966–7	(average) 1968–9	1970	5-year Average
Canada	-1,232	-1,189	-1,046	-1,178
Japan	360	-61	-361	47
U.K. and EC	-745	1,731	529	500
Total, these areas	-1,617	481	-878	-631

The Importance of Adjustment

The deficit in the U.S. balance of payments could not be allowed to continue: (a) It was leading to rapid depletion of U.S. reserve assets and the accumulation of an unstable mass of liquid liabilities. (b) Its nature and extent became so widely recognized as to generate speculation. (c) It led to an intensification of protectionist pressures within the U.S. (d) It intensified the difficulties in maintaining an appropriate share and level of both international assistance to less developed countries and responsibilities in the area of global military security. (e) It subjected the economic foundations of the international monetary system to recurrent shocks. (f) It is not compatible with a sustainable world payments equilibrium required for the fulfillment of mutually shared national objectives.

Because the deficit has been so large and has continued for so long, the solution of these problems now requires a complete and convincing elimination of the deficits; this cannot be achieved without aiming at some period of surplus in the U.S.' basic accounts. Sustained reductions of liquid liabilities would of course require significant surpluses continued for a period of several years.

The world financial community should recognize that a period of unquestioned strength in the U.S. external position is a necessary condition for a strong and stable financial system. Although a U.S. surplus would require temporary deficits (exclusive of SDR allocations) on the part of some countries which have experienced the surpluses which were the mirror image of past U.S. deficits, it should be fully compatible with the legitimate balance-of-payments aims of other nations.

The U.S. cannot be put in the position of running further deficits however reasonable its domestic performance, as a means of reconciling the goals of other countries. Such a result would be financially unsustainable.

The Extent of the Improvement Required to Meet U.S. Needs

In specific terms, the U.S. will need a balance-of-payments position which for some years assures, at a minimum: (a) at least a modest surplus in its basic accounts. Statistically, this is taken in this paper as a surplus of around $3 billion annually on current and long-term capital accounts, or less than $2 billion after allowing for errors and omissions.[3] (b) a surplus on goods, services and private remittances sufficient to finance a foreign aid program appropriate to the United States position and to accommodate foreign demands for U.S. long-term private capital in the absence of U.S. Governmental restraints. Thus, the U.S. requires a surplus on goods, services and private remittances of roughly $2 billion more than the net deficit on government grants and capital, direct investment and other private long-term investment and errors and omissions.

Such a position allows for no net short-term capital outflows, and thus would approximate equilibrium on official settlements and only a modest reduction in official dollar balances. Thus, it appears a minimum target for the initial adjustment.

While a surplus on merchandise trade account is not necessary in theory, there is no prospect at this time, particularly with the current net expenditures on military transactions, that these requirements can be met unless the U.S. has a substantial merchandise trade surplus. Without a surplus on merchandise trade (and therefore in the U.S. current account) and an end to the trend deterioration in the trade balance, payments on foreign investments in the U.S., including interest on liquid liabilities, are likely to rise as much as the income from U.S. investments abroad, eliminating the likelihood of net improvement in the services accounts.

---

[3] A $3 billion surplus on basic balance would be equivalent to less than $2 billion after allowing for errors and omissions because the latter have shown a persistent deficit averaging well over $1 billion annually. This is believed to comprise in the main unidentified current and long-term capital transactions. [Footnote in the source text.]

Before recently announced actions, the U.S. balance-of-payments position and prospects as appraised by U.S. Government experts internally were as follows:

($ billions)

	1970	1971	1972
Goods, services and private remittances	+2.2	-1.0	-2.7
of which:			
Merchandise trade	+2.1	-1.9	-3.5
Government grants and long-term capital	-5.2	-7.4	-6.1
Current and long-term capital account	-3.0	-8.4	-8.8

The U.S. economy has not been operating at a high employment level. Adjusting for cyclical factors—estimating what the figures would be if the U.S. economy and those of all of its major trading partners were operating at levels of capacity consistent with domestic objectives—the U.S. payments position and prospects, prior to the recent actions, were as follows:[4]

($ billions)

	1970	1971	1972
Goods, services and private remittances	-1/2	-2-1/2 to -3	-4
Of which:			
Merchandise trade	-1	-3-1/2 to -4	-5
Grants and long-term capital	-5	-5	-6
Current and long-term capital account	-5-1/2	-7-1/2 to -8	-10
Normal errors and omissions			-1
Total			-11

The foregoing suggests that the U.S., taking account of no adverse trend beyond 1972, needs an improvement in its current and long-term

---

[4] The OECD Secretariat, in CPE/WP3(71)13 suggests that adjustments in the U.S. balance-of-payments figures for 1970 to correct for cyclical factors should be somewhat larger than those used in the U.S. calculations. The Secretariat's cyclical adjustment for the goods, services and remittances balance in 1970 is about $1 billion larger than the U.S. figure, largely because the U.S. estimate provides for a downward adjustment of extraordinarily high interest payments in that year. (The figures for this balance used by the U.S. and the Secretariat also differ because the U.S. includes U.S. Government pension payments whereas the Secretariat does not.) [Footnote in the source text.]

capital account in 1972 of $13 billion to achieve a minimal surplus in its basic accounts (and therefore assured equilibrium in its official settlements accounts) for a period of years. A measure of improvement based on the actual U.S. position in 1970 or even on the cyclically adjusted position in that year would not be adequate. It would not take account of the very serious trend deterioration in the underlying position which must be expected to continue until a fundamental correction is achieved.

If the improvement required to meet U.S. objectives were to be brought about through exchange rate action and U.S. domestic measures or through trade measures, the improvement would have to be found predominantly in the merchandise trade account. Although the dollar income from foreign investment could be expected to rise and travel expenditures might decline somewhat with an exchange rate realignment, the increased dollar equivalent of foreign currency costs of U.S. military expenditures abroad together with increased shipping costs would be likely to offset much of these improvements. The only foreseeable means of reducing to some extent the required adjustment in trade would be a modification of arrangements for financing U.S. military expenditures in NATO countries or in Japan.

An improvement of $13 billion in the U.S. merchandise trade position from the cyclically adjusted deficit projected for 1972 would mean a surplus of only $8 billion. Such a surplus would be little more than the surplus which the U.S. had in 1964 ($6.8 billion) when the total volume of world trade and production was much lower. Prior to recent developments, Germany and Japan were expected to have trade surpluses of around $6 billion in 1971. It would also be much less in relation to U.S. GNP—less than 0.65 percent—than the surpluses which many other countries have been running, none of which has anything approaching U.S. responsibilities for defense nor a role as a major private capital supplier for LDC's and others. In 1970, for example, Germany had a trade surplus in excess of 3 percent and Japan one in excess of 2 percent.

The $6 billion allowance made in the above calculations for net private capital outflows and government aid amounts to about 1/2 of 1 percent of estimated high employment GNP (approximately $1.2 trillion for 1972). As a proportion of GNP, this would represent a substantial *reduction* from earlier years. In the 1960–1964 period, such flows averaged $5-3/4 billion annually or 1.04 percent of GNP; in the 1965–1970 period, with U.S. capital restraints programs in effect, they averaged $5-1/2 billion or 0.65 percent of GNP.

The net outflow on Government grants and capital is expected to rise, from $3.7 billion in 1970, to $3.8 billion in 1971, and $4.1 billion in 1972. If the net outflow on all long-term capital plus government grants is not to exceed $6 billion, net private long-term capital outflows cannot exceed $2 billion. That figure will have to allow for both private investment in developing countries and resort by international lending institutions to the U.S. capital market.

In recent years net flows of capital and government grants to LDC's have averaged over $5-1/2 billion annually. Increased borrowing on the U.S. capital market by international lending institutions is possible. Thus an expected net grants and long-term capital flow in the $6 billion range in 1972 represents essentially a flow to LDC's, without significant net capital outflows to industrial nations. In fact, a level of grants and long-term capital outflow of 1/2 percent of GNP—even though it all goes to LDC's—is likely to be subject to criticism as being grossly inadequate in comparison with 1 percent of GNP targets accepted by a number of other donor countries.

The improvement in the U.S. position to be achieved would thus be:

($ billions)

	Trade	Goods, serv & remittances	Grants & long-term capital	Current & long-term capital
High employment position in 1972 expected in absence of corrective action	-5	-4	-6	-10
Position required for surplus of $3 billion on basic balance*	8	9	-6	3
Improvement required	13	13	0	13

---

*Equivalent to less than $2 billion after allowing for E & O. Does not allow for short-term capital outflow.

The $13 billion estimate for the amount of improvement needed in the goods and services accounts in the U.S. views is a minimum, and may be conservative.

a. The full impact of changes in exchange rates is not felt immediately but only with a considerable lag. The full effects of any such change in 1971 would probably not be realized until 1973 or even beyond. If the trend deterioration in the U.S. position continued through 1972, an additional $1 billion or more would need to be added to the $13 billion figure for the improvement needed to produce the required surplus in 1973.

b. The assumption is optimistic that there will be no net outflow of long-term capital to industrial nations. The U.S. wishes to remove its temporary restraints on long-term capital outflows, and believes any long-term equilibrium must properly assume such removal. We cannot be certain that a change in exchange rates would so shift the attractiveness of the U.S. relative to other industrial countries as a site for investment in manufacturing industries that U.S. restraints on capital outflows (including the interest equalization tax) could be removed without resulting in substantial net flow of long-term capital from the U.S. to other industrialized countries, taken as a group. In particular no allowance is made for repayments of foreign debts incurred by U.S. corporations in financing foreign investments over the past few years when the capital controls program was in effect. Moreover, no allowance is made for future Canadian use of the New York capital market nor for any net use of this market by European borrowers. The U.S. has supplied an average of $1.2 billion per year net of private long-term capital to Canada. If this were to continue the U.S. would need a correspondingly larger goods and services surplus (unless long-term funds moved to the U.S. from the EC and Japan). The possibility that net long-term capital outflows are being underestimated is further supported by the fact that improvements in the goods and services balance have almost always been accompanied by substantial *increases* in net long-term capital outflows. Certainly to the extent that a new increase in exports may involve an increase in outstanding trade credits, an increase would be expected.

c. The estimates take no account of the adverse effects upon U.S. trade of the contemplated enlargement of the European Common Market or any preferential trade arrangements concluded or which may be concluded between the enlarged EC and other nations.

d. No allowance has been made for any offsetting measures or other actions by any other country, or for any automatic effects on foreign business activity and the related foreign import demand. It may be necessary to take measures which are strong enough to compensate for offsetting actions by or developments in other countries in order to achieve the desired improvement in the U.S. position.

e. In previous instances of extended disequilibrium, the normal expectation has been that, in moving for readjustment in exchange rates, countries properly err on the side of safety. A period of sizable surplus to repay debts or rebuild reserves is anticipated. *This statement of requirements makes no such allowance.*

Prudence would suggest that a swing in U.S. goods and services accounts significantly larger than $13 billion should take place to provide for the lags in effectiveness of measures, the possibility of continuing Canadian borrowing, some repayments of U.S. borrowing in Europe, and a margin of safety.[5]

---

[5] On December 16 a longer, revised version of this paper was circulated in the Treasury Department by F. Lisle Widman, Director of the Office of Industrial Nations, who noted that the purpose of the paper was to meet inquiries from the public. (Washington National Records Center, Department of the Treasury, Office of the Assistant Secretary for International Affairs: FRC 56 76 108, US/3/005 Studies and Reports, Volume 9) Volcker was opposed to issuing the paper publicly. (Memorandum from Wilson E. Schmidt to Volcker, December 22, and letter from Volcker to Schmidt, December 28; ibid., US/3/006 Commentaries and Reports Volume 2)

---

77.   Memorandum of Conversation[1]

Washington, September 10, 1971.

PARTICIPANTS

Japan

Mikio Mizuta, Minister of Finance
Takashi Hosomi, Vice Minister for International Finance
Kanzo Tanigawa, Director General, Customs Bureau
Koichi Inamura, Director General, International Finance Bureau
Toyoo Gyoten, Special Assistant to Vice Minister of Finance for International Finance Bureau
Michio Kondo, Counselor (Financial), Embassy of Japan

United States

Secretary of the Treasury John Connally
Under Secretary for Monetary Affairs Paul Volcker
Assistant Secretary John Petty
Deputy Assistant Secretary William Cates

The Secretary began by stressing that although exchange rate changes will have to be worked out on a multilateral basis, it is imperative that substantial changes be made. Another point he wished to emphasize was that the textile matter, which had not received much

---

[1] Source: Washington National Records Center, Department of the Treasury, Secretary's Memos: FRC 56 74 17, Memcons 1971. Confidential. Drafted by Cates on September 13 and approved by Volcker. Copies were sent to Volcker, Petty, Willis, Schmidt, Dale, Meissner, and the Executive Secretary. The conversation was held in Secretary Connally's Dining Room.

attention during the EconCom meeting, was of the utmost importance.[2] The U.S. Government all the way up to the President is seriously concerned about the textile issue. Minister Mizuta asked if textiles would be discussed at the Rogers–Fukuda lunch.[3] Secretary Connally replied he did not know and that the last he heard was that it would not be but he believed that, diplomatic niceties aside, if problems exist between our two countries, they should be fully and frankly discussed.

Secretary Connally suggested the smart thing for the U.S. and Japan to do would be to get off in a corner and agree on a trade arrangement between themselves and invite in other countries, including LDCs. Japan and the U.S. should trade for each other and not in competition. Minister Mizuta replied that in the long future he felt that Japan, the U.S., Canada, and Australia might well get together on the Pacific Basin concept. Secretary Connally pointed out that Europe was forming a trading bloc against the U.S. and Japan. These two countries should protect themselves. However, he posed one condition: that the U.S. get a head start of six months because otherwise we would never catch up with Japan. Mr. Volcker doubted that six months would suffice.

Minister Mizuta said that when Ambassador Meyer visited him two weeks ago he had told the Ambassador that this was his third stint at being Japan's Finance Minister. The first two times Japan was in balance of payment difficulties and the U.S. was very helpful. He is grateful for that help and is the only Japanese Finance Minister who has had that experience. Now he is aware that the U.S. is in difficulty and he is willing to cooperate in turn. The argument he raised yesterday over fundamental disequilibrium was perhaps misunderstood. He meant to say that the Japanese performance in the first two quarters of 1971 has been extraordinary due to cyclical conditions. Discounting this extraordinary performance and adding the yen float and the surcharge, he thinks that the Japanese surplus would be even smaller than the normal surplus Japan should expect.

Secretary Connally replied that Minister Mizuta has had more than his fair share of bad luck in being Finance Minister three different times—once is plenty.

---

[2] In a September 10 briefing memorandum to President Nixon regarding his 7:30 p.m. meeting with Foreign Minister Fukuda just before a dinner for participants in the ECONCOM meeting, Kissinger suggested that the President "express regret that the ECONCOM did not achieve more substantial results." Kissinger then mentioned two items of "overriding importance": substantial revaluation of the yen and Japanese import liberalization. He also suggested the President make clear to Fukuda that there must be agreement on textiles no later than October 15. (National Archives, Nixon Presidential Materials, NSC Files, Country Files–Far East, Box 536, Japan Volume V 7/71–9/71) No record of the President's conversation with Foreign Minister Fukuda was found. Regarding the ECONCOM meeting, see footnote 3, Document 75.

[3] Secretary Rogers hosted a luncheon for Foreign Minister Fukuda on September 10 beginning at 12:45 p.m. (Personal Papers of William P. Rogers, Appointment Books)

Secretary Connally wished to emphasize that regardless of U.S. attitudes in the past the time has come when we must seek correction for our balance of payments difficulties. While we understand Japanese political difficulties and the problems of the party and personalities governing Japan, we hope that Japan and other countries will recognize our problem and will help us now as we helped in the past. It is only fair to say, Secretary Connally went on, without in any way meaning to be threatening, once the President understood the problem and made his decision other countries would be very mistaken to assume that we are not determined to solve our problem. We have seen the U.S. trade account deteriorate steadily from 1964 to 1971. This has been a strong and lasting trend and is a serious warning to the U.S. Secretary Connally added that he, and in his opinion the President, are convinced that we cannot solve this problem with monetary or fiscal policy or exchange rate changes alone. Trade barriers including tariffs, internal taxes, non-tariff barriers, export subsidies, etc. of other nations were tolerated in the past by the U.S. because our position was so strong that we could afford to be tolerant. Now it is time for an appraisal of tariff and non-tariff barriers all around the world.

The Secretary said that he was not singling out Japan, but cited Japanese forecasts of a $12 billion trade surplus in 1975. There are other countries with whom we have similar difficulties—in particular Canada, whose automobile industry we helped set up and which now provides incentives for the Michelin Tire Company to come to Canada to make tires for the U.S. market. The Canadians are going to have to help us too.

The Secretary added that we are aware that thus far there is some question in the minds of governments around the world as to whether the U.S. is really serious in its determination to solve its balance of payments problem. There should be no question. The President is very concerned and completely determined to solve the problem. If other nations do not come to realize this, there will be great difficulties for all of us.

Minister Mizuta replied that, as Fukuda had said yesterday, we are fully aware of the implication behind the President's new economic policy and we are also aware that internal measures—fiscal and monetary—are not enough to solve the U.S. problem. The Japanese are ready to cooperate, but Minister Mizuta is not confident that the current favorable balance of payments for Japan will last another three years. He pointed out that Japan has historically had a balance of payments deficit and that the capital structure and income levels in Japan remain low. If the yen were as strong as others think, the announcement of the President's new policy would not have had such an unsettling effect in Japan. The stock market decline and general concern indicate that Japan is indeed vulnerable.

Minister Mizuta, however, added that he is pleased to be Finance Minister this time around because for the first time he is able freely to spend money in an effort to stimulate the Japanese economy. Minister Mizuta reiterated that Japan was willing to share the burden in an international cooperation effort but re-emphasized that he is not optimistic about Japan's balance of payments.

Secretary Connally said that the problems between the U.S. and Japan could be divisible into three areas: one, the cost of defense; two, trade restrictions; and three, exchange rates. The first two of these are best handled by bilateral negotiations between our two countries, while the third should be worked out in a multilateral context. Secretary Connally added, however, that Minister Mizuta could be very helpful in the latter area by making it clear to other countries that the U.S. problem is serious and that we are determined to solve it. No other Finance Ministers have had the opportunity for such a thorough exposure to the U.S. position as had occurred during this Ministerial meeting. Finally, the Secretary asked the Japanese Government to do some thinking about where we go from here. He pointed out that Common Market developments would change world trading patterns and that we and the Japanese should do some thinking about these developments.

In summary, Secretary Connally said that the U.S. and Japan should set about now to reconcile their first two problems (defense and trade barriers) in a bilateral framework, while the third (exchange rates) should be dealt with in a multilateral context in a different time frame.

Minister Mizuta said that his impression of the recent G-10 Deputies meeting was that the EC is not in much of a hurry to settle things. While the Minister is prepared to speak out for international cooperation, he hoped that the present uncertainty could be removed as soon as possible. What would be the American position at the G-10 Ministers meeting regarding the surcharge, the price of gold, a de facto devaluation?

Secretary Connally replied that although he would be talking to the President he did not expect to have a proposal for the G-10 meeting.[4] The U.S. is reluctant to table any proposal, for one good reason that other nations always complain that we are telling them how to run their business. Other countries kept saying that the U.S. should do something. Now we have done what we could to solve our problem and it is up to the others to cooperate. If we were to make any proposal, within 24 hours every nation in the world would denounce it and us.

Minister Mizuta pointed out that each country has its own domestic political problems and that while the U.S. is asking others to cooper-

---

[4] The G-10 met in London September 15–16; see Document 78.

ate, from the point of view of other countries, it is important for the U.S. to pave the way. If a general realignment of currency parities is made in such a way that one country's parity remains unchanged while all others must change, this makes political decisions very difficult for the others. Therefore, all countries' parities should change. This is a contribution which the Secretary could make at the G-10 meeting.

Secretary Connally replied that realignment of exchange rates is actually only the second priority. Trade restrictions, tariffs, non-tariff barriers which discriminate against American products are the first priority. The yen-dollar parity has nothing to do with the freedom of an American to own 100 percent of a company in Japan nor with the freedom to export to Japan. The Secretary added that he was in no hurry to fix exchange rates until the basic problem was solved because any country could change its exchange rate—against the dollar—three weeks later.

Minister Mizuta said that his reference to realignment as the first priority was based on Secretary Rogers' opening statement at the EconCom 8. Secretary Connally replied that one should not believe what one reads in the public press.

Minister Mizuta said that he understood the U.S. argument about the removal of trade barriers but nevertheless realignment would also be important. Other countries in his opinion were seriously considering this. Secretary Connally reiterated that we do not want to tell other countries what to do. He mentioned the question of grants vs. loans and said that he could tell the Japanese that they should make more of their aid in the form of grants but he wasn't so sure the Japanese weren't right and that the U.S. shouldn't tie its own aid. But in any case although the Secretary could dictate a solution to the balance of payments problems of Japan, Korea, Canada, and every other country, the result would be a world uproar. It is, therefore, up to the other countries to come forward with ideas to solve the problem. In the meantime, the dollar, the yen, and the DM are all floating so we can live for a while until every nation has a chance to evaluate its own position. We are not going to push for anything at the upcoming G-10 meeting. Minister Mizuta replied that though the Secretary had said that the U.S. economy is sick, the sick man is still very strong. He could prescribe the cure but he doubted the sick man would accept the prescription (laughter). Secretary Connally replied that the Minister was right. We probably wouldn't accept it: Japanese prescriptions have usually been in terms of what is good for Japan and we need something that will be good for the U.S.

Minister Mizuta thanked Secretary Connally for the Secretary's excellent explanation of the U.S. position and promised that in international meetings Japan would participate in a spirit of cooperation with the U.S. He looks forward to further exchanges like this.

Secretary Connallly agreed that the present was a very good opportunity for himself and the Minister and their staffs to see more of one another. With the growth in power of Russia, China, and the EC, the Secretary expects that the U.S. and Japan will inevitably be pushed closer together.

William C. Cates

78.   **Editorial Note**

The G-10 Ministers met in London September 15–16, 1971. In his prepared remarks Secretary Connally recognized the difficulties in achieving the $13 billion turnaround in the U.S. current account, but took strong exception to those who thought the U.S. goal overly ambitious. He said it was "important," it was "essential," it was "*absolutely* essential, that a formula be developed in the very near future that would anticipate that the balance of payments would be corrected in a relatively short period of time." Connally's statement, along with those of other Ministers and Governors of the G-10, are in the Washington National Records Center, Department of the Treasury, Volcker Group Masters: FRC 56 86 30, 1971, VG/LIM/71-35.

Connally went on to say that he knew the G-10's purpose was to consider problems "strictly monetary in character" and that he did not want to inject items into the discussion that were not soluble in the G-10, but he thought the G-10 ought to concern itself with other problems that at least were soluble in the Councils of the nations that the G-10 represented. Connally mentioned two: restrictive trade practices and the need to promote free trade and a fair and equitable trading system and defense burdensharing. Concerning the latter, Connally noted that the United States devoted 8.9 percent of its GNP and 36 percent of its budget to defense, and no other industrial nation came close to those magnitudes. Connally asserted this should be discussed and considered as part of the overall realignments that were coming.

Separately, but related to defense burdensharing, National Security Decision Memorandum 133 on "U.S. Strategy and Forces for NATO: Allied Force Improvements" was sent by Henry Kissinger to the Secretaries of State and Defense on September 21. Kissinger noted that the President had decided the NATO Allies should be asked to commit a minimum of $2 billion during the next 5 years, in addition to the commitments already planned under the European Defense Improvement Program (EDIP), to correct deficiencies in NATO's immediate combat capability. (National Archives, Nixon Presidential Materials, NSC Files, Agency Files, Box 289, Treasury Volume II 1971)

79.   Memorandum From the President's Assistant for International Economic Affairs (Peterson) to the Members of the Council on International Economic Policy[1]

Washington, September 28, 1971.

MEMORANDUM FOR

The Secretary of State
The Secretary of Treasury
The Secretary of Defense
The Secretary of Agriculture
The Secretary of Commerce
The Secretary of Labor
The Ambassador-at-Large David M. Kennedy
The Director, Office of Management & Budget
The Chairman, Council of Economic Advisers
The Special Representative for Trade Negotiations
The Assistant to the President for Domestic Affairs
The Assistant to the President for National Security Affairs

SUBJECT

Council Work Program

The President has directed the implementation of the detailed work program for the Council on International Economic Policy, as reviewed at the September 7, 1971, CIEP meeting.[2]

---

[1] Source: National Archives, Nixon Presidential Materials, NSC Files, Agency Files, Box 218, CIEP. Secret. Attached to an October 5 memorandum from Hormats to Kissinger summarizing the memorandum.

[2] Members of the CIEP were invited to the September 7 meeting under cover of an August 30 memorandum from Peterson informing them its purpose was to review the current status of the CIEP's work program and to discuss priorities for the future. (Ibid.) The President chaired the meeting from 8:33 to 10:35 a.m. on September 7. (Ibid., White House Central Files, President's Daily Diary) Attendees included Rogers, Samuels, Connally, Volcker, Laird, Hardin, Stans, Hodgson, Kennedy, Shultz, McCracken, Gilbert, Ehrlichman, Haig for Kissinger, Peterson, Allen, Hinton, Webster, and Hormats. See also Document 174.

Within the next few days, we will be sending you a CIEP Study Memorandum with terms of reference of each project.

Timing of Legislative Proposals

Until significant progress is made on exchange rate realignment and negotiations related to the removal of the surtax, it may not be appropriate to submit important foreign economic and trade legislation. Presently, there is great uncertainty as to how long these negotiations will take. We are to work on the assumption that we should have in the President's hand a comprehensive outline of positive legislative recommendations by year end. Also, we should have defensive or contingency legislative plans in case the Labor Union's programs make major progress in Congress. Another consideration in this timing is the State of the Union Message. We are to assume further that the question of America's position in the world economy will continue to be sufficiently important to warrant emphasis in that message. For these reasons, we are directed to adhere to the schedules as outlined in the work projects.

Work Program—Major Elements

1. Planning a series of major *bilateral* negotiating initiatives—Japan (already completed), Canada, and EC—as well as multilateral initiatives at the OECD, GATT, and UNCTAD.

2. Defining specific policies and programs on *foreign investment* policy (particularly technology transfer, expropriation, multinational corporations and stimulating foreign investment in the U.S.).

3. Major programs on *adjustment assistance* for impacted industries.

4. Intensified *export promotion* program (incentives, financing, East-West trade, trading companies, antitrust, etc.).

5. Trade legislation *contingency* plan (labor unions are pushing ahead vigorously).

6. U.S. *competitiveness, growth and productivity* in the 70s. (Attached are copies of the charts used during our Council meeting to refresh your memories on the specifics.)[3] It turns out these programs are essentially domestic in nature since, without a strong domestic economy, it will be very difficult to have a strong, outward-looking foreign economic policy. This also emphasizes the importance of emphasizing concern with *job* effects of our programs, since concern over loss of jobs due to imports and foreign investments is obviously an increasingly important issue. On most of these points, the Council's role will be to define and

---

[3] Several lists of items related to this topic are attached (none printed) but no charts were found.

stimulate rather than to implement. Thus, we have and will continue to work very closely with the Domestic Council on most of these projects.

   a. Enhancing *U.S. industrial technological position.* (This is nearly ready for Presidential review.)
   b. *Antitrust*—(John Ehrlichman has work well along on this, though we have inputs to make on the international competitiveness aspects).
   c. *Long-term energy and raw material position,* including technological development of raw material substitutes.
   d. *One hundred million jobs by the end of the next ten years*—(U.S. manpower and educational policies).
   e. *Projecting the future development of U.S. economy in this decade—including the kind of industrial manufacturing and employment base the U.S. is likely to have (in basic sectors—steel, automobiles, electronics, etc.), the U.S. wants to have, and what price we are willing to pay for it.*

Other Programs

   7. These include such subjects as the development of improved government information systems on international economic performance, and improved organizational structure.

Outside Consultants

   8. Because of the importance and complexity of these subjects, and the unique value of outside experience and inputs on most of them, the President has asked that a special effort be made to attract the best outside talent from business and universities to work on the various projects. We request that, prior to naming any specific consultant, a list of proposed consultants be sent to my office.

   There is of course opportunity provided for the working groups to suggest additional terms of reference for each project, as well as to suggest specific priorities for the projects.

   I would appreciate your assigning your best people to this effort and emphasizing the importance of meeting these deadlines. With the President's initiatives of August 15, we may well be in a unique position to put forward a positive foreign economic legislative program, something that seemed very unlikely even a few months ago.

Peter G. Peterson

80.   Editorial Note

On October 18, 1971, Peter G. Peterson sent CIEP Study Memorandum 14 to the Secretaries of State, Treasury, Commerce, and Labor; the Attorney General; the President's Assistant for National Security Affairs; the CEA Chairman; the OMB Director; the President's Assistant for Domestic Affairs; and the Federal Reserve Chairman informing them the President had requested a comprehensive study of the issues involved in inward and outward international direct investment, and recommendations for U.S. policy. Peterson noted that Secretary Connally had made Wilson Schmidt available to chair a special, interagency task force to work on the issue. (Department of State, S/S Files: Lot 82 D 126, Box, 5195, CIEP Study Memoranda)

The Task Force's first order of business was to "identify those issues or questions which require further study or more sharply focused responses." Peterson suggested four major topics: A. Trade and Investment in the U.S. Balance of Payments; B. Multinational Corporations; C. Investment Issues in Foreign Relations; and D. Foreign Investment and the U.S. Economy. The Chairman was to issue biweekly progress reports and the final Task Force report was due on December 15, 1971.

Foreign direct investment had a central role in the Nixon administration's foreign assistance/economic development policy and an Expropriation Policy Statement was issued in January 1972, but no evidence of comprehensive work on foreign direct investment issues as envisaged in CIEPSM 14 was found. For documentation, see *Foreign Relations, 1969–1976*, volume IV.

81.   Telegram From the Mission to the OECD to the Department
        of State[1]

Paris, October 20, 1971, 1617Z.

17682. Subject: WP-3 Meeting October 18–19.

1. WP-3 discussion of required balance of payments adjustments was recognized by all as prelude to exchange rate negotiations. Thus members protected their positions with zeal which resulted in wide discrepancies and inconsistencies in estimates of total adjustment required and in allocation of shares to individual countries.

2. Need for $13 billion turn-around in U.S. position[2] (and corresponding adjustment by other OECD countries) was disputed by others on variety of grounds:

A. That U.S. projection of $4 billion C/A cyclically adjusted deficit in 1972 was too high; did not appropriately judge 1971 situation; was based on extrapolation of existing trends without sufficient account of self-correcting factors,

B. That might not be necessary to assume total OECD surplus limited at $11 billion,

C. That other OECD countries would not willingly accept situation whereby U.S. would have C/A surplus of $9 billion out of total OECD surplus of $11 billion,

D. That U.S. surplus of $9 billion was excessive in terms of GNP,

E. That policies needed to be considered to reduce net U.S. long-term capital outflow to contribute to solution,

F. That in calmer international situation, and appropriate U.S. monetary policy, portion of turnaround would be covered by return flows of funds, and by normal demand for dollars by dollar area countries and others,

G. That while small countries needed surpluses to protect currency, situation was different for large country with long-term deficit whose currency not presently convertible,

H. That SDR allocations might cover part of gap,

I. That account not taken of likely change in competitiveness resulting from improving relative price-wage performance of U.S.

3. These points were answered by U.S. and to some extent by Chairman and others.[3] U.S. pointed out reasons why $13 billion turn-

---

[1] Source: Washington National Records Center, Department of the Treasury, Office of International Monetary Affairs: FRC 56 77 68, Briefing Books, 1970–1975, EPC Meeting 11/18–19/71. Limited Official Use. Repeated to Ankara, Athens, Bern, Bonn, Brussels, Copenhagen, Dublin, The Hague, Helsinki, Lisbon, London, Luxembourg, Madrid, Oslo, Ottawa, Reykjavik, Stockholm, Tokyo, and USEC.

[2] See Documents 76 and 78.

[3] Under Secretary Volcker was head of the U.S. Delegation. Emminger was the WP-3 Chairman. Emminger's November 10 report on the October 18–19 WP-3 meeting is in the Washington National Records Center, Department of the Treasury, Office of International Monetary Affairs: FRC 56 77 68, Briefing Books, 1970–1975, EPC Meeting 11/18–19/1971.

around was conservative estimate; noted IMF estimate of starting point close to U.S. estimate of $4 billion deficit for 1972; that aim of $9 billion C/A surplus was for transitional period and not forever; that proposed U.S. share of total OECD C/A surplus was no higher than in the mid-60's; that return flows of funds and increased demand for dollars could not cover adjustment gap since there would be no such flow in absence of convincing elimination of U.S. deficit and in any event would be needed for financing of deficit in interval before impact of rate adjustment was fully felt; that our estimates took full account of expected strengthening of U.S. competitiveness; that no reason to assume every WP-3 member needed the same size surplus relative to GNP; that we looked toward situation of market equilibrium which required less rather than more reliance on capital restrictions. In response to suggestions by some delegates that "interim financing" might be available to ease U.S. transition during adjustment period, U.S. responded that we wanted to cover deficit by reversal of trade position rather than interim financing; i.e., "trade not aid."

4. On discussion of other countries "aims" and allocation of "required adjustment":

A. Germany accepted Secretariat allocation (which called for $1-1/4 billion adjustment by Germany) conditioned on acceptance of Secretariat figures by all,
B. Japan estimated adjustment need in range of zero to $1-1/2 billion (compared with Secretariat estimate of $3-1/4 billion),
C. Canada estimated adjustment need of zero (compared with Secretariat $1/2 billion),
D. Switzerland estimated adjustment need of $1/2 billion, which it said was covered by recent revaluation,
E. Italy estimated adjustment need of zero (compared with Secretariat $3/4 billion) and IMF zero, conditional on acceptance of OECD figures by all others. Otherwise Italians wanted improvement in their position of $.3 billion,
F. Netherlands agreed with Secretariat estimate of zero adjustment need,
G. France and U.K. estimated adjustment need in opposite direction, i.e., they wanted to increase their C/A surpluses (by about $1 billion together, according to Secretariat) whereas Secretariat called for $3/4 billion reduction in surplus for France and zero for U.K.,
H. Belgians appeared to acknowledge no need for adjustment (compared with Secretariat estimate $.6 billion) although statement not entirely clear.

6. In sum, others in total estimated adjustment need of only $3-1/4 billion before reducing that amount by $1 billion to cover France and U.K. estimates. (Secretariat estimated adjustment of $1/2 billion by small OECD countries not represented.) This meant discrepancy of almost $11 billion from U.S. estimate of $13 billion. Total estimates sur-

plus of all OECD countries cyclically adjusted 1972 added to $5-1/2 billion total of targets added to $16-1/2 billion.

7. Revelation of such extreme differences made it clear to all that it was pointless to try to reach agreement on a set of numbers.

8. U.S. pointed out very hard to rationalize discussions with facts in real world; cited articles in papers about large Japanese and Canadian trade surpluses; noted countries apparently trying to use C/A surplus to stimulate domestic growth and expecting U.S. to absorb the unemployment consequences; said no question of dollar gold price arising since number of other OECD countries apparently wanted to devalue their currencies, and apparently U.S. could best help in their view by running deficit.

9. Several delegates (Sweden, Canada, U.K., etc.) and Chairman said results not surprising in view of fact that delegates were deputies, not ministers, and purpose was not to negotiate but to clarify issues. Could not expect agreement on figures at time exchange rate negotiations starting, and meeting had served useful purpose in better understanding of issues and each country's position.

10. Secretariat distributed projections of growth rates for major countries in 1st half 1971 which indicated adjustment could begin in context expanding economies. Conclusions, while not formally accepted, were warmly welcomed and given special emphasis by Emminger in subsequent press conference.

11. Secretariat pressed for experts meeting for further examination of estimates. Although U.S. indicated readiness have multilateral or bilateral review, others showed amusing reluctance to submit to technical examination of their calculations and proposal was dropped.

Greenwald

82.   Telegram From the Embassy in Japan to the Department of
        State[1]

Tokyo, October 23, 1971, 0615Z.

10649. Sub: Japanese reactions on defense burden-sharing. Ref:
Tokyo A-377, May 24, 1971.[2]

Begin Summary: Embassy believes it would be useful to summarize
present state of Japanese views on this subject. Japanese have been casting about for ways to cope with apparent pending US demands on
defense burden-sharing. They see issues as falling into different categories. All Japanese seem to favor idea of increasing economic aid to
Southeast Asia, and GOJ has already started to do this. GOJ expects
double its concessional aid in CY 71 to $700 million. It intends to
increase total financial flows abroad to one percent of GNP by 1975
(about $4 billion). Possible proposal that Japan assume a greater share
than present of US garrison costs in Japan, in ways amounting to
defense support arrangement, has met with categorical opposition.
Question of increasing arms purchases from US is being debated with
increasing intensity. GOJ favors idea, mainly as a means to cut cost of
expensive new weapons programs, and despite probable 8 to 13 percent
cut in fourth defense buildup plan, probably will purchase $800 million
to $1 billion worth of US equipment, or roughly double purchases
under third DBP. *End Summary.*

1. Defense burden-sharing has become one of major concerns of the
Japanese in recent weeks. Japanese are not clear as to what this may
entail or its ultimate cost. They feel they must respond positively in
some manner to placate the US and win concessions on currency and
trade issues, but do so in light their plans to prune already modest
defense budget proposals because of anticipated revenue shortfalls.

2. In GOJ and public mind, defense burden-sharing consists of: (A)
increased economic aid to Southeast Asia to help compensate for US aid
reductions; (B) assumption of a greater share of costs for stationing US
forces in Japan; and (C) increased purchases of US military equipment.
There has been little opposition to point (A). Big business interests favor
increased economic aid as the means for meeting US defense burden-
sharing demands. GOJ not only expects to double concessional assistance this year to $700 million, its objective is to increase its economic

---

[1] Source: Department of State, S/S Files: Lot 73 D 153, Box 124, Morning Summaries,
August 25–December 31, 1971. Limited Official Use. Repeated to the Secretary of Defense,
COMUSJAPAN, HICOMRY, and CINCPAC.
[2] Not printed.

assistance to same level as US (.32 percent GNP CY 70) and other industrial countries relative to GNP as soon as possible. Further, GOJ has declared it intends increase its financial flows to developing countries to one percent of GNP by 1975 (estimated at about $4 billion). Governmental economic assistance would then amount to about $1.3 billion of this sum, and target is 50 percent ODA (concessional) GOJ assistance.

3. On increasing Japan's share of US forces costs:

A. Japanese have publicly and privately expressed categorical opposition to anything which seems reinstitution of defense support arrangements existing under 1952 Treaty. (Department will recall administrative agreement at that time provided GOJ would pay $155 million per year for purpose of procurement by US of transportation and other requisite services in Japan; that GOJ insisted prior to 1960 Security Treaty on omitting such provisions anticipatory to 1960 Treaty.) According to press reports, US has suggested that Japan assume balance-of-payments costs for maintaining troops in Japan amounting to about $650 million per annum. GOJ leaders, including Foreign Minister Fukuda and JDA Director General Nishimura, have stated that no formal request on this matter has been received from the US, but that in any event it would be unacceptable.

B. Other Japanese officials argue that much of US costs are being incurred more for strategic defense of the US than for the defense of Japan, or that a large portion of the $650 million is being spent not on defense but on US forces purchase of goods and services for private personal consumption. (*Comment:* In fact, in CY 1970, 62.5 percent of this sum was from non-appropriated fund sources, so Japanese analysis is correct.) In any case, they state that national sentiment would not permit assumption of such additional cost for US troops, equal to more than one-third annual JDA defense budget. After reversion of Okinawa, they fear this amount might have to be doubled to take care of US forces costs there.

C. Finally, FonOff officials state that SOFA Article 24 would have to be amended to enable GOJ to pay for costs of stationing US troops beyond what is done presently. They are extremely reluctant to make any changes in SOFA for fear of provoking opposition moves against SOFA and Security Treaty. In this connection, it should be noted it is estimated GOJ on annual basis in Japan contributes $110.247 million from budget (JFY 71 estimate) for land rentals on facilities provided US forces, land acquisition expenses, management of facilities, relocation expenses, subsidies to municipalities to compensate for revenue loss or other expenses incidental to presence of US forces, payment of highway tolls, unreimbursed labor administration costs and special contributions to US forces Japanese employees. (This does not take account of similar substantial contributions expected for Okinawa, post-reversion, on which we do not yet have budgetary estimates. It should also be noted US expects to save $30 million per year for local defense responsibilities, which will be assumed by JSDF, and $10 million per year on land rentals, as result of reversion.)

4. Question of increasing arms purchases from US is being debated with increasing intensity between certain GOJ sectors and big business interests. Fukuda and Mizuta have argued in favor of this burden-sharing approach, while warning against GOJ adoption of any clear-cut weapons purchase plan similar to US-West German offset agreement. Both Finance Ministry and Secretariat of National Defense Council have reportedly expressed strong support for purchase of major new weapons systems (such as F5B trainer aircraft in place of Japanese XT-2) mainly in interest of cutting costs. Strong opposition views have come from MITI and industrial organizations such as Keizai Doyukai (Committee for Economic Development) and Keidanren (Federation of Economic Organizations). They claim that increased purchases from abroad would represent a reversal of former JDA Director General Nakasone's "autonomous" defense policy, which has as one of its long-term objectives development of indigenous defense industry capable of meeting all of JSDF's equipment requirements. Business interests also argue that foreign weapons purchases would detract from domestic development of technological know-how and benefits to the economy, and subject JSDF to whims of arms export nations.

5. JDA is now revising 4th defense buildup plan (covering JFY 1972–76) based on views of Finance Ministry and NDC Secretariat. While definitive information is presently unavailable, it appears likely that cost of this five-year plan may be reduced from 5.2 trillion yen ($16 billion at 330:1 current exchange rate), excluding 0.6 trillion yen for pay increases, to about 4.5 to 4.8 trillion yen ($13.6 to $14.6 billion). Defense spending will, therefore, probably range 8 to 13 percent below originally planned level. Heaviest cuts will reportedly be made in supply, service support, and procurement of new equipment. Embassy (MDAO) believes reduction in last category will probably be in neighborhood of 20 to 25 percent.

6. Latest indication is that, partly as result of Finance Ministry pressure, JDA would make little change in revised 4th DBP as regards military purchases from US, despite overall budget reduction indicated above. On 11 October, JDA Director General Nishimura stated that his agency was currently studying possibility of buying $800 million and, "depending on circumstances," up to $1 billion worth of equipment from US under that plan. Relative to purchases from the US under the current 3rd DBP (estimated at $500 million by Nishimura), his latest estimates represent increases of 60 to 100 percent at 360:1 exchange rate, or increases of 45 to 85 percent at 330:1 exchange rate. Thus, even at a

time of budgetary stress, there will still be proportionately large purchases of US military equipment and technology out of total sums available for procuring new equipment.

7. Meanwhile, partly as a sop to business interests, Nishimura has
repeatedly emphasized that JDA would make no basic change in its
"autonomous" defense policy. On 11 October, he said that despite
reduction of total spending under 4th DBP, he hoped to increase R and
D funds above originally planned levels. He said primary effort would
be placed on development of aircraft and missiles.

8. Foregoing represents latest state of play in Japan on defense burden-sharing issue. Underlying GOJ reaction is prevailing mood against
increased government spending in view of anticipated revenue short-
falls. We will have a clearer picture of Japanese response when JFY 72
budget, and possible 4th DBP, are put in final form late this year.

Meyer

---

83.   **Memorandum From Secretary of State Rogers to President
        Nixon**[1]

Washington, December 2, 1971.

SUBJECT

Your High Level Meetings: The Results We Seek

Your meetings with Brandt, Caetano, Heath, Pompidou, Sato and
Trudeau[2] underscore your commitment to full consultation with our Allies
prior to your discussions in Peking and Moscow.[3] These meetings, howev-

---

[1] Source: National Archives, Nixon Presidential Materials, NSC Files, Agency Files,
Box 285, State Volume 13. Secret.

[2] President Nixon met with Prime Minister Trudeau in Washington December 6 (see
Document 85), President Pompidou in the Azores December 13–14 (see Document 219),
Chancellor Brandt in Key Biscayne December 29, and Prime Minister Sato in San
Clemente January 6–7, 1972 (see Document 87). Portuguese Prime Minister Caetano was
the official host for Presidents Nixon and Pompidou in the Azores and gave a dinner in
their honor on January 13. President Nixon met with Caetano for their Summit upon his
arrival in the Azores during the evening of January 12, a largely courtesy/protocol event.
Documentation on the Caetano Summit is in the National Archives, Nixon Presidential
Materials, NSC Files, President's Trip Files, Box 473, PM Caetano 1971.

[3] President Nixon traveled to the People's Republic of China February 17–28, 1972,
and to the Soviet Union May 22–29, 1972.

er, have a significance for the Free World beyond moving further from confrontation to an era of negotiation; they should also establish the basis for resolution of current international economic and monetary issues.

Therefore, our objectives are:

First, seek to assure that your forthcoming summit meetings with the Communist world are undertaken against the background of Free World unity and understanding;

Second, reassure our Allies, both in the Atlantic and the Pacific, that you go to Peking and Moscow with no intention of "dealing over their heads" on any matters where their security or other vital interests might be affected;

Third, stress that, before these summit meetings with Communist leaders, you want to see the pressing trade and financial differences between Free World countries well on the way to resolution; and

Finally, indicate that these consultations are part of a continuing process of discussion with our Allies.

The agenda for the scheduled talks covers your visits to Peking and Moscow, the current international economic and monetary situation, other international issues such as the Middle East and South Asia, and bilateral issues.

Your own discussions should concentrate on your forthcoming visits to the Communist world *and* on resolving the current economic and monetary issues that tend to divide the Free World today. The cabinet-level talks that will be held in tandem can cover in addition other major international issues as well as bilateral problems.

Our Allies should be left with the clear impression that we do not intend to negotiate in Moscow on security issues that affect their interests. They should be disabused of the idea that we intend to negotiate mutual and balanced force reductions or an arrangement for a CES with the Soviets bilaterally. You should alert them to the possibility that some agreements may be reached in connection with the Moscow visit e.g., on SALT and bilateral trade issues.

I believe you should particularly stress that any ally, in going to Moscow, will be most successful if he is backed by the strength of the Alliance. To this end, you should stress your firm intent to maintain U.S. forces in Europe and the need for our Allies to pursue improvements in their conventional force capabilities.

Regarding Peking, you should emphasize that your purpose is the initiation of a dialogue to remove the misunderstanding that has accumulated over the decades. Therefore, no dramatic results or major agreements are foreseen; there is no intention to reach agreements on third party problems or change existing commitments. Sato in particular should be assured that Japan's security and other interests will under no circumstances be undermined.

In addition, you should stress that you want to learn about each Allied leader's views and experiences in dealings with the leaders in Peking and Moscow, stressing that shared knowledge is important to Allied unity. You should also assure our Allies that they will be informed of the results of these visits.

The agenda item on international economic and monetary issues reflects the fact that your August 15 measures have resulted in a critical change of attitude on the part of our major Allies and trading partners.[4] It is now recognized that the imbalance in the international economic system has to be corrected and that fundamental measures are necessary to achieve this. The outcome of recent sessions of the Group of Ten in Rome appears to indicate that we now have an opportunity to reach a near-term settlement involving a major realignment of the principal currencies and some concessions in the trade field. We should concentrate our attention on realignment initially because gains in that area will produce the greatest results both in terms of our international balance of payments and in the strength of the American economy.

The shock treatment used to achieve this major breakthrough, however, has left bruised feelings and concerns about the future direction of American economic policy. The succession of consultations you will have can lead to a strengthening of allied relationships and create a firm basis for going on with the next stage in talks looking toward the creation of new monetary arrangements and negotiations for expansion of trade. Your talks can serve the purpose of beginning this next stage with the firm assurances that the United States, under your leadership, has no intention of retreating into an isolationist or protectionist policy.

Specifically, you should stress the need to:

—move quickly to a new, credible structure of exchange rates which would help bring about a substantial improvement in our balance of payments. We would remove the surcharge and the buy-American feature of the proposed job development tax credit.

—resolve certain trade issues immediately and work intensively on others in the next few months bilaterally and through GATT.

—work together in the Group of Ten and the IMF on a more fundamental reform of the international monetary system, and in the OECD high-level group on preparations for a major—and reciprocal—effort to bring down barriers to industrial and agricultural trade.

Needless to say, movement toward the favorable settlement of these economic issues will strengthen ties with Europe and Japan and strengthen your hand in talks in Peking and Moscow.

In terms of press results from these meetings, I believe we should strive to achieve:

---

[4] Reference is to the President's New Economic Policy; see Documents 168 ff.

a) understanding and support for your visits to Peking and Moscow as efforts to reduce tensions without impairing Free World security;

b) agreement that current economic and monetary issues can be resolved through efforts on the part of the leading allied powers at the political level;

c) recognition that we remain, as a superpower, a nation cognizant of our Allies' interests, prepared to take these into account, and to work with them for reasonable solutions.

William P. Rogers

---

84.   **Memorandum From Secretary of the Treasury Connally to President Nixon[1]**

Washington, December 6, 1971.

At the Rome meetings,[2] we continued to make the point that part of our needed balance of payments adjustment should be an improved arrangement for defense burden-sharing. This point was explicit in your August 15 speech. We took the position that this was a matter that had to be discussed in the NATO forum. Thus, if we fail to carry through with this position at the NATO ministerial meeting in Brussels this week, we will have passed up the obvious time and place. That will leave us in a weak position for pressing the issue later.

This means that we need to decide now whether the Administration is to rely solely on the European Defense Improvement Program, which gives us no financial help, or whether we should also seek some multilateral arrangement for sharing the foreign-exchange burden of defense. The extra effort we are asking our Allies to make with their own defense forces requires only an additional fraction of one percent of their Gross National Product. What we need from them as financial burden-sharing comes only from their excess dollar reserves. It would not require added manpower or use any of their real resources, although it might add to their internal budgets.

I believe we have a proposal we could put on the table along with the European Defense Improvement Program. It is to designate all

---

[1] Source: Washington National Records Center, Department of the Treasury, Records of Secretary Shultz: FRC 56 80 1, JBC Memoranda for the President–71. Secret.

[2] Reference is to the G-10 Ministerial meeting in Rome November 30–December 1; see Documents 200 and 201.

extra-territorial military bases in NATO Europe as "NATO bases." These consist mostly of American, British, and Canadian bases in Germany. The annual costs of about $1.2 billion of operating these bases—though not the pay and equipment of the forces manning them—would be placed in a NATO bases budget, to which NATO members would contribute negotiated shares. An appropriate offer by the United States as to its share of this new budget would be the same 30 percent now borne by the United States in the NATO infrastructure budget.

As a component of a larger settlement with the European nations, the United States could also press France to pay off over a reasonable period of, say, four years the NATO losses of approximately $700 million that resulted from premature termination of the agreement to station NATO forces in France. Four hundred million dollars of those losses were incurred by the United States.

This proposal for a NATO bases budget is reasonable. I believe that other countries would support the principle. There have been many indications from key Europeans, particularly from the German Government, that they are anxious to find some new and more stable basis for continuing the American presence in Europe. In my meetings with finance ministers, I have found philosophical agreement that there needs to be some arrangement of this kind. We can expect resistance when it comes to budgetary impact and negotiating a formula for shares, but there is recognition of the principle. The mood in the Nation and in the Congress makes it urgent that we obtain such an arrangement. The benefit would be political as well as financial.

The merits of the proposal aside, we should not give away this issue for nothing. Even if we fail to get financial burden-sharing, vigorous pressure for it may help us arrive at better economic arrangements in other fields.

Therefore, it would be most helpful if Secretary Rogers emphasizes burden-sharing at the NATO ministerial meetings this week. Indeed, if this issue is to be kept alive, we will need to make a proposal for a multilateral financial arrangement on the table at NATO. If you agree, the attached draft statement outlines our approach for the use of our delegation.[3]

John Connally[4]

---

[3] Not printed. The draft statement was for Secretary Rogers' use at the NATO Ministerial meeting December 9–10. According to the communiqué of the meeting, the European Defense Improvement Program (EDIP) was reaffirmed but a NATO bases proposal was not adopted. (*NATO Final Communiqués, 1949–1974* (Brussels: NATO Information Services), pp. 266–272)

[4] Printed from a copy that indicates Connally signed the original.

85.   Memorandum for the Record[1]

Washington, December 6, 1971, 4 p.m.

SUBJECT

U.S.-Canadian Ministerial Meeting

PARTICIPANTS

Canada
Edgar J. Benson, Minister of France
Jean Luc Pepin, Minister of Industry, Trade and Commerce
Sol Simon Riesman, Deputy Minister, Department of Finance
James F. Grandy, Deputy Minister, Industry, Trade and Commerce
Albert Edgar Ritchie, Under Secretary of State for International Affairs
Marcel Cadieux, Canadian Ambassador to the United States
Peter M. Towe, DCM, Canadian Embassy

United States
Secretary John B. Connally
Secretary Maurice Stans
Under Secretary Paul Volcker
Assistant Secretary of Treasury, John Petty
Assistant Secretary of Commerce, Harold Scott
Acting Assistant Secretary of State, Julius Katz
Deputy Assistant Secretary of State, George Springsteen
William Johnson, Canadian Country Director
Ambassador Adolph William Schmidt
Helmut Sonnenfeldt, NSC
Robert Hormats, NSC
Denis Clift, NSC

Minister Pepin indicated Canada's desire to keep trade discussions outside of the surcharge context and to discuss "trade irritants" of interest to both the U.S. and Canada. Trade irritants for the U.S. were the Canadian-American Automotive Agreement, tourist allowances for Canadian tourists returning to Canada, and the Defense Production Sharing Arrangement.

Canada was concerned with such matters as uranium, petrochemicals and U.S. anti-dumping regulations. Canada believes it must have a balanced trade package in which it also receives something from the U.S. and does not believe the U.S. has helped in developing this package. Mr. Petty discussed Canada's request of changes in U.S. trade programs and indicated what was being done on these matters.

---

[1] Source: National Archives, Nixon Presidential Materials, NSC Files, Subject Files, Box 356, Monetary Matters. Secret. The meeting was held in the Roosevelt Room. Prime Minister Trudeau also met with President Nixon the same day.

Secretary Connally indicated a need for Canada to help the U.S. eliminate its balance of payments deficit. Minister Benson insisted that Canada had a deficit on current account (trade and invisibles) with the U.S. Secretary Connally indicated that the reverse is true and that last year Canada had had a trade surplus with the U.S. of $1.7 billion. (These terms and our figures are illustrated below) Mr. Volcker pointed out that Canada continues to be a strong exporter of goods and a strong importer of capital. Minister Benson maintained that last year Canada's overall surplus on current account was less than one-half of what it was in 1970 and that capital inflows have fallen off steadily. Canada also pointed out that it has engaged in a clean float in which its dollar has floated upwards and that forces currently at play will decrease or eliminate Canada's surplus with the U.S.

U.S. Bilateral Balance of Payments with Canada
1970 (in U.S. $)

U.S. Exports	9,044
U.S. Imports	-10,720
Trade Balance	-1,676
Invisibles	1,080
(shipping, tourism, etc.)	
a) Current Account Balance	-596
U.S. Direct Investment in Canada	-915
U.S. Purchase of Canadian Securities	-475
Other	-19
Canadian Investment and Security Purchases in U.S.	+367
b) Capital Account Balance	-1,042
Basic Balance (a & b)	-1,638

Secretary Connally pointed out that we will have a deficit of $10–11 billion in 1972, and that we would expect some help from Canada in improving our position. He indicated that the Canadian dollar was undervalued. Minister Benson replied that it was not, and that Canada was allowing its dollar to float freely and would re-peg it when it arrives at a sustainable market rate. It had moved upward recently and was now nearly at par. Canada's pulp and paper industry, to cite one example, had been hurt by the exchange rate adjustments, and is now realizing no profits. He indicated that Canada had a deficit of $220 million on current account with U.S. last year. It had had a $2 billion overall current account deficit in 1965 and had steadily progressed to the point where it has a much smaller deficit.

Secretary Connally repeated that the U.S. had a $1.7 billion trade deficit with Canada and a current account *deficit* of $600 million. Canada stated that the U.S. had a current account surplus with Canada, but that its *basic balance* with Canada was indeed in deficit.

Canada strongly asserted its intention to let the market rate determine the value of its dollar and to re-peg when it is sure it has a sustainable rate. It hopes to do this as soon as possible. Canada pointed out that its currency is extremely vulnerable to market crises primarily because big American firms can move huge sums of money across the border almost instantly.

Secretary Connally wanted to know whether, because it was so intent upon floating, Canada would help him at the next Group of Ten meeting to get others to float as well. He said that U.S. would be happy to keep its dollar floating if others agreed to float. Canada indicated that its policy was to float because it would be difficult to re-peg while monetary conditions were uncertain. However, other countries may assess their interests differently. Secretary Connally indicated that Canada should be able to find a viable parity for its currency; and, that, because it has floated longer than anyone else, it should know at what rate the Canadian dollar could be sustained. Minister Benson indicated that Canada did not know, during this period of uncertainty, at what rate its dollar could be sustained and could not afford to re-peg at a rate which would necessitate large-scale Canadian intervention in the exchange market. It would float until it did have enough information to re-peg.

With regard to trade questions,[2] Minister Pepin indicated that Canada was prepared to remove the first two (the requirement that auto manufacturers in Canada produce in Canada approximately 75% of all products sold there, and that their companies maintain specific minimums of absolute values of their production in Canada) of the three "transitional safeguards" of the Canadian-American Automotive Agreement, but is still sticking on the third—no duty-free import of automobiles by individuals, (i.e. Americans are free to import cars from Canada, but Canadian individuals must still pay a 15% duty on cars imported from the U.S.). Minister Pepin indicated that a committee should be set up to look at this tariff, and examine measures to broaden the agreement. Secretary Connally indicated that "symmetry" would dictate imports of American cars into Canada be treated the same way as Canadian cars into the U.S.

---

[2] Sub-Cabinet level meetings on "trade irritants" had been held in Ottawa on November 4 and November 15. Reports on those discussions were sent in telegram 1816 from Ottawa, November 6, and telegram 1871 from Ottawa, November 17. (Department of State, S/S Files: Lot 73 D 153, Box 124, Morning Summaries August 25–December 31, 1971)

On tourist allowances, Canada indicated that it was willing to raise the exemption on duty from $25.00 to $50.00, and would be willing for the U.S. to drop its duty-free allowances from $100 to $50.00. With regard to granting special tariff exemption for Micheline to build a factory in Canada, Minister Pepin indicated that Canada would make no tariff change without first consulting with the U.S. Minister Pepin indicated a desire to develop a package on "irritants" and was willing to continue negotiations to this end. Pepin indicated, however, that it would be politically very difficult to drop the third "safeguard" in the Canadian Automotive Agreement at this time. In fact, he said, the Canadian Government was way out on a limb for having agreed to remove two of three.

Mr. Volcker indicated that the U.S. wanted a solution conducive to expanded trade. Canada had imposed certain trade restrictions when it was in deficit. He proposed that we negotiate to make these arrangements reciprocal, and that we take the necessary political steps to bring this about. Canada indicated, however, that it would have to get a GATT waiver to remove the 15% duty on cars imported by individual Canadians from the U.S.

Secretary Connally indicated that it would be important to reaching a solution to the monetary problem in the near future if Canada could move on these trade issues. He felt that we should try for reciprocity in our trade arrangements. Minister Pepin indicated that this might be possible. Secretary Connally again repeated the importance which this country attaches to resolving our balance of payments and trade problems and indicated that Canada would have to do its share.

The meeting concluded with the understanding that the bilateral committee being established to find solutions to trade irritants would submit its recommendations by December 17.[3]

---

[3] According to an April 12, 1972, memorandum from Assistant Secretary of Commerce Scott to Kissinger, Assistant Secretary-level consultations with the Canadians were held in Washington December 16–17. (National Archives, Nixon Presidential Materials, NSC Files, Country Files–Europe, Box 671, Canada Volume III 9/71–12/72) No record of recommendations was found.

86.   Telegram From Secretary of State Rogers to the Department of State[1]

Brussels, December 10, 1971, 1310Z.

5168. Secto 17. Subject: Offset Negotiations—Agreed Minute.

Following is text of US-FRG offset agreement for FY 1972–73 signed in Brussels December 10 by Deputy Under Secretary of State Nathaniel Samuels and Ministerial Director Dr. Axel Herbst.

Begin Text:

Minute

The Governments of the Federal Republic of Germany and the United States of America agree as follows:

1. Military Procurement

A) Between July 1, 1971 and June 30, 1973, the Government of the Federal Republic of Germany will make payments for procurement of US defense goods and services in the field of defense in the amount of DM 3950 million.

B) Part of such procurement in the amount of DM 1650 million shall be financed through utilization of funds now on deposit in the name of the Federal Republic of Germany with the United States Treasury in accounts entitled "Account No. 20X6409—Secretary of the Treasury, Department of Defense, Military Purchases by Federal Republic of Germany" and "Account No. 20X6415—Secretary of the Treasury, Special Transfer Account, Military Expenditures by the Federal Republic of Germany".

C) The balance of such procurement, which is DM 2300 million shall be financed by June 30, 1973, by the utilization of German funds not on deposit with the United States Treasury on June 30, 1971, which the Government of the Federal Republic of Germany will transfer directly to suppliers of defense goods and services in the United States or which it will deposit with the United States Treasury in Account No. 20X6409. Of this amount DM 81 million was paid before July 1, 1971.

D) All military procurement by the Federal Republic of Germany will be made in the light of German military requirements and budget capabilities, given the availability and economic advantage of procurement in the United States of America.

---

[1] Source: National Archives, RG 59, Central Files 1970–73, FN 12 GER W. Confidential. Repeated to Bonn.

2. Investments for Troop Facilities

A) Between July 1, 1971 and June 30, 1973 the Government of the Federal Republic of Germany will make available an amount of DM 600 million for services and deliveries for the modernization, construction and improvement of barracks, accommodations, housing and troop facilities of the forces of the United States of America stationed in the Federal Republic of Germany. Specific projects will be agreed between the two sides. The disbursement of the funds will be made in portions subject to the progress of the building projects, similarly to existing procedural arrangements. Amounts not utilized prior to 30 June 1973 shall remain available for measures as envisaged under this paragraph of this agreement.

B) Structures, improvements and other alterations including built-in equipment financed in this manner will be treated as property owned by the Federal Republic of Germany used by the U.S. forces within the framework of the NATO Status of Forces Agreement and the supplementary agreement thereto.

3. Bundesbank Credits

A) Arrangements will be concluded between the United States Treasury (in cooperation with the United States Federal Reserve Board) and the Deutsche Bundesbank concerning investment by the Deutsche Bundesbank during the period July 1, 1971–June 30, 1973, in special, 4-1/2 years, 2-1/2 percent, dollar denominated United States Government securities. The objective should be the investment by the Deutsche Bundesbank of DM 2 million during the above mentioned period.

B) The Federal Republic of Germany will pay to the United States of America prior to the date when interest falls due under paragraph 3A above an amount of DM 100 million in settlement of the United States interest obligation. Such sum may be paid out of funds on deposit in the name of Federal Republic of Germany with the United States Treasury in Account No. 20X6415.

4. Detailed Arrangements

Detailed arrangements implementing this agreement shall be made by the responsible agencies or ministries of the Governments of the United States of America and the Federal Republic of Germany.

For the Government of the Federal Republic of Germany

For the Government of the United States of America

Brussels

December 10, 1971. *End Text.*

Rogers

87.   **Editorial Note**

As plans went forward for Japanese Prime Minister Sato's meeting with President Nixon in January 1972, U. Alexis Johnson, Under Secretary of State for Political Affairs, met with Japanese Ambassador Ushida on December 20, 1971. In a letter to Kissinger the same day, Johnson recounted a few highlights of the meeting relevant to the upcoming Nixon–Sato meeting, including their discussion of the People's Republic of China and Taiwan, the Soviet Union, and Okinawa. Johnson then continued:

"On the question of a further cutback on the Okinawa bases, Sato and Fukuda have the impression, on the basis of Kishi's talk with the President and Connally's talk with Sato and Fukuda while in Tokyo, that if they delivered on textiles, monetary reform and trade they could expect some movement on this issue. With their now having delivered on textiles and monetary reform, and what they expect to deliver on trade prior to San Clemente, they will hope for something on the base issue. Fukuda is now concentrating on golf courses and private American beaches and would very much hope to have some word on this prior to San Clemente." (National Archives, Nixon Presidential Materials, NSC Files, Agency Files, Box 285, State Volume 13)

President Nixon had met with former Prime Minister Nobusuke Kishi on October 22 from 3:15 to 4:47 p.m. (Ibid., White House Central Files, President's Daily Diary). No record of the meeting has been found. The reference to Connally's talks in Tokyo is to his visit November 11–12; see Document 193. Regarding textiles, an agreement was reached by President Nixon's October 15 target date; see footnote 2, Document 77. Documentation on the textile agreement is scheduled for publication in *Foreign Relations, 1969–1976*, volume IV.

Johnson's December 20 letter continued:

"Sato very much hopes to avoid trade issues at San Clemente. Tokyo would probably have been willing to give a little more on this if it had been necessary to achieve agreement at this weekend's Washington Group Ten meeting. However, as Japan gave more on the monetary side than it had expected to give, MITI and agriculture were able to prevent further Japanese trade concessions. Both Mizuta (Minister of Finance) and Ushiba are convinced that even though the monetary issue was settled, Japan has a 'moral obligation' to do more on trade."

In preparation for the President's meeting with Sato, Kissinger met with Ambassador Ushiba in Washington on December 22, prior to the latter's traveling to Tokyo. Kissinger told Ushiba that the short-term trade issues should be settled before the President and Prime Minister met. When Ushiba expressed concern, Kissinger informed him that "the

President did not like to discuss economic matters, and in addition, injecting trade into the discussions at San Clemente would make it appear to an undesirable extent that Japan had offered something on trade and had received something in return, e.g., concessions regarding Okinawa." Kissinger said the "Japanese do not need to offer too much; even some fairly limited moves would do." Ushiba said he would take it up with the Prime Minister. (Memorandum of conversation, December 22; National Archives, Nixon Presidential Materials, NSC Files, VIP Visits, Box 925, Japan–Sato San Clemente January 1972)

Following his return to Washington, Ambassador Ushiba met with Special Trade Representative Eberle. In a January 3, 1972, memorandum to Kissinger, Hormats reported that MITI Minister Tanaka planned to discuss trade issues with U.S. representatives in San Clemente with the hope of concluding an agreement that would not be made public until after the meeting to avoid any connection with the Okinawa agreement. The Japanese then wanted no additional trade bilaterals for at least a year to keep friction out of the relationship and wanted further trade discussions to be in a multilateral context. (Ibid.)

In his January 4 briefing memorandum for the President on the upcoming meeting with Prime Minister Sato, Kissinger noted that "the major frictions that have afflicted our relations with Japan in the past year appear to have bottomed out. Textiles are solved, the monetary system is realigned, and arrangements on Japanese trade liberalization should be completed before or during the San Clemente talks." Regarding the latter, Kissinger noted: "you will not need to touch it except in general terms." (Ibid.)

Japanese Prime Minister Sato met with President Nixon January 6–7, 1972, in San Clemente. The memoranda of the President's conversations with the Prime Minister indicate that aside from brief interventions on defense burdensharing and Japan's intention to increase its foreign economic assistance, the two heads of government did not discuss bilateral economic issues.

In a discussion with Sato of present and future high-level talks, the President and Kissinger noted that some European issues were different from U.S. issues with Japan, but the President said, "we must look at the world as a whole . . . in viewing the Free World, the great economic powers, the United States, Japan, Germany, Britain, France and possibly Canada, must consult closely if we are to build a stable and productive Free World economy with trade and monetary stability . . . the development of a 5-power consultative process (adding Italy, perhaps, and Canada) would not only serve the needs of the Free World, but would also contribute to the development of cohesion in policy for handling all the difficult political and security problems that arise." Prime Minister Sato supported the concept of a five-power conference as suggested by the President and, perhaps with the addition of Canada and Italy, saw no need to involve other countries. The records of the discussions are in memoranda for the President's file, January 6 and 7; National Archives, Nixon Presidential Materials, NSC Files, VIP Visits, Box 925, Japan–Sato San Clemente January 1972.

During more than 5 hours of conversations on January 6 and 7 with MITI Minister Tanaka and Finance Minister Mizuta, Secretaries Connally and Stans and Ambassador Eberle made it clear that Tanaka expected the trade negotiations to be completed by Eberle and Ushiba in Washington on January 12. Tanaka indicated he was prepared to discuss other issues, but not agriculture, which Ushiba would have to address on January 12. Pressed by Connally, Tanaka put a proposal on the table that Connally and Stans found disappointing. Connally noted that negotiations with the Canadians were going well and the United States anticipated significant concessions from the EC. "We were not asking more from Japan than we were looking for from others." (Memoranda of conversation, January 6 and 7; Washington National Records Center, Department of the Treasury, Files of Under Secretary Volcker: FRC 56 79 15, San Clemente Talks with Tanaka–1/72)

88.   Editorial Note

On January 19, 1972, George Willis sent Under Secretary Volcker a paper entitled "Alternative Possibilities for Coordinating Balance of Payments Improvement," setting forth conclusions reached at a January 17 meeting in Volcker's office. The paper noted that several departments and agencies had responsibilities in the balance-of-payments area, and concluded they could best be coordinated by a Cabinet-level committee chaired by the Treasury Department. In Willis' first scenario, a Cabinet Committee on the Balance of Payments would replace the Council on International Economic Policy. Other alternatives were also put forward. (Washington National Records Center, Department of the Treasury, Files of Under Secretary Volcker: FRC 56 79 15, BOP–General)

On January 20 former NSC Staff member C. Fred Bergsten, in his capacity as Visiting Fellow of the Council on Foreign Relations and Guest Scholar at the Brookings Institution, wrote Henry Kissinger to express his concern that if Peter Peterson left the White House, the

Treasury Department, under Connally, would seek to monopolize the international economic policy decisionmaking process, making it more difficult for Kissinger to "find handles." (National Archives, Nixon Presidential Materials, NSC Files, Subject Files, Box 309, Brookings Institution) On January 27 President Nixon announced Commerce Secretary Stans' resignation and his intent to nominate Peterson as Secretary of Commerce. (*Public Papers of the Presidents of the United States: Richard M. Nixon, 1972*, pages 107–109) Peter Flanigan was named to replace Peterson in the White House.

On March 31 Michael Bradfield sent Under Secretary Volcker a draft memorandum to the President that set forth Secretary Connally's proposal that the President add to Connally's responsibilities for monetary and tax matters responsibility for overall trade policy as well. The reasoning was that monetary, trade, and tax matters were closely integrated, but international consideration of these issues was fragmented into separate jurisdictional compartments. Connally's proposal was in lieu of legislation pending in Congress to give a broad statutory mandate to the CIEP. (Washington National Records Center, Department of the Treasury, Files of Under Secretary Volcker: FRC 56 79 15, PAV International Monetary Reform 1972) No record has been found that the proposal was forwarded to the President.

89.   Memorandum From the Executive Secretary of the
        Department of State (Eliot) to the President's Assistant for
        International Economic Affairs (Flanigan)[1]

Washington, April 12, 1972.

SUBJECT

Canada

I have seen Paul Volcker's comments of March 29 on the CIEP study on Canada[2] and have the following observations:

1. The difference between Treasury and the agencies that prepared the CIEP study are not necessarily irreconcilable. Thus:

—Treasury's balance of payments forecast is more gloomy than that in the CIEP study. Surely this is an area where agreement should be possible.

—Treasury opposes the establishment of a sub-Cabinet standing group.[3] But Treasury's opposition is based at least in part on a misunderstanding. The proposed standing group is not intended to displace the balance of payments subcommittee (which has not met for almost two years) nor to deal with, or delay in any way the negotiation of, the short-term trade issues between the U.S. and Canada. The proposed standing group would provide a framework for advance consultations on emerging and sensitive matters, such as investment and industrial policy, that cannot be looked at solely in a balance of payments context.

—Treasury believes direct unilateral action may be necessary to deter Canada. Until Treasury spells out the kinds of unilateral action it has in mind, some quantification of the gains to our balance of pay-

---

[1] Source: National Archives, RG 59, Central Files 1970–73, E 1 US. Confidential. Drafted by A. Reifman (E) on April 5 and cleared by Dallas L. Jones (S/PC) and George Springsteen (EUR). Attached is an April 7 memorandum from Assistant Secretary Willis C. Armstrong to Deputy Under Secretary Samuels noting that Volcker's memorandum on the CIEP study on Canada revealed a large difference between Treasury and other agencies on Canada policy.

[2] Neither Volcker's comments nor the CIEP study has been found. A March 20 6:15 p.m. note for Under Secretary Volcker indicates that the draft CIEP paper was scheduled to be discussed in a CIEP Operations Group meeting at 10:30 a.m. on March 21. (Washington National Records Center, Department of the Treasury, Files of Under Secretary Volcker: FRC 56 79 15, CIEP Meetings) No record of the meeting was found.

[3] This was a Department of State proposal that came out of the Department's internal Policy Analysis and Resource Allocation (PARA) exercise that sought to match resources with policy issues. In a January 31 Policy Analysis Decision Memorandum (PADM 10) from Under Secretary Irwin to Assistant Secretary for European Affairs Hillenbrand regarding the PARA review of Canada, the second policy conclusion was that "the Department should propose a sub-Cabinet U.S.-Canadian standing group," which would "deal with the wide variety of political-economic matters arising between the two countries and engage in a systematic dialogue on major long-term problems of common concern." (Department of State, S/S Files: Lot 82 D 126, Box 5195, PADM File Book PADM 1 Thru 32)

ments if the action is successful and some estimate of the risks and costs involved (we have more than $30 billion of investment in Canada), other agencies cannot be expected to subscribe. We do not object in principle to unilateral action—we took such action, for example, on Canadian oil. We do believe, however, that a cost-benefit assessment should be made in each case.

2. If you agree, I shall reconvene the interagency group and instruct it to:

—try to reach agreed forecasts and do the quantification noted above;
—amend the CIEP study where Treasury views can be accommodated; and
—identify areas where differences remain.

I would appreciate your support in assuring Treasury participation.[4]

R. T. Curran[5]

---

[4] In an October 2 letter to Flanigan, Under Secretary of State Irwin referred to the failure to make progress in resolving the disagreement with Treasury. Irwin noted that after discussing the matter with Secretary Shultz, he believed Treasury would cooperate in preparing for negotiations. (National Archives, RG 59, Central Files 1970–73, E 1 US) In his November 15 Evening Report to the President, Secretary Rogers indicated that Under Secretary Irwin and Canadian Under Secretary of State for External Affairs Ritchie had discussed a wide range of issues including bilateral trade problems and preparations for multilateral trade and monetary negotiations. Both reportedly agreed consultations should precede any unilateral actions. (Ibid., S/S Files: Lot 74 D 164, President's Evening Reading Items)

[5] Curran signed for Eliot above Eliot's typed signature.

---

90.   Editorial Note

On May 16, 1972, the White House announced that George Shultz would replace John Connally as Secretary of the Treasury. In his address to the OECD Ministerial meeting on May 25, Paul Volcker opened by expressing greetings and regrets from Secretary Connally "who, as you know, intended, until a certain event last week, to attend the Council meeting here today." See Department of State *Bulletin,* June 19, 1972, pages 827–836, for President Nixon's May 24 message to the OECD, Stein's May 24 statement, Volcker's May 25 statement, Irwin's May 26 statements, and the final Communiqué of the May 24–26 Ministerial meeting. A slightly different text of Volcker's statement was circulated to members of the Volcker Group under cover of a May 31 memorandum from Willis. (Washington National Records Center, Department of the Treasury, Volcker Group Masters: FRC 56 86 30, VG/Uncl. INFO/72–79)

On May 5 Hormats had sent Kissinger a memorandum apprising him of the status of the international economic policy negotiations and recommending that Kissinger discuss the matter with Connally and Flanigan. Hormats told Kissinger that "after much debate, a USG position has been reached on the forum for discussing international monetary and trade reform—the OECD." He continued: "A related matter, which may be the source of an intense interagency conflict centers on the U.S. posture with regard to future trade negotiations. *Treasury* regards the major goal of the U.S. in forthcoming trade negotiations as balance of payments improvement for the U.S., i.e., an attempt to bring about changes which do not provide *reciprocal benefits* to our trading partners. This was the same posture we took in attempting to obtain trade concessions following the August 15 announcement. It produced little real benefit for the U.S. and subjected us to strong foreign criticism for attempting to press our trading partners to undertake measures in the area of trade without our reciprocating." Hormats indicated that Eberle and Irwin thought Connally's position untenable. (National Archives, Nixon Presidential Materials, NSC Files, Agency Files, Box 273, OECD)

On May 25 Under Secretary Irwin sent a cable to Secretary of State Rogers, who was with the President in Moscow, noting that he would probably see sensationalized press reports about differences with other OECD members, particularly France. Irwin concluded, however, that there seemed to be consensus about a link between trade and monetary negotiations and a role for the OECD. (Telegram 10087 from USOECD to Moscow (repeated to the Department of State), May 25; ibid.)

91.   **Report by the President's Assistant for International Economic Affairs (Flanigan)**[1]

Washington, June 20, 1972.

REPORT OF VISIT TO WESTERN EUROPE
May 30–June 10, 1972

There were three main purposes for my trip to Western European capitals. They were: (1) to get to know some of the key European personalities with whom we will be dealing in the forthcoming trade and monetary negotiations; (2) to express my concern over the development of a spirit of economic isolationism or turning-inward on both sides of the Atlantic which, if left unchecked, could drift toward a new kind of dangerous political isolationism which neither side could afford, and (3) to report on the status of the commercial negotiations in Moscow,[2] while emphasizing that these talks in no way diminished the importance of the US-European ties.

In each of my discussions with European leaders (list attached),[3] I made the above points and asked for comments. The following report breaks down my talks into sets of issues which arose out of these talks.

I. Blocism: European vs. Atlantic

Concerns

As examples of the kind of policies which Americans see as moves by Europeans to opt for strictly regional, Europe-oriented solutions rather than to attempt to find more broadly-based, worldwide answers, I cited the Common Agriculture Policy and the developing web of special preferential deals which the EC was working out with non-member European states, the countries in the Mediterranean basin and, according to some recent indications, even with some East European states (e.g., Romania). I made it clear that we were not concerned with generalized preferences for LDC's, though we did object strongly to the system of reverse preferences which the EC worked out with many of them.

---

[1] Source: Washington National Records Center, Department of the Treasury, Files of Under Secretary Volcker: FRC 56 79 15, CIEP. Confidential. Attached to a June 23 transmittal memorandum from Flanigan to Rogers, Irwin, Shultz, Volcker, Peterson, Kissinger, Eberle, Shakespeare, the Ambassadors at the posts Flanigan visited, and CIEP Staff members.

[2] These negotiations were undertaken pursuant to the President's May 22–29 trip to the Soviet Union.

[3] Not printed.

In virtually every case, the response was that the EC was forced into these arrangements for either domestic socio-political reasons (the CAP) or for reasons related to economic or, mainly, foreign policy concerns. Typical of these was my talk with Raymond Barre, Commissioner for Financial and Monetary Policy at the EC Commission.

On agriculture, Barre's defense was that Europe was just now going through the agricultural revolution which the US had undergone during the 1930s. In about 10 years, this process would be complete. Meanwhile, the US and Europe were talking past each other on different levels of understanding about the nature of the problem. On preferences, he (as did others) emphasized the political importance to both Europe and the Atlantic Alliance of keeping the Mediterranean countries closely associated with the West. In Europe, the deals with the EFTA non-applicants were the inevitable consequence of British entry. The new EC could not erect new barriers to trade among the different categories of EFTA countries where trade had previously been free. He thought we should re-examine the problems this creates for outsiders on a reciprocal basis, adding that, even if reciprocity is not full, there needs to be some overall concept of "global reciprocity" to guide the next round of negotiations.

I responded to him, as to others, by noting that the solution to a political problem in one country inevitably creates a political problem for those at whose expense the solution has been imposed. This was especially true in agriculture. I said I'd rather try to find an intrinsically free trade solution rather than to continue to appeal to each side's comprehension of the other's political problem. I said we were not seeking to destroy the CAP, only asking that it be transformed into another kind of common policy which would be fairer politically and more rational economically.

On preferences, I argued in all capitals that, while we understood (even if we did not always accept) the rationale behind any particular deal, what concerned us was the total implication of these deals taken as a whole. Here is a clear case of the whole being greater than the sum of its parts. I stressed that Americans see them as a conscious effort by the EC to discriminate against us commercially to Europe's advantage while calling upon us to accept these disadvantages on the grounds that they serve our common political and security interests. I said that this kind of argument is no longer acceptable in the US, and that Europe should be aware of the fact that the days when we were able to accept almost any commercial costs for political reasons are over.

The response to this line of argument varied among the capitals. My talk with Giscard d'Estaing was frank and not discouraging. However, I cannot be optimistic about a forthcoming French response.

In Belgium, Davignon was positive, Fayat non-committal. The EC Commission was divided, but not encouraging. (Mansholt, for reasons of his own, was not only indifferent but actually hostile. See the attached report of my talk with him.)

The British clearly recognize the dangers involved if the trends I discussed above are allowed to go unhindered. They agree on the need to redress the imbalance between internal European preoccupations and external relations. However, it is also clear they feel a constraint as new members not to move out in front of the Six either too far or too fast.

Within the Six as such, Schiller was most encouraging. While he said Germany was determined to keep the EC outward-looking, even he cautioned against expecting too much. However, he assured me that Germany would work hard within the EC to prevent the rise of blocism in both trade and monetary relations.

The Italians all make sympathetic statements about the problem and were conscious of the need to avoid an Atlantic split. However, the internal situation of political (and Ministerial) uncertainty led me to conclude that, at the moment at least, the best we can expect from Italy is support for someone else's initiative, but certainly no disposition to share a leadership role for an outward-looking reorientation of EC foreign policy.

II. Trade and Monetary Links

My trip took place after the OECD Ministerial session, Paul Volcker's speech to it and the decision that, while the link was recognized by all, there should be no special mechanism created in which to discuss it.[4] I found OECD Secretary General van Lennep satisfied that the organization has been given a mandate to deal with the link, even if the specific forum proposal was rejected. He advised us to be relaxed on the problem for now and to have another look at it after the Rey Group had submitted its report in late June.

The alleged French opposition, he said, was mainly directed against the Schweitzer proposals for terms of reference for the Group of 20, to be created as the main monetary reform body at the September Fund meeting. The French tended to confuse these with the van Lennep proposal.

During my talks in all the capitals, I found that no one questioned the basic thesis of the Volcker speech that there was need for consistency between trade and monetary rules. All agreed on the fact of the link, that this fact had to be addressed and that, in all probability, the OECD was as good a place as any to do so.

---

[4] See Document 90.

In London, Barber apologized for what he admitted may have seemed to us to have been a British let down at OECD. He said he was originally inclined to favor the creation of a special group but, on seeing the clear opposition developing against it, simply had to reverse himself to accommodate to reality.

III. Timing of Monetary Reform Negotiations

During my talk with Barre, it became apparent that the EC, as a unit, is still a long way from any kind of consensus concerning the objectives which "Europe" should seek in reform negotiations. The first meeting at which the Finance Ministers of the 10 will discuss this question has just been scheduled for July 17 and 18 in London. The most optimistic expectation for the emergence of a consensus, according to Barre, would be at or after the September IMF meeting. A more realistic estimate would be not before October or November, at best.

Barre doubted that the October EC Summit would give much attention to this issue. Its main preoccupations, he said, would be on "consolidating" the internal EC system and the development of coordinated economic and social policies linked to monetary union. Thus, the definition of a European position on reform would probably be left in the hands of Finance Ministers for the foreseeable future.

I asked each of the Finance Ministers I saw after the Brussels stop to comment on this scenario. All agreed that it would not be realistic to expect a fully coordinated EC position before year-end, if then. The British even remain skeptical that there will ever be a fully common EC position short of the point of final agreement internationally.

I used these admissions to remind the Ministers that, given the lack of a common EC position, I hoped they no longer believed that it was the U.S. which was dragging its feet on initiating reform negotiations. All agreed that the fault was not ours.

Barber used the occasion of our talk to emphasize his interest in hearing from us any ideas we may have about the kind of reformed system we would like to see come out of the negotiations. He said it would be very useful to him in his talks with both the Europeans and the Commonwealth Ministers. He particularly wanted to avoid the development of a situation later this year in which, in the absence of clear signals from the U.S., the U.K. and others began to find themselves being locked in to a "European" consensus which would prove to be unacceptable to us. He urged us to use him as a sort of honest broker and assured me that he would respect the confidentiality of any ideas which were passed to him that we wished to be so treated. I agreed he deserved a response to his proposal, even if it were non-commital.

IV. External Relations at the EC Summit

I am inclined to agree with Barre's assessment that, at least as of now, external relations is not likely to be an item of great concern to the Europeans at the Summit. Institutional and internal issues are expected to loom much larger by comparison. On external relations, attention seemed to be about equally divided among three areas: relations with developed countries, relations with LDC's and East-West issues.

In countries where I thought it would be useful (UK, Germany and Belgium), I suggested that a declaration from the Summit, recognizing that EC enlargement imposed special responsibilities on members toward their partners outside (and especially toward those in the Atlantic Alliance) and stating the intent of the 10 to move toward major reform of the international system and external liberalization would be very helpful to us in stemming the tide in the US toward the kind of economic and political isolationism of which I warned them earlier.

The response to this proposal was positive from the British, Schiller and Davignon. While I did not make the suggestion as such with the EC Commission, it was clear from the conversations that there was little or no disposition on their part to push for such an outcome. Mansholt in particular had neither sympathy nor comprehension of the problem.

Despite Giscard's attentiveness to the problem and his apparent sympathy with it, I remain skeptical that the French would endorse it unless substantial pressure (and, probably, concessions on other issues) were forthcoming from her EC partners. However, I believe the Italians would support such an initiative if others pushed it, and I was given to understand that the Dutch would do likewise. I have no feel for the Norwegians, Danes, Irish and Luxembourg.

While there are some risks involved, I believe the proposal should be followed up with those who were responsive and I plan to do so.

V. Economic Content of CESC

Though NATO Secretary General Luns told me he did not think that there would be much emphasis on East-West economic issues at the Conference on European Security and Cooperation, Ambassador Kennedy and his staff believe that, with MBFR excluded, most of the content of the conference will in fact be economic. We will need to keep close watch over the preparations for this meeting for at least two reasons: (1) there are indications that some EC countries may be toying with the idea that special ad hoc preferential arrangements could be worked out to promote closer industrial cooperation between East and West Europe, and (2) there is a danger that France may convince her EC partners to go into the Conference as a bloc with common positions, thus introducing a split into NATO coordination.

Luns is particularly conscious of the latter danger and emphasized his determination to see to it that the EC as a group does not preempt decisions which should properly be discussed and taken in NATO. He stressed in particular his opposition to the French attempt to set up an EC political institution in Paris separate from the international organizations in Brussels.

VI. Reactions to Moscow Summit

In each conversation, I discussed the results achieved by the President in Moscow, ending with a reference to his speech to the Congress on his return in which he emphasized the need to maintain and strengthen the Atlantic Alliance. Without exception, the Europeans expressed satisfaction with the Summit results, and were appreciative of the President's speech.

Schiller told me that Gromyko was in Bonn the week before (after the Summit) and mentioned that the Soviets were studying the reaction in the US to the visit. He said it appeared to be "at least 95 percent positive," which, he told the Germans, was very encouraging to him.

VII. Conclusions

1) On monetary reform, I believe we should give careful consideration to the best method of preempting the creation of an anti-US European consensus, and with whom we can work toward this end. It is clear that there are significant differences of view among the member states about both overall goals and specifics, and we may be able to use these differences to our advantage if we move rapidly ourselves.

2) A forthcoming declaration from the October EC Summit, reemphasizing among other things, the importance of strengthening the EC's economic relations with its Atlantic Alliance partners, would be most helpful to us as we prepare to face the Congress with the need for legislation. Indeed, without a strong statement, we could be in considerable trouble. I will discuss ways to work with our friends in Europe on this with Secretaries Rogers, Shultz and others in Washington.

3) We must give careful attention to the preparations for the CESC and the economic content thereof. Specifically, we need to assure that the European desire to improve economic relations with the East does not run counter to our broader trade and monetary objectives that we will be working out in OECD, IMF and GATT during the rest of this year and beyond.

Attachment 2

Brussels, June 1, 1972.

Conversation with EC Commission President Sicco Mansholt

After a discussion of the President's trip to Moscow, I concluded by expressing my conviction that, despite our satisfaction with the progress we were making in improving Soviet-American relations, it is the strengthening of the Atlantic system that deserves our highest priority.

While not directly disagreeing, Mansholt responded with a long speech which began by noting what he believed was a growing sentiment in European public opinion and parliaments about the future of relations between the developed and developing countries. He said that, in comparison with the "minor" economic problems among developed countries, those between developed and developing economies were much more serious.

He had made two trips to the UNCTAD meeting at Santiago. He said that the U.S. attitude there was, to say the least, disappointing. He warned that Europe was becoming deeply concerned about the north-south split and its implications for future peace. It seemed clear, from the U.S. performance in Santiago, that this concern was not shared in America. Thus, a serious confrontation between Europe and the U.S. was in the making over trade and aid policies toward LDC's. He assured me that Europe will meet its obligations, even if the U.S. will not.

Specifically, the EC will begin to develop commercial and industrial policies which will look to the interests of the LDC's. The problems Europe has with the U.S. are not important. The "Eberle negotiations" earlier this year were a big mistake for Europe. It was "silly" to have spent so much time and political capital on a few million dollars worth of trade in citrus fruit, tobacco, etc., when 20 percent of the world was starving.

He assured me that *he* was not the least concerned with soyabeans, ("to hell with your soyabeans") but he was over palm oil because it is an essential LDC export. He said we don't need free trade or even market-determined trade in such products but rather product agreements specifically designed to organize trade in a way to favor LDC exports. If the U.S. does not join in such arrangements, he was sure Europe will go it alone. He even went so far as to suggest that there should be no tariff reductions among developed countries, since it would reduce the advantage of tariff preferences to the LDC's.

On aid, he was highly critical of the U.S. which had consistently failed in recent years to come anywhere near the one percent of GNP aid target. Here again, Europe would meet its responsibilities even if the U.S. did not.

These problems, he suggested, would be the most critical with which the EC summit should deal in its discussion of relations with third countries (implying that relations with the U.S. would be decidedly secondary). He also stated that a large part of the new EC political cooperation talks ("an EC foreign policy") will be devoted to consideration of strengthening economic links between the EC and all developing countries. He recognized that the past concentration on Africa was disproportionate and that these links had to be broadened to include South America, Asia, etc. He concluded that it was the real world he was talking about, not that which occupied so much of the time of our respective governments. He particularly stressed that the U.S. members of Congress with whom he had talked were not aware of this real world.

I replied that the real world in which a U.S. Congressman and Senator lives is one of politics. I then said he should bear in mind that the U.S. has been in the aid business—starting with Europe itself—far longer and that the total of that aid over the years was still the highest by far.

I then said that, in assessing responsibilities, he could not overlook the fact that the U.S. bears the main burden of maintaining the defensive shield of the free world. The percentage of GNP which we devote to this responsibility is substantially higher than that of the Europeans. (He attempted to debate this.) He should look at these—aid and defense—together in judging who was meeting whose responsibilities.

He said that, as a Socialist, he did not agree that the war in Vietnam was contributing to the solution of the problems he had outlined. I said that, even excluding our expenditures on Vietnam, what I said still held up. As regards Europe in particular, it was clear that the burden borne by us was more than disproportionate. If Europe felt it could devote a larger percentage of its resources to aid, that was fine, but it should understand that this was made possible largely because it is not as burdened by defense expenditures as we, even for Europe itself.

I went on to point out to him that, for 20 years, we have been running balance of payments deficits, due largely to our military and aid commitments. Europeans tell us this has to stop; that they don't want any more dollars. Under these circumstances, I didn't see how we could increase our aid as he suggested in the absence of some fundamental readjustments in the monetary and trade systems—reforms which recognize and take account of the fact that all these issues—trade, aid, defense, finance—are interrelated.

Concerning preferences, I suggested his argument might be more convincing in the absence of the reverse preferences which the Europeans required from the LDC's, whose value to the latter I failed to see. Finally, I said I thought we both needed to give at least as much attention to the U.S.-EC relationship as he wanted to give to the developed-developing country problem.

Mansholt agreed that Europe should shoulder more of its own defense burden. However, he said, the real issue is that income from future growth needs to be distributed more extensively to the LDC's to close the gap. This should be done by heavy new taxation in developed countries (even if it resulted in a decline of standards of living in the developed countries, and in the U.S. in particular as the richest), and by trading arrangements to organize markets in favor of LDC exports. We need, he said, to adapt our agricultural and industrial policies to meet their needs. There is no need for developed countries to produce those things which LDC's can, even if the former can do it more efficiently.

I said that his suggestion was not only unrealistic politically but also contrary to all past experience. I said it had been my experience that a prospering country with a high standard of living was both a better market for LDC exports and a more generous giver of aid. I asked how we could be expected to import more—from LDC's or anyone—with falling demand and declining standards of living.

Mansholt did not answer but, reverting to his Santiago experiences, charged that the U.S. was embarked on a deliberate policy of destroying the only democratic regime left in Latin America "in the same way we had destroyed democracy in Cuba." He said that Allende was faced with a serious challenge from both the left and the right in Chile and that, if he went under, the country would give way to anarchy and, ultimately, become another Cuban-style dictatorship.

I said we had in no way interfered in Chile, and denied flatly that we were embarked on any venture to destroy the Allende Government. He fired back a question about our policy of voting against loans by the international institutions to Chile. I replied that we felt that the Chilean Government should discharge its obligations to the companies it had expropriated before we could justify such loans. I said we were not contesting Allende's right to expropriate, but we did believe he should offer prompt and adequate compensation.

Mansholt claimed that Chile owed us nothing because companies like Anaconda had exploited Chile for years, contributing nothing while withdrawing only profits. For example, he said that, as a Socialist, he did not believe that capitalism is effective or desirable as a means of promoting development. He had visited El Teniente while in Chile and could find no schools, no housing, no roads built by Anaconda to serve

the people in all the years it was there. Instead, there were large lati-
fundia, estates, etc. for the managers, while the peasants toiled in mis-
ery.

I asked him how many schools, houses, roads, etc. had been built
by the tax money collected from Anaconda by the governments (eg Frei)
which he professed to admire. He did not answer, contenting himself
with a remark that Allende was right to have not only assessed ex post
taxes but to have offered nothing to Anaconda.

Peter M. Flanigan[5]

---

[5] Printed from a copy that bears this typed signature.

---

92.   Memorandum of Conversation[1]

Washington, July 17, 1972, 11:30 a.m

PARTICIPANTS

United States
Secretary of the Treasury George P. Shultz
Under Secretary for Monetary Affairs Volcker
Schubert Dyche, OINF
Michael Unger, OINF

Japan
Nobuhiko Ushiba, Japanese Ambassador to U.S.
Michio Kondo, Finance Minister, Embassy of Japan

SUBJECT

Summary of Ambassador Ushiba's Call on Secretary Shultz

Ambassador Ushiba stated that he would be leaving for Tokyo
tomorrow morning to meet with the new Prime Minister who takes
great interest in our mutual problems. He also stated that Japan's
exports to the United States had eased very much compared to last year
partly because of voluntary agreements on textiles, autos have leveled

---

[1] Source: Washington National Records Center, Department of the Treasury, Files of
Under Secretary Volcker: FRC 56 79 15, Japan General. Confidential. The meeting was
held in Secretary Shultz' office. Drafted on July 18 by Unger and approved by Volcker.
Ambassador Ushiba also met with Flanigan on July 15 prior to his travel to Tokyo. A
memorandum of that conversation, dated July 17, is ibid.

off and electronics have slowed. However in spite of these changes, a large trade imbalance exists which Japanese business and government is anxious to see reduced. The Ambassador believes that unless the trend is eased by September or October, there will be very strong protectionist pressures in this country.

Secretary Shultz stated that the strong Japanese surpluses were not compatible with a stable world system. It's not only a question of protectionist sentiment but in a broader view it is not compatible with global stability. He further stated that some very substantial changes with real magnitude were necessary. The United States appreciates the goods Japan supplies us with—our consumers want them. The Secretary stated that he had met the new Prime Minister at a breakfast here and stated that the Prime Minister was a strong man and that if he decided to do something, it will get done.

The Secretary commended on the recent go around on the financing of a nuclear power plant in Japan.[2] Japan has the resource and should have financed the plant itself. It's a question that goes beyond exports. What we want is a stable world trading and payment situation and given the income and price elasticities of Japan they are not consistent with a stable world system.

Ambassador Ushiba stated that the Japanese well understand the problem and that they were moving in the right direction by trying to reflate the economy and use foreign exchange for useful purposes. These things take time but Japan is moving in the right direction.

Secretary Shultz stated that it was important to have major things happen to bring about a better trade balance. The magnitudes are gigantic and that while little things are important they add up to numbers like $100 million or so—which is just a drop in the bucket.

The Secretary asked the Ambassador if there was any prospect of Japan setting targets for increased imports from the United States. He felt this was useful for the short run. The Ambassador stated that this was one of the themes to be taken up at the meeting in Hakone.[3] The

---

[2] On July 1 Export-Import Bank President Henry Kearns send a memorandum to Under Secretary Volcker informing him that on June 28 he had communicated with the Chairmen of Tokyo Electric Power and the Japan Atomic Power Company about financing two projects from Japanese dollar sources. Both had responded that it was not possible in the timeframe necessary to line up financing. General Electric Vice President Hoyt Steele also informed Kearns of the need for Export-Import Bank financing "if the United States is to achieve a major supply situation." (Ibid.) On July 7 Federal Reserve Governor Brimmer wrote Volcker expressing his concern over an Export-Import Bank nuclear power loan for Japan, with which he had reluctantly concurred in the National Advisory Committee meeting. (Ibid.)

[3] Special Trade Representative Eberle headed the U.S. negotiating team that met with Japanese trade negotiators at Hakone, Japan beginning July 25. See Document 93.

Ambassador wanted to know if this was a proposal from the U.S. side. Secretary Shultz stated that it was not a formal proposal, but was a substantive thing to talk about.

Ambassador Ushiba stated that Japan was considering some emergency measures such as stockpiling certain commodities.

Secretary Shultz stated that he thought this was a possibility which might be considered but such actions should be considered within the framework of a $3.6 billion trade surplus with the United States and $8 billion overall. The numbers that have to be brought into balance are very, very large.

Ambassador Ushiba stated that he had been informed by his government that the basic trade trend is changing—that trade should be less this year than last. Under Secretary Volcker inquired as to whether the Ambassador was referring to trade with the United States. The Ambassador stated yes. Under Secretary Volcker stated that he didn't believe this was true.

Mr. Dyche stated that the results to date for 1972 indicate a deficit approaching at least $3.6 billion for the year, quite apart from various forecasts that also show deficits in this range. It's difficult to see how a reduction for the year will come about in the next five months.

Ambassador Ushiba stated that he is certain that by end of year— by this fall a change will occur in the trading pattern. The effect of the revaluation is beginning to be felt and it is getting much more difficult to sell in existing markets.

Secretary Shultz stated that we must be realistic—the magnitudes are gigantic and that steps which have potential for real magnitude must be taken.

Ambassador Ushiba inquired as to what steps Secretary Shultz had in mind.

Secretary Shultz said that a few had been mentioned earlier. He thought the revaluation last December should have been greater.[4] Our studies showed a revaluation of 25 percent would have been appropriate, even though we agreed it probably could not be done at one time. Our economy is growing faster this year and our imports will go up. He then reiterated that the problem was a broad world matter and Japan must take actions with real magnitude.

Ambassador Ushiba inquired as to whether Secretary Shultz thought the U.S. economy would continue to expand.

Secretary Shultz replied that he thought so. The building of inventories is beginning and economy moving quite well. The GNP problem

---

[4] See Document 221.

is net negative exports—a problem in the expansion of last year. Basically economic expansion seems to be moving quite well—probably better than we forecast last January. Price indexes with some exceptions are settling down. A major problem is the management of 1973–74 budget, but the President has a way of getting things around to his point of view. He stated he thought the domestic economy looked good.

Ambassador Ushiba asked how the dollar looked.

Secretary Shultz doesn't feel that there should be a new dollar crisis at this time. The U.S. economy is now stronger and prices are settling down. He thinks that the relative position of the dollar abroad if anything, has moved in a more positive direction. However, there remains the big deficit in our balance of payments with Japan and Canada. It's a joint problem and unless there is a better balance, he sees no chance for stability.

Ambassador Ushiba asked a question about when the G-20 would be meeting.[5] Also what happened to G-10?

Secretary Shultz felt the two groups would have continuity and perhaps the two would come together at some point. He indicated that the G-20 is broader to include the developing countries. He stated there are a number of things that have to be worked out—not only in an intellectual sense but in an administrative sense. The United States wants to stay close to Japan as we have a common problem.

Secretary Shultz asked Under Secretary Volcker if he had anything to add. To this Under Secretary Volcker stated that it was only a matter of emphasis. We don't have much time as the foreign exchange markets show. Although the speculation occurs in Europe, one of the main reasons for speculation is the imbalance between the United States and Japan, and speculation won't go away until our problem is resolved.

Secretary Shultz, in concluding, wished Ambassador Ushiba a pleasant trip and asked him to give his regards to Ambassador Ingersoll.

Ambassador Ushiba replied that he would do so.

Michael Unger

---

[5] The C-20 met for the first time on September 23; see Document 244.

93.   Editorial Note

Bilateral trade issues with Japan had not been resolved prior to or during the President's January 1972 meeting with Prime Minister Sato in San Clemente (see Document 87), and a new drive was underway to conclude the trade negotiations before President Nixon and the new Japanese Prime Minister, Kakuei Tanaka, met in Honolulu August 31–September 1, 1972.

Special Trade Representative Eberle led a U.S. negotiating team to trade bilaterals in Hakone, Japan, that began on July 25. The Japanese team was headed by Kiyohiko Tsurumi, Deputy Vice Minister of Foreign Affairs. At the outset of a July 29 meeting with Ambassadors Eberle and Ingersoll, Tanaka said he had just talked with MITI Minister Nakasone and understood the Hakone talks had reached agreement on 60–70 percent of the U.S. expectations. Eberle said the Hakone talks had been "most useful," but added that a major disappointment had been limited progress on the bilateral trade imbalance. Prime Minister Tanaka indicated that he had already issued instructions that the bilateral imbalance should be reduced to less than $3 billion for the Japanese fiscal year ending March 31, 1973 (a U.S. projection estimated it would be $3.6–3.8 billion). Eberle agreed with Tanaka that the trade balance needed to be viewed in a multilateral context, but added that the imbalance was so large it was a "serious distortion of the total market."

Tanaka agreed the two sides should expedite discussions in the uranium and aircraft purchase areas, and Eberle added that expert meetings on agriculture, computers, integrated circuits, and the Japanese distribution system were also required. (Memorandum of conversation, July 29; Washington National Records Center, Department of the Treasury, Files of Under Secretary Volcker: FRC 56 79 15, Japan General) During August a number of cables were exchanged between the Department of State and the Embassy in Tokyo as agreements in these and other areas were sought. These telegraphic messages are in the National Archives, Nixon Presidential Materials, NSC Files, Country Files–Far East, Box 538, Japan Volume 8 5–12/72.

On August 10 Ambassador Ingersoll reviewed with Foreign Minister Ohira what he thought should be the trade results at the upcoming meeting in Honolulu between President Nixon and Prime Minister Tanaka. Ingersoll noted that it would be useful for the "President and PM to announce overall package of increased Japanese purchases, perhaps in $700 million–$1 billion range, which might include items such as agriculture, enriched uranium, uranium ore, wide-bodied aircraft, helicopters, and small aircraft." (Telegram 8543 from Tokyo, August 10; ibid.)

On August 2 Hormats had sent Kissinger a memorandum apprising him of the outcome of the Hakone negotiations and Eberle's reading of the political dynamics of the trade issue in Japan. Tanaka was viewed as not fully in control and reportedly did not want MITI Minister Nakasone at the Honolulu meeting where his image might be burnished. Hormats cautioned Kissinger that the trade issues not be over-publicized lest Nakasone's hand be strengthened and commented that if Tanaka wanted to exclude Nakasone from the Honolulu meeting he might be willing to agree in advance on some issues in Nakasone's domain. (Ibid., Subject Files, Box 404, Eberle)

On August 9 Hormats sent separate memoranda to Kissinger and Haig regarding the trade negotiations, and that evening Kissinger, Flanigan, Eberle, Haig, Holdridge, and Hormats met to discuss strategy, possible outcomes, and trade-related matters that might arise during Kissinger's and Holdridge's forthcoming trips to Japan. The Japanese were to understand that what the United States sought was based on authority at the highest level. Hormats' memoranda and the memorandum of the August 9 conversation are ibid., Country Files–Far East, Box 538, Japan Volume 8 5–12/72.

The President met with Eberle from 10:42 to 11:09 a.m. on August 14 to discuss U.S.-Japanese trade negotiations, a meeting that included a brief opportunity for members of the press and the White House photographer. Flanigan and Haig were present at the outset, but left at 10:55 a.m. (Ibid., White House Central Files, President's Daily Diary)

On August 16 a White House message to Ingersoll and Holdridge in Tokyo informed them of what Washington agencies understood to be already agreed and what additional measures they sought; see Document 95 and footnote 1 thereto.

94.   Paper Prepared in the Council on International Economic Policy[1]

Washington, undated.

U.S. OBJECTIVES FOR TRADE NEGOTIATIONS AND
MONETARY REFORM

I. Premises

A. The primary United States objective in the comprehensive trade and monetary negotiations is to maintain a thrust toward a liberal trading and payments order in a manner that supports our efforts to restore and sustain an external economic equilibrium and equity or fairness in our trading relationships, real and perceived. This objective grows out of the fundamental goals of encouraging competitiveness and efficiency in American enterprises and open, harmonious political and economic relations with other nations, thus offering improvement in our standard of living in a context of the growth and cohesion of the Western world. On the premise that expanded world trade on an equitable basis and monetary and balance of payments equilibrium can benefit all parties through more efficient use of resources, and promote the close economic and political integration of Western economies, the basic goals are in the interest of, and attainable for, all participating countries.

B. Specifically, these interests would be served by an international economic system providing an environment which—

i. facilitated international trade and capital flows among nations; subject only to such safeguards as may be necessary against shifts so rapid as to undermine the stability and sustainability of the system;
ii. involved a minimum of governmental restraints and subsidies on international economic transactions and a maximum of market-directed U.S. and world trade and investment;
iii. preserved the habit of cooperation which has become established in international economic affairs.

C. In the complex task of reshaping the world's economic system, a balanced "package" approach must necessarily be employed in judging specific proposals affecting the system and the adjustment process; the

---

[1] Source: Washington National Records Center, Department of the Treasury, Files of Under Secretary Volcker: FRC 56 79 15, NSDMs. Confidential. Attached to a November 30 memorandum from Flanigan to the Secretaries of State, Defense, Commerce, Treasury, and Agriculture, which indicated the paper was prepared "last summer in cooperation with your departments." Flanigan's transmittal memorandum suggests the paper was prepared in the CIEP, but parts of it are identical to the paper that Treasury Deputy Under Secretary Bennett prepared for the Volcker Group Alternates on June 5; see Document 230.

implications of parts of the proposed system cannot be judged fully until the broad outlines of the whole package are in view; in order ultimately to reach an agreement embracing all major trading nations, the U.S. may have to accept less than full achievement of some objectives.

II. Objectives

1. A Revised Set of International Trade and Monetary Rules—

a) which will both enhance economic competition and efficiency and promote international payments equilibrium through reduction in governmental barriers and subsidies which distort international trade;

b) which will preserve needed freedom of action in domestic macro-economic policies;

c) which will confine use of discriminatory trading arrangements to clearly defined circumstances in which such discrimination is related to broader political economic requirements;

d) which will avoid discrimination against or among investors from abroad while providing host governments with adequate control over business activities within their territories;

e) which will minimize restrictions for balance of payments purposes by industrialized countries generally on long-term capital flows and avoid their use by the U.S.;

f) which will limit distortion of international transaction by tax and other forms of governmental incentives affecting the location of economic activities and the selection of markets for production;

g) which will promote coordinated consideration of trade and monetary problems, and improved institutional arrangements with and among international organizations as well as national governments providing for continuing high level consultation with respect to the operations of and inter-relations among the international monetary and trading systems and national laws and regulations affecting international trade and finance;

h) which will while leaving necessary scope for national and international consultation and decision-making be clearly spelled out in international agreements.

2. To Help Achieve These Ends, the Monetary System[2] Should—

a) encourage the use of price-oriented measures and adequate financing facilities to deal with volatile short-term capital flows;

---

[2] The mechanics of a system meeting these criteria including the exchange rate regime, convertibility requirements, and the reserve role of the dollar are not addressed in this "Objectives" paper. [Footnote in the source text.]

b) encourage the phasing out of gold as a reserve asset;

c) more symmetrically apply pressure to adjust on surplus as well as deficit countries;

d) encourage countries in surplus on current and overall official account to liberalize trade more rapidly than deficit countries as one acceptable means of adjustment.

3. Trade Liberalization

a) We have agreed internationally to seek authority for trade negotiations "on the basis of mutual advantage and mutual commitment with overall reciprocity." The President has defined our general objective as "progress toward free and fair trade" which requires both rule changes and institutional improvements and a more detailed set of objectives for trade negotiations per se.

b) The *"free and fair trade"* concept must extend to agricultural trade as well as to trade in industrial goods and raw materials. It requires elimination or harmonization of NTBs as well as tariffs. It postulates that the enlargement of the EC and the negotiations of preferential arrangements including those with EFTA non-applicants will further adversely affect our trade, and that we should seek to reduce the trade-restricting effects of the Common Agricultural Policy, the new discrimination against our exports resulting from the preferential arrangements, and the ability of the EC or other areas to extend such preferential arrangements.

c) We seek acceptance of the principle that, ultimately, tariffs should be eliminated or at least made the only form of protection at the frontier. If the European Common Agricultural Policy continues to frustrate our ability to exploit our clear comparative advantage in some agricultural products we may be forced to impose countervailing restrictions, or to adjust exchange rate relations, which measures, however, would be costly as they would adversely affect our terms of trade.

d) *Fair trade* implies three related ideas:

1) There must be no discrimination among outside suppliers to any given customs area. This means, in particular, that we seek the end of special preferential arrangements, including reverse preferences, which fall short of full economic unions. Generalized preferences for LDCs should be the only exception, and the exception will be less important as tariffs are progressively reduced.

2) Countries in determining their own economic, commercial agricultural, and industrial policies should endeavor insofar as possible, not to transfer the costs of such policies to other countries, except to the extent to which other countries agree to accept such costs. This principle is particularly important with respect to agriculture, NTBs in general, and export subsidies. A foreseeable exception would be the new orderly market-

ing/market disruption mechanism (see e(2) below) which contemplates mutually agreed use of safeguards. Unilateral invocation of safeguards would be permitted if agreement could not be reached, but compensation or retaliation would also be authorized in that event.

Unfair advantages, conferred on its exporters by a nation's tax system, domestic subsidy programs or other arrangements should be eliminated or harmonized internationally through agreed rules. Similarly, advantages conferred on domestic industry or agriculture, whose effect is to introduce a barrier to imports other than a defined tariff, should also be progressively eliminated.

e) *Exceptions*

In moving toward free trade we and other countries will need defined and acceptable arrangements:

1) to govern and restrict the use of trade or capital controls for balance of payments purposes;

2) to safeguard markets temporarily against disruption by an excessively rapid buildup of imports while domestic adjustment is given time to work with reasonable smoothness;

3) to control indefinitely imports which could compromise national security, health, environment, etc.;

4) to phase reductions in some tariff and non-tariff barriers over longer periods to provide time for easier adjustment; and, perhaps—

5) to maintain moderate tariffs in agriculture since the elimination of barriers to imports of some agricultural products might pose excessively difficult adjustment problems.

f) *Constraints*

The major constraints on our negotiators—as on others—will be political and balance of payments considerations.

1) The political constraint arises largely because import pressures are specific and vocalized whereas the benefits of trade are general and under-represented in the absence of a strong executive attitude. Realistically, a precondition for Congressional enactment of substantial trade negotiating authority probably is declining or low unemployment. Congressional realities also demand that trade liberalization authority result in clear progress in dealing with what we have seen as inequities for U.S. producers.

2) The balance of payments constraint requires that the process of multilateral trade liberalization support to the extent possible an overall equilibrium in our balance of payments and strength in our current account, which are essential to re-establish confidence in the strength of the dollar and monetary stability.

g) *Scope*

The scope of negotiations concerning trade and related matters should be sufficiently broad to make allowance for the overall conditions of doing business internationally and to assure that concessions gained by liberalization in one area, e.g., tariffs, are not offset by new restrictions elsewhere. Thus, variations in tax treatment, policies toward foreign investment, regulation of industrial production and sales activity, and industrial and regional policies which distort competition should be negotiated as well as direct trade restrictions.

95.   U.S. Position Paper[1]

Washington, undated.

U.S.-JAPAN TRADE ISSUES

1. Overall Trade Imbalance

The U.S. has requested that Japan take action to reduce its trade surplus with the U.S. by at least $1 billion in each of the next two years. What we would like is for Japan to reduce from the present *anticipated* surplus of $3.6–$3.8 billion by $1 billion, to be achieved by March 31, 1973—the end of Japan's current fiscal year. Then, in the next fiscal year, we would like Japan to reduce the surplus by a further $1 billion.

2. Increased Purchases over JFY 71

We desire that the Japanese government undertake to *ensure* this in part through an increased level of purchases as follows:

(a) *Agricultural purchases:* Japan has projected an increase of $270 million of purchases. We seek information detailing the components of this category, and to develop language for a commitment. In addition, Japan agreed to make $50 million additional purchases for food agency account. We seek information detailing the components of this category, and to develop language for a commitment; and would like to receive a commitment for another $100 million which might include long staple cotton.

(b) *Forestry and fisheries:* Japan has projected an increase of $120 million of purchases. We seek information detailing the components of this category, and to develop language for a commitment.

---

[1] Source: National Archives, Nixon Presidential Materials, NSC Files, Country Files–Far East, Box 538, Japan Volume 8 5–12/72. Confidential. Attached to an August 15 memorandum from Hormats to Haig indicating that the paper was a "final agreed position paper" and recommending that Haig send it to Holdridge and Ingersoll in Tokyo, because "it is a clear and accurate representation of the U.S. position." Haig approved that recommendation, and a telegraphic text of the message was sent from the White House to the Embassy in Tokyo at 0104Z on August 16. (Ibid., VIP Visits, Box 926, Tanaka 8/31–9/1/72)

3. Enriched Uranium Purchases

The three aspects of this category are subject to discussion by a Japanese team with Atomic Energy Commission officials. We request that the Japanese team arrive in the U.S. as soon as possible.

(a) *Enriched Uranium:* The Japanese have agreed to purchase $160 million of enriched uranium (5,000 special working units). Details to be worked out by U.S.-Japan discussion in the near future. U.S. could supply up to 10,000 special working units, and we would hope that the purchase could approach this amount.

(b) *Uranium Ore:* The Japanese have agreed to $200 million purchases, providing the U.S. price is competitive. Details to be worked out by U.S.-Japan discussions in the near future. (This $200 million figure covers twice the ore necessary for the 5,000 SWU's).

(c) *Enrichment Facilities:* A letter of intent is sought between the two governments to approve the principle of a joint-venture enrichment facility and encourage the respective country's private companies to proceed to work out a program.

4. Commercial Aircraft Purchases

The U.S. seeks assurances of the Japanese to facilitate by financial and other measures the purchase of at least $150 million of commercial aircraft by private companies.

5. Liberalization Measures

The following measures were agreed upon and require written commitments from the Japanese government:

(a) *Retailing:* It was agreed that 100% U.S.-owned retailers could operate in Japan with up to 11 branches. The key element is the definition of the U.S.-made products required for 50% of sales. The language for the commitment is agreed and we are awaiting this letter.

(b) *Processing and Packaging:* Liberalization was agreed on U.S. bulk imports by Japan, particularly cosmetics, film (except color and color-sensitive paper), and pharmaceuticals. The language for the commitment is agreed and we are awaiting this letter.

(c) *Computers:* It was agreed that the U.S. share of the Japanese computer market could rise from 46% to 50%. Also imports of parts and peripherals were to be liberalized to allow Japanese and U.S. firms to import with fewer restrictions. The language for the commitment is agreed and we are awaiting this letter.

(d) *Government Procurement:* The Japanese maintain they have no "Buy Japan" requirements, except on computers and nuclear reactors. A written communiqué by MITI to government agencies or a written commitment in another form is needed.

6. Defense Procurement

While this issue would not be raised publicly or announced, a private commitment is sought to increase such purchases from the U.S. from a level near $200 million per year to $300 million to $400 million per year.

---

96.   Memorandum of Conversation[1]

Karuizawa, Japan, August 19, 1972, 9:20 a.m.–12:25 p.m.

PARTICIPANTS

Prime Minister Kakuei Tanaka
Shinsaku Hogen, Vice Minister of Foreign Affairs
Mr. Kiuchi, Private Secretary to the Prime Minister
Mr. Konaga, Foreign Office
Mr. Ukawa, Head of Economic Section, North American Bureau, Foreign Office (Interpreter)
Dr. Henry A. Kissinger, Assistant to the President for National Security Affairs
Ambassador Robert S. Ingersoll
John H. Holdridge, NSC Senior Staff Member
Peter W. Rodman, NSC Staff

[Omitted here is a discussion of unrelated topics.]

Prime Minister Tanaka: Particularly since I learned you were coming, I have asked my officials to look at the short-term and long-term trade picture. I have looked at your figures myself.

To give you my rather frank estimate of the situation, I do not think it is possible to arrive at a comfortable balance in a half year, or even one year. Perhaps in a period of three years, having studied the issues, we may be able to stabilize our economic relationship, in the sense of a not so uncomfortable imbalance as today. All of us should be seeking to achieve that goal, in that time frame, and I think it is possible.

Dr. Kissinger: What is the Prime Minister's definition of a "comfortable" trade balance?

Prime Minister Tanaka: It is perhaps a rather difficult question to answer in exact terms, because basically you must seek a balance in a

---

[1]   Source: National Archives, Nixon Presidential Materials, NSC Files, Presidential/HAK Memcons, Box 1026, HAK–PM Tanaka 8/19/72. Top Secret; Sensitive. The meeting was held in the Mampei Hotel.

multilateral sense; this can't be achieved just between the U.S. and Japan. In abstract terms, we don't have export or import terms where our going up or down is too abrupt. And if I remember the figures from last year, the imbalance is on the order of $3.2 billion. I have asked my officials to come up with means to reduce it to less than $3 billion by the end of the present Japanese fiscal year, and if this is not possible also to seek other means, in a multilateral sense, to make the situation less difficult. So we may be able to arrive at within not too long a trade balance which is less difficult. Not just between ourselves but also with other areas—the Middle East, Europe—as long as ten years, as well as near-term measures.

Dr. Kissinger: We agree there cannot be an exact balance between our two countries, and that an overall balance has to be solved on a multilateral basis. We also favor a mid-term projection, in the framework which the Prime Minister indicated. At the same time, if our bilateral balance becomes uneven, the pressures within the U.S. for some sort of unilateral steps become so great that we will never have the time to develop the long-term projection.

On the statistics—I'm not an economist[2]—they seem to indicate the imbalance this year between our two countries will be about $3.6–3.8 billion, according to our figures. If that is accepted, if it could be reduced below $3 billion before the end of your fiscal year, that would be a positive contribution. We must think about what base you start with. And then, if we can take another significant step next year, that will be considered a very real progress.

Actually the President's thinking is that, assuming these figures are accepted, we should make an effort to get next year's program settled before Hawaii—because we don't want to spend so much time negotiating on purely commercial matters when we have so many profound political things to discuss between us.

Prime Minister Tanaka: I quite agree we ought to try to be tackling what you described as the profound issues. On this question of the trade balance I have taken an active part in asking my officials to see what measures are possible. Perhaps we can work this out before Hawaii.[3] Perhaps we can ask Ambassador Ingersoll and Mr. Hogen to look into the details. On the Japanese side some of the issues are: purchases of enriched uranium; purchases of civil aircraft; agricultural

---

[2] In a June 12 conversation with Tanaka (when he was still MITI Minister), Kissinger said: "Let me ask the Minister something about economics, which is not a field I usually address in great detail. . . . My major interest in economics is to make sure it doesn't disturb foreign policy." (Memorandum of conversation; ibid., HAK–Tanaka 6/12/72)

[3] President Nixon and Prime Minister Tanaka were scheduled to meet in Hawaii August 31–September 1.

purchases, which was discussed with Mr. Eberle when we agreed to a special purchase of $50 million in addition to an estimated growth of $390 million in the current fiscal year in agricultural purchases, to a total of $440 million. It could reach a figure of $500 million. But I must emphasize that although we can put these figures together, it may not immediately have effect in solving the imbalance problem, because some of this will not show up immediately as Japanese imports. But by the end of March of next year, which is the end of the Japanese fiscal year, we will see if the Japanese officials concerned and a number of private companies might come up with measures that could reduce the imbalance to less than $3 billion. In the main by increased purchases. Also, by lending in foreign exchange terms, and at a cheaper rate of interest. These aren't easy to implement, and take time. But I want to emphasize that I have pressed Japanese officials and Japanese companies to take steps which if they don't have an early effect will come up with a reduced imbalance.

There is also the question of whether we can liberalize our imports of agricultural goods. Theoretically it is correct that if we reduce the restrictions we might be able to purchase more—but it is also possible that we might end up with increased Japanese purchases from Southeast Asia, the Middle East, and even the Chinese mainland. We have to look at a mechanism whereby we can increase purchases from the USA.

On economic issues, as you see, I have a list before me detailing the items that can be increased. Gas turbine generators, for example. Let us see what we can best do, before Honolulu. Ingersoll and our officials can make their best efforts. I don't want to go into details now.

Dr. Kissinger: I agree. May I make one suggestion, Mr. Prime Minister, in the spirit of frankness we have always observed? Some of our differences in the previous period were due to the fact that we had an agreement to do something in principle—but the differences came up in the interpretation of what it means. Therefore I believe that before Hawaii it would be helpful, and will avoid difficulties in the future, if we could have an understanding on what to do in detail, not just in principle. It would help if Ambassador Ingersoll and your officials could work out something concrete and detailed; for example, concretely what a reduction of the trade imbalance to $3 billion means.

Then in Hawaii we can pass over the economic issues except in a general way.

Prime Minister Tanaka: Yes. I think it is important perhaps to look at it through three phases, or through three actions. First of all, we agree in principle that we would seek a more normal economic relationship between our two countries; we acknowledge that as a common goal. As I said, this could not be achieved in a period of one year. It would take until 1973, or 74, or perhaps longer. Secondly it is important to have meetings at the expert level as often as possible. An idea comes to mind perhaps to organize them on a quarterly basis, to look at the trade balance. Not just Ministers, but as at Hakone—with Eberle. Not too much publicity.

Dr. Kissinger [interjecting]:[4] With your press and our leaking?!

Prime Minister Tanaka: That's what comes to mind. Perhaps in Tokyo, perhaps they might be invited to the U.S.

Dr. Kissinger: We could alternate.

Prime Minister Tanaka: The key is closer contact.

Third, the fact of the matter, the problem is we are getting dollars in increased numbers, and don't have much to do with them. We bought short-term Treasury Bills, SDRs, but refrained from buying gold so as not to drive up the price of gold. Perhaps we could make more substantial purchases, perhaps $3–5 billion of bills issued by the Federal Reserve Bank. I understand that the West Germany authorities buy these on five-year terms. Perhaps we could do this for longer, for 10 years. The experts can examine this. I understand the Germans get 5% interest. Perhaps we can pay you more as a means of bridging over the economic balance until we could seek longer term measures, a more basic international balance.

The third idea is a proposal like the man-wife relationship in this country: When they make a savings account they put it in both names, in a joint account. We should be doing the same. We should be saving jointly.

Dr. Kissinger: When they break up, one of them usually runs away with the money!

Prime Minister Tanaka: With the U.S., it is acceptable.

Dr. Kissinger: No, Mr. Prime Minister, I agree. For the long-term problem we need regular consultation, perhaps a mechanism by which the experts could every three to four months meet, with as little publicity as possible, perhaps at alternating locations. As regards your specific suggestion, I think it should be discussed by the appropriate experts. And also at Honolulu we could discuss the basic mechanisms of how to deal with the problem.

But on the short-term problem, as I understand what you have said here, we have agreed that before Honolulu, Ambassador Ingersoll and your officials will work out a specific program to

<hr>

[4] These and all but the last set of brackets in the text of the memorandum of conversation are in the source text.

reduce the deficit to $3 billion this fiscal year.[5] So that that matter doesn't have to be dealt with at Honolulu.

Prime Minister Tanaka: When you mention that we try to arrive at a program to cut it to $3 billion by the end of our fiscal year, this isn't entering figures in a bank account. What is important is that either it can be done or it cannot. What we will do is try. We will attack this problem using that figure as a guide. It is evidence of our forward-looking attitude. It is a guide I have given my officials, and also on the basis of reaching a solution as two family members, against the background of our effort to normalize our relations over a period of two–three years.[6]

Let me use this example, in confidence: I have instructed our authorities to see if they can increase Japanese purchases of arms— this is now estimated in the range of $700 million—to make it, say, $850 million. If you say this must take place, and show in the statistics—which aren't the same in the U.S.—by the end of March, it won't be possible. What I'm saying is, it can be done in the range of, say, five years.

Let me use two more examples: You asked us to liberalize our imports of fresh oranges on a seasonal basis, in Hakone. My officials said no, it was not possible. I asked them to look again, to see if it could be done in a different time period, or with liberalized allocations. These won't show in the figures by the end of next March. I also asked my offi-

---

[5] Later in the day Kissinger discussed a wide range of topics with Foreign Minister Ohira in Tokyo. Concerning the trade balance issue, the memorandum of conversation reads as follows:

"Foreign Minister Ohira: Well, on the question of the trade imbalance which you touched on, it is a question which we in the Foreign Ministry are quite deeply concerned about. Under Prime Minister Tanaka's energetic leadership we hope hard work can continue so that by the time of the meeting in Hawaii we can announce to the peoples of the two countries what we have arrived at. I think we can conclude it.

"One thing on which I am a bit concerned, that is we are now talking about trying to reduce the fiscal year imbalance to a level around $3 billion or a little below that; we are also trying to work out a package between Ambassador Ingersoll and Minister Tsurumi. What concerns me is that these two things we want might not necessarily meet as an exact figure. In the package, we are talking not only about trade, but also about services and imports which extend beyond this fiscal year. So the resulting package may not necessarily be reflected in reductions in the trade imbalance referred to earlier. In our talks you have understood this. I would like to make doubly sure that there is full understanding of the question.

"Dr. Kissinger: The Prime Minister made this point this morning. Ambassador Ingersoll and I have had a chance to discuss it at lunch. We understand that some part of the package will not show up in the trade imbalance until after this year. But we are talking about the spirit and general objectives; we will not do it like bookkeepers. [Laughter.] What we are talking about is reducing the deficit, and we won't be too concerned if some figures don't show up in the trade imbalance." (National Archives, Nixon Presidential Materials, NSC Files, VIP Visits, Box 926, Tanaka Visit 31 Aug–1 Sept)

[6] [text not declassified]

cials about importing a greater quantity of feeder cattle. It is now at 5000 head. We could consider going up perhaps twice or three times that amount, if this is possible to do. Other purchasers are aggressive and competitive, however.

There was also another idea floated at Hakone—on mixed blending orange prices—if we could seek an arrangement where the agricultural people on this side—the opponents—can be made a partner on this, with the American partners.

Dr. Kissinger: We will approach it in a spirit of friendship. And if you approach it, as you have, in a spirit of concreteness, then I am sure it can be resolved.

Prime Minister Tanaka: To put it frankly, during the Sato–Nixon talks on the question of textiles, I believe an Oriental, a Japanese expression was used by the former Prime Minister—*zen sho sru.* [The interpreter indicated that it was difficult to translate, but that it was roughly: "I shall look into this, in a judicious and forward-looking manner," or "in a spirit of goodwill, I will use my greatest efforts to see what can be done."] If someone says this in the Diet, it is accepted as a statement of a forward-looking attitude—but perhaps not between foreign governments. I want to avoid the misunderstanding, which may have been a problem in the past, by saying that we would aim at a reduction of $1 billion, and trying to indicate to my officials an approach in that sense. So if we cannot come up with a reduction by March 31, I do not wish to be accused of not being good at my word. I meant an order of magnitude, a goal.

Dr. Kissinger: That's fair enough. On this basis, no misunderstanding can arise.

Prime Minister Tanaka: The way to put it is, Japan and the U.S., working both together, mutually try to seek whether they can reduce the trade imbalance to less than $3 billion by the end of the Japanese fiscal year. But some measures, some purchases, mentioned earlier on would not show up in the trade figures by that time.

Dr. Kissinger: That's understood. That's understood.

Prime Minister Tanaka: What I try to emphasize is that we try to tackle the problem with the best will in the world.

Dr. Kissinger: That's all we ask. We will blame Ambassador Ingersoll if anything goes wrong!

[There was a brief recess from 11:00–11:03 a.m.]

Prime Minister Tanaka: To try to solve this issue before Honolulu, I nominate Mr. Tsurumi, Deputy Vice Minister of Foreign Affairs—who has led the Japanese group on this. He can be in touch with Ambassador Ingersoll to work out the details.

Dr. Kissinger: Good. Where shall we make the announcement of this decision—at Honolulu or before?

Prime Minister Tanaka: We would have no strong preference. We should aim at the more effective use of this. Therefore, what is your view?

Dr. Kissinger: I think we should aim at announcing it at Honolulu.

Prime Minister Tanaka: Just the confirmation at Honolulu of the details worked out.

Dr. Kissinger: Just confirmation, no details at Honolulu—just confirmation between you and the President of what our Ambassador and your people have worked out.

Prime Minister Tanaka: Taking this into consideration, Ambassador Ingersoll, perhaps you can discuss with us the details on timing and wording and content?

Ingersoll, Kissinger: Yes.

Ambassador Ingersoll [to Kissinger]: You can give me some guidance.

Dr. Kissinger: Yes.

Prime Minister Tanaka: It may turn out that as long as we are agreed in advance on what we are planning to announce, perhaps we could announce it before Honolulu—so we could clearly divide it from what we are discussing at Honolulu?

Dr. Kissinger: Why don't we wait til we have a package, and then decide?

Prime Minister Tanaka: Yes.

Dr. Kissinger: If we can solve the package we can solve the announcement.

Prime Minister Tanaka: Yes.

[Omitted here is a discussion of unrelated subjects.]

97.   Memorandum From Secretary of the Treasury Shultz to President Nixon[1]

Washington, August 25, 1972.

SUBJECT

Economic Aspects of this Month's Negotiations with the Japanese

The effort to achieve a short-term trade and financial package with the Japanese prior to your Hawaii trip is useful and desirable from several standpoints. At the same time, there is a clear danger that, carried too enthusiastically in certain directions for the sake of the *appearance* of a harmonious "big package," our basic continuing economic problem could be aggravated. I find some possibilities under consideration that would be potentially counterproductive by giving a false sense of progress, make it more difficult for the Japanese Government to build the support at home for more fundamental, needed action in the future, and possibly prejudice negotiations in other directions.

These dangers can be avoided if we do not fall into the trap of appearing to enthusiastically accept essentially "window dressing" transactions as a substitute for the hard and continuing effort to produce a lasting equilibrium in Japanese (and, thus, U.S.) payments. All efforts should be made to increase the imports from the United States, and to reduce the trade imbalances. However, prepayment should not be an objective.

Such payments are of little or no help to us in the short-run, since Japan has no alternative at present to holding dollars in any case. To the extent they relieve pressure for other measures to actually increase imports into Japan, they could be counterproductive to our longer-term efforts.

In the strictly financial area, the Japanese have apparently proffered long-term low interest rate loans in *yen*. These should certainly be rejected for they dig us in a deeper hole and are a bad precedent. Long-term *dollar* investments are a matter of relative indifference to us, and should not be accepted as a Japanese concession (although we are willing to talk about it when convenient to them).

Finally, the Japanese are interested in a statement from the highest levels of the U.S. Government that they can use to help sanctify the present yen-dollar exchange rate. Their pressure poses a problem. On the one hand, realistically, a change in the yen exchange rate may soon be nec-

---

[1] Source: National Archives, Nixon Presidential Materials, NSC Files, VIP Visits, Box 926, Tanaka Visit 31 Aug–1 Sept. No classification marking. Attached to Kissinger's August 29 memorandum to President Nixon, Document 98.

essary to achieve balance. On the other hand, in avoiding placing your prestige on the line with respect to the present yen rate, we do not want to give the opposite impression we look to a break-up of the Smithsonian Agreement. Thus, a formula of words must be found that, while supporting the Smithsonian Agreement in general as a useful interim step, avoids a commitment to the specific yen-dollar parity in the future.

George P. Shultz

---

98.   Memorandum From the President's Assistant for National
        Security Affairs (Kissinger) to President Nixon[1]

Washington, August 29, 1972.

[Omitted here are Section I on Purpose, Section II.A, Background, and subsections II.A.1, II.A.2, and II.A.3 on Reaffirmation of the Alliance, Japan's Normalization of Relations with the PRC, and US China Policy, respectively.]

4. *US-Japan Bilateral Economic Relations.* Although Japanese leaders now recognize Japan's major responsibility for reducing the massive trade deficit, they are reluctant to commit themselves to the kind of decisive, short-term ameliorative action we want. They fall back rather on projections that Japan's new economic recovery supplemented by Japanese government fiscal policy and other economic trends now underway will resolve the problem in about two years.

The problem at Honolulu will depend on the progress made in our current economic negotiations following up on Eberle's meetings in Hakone and Ingersoll's discussions preparatory to Honolulu. In these the Japanese are moving to develop a concrete package to meet the Tanaka Government commitment to reduce to below $3 billion the trade deficit by the end of this Japanese Fiscal Year (next March 31). There is greater reluctance to commit Japan to another billion reduction by the end of the following JFY.

We understand that the Tanaka Government's inability to agree at Hakone, and subsequently, on additional measures to reduce the trade

---

[1] Source: National Archives, Nixon Presidential Materials, NSC Files, VIP Visits, Box 926, Tanaka Visit 31 Aug–1 Sept. Top Secret; Sensitive. A stamped notation on the memorandum indicates that the President saw it.

gap further has probably been due to the unexpectedly strong resistance of mid-level bureaucrats in the economic ministries. These officials are loyal to Japanese business and industry interests. Nevertheless, past experience has indicated that we can be most effective by pressing the Japanese Government quietly but firmly to specific commitments that are politically feasible for it domestically. Indeed, US pressure is one of the most effective levers available to a Japanese Prime Minister and the Foreign Office to use with recalcitrant economic bureaucrats. Tanaka, with his currently strong political position (he is supported by over 70% of the people in opinion polls) is by virtue of this and his decisive temperament in a position to use such leverage.

[Omitted here are sections on Participants, Press Plans, and the Schedule.]

Tab C[2]

Economic Issues

The Problem

For the U.S. to: (a) allay protectionist pressure which could be troublesome next year, (b) successfully conclude monetary reform negotiations, and (c) obtain Congressional support for trade negotiation legislation, we must substantially improve our balance of payments position. Realistically, a major part of the improvement must come vis-à-vis Japan. However, our bilateral trade deficit, which was $3.2 billion in 1971 is projected by us to be about $3.8 billion in 1972. (The Japanese are now predicting $3.6 billion.) Japanese Foreign Exchange Reserves rose by over $10 billion in 1971 and today are above $16 billion.

Japan, for its part, recognizes in principle the necessity of reducing its trade and payments surplus which has made it the target of protectionist pressure in Europe and the U.S. However, the Government and the business community are extremely reluctant to translate this principle into concrete actions which are harmful to specific interests in Japan.

Japan's Position

Prime Minister Tanaka has stated that his target is reduction of the trade deficit to below $3 billion by the end of the current Japanese fiscal

---

[2] Secret; Sensitive. Tabs A–I are attached to Kissinger's memorandum. The others are: A. Talking Points; B. Japan's Normalization of Relations with the PRC; D. Korean Peninsula; E. Relations with the Soviet Union; F. US Military Presence in Japan; G. Biography of Tanaka; H. Memorandum to you from Secretary Rogers; and I. Memorandum to You from Secretary Laird.

year (March 31, 1973). [This was the target agreed on in the Tanaka/Kissinger meeting.][3]

Tanaka has put substantial pressure on his bureaucracy to come up with an acceptable package. His objective was to have this ready prior to the Summit so that detailed economic issues would not have to be discussed, and in order to avoid the appearance that Japan had made concessions at Hawaii under pressure from the U.S. Tanaka also did not wish to bring with him his Minister of International Trade and Industry, Nakasone.

In the package put together as the result of Ambassador Eberle's meetings with the Japanese at Hakone and Ambassador Ingersoll's follow-up the Japanese have agreed to purchase $320 million in uranium enrichment services, $320 million worth of civil aviation equipment including wide-bodied aircraft, $20 million worth of helicopters and aviation related facilities, and $26 million worth of special agricultural purchases. Total value: $686 million.

In addition Japan *projects* an estimated increase in agricultural purchases, over last year's level, of $270 million and in purchases of fishery and forestry products of $120 million, plus $24 million in additional purchases of U.S. feed grain resulting from a reduction in sales from Japan's stockpile of feed rice. Total value: $414 million.

Japan has also agreed to allow 100% foreign-owned investment in retail operations totaling up to 11 stores and in limited import-processing activities such as film and cosmetics; also, to permit an increase in the U.S. share of the Japanese computer market. The AEC and the Japanese have agreed to use their best efforts to set up a working group to examine feasibility of a joint-venture uranium enrichment facility to be built in the U.S.

Japan wants to make the announcement of these specifics in a separate press release.[4]

The Japanese allege that—aside from the above and some minor steps to liberalize imports—the Japanese political situation presently precludes a) removal of quotas (34 GATT illegal quotas are still retained) although there is some possibility that the quota levels on oranges, juices, beef, and feeder cattle will be reduced, or b) special budget increases for procurement from the U.S. They argue that last December's yen revaluation, projected Japanese economic growth with an attendant increase in import demand, and orderly exporting prac-

---

[3] See Document 96. Brackets in the source text.

[4] The trade package was announced at the conclusion of the talks in Honolulu on September 1. See Department of State *Bulletin,* September 25, 1972, pp. 332–333.

tices will *with time* move us closer to equilibrium. They might argue that beyond present commitments, it will be difficult at this time to make any formal commitment on specifics or targets for the next Japanese fiscal year.

U.S. Position

This package—containing the purchase of U.S. goods and services of over $1 billion—while helpful in reducing our trade and payments imbalance, contains some items—uranium enrichment, wide-bodied aircraft, helicopters—which are being prepaid. These represent real sales for now and the future but except for agricultural purchases these do not help our *trade* balance *this year.* The package is an indicator of our mutual effort to turn around the growing imbalance in U.S.-Japanese trade. But its significance in this regard is diminished without a Japanese commitment to reductions in the trade imbalance. Accordingly, it is important that we receive in the joint statement a commitment that Japan intends to reduce by March 31 its trade surplus with the U.S. to below $3 billion, or by an amount of roughly $1 billion from the present projected surplus of $3.8 to $4 billion. Further, we want to receive an additional commitment to continue to work for additional concrete measures to reduce the imbalance and, on a longer-term balance of trade objective, that Japan will exert its best effort to reduce the trade deficit by at least an additional $1 billion in the next Japanese fiscal year beginning on April 1, 1973.[5]

We also want to:

—Stress the importance we attach to cooperation with Japan in multilateral trade negotiations and monetary reform.
—Reach agreement with Japan to hold future meetings at a high level to review evolving economic relationships.
—Agree to hold a meeting of the Ministerial-level Committee on Trade and Economic Affairs (ECONCOM) in the first half of CY 1973.[6]

[If Tanaka does not agree to commit himself to reduce the deficit by an additional $1 billion during the next fiscal year, you may wish to get a commitment that we will work to develop *concrete measures* to further reduce our trade imbalance and that we will review progress toward this end at ECONCOM and other high level meetings to be held next year.][7]

Should the Japanese raise the issue of the Smithsonian Agreement in such a way as to seek our agreement that the rates are unalterable or

---

[5] No separate press release has been found. The Joint Statement is printed ibid., pp. 331–332.

[6] These three objectives were affirmed in the Joint Statement.

[7] Brackets in the source text.

to get our support to help defend the present yen rate to prevent another yen revaluation (which Tanaka and Japanese businessmen wish to
avoid because it would cut into Japanese competitiveness), our position
is that the Smithsonian Agreement was a propitious beginning and we
should now work to achieve fundamental reform. We should avoid a
commitment to any specific yen-dollar rate in the future. [George
Shultz' attached memorandum explains this position in detail.][8]

---

[8] See Document 97. Brackets in the source text.

---

99.   Memorandum of Conversation[1]

Oahu, Hawaii, August 31, 1972, 1 p.m.

PARTICIPANTS

Prime Minister Kakuei Tanaka of Japan
Ambassador Nobuhiko Ushiba
Hidetoshi Ukawa, Chief, Second North American Section, American Affairs Bureau,
    MOFA (Interpreter)

President Richard Nixon
Mr. Henry A. Kissinger, Assistant to the President for National Security Affairs
Mr. James J. Wickel, American Embassy, Tokyo (Interpreter)

SUBJECT

Prime Minister Tanaka's Call on President Nixon

[Omitted here are an exchange of pleasantries and discussion of the
Emperor's visit to Alaska and of former Prime Minister Sato.]

The Prime Minister then recalled telling Dr. Kissinger recently that
constant contact, both official and unofficial, is very important.

Dr. Kissinger noted that the Prime Minister said this is important in
both the political and economic fields.

The Prime Minister recalled, in connection with economics, that he
also said Japan must have a strong American economy. The fundamen-

---

[1] Source: National Archives, Nixon Presidential Materials, NSC Files, VIP Visits, Box
926, Tanaka Visit 31 Aug–1 Sept. Secret; Sensitive. The meeting was held in the
Presidential Suite of the Kuilima Hotel. According to the President's Daily Diary, the
meeting ended at 3:15 p.m. and was followed by a meeting of the principals with their
official delegations. Kenzo Yoshida, Director General of the Asian Affairs Bureau,
Ministry of Foreign Affairs, participated on the Japanese side in Ambassador Ushiba's
place. (Ibid., White House Central Files)

tal view of the GOJ is that American prosperity means Japanese prosperity. While the current economic problems could not be resolved in one move, he expressed the belief that constant communication, with meetings between officials and experts every month if necessary, while keeping watch on long-term trends would lead to a smooth solution satisfactory to both sides.

The President noted that one of the reasons he appointed Ambassador Ingersoll is that we need in Japan a businessman with a good economic background. The Prime Minister, he noted, has not only achieved success in business but has the further qualification of having served as Finance Minister and Minister of International Trade and Industry.

The Prime Minister said that he appreciated the appointment of Ambassador Ingersoll, who could foresee problems in all aspects of the relationship, not just economic ones. It was, he said, a happy choice, since he is an expert in economic affairs. The Prime Minister said that he knew Ambassador Ingersoll many years before, having met him through David Kennedy, when he was still head of Continental Illinois. He noted that he had, as Finance Minister some years ago, approved the establishment of Continental Illinois' branches in Tokyo and Kobe.

The Prime Minister cautioned that trade negotiations through government channels only tended to develop into item-by-item negotiations, and pointed out that it is more effective to have consultations between specialists, with a view toward expansion of long-term balanced trade to the mutual advantage of both countries. Therefore, he appreciated the fact that Ambassador Ingersoll does not confine himself to official contacts with himself and the Foreign Minister, but also speaks broadly to the business community in Japan, which understands him so well.

The President said that he knows negotiations to resolve the great imbalance in our trade are difficult. He is glad to hear there is some progress. He also understood that the counterparts are discussing the technical points in the other meeting.[2] He emphasized that a skilled and experienced politician would understand that the present trade imbalance might appear to be advantageous to Japan, but if allowed to grow could lead to rising protectionism in the Congress. We should understand, he said, that it is in our mutual interest to resolve this trade imbalance as much as possible so as to prevent any move toward restriction issues, but rather to provide for freer trade, which is in the interest of both Japan and the United States, which are great economic powers. He realized that some Japanese businessmen, like our own,

---

[2] The results of the trade negotiation were announced in Honolulu on September 1; see footnote 4, Document 98.

would tend to take a negative attitude toward any actions taken which they thought would result in a detriment to their own short-range interests. However, in viewing the long-term, he stressed that we as political leaders must create conditions which encourage the reduction of barriers. This, he said, we can do only if the members of the Diet and of our own Congress are convinced of the long-term interest to both countries of redressing the balance. Japan's businessmen and manufacturers are competitive and efficient, he said, and our own businessmen and manufacturers have that reputation. Therefore, we should welcome competition, and as political leaders he said both of us should do all we can to see that barriers are not raised. Therefore the GOJ moves to reduce the present trade imbalance would have, he believed, a salutary effect on both public opinion and in the Congress.

The Prime Minister said that an excessive imbalance in trade did not serve either nation, and is undesirable. Therefore, he wished to do his best to reduce the current imbalance. Japan would make specific efforts to reduce the imbalance, in order to continue to benefit from expanding trade. However, he did not believe this matter could be solved in half a year, or a year. Having served as Minister of Finance some three years, as an LDP policy-maker, and also as Minister of International Trade and Industry for a year, he felt he is qualified as an expert. While in office, therefore, he said he wishes to bring about an "ideal situation." While continuing to consult between governments, he said the Government of Japan would also continue its efforts to persuade business to accept necessary measures.

The Prime Minister added that the President's term of office is four years, but his own term as LDP President is only three.

The President said that he is young, the youngest to serve as a Minister and also to serve as Prime Minister.

The Prime Minister said that he was also the youngest man to serve as a Diet member, but pointed out that long life does not depend on chronological age. While the President could serve eight years, he could serve as LDP President only six years (two three-year terms).

The President asked if that is all he could serve.

The Prime Minister replied that this is all, unless LDP party regulations are amended, or unless he stepped down after two terms and later ran for another term.

The Prime Minister said that he views Japan-U.S. economic problems as being important. Therefore, he has been meeting with Ambassador Ingersoll, and Ambassador Eberle, and wishes to bring about some conclusion. Japan's entire post-war economic recovery has been based on the dollar, he said, and therefore the maintenance of the value of the dollar and continued growth of the American economy are also in the interest of Japan, insomuch as these contribute to the maintenance of world peace and the position of the free world. Japan, he said, wishes to cooperate in the interest of expanding the American economy.

The President said this is mutual. A strong, healthy Japanese economy is in our interest. He realized that Japan has a special problem with respect to playing a military role in the Pacific and Asia, but Japanese economic influence could be decisive in many areas. Therefore, it is in our interest that there be a strong, vigorous Japanese economy, so that Japan could play a vital role in Southeast Asia, which would help develop the whole region, and would be decisive. He commented that the Prime Minister would read in the press statements reflecting the feeling by some of our political leaders and businessmen that Japan is a serious competitor to be dealt with, but noted that he does not share their feelings. Healthy competition benefits both nations, he believes, except, of course, when the trade imbalance is too great.

The Prime Minister said that he wished to discuss the healthy balance of trade noted by the President. Within two or three years Japan wishes to restrain its surplus on current account to one percent of GNP, which would be used to finance economic aid of one percent of GNP to the LDCs. Moreover, of that amount the Government of Japan wishes to reach the ideal level of 0.7% of governmental developmental assistance as soon as possible. It is said by some that Japan has attained economic affluence, he said, but this is not true. There is an excessive concentration of population in urban centers, such as Tokyo and Osaka, which gives rise to many problems like pollution and inadequate housing. Japan lags behind the United States in social capital formation, he said, and great investments are needed for social capital and to improve living conditions. Thus, great domestic investments must be made, as well as large contributions to economic assistance to the LDCs. He said that the Government of Japan hopes to move forward toward realizing both goals.

In this connection, the Prime Minister added that Japan should cooperate with the Southeast Asian nations and the ROK in providing both aid and investment. When the tensions in Vietnam have been reduced, he said that Japan should also provide aid and investments to help stabilize the lives of the people. He noted Japan's promise at UNCTAD[3] to attain the goal of governmental aid of 0.7% of GNP by the end of the decade. This would equal the entire budget to support the Government of Japan Defense Forces. While this is a difficult objective, he said the Government of Japan should tell the people this aid is essen-

---

[3] UNCTAD III convened in Santiago, Chile, in April 1972.

tial, and gain their understanding. With the cooperation of the United States over the past quarter of a century Japan has achieved great economic progress and Japan now wishes to assume a larger burden in contributing to peace and the development of the LDCs, on the basis of full consultation with the United States.

[Omitted here is a discussion of relations with the EEC, Vietnam, and China.]

100.   Memorandum of Conversation[1]

Washington, September 11, 1972, 10 a.m.

PARTICIPANTS

The President
Secretary Rogers, State
Secretary Shultz, Treasury
Secretary Peterson, Commerce
Secretary Butz, Agriculture
Deputy Secretary Rush, Defense
Caspar Weinberger, OMB
Herbert Stein, CEA
Ambassador William D. Eberle, STR
General Haig, NSC
Peter M. Flanigan, Executive Director, CIEP

SUBJECT

CIEP Executive Committee Meeting

President: This meeting will be devoted to the trade issues relating to the European Community. It will cover these in general but not be specific on particular trade matters. Peter, would you like to start off.

Flanigan: It has been the basic tenet of US foreign policy to support strongly the formation and enlargement of the EC. This was primarily

[1] Source: National Archives, Nixon Presidential Materials, NSC Files, Agency Files, Box 219, CIEP. Secret. Drafted by Hormats; an attached NSC Correspondence Profile sheet indicates it was approved September 18. The meeting was held in the Cabinet Room. A tape of the conversation is ibid., White House Tapes, Cabinet Room. Another record of this meeting, apparently drafted in the CIEP, is attached to a November 3 memorandum from Flanigan to Kissinger on U.S.-European relations. (Ibid., NSC Files, Agency Files, Box 219, CIEP) Background material for this meeting, circulated to the President and CIEP members, is ibid. According to the President's Daily Diary, the meeting ended at 11:06 a.m. (Ibid., White House Central Files)

for political reasons. The economic problems which were raised by the establishment of the EC were not enough to pose a specific threat to us although in the examination of the Rome Treaty several years ago we raised, and still maintain, a variety of objections concerning its compatibility with GATT. But recent EC enlargement and spread of preferences are more questionable legally and more damaging to our trade interests. Bill Eberle has strongly defended our interests. The atmosphere has been one in which the US has been engaged in a growing sense of confrontation with the EC. These can escalate. We are challenging the EC in an effort to limit damage to our interests and obtain cooperation in a broader area. The strategy we engage in has implications for the forthcoming monetary negotiations and our multilateral trade negotiations with Europe next year. We should agree on appropriate responses in dealing with the EC.

There are three examples of how problems will develop:

—The Ten will have to effect a common tariff. We sell $125 million worth of grain to the UK. The EC will argue that we have been compensated by a reduction of their tariff on industrial products. We say "no."

—EC preferential arrangements violate the GATT. There is an issue over dealing with arrangements with Spain and Israel. We have already filed our objections. The issue now is whether we escalate our objections. Or, should we deal with these as part of a broader agreement?

—In January it will be a GATT "open season". Our tariffs are bound for a three-year period. On January 1 of next year we have the right to change them or we can suspend them and see what the EC will do. We need guidance. We must keep in mind our broader objectives which are to reduce barriers to trade and contribute to a reduction in tension in our economic, political, and security interests in Europe.

The STR paper[2] provides 4 options—from doing a little to an out and out confrontation.

—A. *Downplay confrontations* and concentrate on a few things that we can solve such as a standard code for products. We would postpone any development of any major negotiating position until after the election. This assumes that France has maximum leverage at this point and the CAP is popular in certain quarters of Germany. We would wait until the climate is better and not develop a strategy at this time.

—B. *Atlantic cooperation approach.* Under this we would lay the groundwork in the economic and political area for a possible major political initiative next year. Unlike Option A, this adds a definitive positive cost to the way we move over the next few months. We would ease

---

[2] Not further identified.

off of confrontations which are harmful to the climate and avoid rocking the boat, but this would allow current actions by the EC against our trade interests to proceed unchecked.

—C. *Modified confrontation.* Continue to defend interests strongly and bring many problems to a head but stop short of bringing issues to a GATT vote, which we would probably lose. We could deal with major issues at a Summit. We would press for solution of some issues even at the risk of damaging relations. This could be combined with Option B. In our negotiations on EC enlargement we would attempt to get compensation on grain or we could unilaterally unbind tariffs.

—D. *Precipitate a crisis.* This is based on the premise that meaningful solutions cannot be reached unless there is an atmosphere of impending crisis. This would obviously bring us into major confrontation with the EC and spill over into other aspects of our relationship if we cannot get the solutions we want.

In interagency discussions all parties felt we should vigorously promote US interests. Some felt we should do so to the point of confrontation. Others preferred combining Option B and Option C, which was to work more toward a cooperative approach. All felt this should be developed as part of a broader US-European relationship.

President: What do you think of this, Bill?

Eberle: It is imperative for us to carry the major share of the initiative. The EC is not able to do so. We cannot step back. We must carry things through if anything is to be done. Option C permits us to do this and get a major feel for the atmosphere in which these negotiations will proceed.

President: How will the Europeans react?

Eberle: I am "bearish" about prospects now but see hopeful opportunities on the horizon. The German Minister of Finance[3] says that the CAP costs more than the total contribution of agriculture to Europe's GNP. The Germans and French have made "backdoor" suggestions that we all agree in Article XXIV negotiations that there is some trade damage from the CAP and then carry over this agreement to the comprehensive negotiations in settlement. There are forces starting to build up. We should keep pressure on. There is hope. The Europeans feel we should not back away. If we back away, it takes away support from those in the EC who agree with us.

President: Will the new EC be lined up against us?

Eberle: We should assume this. Today the EC is isolated in the GATT on the question of enlargement. The key issue is whether they

---

[3] Helmut Schmidt replaced Karl Schiller as German Finance Minister in July.

will accept more economic cooperation with North America or whether they will back away.

President: Nationalism in Europe is stronger than nationalism in the US and it is damned strong here. They enjoy kicking the US around. Eighty-eight percent of all the European media is violently anti-US. They will cut their own throats economically to take us on politically. We cannot get a very liberal trade program through the US. On these issues our people are very nationalistic.

Eberle: Nationalism is stronger in Europe against Japan than against the US.

President: We need to consider possible Congressional reaction to our failure to press our trade interests. Nationalist pressures are strong pressures in Congress. The Foreign Affairs and Foreign Relations Committees are unrepresentative. They only represent their own Committees. The Foreign Affairs Committee is a little more representative. But they do not represent the feelings of the country. We can't get too far out in front of our constituents. They are very tough on trade. These feelings are strong not only in the labor movement but among a large segment of the business community.

Shultz: In Europe there are different nationalisms—German, French, and British nationalisms, and on monetary policy they sometimes differ. There are different opinions in different countries.

Rogers: It is sort of a mixed-up nationalism. The question is, are they supporting the EC or individual nations. Trade questions will be decided on what is good for everybody. Our position has to be the one that Bill Eberle outlined. Elements of Option B could be combined with C. If we offer to liberalize, it will have a domestic problem. Our dairy policy is the same as the CAP. If we appear willing to make concessions on agricultural policy the dairy farmers would go up in smoke.

President: Let there be no doubt that our position before the election is one of protectionism. We should not indicate that we are preparing any concession not in the interest of the US. If anyone does, we will repudiate it.

Rush: The Europeans protect their domestic interests and their bloc interests. Both European and individual country nationalism is against the US.

President: What is your opinion of the nature of the EC nationalism—European or individual.

Flanigan: When they can do something to protect their national interests they will. When they can't do it on their own (e.g. the development of aerospace industry) they will do it as a group. For instance, they are developing an industrial policy. We should resist the EC effort to subsidize particular industries or develop high technology industries through preferential arrangements.

Peterson: We should confront the Europeans. If we appear to be liberalizing now, Burke–Hartke pressure is likely to develop. We must recognize that there is a security aspect to our relationship. On security and military, the Europeans have the best of both worlds. Trade issues will have to be related to larger issues including our military relationship. They need to be played at the Presidential level. If they fear we will abandon our military support, it will affect the way they deal on trade matters.

Rogers: They are not about to change the CAP. To change the CAP would cause serious problems for them as governments. Likewise, there are preferential trade issues and relations with the EFTA non-applicants which are important to them. At the moment they are only problems of principle for us, but do not hurt us badly. The question of a trade bloc, however, is a serious problem. It will have to be dealt with in the larger context of trade negotiations.

The question is how much do we want to threaten them with them in public. Do we want to go so far as to threaten withdrawal of concessions. This causes many problems. We should not do this in the next two months. We have a strong case but they have some problems with us too. It is not fair to assume they do not have complaints too. Our policy should be tough without any specific threats. We should hit them with a general position but without specific threats. We should also get them to adopt a structure in which we can negotiate with them on a regular basis.

President: In the following months we should not say anything forthcoming on trade. For example, my speech to the IMF meeting will not be forthcoming on trade matters.[4]

However, more is involved here than just questions of "horse-trading" between soybeans and cheese. The question is what Europe wants its position to be vis-à-vis the US and the Soviet Union. We hear about Finlandization of Europe. If Europe should adopt a trade policy which is anti-US, it could affect attitudes in the US—bring about an unenthusiastic attitude toward Europe—and will carry over into the political area. There will be pressure to withdraw divisions and NATO would come apart. The idea that Europe can defend itself without the US is "bull". If NATO comes apart, they will be an economic giant but a military and political pigmy. The USSR will encroach on them. It will not be in the traditional way but a new-style invasion. European leaders are

---

[4] For text of the September 25 address, see *Public Papers of the Presidents of the United States: Richard M. Nixon, 1972*, pp. 907–911.

264 Foreign Relations, 1969–1976, Volume III

terrified at that prospect. European leaders want to "screw" us and we want to "screw" them in the economic area.

But political relationships should be overriding for us and for them. What will matter in trade is its relationship to the total problem—what we want our relationship with Europe to be. Between now and the election we should say nothing, but we should give careful thought about how trade relations fit in the context of our overall relations. We should examine what price we might have to pay on the trade side for this political relationship, and they should do so as well. We should not allow the umbilical cord between the US and Europe to be cut and Europe to be nibbled away by the Soviets. We need to strengthen the bonds of trade, monetary relations, exchanges, etc. As an example of what I mean, you recall that when the Soviet runner won the 100 meter race in the Olympics he said that the race marked the end of an era and now the Europeans are the best. Basically this is just racism, since they are white and our sprinters are black, but the idea of Europe versus the US is a Soviet line. This was an example of a new style, with the Soviets trying to identify themselves with the Europeans and against the US. Brezhnev and Kosygin say almost the same things.

All non-Communist countries in Europe do not want to come under that influence. They know we have divisions and nuclear weapons. It is easy for us to say we will take them out of Europe, but it is definitely not in our interest to do so. Chayes goes around Europe talking about removal of troops, and every time Americans see us take a bad rap in basketball or something they remember. This contributes to the growing sentiment in the US such as "damn the Europeans" and the "foreigners are doing us in". It is true that the foreigners are doing bad things to us and we should do some bad things to them. But we must be under no illusions. We cannot turn isolationist in the broader context.

If we were only looking at trade, we could get along without the Europeans or the rest of the world since trade is much less important to our GNP than to theirs. Trade is the froth on top of the beer, but beer without froth does not taste too bad. But we need to look at the bigger picture. For instance, we should treat Japan with tender loving care because what Europe would become to the Soviets, Japan to China would be even more. Trade is important politically. Trade relationships can benefit political relationships, although wars have been fought between countries with trading relationships with one another. Our interests are served by being as tough as we can without going over the line where anti-US sentiment will cause them to turn against us and break with us. The Europeans recognize that they do not matter in the world any more. They know it. Economic issues are the things they now concentrate on. They are big for them and small for us. That means we will probably have to give more than our interest, strictly construed, would require. However, for the moment we should let the Europeans know that there are a lot of Americans who would welcome our getting out of Europe, and Japan. But we are fighting this. The Europeans should realize why. It is not because our economic survival is at stake but rather because we have a major interest in our overall relations with them, which we value highly, and in the interest of world peace.

The whole area of our economic relations affects our leverage position in the world. In the future our relations will have a larger economic content. This will require more subtlety in the way we conduct our overall relations. We are best to play this game. We are the strongest. However, this is not the time to decide this. After the elections is the time. Then we can do what we have to do. It is going to be very hard to sell trade liberalization to the Congress and the people. We need to make a strong case. We will be prepared to do it because we know that more is at stake than just trade, because our interests require it. But for now we should not talk in public about the political-commercial trade-off.

Peterson: How do you regard the political-commercial tradeoff?

President: There obviously is a link between economics and political-security issues, but we should not link it openly now.

Peterson: What are the possibilities for a longer term political-security link, and the prospects for selling a liberalization bill to the Congress?

President: We need good results in the election and we can get a lot done. We are looking to get a majority. A majority has not happened since 1956. It is difficult for a Republican to get a landslide; a majority will be important. With that we can make a major move to propose what is best for the country and try to educate the country so that it sees the issues in the broader context. It takes time for people to understand an issue like this, but they will come around. What is at stake here is a major shift in the world balance of power, particularly among ourselves, the Russians, the Chinese, and the Japanese. As regards Europe, they will have one hell of a time acting as a bloc. They do not get along with each other. The French don't get along with the Germans, the Germans don't get along with the British. It will be some time before they can learn to act as a group. This means we have to work with the heads of Government in the various countries and not that jackass in the European Commission in Brussels.[5]

---

[5] Presumably a reference to EC President Mansholt. The other account of this meeting (see footnote 1 above) includes the same characterization.

[To Peterson]⁶ It is important that after the elections we look at the long-range relations. We have to tie this in with the whole problem of what we want our relations with Europe to be. Europeans are used to thinking internationally. They argue about Tanzania and their other relations abroad. We have to think internationally. We are it in the Free World. We would be missing a great opportunity if we do not see the broad picture and have such a picture to guide us. Then we can educate the people to support that kind of policy. But they should see how it affects their own self interests.

Peterson: We can get something in the economic area by using political-security leverage.

President: Yes.

Rogers: After the elections we can get down to the business of a formal study but for the moment suggestions should be kept private and not reduce things to writing. They should be discussed orally. If we do have a study made, it will get out.

President: Yes, controversial memoranda are likely to leak. Like the grain deal. You remember how hard we tried to keep the amounts secret. Now we are accused of having told the companies. It is ridiculous.

Everyone should be thinking of how we should achieve what we have talked about at this meeting.

---

⁶ Brackets in the source text.

---

101.   **Memorandum From the President's Assistant for International Economic Affairs (Flanigan) to the Special Representative for Trade Negotiations (Eberle)**¹

Washington, September 12, 1972.

SUBJECT

Trade Negotiations with the European Community

In the light of the discussions in the Council for International Economic Policy of September 11, 1972 relating to your August 21, 1972 memorandum entitled "US Response to Developing US-EC Trade

---

¹ Source: National Archives, Nixon Presidential Materials, NSC Files, Agency Files, Box 219, CIEP. Confidential. A copy was sent to Kissinger.

Confrontation",[2] the President has decided that for the present you should pursue a policy of modified confrontation exerting controlled but mounting pressures on issues involving both our trade interests and the principles of the present system. This should be done bearing in mind the overriding importance of our political relations with Europe and that our trade problems must be resolved in the context of larger policy considerations.[3]

PMF

---

[2] See Document 100 and footnote 2 thereto.

[3] With substantially the same language, Flanigan reissued this text on September 25 as CIEP Decision Memorandum No. 14, with copies to most members of the CIEP. (National Archives, Nixon Presidential Materials, NSC Files, Agency Files, Box 219, CIEP)

---

102. Memorandum From the Deputy Secretary of State (Irwin) to President Nixon[1]

Washington, October 7, 1972.

SUBJECT

Fifth Round of US-EC Consultations, October 5–6

The Fifth Round of US-EC Consultations on October 5 and 6 produced the most candid and in-depth discussion since the initiation of the US-EC Consultations.[2] The US side persistently questioned the Europeans on where the European Community was going, both in its internal development of common agricultural, industrial and monetary policies and in the continued proliferation of preferential trading arrangements going well beyond Europe. We stressed that the seeming lack of concern on the part of Europeans for the difficulties which their actions caused for the United States could have dangerous political repercussions. We particularly voiced concern over the Commission's proposed Mediterranean policy which is to be presented to the Council next Monday. We said that the most important move, both symbolically and practically, they could make to reassure the US was to drop the reverse preference provisions from these and other preferential agreements. We stressed the importance of

---

[1] Source: National Archives, Nixon Presidential Materials, NSC Files, Agency Files, Box 219, CIEP. Limited Official Use. Attached to a November 3 memorandum from Flanigan to Kissinger regarding U.S.-European relations.

[2] The series of consultations was inaugurated in October 1970; see Documents 44 and 47.

obtaining positive signals from the Europeans of a willingness to approach these real issues between us in a spirit looking toward cooperative solutions. A most helpful signal, we said, would be a positive declaration on US-European relations at the European Summit.

The EC group was chaired by Commissioner Ralf Dahrendorf in charge of external relations. I chaired the US Delegation which included Bill Eberle, Herb Stein, and representatives from State, Treasury, Commerce, Agriculture and Labor.[3] Bill Eberle was forceful in stating US concerns and in relating them to the many specifics in the trade field for which he is responsible without ever losing sight of the larger political and security contexts which surround all of these issues.

The EC side reported on prospects for the Summit which they indicated will probably produce only a "minor" or "passing" reference to the need to work on relations with the United States. They said this would be balanced by statements from individual governments around the Summit which would be more forthcoming. I said the need was for a statement from the Summit itself, not from friends in the corridor, of willingness to work with the United States in reordering economic relations through multilateral negotiations on monetary reform and trade liberalization. I also expressed the hope that the Summit can avoid an inflexible position on continuing EC preferential trading arrangements.

In a discussion of agricultural policy, Carroll Brunthaver of Agriculture expressed our willingness to work towards far-reaching liberalization of agricultural trade but pointed out that recent Community actions on agriculture would make it difficult for us to hold the line against our own protectionist pressures and move toward a liberalizing negotiation. In connection with a discussion of the Community's industrial policy, which the EC side described as not likely to develop rapidly, we expressed concern over plans to restructure the European aircraft industry in a manner which may hurt an important American export. The EC side took note of this position, but referred obliquely to our recent action on the GE–SNECMA case as seeming to preclude the possibility of joint ventures with the United States in the aviation industry and, therefore, forcing them to combine among themselves to achieve sufficient size and strength to compete with US firms.[4]

Dahrendorf described the proposed EC Mediterranean policy to be considered by the Council of Ministers as required to deal with the economic problems of the Mediterranean countries caused by the enlargement of the Community and as furthering political interests common to

---

[3] Earlier sessions of the U.S.-EC Consultations had been chaired on the U.S. side by Deputy Under Secretary of State for Economic Affairs Samuels.

[4] Reference is to the U.S. determination in September 1972 not to license the export of sensitive jet engine technology to France.

Europe and the US. Bill Eberle and I made clear that the US favors strengthening the political and economic ties between the Community and the Mediterranean countries as a contribution to the stability in the area. What the United States objects to is the discriminatory aspects of this policy, especially the reverse preferences which can only be interpreted in this country as the continuation of a policy of forming a large preferential bloc around the Community. As a result of this exchange, Dahrendorf has a clearer picture of the objectionable feature of the proposed Mediterranean policy.

With respect to the Community's free-trade arrangements with the EFTA neutrals, we made clear we expect a thorough examination in the GATT and action to protect American interests. We cited paper and other industries as likely to be injured unless the Community takes offsetting action. Dahrendorf indicated that there was a growing realization in the Community that something would have to be done for the US and other third countries as a result of the Community's arrangement with the EFTA countries.

Finally, the two sides held a useful discussion of preparations for multilateral trade negotiations. Bill Eberle outlined in general terms the state of preparations in this country and the timetable we expect to follow leading towards the opening of multilateral negotiations in September of 1973. He stressed the need for expeditious action on the GATT procedures under Article 24 with respect to EC enlargement so that these issues could be disposed of before the beginning of multilateral negotiations. It was agreed that there would have to be further meetings to consult on the content of the respective negotiating authorities of the US and the Community to insure that they are mutually reinforcing.

The main area we were not able to discuss was energy. Commissioner Haferkamp who is responsible for energy matters was unable to come at the last minute in part because he was still in the process of gaining Commission approval for a new policy on energy. Because I believe this will be a particularly important area for US-EC cooperation in the near future, I hope to be able to meet with Haferkamp to discuss the energy situation sometime in the coming weeks.

In sum, these meetings met the objectives we set for ourselves and provided us with an opportunity—coming before the Summit—to get our views across to the Commission on the main current issues in our relationship. By the end of our meetings the European representatives recognized that the US was seriously disturbed over the manner in which the EC was handling the GATT aspects of enlargement and the preferential trade aspects of arrangements with non-member countries.

John N. Irwin II

103.   Memorandum From the President's Assistant for International
        Economic Affairs (Flanigan) to President Nixon[1]

Washington, October 11, 1972.

SUBJECT

    United States-European Community Relations

1. On Thursday and Friday of last week the annual US-EC consultations were held in Washington between Administration representatives
headed by Deputy Secretary Irwin (attached at Tab A is his report) and
representatives of the Community headed by Commissioner Dahrendorf.[2]
The American positions were based on the decision, reached at recent
CIEP meeting, to keep maximum pressure on the Community in respect
to U.S. economic interests, short of creating an irresolvable confrontation.[3]

2. The net result of the consultations confirms your conviction that
the Community, and particularly its bureaucracy in Brussels, is determined to maximize its economic potential regardless of the cost to the
United States and the Atlantic system. While paying lip service to the
importance of Atlantic unity, specific decisions are resolved in favor of
the Community and contrary to the interests of the United States.
Examples of this, that were put forth at last week's meeting, were decisions by the Commission to propose to the Community governments
(a) a Mediterranean policy and (b) an industrial policy.

The Mediterranean policy is based on perceived special political
and economic interests between the Community and the countries of
the Mediterranean basin. The policy would be implemented by special
technological and assistance programs and by trade preferences.
Clearly the latter exacerbate the discrimination against current U.S.
agricultural exports, and potential industrial exports to the Community.
Potentially more harmful would be extension of reverse preferences
given by developing Mediterranean countries to the Community, which
have even less justification.

The Commission's proposed industrial policy uses protectionist
devices, such as R&D subsidies, to foster high technology industries in
Europe. This is particularly designed to strengthen Europe's commercial airplane and computer industries, both being areas of strong U.S.
technological dominance and exports.

---

[1] Source: National Archives, Nixon Presidential Materials, NSC Files, Agency Files,
Box 219, CIEP. No classification marking. Attached to a November 3 memorandum from
Flanigan to Kissinger regarding U.S.-European relations.

[2] The consultations were held October 5–6. Irwin's report is Document 102.

[3] See Documents 100 and 101.

3. The current membership of the Commission is clearly dedicated to a course of action contrary to the U.S. economic interest. Happily, with the enlargement of the Community to nine, plus the elections in Germany and Holland, a new Commission will be formed shortly after the first of the year. Sicco Mansholt will be replaced as President by a Frenchman, and any replacement will be an improvement. The new Commissioners from England, Ireland (your meeting with Hillary should be helpful here)[4] and Denmark, and from Germany should the CDU win, could create a greater awareness of the importance of the Atlantic system and of American opinion. It will be important to schedule a quiet but high level visit to Brussels to meet with all the new Commissioners, especially the new President and the Commissioners for Finance, Trade, and Foreign Affairs very shortly after they are installed.

It will be even more important that the new governments in Bonn and the Hague be visited by high level Administration representatives shortly after their elections to attempt to develop a common position on the economic relationship of the Community to the U.S. Hopefully the makeup of these new governments will be sympathetic. Should the CDU win, both Strauss and Narjes, the proposed German Finance and Economics Ministers, have a reputation for an Atlantic viewpoint. I have preliminary work on such visits underway.

4. If we are to be successful in deflecting the Community from its current course, and in creating a climate in which we can reach meaningful agreement in the broader areas of monetary and trade reforms, we must develop viable solutions to the two major US-EC problems, the Common Agricultural Policy and the Community's growing number of Preference Agreements with non-Community countries.

Regarding preferences, every effort will be made to get agreement from the Community not to extend preferences to additional countries, though this horse is largely out of the barn.

With regard to preferences already granted to developed countries, largely European, our policy should be to (a) in the short run, get special tariff relief where an existing U.S. industry is hurt, such as our wood products industry, whose $600 million of annual exports to the Community are in danger, and (b) in the long run, reduce industrial tariffs multilaterally so that the tariff preferences are ineffective against U.S. exports.

With regard to the Community's preferences for developing countries, these should be subsumed in a multilateral program of general-

---

[4] The President met with Irish Foreign Minister Patrick Hillary on October 6. (National Archives, Nixon Presidential Materials, White House Central Files, President's Daily Dairy)

ized preferences, which the U.S. already supports. Reverse preferences, however, which are of no benefit to the developing countries, should be phased out. Several Community members have evidenced sympathy for this position. For these developing countries to which the Community wants to show a special interest, it can undertake a special program of aid, investment and technological assistance. So long as this special program does not include additional trade preferences which discriminate against the United States, this country would have no reason to object—rather it would applaud.

In the area of agriculture, the U.S. could direct its rhetoric more at international agricultural *trade* than at the Community's overall *agricultural policy*, which they consider to be an internal matter, though this is only a semantic difference. The Europeans must indicate a willingness, first, to reduce their subsidies to agricultural exports to third markets, and subsequently to reduce the protection in the future against agricultural imports into the Community. These, rather than a Common Agricultural Policy, are our rightful goals and could possibly be attainable.

5. In the broadest context, the strategy for our economic relations with Europe can only be a part of our overall relations with Europe. As agreed in the CIEP meeting, a review of these relations by NSC and CIEP is at the top of the work plan.

---

104.   **Action Memorandum From Helmut Sonnenfeldt and Robert Hormats of the National Security Council Staff to the President's Assistant for National Security Affairs (Kissinger)**[1]

Washington, October 16, 1972.

SUBJECT

Flanigan's Report to President on US-EC Relations

Bruce Kehrli has requested your comments and/or recommendations on the attached memorandum from Flanigan to the President on US-EC relations (Tab A).[2]

---

[1]   Source: National Archives, Nixon Presidential Materials, NSC Files, Agency Files, Box 219, CIEP. Limited Official Use.

[2]   Document 103.

The Flanigan Memo

The memorandum summarizes the salient issues of last week's annual US-EC consultations in Washington.[3] Irwin headed the US side; Dahrendorf, the European side. The US position—consistent with the results of the recent CIEP meeting—was to keep maximum pressure on the EC on economic matters but not create an irresolvable confrontation.[4]

Flanigan feels that the EC is determined to maximize its economic potential regardless of the cost to the US and the Atlantic system. Specific decisions are resolved in favor of the EC and contrary to US interests. Examples are (a) the Commission's proposal for a Mediterranean policy which would include trade preferences and (b) an EC industrial policy. The former exacerbates the discrimination against US agricultural exports and contains provisions for reverse preferences which discriminate against American exports to Mediterranean countries. The proposed industrial policy also contains protectionist devices, particularly in behalf of Europe's commercial airplane and computer industries.

Membership of the Commission—now dedicated to action contrary to the US economic interests—should change. Mansholt will be replaced as President by a Frenchman. Britain, Ireland and Denmark will also have Commissioners. It will be important to schedule a quiet but high-level visit to Brussels to meet with all the new Commissioners shortly after they are installed and visit the new Governments in Bonn and the Hague to attempt to develop a common position on our relationship with the EC.

We must develop viable solutions to the two major US-EC problems: the Common Agricultural Policy and EC preferential arrangements with non-Community countries. On the latter the "horse is largely out of the barn." Our policy should be (a) in the short run to get special tariff relief where a US industry is hurt, (b) in the long run to reduce industrial tariffs multilaterally so that tariff preferences do not discriminate against US exports. Preferences for developing countries should be subsumed under a multilateral program of generalized preferences, which the US supports. Reverse preferences should be phased out. The EC's development contribution to the developing countries should be made through special programs of aid, investment, and technical assistance.

In the area of agriculture the US should concentrate more on international agricultural trade rather than attacking the Community's agricultural policy, which they consider to be an internal matter. The Europeans

[3] See Document 102.
[4] See Documents 100 and 101.

must indicate a willingness to reduce subsidies to agricultural exports and reduce the protection against agricultural imports into the Community.

The strategy for our economic relations with Europe can be only a part of our overall relations. As agreed in the CIEP meeting, a review of these relations by NSC and CIEP is at the top of the work plan.

Our View

We believe Flanigan's view of European attitudes is oversimplified. There are plenty of people in Europe, if not in the Commission then in top spots in various Western Governments, of whom it cannot be fairly said that they are "determined to maximize economic potential regardless of the cost to the US and the Atlantic system." There are on both sides of the Atlantic important and senior leaders and officials who are eager to find a way to manage our admitted economic problems in ways that will not destroy those common interests we share.

Purely economic "solutions" in most cases (especially regarding fundamental issues such as preferential arrangements and agriculture) may be impossible without a heavy political component. The Mediterranean and Africa are cases in point. It is we, after all, who have urged the Europeans to raise their sights and assume responsibilities around the world which we no longer can or should assume to the extent we used to. However, it is true that so far the Europeans seem bent on doing so almost exclusively by economic and commercial devices, which are discriminatory in nature and are bound to bring them into conflict with those responsible for our economic affairs and with potent US economic interest groups.

Apart from this Flanigan makes a number of valid and constructive recommendations. His general conclusions are consistent with those expressed in Hormats' memorandum to you of October 11, a copy of which is attached (Tab B).[5] We both agree that a major US effort will be necessary to construct a will and a means of solving our problems with the EC in a way which will strengthen and make more sustainable the US-Europe political relationship. An NSC/CIEP study to develop strategy for this effort is of course a good thing provided that in the interim things are not done that deprive the President of any option but confrontation.

Recommendation:

That you authorize us to indicate that you have no objection to Flanigan's memo (Tab A) going to the President.[6]

---

[5] Not printed.

[6] Haig initialed his approval of the recommendation.

105. Memorandum From Acting Secretary of State Irwin to President Nixon[1]

Washington, October 20, 1972.

SUBJECT

European Community Trade Agreements with Spain and Israel

The Problem

The European Community seems intent on continuing to proliferate preferential trading arrangements with non-member countries which are contrary both to the non-discriminatory trading principles we favor and to specific U.S. trading interests. We have consistently stated that we will object to any of these arrangements which are inconsistent with GATT and that, where our trade interests are damaged, we will seek specific compensation. These arrangements include (1) existing ones with the EFTA non-applicants, (2) existing ones with former colonial states, (3) existing ones with Greece and Turkey, (4) proposed new arrangements with Mediterranean states and others, and (5) existing arrangements with Spain and Israel which are special cases.

On the agreements with Spain and Israel, there is general interagency agreement that we should, as we have told the EC, Spain and Israel we would, invoke the procedures of Article 23(1) of the GATT. In doing so we would propose that the EC, Spain and Israel make adjustments to the agreements to eliminate or greatly reduce the discrimination against U.S. exports, and to the extent that U.S. trade continues to suffer damage we would seek compensatory duty reductions on other products of interest to the U.S. The claim of U.S. trade damage resulting from the agreements should be both defensible and substantial enough to demonstrate the seriousness of our concern over this discrimination against U.S. trade interests so to act as a deterrent to the further proliferation of preferential arrangements. Negotiating instructions consist-

---

[1] Source: National Archives, Nixon Presidential Materials, NSC Files, Subject Files, Box 322, European Common Market Volume II 1971–72. Confidential. An earlier draft of the memorandum is attached to an October 12 memorandum from Deputy Under Secretary of the Treasury Bennett to Under Secretary Volcker for use at his October 13 lunch with Flanigan. (Washington National Records Center, Department of the Treasury, Files of Under Secretary Volcker: FRC 56 79 15, October 13, 1972 Flanigan Working Lunch) The lunch was also attended by Irwin, Stein, and Eberle. In an October 17 memorandum from Flanigan to Irwin, Volcker, Stein, and Eberle regarding follow-up to the October 13 luncheon, Flanigan noted that there had been no agreement on how the negotiations should be conducted; the State Department would develop a paper for Treasury Department and STR comments, and the issue would then go to the President for decision. (Ibid.)

ent with the guidance laid down in your decision on controlled confrontation with the EC (CIEP/DM 14 of September 25, 1972)[2] have been
agreed between State, Treasury, STR and the CIEP Staff.

The Issues for Decision

The issues for your decision are two:

(1) Given the political problems which the course of action we propose will raise, and which are discussed more fully below, we feel we
should seek your authorization to proceed. We would propose to do so
immediately after the U.S. election.

(2) State and Treasury have agreed on the amount of the initial
claim we would present. State, within the context of the policy you set
forth in CIEP/DM 14, would leave to the discretion of the negotiator
when and how to recede to the fallback positions discussed below.
Treasury would not authorize at the outset any fallback position from
the original claim.

Discussion

Preferential trade agreements between the European Community
and Spain, and between the European Community and Israel went into
effect in 1970. Each agreement is composed of two principal elements:

(1) *special preferences*—by which the European Community, following a brief phasing period, will extend to all but about 15 percent of its
imports from Spain and Israel duty reductions of 60 and 50 percent,
respectively; and

(2) *reverse preferences*—by which Spain, after a five year phasing
period, will extend to around four-fifths of its imports from the
European Community duty reductions ranging from 25 to 60 percent;
and Israel, after a similar phasing period, will extend to nearly three-
fourths of its imports from the European Community duty reductions
of 10–30 percent.

Meaning of Preferential Arrangements to the Participants

The European Community sees its agreements with Spain and
Israel as part of its general policy to strengthen its political and economic ties in the Mediterranean. The agreements are intended to promote trade with Spain and Israel and contribute to the latter nation's
economic development. Finally, the two trade arrangements are considered to be the inevitable consequence of preferences which the
European Community has granted to former colonies (Morocco and
Tunisia) and NATO members (Greece and Turkey) in the Mediterranean
area.

---

[2] See footnote 3, Document 101.

Spain has made integration into Europe a prime foreign policy objective. Full membership in the European Community is regarded by the Spanish as essential for promoting modernization and liberalization. The current preferential arrangement is seen as a big step toward full membership.

Israel seeks closer ties with the European Community as compensation for its lack of ties with its Middle East neighbors and as a means to promote economic growth.

Action to Date

The United States has taken a firm stand in GATT that the agreements violate GATT rules and are likely to damage our trade. The three participants have been unwilling to accept the contention that the agreements are inconsistent with GATT. Neither side has been able to persuade a sufficient number of the GATT members to support its position. There is little prospect of getting a satisfactory resolution of the legal issue.

We have notified the European Community, Spain and Israel that we will invoke GATT procedures to obtain adjustment of the agreements to reduce the preferential margins or, failing satisfaction, to receive compensation in the form of other trade concessions of interest to the United States.

Nature and Amount of Our Proposed Claim

The Departments of State and Treasury have reached agreement that the United States should claim that, with limited exceptions, its trade will be adversely affected in cases where the preference margin is four percent or more and U.S. exports to the participants have amounted to $50,000 a year or more. On this basis, we would ask the participants to make adjustments in the agreements or provide compensatory benefits covering approximately $750 million of trade.

An initial claim of this magnitude will demonstrate the seriousness of U.S. objections to these and other special and reverse preference arrangements. However, the course we advocate involves serious political risks. Our demands are likely to be met with shock and resentment by the EC, Spain and Israel. Particularly in Spain and Israel our claims will touch sensitive political nerves and sharp reactions are possible. We should also realize there is virtually no chance that the participants will agree to offsetting trade concessions of this size. In part this would be because the other parties would argue that our initial claim was completely "theoretical" and that even a generous estimate of the potential real damage to our trade would have to be far smaller. If we desire to reach agreement on concrete measures of importance to United States exports, we shall have to be prepared to settle for less, and probably substantially less, than the full claim. Even if our main purpose is to maintain pressure on the EC in preparation for the 1973 trade negotiations, it may be advisable, in order to avoid a confrontation getting out of control, to signal at an appropriate moment a willingness to retreat from our initial claim.

Possible Retreat Positions

There are a succession of retreat positions that we could adopt during the negotiations to reduce the amount of our bill and increase the possibility—although limited—for a satisfactory settlement.

The first retreat position would be to drop from our bill commodities covered by the European Community's system of *generalized preferences*. Exclusion of these commodities would reduce our claim to around $500 million.

The second retreat position would be to limit our claim to the trade damage caused or likely to be caused by *reverse preferences* (preferences which the EC enjoys in Spain and Israel) and *hard-core special preference* items, such as citrus, where we can make our most convincing case of actual damage. On this basis, over $300 million of U.S. exports to Spain, around $40 million to Israel and about $22 million to the EC would be listed by the U.S. as adversely affected by the most objectionable feature of the agreements. We would indicate that we would be prepared to settle for tariff adjustments by Spain and Israel to eliminate the discrimination against U.S. goods which benefit the European Community or for compensation benefiting U.S. trade interests through changes in European Community tariffs.

The Risks Involved

There are serious economic and political risks involved in whatever action or combination of actions we might take.

The proposed initial U.S. impairment claim against the European Community, Spain and Israel covering three-quarters of a billion dollars of trade will be seen by these parties and others as a frontal attack by the United States against the agreements. They will think our objective is not offsetting trade concessions but the abrogation of the agreements. The United States is likely to be accused of attempting to block Spain's integration into Europe and of having suddenly reduced its concern for the welfare of Israel. The European Community might become less cooperative on matters of general importance to the United States, such as the forthcoming multilateral trade negotiations.

These risks can probably be reduced or controlled by quiet diplomacy, and by a skillful negotiator, particularly if armed with authority to retreat to the fallback positions described above when he deems it necessary. However, Spain, Israel or the European Community may choose to make a major public issue of the matter.

On the other hand, if the United States does not submit a substantial claim, the impression may be created that our objections to special preferential arrangements, while firmly held, will not be backed by determined action.

Recommendation:

That you authorize us to submit, soon after the November elections, the initial claim indicated above against the parties involved and to seek maximum trade advantage for the U.S. in negotiations, scaling down our initial claim as appropriate.

John N. Irwin II

---

106.   Editorial Note

On November 18, 1972, Kissinger sent National Security Study Memorandum 164, "United States Relations With Europe," to the Secretaries of State, Defense, Commerce, Treasury, and Agriculture, with copies to the Director of Central Intelligence, the Chairman of the JCS, the ACDA Director, and the President's Assistant for International Economic Affairs. NSSM 164 noted that the President had directed the preparation of a basic study of U.S. relations with Europe, particularly Western Europe, setting out goals and priorities for the second Nixon administration. The study was to be completed by January 1, 1973, for consideration by the NSC Senior Review Group.

NSSM 164 concluded: "The existence of this directive and the content of the study must be regarded as extremely sensitive. All officials involved will see to it that proper security precautions are taken to avoid public speculation about changes in our European policy." (National Archives, RG 59, S/S Files: Lot 80 D 212, Box 1113, NSSM 164) For the Department of State's response to NSSM 164, see Document 108.

On November 27 Secretary of Commerce Peterson sent a memorandum to Kissinger and Shultz entitled "Some Thoughts on the Dual Position of (1) Ambassador to NATO and the European Community Operating as a Senior Representative to Europe and (2) The Official

Responsible for East-West Trade." Peterson noted there were two phases to dealing with the challenges the U.S.-European relationship would pose in the President's next term: planning the strategy, and then implementing it. He referred to the NSSM 164 exercise as kicking off the first phase, which must be carried out in Washington, and concluded "that we are putting the cart before the horse in talking about an assignment now in Brussels to act as the President's man in Europe before we have decided what it is we plan to propose to the Europeans."

At several points in his November 27 memorandum Peterson pointedly noted that Kissinger and Shultz were the President's key advisers. He recommended a small European Planning Group, with close liaison with them, to work out a strategy on military, political, economic, and other matters before turning to implementation. Peterson included the following summary of a proposed 10-year strategy on security, economic, and political issues for the Planning Group to consider, which would "reflect the President's–Kissinger's–Shultz's views":

"1. It must originate with and address itself to the highest level of government where we must generate the political will to solve our growing economic problems. It must, in all likelihood originate with the President of the United States.

"2. The strategy must take a *long-term* view in order to give the relationship a sense of durability and permanence. We might seek a long-term, perhaps 10 years, compact or covenant of a cross-sectoral nature in which agreements on trade, defense, energy, monetary and other policies would be pulled together and which we would articulate a new set of principles to govern our relationship—a new Atlantic Charter, as it were.

"3. In putting together any such comprehensive agreement, we must play our negotiating cards where they have the greatest impact—not administrative cubby holes. I suspect that our best trump card could be long-term *security agreements.*

"4. Our strategy should also involve a realistic ordering of economic priorities so that, when the trading starts, we will be in a position to get the trade-offs which maximize the return to us. In the past, we have scattered our economic negotiating shots too much.

"5. Our strategy should be to seek agreement on some joint policies for dealing with the growing *energy* shortage. The incentive for such agreement should be strong since the United States and Europe both have interest in avoiding cut-throat competition either for energy or for foreign exchange earnings to pay for the energy.

"6. Our strategy must take note of the danger that our new commercial relationships with Eastern Europe and the Soviet Union could serve as a wedge between us and our traditional Western European allies. Participations for European capital in some of our Soviet energy ventures could help avert this. Using additional trade with Eastern Europe as a political lever to achieve joint objectives is still another thing we should do.

"7. The strategy might look toward far broader forms of cooperation between the U.S. and Europe, cooperation in areas such as medicine, drug control, crime, transportation and pollution abatement.

"8. Finally, in our approach, we must examine closely the need for new institutions and new methods of consultation to meet the problems of the 1970s and avoid the apathy and even hostility that is building up on both sides."

Peterson's memorandum then developed each of the eight points in greater detail. On the economic side he thought U.S. and European economic interests were not in conflict in the long run, but that in the short term Europe sought trade advantages and responded to political needs that were frictions in the relationship. He expressed his concerns about a coming energy crisis with "massive" U.S., European, and Japanese energy trade deficits that could have "traumatic effects on the international monetary system" and a "cannibalistic scramble not only for energy but for export earnings to pay for it," which would hardly contribute to stability in the Western Alliance.

In the implementation phase Peterson saw three possibilities for an Ambassador. First, the Ambassadors to NATO, the European Communities, and the OECD could be combined in a super-ambassador based in Brussels. Another possibility would be an Ambassador at Large stationed in Europe with coordinating responsibilities for NATO, the EC, and the OECD. Finally, should the President and European leaders decide a conclave of "wise men" would be helpful in resolving problems, an Ambassador at Large or another designee could assume this role. (National Archives, Nixon Presidential Materials, NSC Files, Agency Files, Box 214, Commerce Volume IV July–December 72)

On November 30 Haig forwarded to Shultz a paper entitled "Peterson Assignment," under cover of a memorandum indicating the paper was to be delivered in a sealed envelope. (Ibid., Box 290, Treasury Volume III) The paper outlined Peterson's prospective duties as the "President's European Representative": Ambassador to the OECD, NATO, and the EC with responsibility for coordinating the U.S. role in and relations with these institutions. He would report to the President through Kissinger and Shultz. His deputies would have day-to-day operating responsibilities for the three missions and would report to Washington agencies on day-to-day matters in the normal way.

No "super-ambassador to Europe" was appointed. During the second Nixon administration each of the three missions continued to have its own Chief of Mission, and no Ambassador at Large with coordinating responsibilities for Europe was designated.

---

107.   Editorial Note

On December 1, 1972, in Key Biscayne, Florida, Press Secretary Ron Ziegler announced on the President's behalf that George Shultz would remain as Secretary of the Treasury in the second term. The President also named Shultz an Assistant to the President to be "the focal point and the overall coordinator of the entire economic policy decisionmaking process, both domestically and internationally." Shultz' duties as Assistant to the President would include chairing a new Cabinet-level Council on Economic Policy. (*Weekly Compilation of Presidential Documents*, Volume 8, No. 49, December 4, 1972, page 1711)

In remarks following Ziegler's announcement, Shultz noted that the primary membership of the Council on Economic Policy would be the Department of Labor, Commerce, Agriculture, and Transportation and in the field of international economic policy the Department of State. Within the Executive Office of the President, the OMB Director, the CEA Chairman, the CIEP Director, and the Cost of Living Council Director would be key members. Shultz noted that the Council on International Economic Policy and the Cost of Living Council were examples of "continuing working groups that worry about essential aspects of policy." (Ibid., page 1712)

On December 22 Clay T. Whitehead, Director of the White House Office of Telecommunications Policy, sent a memorandum to Shultz proposing that OTP be a member of the new Council. Melvin Laird, in a letter to Shultz and a January 5 memorandum to the President, also proposed the Secretary of Defense as a member of the new Council. (Washington National Records Center, Department of the Treasury, Records of Secretary Shultz: FRC 56 80 1, GPS, Dam, Kenneth 1971–1974)

108. Paper Prepared in the Department of State[1]

Washington, undated.

NSSM RESPONSE

Part I

II. The US and Europe in Transition: Background for the Future

[Here follows discussion of subjects unrelated to economic policy.]

Developments in the US, meanwhile, create uncertainties and concerns among the Western Europeans: Congressional efforts to reduce US forces in Europe, increased preoccupation with domestic issues, balance of payments problems, budgetary stringencies, and the appearance of growing isolationism and protectionism are seen as affecting US policies toward Europe.

[Here follows discussion of subjects unrelated to economic policy.]

Economic problems on both sides of the Atlantic, deriving in part from domestic concerns, exert serious pressure on US-European relations generally and US-EC relations specifically. In the United States, there is major concern about unemployment, and many fear that the US is losing its competitiveness in international markets, that US corporate giants are exporting jobs through their investments in Europe, and that American industry will suffer from waves of cheap goods from Asia. There is growing sentiment that other countries have been dealing unfairly with us in the economic field to their own advantage. The conclusion by the EC of preferential trade agreements with a widening circle of countries has fed this sentiment. An important complaint also has been the Community's protectionist agricultural policies.

European economic concerns also are affecting our relationships. While Europe experiences unabated strong inflation, some countries and regions continue to suffer from economic stagnation. Europeans, too, are chafing under the accumulation of unneeded and inconvertible dollars, which add to inflationary pressures and nullify monetary policies. Resentment over American private investment is rising. Europeans

---

[1] Source: National Archives, RG 59, S/S Files: Lot 80 D 212, Box 1113V, NSSM 164. Secret. The paper was prepared as a response to NSSM 164; see Document 106. A December 18 transmittal memorandum from Stoessel to Kissinger forwarding the 53-page NSSM Response indicates the paper was discussed in the NSC Interdepartmental Review Group for Europe and took into account views of its members and other recipients of NSSM 164. The paper and Stoessel's memorandum are attached to a January 29, 1973, memorandum from Stoessel to Deputy Secretary-designate Rush, explaining that the paper was drafted in EUR taking into account other agency views but it did not represent interagency consensus.

see the US as adopting aggressive foreign economic policies. They complain about our tough application of anti-dumping and countervailing duty provisions. More importantly, they continue to fear that the US seeks to extort unilateral trade concessions by our preponderant leverage in the monetary field.

[Omitted here is discussion of subjects unrelated to economic policy.]

Part II

IV. Issues and Goals

The following are specific issues confronting us in the economic, political, security, military, scientific and technological fields. Many of these issues will require additional detailed study before decisions relative to them can be taken, and goals established. Each should be examined in its specific terms, with consideration carefully given to its impact in other fields.

A. *Economic*

US policy has been to:

—support Western European economic integration as a means to strengthen Western European ability to share responsibility for maintaining a stable and prosperous world order.

Americans and Western Europeans both have the same overriding economic goal of maximizing their prosperity. The open, interdependent economic system, with free movement of goods and services has been an important element of Atlantic economic prosperity. It is important to restate this basic goal because government policies which affect economic conditions on one side of the ocean will also affect the other. An atmosphere of orderly international cooperation is as important to maintain business confidence as is a climate of sound domestic management.

American business has done well within this open system and now has a very large economic stake in Western Europe. US direct and indirect investment assets in the enlarged EC amount to some $36 billion. Western Europe is also our largest customer. Our exports to the enlarged EC and its Western European associates in 1971 were about $13 billion or 30% of our total exports.

In other words, despite some important problems and irritants, we have had and have a highly profitable economic relationship overall with Western Europe, and the opportunity exists to enhance this relationship in the long term.

Issues to be Addressed

—how to deal with the series of new and emerging economic problems which are creating pressures on both sides to restrict the open economic system. These are now being addressed in various US fora, such as CIEP and STR.

1. *Monetary:*

US policy has been to:

—press major surplus countries to revalue or to take other measures to bring their payments balances into equilibrium;
—develop a new multilateral monetary system based on a more symmetrical adjustment process that facilitates freer trade and capital flows;
—favor EC movement toward a closely integrated monetary union consistent with the foregoing US aims.

The 1971 monetary crisis represented the culmination of several major trends, especially the serious, long-term balance of payments problem. That crisis was brought to an end by the Smithsonian agreement, but the international payments imbalance persists despite the fact that the US now has better control over its inflation than Europe. The Western Europeans at present have the choice of continuing to accept non-convertible US dollars, changing their exchange rates in our favor, and/or instituting capital controls. The US economy is not seriously hampered by the continued payments deficit. However, progress towards a new system must be made to avoid further financial crises which could seriously undermine business confidence and lead to governmental restrictions on trade and capital movements. In order for the US to restore some form of convertibility, however, all the other elements of the system must be compatible. Most importantly, it must provide for satisfactory adjustment by surplus and deficit countries.

Here is perhaps the single most important area of potential tension between the US and Europe. The Western European countries, which are more dependent on exports than the United States, have been accustomed to growth based upon increased exports and would tend to resist measures or rules that would erode their export surplus, which has ensured high levels of employment. Yet they will have to move in this direction if they wish to end the present situation which is so psychologically frustrating to them.

Because we are dealing with an area of extreme domestic sensitivity to Western Europeans and Americans alike, such as jobs and farm income, the task of constructing a new and equitable monetary system will require skill. A complicating feature is that the EC members have committed themselves to the goals of achieving economic and monetary union (EMU), but are only on the threshold of this development. In the short run, EC moves towards EMU may complicate the task of achieving a new world system. In the longer run, if the EC members can adopt a genuine single currency area through harmonization of policies, it may facilitate the adjustment process between the US and them.

Issues to be Addressed

—how to achieve US-Western European agreement on an adjustment process in which surplus and deficit countries have symmetrical responsibilities.

—construction of a new and equitable monetary system that facilitates free trade and capital flows, while permitting the EC to form a monetary union. Like economic issues, these are being addressed today in various fora of the US Government.

2. *Trade:*

US policy has been to:

—exert controlled but mounting pressure to obtain Western European cooperation on both specific trade problems and the 1973 multilateral trade negotiations.

The vast bulk of our trade moves in a liberal, open system. More than ever trade flows are responsive to economic and business conditions on both sides of the ocean.

The most important exception, of course, is agriculture where the Community's Common Agricultural Policy has been protectionist and restrains the development of our exports. Though our agricultural exports to the enlarged EC were at an all-time high totalling $2.4 billion in 1971, it has been estimated that these exports could amount to $5–7 billion in 1980 if the major agricultural producers and importers including Western Europe and Japan were to follow more liberal policies. This of course means that the Community would have to find a way to meet the political interests of their inefficient grain producers in Germany and we would have to override the interests of our dairy lobby.

However, the whole open trading system is jeopardized by the accumulation of tensions over developments, policies and practices. These tensions generate much heat and feed protectionist forces which seek to pressure governments to take restrictive actions. There is an important danger of an escalation of restrictive measures and counter-measures which added together would constitute a "trade war," leading to a significant erosion of the open, interdependent system and threatening economic prosperity.

A priority task, therefore, is to move to control these pressures by solving some of the troublesome short-term issues, but more importantly to move into a major new round of trade negotiations which will subsume many of the problems and provide an effective counter-thrust to protectionist pressures. In doing so, it must be borne in mind that the trade problems are disparate. Some have more economic impact than others, while some generate more political heat than others. This argues for a sound appraisal of our priorities in the trade field.

Obtaining a long-term liberalization of agriculture is in our interest both on economic grounds (a large balance of payments pay-off) as well as in terms of political advantages (the farm bloc is important to maintaining a liberal trade posture).

Lowering the common external tariff of the EC in reciprocal trade negotiations is important on both economic and political grounds. It would reduce the tariff discrimination inherent in the enlarged Community, and its free trade arrangements with EFTA and preferential arrangements with others. It would heighten the real and perceived interdependence of the two areas and would confirm that the two continents are being tied closer together rather than drifting apart.

The US and other countries not members of the enlarged EC will be engaged in the GATT in renegotiating with the enlarged EC the trade concessions accorded them in the past 25 years by the UK, Denmark and Ireland. The dissolution of the British Commonwealth trading system and the lowering of the UK tariff to the level of the EC's common external tariff will provide us benefits. However, accession of the UK to the Common Market will have some important unfavorable consequences, particularly for exporters of agricultural commodities. It will be a delicate matter to obtain enough for US agriculture in these GATT renegotiations to maintain US agriculture's support for further trade liberalization without jeopardizing Western European willingness and ability to include agriculture in the multilateral trade negotiations.

Eliminating the reverse preferences of the Community in non-European areas is more important politically than economically. While the trade impact may be small, the reverse preferences create the impression in this country that the Community is carving out a vast discriminatory trading bloc, and therefore undermine public and Congressional support both for our European political and security objectives and liberal trading policies. We have had some success in counteracting the spread of reverse preferences in the Mediterranean, and we must keep up the pressure.

There are many other issues in the trade field that require management both in the short run and during the negotiations, but the above are the immediate priorities.

One may wish to build up pressure through some of the short run issues, e.g. by taking GATT action on the EC agreement with Spain and Israel, or in the negotiations on EC enlargement, but we must keep the priorities in mind and not permit the pressure on short-run issues to get out of hand and interfere with these priority objectives.

Issues to be Addressed

—solving or controlling short-term trade problems.
—obtaining industrial and agricultural concessions from Western Europe in 1973 multilateral reciprocal trade negotiations.

3. *Other Economic Issues*

US policy has been to:

—seek to protect US economic interests on an ad hoc basis or in discussion of these issues in multilateral organizations.

Another potentially important area of confrontation involves investment and industry. At present, US investment in Western Europe enjoys non-discriminatory treatment and a generally favorable climate. But it is a sensitive issue and looms large in key sectors like computers and aircraft. The Western Europeans want to encourage the development of European firms which can match the efficiency and financial power of the giant American-based multinationals. Some would subsidize research and development on a broad scale in Western Europe and adopt "Buy European" policies which might adversely affect US exports and/or either limit or control US investment in favor of European-owned companies.

Given these dangers and our economic stake in Western Europe, we must choose our tactics carefully. Fortunately, the climate for US investment is still relatively favorable despite the vague and possibly mounting resentment over the large American investment. We have begun an exercise in the OECD to examine this whole area of policies and practices affecting investment including also the practices of multinational corporations. The object of this exercise should be to move towards sensible common rules of the game which will guide the major industrial powers in the investment field so as to minimize distortions to the international adjustment process and the rational allocation of resources.

Important to dealing with these problems should be the realization that the European governments identify their access to advanced technology as a crucial element of their economic strategy. This clearly affects their policy toward trade and investment.

Energy policy, too, is a potentially divisive issue between the US and the EC. The Western Europeans are concerned about security of supply and the EC is developing a common energy policy. Given the large US stake in the European energy market in both trade and investment terms, it is in our interest to avoid a competitive scramble for limited oil resources and to reach a broad understanding with the Western Europeans on a cooperative approach to the long-term energy problem and on arrangements to share supplies in the event of an emergency.

A coordinated policy should include not only agreement on supply policies but also an agreed approach to technical solutions to the energy question, i.e., the development of alternate energy sources, the improvement of environmental control, the increased efficiency of power production and utilization and the institution of methods to con-serve energy. The United States is negotiating an agreement with the USSR for cooperation in some of these energy technologies. Western European nations will undoubtedly demand at least equal treatment, and we might wish to consider this in the context of energy programs being developed in the European Community and OECD.

In the environmental sphere, the US should continue the coopera-tion on environment already begun in the NATO Committee on the Challenges of Modern Society (CCMS), the OECD and bilaterally with individual states and the EC. By developing similar environmental standards, similar methods of environmental control, and common rules of the game on handling the costs of environmental control (the "polluter pays" principle), we may prevent either side from interpret-ing the environmental protective actions of the other as disguised trade barriers.

The Federal Water Pollution Control Act Amendment of 1972 requires that the President undertake to enter into international agree-ments to apply uniform standards of performance for the control of pol-lutants from new sources, toxic pollutants, and discharge of pollutants into the oceans. One of the principal objectives of this provision is to avoid handicapping US industry, to which stricter and more costly environmental control requirements might be applied. Problems may arise where European priorities and interests differ from ours.

[Omitted here is the remainder of Section IV dealing with political, security, military, and science and technology issues; the conclusion of Part II; Part III, "The U.S. Role: Priorities, Interrelationships, Institutions and Their Implications for the US"; and Part IV, "Issues and Goals."]

International Monetary Policy, 1969–1972

109.   National Security Study Memorandum 7[1]

Washington, January 21, 1969.

TO

The Secretary of State
The Secretary of the Treasury
Chairman of Council of Economic Advisers
Chairman of the Federal Reserve Board

SUBJECT

U.S. International Monetary Policy

The President has directed the creation of a permanent Working Group to make recommendations on U. S. international monetary policy to the NSC and to implement policy decisions. It will be chaired by the Under Secretary of the Treasury for Monetary Affairs and comprised of the Deputy Under Secretary of State for Economic Affairs, a member of the Council of Economic Advisers, a member of the NSC staff, and a member of the Board of Governors of the Federal Reserve System, and/or their alternates. As appropriate, the chairman of the Working Group may invite other agencies to send representatives to specific meetings.

The President has also directed the preparation by the Working Group of a paper on U. S. international monetary policy for early con-

---

[1] Source: National Archives, RG 59, S/S Files: Lot 80 D 212, NSSM 7. Secret. NSSM 7 established what became known as the Volcker Group after its Chairman, Under Secretary of the Treasury for Monetary Affairs Paul A. Volcker. The Volcker Group was the successor to the Deming Group in the Johnson administration, chaired by then Under Secretary of the Treasury for Monetary Affairs, Frederick L. Deming. From 1969 to 1974 various U.S. Government, foreign government, IMF, and academic papers were distributed, in several numbered series, to members of the Group for their consideration, often at scheduled meetings. A set of these papers is in the Washington National Records Center, Department of the Treasury, Volcker Group Masters: FRC 56 86 30. A duplicate set of Volcker Group papers, bound into folders and indexed, is ibid., Office of the Assistant Secretary for International Affairs Central Files: FRC 56 86 24, The World/1/555 Volcker Group 1969. The papers were most often distributed under cover of a memorandum from George H. Willis, Deputy to the Assistant Secretary of the Treasury for International Affairs. Willis attended Volcker Group meetings and many international meetings on international monetary issues, such as G-10 and C-20 Deputies meetings. Spiral notebooks with his handwritten notes from some of these meetings are ibid., Deputy to the Assistant Secretary for International Affairs: FRC 56 83 26, Willis Notes.

sideration by the National Security Council.[2] It should consider our policy alternatives with regard to the U.S. balance of payments, the functioning of the international monetary system, and contingency plans for response to potential currency crises such as a franc devaluation and/or a British resort to a freely flexible exchange rate for the pound.

The paper should be forwarded to the NSC Review Group by February 15, 1969.

Henry A. Kissinger

---

[2] Drafts of this paper are ibid., Volcker Group Masters: FRC 56 86 30. The drafts were circulated to members of the Group by C. Fred Bergsten, VG/LIM/69–11, on February 5, and by Hendrik Houthakker, VG/LIM/69–26, on February 27. No final text was found and the subject was apparently taken off the NSC agenda; see Document 16.

---

110.   Editorial Note

In the late 1960s and early 1970s, U.S. policymakers gave advanced thought to the nature of the U.S. response to international monetary crises and the need to restructure the international monetary system. Papers on these matters looked at such issues as currency devaluations and appreciations, suspending the dollar's convertibility to gold, and changing the official price of gold, all policy issues that, if their consideration became public knowledge, could lead to intense, destabilizing speculation in foreign exchange and commodity markets. Papers on such issues, therefore, were usually classified and received very limited distribution.

Records pertaining to anticipatory, long-term international monetary planning during the Nixon administration in the Washington National Records Center, Department of the Treasury, Deputy to the Assistant Secretary for International Affairs: FRC 56 83 26, Contingency Planning 1965–1973. (This also contains documents on planning for currency crises during the Johnson administration.) Included are papers on possible foreign exchange crises in 1969 and 1973, a possible float of the pound, and an "excessive" devaluation of the French franc. In 1972 concern centered on a possible breakdown in 1973 of the December 1971 Smithsonian Agreement on exchange rate realignment. The sole contingency planning paper regarding the U.S. Negotiating Position on Gold is printed as Document 153.

Several "contingency" papers prepared in late 1970 and early 1971 out of concern with the continuing balance-of-payments deficit and as the foreign exchange markets heated up in May 1971 are in the Washington National Records Center, Department of the Treasury, Files of Under Secretary Volcker: FRC 56 79 15, 1971 Contingency Planning Papers. These papers, dating from November 23, 1970, to May 9, 1971, anticipate the suspension of the dollar's convertibility to gold announced as a part of President Nixon's New Economic Policy on August 15, 1971.

During the Nixon administration much of the early work on contingency planning was done in the Volcker Group and many of the documents are ibid., Volcker Group Masters: FRC 56 86 30. Volcker Group documents from the Spring and Summer of 1971 focus on such issues as limited exchange rate flexibility, and none of the documents from that time presage the 10 percent import surcharge and suspension of the convertibility of the dollar to gold the President announced on August 15, 1971.

111.　Volcker Group Paper[1]

VG/LIM/69-2　　　　　　　　　　　　　　　　　Washington, undated.

LONG-TERM ASPECTS OF U.S. INTERNATIONAL MONETARY AND EXCHANGE POLICIES

This subject is discussed in this memorandum under these headings:

1) Activation of Special Drawing Rights
2) Gold Price Problems
3) Interchangeability of Dollars, Gold and Other Reserve Assets

---

[1] Source: Washington National Records Center, Department of the Treasury, Volcker Group Masters: FRC 56 86 30, VG/LIM/1–VG/LIM/30. Confidential; Limdis. A January 30 draft indicates the paper was drafted by Willis. (Ibid., Deputy Assistant Secretary of the Treasury for International Affairs, Contingency Planning 1965–1973: FRC 56 83 26) Two other papers, VG/LIM/69-3 ("U.S.-U.K. Arrangements for Joint Contingency Planning," dated January 31) and VG/LIM/69-4 ("Possibilities for Dealing with Situation Created by 'Aggressive' Exchange Rate Action by the French," dated January 31), are attached. The three papers were to be discussed at the Volcker Group's February 3 meeting. No record of the discussion was found.

4) Exchange Rate Policies and Principles—Fixed Parity or Limited Flexibility

Activation of Special Drawing Rights.—The U.S. looks forward to an early activation of the Special Drawing Rights Plan. Mr. Schweitzer has indicated that it might even be possible to consider activation at the September Annual Meeting of the Bank and Fund. He believes, however, that a Ministerial Meeting of the Group of Ten would probably have to take place, possibly at the Annual Meeting itself. Presumably such a Ministerial Meeting would include the French, even though they might not be participants in the SDR scheme.

Any such timetable would probably mean that the Deputies of the Group of Ten would need to begin work on the problem of activation fairly soon in order to recommend a course of action to the Ministers. We might make a tentative suggestion to Mr. Ossola that he convene the Deputies to begin this work either at the February session of the OECD or on the occasion of the next meetings in Europe in the spring.

The following points are suggested for further exploration in the Volcker Group as to the U.S. position and posture on this problem.

Amount of Reserve Creation.—It has been suggested that the United States would like to see reserves created in the amount of $3 to $4 billion a year, amounting to a 4 or 5 percent annual increase in global reserves. It is not clear whether this target would be the initial asking price, for SDRs alone, or whether it would be adjusted downward (or upward) in the event of a continuing addition to (or subtraction from) world reserves through deficits (or surpluses) of the reserve centers. One question to be examined is whether we should continue to envisage a constant annual amount of reserve creation during the five-year period, or a larger figure in the early years, followed by smaller figures in the later years of the initial five-year period.

U.S. Balance of Payments and European Attitudes.—The question arises as to whether the Europeans will be prepared to move to an early activation if the U.S. resumes a substantial deficit on official settlements account in 1969 and in ensuing years. The sources of reserve creation can become complex, and more than $2 billion was apparently added to world reserves outside the United States in 1968, despite an official settlements surplus of $1.6 billion in the U.S. In order to prepare our position on activation, it will be necessary to make a projection of world reserve creation for five years in the absence of any activation. This projection will depend in part on a corresponding projection of the U.S. balance of payments position during the period. Are we to assume no change in official dollar holdings during the next five years, or an upward trend in these holdings at a moderate figure?

2) *Gold Price Problems.*—While an early activation of the SDRs would help to set at rest speculation for an increase in the official price of gold, we cannot be sure that an aggressive devaluation by the French would not bring this problem to the center of the stage. Minister Schiller's continued references to a "realignment of currencies" might also envisage a change in the official monetary price of gold, and hence references to it continue to keep up the hopes of speculators.

The Schiller realignment problem might become serious if the Germans and other Europeans were to delay activation of the SDR and give the French support for a rise in the official gold price. We hope that this technique will not be adopted, and Schiller indicated last November that he was in favor of activation of the Special Drawing Rights. But it seems possible that he is seeking a general realignment of currencies to facilitate and cover a Deutschemark revaluation, and it is reported that he has expressed the view that the dollar is overvalued.

An aggressive French devaluation, which carried with it at least some depreciation of the pound sterling and other European currencies, could present a problem to the U.S. in choosing its future gold and exchange policy. This would be especially true if Germany, Italy, and Japan, for example, were to follow the French with some depreciation. Presumably these strong currencies would move only if the French depreciated by such a large percentage that they would be fearful of the impact on their trade. However, if by any chance there were such a general depreciation by the major countries, the United States would seem to face a decision on these basic alternatives:

a) Elimination of full convertibility and aggressive negotiations with other countries on mutually acceptable exchange rates for all major currencies in terms of the dollar. Such an aggressive negotiation might have to be backed up by threats to make illegal transactions in dollars at any other than a mutually agreed exchange rate.

b) The adoption of a general system of export subsidies and import taxes to offset foreign depreciation or even gain some advantage for U.S. exports in terms of some countries.

c) Depreciation of the dollar in terms of gold and other currencies, which would imply a rise in the official monetary price of gold.

3) *Interchangeability of Dollars, Gold and Other Reserve Assets.*—Assuming that the problem of the gold/dollar relationship is not brought to a head by some monetary crisis, as mentioned in the preceding section, there is a more fundamental question of the long-term U.S. policy with respect to convertibility of dollars into gold. Various approaches have been suggested which have the effect of limiting the potential strain of convertibility. One of these is the freezing in some way of foreign dollar balances. One is the reserve settlements account of Mr. E.M. Bernstein, which is an advanced method of eliminating con-

vertibility that would present very difficult if not impossible negotiating problems. The third is a continuation of the rather informal way in which convertibility has been to some extent limited through central bank cooperation, the re-channeling of reserves into the international money market, through commercial banks, and other ways of holding down the growth in official dollar reserves.

The fourth approach is the suggestion for a dollar bloc and a gold bloc, with a flexible exchange link between the two.

These various proposals may be judged against the long history of monetary evolution. The convertibility of money into a metallic asset has been steadily restricted until it no longer exists domestically in most advanced countries. For a number of years convertibility into gold has been limited to international transactions. Last year, the two-tier system took a further step, and eliminated the convertibility of dollars into gold at a fixed price for foreign private holders of dollars.

What remains is the convertibility link for foreign monetary authorities. It is this link, and the possible loss of gold associated with it, that provides the major remaining impetus to international adjustment arising out of the balance of payments. But this link also threatens the stability of the monetary system, by permitting a run on the U.S. gold reserve on the part of foreign central banks.

Perhaps one of the most important long-term problems facing the U.S. is how to move out of this commitment in a graceful manner without causing undue disturbance to the monetary system and with a fair measure of international approbation, at some time in the future. It is not yet clear whether this can be done, and a breaking of the link may have to come in the context of some crisis and a threatened run on the dollar.

One possibility, over time, is that the nations of the world come to accept Special Drawing Rights in lieu of gold when they convert dollars into other reserves. Such preference for SDRs over gold may be a long time in coming. The preference of many monetary authorities for gold would be to some extent weakened if it became clear that the commodity gold price could dip below the official price of $35 per ounce.

A partial approach to the problem of reducing our vulnerability to convertibility would be the freezing of dollar balances in some form. Most experts believe, however, that this would not be acceptable to foreign countries without some kind of commitment to the effect that the U.S. would no longer have the flexibility of settling its deficit initially with dollar liabilities instead of reserve assets. There is a feeling in many quarters that it would be dangerous for the U.S. to give up the more favorable bargaining position which it now has, when it can pay out dollars initially and then discuss with foreign monetary authorities the various techniques for handling these dollars if the central bank does not want to hold them in its reserves. The reason for this feeling is that, with the U.S. unable to create new reserves in this form, the European countries might use too harshly their veto over the creation of Special Drawing Rights so that the growth in reserves that would be permitted might fall heavily short of the amounts needed to prevent a steadily tightening shortage of world reserves.

The same considerations apply to the Bernstein plan, which makes no allowance for the role of the U.S. as a continuing reserve center with the potential power to create additional reserves in the form of dollar liabilities. Under that plan, there would be no increase in dollar liabilities held as reserves.

The U.S. still has to develop a clear position as to its long-range objective with respect to the maintenance of convertibility and the interchangeability of dollars and gold.

4) *Exchange Rate Policies and Principle—Fixed Parity or Limited Flexibility.*—This subject has attracted especial attention during the past year.

Particularly among academic economists, it has been argued that the system of fixed exchange rates has come to place too much pressure on deficit countries to conform to rates of growth and rates of costs and price inflation in the rest of the world. It is argued that, because the pressure to conform is markedly stronger in deficit than in surplus countries, the latter have an exaggerated weight in determining the rate of growth of aggregate demand in the world as a whole, and, consequently, the rate of economic progress.

Against this, the practitioners of the fixed exchange rate system argue the uncertainties for trade and investment under a system of limited flexibility. However, perhaps more important is their fear that limited exchange flexibility would reduce the resistance of governments to inflationary pressure. Many central banks feel that the public and the government can be to some extent aroused to the danger of inflation through the necessity to protect reserves and maintain an established exchange rate.

The November meeting of the Ministers of the Group of Ten in Germany marked perhaps the first occasion on which the finger was clearly pointed at a surplus country by Ministers of other major countries, with a strong implication that an appreciation of the exchange rate was desirable on international grounds. True, the Ministerial Meeting in a sense symbolized this pressure, because the Germans acted in fact just before the Ministerial Meeting. They found a substitute for exchange rate appreciation, as a compromise measure within the German government. This was the border tax adjustment. It is generally believed that an important reason for using this technique instead of exchange rate appreciation was the common agricultural policy in the Common Market, and the effect of a German appreciation on the German budget in the form of additional subsidies to German farmers. These problems were avoided by eliminating the affected agricultural commodities from the proposed adjustment.

Some brief comments on the particular techniques of limited exchange flexibility are included in Attachment A.[2]

Both the British devaluation of November 1967 and the more recent German corrective border taxes have brought to the fore an additional consideration. In both cases supplementary measures appeared to be necessary affecting domestic demand in order to avoid quick dissipation of the adjustment effects of the action taken.

This calls to mind that any form of international adjustment in the trade and service accounts tends to cut down profit margins in surplus countries and to reduce real income in deficit countries. Both can be resisted by those affected. Also, deficit countries need to shift resources from non-competitive to internationally competitive activity; the reverse movement is needed in surplus countries. There may very well be important differences among countries in the ease of shiftability of their resources. (Compare the U.K. and Japan.) One possible hypothesis is that shiftability is low where there is a) strong resistance to a reduction in real income on the part of the working population, and b) where a relatively small proportion of resources is engaged in internationally competitive activities as against non-competitive production for the internal market.

These two experiences do suggest that it may be easy to over-estimate the effect of limited exchange flexibility in permitting countries to follow more diverse policies with respect to rates of growth and rates of inflation of costs and prices. The further unfolding of the German experience under the border tax arrangements may be instructive in this respect.

It has been suggested that limited exchange flexibility might not make a very large contribution to changing the U.S. trade and current account position. If this were to be the case, the principal effect might be to ease somewhat the pressure on deficit countries abroad, which have smaller economies with a larger segment of total production devoted to foreign trade.

---

[2] Not printed. The paper explored six options: 1) maintenance of the present Bretton Woods system of fixed exchange rates, subject to adjustment for fundamental disequilibrium; 2) use of border taxes to facilitate adjustment in trade accounts, while maintaining fixed exchange rates; 3) adoption of crawling pegs on a mandatory or discretionary basis; 4) adoption of wider margins, 2 percent or less to 5 percent or more; 5) combination of 3 and 4 above; and 6) a gold bloc and a dollar bloc with a flexible exchange link.

It has also been suggested that limited exchange rate flexibility might have significance for the U.S. in other ways than through the effect on our current account deficit. Conceivably, such flexibility might in fact worsen our current account deficit if it resulted in a gradual depreciation of other currencies as a whole against the dollar. One suggestion is that the adoption of these limited flexibility techniques might be useful because it might permit public attention to be focused on the exchange rate rather than on balance of payments and reserve figures, as at present.

---

112.   Telegram From the Department of State to Selected Posts[1]

Washington, January 31, 1969, 0115Z.

15720. Subject: Special Drawing Rights.

1. New Administration reaffirms U.S. interest in the Special Drawing Rights Amendment to International Monetary Fund.[2] You should make this clear to government and central bank officials.

2. As of now 34 countries with a little over 50 percent of the voting power in the Fund have ratified the Proposed Amendment, as against 67 countries and 80 percent of the voting power required for Amendment to enter into force. Only 13 countries representing 41.5 percent of the total quotas have deposited with Fund instruments of participation indicating their ability to assume responsibilities of participant. SDR facility can be activated only when countries representing 75 percent of Fund's quotas have completed this as well as preceding step.

3. Administration believes it is important that requisite number of countries complete both of above steps as soon as possible—our goal is end of first quarter—so that discussion and decision on activation can follow promptly.

---

[1] Source: National Archives, RG 59, Central Files 1967–69, FN 10 IMF. Limited Official Use. Drafted by Thomas O. Enders (E/IMA) and L.P. Pascoe (Treasury), cleared at Treasury by Volcker and Willis and at the IMF by Dale, and approved by Enders. Sent to all posts except Bathurst, Bujumbura, Gaborone, Kigali, Maseru, Mbabane, and Port Louis.

[2] In Fall 1968 the United States had joined in supporting creation of Special Drawing Rights (SDRs) by the IMF as a new source of international liquidity. See *Foreign Relations, 1964–1968*, vol. VIII, Document 193. A first allocation of $9.5 billion equivalent of SDRs over a 3-year period was approved at the 1969 Annual Meeting of the IMF at Washington in September 1969. See footnote 5, Document 140.

4. *For Bonn, Brussels, The Hague, Rome, Luxembourg, Vienna, Stockholm, Kuwait, Jidda:* In discussions with host country officials, you should avoid mention of U.S. desire for early decision on activation of SDR facility.

5. *For Bern, Paris, Pretoria:* Use above information, but presumption here is that would be unwise to make specific approach to government or central bank officials.

Rogers

---

113.   **Memorandum From the Deputy to the Assistant Secretary of the Treasury for International Affairs (Willis) to the Under Secretary of the Treasury for Monetary Affairs (Volcker)[1]**

Washington, February 6, 1969.

SUBJECT

Note on Justification for SDR Activation

The overall preliminary impression that I have from our useful round of talks with Ossola and van Lennep[2] is that we have a fair chance to get an activation of SDR somewhere in the range of $1 to $2 billion by sometime in the fourth quarter in 1969. I am left somewhat uncertain as to what kind of performance on our balance of payments figures would have to be shown to achieve this. On the whole I don't believe that the amount of activation will vary too much if we show a better performance, but activation could be deferred if our results are too bad.

The main result of van Lennep's effort to find a role for WP-3 in the activation process will probably be that he himself will have to be consulted by Schweitzer, and will have a somewhat stronger voice in deter-

---

[1] Source: Washington National Records Center, Department of the Treasury, Deputy to the Assistant Secretary for International Affairs: FRC 56 83 26, Contingency Planning 1965–1973, Sensitive Documents 1–4/69. Confidential; Limdis. Sent through Assistant Secretary Petty. Copies were sent to Daane at the Federal Reserve, Dale at the IMF, and a number of others in Treasury. The memorandum is marked "For information."

[2] Ossola and Van Lennep met with Treasury Secretary Kennedy, Volcker, and Willis at 3 p.m. on February 5. At 4 p.m. they met in Volcker's office with Volcker, Federal Reserve Governor Daane, and Willis. Memoranda of these conversations are ibid., Secretary's Memos/Correspondence: FRC 56 74 7, Memcons 1969.

mining the amount and timing under Schweitzer's proposal. On the whole this influence will probably be exerted to delay the activation somewhat and hold the amount down to the range that van Lennep considers desirable. On the other hand, his endorsement may be of some value in influencing the Dutch position favorably and possibly that of some other countries, although the latter should not be exaggerated. The key factors remain the attitudes of Schiller, Colombo, Carli, Blessing, Emminger, and Ossola. Schoellhorn of Germany, the Adviser to Schiller, is also important.

After September 1969, van Lennep will no longer be a representative of the Dutch Government, so his personal influence will be increasingly limited to the role of WP-3 and OECD in general.[3]

We are working on a paper to build up the argumentation for a large activation figure in 1969–70. I believe it is important to base our argumentation on the two legs. The first is the fundamental justification which has been built into the SDR plan and is now accepted by most of the Europeans. This is that SDR creation is required to meet the secular need for growth in reserves. This should provide a basic minimum figure every year of something like at least 3–4 percent of reserves.

The second justification would be a temporary one, that of providing reserves to cover the losses of reserves in recent years through gold sales, and to replace reserves cancelled by repayment of short- and medium-term credit. My worry is that van Lennep will try to overemphasize this second reason. Throughout the negotiations, van Lennep and McKay of the Netherlands Bank have had a strong tendency to favor this second approach and to reject or play down the first justification. I think this is dangerous for us, because it leads to the conclusion that reserves are created only when there is clearly evidence of serious disinflation in the world, as a kind of cyclical interjection of purchasing power on a fine tuning basis in the world's economy. We struggled a long time to get away from this view and to build up the need for a secular trend of growth in world reserves.

I would strongly urge that we maintain the primary emphasis on the first justification and not allow van Lennep and his concern with the adjustment process to push us too far into the second philosophy.

---

[3] Van Lennep was slated to become Secretary General of the OECD in September. At the time of the February 5 conversations in Washington he was a senior Finance Ministry official in the Netherlands Government and Chairman of the OECD's WP-3 that studied balance-of-payments adjustment needs and policies.

114.   Telegram From the Embassy in France to the Department of State[1]

Paris, February 9, 1969, 1222Z.

1904. For Treasury for Secretary Kennedy and Petty from Volcker. Full day of frank discussion in London raises a few questions on which guidance would be appreciated for subsequent contact in Paris.[2]

1) Chancellor expressed great firmness on sterling parity even in face of conceivable franc move within "justifiable" range should March labor negotiations in France result in large cost increases.[3] French move not felt to be present contingency. However, Chancellor recognizes "speculative" pressures at any time could require new credit to support sterling parity. I responded this raises very difficult question, with continentals apparently negative and US not in position to assist unilaterally, if at all. At same time, we agreed on extreme hazards of "float," both in terms of international monetary stability and internal British position. Question of US help in funding UK debt not raised.

2) This discussion against background of Chancellor's restrained optimism on British balance of payments. He is looking to erratic but noticeable improvement in trade figures, taking one month with another. While no figure put forth, current account surplus for year clearly significantly smaller than previous official estimates (as outside observers already predict); nonetheless felt to be moving slowly in right direction. There is clear recognition of narrow range of tolerance for short-falls in trade results.

3) Much more concern here over resumption of speculative move into Mark prior to autumn German election than any other contingency, but they feel this danger should not materialize before summer. Consequently, hope period of calm will last for some months, but in view of tenuous nature of situation extremely reluctant to engage in any multilateral discussion that could incite market rumors of imminent changes in parities. Discussions on SDR activation felt possible, but little else in "reform" area practical in view of speculative dangers.

4) Chancellor firm on position vis-à-vis South Africa. (Bank of England, on other hand, would like compromise.) I took line that while

---

[1]   Source: National Archives, Nixon Presidential Materials, NSC Files, Country Files–Europe, Box 674, France, Volume I 1/20–4/14/69. Confidential; Exdis.

[2]   Volcker traveled to Europe in February for introductory calls on Ministry of Finance and Central Bank officials following his assumption of duties as Under Secretary of the Treasury for Monetary Affairs and U.S. G-10 Deputy.

[3]   In February 1969 Roy Jenkins was Chancellor of the Exchequer.

I had not examined question in detail, September 9–10 position appeared sound.[4] Said we are perfectly willing to talk to South Africa without acrimony to clear up interpretation and ambiguities through Washington contact.

5) Chancellor also inquired about visit to you, saying reluctant to leave before March–April budget decisions. Early visit barely possible, but would otherwise have to wait until after budget. Told him you glad see him any time, but no urgency on your part. Frank Figgures, Treasury external man, wants to come promptly in any event.

6) I propose sticking to (A) line that further credit extremely difficult and dependent on continental participation, while not actually shutting door in case of speculative flurry, (B) urging key importance of control of UK domestic situation, (C) above position on South Africa. Also, with your approval, will confirm you would be glad to see him as early as the latter part of week of Feb 17, if he feels able to come—otherwise wait until April. Will call you Tuesday afternoon to discuss further.[5]

Shriver

---

[4] See Document 145.
[5] No record of a call on Tuesday, February 11, was found.

115.   Talking Paper Prepared in the Department of the Treasury[1]

VG/LIM/69-17 (Corr.)   Washington, February 18, 1969.

PRESIDENT NIXON'S TRIP TO EUROPE
February–March 1969

International Monetary System
(for use in United Kingdom, Germany, Belgium, Italy;
see separate talking paper for France)

1. We are both interested in improving the international monetary system.

2. In this context, it is essential to bring inflation under control in the United States. This is a major goal of my Administration.

3. We have been looking in a preliminary way at a number of proposals to see whether there are responsible improvements that can be made in the system. On most of these we have no final view. I would be glad to hear what is in your mind.

4. We have decided that an early and substantial activation of the Special Drawing Rights would be extremely useful. This would be a demonstration to the exchange and gold markets that we "mean business", as we say in the United States. A hesitant approach in timing or magnitude would encourage those who profit from uncertainty. It would leave individual monetary authorities under political pressure to build up their gold reserves to an unnecessary and undesirable degree. I want to make clear that we do not regard activation of Special Drawing Rights as absolving us from the fiscal and monetary discipline needed to improve our balance of payments position.

5. (If the discussion proceeds to more specific questions as to where and how many Special Drawing Rights we would like to see created, the following might be added.) I understand that during the negotiations, illustrative figures were mentioned for activation at the rate of about $1.5–$2 billion a year for the initial period of five years. My advisers say it would be the part of wisdom to begin with a substantially

---

[1] Source: Washington National Records Center, Department of the Treasury, Volcker Group Masters: FRC 56 86 30, VG/LIM/1–VG/LIM/30. Confidential; Limdis. An attached cover note from Willis to members of the Volcker Group, dated February 19, indicates that page 1 was a corrected copy. A February 17 draft, labeled "2nd draft," indicates Willis prepared it. (Ibid., Deputy to the Assistant Secretary for International Affairs: FRC 56 83 26, Current Problems and Contingency Planning 11/68–4/69) President Nixon traveled to Belgium, the United Kingdom, the Federal Republic of Germany, Italy, and France February 23–March 2. See Document 116 for a Talking Paper prepared for the President's use in France.

higher figure, particularly in 1969 and 1970. Ideally we would like to see activation before August, to be announced at the end of September at the IMF Annual Meeting.

6. There is a second problem that concerns us. The process of international adjustment of balances of payments has become too dependent upon selective controls and restraints. We would like to stop the drift in this direction and search for other methods of reducing excessive and persistent deficits and surpluses.

7. We owe it to ourselves to explore every possible new proposal for improving the system, including those under discussion in academic circles. We must be careful to do so without upsetting confidence.

8. Whatever changes we might encourage in the monetary system, none will avoid periodic crises affecting individual currencies. As a result, we will continue to need intensive financial cooperation.

8a. (*Only for Germany and Italy*) We appreciate the efforts made by your country to channel excessive inflows of capital out of reserves and into international monetary and capital markets, as well as your participation in financial assistance for countries facing exchange difficulties.

9. I share the view that, unless we have reached a closer meeting of minds, it would be dangerous to undertake a formal international monetary conference.

10. Finally, you should know that I am not going to seek an answer to these problems through a change in the monetary price of gold.[2] I do not see the need or reason for such action.

Final Note

11. If any interest is expressed in pursuing bilateral discussions with the United States, you might say that Secretary Kennedy would be

---

[2] On February 20 Chairman of the Council of Economic Advisers McCracken sent President Nixon a memorandum regarding De Gaulle and the price of gold. McCracken saw no need for the President to respond directly to an anticipated request, "on a metaphysical level," to increase the price of gold but to emphasize "our interest in a better monetary system, and our concern about growing controls over trade and capital movements." McCracken saw no advantage to increasing the gold price but concluded: "It is equally important not to allow the French, or anyone else, to see any signs of flexibility on gold except in the context of our general position. If we are to be cooperative on gold, there must be a total package that makes it worth our while." (National Archives, Nixon Presidential Materials, NSC Files, President's Trip Files, Box 442, Feb–March 69 Trip to Europe) On February 22 Arthur Burns also sent the President a memorandum on gold. Burns wrote: "you have been correctly advised to show no interest on our part in an increase in the price of gold. . . . By all means let us try to keep the official price as it is, but let us also watch carefully the costs that we may incur through such a policy. And whatever else we may do, let us not develop any romantic ideas about a fluctuating exchange rate: there is too much history that tells us that a fluctuating exchange rate, besides causing a serious shrinkage of trade, is also apt to give rise to international political turmoil." (Ibid.)

glad to meet with representatives of the country concerned in Washington.

---

116.   Talking Paper Prepared in the Department of the Treasury[1]

VG/LIM/69–18   Washington, February 19, 1969.

PRESIDENT NIXON'S TRIP TO EUROPE

February–March 1969

FRANCE

International Monetary System

Warning:

Conversations on monetary reform with the French pose special dangers:

1. The basic French attitude towards the international monetary system is fundamentally different from ours. Their persistent underlying objective has been (a) a substantial increase in the price of gold, large amounts of which are in French hoards, and (b) the imposition of very stern discipline on the U.S. through severe limitations on the future of the dollar as a reserve currency. Recent hints to U.S. officials of French views on reform maintain these two elements.

2. Certain elements in the French regime especially eager to see a rise in the official price of gold will deliberately stir speculation to their advantage. Great care must be taken in any allusions to monetary "reform", as the French will tend to associate "reform" with an increase in the official gold price. If at all possible, *attempts may be made to imply your endorsement of such an approach in any Communiqué.* Leaks to the French press designed to promote this objective following your talks are likely unless the U.S. team is alert with denials.

3. We believe there is some danger that the French might undertake at some time in the future, possibly this year, a large unilateral devalu-

---

[1] Source: Washington National Records Center, Department of the Treasury, Volcker Group Masters: FRC 56 86 30, VG/LIM/1–VG/LIM/30. Confidential; Limdis. Presidents Nixon and de Gaulle met in Paris on February 28, March 1, and March 2. International monetary issues reportedly were discussed in an expanded meeting on March 1, but no record of that meeting was found. Regarding their final meeting on March 2, see Document 7.

ation of the franc aimed at disruption of the monetary system and achieving a higher price of gold. They may hint at the desirability of some package deal with the United States to avoid such disruptive action on their part. Any such proposal should be approached very cautiously, even though some elements might be acceptable.

4. In general, it is important to refer details for future discussion, while preserving our subsequent bargaining position by maintaining a firm position on gold price.

Talking Paper

First Alternative Approach (assuming that President de Gaulle invites you to speak first on the international monetary system)

1. We are both interested in improving the international monetary system.

2. In this context, it is essential to bring inflation under control in the United States. This is a major goal of my Administration.

3. We have been looking in a preliminary way at a number of proposals to see whether there are responsible improvements that can be made in the system. On most of these we have no final view. I would be glad to hear what is in your mind.

4. We have decided that an early and substantial activation of the Special Drawing Rights would be extremely useful. We hope that France will look again at this instrument, and become a participant.[2]

5. But there is a second problem that concerns us. The process of international adjustment of balances of payments has become too dependent upon selective controls and restraints. We would like to stop the drift in this direction and search for other methods of reducing excessive and persistent deficits and surpluses.

6. We owe it to ourselves to explore every possible new proposal for improving the system, including those under discussion in academic circles. We must be careful to do so without upsetting confidence.[3]

---

[2] Telegram 27105 to posts in franc zone countries, February 20, notified the Embassies that the IMF had been informed that, at a forthcoming Yaounde meeting, France would tell franc zone Finance Ministers that ratification of SDRs would be considered an unfriendly act. Without revealing knowledge of this information, the Embassies were requested to report any information they could develop about French actions and host country reactions. (National Archives, RG 59, Central Files 1967–69, FN 10 IMF)

[3] On February 19 Willis circulated to members of the Volcker Group VG/LIM/69-20, which contained revised language for this paragraph because of concerns the French press might take the original out of context and conclude the United States was prepared to explore proposals for a change in the price of monetary gold. The suggested, "safer" version reads as follows: "6. We owe it to ourselves to explore a variety of new proposals for improving the system, including those under discussion in academic circles. We must be careful to do so without upsetting confidence, or casting any doubts on the monetary price of gold." (Washington National Records Center, Department of the Treasury, Volcker Group Masters: FRC 56 86 30, VG/LIM/1–VG/LIM/30)

7. Whatever changes we might encourage in the monetary system, none will avoid periodic crises affecting individual currencies. As a result, we will continue to need intensive financial cooperation. Drastic unilateral action by any country with major financial responsibilities poses grave dangers for all.

8. I share the view that, unless we have reached a closer meeting of minds, it would be dangerous to undertake a formal international monetary conference.

9. Finally, you should know that I am not going to seek an answer to these problems through a change in the monetary price of gold. I do not see the need or reason for such action. I am well aware that this has been a difference of view between our two countries. But I am convinced that this would be disruptive and wrong.

Final Note

10. If any interest is expressed by General de Gaulle in pursuing bilateral discussions with the United States, you might say that Secretary Kennedy would be glad to meet with his representative in Washington.

Second Alternative (if General de Gaulle takes the initiative to spell out the French view on international monetary reform)

11. We are quite willing to discuss with the French, as with other countries, responsible improvements in the international monetary system. (If it appears appropriate to do so, you may wish to say that Secretary Kennedy would be glad to see Minister Ortoli if he wishes to come to Washington.)

12. You could then draw on the material set forth under the first alternative above to the extent that seems appropriate. Several points at least should be made clear to the General:

(a) It is important that General de Gaulle understand our position with respect to the monetary price of gold.

(b) Any discussions of international monetary reform ought to be carried on in a quiet manner to avoid stirring up exchange speculation.

(c) If the General drops a hint or issues a warning concerning the possibility of a unilateral decision to devalue the franc, it might be helpful to indicate that we should all try to avoid drastic unilateral actions that would be disruptive to the monetary system.

117. Telegram From the Department of State to the Mission to the OECD[1]

Washington, February 19, 1969, 0222Z.

26395. 1. White House has decided after all to release text of informal remarks at Treasury February 14.[2]

2. Following are President's remarks on international monetary affairs: "There are indications that the problems affecting the international monetary system are very possibly going to be a subject of not only major discussion on the immediate trip but also they are going to be a subject of major concern in this next year and perhaps within the next two years.

Now is the time to examine our international monetary system to see where its strengths are, where its weaknesses are and then to provide the leadership, leadership which is responsible, not dictatorial, leadership which looks to the good judgment and the good advice that we can get from our friends abroad who will have a similar view about the necessity for a sound international monetary system. . . . Here in this department, I see you here at a time that is very exciting, very exciting because whether it is in the field of tax reform, whether it is in the field of international monetary policies, there is a need for new approaches."

3. Missions should use above on if asked basis.

Rogers

---

[1] Source: National Archives, RG 59, Central Files 1967–69, FN 17. Unclassified. Drafted by Enders (E/IMA), cleared by Rogers (EUR/RPE) and Widman (Treasury), and approved by Enders. Repeated to Bonn, Brussels, The Hague, London, and Luxembourg.

[2] At Secretary Kennedy's request, President Nixon visited the Department of the Treasury on February 14 and addressed employees at 3:25 p.m. Telegram 25595 to Paris (repeated to other EC capitals), February 18, informed addressees that the President's reference to international monetary reform had come up in an informal "pep talk" to Treasury staff and the President had no specific proposal in mind. No text of the President's remarks had been released by the White House. (Ibid.) The full text of the President's remarks, dated for release by the White House on February 14, was distributed to the Volcker Group as VG/INFO/69-10 on February 18. According to that text, early in his remarks the President said: "I am going to speak very carefully now, because I realize that when a Secretary of the Treasury, let alone a President of the United States, says something about tax programs or international monetary matters that it can have the effect of changing the price of gold or, for that matter, changing the price of stocks and so forth and so on." (Washington National Records Center, Department of the Treasury, Volcker Group Masters: FRC 56 86 30, VG/INFO/69-1–VG/INFO/69-22) The President's remarks are printed in full in *Public Papers of the Presidents of the United States: Richard M. Nixon, 1969*, pp. 101–105.

118.   Editorial Note

The Volcker Group met on March 11, 1969, to discuss international monetary issues and international monetary reform. Three papers had been distributed by Willis to members of the Group on March 10 and 11 as a basis for discussion at the meeting.

The first paper was entitled "Strategy for Improving International Monetary Arrangements" (VG/LIM/60-37, dated March 10). An earlier draft, dated March 6, indicates it was drafted by Willis. The transmittal memorandum on the March 10 paper notes that it was Part I of a Strategy paper and had been revised based on suggestions made during a Volcker Group meeting on March 8.

The second paper was Part II, the unilateral approach of the "Strategy for Improving International Monetary Arrangements." The undated paper (VG/LIM/69-38) contains handwritten notations, presumably by Willis, many of which appear to relate to the views of Daane, Bergsten, Solomon, and others expressed during the March 11 Volcker Group meeting. A March 6 memorandum from Willis to T. Page Nelson indicates that Volcker had suggested reducing the alternatives for improving international monetary arrangements to two: A. move in the direction of the Bergsten approach of a dollar, and possibly other currency, blocs; and B. the Bernstein approach that would put the dollar on the same footing as other currencies. (Washington National Records Center, Department of the Treasury, Deputy to the Assistant Secretary for International Affairs: FRC 56 83 26, Contingency Planning 1965–1973, Current Problems and Contingency Planning 11/68–4/69) A revised version of Part II, attributed to Nelson, was distributed to the Volcker Group on March 17 (VG/LIM/69-47).

The third paper was Part III of the "Strategy for Improving International Monetary Arrangements," subtitled "Procedure in the Event of Exchange Crises."

The three papers, drafts, and transmittal memoranda are in the Washington National Records Center, Department of the Treasury, Volcker Group Masters: FRC 56 86 30, VG/LIM/31–VG/LIM/50. Other copies of the papers are ibid., Deputy to the Assistant Secretary of the Treasury for International Affairs: FRC 56 83 26, Contingency Planning 1965–1973. VG/LIM/69-48, Document 119, is presumably a synthesis of these three papers.

119. Volcker Group Paper[1]

VG/LIM/69-48   Washington, March 17, 1969.

SUMMARY OF A POSSIBLE U.S. APPROACH TO IMPROVING INTERNATIONAL MONETARY ARRANGEMENTS

1. Unless there are some changes in the international monetary and payments system, cumulative strains could develop over the next few years that could result in increasingly serious disturbances in the framework of international monetary relationships. One aspect of this strain on the monetary system could be heavy reserve losses for the United States, through the conversion of dollars into gold by foreign monetary authorities. The balance of payments on the liquidity basis may well continue at $2–3 billion a year. A strong anti-inflation program, though absolutely necessary, may not be sufficient to shrink our liquidity deficit in a highly competitive world. This prospect would be underlined by a vigorous program of relaxing restraints on capital outflow, in a future situation of relative monetary ease. The present official settlements surplus results from heavy short-term borrowing by United States banks, which pulls money out of foreign official reserves. This is a factor related to credit stringency here, and may prove to be temporary. We may face attrition of our reserves, and periodic currency crises can add to our gold losses.

2. Our strategy therefore calls for either (a) negotiating substantial but evolutionary changes in present monetary arrangements, or (b) suspending the present type of gold convertibility and following this with an attempt to negotiate a new system, in which the United States would undertake a more limited and less exposed form of convertibility of the dollar. The second course, which would necessarily imply unilateral action by the United States, would involve an initial shock to other countries. The extent of the shock would vary with the circumstances preceding such a decision. The reaction abroad might be less nervous if the decision were made at the time of an exchange crisis and after large U.S. gold losses.

3. In our judgment, substantially more needs to be done in 1969 and 1970 to improve the monetary system than the European monetary

---

[1] Source: Washington National Records Center, Department of the Treasury, Volcker Group Masters: FRC 56 86 30, VG/LIM/31–VG/LIM/50. Confidential; Limdis. The paper is marked "Treasury Draft." Another copy is ibid., Deputy to the Assistant Secretary for International Affairs: FRC 56 83 26, Contingency Planning 1965–1973. This paper was presumably the result of discussion at the March 11 Volcker Group meeting; see Document 118.

authorities realize. Their present horizon is limited to a cautious activation of Special Drawing Rights in an amount of no more than $2 billion a year for five years. While we cannot of course expect negotiations on a more far-reaching package of improvements to be completed within a few months, we do believe that the United States needs to reach its own judgment before June 1969 as to whether there is a reasonable prospect of carrying on with our present responsibilities in an improved system.[2] That is, on the basis of soundings taken with officials of other major countries, we should decide by late spring whether or not we have a fighting chance to obtain European support for our program of improvements by stages in 1969–70. Aggressive negotiations, with high level support, would be essential to push such a campaign forward, should we decide to undertake it.

4. The elements in the first approach are set forth briefly below:

a) An activation of Special Drawing Rights of $15–20 billion during 1969–73, beginning in September 1969, with a front-end load factor in 1969 and 1970. This is substantially more than the maximum amount of $10 billion in 1969–73 that has been mentioned in the past as an illustrative figure, and has been regarded by some observers as the European maximum. We would be prepared to compromise to some extent, but $10 billion would not be enough.

b) We would support a general increase in IMF quotas in 1970, but not at the expense of postponing SDR activation beyond 1969. We would not now join in putting pressure on Continental European creditor countries for a quota increase (which may be desired by the IMF staff, the developing countries, and the French, but resisted by the surplus countries).

c) We would seek an appreciation of the Deutschemark and either exchange appreciation or some substitute such as border tax adjustments from other surplus countries. We would accept, as part of such a program of exchange rate adjustment, a moderate but not excessive depreciation of the French franc.

d) We would determine by June of this year whether intensive consultations should begin with other leading countries on the proposals for limited exchange flexibility—moving parities or wider bands, or a combination of the two. We feel that these may be important to facilitate longer-term adjustment of imbalances, but have not taken a decision. At the present time the Europeans are negative, and it might take two years or more for their attitudes to thaw. What we have to determine this spring is whether we think they will thaw, and whether we want them to.

---

[2] The President met with his advisers to discuss international monetary issues on June 26; see Document 131.

e) This program would be supplemented by a strong drive to achieve a more satisfactory NATO offset; and by the adoption of border tax adjustment techniques by the United States, without a change in the U.S. tax structure. The latter would be a substitute for exchange adjustments, which is not feasible for the United States so long as other currencies peg their exchange rates to the dollar.

f) In return for European cooperation in (a) to (e) above, the United States would undertake to relax controls on capital outflow only in accordance with progress on the anti-inflation front.

g) The United States would resist European pressure to agree in advance to convert enough dollars into gold in future years to prevent a rise in global dollar reserves. If absolutely necessary to reach an understanding with the Europeans, we might undertake to do so if dollar reserves were to reach the outside limit of some range that would allow considerable flexibility to cover the substantial swings in dollar holdings that can occur, as well as a reasonable growth in dollar holdings desired by some countries.

h) An increase in the official dollar price of gold would not be part of either approach. Our bargaining position hinges importantly on firm resistance to an increase in the official gold price.

5. The second approach would begin with unilateral United States action to remove the privilege of gold convertibility at the initiative of foreign monetary authorities. We could then allow some time to elapse to see how foreign countries reacted. Presumably many countries would continue to peg to the dollar and no basic change would take place. With others, reluctance to hold dollars might lead to appreciation of exchange rates, to floating rates for capital transactions, to direct measures cutting down the inflow of dollars or to the use of central banking techniques for rechanneling dollars into international money markets. In the political sense, the world might tend to split into a dollar area, comprising (a) those countries that were quite willing to accumulate dollars, and (b) countries, principally in Europe, that would prefer to hold down their dollar accumulations. In the light of developments, we would proceed with calm and unhurried negotiations looking toward all of the elements of paragraph 4 above, but with generally less emphasis on the speed of decisions. However, it would still be desirable to activate Special Drawing Rights in September 1969.

6. In the transitional phase, following the suspension of convertibility at foreign initiative, there could be some initial confusion in the exchange markets, until the policies of the major countries had been clarified. It has been suggested that some private and official holders of dollars might move into Swiss francs, Deutschemarks or other strong currencies. If this happened, the United States and these countries

would have to consult to determine whether the United States would be willing to repurchase any of these dollars with gold or drawings on the IMF. If the United States did not wish to do so, the countries concerned might decide to appreciate their exchange rates or take other steps to hold down their dollar accumulations. All in all, during the transition period the United States might not wish to relax restraints on capital outflow or ease monetary policy, to avoid adding to the flow of dollars with which the stronger currency areas were coping.

7. The most difficult question under this second approach is whether the United States would go back to convertibility, and, if so, what type of convertibility the United States would be willing to resume. Presumably this would mean that the United States would pay out gold and/or Special Drawing Rights for dollars under some new convertibility principles. Presumably most of the present official dollar holdings would be exchanged for Special Drawing Rights or some special type of reserve asset, so that the United States would not be exposed to the risk of large-scale conversions. Establishing the new principles might require intensive monetary negotiations, which might take months or years. A specific United States position on the new type of convertibility has still to be formulated.

8. One reason for deciding on our basic strategy before June is to try to turn to our advantage any international consultations that may result from exchange crises affecting the French franc, the pound sterling or the Deutschemark. If we are agreed upon our objectives, we might be able to accelerate progress in the desired directions, since important decisions sometimes emerge in the heat of crises.

9. *General Conclusions*

a) Suspension of gold convertibility is not proposed now. Moral suasion would continue to restrain gold losses.

b) We propose taking some risks by negotiating hard to raise the European horizon on the monetary system. There is a risk that they will drag their feet on SDR activation, because they think we are too greedy and want too many SDRs to help finance a continuing deficit. There is a risk that some countries will ask for gold, fearing that we are heading toward a suspension. We believe these risks are justified, as we must see a chance to improve the system so as to:

(i) give the United States more flexibility for domestic and foreign policies,
(ii) halt the spread of selective restraints and restrictions.

c) We don't believe we should become locked in to the evolutionary approach for too long.

d) If it becomes clear that progress on evolutionary improvements is too halting, this year or next, we should resign ourselves to the need for suspension of convertibility and a resumption of negotiations with the Europeans from that different posture.

---

120. Telegram From the Embassy in Italy to the Department of State[1]

Rome, March 27, 1969, 1445Z.

1809. Pass Treasury for Petty.

1. Following is summary (cleared with Volcker) of conversation held March 26 by Volcker, Danne and Willis with Treasury Minister Colombo (including Treasury DirGen Nuvoloni and Treasury official Palumbo). Meeting took place at Chamber of Deputies where Colombo had to be on hand for vote of confidence.[2]

2. Volcker asked about Italian timetable for ratifying SDRs. Colombo replied subject had been scheduled for discussion this very day in Chamber Committee but had to be postponed because of confidence vote issue. Hoped would be approved at next meeting of committee and then go to floor, with approval both Chamber and Senate as soon as possible before end of spring.

3. Volcker explained US thinking on SDR activation, stressing that while SDRs could not be looked upon as answer to all problems besetting monetary system, would be important contribution to stability if activation decision would be taken at September meeting IMF. If this to be achieved would be useful for leading countries to begin to discuss matter so as to reach consensus among themselves by say June, or at least before vacation period begins. Volcker also emphasized that while US by no means feels SDRs are method of solving US balance of payments problems, US does have need, over time, to increase its own reserves and SDR creation would help achieve this. In terms amount SDR creation, Volcker indicated had no specific number in mind, but

---

[1] Source: National Archives, RG 59, Central Files 1967–69, FN 10. Confidential; Limdis; Greenback.

[2] Volcker visited a number of European capitals to consult with officials there on revisions in the U.S. balance-of-payments program (see footnote 4, Document 8 and Document 14) and to take soundings on SDR activation, limited exchange rate flexibility, and other matters. Telegrams reporting on Volcker's conversations in Bern, Bonn, Brussels, The Hague, and Stockholm are in the National Archives, RG 59, Central Files 1967–69, FN 10.

argued average annual amount to be created should be significantly larger than two billion dollar figure that has been mentioned widely. This would show governments are willing to act boldly to combat tensions in monetary system and would provide needed liquidity to compensate for fact gold had not recently been flowing into monetary reserves and that much of recent liquidity creation has been crisis borne, e.g., credits extended to assist sterling and franc.

4. Colombo replied he shared belief that SDR creation, while not panacea, would have both psychological value in alleviating speculation and other strains and constituted innovation which gradually can bring about change in monetary system. In beginning Italy had shared view that achievement US balance of payments equilibrium should be precondition to activation, but at last year's IMF meeting Italy stated that SDR creation and re-establishment US B/P equilibrium should take place simultaneously. If US and other deficit countries were to achieve B/P equilibrium, without SDR creation, repercussions on world liquidity would be too drastic. Italy ready to begin talks among G-10 countries on activation, even in advance of completion of requisite number of ratifications, but question of amount, of whether creation should be on one-year or on multi-year basis and of how creation should be distributed over years must be carefully considered. There is a range of divergent views in Europe. Kind of magnitudes Volcker had alluded to could be discussed on way to achieving a compromise. By way of "friendly advice" Colombo urged that question of activation should not be pushed so hard and fast within G-10 as to create new obstacles to idea of activation, since there were countries in Europe that did not look at this question "with same objectivity as Italy."

5. Volcker emphasized that major problem in US was getting control of inflation and thereby placing US balance of payments on a healthy, long-term basis. This is intention of administration. Colombo said he shared this view, and did not wish to suggest US had any other alternative. He did want US to know that Italy is somewhat concerned about difficulties for its own B/P caused by lop-sided structure US payments. High world interest rates caused by tight money in US are attracting capital from Italy. On other hand, if US should re-establish B/P equilibrium too abruptly, this would have adverse effects on Italy's exports and trade position. These double dangers argued for gradualism in US action to achieve better balance.

6. Volcker described US thinking on proceeding soon to a limited relaxation of controls on capital exports, mentioning that liberalizing move in this direction would also help in stemming pressures for trade protectionism in US, which new administration determined to combat. Colombo replied that if such measures could be taken without substantial detrimental effect on US B/P and if thereby protectionist pressure in

US could be resisted more successfully, Italy could have no reservations about such step.

7. Colombo asked Volcker to keep in mind Italian views on two matters (said would not raise question of flexible rates, et cetera, since Volcker would undoubtedly discuss this with Carli at meeting scheduled for afternoon). First he would like us to study Italian proposal of making available to LDCs, through IBRD and IDA, a contribution in dollars corresponding to given proportion of SDR allocations received by industrialized countries (mentioned as purely illustrative example that if Italy received $100 million equivalent SDR allocation, could agree set aside $10 million from its non-SDR reserves in favor LDCs).[3] Colombo said did not have any preconceptions about how contribution should be determined, e.g., as straight proportion of SDR allocations or mixture of proportion allocations combined with factor taking account of balance of payments situation of donor country. Believe would be good idea study this proposal in G-10 forum. Secondly, Colombo wanted US to know that Italy interested in having its IMF quota increased. Italy knows Japan interested in increasing its quota. Italy believes its place should not be lower than seventh among IMF countries. It will ask for this and hopes US will support.

8. Volcker said, in principle, Italian idea of contribution to LDCs at time SDR creation could be studied, but he was fearful this would complicate question of proceeding with SDR activation. Just as Colombo had asked US not to press too hard on question of amount of SDR activation, Volcker wanted to ask Colombo not to press too hard on examination contribution to LDCs before activation question settled. On IMF quota matter, Volcker said US had not had chance think about this question, but we would proceed to examine it and look at as sympathetically as possible. Again, however, while this should be examined on its own merits, he did not want to burden activation question by tie to quota question.

Ackley

---

[3] The Italians took the lead in official international monetary circles in promoting the SDR–aid link. The Nixon administration was not opposed to the idea but did not want to weaken its priority for SDR activation by linking it to aid.

121.   Telegram From the Department of State to the Embassies in Belgium, the Netherlands, Italy, Sweden, and Switzerland[1]

Washington, April 12, 1969, 0127Z.

56540 1. During his recent discussions in Europe, Treasury Under Secretary Volcker indicated to key monetary officials (including Snoy and Ansiaux, Witteveen and Zijlstra, Wickmann and Joge, Stopper and Carli) that U.S. would be willing to explore bilaterally at technical level, problems involved in suggestions concerning limited increase in exchange rate flexibility.[2] Following proposal was put forward, in varying detail:

a. It is to be understood that U.S. Government has not as yet developed an official view on any of these suggestions, or on general question whether any formal or informal change is required in present exchange rate regime. At same time, interest in these ideas is sufficiently widespread so that we believe careful exploration of some of issues involved is desirable. Our interest at this stage is in elucidation, at technical staff level, of technical and policy issues that would be posed if any such changes were to be decided upon. Object would be to increase our understanding of issues involved, and to obtain some indication of tentative views of authorities of important countries, as input to reaching official U.S. views of these ideas.

b. We would be glad to engage in series bilateral technical talks on these questions, in great secrecy, if authorities these governments would find it useful. Have no wish to press if authorities are not interested. Same offer being made to all G-10 countries.

2. Our impression is that most if not all G-10 countries will wish to accept offer if they are satisfied talks will be adequately protected against leaks. Extraordinary care should be taken to limit knowledge of this offer to those with absolute need to know.

3. As means of implementing our proposal request addressee posts review foregoing with D'Haeze, De Strycker, Van Lennep and Kessler, [illegible], and Joge, Leutwiler and Ossola (Palumbo if Ossola thinks

---

[1]   Source: National Archives, RG 59, Central Files 1967–69, FN 10 4/1/69. Confidential; Limdis; Greenback. Drafted by William Dale; cleared in Treasury by Widman and Willis (in draft), in the Federal Reserve by R. Wood, in the Council of Economic Advisers by Wonnacott (in substance), and in State by E. Heginbotham (E/IMA); and approved by Robert M. Beaudry (EUR/NSC–IG).

[2]   Pursuant to discussions between Volcker and French Director of the Treasury René Larre, arrangements were also being made for consultations with the French on limited exchange rate flexibility. The talks would take place on the fringes of an April 24–25 meeting of the OECD's WP-3 that would provide cover for U.S. officials' travel to Paris, minimizing the possibility of press leaks. (Telegram 58690 to Paris, April 16; ibid.)

advisable) and indicate that if government wished pursue such studies, our feeling is useful way to conduct talks would be for one or two teams of U.S. Treasury and Fed technical personnel (one each) to visit host authorities in near future. We envisage discussions as being distinctly below level of Deputies or Alternate Deputies. U.S. technical people will be prepared for visit as early as week of April 21. We envisage talks would require about one full working day per country, though perhaps some leeway might be left for a little more. If at conclusion of this discussion discussants feel a second round would be useful, arrangements could be made for foreign discussants to visit Washington for this purpose at some time during May. We hope to finish any such bilateral technical talks before end of May.

5. As background material for discussion, we would suggest three IMF staff papers which host authorities (except Switzerland) should have, or which we prepared supply. These are DM/69/2, Fleming paper on wider margins; DM/69/4, Hirsch paper on sliding parities; and DM/69/10, Kuczynski paper describing various sliding parity proposals.[3] In addition, we would supply series of annotated questions on which we believe it would be useful to center discussion.

6. If authorities are interested in proceeding on this basis, would appreciate indication of date or dates when could be ready for visit of U.S. technical personnel, and, if available, name(s) of host persons who would participate in discussion. Widman, Treasury, will coordinate schedule. (FYI. Would you see any disadvantages in having team visit four or five countries in sequence?)

For Rome: Re Ossola's views reported Korp–Willis letter April 3,[4] Washington visit by BOI official suggested by Ossola could be in lieu of Rome visit by U.S. team or could follow team's European tour, at option of Italians. Inclusion in talks of a second Italian expert from BOI Foreign Exchange Dept. also optional with Italians.

Rogers

---

[3] DM/69/2 is a paper by J. Marcus Fleming entitled "Wider Margins of Exchange Rate Variation," January 8, circulated to members of the Volcker Group as VG/WG/69-8. DM/69/4, a paper by Fred Hirsch entitled "The Usefulness of Small Changes in Exchange Rates in the Case of Industrial Countries," January 9, was circulated as VG/WG/69-9. DM/69/10, a paper by Michael Kuczynski entitled "Proposals for Small and Perhaps Frequent Changes in Par Values," February 3, was circulated as VG/WG/69-20. (All in Washington National Records Center, Department of the Treasury, Volcker Group Masters: FRC 56 86 30, VG/WG/69-1–VG/WG/69-22) The VG/WG (later VG/WG I) series of Volcker Group papers pertains to the Working Group of the Volcker Group that worked on limited exchange rate flexibility. The WG papers were also circulated to members of the Volcker Group in the VG/INFO series. The DM series numbers were given to papers by the IMF staff.

[4] Ralph V. Korp, Treasury Attaché at the Embassy in Rome. The April 3 letter was not found.

122. Memorandum of Conversation[1]

Washington, May 1, 1969, 10:45 a.m.

PARTICIPANTS

The President
Chancellor of the Exchequer, Roy H. Jenkins
Secretary of the Treasury, David M. Kennedy
British Ambassador, John Freeman
Chief of Protocol, Emil Mosbacher
Henry A. Kissinger
C. Fred Bergsten

The meeting took place on the terrace outside the President's office on a beautiful spring morning. The discussion was extremely cordial and freewheeling and was largely a get-acquainted session between the President and the Chancellor.[2] A UPI photo of the group appeared in the *Washington Post* on May 2.

The President opened the discussion by commenting that recent developments in Europe made even more imperative the maintenance of a common ground between the U.S. and the UK. Our two countries will not always agree on specific issues but will generally fully understand each other's views. The President expressed the hope that the Chancellor and Secretary Kennedy would develop a close relationship with complete candor its hallmark. Given the latest French development (note: the departure of General de Gaulle),[3] we can expect a period of uncertainty and potential instability for as long as three months. During this period, as well as into the future, the U.S. does not wish to be alone.

Secretary Kennedy reported that he and the Chancellor had already developed such a relationship.[4] In addition, he would be talking with

---

[1] Source: National Archives, RG 59, Central Files 1967–69, POL UK–US. Confidential; Nodis. Drafted by Bergsten. According to the President's Daily Diary, the meeting lasted from 10:37 to 11:25 a.m. (National Archives, Nixon Presidential Materials, White House Central Files, President's Daily Diary) The Diary does not record Ambassador Freeman and Bergsten as attendees, but does list John Harris, an aide to the Chancellor.

[2] An April 30 memorandum from Secretary Kennedy to the President informed Nixon that the May 1 meeting with the Chancellor would be a courtesy call where no issues of substance would be raised. (Washington National Records Center, Department of the Treasury, Secretary's Memos/Correspondence: FRC 56 74 1, Memo to the President Jan–April 1969)

[3] Georges Pompidou gained a plurality in the first round of French elections on May 1 and was elected President in the second round on May 15.

[4] Kennedy and Jenkins met at Camp David on April 28 and discussed prospective exchange rate changes, particularly the need for an appreciation of the German Mark, SDR activation, and South African gold. A memorandum of their conversation is ibid., Memcons 1969.

the Germans in the same way. Minister of Economics Schiller wants to visit the Secretary for a day or two in mid-May.[5]

The Secretary reported that he and the Chancellor had discussed the prospects for German revaluation and the French currency problem. The Germans wanted company for their upward move but had not yet received any. The President asked whether the Italians were not strong enough to move, though he recognized their political problems. The Chancellor noted that Italy has a strong current account position, which would get even stronger if Germany revalued, but they face recurring capital flight which reflects their political uncertainties.

The Chancellor expressed the view that German revaluation was inevitable and, in that case, should be done sooner rather than later. The current problem is that the Germans are talking about it but taking no action. The President asked why Strauss is doing so much talking, to which Dr. Kissinger guessed that Strauss wants to delay the revaluation as long as possible and accomplish it at his own initiative.

The Chancellor noted that the Germans can talk without hurting themselves but that the talking hurts others, especially the French and the UK. He expressed the hope that Schiller would not say much publicly unless he was ready to do something. Dr. Kissinger noted that Schiller was not very strong. The Chancellor thought he was a clever man and in many ways not bad, but that he was the worst chairman he had ever seen.

The President then asked the Chancellor for his views on the French situation. Did the Chancellor think that it would change much post-de Gaulle or would the governing establishment simply carry on?

The Chancellor responded that the French bureaucracy was very strong and capable. It had held up the Fourth Republic and would continue to be effective. He was uncertain, however, of Couve's ability to make decisions during the interim period.

The President noted that one of our academic experts foresaw little change. Dr. Kissinger agreed that there would be little change if Pompidou was elected, but he was not sure of this outcome. If the Left decides to back the Center, the candidate of the Center (presumably Poher) could win. This could occur even if the Leftist ran second on the first ballot, with Poher running third. The Center would not be able to

---

[5] Kennedy and Schiller met at Camp David June 1–2; see Document 128. Kennedy had met earlier with Economics Ministry State Secretary Johann Schoellhorn and Bundesbank Director Otmar Emminger on April 29. A memorandum of their conversation, which focused on exchange rates, is in the Washington National Records Center, Department of the Treasury, Secretary's Memos/Correspondence: FRC 56 74 1, Memcons 1969. On May 10 Secretary Kennedy informed President Nixon that the German Cabinet had decided not to revalue the Mark; see Document 126.

deliver its votes to the Left, but the reverse could occur. The Left might wish to support Poher in order to dilute the power of the Presidency and shift power back toward the Assembly.

The Chancellor thought this would represent a return to the Fourth Republic and Dr. Kissinger fully agreed. The Chancellor was not sure that the Left would support the Center, but Dr. Kissinger responded that the interest of the Left was to destroy a strong presidency in order to produce a fairly weak government. The Chancellor did not think the Communists would clearly opt for a centrist over Pompidou, but he admitted that they would like to see a weak government emerge. Dr. Kissinger agreed and thought this argued for the thesis he had just outlined. The Gaullists would not hold together without de Gaulle, but if Pompidou wins there will be little change in the short run.

The President then asked about French economic policy. Secretary Kennedy thought that it would improve because General de Gaulle's interference had been a major problem. Mr. Bergsten noted that the outcome of the wage negotiations was one key element in the situation and a key question was whether the new government could hold them down. The Chancellor and Secretary Kennedy agreed that these were key questions for the longer term but thought they were not decisive for the short run viability of the franc.

The Chancellor asked Secretary Kennedy whether he assumed there would be no French devaluation until their elections. The Secretary replied that the timing was very tight. Germany must move soon in view of their election and perhaps that is why Schiller wants to come earlier than originally planned.

The Chancellor noted that Strauss would be visiting him at the same time and that the U.S. and UK should therefore keep in close touch. If Strauss says the Germans will move but not until the French election, there will be massive speculation between mid-May and mid-June. The Chancellor thought it would be hard for Germany to revalue sufficiently and there was no real pressure on them since they were taking in money. The Secretary noted that such a scenario would bring sterling under pressure, given the British reserve position. The Chancellor noted that sterling had done all right today (May 1) despite flows into Germany, but he reiterated his concern about the Germans' talking and not acting.

The President noted that this could be an explosive year in Europe politically. We do not know who the players will be by the end of the year. We must all therefore remain flexible in our policies while at the same time retaining a force for stability. The Chancellor affirmed that there was now a new political situation in Europe.

The President remarked that it was his understanding that Prime Minister Wilson now wishes to delay his visit to Washington. The

Chancellor made it clear that the Prime Minister wishes to come when he can, and the President added that it might be better for the visit to follow the French election. The Chancellor agreed.

The President asked whether the Prime Minister would be able to keep the unions in check with his proposed new legislation. The Chancellor replied that the legislation was the right thing to do and was necessary. He thought they could get it through by the end of July although it will be a battle. (The President commented that such a proposal was "gutsy.")

Ambassador Freeman commented that public opinion including labor was with the government on this issue. He cited a recent poll showing 60 percent support for the government's proposal. In reply to the President's question of why there was support, the Ambassador commented that the rank and file union members were fed up with their leadership, with the inconvenience of periodic work stoppages, and that they were beginning to understand economic problems. The Chancellor added that the great worry of union members was unofficial strikes. The UK does not lose as many man-days of work per year as does the U.S., but their strikes were less orderly. This particularly incensed the wives of the union members. One advantage of the British balance of payments problem is the development of widespread appreciation of their economic difficulties; the monthly trade figures are widely followed and the people are impatient for progress. Nevertheless, there are significant problems within the union leadership and the Parliamentary Labor Party, which includes 80 to 90 of their 330 MPs.

Dr. Kissinger noted that these back benchers would not vote against the government. The Chancellor said that some would although they would hope others would keep them from voting themselves out of power. The risk is that they would miscalculate on the offsetting votes.

The President said he was interested in discussing the question because popular attitudes reveal something about the character of a country. It was encouraging to him that the British people were undaunted. Governments could do things if their people were willing to take bitter medicine. Many experts said that the UK was finished, but he had said on his last telethon during the campaign that no one should under estimate the resilience of Britain, which asserts itself at unexpected times.

The President then commented that we might be at a watershed in history. With de Gaulle gone we have a great opportunity and need to develop new areas of strength. The character of people, including the U.S. were critical in the making of difficult decisions. Any one nation can affect others significantly by standing up for what is right.

The Chancellor thought that Europe [*Britain*] might now achieve entry into the EEC, although it still might take a year or so. Progress toward this goal would have a great impact on UK morale. Morale was not low at the present time, however, despite the balance of payments, because the economy was in good shape otherwise.

The President commented that we should be thinking of new approaches on several fronts when the situation is as fluid as this. He would take a gingerly approach to improving the international monetary system since we can't talk too much without exacerbating our problems. He did hope, however, that we could do some imaginative thinking in this period and not just react to crises. We need to decide on what kind of Atlantic Community we wish. It could not develop as originally conceived and the passing of de Gaulle would not make it an easy task since there would still be Gaullists in all countries. It was his hope, however, that we could make some attacks on these problems. If not, more fragmentation would set in due to lack of leadership and the world situation could become quite difficult. He admitted that this discussion might sound esoteric, but he thought strongly that we should not miss such an historical opportunity.

The Chancellor agreed and noted that we must keep monetary questions in their proper place, within the broad political framework. He said that Britain would try to find its way through to its relationship with Europe. The failure to do so to date had meant a total loss of momentum for the European movement. Dr. Kissinger noted that Poher would favor UK entry and that even Pompidou was less hostile than the General. He saw this as the major change likely in French policy.

The President added that the real question is the Atlantic world that would result. The Chancellor replied that the UK wants to enter Europe to strengthen the Atlantic Community. Ambassador Freeman noted that this was precisely the source of de Gaulle's opposition to UK entry, which must now be probed.

The President said that he had reminded the State Department of their argument that our problems with Europe would disappear if de Gaulle were gone, and had asked for a paper on the subject. We needed to do some hard planning and thinking. A real opportunity existed given a new French government, the German election, and the Italian problem. We cannot seize the opportunity with the old stereotyped approaches, however. A new breakthrough is required. A key element is for us to remain flexible. The President expressed an interest in any new approaches, which the UK might suggest, not just in the financial field. If we develop no new approaches but just react to developments, we might see Europe fragment—this tendency was the virus of the day.

Secretary Kennedy stated that he hoped to explore quietly with French officials what the French could do on the exchange rate before their election. He would avoid any intrusion in the political scene. The President asked whether such an approach could be private, and Dr. Kissinger asked whether it would be conducted at the expert level. The Chancellor thought an approach could be kept private. Secretary Kennedy said he would do it via Under Secretary Volcker. Secretary Kennedy encouraged the British to make an effort to find out as well, perhaps through Governor O'Brien, who is also close to the French. A discussion ensued on how best to approach the French.

The President concluded with a reminder that we should not let the movement of history pass us by while important situations change. The Chancellor agreed and Dr. Kissinger concluded that the situation had become unfrozen.

---

123.   Action Memorandum From the President's Assistant for National Security Affairs (Kissinger) to President Nixon[1]

Washington, May 2, 1969.

SUBJECT

U.S. Policy Toward the Present European Currency Situation

The attached memorandum from Secretary Kennedy summarizes the European monetary situation and suggests a possible course of US action.

Speculation on a revaluation of the German mark has increased tremendously in the past two days, in response to statements by Strauss openly raising the possibility of an early German move "in a period of calm, and in company with other countries".[2] Renewed speculation on a French devaluation has resulted from the exit of de Gaulle plus the expected DM revaluation. The main danger, however, is that both events—which are probably inevitable—will not occur soon enough to prevent a massive run on the British pound, which could force the UK

---

[1] Source: National Archives, Nixon Presidential Materials, NSC Files, Agency Files, Box 289, Treasury, Volume 1. Secret. A stamped notation on the memorandum reads: "The President has seen," and the President wrote: "Excellent analysis."

[2] Strauss' statements were not further identified.

to abandon its fixed exchange rate, devalue by a sizable amount, and/or apply import restrictions.

The direct economic effect on the US of any or all of these changes would be small and certainly manageable. A major problem for us would arise only if a forced British move disrupted confidence in the functioning of the entire international monetary system, which could lead to efforts by foreign monetary authorities to convert their dollar reserves into US gold. A failure of the three main foreign governments to respond responsively to the situation could, in the extreme, generate widespread financial chaos with deleterious political and economic effects on the US. (The economic effect would be much more serious in all other countries than in the US. However, the plain fact is that only the US will take responsibility for the functioning of the entire system.)

Secretary Kennedy proposes that we encourage the Germans and French to change their exchange rates as soon as possible and by appropriate amounts. The amount cited in the Treasury memorandum—a move of 10 percent by each—is about right. It would be desirable for the Germans to revalue by a bit more, but it would be undesirable for the French to devalue by very much more.

Secretary Kennedy's memorandum recommends only that we try to energize the French and Germans to reach bilateral agreement on the questions, and asks for approval to indicate your support for the approach.

I will not dispute the economic analysis involved in making this recommendation. The basic issue is how close Western Europe is to a financial panic. But any move toward French devaluation and German revaluation will be extremely difficult politically for both countries.

In my judgment Strauss would not have publicly mentioned revaluation (*before* discussing it with the Chancellor) if he were willing to move quickly. Furthermore, it is highly doubtful that France will devalue one or two weeks after de Gaulle unless forced to do so by a financial panic. A basic question is who would make the decision: Couve would not reverse his mentor and Poher's position is clearly not sufficiently strong. And neither Germany nor France will act in order to save Britain. The threat to Britain and ultimately the U. S. could thus develop as outlined above. (I have checked my political judgments with the State Department, which agrees.)

If massive speculation becomes a virtual certainty, it may become necessary for us to weigh in with an effort to convince the Germans and/or French to move in order to avoid the major risk already cited, despite the political risks of so doing. Such an effort might require your personal involvement. Our main pressure would probably have to be applied to Germany, and the offset negotiations which began yesterday would provide an opportunity to give them something in return.[3] (NSDM 12 has already directed that we indicate to Germany our willingness to broaden our offset negotiations in future years to include overall monetary cooperation, and you asked to review this year's negotiations for the possibility of doing so sooner. The timing may prove to be extremely fortuitous.)

But such a U.S. effort would have highly sensitive foreign policy implications—since we would in essence be trying to get other countries to change their exchange rates—and the politics of any move to do so should be considered extremely carefully before you decide to pursue it. Until it is clear that we face a major crisis, we should keep our profile as low as possible, since any major U.S. involvement—no matter what its purpose—would almost inevitably be used by the French left as an example of U.S. involvement in France's internal affairs.

Recommendations[4]

1. That you authorize a low-key effort to encourage the French and Germans to get together to work out a solution, without, however, trying to tell them what that solution should be or using your name explicitly.

2. That you direct Secretary Kennedy, that if your low-key approach fails, he must come back to you for explicit approval before taking further steps.

3. That you direct him to develop a contingency plan for use if a crisis were to develop and further U. S. action were needed, and assure him of your personal intervention if and when needed.

---

[3] See Document 18.

[4] There is no indication the President approved or disapproved these recommendations.

Attachment

Memorandum From Secretary of the Treasury Kennedy to President Nixon[5]

Washington, May 1, 1969.

The unsettling effects of the French election on the exchange markets were greatly aggravated yesterday by statements of German Finance Minister Strauss openly raising the possibility of an early German revaluation. While the May Day holiday on the Continent is providing limited respite today, it now seems likely that speculation will gather force until the anticipated revaluation (and French devaluation) takes place. The main danger is that, unless the impasse is broken shortly, there may be a forced devaluation of the British pound, posing a clear risk of a series of other devaluations at the expense of the dollar and exchange stability generally.

This potential crisis comes at a time when intensive conversations with the British and Germans give us a clear sense of their own objectives and possible actions.[6] On the other hand, contact with the French Government has been circumscribed by their transition and the difficulty of identifying those currently most influential in this area.

We are initiating contacts with all the principal parties against the background of the following objectives:

1. The German mark should be revalued by 10 percent. The French franc should be devalued by 10 percent. The Netherlands guilder and Swiss franc should be revalued (by lesser amounts), if possible, recognizing this probably cannot be achieved before German action.
2. The French-German action should take place as early as this weekend, or as soon as possible thereafter.
3. The British pound should hold at its present parity.

Our contacts would be directed at energizing the main parties at interest—the French and Germans—to reach a bilateral accommodation on these lines.

---

[5] Secret. Volcker, Bergsten, Samuels, Houthakker, Daane, and Cooper discussed the substance of this memorandum on May 1. (Note to Willis; Washington National Records Center, Department of the Treasury, Deputy to the Assistant Secretary for International Affairs: FRC 56 83 26, Contingency Planning, Current Problems and Contingency Planning 4–10/69)

[6] See Document 122 for a record of talks with British officials. Otmar Emminger and Johann Schoellhorn, accompanied by Ambassador Pauls, met with Secretary Kennedy and Under Secretary Volcker on April 19. A memorandum of their conversation is in the Washington National Records Center, Department of the Treasury, Secretary's Memos/Correspondence: FRC 56 74 7, Memcons 1969. Kennedy met with Emminger and Schoellhorn again on April 29; see footnote 5, Document 122.

The main stumbling blocks are (1) German insistence heretofore that their revaluation must not be in isolation, (2) French paralysis during the transition, and (3) the unwillingness of the Dutch or Swiss to "make company" for the Germans at this time. As part of our effort to meet German resistance, we would indicate to them our willingness to accept a relatively "soft" military offset, along the lines of their present proposal. We have also initiated other contacts with finance ministers and central banks. However, it would be desirable if we could indicate your personal knowledge and support of this approach. While we hope it will not be necessary, we also hope we could count on your personal intervention, if required at a critical point.

This approach has been discussed with and is supported by the State Department, the Federal Reserve, and the Council of Economic Advisers.

David M. Kennedy

---

124.   **Action Memorandum From the President's Assistant for National Security Affairs (Kissinger) to President Nixon**[1]

Washington, May 7, 1969.

SUBJECT

The Present International Monetary Situation

Issue

Attached at Tab A is a memorandum from Paul McCracken which reviews the present status of the international currency difficulties and makes three recommendations:[2]

---

[1] Source: National Archives, Nixon Presidential Materials, NSC Files, Subject Files, Box 309, Balance of Payments. Secret. Drafted by Bergsten.

[2] McCracken's May 5 memorandum is not printed. McCracken began by referring to a May 2 meeting at the Treasury Department that "brought out the political difficulties in getting France to devalue, a solution about which we had no doubts in any case." McCracken noted that the action Kennedy had proposed on May 1 (see the attachment to Document 123) was therefore ruled out for the time being. In a May 6 memorandum to Kissinger, Bergsten characterized some of McCracken's analysis as inadequate and some of his recommendations as extremely dangerous politically, and recommended Kissinger sign the May 7 memorandum to the President. (National Archives, Nixon Presidential Materials, NSC Files, Subject Files, Box 309, Balance of Payments)

1. That we inform the United Kingdom, which is the main potential crisis point, that:

(a) We hope they will continue to defend their present exchange rate.
(b) We are opposed to their adopting any new import restrictions.
(c) We are willing to help them manage a floating exchange rate for the pound, if they are forced to abandon their present parity, presumably by making available to them enough money to moderate any decline in its value.

2. That we make no statements supporting the present structure of exchange rates (except for the gold-dollar price) or minimizing the seriousness of the situation.

3. That we come out more openly for the "crawling peg", a basic reform of the international monetary system which would permit gradual adjustment of exchange rates and hence help avoid future crises.

Present Situation and Analysis

Dr. McCracken's memorandum is contradictory on one of the crucial elements of the situation. It states at one point that "there are no indications" that Germany will revalue unilaterally, and at another that they "will probably change their view if more money flows in". I share the former judgment; the present monetary system puts very little real pressure on surplus countries to act short of intense political pressure from the rest of the world. In the case of Germany, this means in practice that the US would have to involve itself deeply—probably including your personal intervention—to change their minds.

Second, the memorandum indicates only by omission that the US is well shielded from any direct effects of the present European currency problems. Our exceedingly tight monetary policy is keeping the dollar extremely strong in the exchange markets. Thus our only purely national worry is the possibility that a real financial panic will ensue and lead foreign monetary authorities to lose their nerve and seek to convert their dollars into US gold. We might then be forced to suspend the convertibility of the dollar into gold, which would risk major foreign policy problems as outlined in my memo last Friday.[3]

Third, I fully endorse Dr. McCracken's conclusion that the UK is the major potential crisis point in the system and therefore agree with his recommendation that we express our hope that the UK will hold its present exchange rate.

However, I do not agree with his recommendation that we tell the UK that we would prefer a floating exchange rate for the pound to new import restrictions, if they are forced to do something. Even on purely

[3] Document 123.

economic grounds, it is not clear that our balance of payments would be hurt more by restrictions than by a change in the exchange rate of sterling. More important, however, a UK decision to float would represent a major break with the present monetary system and is much more likely than new restrictions to induce other countries to follow. Thus, a decision to float is much more likely to touch off a panic. It is true that import restrictions would only buy time for the UK, but there is good economic reason to believe that they are finally on the right track and that a bit more time will permit them to hold their present exchange rate.

Finally, I agree that we need to move specifically toward reforming the monetary system so that such crises will not recur continuously and that the "crawling peg" is a desirable element in such reform. There are two problems with his recommendation that we come out more openly for such an approach, however.

One problem is that we should be very cautious about openly advocating the "crawling peg" at the present time. Any US statement on exchange rates would increase market nervousness and run counter to Dr. McCracken's other recommendation that we avoid making any statements on the present situation. (We should, however, be alert to opportunities afforded by the present situation to increase support for our reform ideas.)

The other problem is that you have not yet received the options paper on monetary issues which you asked the Treasury to provide a month ago. As a result, you have not had an opportunity to consider the subject systematically and we have no agreed policy. We need to move on this quickly before a real crisis overtakes us.

Recommendations:[4]

1. That we inform the UK, in low key, of our hope that they can maintain their present exchange rate.

2. That we go no further in our policy recommendations to the UK.

3. That we make no statements at all concerning the present European currency situation, or, for the moment, our specific proposals for international monetary reform.

4. That you convene an early meeting to consider overall US international monetary policy.[5] I recommend that such a meeting include the Secretary of Treasury, the Secretary of State, the Chairman of the Federal Reserve Board, the Chairman of the Council of Economic Advisers, and myself.

---

[4] The President approved all four recommendations and wrote "OK" at the end of the memorandum.

[5] Such a meeting convened on June 26; see Document 131.

125.   Editorial Note

As currency uncertainties emerged in early May 1969, due to the imminent change in the French Government and renewed speculation that the German Mark would be revalued and the British pound devalued or allowed to float, policymakers began to consider options for actions by the U.S. Government.

A May 7 paper entitled "Policy Considerations in Current Monetary Situation" had a short-term focus related to the current crisis, while a May 10 draft memorandum to the President on the Secretary of the Treasury's letterhead entitled "U.S. Policy Options With Respect to International Monetary Evolution" looked to the longer term evolution over the next decade. Both papers are in the Washington National Records Center, Department of the Treasury, Deputy to the Assistant Secretary for International Affairs: FRC 56 83 26, Contingency Planning 1965–1973, Current Problems and Contingency Planning 4–10/69. There is no indication that the draft memorandum went forward to the President, but many of the ideas in the memorandum are included in the paper prepared for the meeting with the President on June 26; see Tab B to Document 130.

On May 10 Bergsten sent Kissinger a memorandum that reads as follows: "Following is the memorandum which you requested, which Dick Cooper (who flew down for the day) and I wrote today. Volcker would not commit himself to prepare an options paper so we proceeded fully on our own. The Volcker Group will meet tomorrow night." (National Archives, Nixon Presidential Materials, NSC Files, Subject Files, Box 309, Balance of Payments) The paper Bergsten referred to has not been found, but attached to another copy of his May 10 memorandum is a May 2 memorandum from Cooper to Kissinger on "Implications of Gold Suspension and a Floating Pound." In a May 13 memorandum to Kissinger on "The International Monetary Situation," Bergsten indicates that his and Cooper's May 10 paper set out options for the current crisis. (Both ibid., Agency Files, Box 215, Council of Economic Advisers—Secret) No record of a May 11 Volcker Group meeting has been found.

126. Memorandum From Secretary of the Treasury Kennedy to President Nixon[1]

Washington, May 10, 1969.

The decision of the German Cabinet not to revalue the mark will leave an air of uncertainty over international financial developments for some time. The immediate outlook for the exchange markets is highly uncertain, and turns on the credibility of the German position. This will depend, in large part, on what other tax and financial measures the Germans are prepared to take. The Germans have been extremely vague on this, and no decisions are expected until the middle of next week, at the earliest.

While the German position on the mark parity is unsatisfactory, I see no alternative but to accept it as an accomplished fact for the time being, and to work as best we can within that framework in the days ahead.[2] Revaluation has become a straight party issue, with Strauss leading the CDU opposition. While some reports indicate the Chancellor himself has some sympathy for revaluation, in the last analysis there seems little chance that he would reverse the decision, unless or until external conditions and pressures change. In practice, this would require an even more severe crisis in the exchange markets or changes in parity by other countries so the Germans have "company."

Our interest for the short run lies in (1) promoting a reversal of the recent speculation into marks, and (2) building protection against the possibility that new speculative pressures will converge on sterling. To help achieve the former, in press statements and contacts we will cast no doubt on the ability of the Germans to sustain their position, accept it as a fact, and make plain the necessity for supporting measures to repel speculation.

The second objective is supported by the agreement now reached under pressure from events and the U.S., between the U.K. and the

---

[1] Source: National Archives, Nixon Presidential Materials, NSC Files, Subject Files, Box 309, Balance of Payments. Confidential.

[2] According to a May 13 memorandum from Bergsten to Kissinger, the United States sought to influence the German Cabinet's decision. Bergsten wrote: "the only feedback I have gotten from our intervention on Friday night [May 9] is that it came too late and hence was of no help. I do not know whether this means that the decision had really been made before the Cabinet meeting, as reported in some press stories, or that Ambassador Pauls failed to convey it to Kissinger promptly enough. This report came from Bundesbank Director Emminger, who with the rest of the Bundesbank firmly supported Schiller's effort to get revaluation, to Federal Reserve Board Governor Daane at the Sunday meeting of central bankers in Basel." (Ibid., Agency Files, Box 215, Council of Economic Advisers)

IMF in negotiations on a $1 billion credit package. This will be leaked to the press in London in time for the Monday papers.

The question of additional credit facilities for the British, by the U.S. and other countries, will also arise, especially if speculative pressures on sterling are not reversed. The Federal Reserve, in contacts this weekend at the regular Basle meeting of central bankers, will test sentiment on this difficult issue. With respect to "recycling" recent German gains, the question of a German government guarantee may arise.

If a calmer market atmosphere prevails in the days and weeks ahead, some orderly realignment of exchange rate parities still may be possible this summer. This would be a prelude to our efforts to achieve more fundamental reforms. But it is clear we will continue to face formidable uncertainties until the politically-charged impasse on exchange rates is resolved.

David M. Kennedy

---

127.   Editorial Note

On May 27, 1969, George Willis circulated a summary of a series of consultations on exchange rates that had been taking place since March 25. The summary was sent to members of the Volcker Group and the Working Group as VG/WG/69-65. (Washington National Records Center, Department of the Treasury, Volcker Group Masters: FRC 56 86 30, VG/WG/69-61–VG/WG/69-77) Technical level consultations were held in London March 25–26. (VG/WG/69-36, April 1) Further consultations were held in Europe in late April, U.K. officials traveled to Washington for a second round of talks on May 13 and 14 (VG/WG/69-73, June 6), and talks were held in Stockholm, Amsterdam, and Rome during the week of April 21. (VG/WG/69-59, May 12) Governor Daane, Willis, and Embassy officers in Paris had consultations with the French on April 24 (VG/WG/69-53, May 7), and Donald C. Templeman of Treasury and Wood had consultations in Zurich and Brussels on April 29 and 30. (VG/WG/69-77, May 22) (All ibid., VG/WG/69-21–VG/WG/69-39; VG/WG/69-40–VG/WG/69-60; and VG/WG/69-61–VG/WG/69-77)

The May 27 summary of these consultations included the following points:

"Prevailing attitude toward greater exchange-rate flexibility: negative, especially if allowance is made for the veil of courtesy and friendliness which lead many to soften their criticisms and doubts; in the second round with the British they wanted to be sure the U.S. was not misled by their willingness to engage in constructive discussion and made clear their attitude was basically negative.

"Role of the dollar: other side invariably raised and we could see no practical alternative to continuation of the present system, i.e., the dollar pegged to gold at the $35 price, and other currencies 'flexing' around the dollar.

"Discrete changes: no one disagreed and some insisted that large 'one time' parity changes could not be ruled out.

"Discipline: widespread concern that greater exchange-rate flexibility would weaken 'disciplinary' pressures on deficit countries.

"Wider margins: no strong support and considerable opposition, especially from EC countries that seemed unanimous in regarding wider margins as posing more of a problem for their agricultural system (CAP) than would a moving-parity system."

The full report on the limited exchange rate flexibility consultations, including additional ones later in the year, was sent under cover of a letter from Under Secretary Volcker to his European, Canadian, and Japanese counterparts on December 12, and circulated to members of the Volcker Group and the Working Group as VG/WG/69-112 on December 23. (Ibid., VG/WG/69-99–VG/WG/69-112)

---

128.   Telegram From the Department of State to the Embassy in Germany[1]

Washington, June 3, 1969, 2316Z.

89501. Subject: Kennedy–Schiller Talks on Monetary Cooperation. Pass to Deputy Under Secretary Samuels. Although no attempt was made to reach any firm agreements on controversial questions, we are convinced that Secretary Kennedy's meeting with Schiller was extreme-

---

[1] Source: National Archives, RG 59, Central Files 1967–69, FN 10. Confidential; Priority; Limdis; Greenback. Drafted by Widman (Treasury); cleared by Volcker and Willis (Treasury), Heginbotham (E/OMA), and Kornblum (EUR/GER); and approved by Quinn (S/S-O).

ly useful. Schiller was apparently pleased with his reception, and enjoyed the atmosphere of Camp David. He also seems to have "hit if off well" with Secretary Kennedy.[2]

Separate cable being sent covering references to military offset negotiations[3] and memcon will be forthcoming at later date. Following highlights may be useful to Under Secretary Samuels for scheduled meetings with Blessing and with Schiller if he returns in time.

Talks concentrated on improvement of international monetary system. Schiller would like to see three major actions—(1) activation of SDR, (2) general realignment of exchange rates, and (3) increased rate flexibility. While his preference would be for simultaneous action on these measures, he recognized this unrealistic. Schoellhorn indicated belief that activation could be made acceptable in Germany provided there was public acknowledgement that other steps to strengthen monetary system were contemplated. In drafting a brief communiqué, key point for Schiller was that "establishment of the special drawing rights facility in the IMF will be *one* important step in the orderly evolution of that system." Germans were particularly concerned to get proper translation of word "one." Word "establishment" is also interpreted by Schiller to include both ratification and activation.

No effort made during talks to reach agreement on amount of activation. Volcker explained rationale for figures used in document which U.S. has submitted to G-10 Deputies[4] and urged Germans to focus on arithmetic. Schiller did not press case for only small amount, or for delay, but neither did he respond positively to U.S. arguments.

Schiller is still looking for sizable family of fellow travelers for proposed currency realignment, but ideas not concrete. Mentioned U.K. (where he seems to be pushing for further small devaluation), plus France, Japan, Switzerland, and Austria. Made vague references to "special position of United States" but gave no indication that he was advocating change in price of gold.

---

[2] Secretary Kennedy and Under Secretary Volcker, accompanied by Willis and Widman, met with Minister Schiller and Johann Schoellhorn at Camp David June 1–2. A memorandum of conversation, dated June 13, is in the Washington National Records Center, Department of the Treasury, Secretary's Memos/Correspondence: FRC 56 74 7, Memo of Conversation (1) 1969.

[3] Not found.

[4] The paper, entitled "The Need for Reserve Creation in the Next Five Years," dated May 28, was distributed in Washington to members of the Volcker Group and Working Group II as VG/WG II/69-8 on May 29. (Washington National Records Center, Department of the Treasury, Volcker Group Masters: FRC 56 86 30) Earlier drafts, beginning on May 12 and including one dated May 26 revised by Volcker, are ibid., VG/WG II/69-1–VG/WG II, 69-13. Volcker Group Working Group II was concerned with reserve asset creation, particularly SDR activation. Several different scenarios were examined in the papers, and in one, where all additions to reserves were to be SDRs, the annual SDR requirement was put at $4.5 billion. According to the memorandum of conversation of the June 1–2 meeting (see footnote 2 above), Schoellhorn found the higher estimates "shocking."

Schiller also appeared to be thinking that it might be possible to reach agreement on some form of crawling peg system after realignment. He recognized there is still need for extensive technical studies on flexibility proposals, and Kennedy urged concentration on getting decision on activation at end-September IMF meeting. Timetable would necessitate ratification by 67 countries by end-June, or early July, and completion of preliminary steps before summer vacations. Schiller indicated that he was prepared to work on matter through July, but not available in August or September, the months of active political campaigning. Schiller hoped no G-10 Ministerial meeting would be needed, but expressed concern at Italian delay in ratification. Schiller considered activation of SDR could be expected "this year."

It was agreed that timing of rate realignment question dependent on further education of German opposition and in any case not likely before German election except in dramatic international crisis. Technical studies on flexibility should proceed though no technicians yet designated by Schoellhorn. Secretary Kennedy cautioned that several countries were still very anxious that nothing be said publicly about these studies or to indicate that serious consideration being given to flexibility. Believe Germans are prepared proceed on this basis.

Significantly, Schiller indicated that while his position with respect to three steps in reform of monetary system shared by Bundesbank and academic institutes in Germany, same elements in Cabinet and public, which strongly and effectively opposed revaluation, oppose all proposals on flexibility. Nevertheless, he saw merit in proceeding with studies and plans, which he agreed to keep secret until after IMF meetings.

Schiller indicated that, if at all possible, he would attend American Bankers Association meetings in Copenhagen week of June 15 in anticipation that he and Secretary Kennedy might discuss these problems further with each other and with other key Ministers.

Rogers

129.   Action Memorandum From the President's Assistant for National Security Affairs (Kissinger) to President Nixon[1]

Washington, June 6, 1969.

SUBJECT

> The International Monetary Situation

Memoranda from Paul McCracken

Attached at Tabs A and B are information memoranda from Paul McCracken on the international monetary situation.[2] Their major points are:

1. The U. S. balance of payments was in deficit by the incredible amount of $2.1 billion in the *two weeks* ending May 14. (The deficit has never been more than $4 billion in any previous year.) The U. S. was thus the source of about one-half the money which flowed into Germany during that period. For the year to date, we are now in small surplus on one of our payments definitions and in deficit by about $4 billion on the other.

2. Germany has lost about $1.2 billion of the $5 billion inflow of those two weeks. The market is not convinced that the DM will not be revalued and most of the speculative money is sitting tight to await further developments.

3. The UK has regained about $400 million of its $600 million loss. France has regained about $100 million of its $500 million loss.

Memorandum from Secretary Kennedy

Attached at Tab C is an earlier information memorandum from Secretary Kennedy which gives his views on the international monetary situation.[3]

The Secretary concludes that our short-term interests lie in promoting capital reflows out of Germany and into the UK. He thus:

1. Sees no alternative to accepting the German decision against revaluation, privately as well as publicly.

---

[1] Source: National Archives, Nixon Presidential Materials, NSC Files, Subject Files, Box 309, Balance of Payments. Secret. Drafted by Bergsten. A stamped notation on the memorandum reads: "The President has seen," and a handwritten notation indicates that it was returned from the President's office to Kissinger on June 11. The President wrote on the memorandum: "High priority."

[2] Not printed. These were two of the more or less weekly memoranda from McCracken to the President apprising him of recent developments in international monetary or financial affairs.

[3] Document 126.

2. Notes that the issue of additional credits to the UK is bound to arise; their "new" $1 billion credit from the IMF contains at best $300 million of really new money.

3. Feels that the German decision will change only if an even more severe crisis develops or if other countries decide to change their exchange rates as well.

4. Suggests that an orderly exchange rate realignment may be possible this summer, implying (per 3) either that a severe crisis lies ahead or that countries other than Germany *will* decide to change their rates.

5. Judges that we will continue to face formidable uncertainties until the exchange rate situation is resolved.

Further developments

Developments since the German decision give little hope that the immediate problem of exchange rate disequilibrium has been solved.

First, the "recycling" of speculative funds agreed upon by the central bankers at Basel on May 11 is very meager. The Bundesbank has agreed only to recycle $500 million to countries other than the UK and $120 million to the UK. They will not agree to any recycling for the UK unless the German government guarantees the credit against UK default. Coming against the total inflow of $5 billion since the French referendum, the amount is thus grossly inadequate and, unless Britain is better provided for, may not be adequately distributed.

Second, as noted by Dr. McCracken, the market is clearly skeptical that exchange rate changes will be avoided. Only about 25 percent of the inflows have moved back out through the market. Most of the speculative money, at least for the moment, is awaiting further developments.

Third, there are additional uncertainties:

—Dr. McCracken relayed the bad U.S. balance of payments figures.

—The British trade figures are bad for the third month in a row and will heighten doubts that Britain has solved its balance-of-payments problem.

—The French trade figures for April are also bad and have intensified the view that devaluation of the franc must occur fairly soon.

—The additional German economic measures, adopted "in lieu of revaluation", are aimed mainly at their domestic inflationary pressures and hence will further increase their external surplus; their measures to deal directly with the external position are puny.

Outlook

The one ray of hope is that Germany, despite its public avowals that its decision not to revalue is "eternal", has already indicated privately that it will still consider revaluation if it can get company from other countries. But no "company" seems interested and the Germans have also indicated that "eternal" means "until after its election in

September." There is virtually unanimous agreement that a DM revaluation is inevitable; hence a new speculative crisis is certain to develop as the election approaches.

What France will do regarding devaluation, after the runoff election, is unclear. Some experts think that Pompidou would devalue quickly and pin the blame on de Gaulle. And Poher has begun to echo the Strauss call for a "multilateral realignment".

Any new French government, however, would probably wish to deal with the pending wage negotiations before devaluing and would also need time to prepare a plan for supplementary domestic measures to make any devaluation work. (Such a position is quite defensible.) By the time these two problems are met, the Bonn elections may be close at hand and Germany will probably not wish to move even in concert with others. In short, there is no certainty that France will provide Germany with its desired "company" very soon.

The UK will also remain on the margin, with liquid debts swamping its meager reserves, especially if the Wilson Government continues to face major political problems. There is little chance of a discreet UK devaluation, however, which would provide "company" for Germany. The British would be more likely to impose additional import controls or let the pound float freely. A French devaluation without a German revaluation could force such action on the UK.

General uneasiness about exchange rates, especially if coupled with large U.S. deficits, could also jeopardize European agreement to early and sufficient activation of Special Drawing Rights and thereby exacerbate the jitters surrounding the system.

The United States has two tactical options in the present situation:

(1) We can attempt to apply pressure soon, during a period of relative calm, to try to pre-empt future crises. The pressure would be mainly on the Germans to revalue or take decisive alternative steps to reduce their payments surplus, but might have to extend to other countries to provide "company" for them.

(2) We can simply await the next crisis, which is virtually certain to occur by September and could come much earlier, and seek the desired changes then.

Experience shows that intervention in a period of relative calm—unless handled extremely deftly and with extremely good luck—can create the very crisis it seeks to pre-empt. Intervention during a crisis, however, could plunge us even more deeply into the midst of a major domestic political struggle in Germany.

Embassy Bonn has recommended against any U.S. intervention due to the possibility of fanning "nationalistic sentiments" in Germany and strengthening the right wing there. Our approach prior to the decision not to revalue was, of course, unsuccessful. We are thus threatened with policy paralysis in dealing with the immediate situation.

However, inaction carries serious risks. The certainty of renewed crises and the nearness of the UK to bankruptcy means that the system could suffer severe disruption. This could lead to renewed pressures on the U.S. gold stock, especially if our balance of payments were to deteriorate sharply, and force us to make some difficult decisions on our own international monetary policy.

And even if the system does not face fundamental disruption, there is likely to be a further escalation of restrictions on international trade and payments by other countries unless the necessary exchange rate realignment occurs *and* there is reform of the overall system.

Conclusion

The short-term threat of renewed crises highlights the more fundamental problems of the international monetary system. In fact, the short-term problem of exchange rate realignment probably must be solved before we can get the type of long-range reform favored by most of our officials—greater flexibility of exchange rates—or even before this kind of reform can be openly discussed internationally, because of the probability of kindling speculation if rates are out of line when such reform is discussed.

The time has thus come when the United States needs to define clearly its strategy on both the short-term and longer-term aspects of the monetary problem and pull the two together.

There are a number of important international monetary meetings in June. In addition, Secretary Kennedy's speech to the American Bankers Association on June 20 provides an excellent opportunity for a major statement of the Administration's international monetary policy. If we do not begin to move now, it will be difficult to do so before September. At a minimum, we should be ready to take major initiatives in the fall after the key European elections are over. We should thus try to make our decisions fairly quickly.

In early April, you asked the Secretary of Treasury to coordinate for you an interagency options paper on monetary reform.[4] Two weeks ago you agreed to my recommendation to convene an early meeting to discuss overall international monetary policy, to be attended by the Secretaries of Treasury and State, Chairman Martin, Paul McCracken and myself.[5]

Recommendation:

I now recommend, that you authorize me to:

---

[4] See footnote 6, Document 16.
[5] See Document 124.

1. Set up a meeting in about ten days to consider U. S. international monetary policy, both short-term and toward longer run reform of the system. (If our meeting slides beyond that point, it will be difficult to take any initiatives you might decide before summer.)

Approve[6]

Disapprove

2. Ask Treasury to submit, as the basis of discussion for that meeting and sufficiently prior to it, the interagency paper you asked for earlier.

Approve[7]

Disapprove

See me

---

[6] The President initialed this option. The meeting was held June 26; see Document 131.

[7] The President initialed this option. See Document 130 for a discussion of the paper submitted for the June 26 meeting.

---

130.   **Memorandum From Secretary of the Treasury Kennedy to President Nixon**[1]

Washington, June 23, 1969.

I am transmitting herewith a memorandum (Annex I) prepared by an interagency group under the chairmanship of Under Secretary Volcker, setting forth your basic options in international monetary affairs.[2] The

---

[1] Source: National Archives, Nixon Presidential Materials, NSC Files, Agency Files, Box 215, Council of Economic Advisers. Confidential. Another copy is attached to Document 131.

[2] The 48-page, double-spaced Annex I, entitled "Basic Options in International Monetary Affairs" and dated June 23, is not printed. An earlier, 33-page version was circulated to members of the Volcker Group as VG/LIM/69-66 on June 19 for discussion in a meeting of the Group on June 21. (Washington National Records Center, Department of the Treasury, Volcker Group Masters: FRC 56 86 30, VG/LIM/62–VG/LIN/70) On June 20 Bergsten provided Willis with written "Comments on Draft Options Paper." (Ibid., Deputy to the Assistant Secretary for International Affairs: FRC 56 83 26, Basic Options 3–6/69–Confidential; LIMDIS) A revised version was circulated as VG/LIM/69-68 on June 22 for discussion by the Group on June 23. (Ibid., Volcker Group Masters: FRC 56 86 30, VG/LIM/62–VG/LIM/70)

complexity of the issue will require some extended discussion. It may be useful to highlight a few points on which early guidance will be particularly useful.

The document suggests three major alternatives, which are discussed in paragraphs 25 to 50, and summarized in Attachment A.

The principal question for decision arising here is whether we should conclusively rule out any option at this stage.

Assuming that for the present Option I (a series of multilateral negotiations pointing toward a fundamental, but evolutionary change in the existing system) is to be pursued, these negotiating issues either will or may be faced in days or weeks:

(a) The SDR question: negotiations are beginning on June 27, and we should reach a decision on the amounts that we should propose to be activated for the first five-year period.
(b) The question of adjustment of exchange rates may be precipitated at any time by a French move; we need guidance on the extent to which we might bring political pressure on one party or another to achieve the desired result.
(c) A speculative crisis may at any time require additional credit support for the pound, to prevent a further depreciation; Europeans are very reluctant to go further, and additional extension of Federal Reserve short-term credit may ultimately require Congressional funding. What is our attitude?

What should our public posture be on proposals for limited exchange rate flexibility and how is it to be timed and handled?

These issues are discussed in paragraphs 51 to 65 of the attached memorandum.

Also, paragraphs 62 to 65 allude to the fact that payments of gold to the IMF in 1969–71, partly in connection with quota increases, and "nibbling" gold sales to central banks could possibly reduce our gold reserves as low as $8 billion. It is important for negotiating purposes to know whether this prospect is acceptable.

While I hope you will be able to read the memorandum to get the full flavor, I thought it would be useful if we started the meeting on Thursday[3] by having Under Secretary Volcker review the main points orally, with the assistance of some charts, before proceeding with the general discussion.

I know you are aware of the sensitivity of some of the material included here, and we have safeguarded copies accordingly.[4] Subject to

---

[3] June 26.

[4] On June 23 Under Secretary Volcker sent a memorandum to the six principals listed below to the effect that Secretary Kennedy wanted the existence and contents of the Basic Options paper limited to the recipients, and that all earlier drafts should be destroyed or returned to his office. (National Archives, Nixon Presidential Materials, NSC Files, Agency Files, Box 215, Council of Economic Advisers)

your approval, I believe that the attendance should be kept very limited. The following are now expected to attend:

The Secretary of State
Federal Reserve Chairman Martin
Dr. Arthur Burns
Dr. Henry Kissinger
Dr. Paul McCracken
Budget Director Mayo

David M. Kennedy

Attachment A[5]

SUMMARY OF BASIC OPTIONS

[Paragraph notations refer to the basic document (Annex I)][6]

I. Paragraphs 30 to 32. *A series of multilateral negotiations pointing toward a fundamental, but evolutionary, change in the existing system.* This would include:

(a) Early activation of Special Drawing Rights in a substantial amount. The U.S. asking figure would be $4 to $4-1/2 billion, as against a possible European starting point of around $2 billion a year, for 5 years.

(b) Realignment of exchange rates, with emphasis on a substantial appreciation of the Deutschemark (and other strong currencies if possible). We would acquiesce in a moderate French depreciation, which may be inevitable and perhaps imminent.

(c) After SDR activation, an active and sympathetic exploration of various forms of limited exchange rate flexibility designed for the longer term.

(d) Negotiations to expand IMF quotas in 1970.

(e) At some stage, possible exploration of the feasibility and desirability of "reserve settlement account" proposals designed to consolidate dollar balances and gold in a common reserve pool.

(f) Continued and strong efforts to remove structural impediments to our trade and to achieve better offset arrangements on military expenditures.

This approach, if successful, should restore considerable flexibility for U.S. policies and preserve a united world monetary structure. The main disadvantage is that the cautious pace of multilateral agreement

---

[5] Confidential; Limdis.

[6] Brackets in the source text.

may fail to move rapidly enough to achieve the objective and relieve the present strain.

II. Paragraphs 33 to 39. *Suspension of the present gold convertibility at the request of foreigners.* This might be forced upon us by reserve losses, or considered necessary because of insufficient results under Option I. It could take various forms ranging from continuing some convertibility on a negotiated basis, using gold, IMF drawings or other assets, to an entirely passive role that would make all foreign dollar holdings inconvertible. If successful, this move to a "dollar standard" would reduce gold losses, stimulate favorable currency realignment, and retrieve flexibility in financing U.S. deficits and influencing the international monetary system. Disadvantages would be the possible acceleration of divisive tendencies leading towards a dollar bloc and a European gold bloc, a general European reaction against financial cooperation, the possibility of foreign controls to limit dollar receipts from U.S. investment, and undesirable special exchange arrangements.

III. Paragraphs 40 to 50. *A small or large increase in the official gold price.* This would require formal Congressional approval, against probable strong resistance from important Congressional quarters in both parties.

The purpose of a small change would be to facilitate limited exchange realignment, but this would be achieved only with serious international political problems and at the risk of a run on our gold stock in anticipation of further changes.

A massive increase would be designed to strengthen our reserve position and flood the world with liquidity, thus potentially "buying time" for financing future deficits. On the other hand, such a change would add to the current world-wide inflationary potential and present extremely serious problems of equity for Japan, Canada and other dollar-holding countries. Progress toward the more basic monetary reforms under Option I would be shelved indefinitely, and any added financing flexibility could be short-lived. For these reasons, this option had no support in the "Volcker Group."

131. Action Memorandum From the President's Assistant for National Security Affairs (Kissinger) to President Nixon[1]

Washington, June 25, 1969.

SUBJECT

Your Meeting on International Monetary Policy on June 26 at 10:30 a.m.

The following memorandum outlines the policy choices which you face in the international monetary area, summarizes the options for implementing them presented in the paper submitted by Secretary Kennedy (Tab A),[2] provides a political assessment of the options, and makes recommendations. Comments by Paul McCracken are at Tab B.[3]

U.S. Policy Issues

The U. S. balance of payments is a problem because it can place constraints on both our domestic economic policy and our foreign policy. Our basic objective is to minimize those constraints. In addition, we seek a smoothly functioning international monetary system because it will promote world economic development and our basic foreign policy objectives. We have four broad alternatives, which in practice can of course be combined, for dealing with the problem:

1. We can try to *finance our deficits.* There are four ways to do so:

(a) Borrow explicitly, from the International Monetary Fund or elsewhere. This would subject us to increasing foreign influence over our domestic economic policy and would only postpone the problem since all explicit loans of large magnitude would have relatively short maturities.

(b) Borrow implicitly by inducing other countries to build their dollar holdings. At the extreme, this would mean getting (or forcing) the world to go onto a "dollar standard". The probable magnitude is much greater here and would carry no fixed maturities. However, the outstanding dollar balances would always represent a threat to our reserves. They could also be a source of instability for the overall system unless the "dollar standard" were formalized, which could cause serious political problems.

---

[1] Source: National Archives, Nixon Presidential Materials, NSC Files, Agency Files, Box 215, Council of Economic Advisers. Confidential.

[2] Document 130.

[3] No record of the June 26 meeting was found. During an August 25, 1997, interview with the editor, Bergsten characterized it as, in effect, the NSC meeting that had been contemplated in NSSM 7, which had been canceled (see footnote 2, Document 109 and Document 16). According to the President's Daily Diary, Kennedy, Rogers, Martin, Mayo, Burns, Kissinger, McCracken, Volcker, Samuels, and MacLaury attended the meeting, which was held in the Cabinet Room from 10:40 to 11:36 a.m. (National Archives, Nixon Presidential Materials, White House Central Files, President's Daily Diary)

(c) Get large enough creation of Special Drawing Rights (SDRs). The scope here is decidedly smaller, since we are likely at best to get about $500 million of freely usable SDRs annually for the first five years of the scheme, compared with payments deficits which may run to several billion dollars.

(d) Sharply increase the price of gold. This would give us a windfall reserve increase of $10 billion if the price were doubled. Some or most of it might, however, have to be used to convert outstanding dollar balances, which now exceed $15 billion in official hands and another $20 billion in private foreign hands. Foreigners might be unwilling to add to their dollar holdings in the future—cutting off our main present avenue of financing. The net effects are thus not clear even in a financing sense. (I discuss this option in broader terms below.)

2. We can seek equilibrium in our balance of payments by *deflating our domestic economy* sufficiently. All the experts think this would require much more than the disinflation which is needed for purely domestic reasons. It is thus rejected outright in the paper. I agree with this conclusion and note also that a severe U.S. recession—which would probably be necessary—would be disastrous for foreign policy as well as domestic economic reasons since it would so drastically affect the living standards of so many other countries.

3. We could continue to *apply controls* to some or all of our external transactions. The paper concludes that we will probably have to maintain some controls whatever path we follow. I am not sure that this is right. I am sure that reliance on controls would require us to extend them well beyond where they are now—to cover all capital movements, Government transactions, and probably trade itself. Such reliance would increase greatly the pressures to bring back troops from Europe and cut aid. It would increasingly poison our international relations as well as be contrary to our basic economic philosophy.

4. We could seek a *change in the exchange rate* of the dollar vis-à-vis at least some of the other major currencies. This is probably the only lasting way to really move toward equilibrium in our payments position. It could be done either by:

(a) A small increase in the U.S. price of gold without comparable increases by at least some other countries. (A change in the price of gold per se does not mean a change in the exchange rate between the dollar and other currencies if they maintain their present peg to the dollar and simply accept the higher gold price in terms of their currencies as well.) The Kennedy paper rightly points out that this course has so many economic disadvantages that it should be rejected.

(b) Upvaluations of their exchange rates by other countries, notably Germany. This is a necessary step under any satisfactory reform scheme and is probably a prerequisite for the next item. The problem is getting enough other countries to upvalue by enough.

(c) Adoption of a system of greater flexibility of exchange rates. (b) is a one-shot change while this would provide a fundamental reform aimed at maintaining the new equilibrium. It could either be negotiated multilaterally, adopted by some key countries unilaterally, or forced on the world by a unilateral U.S. action to suspend convertibility of the dollar.

Options in the Kennedy Paper

The paper presents three alternative policy courses for the United States:

1. A negotiated multilateral solution which would essentially include:

(a) Sufficient activation of SDRs. Large amounts are needed both to give us adequate financing and to help remove the present tightness in the overall system. The paper recommends that we ask for $4.5 billion annually but be prepared to accept a smaller amount, probably around $3 billion.
(b) A realignment of existing exchange rates, particularly upvaluation of the German mark. It is recognized that we will probably have to accept French devaluation to get the mark upvalued. The paper is not sanguine about getting additional upvaluations which would help the United States.
(c) Active and sympathetic exploration of greater flexibility of exchange rates. This would be the hope for lasting equilibrium in the system over the longer run.
(d) Willingness to help "buy" the package by permitting an orderly decline of our gold stock by another $2 billion, to about $8 billion.

2. Unilateral U.S. suspension of gold convertibility. This would force other countries to take action which would lead to one of the following:

(a) Greater flexibility of exchange rates and hence lasting adjustment of our position.
(b) Financing for the U.S. via dollar accumulation by others. It is the most likely route to a near-global "dollar standard".
(c) Imposition of controls by other countries to avoid (a) or (b). We would thus be back about where we started, except for the important difference that other countries would be applying the controls.

3. An increase in the price of gold which would increase world liquidity and hence provide some additional financing for the United States. It would achieve no other objectives and hence represent at best a temporary "solution" to the problem.

Political Assessment

The negotiated multilateral option is most consistent with our overall foreign policy. It would seek a solution through working together with our allies, mainly those in continental Europe. Success in this effort could mark a major milestone in building a truly cooperative Atlantic Community and represent a major foreign policy achievement for this Administration.

Either alternative approach would represent a unilateral move by the United States which would antagonize a number of major countries. It might thus be less costly, in political terms, to apply considerable pressure on the Germans and others in an effort to carry off key parts of the multilateral approach if by so doing we could avoid the need to use one of the unilateral routes.

This sharp distinction becomes very much blurred in practice, however. It will undoubtedly take a great deal of negotiated effort—including your personal intervention—to achieve a satisfactory solution through multilateral negotiation. This is because external constraints on the U.S. can be reduced to a safe level only if we get much greater allocation of SDRs than most Europeans want, much more realignment of exchange rates than most Europeans are willing to do, and much faster movement toward greater flexibility of exchange rates than most Europeans are even contemplating at the moment.

At the same time, we have already moved a long way towards suspension of the gold convertibility of the dollar. Germany has explicitly agreed not to convert (under the implicit threat of troop withdrawals as part of an earlier "offset" agreement). All other major countries are afraid to queue up for gold for fear that we will close the window. We are thus already achieving much of the gain from suspension—essentially through accumulation of dollars by others—while minimizing the political costs of blatantly unilateral U.S. action. We are compromising, however, because we maintain controls, offset agreements, tied aid, etc. to try to avoid a crunch by minimizing the amount of dollars that they will be forced to accumulate.

In addition, formal suspension could have a desirable political effect. It would force the Europeans to make the difficult choices which they can avoid under the present system. It might thus provide a major impetus toward closer European integration, much as our Kennedy Round initiative forced them to make basic choices on their trade policy. And it might even help UK entry since the continentals would feel forced to band together to "counter a unilateral U.S. initiative" and could well decide that maximum size was desirable in doing so. On the other hand, it must be recognized that they might not be able to get together and the result could be a further atrophy of the integration process with some of them linking to the dollar and others going their own way.

The main political effect of either suspension or an increase in the gold price is to break a U.S. commitment which dates to 1934. It is not clear which would be worse from a foreign policy standpoint.

Suspension could cast doubt on the dollar value of countries' gold holdings but this is not very serious since the free market price of gold is above the official price. The main effect would be on the major gold holders: the continental Europeans, South Africa, and the Soviet Union.

An increase in the official gold price would break faith with all those who have helped us for a decade by holding large amounts of dollars, meaning most of the world outside continental Europe and even some of the latter (e.g. Germany). It would raise domestic political problems in many countries and the Japanese say that their government would fall if we raised the gold price.

I would guess that the short-term political costs of suspension might be greater, precisely because it would force the Europeans to make hard choices. But because they would have to make these choices and get the system reformed, suspension would probably lead to a better political result over the longer term.

An increase in the gold price would effectively eliminate the impetus to basic reform by appearing to solve the problem and would also stimulate general belief that any future crisis would be met by another gold price increase—increasing the instability of the system and the likelihood we could no longer get much, if any, dollar financing.

The key countries in any reform effort are Germany, because it is the strongest surplus country and will undoubtedly stay that way short of major new East-West tensions, and France, because of the desire of the rest of the Six for a common position. In fact, only France could probably play a leadership role in forging a common U.S. position since the others would fear and resent any German effort to "impose its view" and the others do not have the necessary strength. The UK is not a factor because it is financially prostrate and Japan simply does not play a role commensurate with its economic power.

The outlook for German cooperation is cloudy. Their recent decision not to revalue may be blamed on the coming election but it is not clear that they will move even thereafter. The Germans are also moving very cautiously on the size and even timing of SDR activation.

If Strauss remains important in financial affairs after the September election, there can be only a limited prospect of sufficient German cooperation to make the negotiated multilateral approach succeed. On the other hand, the bulk of informed German opinion—including many businessmen and bankers—are coming to understand that only upvaluation of the mark and greater flexibility of exchange rates will enable Germany to avoid inflationary pressures from abroad. SPD victory would hasten the likelihood of implementation of these views but even then it would be uncertain.

Pompidou's approach to these issues is certain to be less dogmatic than de Gaulle's and the weakness of France's external financial position will circumscribe him a great deal. Pompidou reportedly argued with the General that France should support SDRs and Giscard d'Estaing is one of the intellectual fathers of the scheme. Nevertheless, the French are unlikely to move very fast from the General's positions and will thus probably not accept large activations of SDRs, let alone move on to other basic reforms.

Issues for Decision

Political realities thus suggest that it will be extremely difficult to reach a negotiated multilateral agreement on a sufficient scale within a relevant time period unless the alternatives are clearly perceived as worse by the key Europeans.

There are three key operational questions:

1. Should we even attempt to pursue the negotiated multilateral approach and, if so, how long should we persist?
2. What should be our balance of payments policy while we pursue this approach?
3. If we abandon the multilateral effort, which alternative—suspension or an increase in the gold price—should we pursue?

The answer to the first question depends on the cost of pursuing that alternative. If we resolve not to let the present system constrain us seriously—meaning that we are prepared to move to one of the other options if it does—then I see no harm in doing so.

In practice, this means that we would answer the second question by continuing to reduce our controls over private capital and our aid programs and perhaps taking a more relaxed position on issues like the German offset. We would not let external pressures force us into policies undesirable in and of themselves. Resolve to pursue this course will require steady nerves.

If forced to move to one of the other approaches, I would opt strongly for suspension. I agree with the economic case made in the Kennedy paper and would add that it would seem to me less politically harmful in the longer run than an increase in the gold price—and by forcing the Europeans to face some difficult choices could perhaps even provide a new impetus toward European integration.

Recommendations:

I therefore recommend that:

1. You authorize continued pursuit of the negotiated approach to international monetary reform. Specifically, we should:

(a) Seek a large amount of SDRs;
(b) Support exchange rate realignment without bringing coercive pressure;
(c) Provide crisis financing for the British as needed;
(d) Take a public position in favor of greater exchange rate flexibility as soon as our negotiators think the time is ripe.

2. You make clear that you are not prepared to purchase such agreement by tightening controls over the U.S. economy and our foreign policy, and that you wish to continue the process of relaxing those controls. We should pursue a passive balance of payments policy while pursuing the negotiations for monetary reform.

3. That you accept the recommendation of the Kennedy paper that we suspend gold convertibility of the dollar if the effort toward a negotiated multilateral solution breaks down or if we are forced to take defensive action as result of a crisis.[4]

Tab B

Memorandum From the Chairman of the Council of Economic Advisers (McCracken) to President Nixon[5]

Washington, June 25, 1969.

SUBJECT

"Basic Options in International Monetary Affairs"

The "Basic Options" paper prepared by the Volcker Group is a clear and perceptive summary of the major international financial issues.[6]

I

The Council of Economic Advisers, which has participated in the drafting of this paper, is in general agreement with its formulation of the options and with its recommendations. In particular, I agree that the evolutionary approach now being followed (option a) should be pursued. I take a more positive view of the merits of limited exchange rate flexibility than the paper does, but since the U.S. dollar would not move under such a scheme, our bargaining position in advocating this scheme is admittedly limited. It should nevertheless be stressed that our hopes of establishing a less crisis-prone international monetary system rest primarily on achieving limited flexibility. The fear that an endorsement of limited flexibility would further unsettle the foreign exchange markets seems exaggerated, and it tends to induce inaction on this matter.

---

[4] Presumably at least Recommendations 1a, 1b, and 1d were approved during the June 26 meeting; see Document 140. Recommendation 3 was one plank in the New Economic Policy President Nixon announced on August 15, 1971.

[5] Confidential.

[6] See footnote 2, Document 130.

I also agree with the paper in regarding the suspension of gold convertibility (option b) as a major break in international cooperation, and therefore not to be undertaken unless the evolutionary approach turns out to be unpromising. In particular, I do not support the view, implied in para. 56, that we should suspend convertibility if the other countries are unwilling to activate more than $2 billion in SDR's (Special Drawing Rights) per year. Although SDR's will no doubt be an important addition to international liquidity, this additional liquidity can make only a modest contribution to the adjustment process by which nations with different rates of price movements, different objectives of economic policy, and different rates of technological development adjust to each other. It is the present system's inability to effect these adjustments, by excessive rigidity of exchange rates, that is the main cause of current troubles. Consequently I do not believe that a large amount of SDR's, while desirable, should be regarded as the touchstone of success for the evolutionary approach.

I agree with the report's rejection of an increase in the gold price, whether large or small. If it ever comes to a choice between options b and c we should demonetize gold, which is what option b amounts to.

II

There are a number of points not fully covered by the paper which you may wish to pursue in the meeting on Thursday.

1. *Public posture and Presidential leadership.* The paper does not give you anything to say for public use, even though an insufficient sense of direction on the part of the financial and business community is a current problem. If you agree to the evolutionary approach, it might be desirable to recognize publicly that flexibility of exchange rates must be part of achieving a less brittle system. Of the two other components of the evolutionary approach, SDR's are by now somewhat shopworn and a realignment of parities cannot be mentioned in public.

2. *Balance of payments controls.* The paper does not hold out any hope for a further relaxation of controls in the immediate future. While maintenance of controls is seemingly justified by the precarious state of our balance of payments, it is not clear that relaxation must await a return to equilibrium. In fact it is not clear how much controls contribute to reducing the deficit, and they do come at a heavy cost in other matters. A subcommittee of the Volcker group is working on this subject and you may want to express an interest in its results. Indeed, we might want to consider a phased relaxation of controls as a major policy objective in its own right. If this puts a strain on the international monetary system, it would be evidence that the system needs modification. If we do not press forward here, the momentum generated by the April 4 relaxation may be lost, and this Administration may become no less committed to controls than its predecessor.

3. *Sterling*. Although I agree that for the moment (say, through the summer) sterling should hold at its present parity, it would be most unwise to supply Britain with further credit. This would require Congressional approval. And it is probably not in the interest of the United Kingdom to go even further into debt. Moreover, there are indications that sterling has a long-term tendency to depreciate, which makes it an ideal candidate for the so-called crawling peg form of exchange rate adjustment. Whenever the next sterling crisis erupts, Britain should be encouraged to adopt such a device in order to avoid resorting to direct controls.

Paul W. McCracken

---

132.   Telegram Fom the Embassy in France to the Department of State[1]

Paris, June 30, 1969, 1100Z.

9840. From Under Secretary Volcker and Governor Daane to Treasury Secretary Kennedy, for Petty and Dale, US Executive Director, IMF, and to FedRes for Chairman Martin. Section I of II.

Subject: Meeting of Deputies of G-10—SDR Activation, June 28.[2]

1. Outcome of first full day's negotiations on SDR's satisfactory, with a number of European delegations adopting initial negotiating position at somewhat higher level than anticipated.

2. Chairman (Ossola, Italy) summarized initial positions, characterizing them as not firm national positions, but indications of emerging national positions, as follows (amount per annum in billions of dollars, followed by number of years for first decision):

---

[1] Source: National Archives, RG 59, Central Files 1967–69, FN 10. Confidential; Priority; Limdis; Greenback. Repeated to the Embassies in G-10 capitals (sent to the Treasury representatives in Bonn, London, Rome, Tokyo, and USOECD in Paris) and to USEC.

[2] George H. Willis was a member of the U.S. delegation. His handwritten notes on the meeting are in the Washington National Records Center, Department of the Treasury, Deputy to the Assistant Secretary for International Affairs: FRC 56 83 26, Willis Notes. SDR activation was also discussed in the OECD's WP-3 June 27–28. A report on the WP-3 meeting is in telegram 9836 from Paris, June 29. (National Archives, RG 59, Central Files 1967–69, FN 10 1 IMF)

U.S.—4.5—5 years (strong presumption)
Netherlands—2.0—5 years (preferably with low first year)
Germany—3.0—2–3 years
Italy—3.0—3 years
Belgium—2–2-1/4—2 years
Japan—3–4—2 years
Sweden—3.0 plus—5 years (tolerate 3 years)
U.K.—middle figure—2–5 years (with large initial year)
Canada—upper range—5 years
France—not participating
Switzerland—not participating

3. Chairman stated general consensus in favor of activation around time of September annual meeting of IMF. This required Group of Ten to reach decision by end August to be communicated to Managing Director of IMF as part of consultations preceding his formal proposal. Either Deputies (acting for Ministers) or Ministers might have to meet in late August if matter not settled in July. Belgian Deputy entered only reservation among participants as to ability to commit his government within a few weeks. General preference for settling matter in Deputies if possible, with British and French making strong plea against Ministerial meeting. U.S. took position they strongly hoped Ministerial meeting could be avoided, but were fully prepared for such meeting if required to reach agreement.

4. For guidance U.S. Missions in discussions of subject with officials, our view is that satisfactory consensus can be reached in July, or latest in August. It is natural that initial discussion of activation amounts shows some range in initial positions. We continue to believe that $4.5 billion a year for five years is amount called for (a) to achieve reasonable reserve growth objectives of both industrial and developing countries, (b) to facilitate adjustment process, and (c) to assist in repayment of reserve credits extended in past five years. Further progress toward this view is needed, but seems achievable as various governments focus on arithmetic of reserve needs and its implications.

5. FYI: A number of delegations accepted $4.5 billion a year as amount of new reserves needed in all forms, but deducted anticipated net new reserve creation due to anticipated resumption U.S. official settlements deficits and possible net growth of reserve credit. This contrary to our projections, which imply net reductions in reserves on these two counts taken together. Further negotiations will explore these differences of view. At this point we believe that possibilities of agreement between present German-Italian $3 and $4-1/2 billion in early years are good, and that we can hope to reach some agreement for full period of five years. In latter connection Japanese have emphasized and we concur that it is important that legal staff of Fund produce promptly paper on options open to Fund to adjust allocations for later years to allow for subsequent selective quota increases. End FYI.

6. We understand Finance Ministers of European Community meet on July 21–22 prior to Deputies' meeting July 23–24. U.S. Missions should bear in mind importance of meeting of the Six and our interests in avoiding inflexible EC group position. Believe Italians and Germans will be sympathetic to desirability of retaining flexible negotiating position at reasonable levels of SDR activation.

7. Section II will follow on subject of IMF quota increase.[3]

Shriver

---

[3] Section II was sent in telegram 9871 from Paris, June 30. Governor Daane reportedly argued "that issues involved in working out quota increase very complex and delicate, and should not be allowed intrude on priority business of SDR activation." Paragraph 3 reports on a short discussion of Italian Minister Colombo's proposal for an SDR–aid link. The Netherlands, Belgian, French, Canadian, Swedish, and Japanese representatives reportedly all said they had great conceptual difficulties with the link. Governor Daane shared their concern but felt "that in case of some donor countries voluntary pledges of type suggested by Colombo could be appropriate, and that Group should continue study how achieve without linking liquidity creation and capital requirements." (Ibid., FN 10)

---

133.   Volcker Group Paper[1]

VG/WG II/69-24   Washington, July 16, 1969.

DRAFT SUMMARY OF ALTERNATIVE U.S. POSITIONS
FOR DISCUSSION AT VOLCKER MEETING
July 17, 1969

SDR Activation

The following alternatives are suggested for the consideration of the Volcker Group:

Alternative A—Minimum Position

$4 billion in Year I; $3 billion in Years II and III; Years IV and V left open, but with understanding that decision will be made on Years IV and V no later than the September Annual Meeting in 1971.

---

[1] Source: Washington National Records Center, Department of the Treasury, Volcker Group Masters: FRC 56 86 30, VG/WG II/69-14–VG/WG II/69-35. Confidential. The paper is marked "Willis Draft." VG/WG II/69-24 was circulated to members of the Volcker Group and Working Group II under cover of a July 17 memorandum from Willis indicating the draft paper would be discussed at a 4:30 p.m. meeting of the Group that day, prior to the meeting of the G-10 Deputies in Paris July 23–24.

Discussion

Chairman Ossola of the Deputies appears to have indicated some willingness to try to reach agreement on this proposal, if it would be acceptable to the United States. The United States has not given him encouragement to do so. The amount, totaling $10 billion in three years, is somewhat larger than the figure of $3 billion for two or three years mentioned by the German Delegation at the June Deputies Meeting. It is considerably above the Belgian and Dutch figure, though it applies to a shorter period than the Dutch proposal. It could conceivably be defended by the Europeans as coinciding with the $10 billion figure discussed last year, even though telescoped into a shorter time period. It is conceivable that, if the Finance Ministers of the Six do not agree on a more stringent position in their meeting on July 21–22, this alternative could be accepted by the Deputies without an August Deputies Meeting or an appeal to the Ministers. It is not certain that this could be done, however, because of Dutch and Belgian resistance. There is no clear additional sweetener for the Dutch and Belgians, unless it lies in support for a conservative approach to quota increases, discussed below.

Alternative B—Intermediate Position

$4 billion in Year I, $4 billion in Year II, and $4 billion in Year III. Decision Years IV and V no later than September 1971.

Discussion

This position would result in $2 billion more of SDRs than Alternative A in the first three years. The U.S. share would be approximately $500 million, or conceivably more if some members of the Fund did not participate in the SDRs. (It is assumed in Alternatives A & B that the amount of activation is fixed absolutely, and would not be increased if additional participants joined in at a later date.)

While this position might conceivably be sold to the Europeans in July, it seems more likely that adoption of Alternative B would lead to a Deputies Meeting at the end of August 1969, for further negotiation. An important question is whether the U.S. is likely to lose or gain if agreement is postponed in July.

There are several reasons why postponement may prove disadvantageous to the U.S. In the first place, allowing more time to elapse before committing the European Deputies permits opposition elements in those countries to organize more effective pressure against a substantial activation figure. This opposition may result from political rivalries, electoral strategy, or genuine fear that a large activation would contribute to inflation or unduly impair international monetary discipline. In the second place, by mid-August, if not earlier, the unprecedentedly large U.S. liquidity deficit will become known to the Europeans. This could be embarrassing to the European Deputies who are most inclined to take a liberal view of activation, and cause them to be less venturesome in leading their own governments. It appears to be well substantiated, for example, that Emminger, Schoellhorn and Schiller have already mentioned activation figures which are about twice as high as the figures generally talked about in other German Ministries and at lower levels in the Bundesbank.

On the other hand, the possible advantages of deferring a decision until August relate to the uncertain results of an appeal to Chancellor Kiesinger during his August 7 visit to Washington and a judgment as to the effectiveness and usefulness of a threat to insist upon a Ministerial Meeting at the end of August.

Alternative C

In this alternative a different approach would be taken arithmetically. The amount proposed for SDR activation would be based on the assumption that all members of the Fund would participate, and the amount would be written down proportionately if the actual participation were less than 100 percent of IMF membership. If at a later stage other countries opted in, the amount allocated would be increased and the same procedure would be followed if there were selective quota increases. This means that the figures cited would not be a maximum, but could be exceeded if there were selective quota increases, though presumably not by a large amount. Under this alternative, the U.S. might propose $4-1/2 billion a year for three years, with decision on Year IV and Year V to be taken before September 1971. The United States share would be about $1,125 mil., and would not vary depending upon the number of participants in a given year or the adoption of selective quota increases.

Discussion

It may be recalled that the United States at present has legal authority to participate during the initial activation in an amount up to our present quota of $5,160 million. Over a five-year period, an annual allocation of $1,125 million a year would be beyond our present authority. This was pointed out to Mr. Dale by the Japanese Executive Director, whose legislation apparently parallels ours. This may be true of some other countries as well. For this reason it would be desirable to reduce the U.S. asking figure to bring it within our present legal authority. In this alternative, this is done by reducing the period to three years.

This alternative also would quite probably mean no agreement at the July meeting and a continuation of negotiations in August. At the August meeting the United States would probably have to move toward Alternative A in order to reach agreement, by reducing the amount. Under no conditions should the U.S. agree to any activation period shorter than three years.

The considerations noted in Alternative B above would apply to this alternative.

Alternative D

In the initial discussion in the Executive Board, Mr. Schweitzer suggested the possibility of an allocation for five years at the mid-point of a range between $2.5 billion a year and $4.0 billion a year, or about $3.25 billion a year for five years. He indicated that an additional amount might be added at the beginning of the period to make up for deficient permanent reserve creation in recent years.

Discussion

The Fund Staff has been very reluctant to give up the principle of five-year allocation. The reasons cited for this view are that:

(a) three years is too short a time to provide adequate experience with the reconstitution provisions and with the SDR transactions in general, and
(b) the governments would find themselves in a rather awkward position to take a decision for the remaining two years without casting doubt on the value of the SDR, if the annual allocations were reduced.

A possible unspoken consideration is the desire to associate SDR allocations with quinquennial quota increases.

Alternative Positions on IMF Quota Increase

While the United States would have preferred to postpone a substantive decision on the amount of general and selective quota increases in the Fund, it now looks as though it may be necessary to reach a substantive agreement on the main outlines of a quota increase in order to settle the issue of SDR activation in July or August of this year. Several alternative U.S. approaches are briefly summarized below.

Alternative A

General increase of 15 percent in IMF quotas with selective increases totaling not more than 10 percent of present quotas, or about $2.1 billion. The United States could either (1) take no selective increase, (2) take enough increase to maintain its voting power, or (3) take its proportionate share of an overall 10 percent figure for world-wide selective increases. It is estimated that Alternative A (1) might result in gold sales of about $600 million, with Alternative A (3) adding another $75 million, for the U.S. selective increase, for which the United States would receive gold tranche claims. A

15 percent increase in our gold tranche would amount to about $193.5 million. The net reserve loss we could suffer could therefore be about $400 million, though our conditional drawing right would be enlarged by about $775 million. These estimates are based on the assumption that about 18 countries would not convert dollars into United States gold to make the requisite payments to the Fund, but would use their own resources.

Discussion

This approach follows the suggestions of major European countries at the last meeting of the Deputies. It should be readily saleable to the Europeans, but could encounter rather strong opposition from the IMF staff and the Executive Directors of the non-Ten countries. Mr. Dale indicates that the Executive Directors of these non-Ten countries appear to be insistent on a 20 to 25 percent general increase for their own countries. While he does not think that they would openly refuse to go along with SDR activation if we supported Alternative A, the Europeans would probably realize that no agreement on quotas might be reached on this basis, at least without long and acrimonious negotiations. This might affect the willingness of the French, Italians, Japanese and Canadians to reach an understanding on SDR activation.

Alternative B

Under this approach there would be a general increase of 15 percent for the members of the Group of Ten plus not more than their share of selective increases totaling globally no more than 10 percent of existing quotas, or about $2.1 million. The rest of the world, however, would receive uniform quota increases of 20 percent, plus a proportionate share of the overall 10 percent selective increase.

We would estimate that this alternative would cost the United States approximately $770 million in gold, with our gold tranche and credit tranche drawing rights the same as in Alternative A above.

Discussion

Mr. Dale has advised me[2] that this suggestion has come up recently in the IMF staff, in an effort to deal with what is felt to be a European objection to a substantial increase in the United Kingdom quota. It is also felt that the United Kingdom is not enthusiastic about a substantial rise in its quota.

The advantages of this approach would be to satisfy both the Europeans and the non-members of the Ten with respect to the size of their general quota increases.

---

[2] Willis.

On the other hand this approach continues and emphasizes a trend in the Fund towards expanding the drawing rights of the non-G-10 more rapidly than those of the Group of Ten countries, and thus probably reduce the liquidity of the Fund. To some extent this tendency would be offset by large selective increases to some G-10 members. The United Kingdom would find its voting power reduced, and the United States would also be in this position unless it elected for some share in the selective quota increases. To maintain its voting power, it would need to take a selective increase of something like $400 million. It is also worth bearing in mind that a reduction in the relative share in IMF quotas for the United States means over time a fairly significant cumulative loss of SDR allocations, which are proportionate to relative quota shares.

Alternative C

A uniform general increase of 20 percent for all members, accompanied by selective increases not exceeding 10 percent of existing quotas or about $2.1 billion. Again the United States would have three options open to it with respect to its own selective quota.

We estimate that this approach would cost the United States approximately $810 million in gold sales to the Fund, against which the United States would receive an additional gold tranche claim of $258 million plus any allowance for selective increases, and additional credit tranche drawing rights of $1032 million plus any adjustment for a selective quota increase.

Discussion

This approach would maintain the principle of uniform treatment of all IMF members for a general quota increase, and could probably be made acceptable as a minimum figure to the Executive Directors of non-G-10 countries.

On the other hand some difficulty might be encountered in gaining European acquiescence to such a figure, resulting in European delay in decision on SDR activation on this score. Adoption of this position might increase the likelihood of an appeal to Ministers to resolve the SDR and quota questions, although it is true that in the past the Europeans have proved reluctant to maintain a strong position in the face of a fairly determined stance on the part of the developing countries.

Alternative D

This would be a frankly compromise position, calling for a general quota enlargement of 17-1/2 percent, midway between the European maximum and the indicated minimum of the non-Ten countries. As before, the selective increases would be held within 10 percent of quotas.

We estimate the United States gold loss under this alternative at about $750 million. Our gold tranche claim would rise by about $225 million, plus any allowance for selective increases and our credit tranche drawing rights by something over $900 million, plus adjustment for a selective quota increase.

Discussion

This alternative would preserve the principle of uniform treatment of IMF members in general quota increases. It would appear to be a reasonable compromise between the initial positions of the two factions and the Fund.

134. Telegram From the Embassy in France to the Department of State[1]

Paris, July 24, 1969, 1850Z.

11272. Subj: July 23 call on Pompidou: international economic and monetary situation.

1. Pompidou said at our July 23 meeting that the most urgent problem facing the West at this point was the international economic and monetary situation, and in that general picture the strength and position of the dollar was crucial. He alluded specifically to the so-called French war against the dollar and smilingly he said that the possibilities of any such war at this time were non-existent; that the franc was in no position to challenge the dollar; and that, in fact, the economic strength of the US and our determination to prevent inflation and protect the status of the dollar was crucial to all the Western countries. [Omitted here is a discussion of the Euro-dollar market and domestic economic policy in the United States.]

3. I asked Pompidou whether the French would be of a mind to facilitate international monetary equilibrium by participating in the Special Drawing Rights. Pompidou responded that there were two aspects to this question: one was the principle involved, and the second was the quantity. With regard to the principle, he pointed out that

---

[1] Source: National Archives, RG 59, Central Files 1967–69, FN 17. Confidential; Priority. Repeated to Bonn, Brussels, The Hague, London, Rome, and USEC.

France has consistently emphasized the usefulness of gold as an instrument which enforces discipline. He himself was not a devoté of the extreme theories on gold: i.e., he was not a doctrinaire supporter of Jacques Rueff's ideas, but that in lieu of gold, self-disciplinary actions had to be taken. In this connection, of course, he reemphasized the necessity for US to do something because the whole of the Western world's economic and monetary situation depended upon US and not upon actions taken by anybody else. In response I repeated my personal conviction that the US had already taken a number of significant actions to stem inflation and that our country was preparing to take even more. And in this connection I pointed out that Under Secretary Volcker would be meeting with Finance Minister Giscard d'Estaing today[2] and that I was sure Volcker had ample authority to provide the French Government with all of the current details as well as the philosophical foundations of our policy.

4. On this subject Pompidou appeared to me like a man who wants us to succeed in our own struggle for economic stability and as a person who would react favorably to the SDRs if and when he saw sufficient disciplinary actions on our part to overcome any doubts his own theorists might have stemming from their preoccupation with gold. He gave me the impression that we were dealing more with a Rothschild banker than with a Sorbonne professor of economics. In other words, I gained the impression from Pompidou's rather jocular manner in referring to the gold theorists in France, but not from any explicit statement he made, that Pompidou is searching for practical answers to the practical monetary problems, and that he is not going to insist on a change of the price of gold in the doctrinaire way in which de Gaulle and Jacques Rueff did.

Shriver

---

[2] During his July 24 meeting with Volcker, Giscard d'Estaing "asked how, in a world beset with inflation, it was possible to justify the creation of liquidity in additional large amounts through the SDR method." He continued nonetheless to say that when he attended the annual meeting of the IMF and the IBRD at the end of September in Washington he planned "to state a French position in favor of SDRs, and he would prefer doing so first in the less formal atmosphere of the Group of Ten." (Memorandum of conversation; Washington National Records Center, Department of the Treasury, Files of Under Secretary Volcker: FRC 56 79 15, France) On June 26 an April 28 research paper prepared in the Federal Reserve Bank of New York was circulated as VG/WG 11/69-14 to Members of the Volcker Group and Working Group II. (Ibid., Volcker Group Masters: FRC 56 86 30, VG/WG 11/69-14–VG/WG II/69-35) The research paper contained an analysis of an article by Giscard in the March 1969 edition of *L'Expansion* in which Giscard compared his 1964–1965 proposal for a collective reserve unit (CRU) with the SDR and strongly supported SDRs and opposed any change in the price of gold. In a July 2 letter to Ambassador Shriver, Samuels called Giscard "the father of the present SDR arrangement," because the CRU, although different from the SDR, "envisaged liquidity creation to be a matter of international agreement." (National Archives, RG 59, Central Files 1967–69, FN 10 IMF)

135. Telegram From the Embassy in France to the Department of State[1]

Paris, July 25, 1969, 1230Z.

11295. From Under Secretary Volcker and Governor Daane for Treasury Secretary Kennedy, for Petty and Dale, US Executive Director, IMF, and to FedRes for Chairman Martin. Subject: Meeting of Deputies of G-10—July 23–24.

1. Deputies of Group of Ten carried on day and a half of hard bargaining over question SDR activation and IMF quota increases which ended in consensus on both matters, subject to Ministerial approval.

SDRs

2. As summarized by Chairman (Ossola, Italy), agreement on SDRs is as follows:

(A) For first period of activation of three years global amount to be created of $9.5 billion, of which $3.5 billion in first year and $3.0 billion per year in second and third years.[2]
(B) Representatives of all countries having accepted amendment (this formulation designed exclude France, which did not associate itself with decision—see para 4 below) have declared their willingness strongly to recommend these figures to their authorities and to confirm Ministerial approval within one week.[3]
(C) Agreement will be considered to be in effect when approval received from all parties. At this point Ossola will notify participants

---

[1] Source: National Archives, RG 59, Central Files 1967–69, FN 10. Confidential; Priority; Limdis; Greenback. Repeated to the Embassies in G-10 capitals (sent to the Treasury representatives in Bonn, Rome, Tokyo, and USOECD), and USEC.

[2] In a July 26 memorandum to the President, Acting Chairman of the Council of Economic Advisers Herbert Stein wrote: "While the agreement does not give as much as we wanted [see Document 133], it is nevertheless considerably better than anyone would have expected six months ago. This is due in large measure to European confidence that the U.S. will bring inflation under control. It also reflects the persistence and bargaining skill of Treasury Under Secretary Paul Volcker. With the SDR agreement the part of your April 4 call for international monetary reform [see footnote 5, Document 16] that deals with liquidity has been advanced decisively. The other part, improving the adjustment process, is as necessary as ever but has not yet been pushed. Now that the SDR question is settled and the markets are quiet it would be a suitable moment for Secretary Kennedy to make the speech on international monetary reform that was agreed upon at the meeting of June 26 [see Document 131]." The accompanying undated cover memorandum from Kissinger to President Nixon indicates that Stein's memorandum did not go to the President. (National Archives, Nixon Presidential Materials, NSC Files, Agency Files, Box 215, Council of Economic Advisers)

[3] Telegram 125335 to Rome, July 29, reported that Volcker confirmed to Ossola, on behalf of Secretary Kennedy, U.S. agreement to the consensus on SDRs and increases in IMF quotas. (Ibid., RG 59, Central Files 1967–69, FN 10)

and, with approval of German Economics Minister Schiller as Chairman of G-10 Ministers, will inform IMF Managing Director Schweitzer, who under SDR amendment to IMF articles makes formal proposal for activation after consultations, of which G-10 consensus is one element.

3. During negotiations leading up to consensus, Common Market (minus France) first put forward proposal for $2.5 billion per year for three years. U.S. pulled them up to $3 billion per year for three years and in final round of bargaining got first-year figure up to $3.5 billion in interest of psychological effect on exchange markets. While all nine parties to agreement will confirm Ministerial approval to Chairman Ossola, in fact only four are on ad referendum basis: U.S., Canada, Germany and Netherlands.

4. Strictly FYI: As indicated para 1 above, France did not associate itself with agreement. However, informal talks suggest French adherence in September, although agreement on figure which is relatively high by Common Market standards may introduce complication into this timetable.

Quota Increase

5. Chairman proposed consensus along following lines. Members of G-10 will support an over-all increase in quotas in the order of magnitude of 30 percent (plus or minus three percentage points). This would support selective increases that would bring quotas more in line with the economic position of countries. Chairman said this consensus also implied (A) that quotas should be raised as soon as possible and that annual SDR allocations would then reflect the new quota distribution and (B) that the increase in quotas should not affect the General Arrangements to Borrow.

6. In discussion, Van Lennep (Netherlands) made effort to narrow the parenthetical range of 6 percent with 30 percent as center to range of $28.5 billion to $31.5 billion. Daane (U.S.) stressed need for wider 27–33 percent range to have needed flexibility to work out individual quotas in IMF executive board. Van Lennep accepted wider margin on interpretation by Morse (U.K.) that restraints to increases would increase as figure moved farther from 30 percent within 6 percent range.

7. De Strycker (Belgium) stressed that the consensus (A) did not imply any approval of the "split-level" method of general increase or any other formula for dividing total quota increases; (B) no understanding was implied as to any specific national quota increase and none was approved; and (C) no quantitative figure of any kind was being approved, except the 30 percent order of magnitude. Daane (U.S.) supported Belgians and entered reservation as to any sharp reduction

in U.S. own relative share, such as that shown in some Fund tables that had been discussed on previous day. While we would accept the over-all 30 percent with its range, the only agreement on individual quotas that we would accept was that we would inform our Executive Director as to specific quantitative position on all figures. Larre (France) complained that G-10 should be more specific, and that increase of 33 percent was needed to reach over-all increase of $7 billion. Larre felt that consensus left too much flexibility. Chairman, nevertheless, concluded there was consensus on the flexible position he had outlined.

Press Relations

8. Chairman pointed out it would be impracticable expect that he and other Deputies could avoid saying anything to press re outcome of meeting. He therefore proposed common line, which was agreed as follows:

(A) No figures will be released either on amounts or time period, in deference to position of G-10 Ministers, who must approve Deputies' consensus; IMF Managing Director, who must make formal proposal for activation; and non-G-10 members of Fund. (It was, of course, recognized figures will certainly become known to press.)

(B) It would be indicated simply that Deputies have reached consensus—subject to approval by Ministers—on SDR activation and on size of over-all increase in IMF quotas within framework of quinquennial review of quotas. After Ministerial approval, this consensus will be communicated to IMF Managing Director, and it will be for him to take into account within context of his world-wide consultations on activation.

(C) Would be indicated that "one country which has not accepted SDR agreement" (i.e., France) has not associated itself with consensus.

9. In view of fact that agreement has not yet been approved by Ministers, and sensitivity of Europeans on this point, it is extremely important that U.S. spokesmen not indulge in unauthorized release of figures.

Next Meeting

10. Next meeting of Deputies scheduled take place in Washington on Sept 27 with following tentative agenda: (A) draft communiqué for meeting of G-10 Ministers and Governors; (B) election of new Chairman of Deputies; (C) brief discussion of future work program of Deputies. G-10 Ministerial meeting tentatively scheduled for afternoon October 1 in Washington.

Shriver

136.   Editorial Note

France devalued the franc by 11.1 percent on August 8, 1969. German Chancellor Kiesinger was in Washington at the time, and Henry Kissinger sent President Nixon a brief memorandum on August 8 asking him to discuss the devaluation with the Chancellor before he left Washington. (National Archives, Nixon Presidential Materials, NSC Files, Country Files–Europe, Box 675, France, Volume III Jan 69–10/31/69) No record of any discussion with Kiesinger on the franc devaluation and his plans for the mark was found.

Policymakers considered the impact of the franc devaluation on other currencies, including the dollar. In his August 9 weekly report on international finance to the President, Council of Economic Advisers Chairman Paul McCracken thought the dollar would be unaffected, doubted the mark would be appreciated, mused on how much support the United States should give the pound, and wondered how the devaluation would affect planning for Secretary Kennedy's speech on monetary reform, including improvement in the exchange rate system. (Ibid., Box 215, Council of Economic Advisers) (Regarding Kennedy's speech, which was given on September 30 at the annual meeting of the IMF and IBRD in Washington, see footnote 7, Document 139.) The opinion that the mark would not be revalued until after the German elections in September proved correct. Following heavy speculative flows on September 22 and 23, Chancellor Kiesinger on September 24 called for a closing of German foreign exchange markets through the election on September 28, and the mark was allowed to float on September 30.

According to a September 3 memorandum from Secretary Kennedy to the President, foreign exchange market issues had been discussed during a Quadriad meeting on August 28 in San Clemente. For the President's information, Kennedy attached an undated Contingency Planning paper to his September 3 memorandum, which, inter alia, recommended providing up to $500 million in support for the pound. The paper also indicated that contingency plans were being developed to suspend the dollar's convertibility to gold, and recommended that the United States should be prepared for prompt action, but that the gold price should not be increased. (National Archives, Nixon Presidential Materials, NSC Files, Agency Files, Box 289, Treasury, Volume I) A copy of the Contingency Planning paper, with the handwritten date of May 1969, is also in the Washington National Records Center, Department of the Treasury, Deputy to the Assistant Secretary for International Affairs: FRC 56 83 26, Contingency Planning 1965–1973. Kennedy's September 3 memorandum went forward to the President attached to Kissinger's September 24 memorandum on policy options, Document 139.

Kissinger concluded a September 6 memorandum to President Nixon transmitting another weekly international finance report from Chairman McCracken to the President with a paragraph explaining that the Treasury Department had backgrounded key financial writers on Secretary Kennedy's forthcoming speech on international study of greater exchange rate flexibility. He referred to a *New York Times* front-page story of that day that noted the President's personal involvement in the initiative. He concluded: "we are now fairly clearly on the record as seeking a negotiated solution to one of the key problems of the system." (National Archives, Nixon Presidential Materials, NSC Files, Agency Files, Box 215, Council of Economic Advisers)

A draft of Kissinger's September 6 memorandum to the President was sent telegraphically to Alexander Haig in San Clemente on September 4 with a reference to a memorandum discussing unilateral actions, presumably an undated and unsigned memorandum from Kissinger to the President entitled "The Imminent International Monetary Crisis." The memorandum discussed scenarios for suspending the convertibility of the dollar to gold; there is no indication that it went forward to the President. (Both ibid.)

---

137.   Memorandum From the Chairman of the Council of Economic Advisers (McCracken) to President Nixon[1]

Washington, September 8, 1969.

SUBJECT

A U.S. Initiative on International Monetary Reform

In the remaining weeks prior to the German election, it is evidently important to avoid initiatives which might be construed as exerting pressures on the German electorate.[2] It is no less important, however, to

---

[1] Source: National Archives, Nixon Presidential Materials, NSC Files, Agency Files, Box 215, Council of Economic Advisers. Confidential. This memorandum was sent to the Treasury Department under cover of a September 9 memorandum from Ken Cole. It is attached to a copy of Secretary Kennedy's September 19 memorandum to the President (Document 138). A September 8 draft, which forms Tab D to Document 139, is identical to the text printed here but without the final paragraph. (National Archives, Nixon Presidential Materials, NSC Files, Agency Files, Box 215, Council of Economic Advisers)

[2] The election was scheduled for September 28.

maintain the momentum which has been built up for international monetary reform, to assert U.S. leadership, and to prevent the reassertion of natural tendencies to avoid rocking the boat while nebulously hoping for the best. As decided at your June 26 meeting,[3] a major initiative towards greater exchange rate flexibility should be presented at the IMF meetings (which take place immediately after the German elections). While avoiding advocacy of any particular scheme, this initiative should suggest that the United States considers such a reform to hold promise for eliminating some of the patent defects in the present system.

Because of the central position of the United States in the international monetary system, and our great interest in monetary stability, it is essential for us to provide leadership in the quest for a better adjustment mechanism. Without our leadership, there is a tendency for other countries to hold back from innovations. At the same time, we should recognize that, because we want the dollar to remain the pivot of the entire system (and hence not subject to flexibility), we would in effect be suggesting to other countries that they consider amending their exchange rate policies without our having to make a similar change. In this situation, it is appropriate for us to make our view clear, but to avoid exerting strong pressures on other countries to adopt the innovations which we consider desirable.

The circumstances are favorable for a U.S. initiative at the IMF meeting later this month. There is widespread recognition that present methods of balance of payments adjustment are inadequate. The exchange markets are temporarily quiet, but strong doubts about the future of the German mark and the pound sterling remain. The liquidity problem has become much less urgent, thanks to the recent agreement on Special Drawing Rights.[4] Several authorities in Italy, Germany, Japan and France have expressed interest (sometimes amounting to explicit advocacy) in greater flexibility of exchange rates. American businessmen and bankers have become increasingly aware of the disadvantages of frequent monetary crises and are willing to consider alternatives to present arrangements. The press is full of rumors and speculation on our official attitude towards reform.

Finally, I should mention that a U.S. initiative on the exchange rate mechanism would be truly an achievement of your Administration. Although the final agreement on international liquidity was completed this year, the original initiative is generally credited to the previous Administration. Consequently unfavorable comparisons would be

---

[3] See Document 131.

[4] See Document 135.

invited if we did not come up with new ideas at the IMF meeting. Needless to say a more compelling argument for these ideas is that they will serve our own interests and those of the world as a whole.

Accordingly, I suggest that the Administration make a strong and forward looking statement, at the forthcoming annual meetings of the International Monetary Fund, on needed changes and strengthening of the international monetary system. Secretary Kennedy could make such a statement timed to avoid any relationship to the German election. It would, I believe, be received sympathetically by member nations generally.

Paul W. McCracken

---

138. Memorandum From Secretary of the Treasury Kennedy to President Nixon[1]

Washington, September 19, 1969.

SUBJECT

U.S. Initiative on International Monetary Reform

We have now had an opportunity to sound out our partners in the Group of Ten on their likely reaction to a U.S. call for study of limited exchange rate flexibility at the forthcoming World Bank/International Monetary Fund Meetings. Their responses, as given to Under Secretary Volcker on a trip to Europe and as volunteered by central bankers meeting in Basle,[2] are summarized in the attached table.

As you can see, in official circles there is widespread reluctance to deal with this issue. Except for the Italians and certain of the German

---

[1] Source: National Archives, Nixon Presidential Materials, NSC Files, Agency Files, Box 289, Treasury, Volume I. Confidential. An attached September 24 note from Haig to Bergsten requested, "as a matter of urgency, a cover memorandum from Henry to the President," presumably Document 139, to which a copy of this memorandum is attached as Tab E. Another copy is attached to a copy of the September 8 memorandum from McCracken to the President (Document 137) proposing a more forthcoming approach at the IMF and IBRD annual meeting, and this memorandum by Secretary Kennedy is presumably the Treasury Department reply.

[2] Volcker's itinerary has not been fully identified, but he apparently met with Chancellor of the Exchequer Roy Jenkins. (Paul A. Volcker and Toyoo Gyohten, *Changing Fortunes: The World's Money and the Threat to American Leadership* (Times Books, 1992), p. 69) The reference to the central bankers meeting is presumably to a meeting of the Bank for International Settlements attended by Daane and possibly Volcker as well.

officials, financial authorities in the rest of the Group of Ten countries are currently opposed to greater exchange flexibility in substance, and some are fearful that even study of the issue will be destabilizing.

To some extent, the adverse tone of the comments was an out-growth of some unfortunate leaks to the U.S. and foreign press about our intentions,[3] which failed to place the matter in appropriate per-spective. In substance, the opposition has differing origins. Some offi-cials simply think that greater exchange rate flexibility will create more problems than it will solve. Others, particularly those whose currencies are under pressure, are concerned that open discussion of greater flexi-bility will expose them to increased speculation and reserve losses. Still others are suspicious of our motives in raising this issue at this time, reading into our interest in exchange rate flexibility a defeatist attitude toward dealing with our internal inflation.

In contrast to these foreign official views, greater exchange rate flexibility has wide support in the academic community, has attracted interest in the business community, and has strong appeal to certain members of Congress. In the end, I believe most—if not all—of the lead-ing countries will accede to our request for international study. I believe that our interests, and indeed theirs in the longer run, will be served by proceeding with such an exercise. However, the foreign official response does emphasize the importance of proceeding in this matter with considerable care respecting the reservations and sensibilities of our friends to elicit their cooperation.

For that reason, in asking for study, I plan to emphasize (1) that careful study is required, and this means that no one need fear early and potentially disturbing changes; (2) that we do not have preconceived ideas as to the "best solution"—at the same time we must rule out cer-tain alternatives that would clearly be unworkable or work to the dis-advantage of the United States; and (3) that the U.S. does not look upon greater exchange flexibility as an alternative to continued pursuit of anti-inflation policies domestically. I am now working on a draft speech for the Bank/Fund Meetings which I trust will make these points clear.

David M. Kennedy

---

[3] Not further identified.

Attachment

	Concept of Flexibility	Willing to Study
U.K.	Strongly opposed	Yes, but dangers
Germany	Split internally; strong pressures on both sides	Yes
France	Minister's position uncertain; technicians opposed	Probably
Italy	Sympathetic	Favor
Netherlands	Strongly opposed	May oppose
Belgium	Strongly opposed	Probably
Sweden	Opposed	Yes
Canada	Opposed	Yes
Japan	Opposed	Yes
Switzerland	Strongly opposed	Yes

---

139. Memorandum From the President's Assistant for National Security Affairs (Kissinger) to President Nixon[1]

Washington, September 24, 1969.

SUBJECT

International Monetary Situation—U.S. Policy Options

Secretary Kennedy has provided you with a contingency paper on the international monetary situation (Tab C).[2] He regards it as an information memo, not requiring action at this time, although it does make several specific recommendations. It has not been approved by any other agencies. (See cover note at Tab B.)[3] Paul McCracken has also written to you on the subject (Tab D).[4]

---

[1] Source: National Archives, Nixon Presidential Materials, NSC Files, Agency Files, Box 215, Council of Economic Advisers. Secret.

[2] Not printed, but see Document 136.

[3] Tab B, not printed, is Kennedy's September 3 memorandum to the President; see Document 136.

[4] See Document 137 and footnote 1 thereto.

Present Situation

Another major international monetary crisis is quite possible in the next few weeks.

Speculation that Germany will revalue after its election on September 28 has already begun to precipitate massive new inflows into Germany ($1 billion in the last two weeks) and they are likely to accelerate immediately after the election. The SDP, which openly favors revaluation, is doing well at the polls and there is a growing belief that it may gain in strength. This would give it a greater voice in an eventual coalition government, which is still the most probable outcome. There will be widespread speculation whoever looks like a winner, however, because the economic (if not the political) case for revaluation is so clear.

The UK and Belgium continue as the potential weak spots, although the UK is doing well for the moment as the result of good trade figures.

Italy is the latest problem, losing $250 million so far this month. Sweden has also been suffering losses which are large for it. And France has begun to lose again, only a month after its devaluation.

Any of these countries might conclude—as did France last month—that it is useless to defend exchange rates which are unviable in the long term without German revaluation. If any of them devalue or float their exchange rates, numerous other countries would follow. Only a few countries beside Germany could then avoid devaluation. The result would be a severe disruption of the international monetary system and a further weakening of the U.S. competitive position, already jeopardized by inflation.

Strategic Choices and Broad Options

We face a strategic choice whether to attempt to forestall the development of a monetary crisis or to let it develop and respond afterwards. We have three options under each of these two strategies. We cannot approach Germany just before its election, of course, and our ability to do so thereafter will depend on the balance of political forces which emerges from it.

Preventive Action

1. We could pressure the Germans for immediate revaluation.

2. We could seek immediate assurance that revaluation will be undertaken as soon as it becomes possible politically and finance weak countries through the interim period.

3. We could urge weak countries to hold their exchange rates even without any assurance of German revaluation, financing them as nec-

essary, and be prepared to press Germany very hard on revaluation after a new government is formed. (This could require much larger loans than Secretary Kennedy mentions.)[5]

Response to Crisis

4. We could suspend convertibility of the dollar into gold as soon as we learned that any major country planned to devalue or float, announce our support for any sound currencies under pressure, and call for basic reforms of the monetary system. This would be an effort to pre-empt the collapse of the system by heading off the initial trigger.

5. We could suspend gold convertibility of the dollar in response to a forced devaluation or float of the British pound or another major currency, declaring our readiness to support financially other major currencies while basic reforms of the system are worked out. This would be an effort to limit the scope of the breakdown of the system. Secretary Kennedy's paper implicitly favors this course.

6. We could suspend gold convertibility of the dollar after devaluation or floats by a number of the countries calling for urgent reform to regain stability. This approach would be the easiest to justify and would minimize charges of a unilateral U.S. "power play."

7. We could double or possibly triple the official price of gold.

Conclusions

We cannot decide on a precise course of action in advance of the crisis. However, we should have a clear idea of the direction in which we want the international monetary system to move and, in light of that, how we should respond in a crisis situation.

You therefore need an interagency paper on the options we face and our choices in choosing among them. And you need it soon, because the crisis may be upon us quickly and because our position should be set before next week's annual meeting here of the IMF, as background for the many talks our people will be having with foreign financial officials.

There is also one immediate problem. It was agreed at your June 26 meeting with your top financial and foreign policy advisors that Secretary Kennedy should make an early public call for an intensified official international study of greater exchange rate flexibility.

The Secretary has not implemented this decision, however. And— in response to criticism from some foreign central bankers—he is now wavering over how firmly to do so even at the IMF meeting. (See his

---

[5] Secretary Kennedy mentioned up to $500 million for sterling; see Document 136.

memo at Tab E.)⁶ To pass by this obvious opportunity would clearly indicate that the U.S. is not going to take a lead in this area, and Paul McCracken urges at Tab D that the earlier decision be implemented rigorously.

Recommendation:

That you sign the memorandum to the Secretary of the Treasury at Tab A, directing him to submit (a) an interagency options paper by September 30 and (b) his proposed IMF speech by noon September 29.⁷

Approve⁸

Approve options paper only

Approve proposed speech only

Disapprove

---

⁶ Document 138.

⁷ Tab A, a two-paragraph memorandum, is not printed. No options paper was found. The annual meetings of the IMF and IBRD were scheduled to be held in Washington September 29–October 3. A first draft of Secretary Kennedy's speech was circulated to members of the Volcker Group as VG/LIM/69-74 on September 25. (Washington National Records Center, Department of the Treasury, Volcker Group Masters: FRC 56 86 30, VG/LIM/71–VG/LIM/77) In an unsigned September 27 memorandum to Kissinger, Bergsten commented on a revised and expanded "near final draft" that "proceeds very cautiously." He noted that the sense of the June 26 meeting with the President "was for a much clearer and more urgent call to action on this issue and three months have already elapsed." Bergsten regretted rejection of the option for widening margins within which exchange rates could fluctuate but nonetheless recommended that Kissinger sign an attached memorandum to the President requesting authority to approve the proposed speech. No record of the President's action was found. (National Archives, Nixon Presidential Materials, NSC Files, Agency Files, Box 289, Treasury, Volume I) Separately, on September 27 the Department of the Treasury forwarded to the White House draft welcoming remarks for Secretary Kennedy to read at the opening of the IMF–IBRD meeting on the President's behalf. In his covering memorandum to Kissinger, Bergsten commented that the President's decision not to address the meeting was "a needless affront to these two valuable organizations." He continued, "No US President in history has heretofore failed to address the meetings personally when they were in Washington." Kissinger approved the text on the President's behalf. (Ibid., Box 306, IBRD/IMF) See Department of State *Bulletin*, October 27, 1969, pp. 353–358, for text of Secretary Kennedy's September 30 speech.

⁸ This option is checked and a note written next to it reads: "done via phone." The memorandum for Secretary Kennedy (Tab A) did not go to the President for his signature.

140.   Information Memorandum From the President's Assistant
        for National Security Affairs (Kissinger) to President Nixon[1]

Washington, October 14, 1969.

SUBJECT

International Monetary Developments

Recent Developments

Attached are memoranda from Secretary Kennedy (Tab A) and Paul McCracken (Tab B) on the international monetary developments of the past ten days:[2]

1. Germany's floating of the mark. The mark has now risen in value by about 6%.[3] The first act of the Brandt government is likely to be to fix a new parity 6-1/2–8% above the old rate of four DM equal $1.00. They will almost certainly also remove the 4% border taxes on trade which they adopted in November 1968 as a substitute for revaluation at that time—so the effective revaluation will be 2-1/2–4% on exports and imports and the full 6-1/2–8% on all other international transactions.[4]

2. The formal IMF decision to create $9.5 billion of Special Drawing Rights (SDRs) in 1970–1972.[5]

3. Laying of the groundwork for serious international consideration of greater flexibility of exchange rates.

Implications

Two of the three components of the U.S. international monetary policy agreed at your June 26 meeting with your financial and foreign policy advisers are now completed: a large amount of SDRs has been decided and a tenable exchange rate structure has been achieved through the French devaluation, German revaluation, and UK turnaround into sizable surplus.

---

[1] Source: National Archives, Nixon Presidential Materials, NSC Files, Agency Files, Box 216, Council of Economic Advisers. Confidential.

[2] Tabs A and B, both dated October 4, are not printed.

[3] Following the West German elections on September 28, the Mark had been allowed to float on September 30.

[4] After assembling a Parliamentary majority on October 3, Willy Brandt became Chancellor on October 21. Documentation on the German measures in November 1968 is in *Foreign Relations, 1964–1968*, vol. VIII, Documents 215, 216, and 219.

[5] The IMF Board took this decision on October 3.

In addition, the third point—greater exchange rate flexibility—has moved on to the front burner of the international monetary agenda.[6]

There is thus an excellent chance that the international monetary system will remain calm for at least six months and perhaps much longer. The task now is to use the available time to improve the basic structure of the system so that relative calm can prevail indefinitely. That task is underway with the study of exchange rate flexibility.

Another significant effect of the recent developments is that both France and Germany have now effectively withdrawn from the Common Agricultural Policy by fully offsetting the impact on their agricultural sectors of their exchange rate changes. The CAP—which many regard as the major impetus toward closer European integration now that their customs union is completed—is thus suspended for all practical purposes. It is quite unclear how and when the Europeans can put it back together. This raises important questions (and perhaps opportunities) for British entry to the EC, our own agricultural exports, and numerous other international political and economic questions.

Remaining Problems

A few problems remain, although they are of decidedly lesser magnitude at present:

1. Our own balance of payments deteriorated significantly in the third quarter. It will continue to deteriorate if we are able to ease our domestic monetary policy as inflation is brought under control. The deterioration will be exacerbated as we continue to liberalize our controls over capital exports.

McCracken in fact cites the need to improve our balance of payments as the main reason why we should push hard for greater exchange rate flexibility. Secretary Kennedy reports that he is working on export incentives and possibly other measures to help our payments position.

2. Germany's revaluation may not be enough to hold speculation on the mark at bay for very long. A few other currencies, notably the Dutch guilder but perhaps also the Japanese yen, could come under pressure to revalue too. And the French franc is by no means safe, given widespread skepticism that the measures it has taken so far will bring its balance of payments into equilibrium.

3. We remain at loggerheads with South Africa over how its gold production should be marketed.[7] Secretary Kennedy regards this as merely an "annoyance", however.

---

[6] Secretary Kennedy discussed the question of "limited flexibility" of exchange rates in his September 30 speech at the IMF; see footnote 7, Document 139.

[7] See Document 145.

141.   Telegram From the Department of State to the Mission to the United Nations[1]

Washington, October 24, 1969, 2330Z.

181169. Subject: GA Committee 2—Comments Relative to Syrian Statement on International Monetary Reform and Link between Economic Assistance and SDRs. Ref: US/UN 3621.[2] Concerning link of SDRs to assistance, recommend U.S. spokesman avoid volunteering comment on this subject in speeches or addresses. If public statements necessary suggest US Del confine itself to reference to approach taken by Secretary Kennedy in his press conference on the record October 3, 1969 in Washington. This statement follows:

"Question: Do you think, sir, that the creation of Special Drawing Rights will enable you to give some additional aid to developing countries, efforts to assist them, inasmuch as the system has become richer?

Secretary Kennedy: Well, I should think that adding to their volume of reserves does have an indirect relationship to what the nations can do in the way of developing. That doesn't mean a linkage, such as they are talking about, of SDRs with the developing process. I think at the present time the effort should be made to get these SDRs activated and handled and managed in such a way that they contribute to international stability, and that those questions can be looked at and deferred until later."

In private conversations with other delegations US Del may draw on following as and when appropriate:

(1) During the negotiation of the Special Drawing Rights Amendment there was very strong sentiment against any direct linkage of an organic character between the Special Drawing Rights and the provision of assistance for development. It was felt that decisions to create Special Drawing Rights should be entirely governed by monetary considerations and should not be subjected to the pressures that arise for a steadily enlarging flow of real resources from industrial countries to developing countries.

(2) It is important that the Special Drawing Rights become well established as an international monetary asset and this should be our

---

[1] Source: National Archives, RG 59, Central Files 1967–69, FN 17–1. Limited Official Use. Drafted in Treasury by Willis and cleared by Volcker and Petty; cleared in State by Trezise and Kerrigan (IO/OES) and approved by Assistant Secretary of State for International Organization Affairs Samuel De Palma. Repeated to the Mission in Geneva and the Consulate in Vancouver for the U.S. delegation to the Colombo Plan meeting in Victoria.

[2] Not printed. (Ibid.) Cables between the Department of State and USUN on the Syrian proposal in Committee 2 are ibid.

primary consideration during the period ahead. It would be most unfortunate if the question of linkage with economic assistance should lead to reluctance on the part of industrial countries to carry on in future the work that has begun of establishing a facility to provide an adequate rate of growth in world reserves. The latter is a key to adequate growth in world trade and investment and a healthy world economy is vitally important to economic growth of developing countries.

(3) The allocation of Special Drawing Rights is made in proportion to quotas in the International Monetary Fund which was generally accepted as an equitable and reasonable method of allocation. This will make available to the developing countries nearly $2.7 billion in additional reserves during the next three years, a very substantial sum. (FYI. This is about 28% of allocations to be made in three tranches of $3.5 billion in Jan. 1970, and $3 billion each in January 1971 and 1972. End FYI)

(4) Special Drawing Rights involve both rights and obligations, and the obligation for surplus countries is twice as large as the drawing right.

(5) Economic assistance is a matter of political decision in donor countries. Most countries have budgetary and parliamentary procedures governing the provision of development assistance. There are major questions whether countries should abandon these regular procedures, and whether Parliaments would be receptive to doing so. Attempts to introduce new procedures related to SDRs would need to be assessed against the complications introduced into considerations governing the provision of international liquidity.

Rogers

142. Airgram From the Department of State to Treasury Representatives at the Embassies in the United Kingdom, France, Germany, Italy, and Japan[1]

CA–6044   Washington, November 6, 1969, 5:17 p.m.

SUBJECT

    Meeting of Deputies of Group of Ten, Paris, Oct. 31, 1969, on Quota Increases in IMF

Chairman Ossola recalled the September agreement of the Deputies for a total increase in IMF quotas of about 30 percent plus or minus 3 percent.[2] It was implicit that new quotas should be the basis for the second annual allocation of Special Drawing Rights. It was also desirable not to modify substantially the relationship between Group of Ten countries and the developing countries in the IMF. In September figures had been mentioned by a number of countries, and a tabulation has been discussed which showed the U.S. at $6300 million. The United States, the Belgians, and some others did not accept the figures given for them in the September IMF table. Revised figures for these countries, plus the earlier objectives of France, Italy, Japan, and Canada would call for a larger global increase than the amount agreed upon in September.

Chairman Ossola suggested a possible avenue of agreement involving two principles:

(1) Accepting a two-tier approach that was more favorable to the developing countries than to the industrial countries, even though this discrimination was rejected by some developing countries as a bad precedent, and
(2) enlarging the total increase despite the adamant position of Germany against this, taking into account the political advantage of so doing to avoid resentment in other countries of G-10 dictation on Fund matters.

The Chairman said he had asked the Fund staff to prepare a table which provided:

(a) A general increase of 25 percent (for all countries except China);
(b) Distribution of $5 billion in selective increases proportionate to present shortfalls in quotas relative to BW calculations;

---

[1] Source: National Archives, RG 59, Central Files 1967–69, FN 10 IMF. Confidential. Drafted in Treasury by Willis on November 5 and cleared by Volcker; approved in State by Weintraub. Repeated to USOECD and USEC and the Embassies in Brussels, The Hague, Bern, Stockholm, and Ottawa.

[2] For information on the discussion of IMF quota increases at the G-10 Deputies meeting, see Margaret G. de Vries, *The International Monetary Fund 1966–1971: The System Under Stress*, Volume I: *Narrative* (Washington, D.C.: The International Monetary Fund, 1976), pp. 287–305.

(c) A reduction of 8 percent of sum of (a) and (b) for G-10 countries. With some rounding, this produced figures satisfactory to most G-10 countries, and would result in an overall increase of about 35 percent. A table showing these results was distributed.[3]

Inamura (Japan) accepted the proposal. Nield (U.K.) said the U.K. would accept the two-tier principle in the Chairman's ingenious variation. Handfield-Jones (Canada) called attention to the fact that the 8 percent reduction factor had not been applied to the middle group of industrial countries not included in the Group of Ten. If this were done, the total increase might be reduced to about 34 percent. Chairman Ossola favored this suggestion. Larre (Fr) would accept the table if all other members of G-10 accepted it.

Pieske (Ger) said the Group of Ten should abide by the agreement of last July. This agreement was part of an overall understanding on SDR allocations.[4] We should not change this agreement after the SDR part of the understanding has been implemented. There is no need to go beyond 30 percent plus or minus 3 percent. Any G-10 ceiling appears like dictation to other IMF members, regardless of the amount. The Canadian proposal provides no guarantee that intermediate countries would really accept the 8 percent reduction. To the Germans, the proposal put forward some time ago by Mr. Roelandts of Belgium in the Fund calling for a 31 percent overall increase would be acceptable. The Germans would favor adopting a two-tier system openly rather than in the disguised form proposed by the Chairman. Countries which have raised their quota targets since last July bear heavy responsibility for breaking down the agreement of last July.

Chairman Ossola pointed out that Belgium, the Netherlands, Sweden and the U.S. did not accept the figures put forward last July for their countries. The July proposal was put forward under great pressure and we had not realized all of the implications. If necessary, we could force the non-G-10 members of the Fund to accept a reduction of 8 percent since we have a majority in the Executive Board.

Palumbo (Italy) accepted the Chairman's proposal, noting that it provided for a $1 billion figure for the Italian quota, as requested in July. Joge (Sweden) said he would have preferred to limit selective increases to only a few countries. However, because the great majority want selective increases, he would accept the $325 million figure shown for Sweden. He thought the other Nordic countries would accept a reduction of 8 percent, and would be glad to have the two-tier system concealed as in this proposal.

---

[3] Not printed.

[4] See Document 135.

De Strycker (Belg) continued to object to the two-tier system, but this proposal could be modified to avoid two classes of countries. 35 percent was a very high percentage increase. The world was not in a phase of general deflation. To reconcile differences, he suggested a two-stage quota increase, with a first stage covering only three years and the second stage the following two years. This would mean taking the proposal of the Chairman, but giving each country only 3/5ths of its total now. The Chairman thought the two-tranche idea of Belgium might be attractive.

Kessler (Neth) also was against going beyond the 33 percent limit. In the selective quota calculation, the $5 billion or 23 percent of the quotas was so divided that the developing countries got less than 23 percent and the Group of Ten got far more than 23 percent, amounting to about 30 percent. The scheme has the merit of making it possible for the U.K. to go down to 15 percent overall increase. He had no quarrel with the mechanism of the scheme, but the 8 percent reduction was too little. The Netherlands would go down to $675 million, or about a 30 percent increase. In response, Polak (IMF) argued that the selective calculation is not as arbitrary as Kessler suggested. The 25 percent general increase is important to non-members of the Ten.

Emminger (Ger) urged the necessity of insisting on pursuing the Canadian suggestion and reducing the middle group of industrial countries by 8 percent. However, 8 percent was still too small a reduction, and he suggested a reduction of 10 percent with some rounding up here and there, to be applied also to the middle group of countries. Ossola (Italy) thought that Italy and some others would not be satisfied with a 10 percent reduction, but asked for the table to be prepared and circulated.[5]

Volcker (U.S.) reminded the group that the U.S. had been reluctant to agree to the earlier ceiling because of a feeling that more leeway would be needed, but was equally reluctant to abandon the agreement on the 33 percent limit, related to the SDR allocation understanding. The U.S. had never agreed to the figure proposed for it in July. All objective calculations show the United States entitled to a substantial increase. The United States concluded that the earlier figure would erode our relative position in the Fund too much. Any solution along the lines of Roelandts' proposal, mentioned by the Germans, would bring the U.S. down too low and was entirely unacceptable.

Volcker said the U.S. was willing to live within 33 percent, and this could be done by G-10 accepting small adjustments all around. While no one would obtain his target figure, the desired relative position of

---

[5] Not printed.

G-10 members could be attained. The U.S. might consider a small reduction in the U.S. figure to get within the 33 percent limit. Volcker saw problems with the Canadian suggestion. He thought the middle countries would not accept it without supplementary concessions by the Group of Ten.

Volcker said that we had never liked the two-tier system, but this was not a matter of life and death. We preferred the disguised two-tier system and had no difficulty with the proposed approach to calculating quotas. We would not stand in the way of a solution.

Volcker said the quota increases also raised the matter of gold mitigation.[6] It was of some direct concern to the U.S., and any solution here was dependent on a satisfactory solution of the mitigation problem. He suggested a discussion of mitigation at this point before returning to the quota question.

Chairman Ossola accepted this suggestion, and said he was greatly encouraged by the first exchange of views. In view of the short time available before lunch, he suggested another meeting of the Deputies in the afternoon.

Emminger (Ger) said he was not sure there was any chance of getting any further this afternoon, but he and Ossola could talk to Schoellhorn, who was arriving about 2:45 p.m. We should not have a meeting unless we could make further progress.

Ossola argued the great importance of reaching agreement today.

Larre (Fr) complained that the G-10 discussion was on the verge of breakdown. This should not be allowed to happen because of the small difference between 33 percent and 34.8 percent under the scheme.

Chairman Ossola then brought up the subject of mitigation. Primary mitigation had been to some extent handled by installment payments and special drawings during the previous quota increase. There should be credit tranche drawings only if justified for other reasons. Installments might be permitted if requested, but he thought most countries would not so request because of their desire to have their quotas adjusted quickly in order to receive their full share of SDRs. Secondary mitigation had cost the reserve centers about $500 million last time, and this had been mitigated by special deposits of gold in the amount of $350 million and by special gold operations

---

[6] IMF members were expected to subscribe 25 percent of any quota increase to the Fund in gold, sometimes a problem for members that did not hold significant gold reserves. IMF quota increases sometimes led countries to exchange currency holdings for U.S. monetary gold, creating a drain on the U.S. gold reserves. Mitigation concerned strategies and procedures for dealing with meeting the gold subscription of any quota increase. See de Vries, *The International Monetary Fund 1966–1971: The System Under Stress,* Volume I: *Narrative,* pp. 297–298.

under which countries bought gold from a country having a super gold tranche claim on the Fund, and the Fund restored the positions of these countries by selling gold back to them in return for their currencies. The previous deposit scheme was unpalatable to some of the Group of Ten now, but perhaps the triangular arrangement could be agreed upon. The amount of secondary mitigation was somewhere around $600 million.

Polak (IMF) explained that the suggested mitigation gold sale procedure comprised three stages. For example, India might buy gold from Germany with dollars and pay the gold to the Fund. In the second stage the IMF would purchase DMs with gold. The third stage would be stretched out over time and would permit more DMs to be used in drawings than would otherwise be the case so that Germany could restore its IMF position and reduce its dollar holdings. The end result is that the IMF receives payment in usable currency rather than in gold, equivalent to 25 percent of the quota increase.

Volcker (U.S.) said the problem is not primary mitigation though this may arise for some countries. Our concern is to have a permanent form of secondary mitigation. The most natural solution would be to pay out Special Drawing Rights directly to the Fund instead of gold. Minister Colombo had regretted that this was not now possible. It would be feasible, if generally supported, to amend the Fund Articles to make this possible and to obtain legislative sanction simultaneously with legislative approval of quotas. This would tidy up the SDR agreement. He put this idea forward for consideration of the Group.

Volcker also recognized that the recent Fund Staff proposal would be adequate. The drawings in the third step cited by Polak could in fact begin in advance of the gold payments to the Fund. A number of countries could be used as intermediaries. The United States might or might not play such a role dependent upon the wish of others. What we need is agreement in principle that the Executive Board will work out a mitigation plan on this basis.

Emminger (Ger) thought it might be better that the Fund take in SDRs instead of useable currency, but it would be odd to amend the new SDR plan so quickly to permit this. He was not sure this was a practicable procedure. We should, however, explore the method suggested by the IMF Staff. Germany has participated in these mitigation gold transactions before and would have no difficulty in permitting the DM to be used as an intermediary. Volcker (U.S.) intervened briefly to clarify the point that we could obtain much the same result as an amendment by encouraging countries to repay the Fund in SDRs. Then the Fund would end up with SDRs instead of gold, and this provided a certain degree of logic to the whole procedure.

Morse (U.K.) thought it would be logical for the present gold payment to the Fund to be made in SDRs, but this had been specifically eliminated during the negotiations. He would now be content with the procedure outlined by Mr. Polak.

Larre (Fr) saw a contrast between the rigidity of quota positions and the laxity with which people contemplated amendments to the SDR plan. The ink on the SDR amendment was barely dry and we were talking about amending the earlier understanding. Such an amendment is premature. After three years, we can tell whether the SDR has replaced gold in central banks. The only feasible proposal is the Polak procedure which (a) conforms to the IMF rules, (b) has been used in the past, and (c) avoids disruption for gold holders. However, every member of the IMF that holds gold should be eligible as an intermediary.

Chairman Ossola noted that at least two countries have spoken favorably of the amendment to permit payment in SDRs.

Larre (Fr) suggested that countries must give up something of value when they receive a quota increase. Kessler (Neth) suggested that countries be permitted to purchase gold from the intermediary only when they have no gold or have a rather small percentage of gold in their reserves. He added that we might provide for some gold transactions with gold producers in connection with mitigation. In this way, the IMF could recover gold.

De Strycker (Belg) saw prima facie logic to permitting quota payments in SDRs, but there are two major drawbacks. This could mean that $1.7 to $2 billion of SDRs would be paid into the Fund and thus a very large amount of SDRs would move rather quickly from the Fund to be absorbed by surplus countries. Secondly, the IMF would be deprived of gold, which gives a guarantee that the IMF can get the currency it requires.

Joge (Sweden) had no objection to the IMF Staff method. Permission for direct payment in SDRs would be a more direct method. The world's attitude toward SDRs will be largely determined by the attitudes of the Group of Ten authorities. If such payment were permissible, however, he was not sure he would recommend payment in SDRs instead of gold.

Emminger (Ger) strongly supported the Swedish view that the status of SDRs depends on the attitude of the G-10 countries. He was not absolutely certain that Germany would choose SDRs instead of gold if permitted to do so since the SDR is a gold certificate bearing 1-1/2 percent interest. The Fund could procure usable currencies with SDRs just as well as with gold. There is no real danger that SDRs will become illiquid because of reaching the acceptance limits. However, it is not necessary to push the amendment now. It is satisfactory to obtain pragmatic results.

Volcker (U.S.) said the inclination of the U.S. might well be to pay gold rather than Special Drawing Rights even if the latter were permissible. The mitigation problem was not essentially a matter of gold as such but resulted from the circumstance that quota payments to the Fund would produce pressure on U.S. reserves, however composed. Concerning arrangements with gold-producing countries, Volcker referred to having spent some time during the year exploring the problems of the gold producers with them. This had made it plain to him that we cannot link that problem with mitigation at this stage. He saw no practical way to do so at this time.

Chairman Ossola summarized the results of the meeting as follows:

(1) Primary mitigation is not a problem with which the countries around the table are concerned;

(2) There was a rather widespread desire that Special Drawing Rights be usable instead of gold, but a recognition that it is impracticable to insert such an amendment into the ratification of quota increases. It was not clear that countries would in fact use Special Drawing Rights instead of gold if permitted to do so. We should use the IMF Staff technique of mitigation gold transactions without restricting its use to a particular country. The Fund should be left to determine which countries were entitled to use this procedure and which currencies could serve as intermediaries;

(3) There should be no connection between mitigation and arrangements with gold-producing countries, which is a separate problem.

Chairman Ossola then pressed again for an afternoon meeting but Emminger (Ger) again suggested that this matter be left open until it could be ascertained whether it would be useful to have the meeting. The Chairman suggested that the matter might be taken up again at the time of the EPC meeting. Polak (IMF) said this would be very difficult. The IMF could make a proposal along these lines, but it would take a few weeks to clarify the reaction of the other developed countries. There was little time left to reach agreement by December 31. Chairman Ossola was very reluctant to leave the decision to be worked out in other bodies without reaching unanimous agreement in the Deputies. Polak (IMF) said that if the group wanted to agree they should do so today. He did not think the Executive Directors could be asked to delay further consideration of the matter until after the EPC meeting.

Volcker (U.S.) noted that he recognized the procedural and psychological difficulties of presently introducing an SDR amendment. However, he did not want to associate himself at this point with the Chairman's use of the term "impracticable." The Chairman agreed that "difficulty" could be a better description.

Rogers

143.   Information Memorandum From the President's Assistant for National Security Affairs (Kissinger) to President Nixon[1]

Washington, November 17, 1969.

SUBJECT

International Monetary Situation

At Tab A is Paul McCracken's weekly report on the international financial situation.[2] It repeats the points which I have already made to you about events which followed the German revaluation:[3]

1. The Netherlands and Austria decided not to follow the German move with revaluations of their own, and speculative money which had entered those countries in anticipation of revaluation has now flowed back out.

2. $1.25 billion flowed out of Germany as speculators took their profits from the revaluation of the mark.

3. France and the United Kingdom each picked up about $100 million of this outflow.

4. The exchange markets are likely to be relatively quiet for some months as a result of the German action.[4]

---

[1] Source: National Archives, Nixon Presidential Materials, NSC Files, Agency Files, Box 216, Council of Economic Advisers. Confidential. The date is stamped under the handwritten note: "Back from Pres."

[2] Not printed.

[3] The Deutschmark, which had been allowed to float on September 30, was formally revalued 9.29 percent from $0.25 to $0.273224 on October 24.

[4] The President wrote at the end of the memorandum: "This again shows we were right in *not* following Treasury's recommendation for urgent action." No Treasury recommendation for urgent action has been found. The President may be thinking back to May when Secretary Kennedy wanted to press hard and Kissinger advised going slow. A November 3 memorandum from Director of the Office of Industrial Nations Widman to Assistant Secretary Petty on "Suspension of Gold Convertibility," concluded that a large projected balance-of-payments deficit in 1970 could lead to a crisis of confidence in the dollar by mid-1970 and that suspension of the convertibility of the dollar to gold would be "the least undesirable" action, but there was no call for urgent action. (Washington National Records Center, Department of the Treasury, Deputy to the Assistant Secretary for International Affairs: FRC 56 83 26, Contingency Planning 1969)

144. Memorandum From Secretary of the Treasury Kennedy to President Nixon[1]

Washington, December 29, 1969.

SUBJECT

Quota Increases in the International Monetary Fund

Following considerable informal negotiation, the Executive Directors of the Fund were formally charged at the Annual Governors' Meeting early in October to complete a general review of Fund quotas by the end of December and to make recommendations for appropriate increases. The Directors completed this process on December 24. The Fund will probably announce the results tomorrow, for December 31 newspapers.

The over-all increase in quotas recommended will be approximately $7.6 billion, compared to present quotas of some $21.4 billion. The potential increase will thus be about 35 percent.

This proposed increase is consistent with our broad program for international monetary reform, as outlined to you last Summer.[2] It is a logical (but less important) complement to the activation of Special Drawing Rights. Larger quotas provide greater scope for balance of payments financing for all countries through the IMF more or less in line with the growth in the world economy.

The new quota recommended for the United States is $6,700 million, an increase by almost 30 percent from the present quota of $5,160 million. Since the U.S. quota will increase by a smaller than average proportion, the U.S. share of total Fund quotas will be modestly reduced, from the present 24.2 percent to 23.2 percent.

The share of the main industrial countries (the Group of Ten) in total quotas will be approximately the same in the future as now, approximately 61 percent. This reflects an increase in the weight of the Common Market countries. The quota share of the developing countries has been protected against much of a reduction, although the statistical calculations traditionally used by the Fund in determining quotas would have indicated a significant reduction. The share of developing countries will fall from 28.3 percent to about 27.3 percent.

---

[1] Source: National Archives, Nixon Presidential Materials, NSC Files, Agency Files, Box 289, Treasury, Volume I. Confidential. Attached to internal National Security Council memoranda and a transmittal memorandum to the President indicating that Kissinger approved Secretary Kennedy's recommendation on the President's behalf since the quota increase was consistent with policy decisions already taken.

[2] Presumably a reference to the June 26 meeting with the President; see Documents 130, 131, and 140. An IMF quota increase would complement SDR activation in adding to the stock of international liquidity.

Quota increases must normally be paid for 25 percent in gold and 75 percent in the member's own currency. The U.S. quota increase will require a gold payment of $385 million and a payment in dollar instruments of $1,155 million. Many other countries, especially the larger industrial countries (except perhaps Japan), expect to make the required gold payment from their own holdings. However, a number of smaller countries would have to buy gold to make the payment, presumably from the United States. In order to mitigate the effect of such gold purchases on U.S. reserves, the Fund has worked out rather complex procedures to "steer" the gold back to where it was bought.[3] These arrangements will avoid a fall in U.S. gold holdings of up to an estimated $600–$700 million, which would otherwise have occurred.

The U. S. quota increase in the Fund will require authorizing legislation in 1970. However, these operations are considered as an exchange of monetary assets and have no budgetary impact.

The established practice is that countries, especially the more developed countries, receiving quota increases in the Fund should increase their subscription to the capital of the World Bank by a corresponding amount. We believe this tradition should be maintained, in the light of our desire to strengthen multilateral lending institutions. This will require authorizing legislation and have a budget impact of $24.6 million in Fiscal 1971, corresponding to a 10 percent paid in portion of a $246.1 million capital subscription. Allowance has been made for this in your prospective 1971 budget.

With your approval, I plan to vote the United States in favor of the proposed increase in IMF quotas and to support corresponding selective increases in World Bank capital in forthcoming discussions in the World Bank.[4]

David M. Kennedy

---

[3] See Document 141 and footnote 6 thereto.

[4] The memoranda attached to this memorandum (see footnote 1 above) indicate that Kissinger's approval on the President's behalf was being passed to Treasury by Robert D. Hormats on January 5, 1970, in time for a World Bank meeting on January 6.

145.   Editorial Note

The gold communiqué of March 17, 1968, established the two-tier gold market where monetary gold would be exchanged among official authorities at the official price and the free market would determine the price for all other uses. Monetary authorities would no longer buy gold from the private market, including new production. See *Foreign Relations, 1964–1968*, volume VIII, Documents 187–191 for background on the creation of the two-tier gold market.

How gold from South Africa, the largest producer, would be marketed was not settled at the time of the March 1968 communiqué and was under discussion until resolved in December 1969. In fact, all signatories of the communiqué and most other members of the IMF eschewed purchases of gold from South Africa but, according to a July 30, 1969, memorandum from T. Page Nelson, Director of the Office of International Gold and Foreign Exchange Operations, to Treasury Under Secretary Volcker, there were at least three exceptions, Portugal, Congo (Kinshasa), and Singapore. Nelson suspected the South Africans had made a vigorous effort to sell gold to monetary authorities and concluded the amount sold, perhaps $80 million, was a very poor showing. This memorandum, documentation on exchanges between Under Secretary Volcker and South African authorities, and a December 9 report to the President from Acting Treasury Secretary Charls Walker entitled "Possible Understanding with South Africa on Handling of Gold" are in the Washington National Records Center, Department of the Treasury, Files of Under Secretaries Deming and Volcker: FRC 56 79 14, Subject Files, South African Gold.

During 1969 there was an active exchange of cables between Washington and the Embassy in Kinshasa with instructions for the Embassy to protest Congolese purchases of South African gold with Congo's Central Bank Governor Ndele and, on at least one occasion, President Mobutu. This exchange of cables and related memoranda are in the National Archives, RG 59, Central Files 1967–69, FN 19, FN 17, FN 10, and FN 10 IMF. Some of the outgoing messages were drafted in the Treasury Department and forwarded to the State Department for clearance and transmission; others were drafted in State and cleared with Treasury.

Early in the exchange Washington agencies noted, for Ndele's information, that the purchase by the Congo Central Bank was in violation of the U.S. understanding of Congo's intentions and was upsetting the international monetary system. In addition, Congolese gold purchases might cause problems elsewhere in the bilateral relationship as

Congress, questioning the propriety of a less-developed country holding its reserves in a non-earning asset, had sometimes considered amendments to the Foreign Assistance Act prohibiting aid to countries buying monetary gold. Since Congo had purchased the South African gold at $35 per ounce and the free market was then at $42, the Embassy was instructed to request that Ndele resell that gold in the free market, reap the profit, and be in conformity with the communiqué. (Telegram 17644 to Kinshasa, February 4, 1969; ibid., FN 19)

In their rebuttal to Ndele's negative response to the Embassy's initial démarche, Washington agencies explained on February 19, in telegram 26264 to Kinshasa, that the position on purchase of newly-mined gold was not specifically spelled out in the March 17, 1968, communiqué because Canada and Switzerland had been unclear about their legal authority to refuse to purchase. Shortly after the two-tier system was established, however, four of the largest gold-producing countries after South Africa (Canada, the United States, Australia, and Japan) took steps to have their new production go into the free market and not into monetary reserves. Washington agencies pointed out that the signatories recognized that the two-tier system could not operate effectively if the world's largest gold producer could channel its output to either market depending on which would give it the greatest benefit. In support of that point they quoted from an August 1968 speech, which was not further identified, by Bundesbank Director Otmar Emminger:

"At present it seems to be South Africa's main objective to obtain the right to sell gold at the fixed official price to the IMF at its own discretion. If this privilege were granted to South Africa it could decide at will what share of its newly mined gold to sell on the free market and what share at the fixed official price. As a monopolist it could thus reap the highest possible profit. Much more important, and objectionable from a monetary point of view, would be the possibility for South Africa, by manipulating its sales of gold on the free market in an erratic way, to keep the gold market in a state of constant unrest and thus make the gold price a subject of permanent discussion and speculation." (Ibid.)

The exchange between the Embassy and Ndele continued amid reports of additional Congolese gold purchases, and at one point it seemed agreement might be reached for Congo to sell its South African gold purchased after March 17, 1968, on the free market and replace that gold with monetary gold from the United States.

On the fringes of the 1969 annual meetings of the IMF and the IBRD in Washington, Ndele met with Under Secretary Paul Volcker and Federal Reserve Board Chairman William McChesney Martin on October 1. According to the report of this meeting, Ndele told Volcker and Martin that he thought he was doing the United States a favor by not asking to buy U.S. gold in view of the pressure France and other governments were applying to U.S. gold reserves. Regarding the U.S. suggestion that Congo sell on the open market gold already purchased from South Africa and then purchase an equal amount from the United States, Ndele said he could not do that because he had given his word to the South Africans. Going back on his word, even to South Africans, would blot his personal integrity in international banking circles. Nonetheless Ndele said that he had no special interest in South Africa and would much prefer dealing with friends as long as he could be assured of having future gold needs met under the same conditions. Volcker said the United States would be happy to consult with Congo about future gold requirements, including buying and selling arrangements, provided Congo agreed to operate within the limits set by the two-tier system with respect to purchases from South Africa. Ndele finally agreed, and following a review of Congolese gold policy, during which Ndele revealed that gold was 40 percent of Congolese reserves, Ndele ended the discussion saying at that point he had no intention of purchasing more gold. (Telegram 170804 to Kinshasa, October 8; ibid., FN 17)

As discussions with South African officials on marketing new production and sales from South African reserves and the dialogue with the Congolese were ongoing during 1969, the free market price of gold declined, causing concern in some official circles that it might fall below the official monetary price of $35 per ounce. In early December 1969 Treasury Secretary Kennedy, accompanied by Under Secretary Volcker, traveled to Europe as part of the U.S. delegation to the December 4–5 NATO Ministerial meeting. They met with Belgian and European Commission officials in Brussels and, on side trips, Finance Ministers and Central Bank Governors in London, Paris, Bonn, The Hague, and Rome (Volcker only). The gold price and the marketing of South African gold featured prominently in their consultations. Memoranda of those conversations are in the Washington National Records Center, Department of the Treasury, Secretary's Memos/Correspondence: FRC 56 74 7, Memorandum of Conversations–1969.

Volcker met with South African officials in Rome on December 13–14, and the agreement they reached was ratified by the IMF on December 30. In effect, whenever the gold price was above $35, South Africa would market gold on the free market in amounts needed to meet its need for foreign exchange, and any additional production would be added to South African reserves. When the price was at $35 or below, South Africa would market newly-mined gold to the IMF at $35 to meet its foreign exchange needs, and if new production was less than adequate to meet current foreign exchange requirements, South Africa would be permitted to sell the IMF gold accumulated in South African reserves since March 17, 1968. See Margaret de Vries, *The International*

Monetary Fund 1966–1971, Volume I: *Narrative,* pages 409–415, for the IMF's history of the resolution of the South African gold problem.

A number of U.S. Government, foreign government, and IMF papers on South African gold are also in the Washington National Records Center, Department of the Treasury, Volcker Group Masters: FRC 56 86 30.

---

146. Memorandum of Conversation[1]

Camp David, Maryland, May 3–5, 1970.

PARTICIPANTS

France
Valery Giscard d'Estaing, Minister of Economy and Finance
Olivier Wormser, Governor of the Bank of France
René Larre, Director of the Treasury
Georges Plescoff, Finance Minister, French Embassy
Claude Pierre-Brossolette, Special Assistant to Giscard d'Estaing

United States

Secretary Kennedy
Under Secretary Volcker
Assistant Secretary Petty
Deputy Under Secretary MacLaury
Donald J. McGrew, U.S. Treasury Representative, Paris.

SUBJECTS

Part I: French and U.S. Economic Prospects
Part II: Interest Rates
Part III: Outlook for International Payments Equilibrium
Part IV: Future of the International Monetary System
Part V: European Monetary Union
Part VI: SDR Link to Development Finance and Use
Part VII: IDA Replenishment
Part VIII: Bank Secrecy
Part IX: Approval by Under Secretary Volcker

[Omitted here are Parts I and II.]

---

[1] Washington National Records Center, Department of the Treasury, Files of Under Secretary Volcker: FRC 56 79 15, France. Confidential. Drafted by McGrew and approved by Volcker on May 20. Copies were distributed within Treasury and to the Executive Secretariat at State, Chairman Burns at the Federal Reserve, and Chairman McCracken at the Council of Economic Advisers.

III. Outlook for International Payments Equilibrium

Secretary Kennedy suggested that Mr. Volcker should lead off on this topic.

Mr. Volcker said that in the first quarter of 1970 our official settlements deficit was about $3 billion. This resulted partly from a reversal of year-end window dressing by U.S. corporations to meet the direct investment control requirements. About one-third of the deficit was accounted for by a reduction of U.S. bank borrowing from overseas branches. The liquidity deficit in the first quarter was around $2 billion. It also was influenced by the window dressing operations. A better picture is given by averaging the fourth and first quarters. This gives an official settlements deficit of just over $1 billion per quarter and a liquidity deficit of several hundred million dollars.

In other words, we got what we had anticipated. With the downward movement of U.S. interest rates, there was a reversal of capital flows. This would continue if there were to be a continued downward movement in our rates. However, with the recent rise in U.S. interest rates there has been no further drop of U.S. bank borrowings from overseas branches. In fact, there has been some increase. The slowdown in the U.S. economy has had the natural result of improving our trade balance. The trade surplus for the first quarter was about $500 million, or an annual rate of $2 billion. Repayment of foreign bank loans also helped our situation in this period.

Looking further ahead, we want to see an increase in our trade balance over the next several years, so as to restore the level of the mid-1960's. This together with gains on remittances of profits should lead to an improvement of the current account. While the capital accounts have been abnormally favorable in the recent past, we would not expect them to be so adverse as they were in the early 1960's. The development of foreign capital markets means that there should be less reliance on the American market. The narrowing of the interest rate spread between the U.S. and the rest of the world works in the same direction. We do, however, expect a chronic deficit on the capital and aid accounts.

In summary, our long-term outlook is for a stronger trade position and current account, with some capital outflow but less than in the early 1960's. We have no illusion that this objective can be achieved this year or next. We will continue to have an underlying deficit, and the question is whether or not it will be aggravated by abnormal outflows of short-term money.

Our basic accounts are showing an improvement. Whether or not this will continue depends upon what happens abroad. All of the major countries except Canada want to run current account surpluses. Even Canada wants to move from deficit to equilibrium. Japan, the other country which affects us most, is moving from equilibrium to a large surplus. European countries are also seeking to strengthen their position.

The fundamental question is whether or not we can restore our traditional competitive position by better price policies than elsewhere. In 1959 our trade position was similar to the present situation. Some five years later we have built our trade surplus back up to $6.5 billion. However, that was a period of underemployment of U.S. resources, and the prospects are admittedly less favorable today.

We do not want to restore our trade position through the use of import restrictions, and the President is determined to resist pressures in the U.S. for such restrictions. We are concentrating on two areas to help improve our trade balance:

1. In the field of export credit, we have traditionally placed great reliance on the fact that our interest rates were lower than those prevailing elsewhere. With the present high rates in the United States this advantage has been lost. We are therefore providing more budget money to the Export-Import Bank, which is also undertaking to liberalize its lending policies.

2. During his visit to Paris last December, Secretary Kennedy mentioned our concern about the effect on our export position, stemming from the differences between the U.S. tax system and foreign tax systems. At that time we indicated that we were studying the possibility of providing the same facility for exports as we give to a U.S. subsidiary manufacturing abroad. This means taxing the profits only when they are remitted to the parent company. We have now developed a concrete proposal in this regard, and we hope it will help shift the focus of our producers somewhat from the domestic to the export market. This is a chronic problem for us. U.S. producers have tended to look upon the export market as marginal, whereas in many European countries it is the market towards which producers make their major effort. The proposed measure is designed to bring about a change in U.S. business psychology, and in the short run this will certainly be as important as any real results.

Our very heavy military expenditures abroad are also an important element in our balance of payments outlook. They have tended to increase in recent years because of rising costs and the Vietnam effort. Even if we succeed in disengaging ourselves from Vietnam, there will still be outlays of about $1.5 billion a year in Europe, mostly in Germany. It would be our hope to get some better offset to that than we have had in the past.

Secretary Kennedy said he had had talks on these matters with a number of countries. Take the case of Japan. They have become a world economic power, but their people have not yet grasped the implications of the change in their position. Whereas before, our trade with Japan was in equilibrium or even in surplus, it has now moved into deficit.

There are a number of problem areas. In the field of electronics, they have taken the entire U.S. market for radios and most of the market for black and white T.V. sets. They are even moving into the colored T.V. market. We find that their producers follow different pricing policies as regards the domestic and export markets. We have emphasized to them the difficulties of resisting pressures in the U.S. for quantitative restrictions in the face of such practices.

The point is that a country can't have closed markets at home and expect to enjoy open markets elsewhere. Capital and equity markets should be open. Similar considerations apply in the case of development aid. With respect to the Asian Development Bank, we are keeping our share equal to that of Japan rather than taking the lion's share.

Then look at the question of defense expenditures. Japan has virtually no defense budget. Likewise defense expenditures in Europe are much smaller proportionately than those of the U.S. We are working on this matter in NATO, but it is an uphill struggle. It is always difficult to bring about a shift, when that means budget increases for others.

In the matter of trade, as Mr. Volcker said, U.S. producers are oriented towards the domestic market. Their approach to foreign markets has been to put plants abroad instead of direct selling of U.S. products. We have done quite of bit of work during the past year to find some tax techniques which would encourage a shift in attitudes. However, this is not much of an answer if other countries do better at controlling inflation than the U.S. We recognize that success on this front is fundamental.

In conclusion, it is simply not possible for all countries to realize surpluses simultaneously. If all industrial countries are in surplus, it would simply have to come out of the hide of the developing countries.

Mr. Giscard d'Estaing asked whether or not the U.S. authorities regarded the level of U.S. prices as being competitive.

Secretary Kennedy said the situation varied from product to product. Our prices certainly are competitive in the case of sophisticated products and primary products. We were less competitive in many other lines. Agriculture gives us great concern, for as the EC moves to the CAP, high prices in Europe affect our agricultural exports. If the U.K. enters the Common Market, there would be a big problem for us were we to lose the British market for agricultural commodities.

Mr. Volcker said our agricultural exports were down slightly over the past five years. Japan is a good example. They have insisted on achieving self-sufficiency in rice, even though their price is about double the world price. In other commodity areas our exports have held up well. The root of our trade account problem has been the growth of imports.

Mr. Giscard d'Estaing said the American people seem to think that the U.S. trade problem is with the Common Market. The figures show the contrary, however. Between 1958 and 1969 U.S. exports increased by 118 percent to the rest of the world, 145 percent to EFTA, and 182 percent to the EC.

Secretary Kennedy said he was sure that this attitude was not prevalent in U.S. official circles. He had already cited Canada and Japan as major problem areas for us in the trade field. Of course, there were a few dramatic cases which had had a considerable influence on public attitudes. For example, when our poultry exporters were shut out of the EC market, this got considerable publicity and certainly was an irritant. However, we always supported a strong community with the idea that there would be an increase in demand in which all would share. This definitely remains our policy.

Mr. Volcker pointed out that in recent years trade in general had shown substantial increases. This particularly was the case as regards U.S. imports, including U.S. imports from the Common Market.

Mr. Giscard d'Estaing said that was the result of what had been happening in the U.S. and could scarcely be blamed upon the Common Market.

Mr. Larre asked if we had in mind a target surplus for our current account.

Mr. Volcker said we did not, but we certainly hoped that it would grow.

Mr. Petty said that it would, of course, not be one percent of GNP as in Japan.

Mr. Plescoff said he presumed we would be happy with one-half percent of GNP.

Mr. Volcker said that was true for the moment, but he not sure it would be enough over the longer run.

Mr. Larre asked what were our estimates of the current account for 1970.

Mr. Volcker said we were projecting a trade surplus of $2 billion or $2.5 billion and a surplus on goods and services of $3 billion. This would leave us with a current account surplus of $1.5 or $1.6 billion.

Mr. Petty said, with respect to the Minister's question, that studies showed demand for our exports to be relatively inelastic. Secondly, U.S. opinion certainly does not attribute all of our problems to the Common Market. It is recognized that part of the difficulty stems from our inflation and from the Japanese problem.

Mr. Volcker said that over the last five years there had been a substantial deterioration of the U.S. trade position with Japan, Canada,

Germany and Italy. With other countries the total had been steady, and there had been some gains.

Mr. MacLaury said that this pattern did not suggest that the dollar was overvalued.

Mr. Petty said that the problem with Japan arose from the restrictions which they maintained against outsiders and that in the case of Canada the automobile agreement had an asymmetrical effect, because U.S. cars imported into Canada were still subject to a 15 percent tariff.

Secretary Kennedy said there was a feeling of concern in Congress, which he shared, about the effect on trade of the differences between the U.S. and European tax systems. We have been studying what we might do in this regard, but it is hard to make a change in our system, which relies heavily on income taxes. Some people have suggested that we ought to introduce a value-added tax and some people think that we should adopt border taxes. However, we have not taken any decisions on these matters. So far the only proposal to be adopted is the DISC proposal.

Mr. Giscard d'Estaing said the value-added tax had considerable merits as a substitute for an ordinary sales tax. However, it was complicated and lent itself to fraud.

Secretary Kennedy expressed surprise at the Minister's statement. He said that one of the arguments put forward by U.S. proponents of the tax was that it was difficult to evade.

Mr. Giscard d'Estaing said that was true for large industrial corporations but not in a number of other areas. He then referred to the situation of several years ago when the U.S. authorities repeatedly predicted that the deficit would be over in a year or so. At that time the problem was expressed in terms of much narrower margins. Now, however, the figures we hear are much higher, $5 billion or $10 billion. And in point of fact the U.S. had a surplus last year. Is there any way in which the problem could be put that would make it more understandable?

Mr. Volcker said the question raised by the Minister was a complicated and difficult one. There is no easy answer. It is true we had a surplus last year and the year before, but that surplus was unsatisfactory. It resulted from inflows of short-term money. It was interesting to see the problems which that surplus created for the rest of the world. The result was that we drew reserves from the rest of the world, and there were many complaints in WP-3 that our surplus was too large.

How should the U.S. basic position be measured? It is not easy to say. We should think in terms of a current account surplus, but we cannot say exactly how large this surplus should be beyond saying several billion dollars more than in the past. We had an overall surplus in 1968, but in fact our basic accounts were deteriorating. Last year we held our own, and this year we will show some improvement. Over a period of years official dollar holdings should not be increasing, and this will be a valid position if we create enough liquidity in other forms. Neither the liquidity nor the official settlements basis provides a figure that is understandable to the general public. We need to do much more work on this matter.

Mr. Giscard d'Estaing said it was important for the world to know where the U.S. was going. He hoped the U.S. authorities could find a meaningful balance of payments presentation.

Mr. Volcker said he thought attention should be focused on the current account. However, with a current account presentation it was important to keep in mind that equilibrium was not zero but a big positive number.

Secretary Kennedy said that we would have to spend a lot more time on this question.

Mr. Giscard d'Estaing said he would like to make a few remarks about the French balance of payments outlook. The trade account now shows a small surplus. This state of affairs will probably continue for several months but change later in the year. The swing to exports since the devaluation seems to have been abnormally high, and it would be reasonable to expect some downward correction. Other items will probably be about in balance for 1970. The present French projection is for an overall surplus of about $1 billion, or perhaps a little more, in 1970. However, if the present rate of foreign exchange inflows continues, the figure could turn out to be much higher.

For the next five years, the target is to keep a small trade surplus and to cut the deficit in services, mainly by improving the insurance and shipping accounts. The result would be a surplus of $500 million to $700 million per year in order to permit the outward flow of French investments. As Secretary Kennedy and Mr. Volcker remarked, France, like all other countries, is looking for a surplus.

Mr. Volcker said that with the devaluation of the French franc and the revaluation of the Deutschemark, financial opinion seems to feel that France has restored a strong competitive position.

Mr. Giscard d'Estaing said that French exporters generally agree with this assessment. In his talks with them, for virtually the first time, he hears no complaints about their competitive position.

IV. Future of the International Monetary System

Secretary Kennedy referred to the work which the IMF has been doing on the question of limited exchange flexibility. He commented that the techniques under consideration would involve no wide changes in the present exchange rate system. One matter which would have to be decided was whether these techniques could and should be put into effect without an amendment of the present Articles, or whether such an amendment was necessary or desirable. He asked Mr. Volcker to present the U.S. view of the matter.

Mr. Volcker recalled that the proposals under consideration involved widening exchange margins somewhat, the possibility of small and frequent changes in exchange parities, and facilitating transitional floating rates for countries moving to a new parity. A fourth possibility, some method of formal Fund approval for the so-called "trotting" rate systems, had found no support outside of the countries resorting to such techniques. In the G-10 Deputies Meeting in Paris last month there seemed to be fairly wide agreement that the first three possibilities might be permitted on the basis of the present Articles. The question is whether there should be an amendment to permit them more explicitly. Another point is whether or not the Fund can develop criteria for determining when small and frequent changes in parity might be appropriate. This is not something which can be solved quickly, but in the U.S. view it deserves further study.

It is important to recognize that we are not talking about freely floating rates or highly automatic systems. The initiative for rate changes would remain with the countries concerned, subject, of course, to Fund approval. Alternatively, the Fund might give a country a general authorization to move its parity within a limited range. Thus the proposals do not involve any change in fundamentals but they do involve a change in attitudes. The idea would be to try to develop a less rigid attitude toward exchange rate changes. Of course, no one can tell how much these proposals would be used if they were adopted. If they were not used very much, the result would be not much change in the system. The change would be greater if more use were made of them. In any case, it seems to us that there would be a net gain if the matter of exchange rate adjustments could be made less political.

The timetable calls for a report by the Fund in July or early August, which would spell out the three proposals for which there is support and make clear that the fourth is excluded. This would be a chance to state conclusions on limited flexibility modestly but positively. Then it would have to be decided whether the proposals would be given effect through amendment of the Articles or through a decision by the Executive Board to provide guidance for member countries on limited parity changes. The matter of amendment is in the first instance one of symbolic importance, but if it led to greater use of the facilities, it could have substantive implications for the future.

Another meeting of the Deputies is scheduled for early July. This would give them a chance to take up any hard core questions on the matter, so that the IMF Board could finish its report by the end of that month. The report would be transmitted to the Governors, and would be the subject of a G-10 Ministerial Meeting in Brussels on Saturday, September 19. Then the Ministers would be in a position to voice their opinions on the question at the IMF Meeting in Copenhagen the following week. Presumably the major issue in Brussels would be whether to undertake an amendment of the Articles or not.

Mr. Larre commented as follows regarding the French views:

1. It is not clear whether widening exchange margins would discourage or encourage speculation. Both official and academic opinion are about evenly divided. The EC has a special interest in this particular matter. The Six have the feeling that if they could reach a certain degree of monetary union, their currencies might fluctuate as a bloc against the dollar. In the interim they fear that a facility for widening exchange margins could work havoc with the CAP and with their efforts towards economic union. They realize that the facility would be permissive, but if there were troubles within the EC, some countries might wish to make use of the facility with resulting tensions. Moreover, some countries might seek to make use of the facility to gain an advantage for trade purposes.

2. The present Articles are no obstacle to putting into effect the proposal for small and frequent changes in parity. For years the Fund pressed the U.K., Germany, Japan, the Netherlands, and others, on the matter of exchange rates. The Articles did not prevent changes from being made. The real obstacle was internal political problems in the countries in question. In the French view there would be no harm in saying that there can be small and frequent parity changes.

3. There seems to be more substance to the proposal for a transitional floating rate. We saw in the German case that it was useful. However, it was accomplished with the Articles as they are. The Fund could say that such transitional arrangements would be encouraged, provided they were kept within certain limits and did not upset the general exchange rate situation.

4. In summary, the French authorities see no need for a change in the Articles in connection with the limited flexibility exercise. They do not share the view that it would be useful to dramatize the issue through amendment of the Articles.

Mr. Volcker recalled that the EC had been discussing narrowing intra-Community margins within the framework of the present system. If they solved the technical problems, which are admittedly difficult, it would appear that they could also do so if there were a facility for widening margins generally.

Mr. Larre said that the technical problem could be handled. But there is also an economic problem: What will be the level of the six currencies in relation to the rest of the world? With harder and softer currencies within the Six, the level chosen will inevitably place strain on some of those currencies as against others. Such strain would not be welcome to the EC.

Mr. Giscard d'Estaing said that obviously when countries decide to achieve common monetary policies, they accept the political consequences. However, if there is a widening of margins in the rest of the world and if the EC maintains margins or narrows them within the Six, and if there is only a halfhearted monetary union, there will be difficulties. It does not seem likely that there will be a common monetary policy very soon. This is mainly due to the troubles in Italy. There is also the matter of the U.K. They have said that they are ready to take a view similar to that of the EC and not open the margins. Thus the technical and political aspects are mixed together.

Mr. Volcker said it was clear that the proposal for wider margins was not of much interest if neither the Common Market nor the U.K. wanted to make use of it. That left nobody.

Mr. Giscard d'Estaing said it left the U.S.

Mr. Volcker said the U.S. in effect maintained no margins. Our exchange rate is the result of what the others do. With the U.K., the Common Market, and Japan out of the wider margin proposal there was no important country left.

However, the proposal took on greater interest in combination with the proposal for small and frequent parity changes. That proposal also appears to create difficulties for the Common Market. However, if there are no common policies for a number of years or for as long as a decade, it must be assumed that there will be parity changes. With the high degree of discipline they will have, the Six may be one group that would be able to make a crawling peg system work fairly well, but there is a philosophical problem. The crawling peg seems to run in the opposite sense to the EC objective of fixed parities. It does not offer the same incentive to harmonization of policies. It is hard to see how this philosophical problem can be solved.

Mr. Giscard d'Estaing said the two recent rate changes within the EC had greatly disturbed the Common Market. Admittedly, the disturbance might have been less if the magnitude of the changes had been smaller.

Over the next five or ten years the EC will be moving towards fixed parities, and this will take the monetary variable out of the system. It is true that with no coordinated policies, as now is the case, events could force a substantial parity change. The remaining problem is Italy, and that is almost purely a political problem. Who could forecast the Italian outlook for the next ten years? For the EC members, a change of 2 or 3 percent per year does not seem a very valuable tool. The normal aim of economic policy is to accommodate adjustments of 2 or 3 percent a year. For trade and the common farm prices it is much easier to have a fixed parity. Therefore, the EC has to keep open the possibility that there may be one major rate adjustment, but they have no interest in small parity changes. This was the view expressed at the last EC Finance Ministers Meeting in Paris.

As for the rest of the world, exchange rate changes have been delayed too long in the past with bad results. However, France does not want a system where currencies move against one immovable currency: the dollar. In the recent Deputies Meeting this was the U.S. thesis, and it is just not acceptable to France. The French authorities recognize that it is often difficult to determine whether an imbalance is the responsibility of the deficit or the surplus country. However, if as in 1968 the imbalance is clearly due to the U.S., France would not accept that the deficit situation be dealt with by moving currencies against the dollar.

France does not want its exchange rate always being corrected to keep French products in an under-competitive position. If they have an abnormally large surplus because they had followed policies that were too deflationary, of course it would be up to them to revalue. But if their policies and payments position are normal, and if the imbalance is created by inflationary demand in the U.S., it would be unfair to expect France to cut its surplus by revaluation.

The French authorities want to know whether the U.S. stands by the basic principle that it is up to the country where the imbalance arises to adjust, either through its fiscal and monetary policies or through an exchange rate change. If this principle is accepted, then we can study ways in which the change might be facilitated—for example, the transitional floating rate. However, this does not seem to be Mr. Volcker's point of view. His ideas are very plausible, but France will not accept the proposition that in a system with only one reserve currency all parities have to be corrected to make the system function.

Secretary Kennedy asked how, with such a position, there would be a revaluation. Why with their good record would the Germans ever revalue? In such a world there could only be devaluations by countries said to be causing the imbalances. Why should countries ever revalue?

Mr. Larre said the reason would be to protect themselves, not to relieve others of the necessity to devalue.

Mr. Giscard d'Estaing said he recognized it was difficult to say where the responsibility for imbalances lay. However, during the last 18 months the growth of European exports had been due more to the U.S. inflation than to the economic position of the European countries. In such a case it was clear where the responsibility lay. Or take the French situation. If there were reserve gains due to hot money, France would look like a surplus country and would have to revalue.

Mr. Volcker said that was not correct. Whether or not to revalue would be a decision for France. If the reserve gains resulted from inflows of hot money there would be no reason to revalue. On the other hand, the French authorities might want to revalue if the French competitive position was strengthening and the rise of exports was creating a danger of inflation.

Mr. Larre said that a rate change of this kind would be acceptable under the present Articles.

Mr. Giscard d'Estaing asked what was new in the limited flexibility proposals.

Mr. Volcker said that the present Fund Articles specified that a rate change could be made only to correct a fundamental disequilibrium. A change of one or two percent a year could not be called a fundamental disequilibrium. Take the German case. They expect to achieve a better price performance over time than other countries. In that situation it would be better not to let the gap accumulate. It would be better to make changes of one or two percent a year. Such a change could be made in the first year, and then if the price performance was not so good in the following year, the rate could be held. This could be a desirable option for some countries.

Mr. Giscard d'Estaing referred to the argument that the proposal for small and frequent parity changes would discourage speculation. It seemed to him that, on the contrary, the speculators would come to expect small and frequent changes, and speculation would thus be encouraged. At the last IMF meeting the French delegation said there could be a study of wider margins, but they are reluctant, for general philosophical reasons, about the proposal for small and frequent parity charges.

Mr. Volcker said that was why the two proposals were in a single package. The wider margins would tend to offset any encouragement given to speculation by the technique of small and frequent parity changes.

Governor Wormser said that in his view the present Articles gave latitude to put into effect all the proposals. He also felt an amendment would have to be symmetrical to allow for revaluation as well as devaluation. However, the U.S. seems to be shifting the emphasis. The principle laid down at Bretton Woods was that fixed parities should be defended to the end. The idea was that the national economy and the level of prices should be adapted to fixed parities through the adjustment process. Such a process will always be painful.

An amendment on limited flexibility would lead countries to give up the adjustment process. It would offer them another way out of their difficulties. Henceforth they could adjust parities to their prices. This would be a very serious change. It would destroy the forces against a permanent system of devaluation. When Mr. Giscard d'Estaing devalued the franc in 1969, he also put into effect stringent adjustment policies. What would be the behavior of a Finance Minister ten years hence where parity changes had become the habit? These proposals for limited flexibility are very dangerous ground.

Secretary Kennedy said the discussion had been very helpful. It was the clearest exposition he had heard of the doubts about the limited flexibility proposals. The French authorities had some reservations on the matter of amendment, and not a closed mind to the idea of small and frequent parity changes. Perhaps this would do it.

Mr. Volcker said that on the matter of symmetry the U.S. certainly agreed that the limited flexibility techniques should not be asymmetrical. On the other hand, we had the feeling that the present system worked asymmetrically against us. Countries that are forced to the wall do devalue. But a country with a good performance rarely revalues. If this could be changed, it would be a net gain to get rid of the devaluation bias against the dollar. Mr. Giscard d'Estaing asked why an exception was made for the U.S. as regards the limited flexibility proposals.

Mr. Volcker said that the U.S. can change the price of gold but it cannot change its exchange rate. That can only be done through the decision of others.

Mr. Giscard d'Estaing asked why there could not be small and frequent changes in the price of gold.

Mr. Petty referred to the possibility that the U.S. economic performance might be better than other countries. He asked whether in this hypothesis the Minister would be willing to see the dollar price of gold crawl downward.

Mr. Giscard d'Estaing said he did not see why not.

Mr. Volcker said we should be careful not to confuse the question of gold price and the question of exchange rates.

Mr. Larre said that technically the devaluation of the franc last August was a change in the franc price of gold.

Mr. Volcker said that if other countries had followed France by increasing the price of gold in their currencies, France would have had to devalue all over again.

Mr. Larre said that if the U.S. felt the problem of the dollar was a matter for discussion in the G-10, that would be all right with France. However, he presumed that U.S. did not want such a discussion.

Secretary Kennedy said that a change in the price of gold would require Congressional action. There was absolutely no doubt on that score. If the objective was to upset markets this would certainly be an effective way to do it, for Congressional action would require considerable time. Indeed, a proposal for a major change in the gold price could well lead Congress to impeach the President. This was less an economic than psychological and emotional matter.

Mr. Giscard d'Estaing said that if these limited improvements are intended to make for easier rate changes and if there is no need for amendment of the Articles, that could be a matter of practical discussion. But the U.S. presentation evokes another atmosphere. It seems to involve a fundamental change from Bretton Woods. If there is an intention to depart from support of the adjustment process, it ought to be presented as such.

Mr. Volcker said these proposals were not regarded as a great solution for the U.S. competitive position. We couldn't stand repeated revaluations against the dollar. The proposals would be helpful to us directly if they squeezed out the devaluation bias in the present system, but they stand or fall on whether they could help the system as a whole in terms of speculation and in terms of the adjustment process.

[Omitted here is Part V.]

VI. SDR Link to Development Finance and Use of SDR in Lieu of Gold

Secretary Kennedy referred to the proposal for using SDRs to provide financing for economic development. Our view has been that it is premature to consider such a link. We have felt that it was better first to get SDRs established as a new supplement to international reserves. Therefore, we have taken the position that there should be no action now on the link proposal and perhaps not even in the future.

Mr. Volcker said that we are committed to the idea of amending the IMF Articles at some future date to permit the use of SDRs as well as gold in payment of IMF quota subscriptions. For us the question was one of timing.

Secretary Kennedy said that Congressman Reuss has been pushing us very hard on this question. At the time of the SDR legislation he wanted to introduce a provision that would have required us to take SDRs instead of gold.

Mr. Volcker said that he thought there was a consensus for such an amendment and that it ought to be done at some convenient time prior to the next increase in Fund quotas. This change would make it possible to avoid gold payments to the Fund and the problem of mitigation.

On the matter of the SDR link to development financing, the proposal has been that this should be studied in an appropriate international forum. We are reluctant to get into such a discussion with a large group of developing countries at this time for fear of where it might lead. However, when this matter comes up in international meetings, we have sometimes felt that we were the only country resisting the idea of a study. If the French authorities agree with our position, we hope they will instruct their delegations to support us.

Mr. Larre said the French feel they have a good control over their delegations. The U.S. may be sure that it is not alone in opposing discussion. As a matter of fact, their delegations have sometimes reported to them the fear that the U.S. delegation would be the one to give ground on this point.

VII. IDA Replenishment

Secretary Kennedy said he had talked recently with Mr. McNamara, who may also have talked to the Minister. He would like to ask Mr. Petty to make a few comments on where the problem stood.

Mr. Petty said that at the recent meeting in Vienna Mr. de Larosiere had made an excellent presentation of the special problems confronting France because of its large aid program as a percentage of GNP and because of the difference between its share in IDA and its voting rights in the IBRD. However, it would be difficult to achieve a $1 billion replenishment if the final French position were limited to an annual French budgetary expenditure of $40 billion. Perhaps the way out of the difficulty would be for France to take a selective increase in its IBRD capital subscription and for the increase in its IDA contribution to be limited to 90 or 100 percent compared to the increase of 150 percent which other countries are accepting. Such an increase for France would greatly help us to reach the replenishment target. A $1 billion replenishment would mean more IDA money for the franc area countries, and this would rebound to the benefit of France.

Secretary Kennedy said that another possibility would be to do something on the timing of the French payments. They would not necessarily have to be the same amount each year.

Mr. Giscard d'Estaing said the matter of IDA replenishment was discussed at the last meeting of the Common Market Finance Ministers. Mr. Schiller proposed that the Six support a level of $500 million, and the others decided to accept his proposal. Subsequently, the French had heard at Vienna that the Germans had moved to support a higher figure. The Ministers will meet again at the end of the month. If this report about the change in the German position is confirmed, the Ministers from the other EC countries will have to decide what position they should take.

Mr. Petty said that Italy had now indicated support for the $1 billion figure, and the Netherlands had confirmed their support of that level of replenishment. The Belgians had not yet taken a decision. The Japanese said they could support $1 billion if all Part I countries did. We pointed out to the Japanese that the French had a unique position, and they said they recognized this. Therefore, the outcome turns on what the French and the Germans do.

Secretary Kennedy said we could not settle the matter today. However, we were getting close to an agreement. The U.S. has supported the $1 billion figure because of our feeling that it was important to have a large volume of aid through multilateral channels. Our purpose in raising the question was to ask the French to think about what they could do to help us reach a satisfactory agreement.

[Omitted here are Parts VIII and IX.]

147.   Editorial Note

On May 31, 1970, Canada floated the Canadian dollar, in large part because of large capital inflows and concerns about inflationary consequences. Secretary Kennedy informed President Nixon of the float in a May 31 memorandum. (National Archives, Nixon Presidential Materials, NSC Files, Country Files–Europe, Box 670, Canada, Volume II 3/70–8/71) On June 5 Acting Secretary of the Treasury Charls Walker sent a follow-up memorandum to the President informing him that exchange markets were settled and the Canadian dollar was now trading about 5 percent above its previous par value. Walker debunked suspicions that the United States may have influenced the Canadians to float. (Ibid.)

Foreign exchange markets were otherwise relatively quiet following the major currency adjustments in 1969, and remained so until the spring of 1971. During this time U.S. policymakers' concerns with international monetary reform focused on limited exchange rate flexibility. In January 1970 the Department of State sent an airgram to the Embassies and Consulates in major financial centers and industrial countries, as well as the Missions to the OECD and the European Community, informing them the United States fully supported discussion of limited exchange rate flexibility in the IMF. The addressees were cautioned, however, that the United States had no fixed views on what the outcome of the discussions should be and was not seeking systematically to initiate bilateral discussions at that time. The airgram then provided extensive background material addressees could use sparingly to underscore U.S. interest in the subject, but requested that specific issues or technical points raised by host country officials be referred to Washington for reply. (CA–279, January 16, 1970; National Archives, RG 59, Central Files 1970–73, FN 10–1)

On February 25 U.S. Executive Director Dale made a statement in the IMF Board setting out five areas in which the United States thought efforts should be concentrated: somewhat wider bands, flexible authority to depart from generally applicable rules of the game, the concept of fundamental disequilibrium, upward and downward bias in the system, and presumptive criteria for changes in exchange rates. Dale said he entered the discussions "with the view that rate changes should not be the only—and perhaps seldom the primary—element of the adjustment process, but that governments should consider exchange rate adjustment in appropriate circumstances as an entirely respectable and useful policy measure." Dale then elaborated on each of the five areas, without taking a position, and concluded by saying that the United States expected to benefit from the views of other Fund members. The full text of Dale's statement was sent to the Embassies in G-10 capitals and to USOECD and USEC in telegram 28440, February 26. (Ibid., Nixon Presidential Materials, NSC Files, Agency Files, Box 216, Council of Economic Advisers)

The G-10 Deputies met in Paris on April 23 to discuss limited exchange rate flexibility. The opening paragraph of a summary of the meeting read: "The general consensus was that this one-day meeting had given a significant new impetus to the international discussion of limited exchange flexibility. Though there continue to be negative and cautious views within the Group of Ten, positive views were expressed by important members (Germany, U.S., Italy). General agreement was reached to pursue the subject further in the Deputies and to bring it before the Ministers of the Group of Ten on September 19 in Brussels, prior to the IMF Annual Meeting." (Airgram CA–2600 to Bern, Bonn, Brussels (also for USEC), The Hague, London, Ottawa, Paris (also for USOECD), Rome, Stockholm, and Tokyo, May 9; ibid., RG 59, Central Files 1970–73, FN 10 IMF)

At the April 23 meeting Under Secretary Volcker "stressed the importance of a change in attitude towards exchange rate adjustment . . . . Under Secretary Volcker favored a wider band of an approximately 2 percent margin for countries that wish to use it. This was not essential but would be helpful as an adjunct to small and frequent parity changes in the form of a discretionary crawling peg at the rate of about 2 to 3 percent over a 12-month period. . . . The crawling parity raises two important sub-points. First, can criteria be developed. . . ? The second sub-point is the concept of fundamental disequilibrium. . . . As to a transitional period of flexibility, should there not be a legal option for a move like the recent German one? We do not have views as to the length of a transition period or how firmly it should be limited in time and extent." (Volcker Group Paper VG/LIM/70-14, April 29; Washington National Records Center, Department of the Treasury, Volcker Group Masters: FRC 56 86 30, 1970, VG/LIM/70-1–VG/LIM/70-)

Of the 92 papers distributed during 1970 to the Volcker Group Working Group (in effect WG I as there were three others whose records are listed as WG II (reserve asset creation), WG III (balance of payments current account objectives), and WG IV (balance of payments statistical presentation)) on limited exchange rate flexibility, at least 90 were circulated before completing the September 10 U.S. Position Paper, Document 148, for use at the September meeting of G-10 Ministers in Brussels and at the IMF Annual Meeting in Copenhagen. These papers helped establish the context for the U.S. position in Brussels and Copenhagen. (Washington National Records Center, Department of the Treasury, Volcker Group Masters: FRC 56 86 30, VG/WG/70)

During the summer of 1970 there were numerous bilateral and multilateral consultations on limited exchange rate flexibility. Reporting cables on these consultations, as well as a number of cables reporting on consultations and positions regarding the SDR–AID link, are in the National Archives, RG 59, Central Files 1970–73, FN 10.

---

148.   Volcker Group Paper[1]

VG/LIM/70-24   Washington, September 10, 1970.

POSITION PAPER ON LIMITED EXCHANGE FLEXIBILITY

(For meeting of Group of Ten and IMF Annual Meeting)

Problems

1. Decisions are needed on three questions:

---

[1] Source: Washington National Records Center, Department of the Treasury, Volcker Group Masters: FRC 56 86 30, 1970, VG/LIM/70-1–VG/LIM/70. Confidential. Circulated to members of the Volcker Group under cover of a September 14 note from George Willis that indicated a shortened version of the paper was contemplated for use by the delegations in Brussels (G-10 Ministerial) and Copenhagen (IMF Annual Meeting). No shortened version was found. On August 7 Willis had circulated to members of the Group (VG/LIM/70-21) papers by Bergsten and Wonnacott advocating, respectively, the aggressive and low key approaches. (Ibid.) On August 28 Volcker had sent a copy of the Position Paper, dated August 26, to Secretary Kennedy for his approval, under cover of an August 28 memorandum indicating it had been thoroughly discussed in the Group where there was general agreement on the low key approach. (Ibid.) Volcker also told Kennedy he was sending copies to all members of the Group for concurrence, and did so on August 31. (Ibid.) There are no significant differences between the August 26 and the September 10 versions of the paper.

(a) Should the United States push for an early Amendment[2] at this fall's meetings?

(b) What instructions should the G-10 Ministers and Governors give their Deputies?[3]

(c) What posture should the Secretary take at the IMF meeting in commenting on the IMF Report on Exchange Flexibility?[4]

2. Underlying all three of these questions is a basic decision as to whether the United States is pushing hard for some positive action in the form of an Amendment (or possibly a formal IMF decision) in 1971, or whether it is prepared to accept no formal action in 1971 and to rest for the time being on the existing IMF Report, with or without some relatively low-key additional studies or discussion in the IMF and/or the Deputies.

3. All of these questions are related to our underlying objective with respect to exchange flexibility as part of the continuing process of improving the functioning of the international monetary and exchange system. This has two aspects—(a) strengthening the process of balance of payments adjustment by facilitating the ready use of exchange rate changes in appropriate circumstances, and (b) enabling the major countries to cope more effectively with mobile capital movements and exchange speculation, through somewhat wider margins and other changes to facilitate more timely parity changes when necessary. These broad objectives should be as important to other countries as to the United States.

4. In recent years exchange rate policy has played a difficult and frequently disturbing role in the process of balance of payments adjustment. There has been a growing feeling among economists and some officials that more prompt adjustment of exchange rates might have been helpful, if the rigidity resulting from publicized political commitments and Cabinet decisions could have been tempered by the techniques of wider margins, or small adjustments, or transitional floats. Such limited decisions might, for example, be made by monetary

---

[2] Reference is to an Amendment of the IMF Articles of Agreement. Several papers circulated to the Volcker Group Working Group examined whether or not amendment of the Articles of Agreement would be legally required to permit greater, limited exchange rate flexibility.

[3] The G-10 Ministers were to meet in Brussels on September 19; see Document 149.

[4] "The Role of Exchange Rates in the Adjustment of International Payments: A Report by the Executive Directors" was circulated by Willis to members of the Volcker Group and the Working Group as VG/WG/70-90 on September 2. (Ibid., VG/WG/70-82–VG/WG/70-) Willis noted that the IMF report was for release September 13 at 6 p.m. Washington time. Several earlier drafts of the IMF report, along with commentaries on the drafts, are ibid. See Department of State *Bulletin*, October 12, 1970, pp. 431–435, for Secretary Kennedy's September 22 statement during the September 21–25 IMF Annual Meeting in Copenhagen.

authorities rather than dramatically announced by heads of state. There has, however, been as yet only limited official acceptance of the arguments put forward by private economists for this point of view. The Fund report is a first and useful step in giving formal official consideration to these possibilities.

5. The second aspect is related to the first, but is less dependent upon the element of prompt action. Here it is argued that the techniques of limited exchange flexibility, and especially wider margins and/or other techniques for changing parities can be technically helpful in inhibiting disequilibrating movements of relatively liquid funds, and in decreasing speculation by increasing the risks associated with it.

6. The United States would not look to the techniques envisaged in the Fund report as an active tool for improving its basic balance of payments position. To the extent that a bias toward devaluation has existed, these techniques may be useful in reducing this bias, and hence would tend to be a favorable factor in our longer-term need to adjust our balance of payments position. However, looked upon as an active means of correcting our own position and a substitute for other action, these techniques would have serious offsetting disadvantages to the United States. Specifically, repeated use of these techniques among other important industrialized countries in the direction of appreciation against the dollar could easily create a strong presumption of further changes adverse to the dollar, eroding the dollar as a vehicle and reserve currency, sharply curtailing our financing flexibility in a monetary regime in which large financing capability would still be required, and possibly fomenting renewed speculation in gold. Consequently, our approach must stand on more general considerations than on any presumption that these techniques—or any series of revaluations—provide an acceptable means for escaping balance of payments constraints. [In presenting the U.S. position, U.S. officials should counteract any impression that these small changes are being encouraged by the United States as a substitute for corrective measures on our part.][5]

7. The appropriate posture for the United States is to continue to seek the objective of a more receptive international attitude toward the use of the techniques of limited exchange flexibility. However, because of the still substantial resistance to limited exchange flexibility in most developing and developed countries, conscious of the efforts to interpret the U.S. position as a desire to avoid other balance of payments constraints, the United States pursuit of this objective would best be carried on persistently but in a low key. Such an approach also carries with it the advantage of minimizing bargaining tactics by the French and the

---

[5] Brackets in the source text.

developing countries, which would otherwise be placed in the position of being able to demand substantial rewards in other areas for not exercising a "veto" power.

Elements of An Aggressive Approach

8. An aggressive drive for action in 1971 could ideally follow a sequence along the following lines:

(a) The EC countries would be told that they should try to agree on a position favoring an Amendment, prior to September 18 (which is regarded as very unlikely in any case, because of resistance from France and Belgium).

(b) An appropriate instruction to the Deputies in the Communiqué of the Group of Ten at Brussels, directing them to work toward an Amendment in 1971. The French, Belgians and Japanese (?) might reserve on this paragraph.

(c) Positive references to an Amendment in G-10 Governors' speeches at Copenhagen.

(d) A negotiated report by the Deputies supporting an Amendment. Here the question could be what concessions would persuade the French, Belgians, and possibly other unenthusiastic members to acquiesce in a positive report.

(e) Further negotiations with the developing countries, which would be likely to press for an Amendment establishing an SDR link and possibly other concessions.

9. The listing of these points makes rather clear that a successful push for an Amendment would be a very difficult bargaining process.

Elements of a Low-Key Approach

10. A low-key approach in 1971 is more difficult to chart in its specifics. Perhaps the main question is whether or not to give the subject the mild emphasis of a technical report of some kind by the Deputies. If this were to be done, the following would be the steps in a low-key approach:

(a) Ossola, Chairman of the G-10 Deputies, would be advised that it is not necessary to push hard for an agreed EC view on an Amendment by urging German and Italian concessions to the French "monetary" view of European unity, as he has been doing up to now.

(b) The Group of Ten Ministers in their Brussels Communiqué would note the importance of and welcome the IMF report and ask their Deputies to keep the subject under review, in particular appraising on the basis of experience the possible future need for amendment. The Deputies might also analyze the advantages and disadvantages of the three techniques in restraining disequilibrating capital movements, and their effects on the degree of independence possible in national monetary policies among the Group of Ten countries without offsetting capital movements.

(c) The U.S. would welcome the positive aspects of the Fund report and note flexibility within present Articles. References to the subject in

Ministers' speeches at Copenhagen should avoid staking out hard positions.

(d) The report of the Deputies could be a divided report, with no strong effort to reach a consensus, but with the hope that further exposure to the subject would lead to more receptive and less dogmatic attitudes.

11. *Principal General Arguments for an Aggressive Approach*

(a) There is danger that momentum will be lost and public and official attitudes toward exchange flexibility will retrogress, in the absence of U.S. pressure for an Amendment to focus discussion and marshall public support.

(b) Wider margins are useful in themselves to help deal with capital movements and permit more independence in national interest rates; as well as facilitating moving parities; wider margins require an Amendment.

(c) If it is subsequently forced by pressures on our gold stock to take abrupt action, the U.S. can point to its efforts to develop a cooperative system of limited flexibility.

(d) At least one other amendment seems desirable, such as one permitting use of SDRs in lieu of gold at the time of the next IMF quota increase, so the "flexibility" amendment need not be presented to governments "naked."

(e) Even if an amendment does not prove feasible, overt and strong U.S. pressure might help move world attitudes toward receptivity to exchange adjustments in appropriate situations and encourage officials to use exchange rates more promptly to correct imbalances.

12. *Arguments for "Low-Key" Approach*

(a) The only support for an amendment now comes from some quarters in Germany and Italy, and an aggressive push would be resented and would entail bargaining in other areas (e.g., SDR link, Fund voting, and Common Market exchange rate and reserve management policies) that could be against our interests. Most specifically—almost certainly—an amendment "bargain" would rule out unilateral action by an individual EC country, and that group (as expanded) has the only important candidates at present.

(b) The Fund report and recent exchange actions already signalize substantive changes in attitudes. Thus, much of our objective can potentially be achieved by a case-by-case approach over time. In a struggle over a specific amendment, the progress made toward a more fluid interpretation of a fundamental disequilibrium could be reversed, and tight interpretation of a limited amendment could produce retrogression rather than advance in world practices toward exchange flexibility.

(c) Immediate action on limited rate flexibility is not worth the risk of failure of a major U.S. effort; failure would set back chances of practical application within present Articles and public failure could strengthen protectionist sentiments at home.

(d) An aggressive U.S. approach creates strong suspicion abroad as to our motives and the value of the dollar, leading to counter pressure for an overt depreciation of the dollar in terms of gold and exchange market instability.

(e) U.S. pressure for an amendment enables the French to exact concessions from the Germans and Italians in the EC negotiations for European unity.

(f) An aggressive U.S. push opens the way to strong and premature pressure for the SDR link by the developing countries as a bargaining tactic and other undesirable amendments such as changes in voting rights in the IMF.

The Special Factor of the Effects on European Monetary Unification

13. One strand of thought in Europe is typified by Mr. Ossola, Chairman of the Deputies. This is a proposal for a common EC position on limited exchange flexibility. It is designed to get agreement of the French and Belgians to support an IMF Amendment permitting all three types of limited exchange flexibility, by bartering in return a commitment within the EC to use not only wider margins but also moving parities and transitional floats *only* when the EC countries move together as a unit, with decisions to move taken by some as yet unspecified procedure within the Six. This approach may well prove unacceptable to the French and Belgians, who, for example, could bargain to restrict the Amendment to cover only wider margins.

14. To some extent, the motivation for pushing rapidly toward an EC position may be related to the degree of pressure the U.S. exerts for an Amendment. It can be argued that the price being offered to the French is rather high. It appears to embody commitments among the Six going well beyond the present commitment not to use wider margins within the Six. That is, the ability of an EC country acting alone to use a moving parity or a transitional float would apparently be given up right now, instead of some years hence.

15. The proposal also would include a move toward the establishment of narrower margins among the EC currencies than those applicable to the dollar. This would enforce some adjustment of individual dollar intervention points to conform to EC limits, and open the way to an EPU type of EC credit system, concerted intervention, and not far off, common reserve management policies. The French apparently consider that this would help to dethrone the dollar both as a reserve and vehicular currency. This suggests that the U.S. needs to determine whether it is in its interest to expedite this process, recognizing that this will probably be the course of evolution over time within the EC countries.

Recommended Position

A. The United States regards the Report of the Fund as fairly representing the prevailing state of opinion—which has moved forward by quite considerable steps:

(1) It recognizes that there is a place in the monetary system for very limited changes in parities. Smaller and more frequent changes in parity can be approved by the Fund.

(2) It recognizes that the transitional float has been useful in some circumstances.

(3) Members do not need to wait for crises to adjust exchange rates. The concept of fundamental disequilibrium is broad enough to allow members to anticipate maladjustment.

B. The Fund report indicates that there is a good deal of leeway under the present Articles, except for the widening of margins. As for the other two techniques, questions remain as to the adequacy of the present scope, and these questions will need to be looked into over time to determine whether the scope now available is broad enough under today's conditions. The United States is prepared to suspend judgment now on the need for amendment, until experience can answer these questions. Fund procedures can presumably be adapted so as to give more encouragement than in the past to countries proposing to make small and frequent changes in their parities, or to adopt a transitional float under appropriate safeguards.

C. The United States would suggest that the Ministers of the Group of Ten, in their Communiqué:

(1) Take note of and welcome the important contribution of the IMF report to the objective of a more smoothly functioning international monetary system.

(2) Request their Deputies to keep the subject under review (or at least welcome such a review by the ED's), in particular appraising on the basis of experience the possible future need for Amendment. The Deputies might also analyze the advantages and disadvantages of the three techniques in restraining disequilibrating capital movements, and their effects on the degree of independence with which national monetary policies can be pursued without offsetting capital movements. The Deputies should keep the Ministers and Governors informed of their collective views on these matters during the ensuing year.

D. The United States would urge the Fund to present a supplementary progress report in 1971.

149.   Telegram From the Embassy in Belgium to the Department of State[1]

Brussels, September 20, 1970, 1123Z.

4303. Subject: Highlights of Meetings of Group of Ten. From: Treasury Under Secretary Volcker for MacLaury.

1. Ministers and Governors of Group of Ten met for three hours and issued communiqué reported separately.[2] Following report by Chairman Ossola of Deputies, which termed problem not urgent or ripe for final decision and indicated main differences of emphasis among Deputies, they termed IMF report[3] "useful" and agreed to further study by Executive Directors of Fund. They also directed their Deputies specifically to continue work on this subject, as well as to review from time to time working of international monetary system more generally.

2. French and Belgians most guarded in approval of report and wanted social and economic consequences of exchange policies examined and also effect of proposed techniques on sharing of burden of adjustment between surplus and deficit countries. Also, Deputies should follow up SDR and international liquidity developments in relation to forecasts made at time of initial allocation decision. EC countries noted lack of fully agreed EC position which hoped to achieve later.

3. Secretary Kennedy commented on flexibility along following lines (not verbatim text):

"My delegation welcomes the report by the Executive Directors on the role of exchange rates in the adjustment of international payments. We are glad to see that this subject has been examined in the executive board for the first time since Bretton Woods in a thoroughgoing way, and through a special report. This report puts the subject in proper perspective. During the past five years there has been some evidence of rigidity in the system, and delay in the use of exchange rates for adjustment purposes on occasion. A study of this sort was long overdue, and we must not take it up and then simply drop it. We must face up to this question.

4. The report is judicious and in no sense radical. It stresses the preservation of the basic principles of exchange stability, so long as they

---

[1]   Source: National Archives, RG 59, Central Files 1970–73, FN 10. Confidential; Limdis; Greenback. Repeated to London, Stockholm, Bonn, Paris, USOECD, Tokyo, The Hague, Bern, Ottawa, and Rome.

[2]   The G-10 Ministers met in Brussels on September 19, prior to the IMF–IBRD Annual Meetings in Copenhagen September 21–25. The communiqué has not been found.

[3]   See footnote 4, Document 148.

correspond to economic realities. The report is the kind of analysis we expect to have clarify many of the issues with which we must deal. It rejects extreme measures but does broaden the concept of the adaptability of the par value system. It recognizes that the transitional float has been and may be useful in minimizing economic disruption and helping restrain domestic inflation in those cases where a change is necessary.

5. As the report suggests, my delegation is prepared to suspend judgment on the legal questions related to possible future amendments, so that we may determine whether the scope now available under the Fund's articles will prove adequate. In this connection, I hope the Deputies will keep the subject under review as it is examined by the Executive Directors and inform the Ministers and Governors of their collective or individual views on the need for an amendment during the ensuing year.

6. I think that we will all agree that the work of the Deputies has been very useful. I hope they will continue to meet and to report to us. It has been demonstrated that they can do so without giving the appearance of crisis.

7. Members of my delegation have made it clear that the United States does not look to the techniques examined in the report as a means of bringing about major improvements in our own balance of payments or those of other countries. We rather think of them as helping to loosen tendencies towards excessive rigidity in the exchange structure, and possibly leavening past tendencies for exchange depreciation to be more frequent than appreciation. In a broader sense, we believe these exchange techniques deserve our more careful consideration to make us better prepared to deal with the strains arising from international movements of funds. I believe that it is most helpful to have any differences of view expressed.

8. The United States fully appreciates that the Community wishes to progress toward exchange stability within that group."

9. Chairman Emminger (German) of WP-3, in general review of world monetary situation, noted recent tendency for inflationary pressures to continue stronger in Europe than in North America, increasingly severe international limitations on autonomy of national monetary policies, and that outflow of dollars into foreign reserves would no longer be offset as in January–June 1970 by "mitigating influences" of repayment of official reserve credits. Ministers and Governors commented at some length on economic and monetary situations their countries. Secretary Kennedy expressed belief United States on way to resumption of growth without excessive price rises, though adjustment had been long and hard. Said U.S. not satisfied with balance of pay-

ments situation, though trade position improving, and exerting efforts expand exports. Chairman Burns stressed recent "dramatic" improvement in productivity and said policy objective is gradual rather than too rapid recovery. He looked forward to a prosperous world and did not want to see very high interest rates much longer. Over two-year period U.S. balance of payments not as bad as it looks in last six months. Canadian Minister said Canada hoped to return to fixed level when a sustainable level reached, and not wise attempt to do so now.

10. Netherlands Minister said Bretton Woods philosophy was that stability of exchange rates should not require countries to deflate or inflate domestically and that exchange adjustment could therefore be used to avoid inflationary domestic policies as it has in past been used to avoid deflationary policies.

11. At meeting on September 18, Deputies discussed position of industrial countries on possible pressure by LDCs for study of SDR–aid link in IMF or elsewhere. All Deputies supported U.S. view that study is clearly premature until SDRs firmly established as monetary instrument. Germans, Dutch, Japanese, French felt U.S. position not strong enough, question decided in 1968 and should not be reopened, and study of link should not be undertaken at any future time. U.K. position weakest and could not commit Chancellor. French and some others noted that positions expressed in other international forums, especially UN bodies, did not always coincide with views of Treasuries.

12. We are told here that communiqué of Commonwealth Finance Ministers meeting at Cyprus endorsed study of SDR–aid link prior to 1972 allocation. British say resolution for IMF study may be put in by Latin Americans or others at Copenhagen, but no confirmation this from Fund staff here at present time.

Eisenhower

150.   **Memorandum From the U.S. Executive Director of the International Monetary Fund (Dale) to the Under Secretary of the Treasury for Monetary Affairs (Volcker)**[1]

Washington, November 23, 1970.

SUBJECT

Contingency Planning

I did the attached note over the weekend mainly because of a feeling that a very large one-time SDR allocation as a part of Scenario II[2] looks pretty unrealistic. But a substantial U.S. official settlements surplus combined with a much larger *rate* of SDR allocation—both of them by virtue of international agreement—might not be so wholly unrealistic.

Attachment

A Rationale for a Major Exchange Rate Realignment[3]

The relationship between the *stock* of total U.S. international reserve assets and the *stock* of U.S. reserve liabilities is not satisfactory, either for the United States or for the international community. Except for 1968 and 1969—when this result was clearly seen as a temporary aberration—the trend in this relationship has not been satisfactory for a number of years. Both of these factors make the international monetary system vulnerable to speculative influences.

It has been accepted for some time that a *necessary,* though in itself perhaps not a sufficient, condition for a sustained zero balance of the United States on the official settlements basis would be the satisfaction of the world's "demand" for official reserve assets from a source other than an official settlements deficit in the U.S. external balance. That source of satisfaction is now available in the SDR.

---

[1] Source: Washington National Records Center, Department of the Treasury, Files of Under Secretary Volcker: FRC 56 79 15, 1971 Contingency Planning Papers. Confidential; Limdis.

[2] Presumably reference is to one of several scenarios in an options paper. The paper has not been found.

[3] A substantially expanded version of this paper, dated January 28, 1971, entitled "Scenario III—Exchange Rate Realignment and Related Matters," is in the Washington National Records Center, Department of the Treasury, Files of Under Secretary Volcker: FRC 56 79 15, 1971 Contingency Planning Papers.

We can, if we and the rest of the world agree on it as a mutual objective, go much further. What is now necessary is a large and sustained U.S. official settlements surplus, so that both the relationship between our reserve assets and liabilities and the *stock* position will be greatly improved. What I would suggest is that:

1. It should be agreed internationally that for a sustained period of time—say, five years at a minimum—the United States and the world should aim for a U.S. official settlements *surplus* in the range of $2–3 billion per year, abstracting from short-term deviations.

2. This should be aimed at by an immediate major realignment of exchange rates, and any exchange rate changes proposed later during the quinquennium should be judged importantly against this generally-agreed objective. Adding up the "underlying" U.S. deficit (i.e., abstracting from existing cyclical and random factors in the present deficit) together with the balance of payments cost of completely liberalizing capital flows and other transactions as well as allowing for an average surplus of $2.5 billion per year, this would probably mean the need for an annual improvement in our balance of payments on the order of $6–8 billion. It is this range of figures at which a realignment of exchange rates must be targeted.

3. The present rate of SDR allocations is undoubtedly too small. In addition, it is based on the assumption that net additions to world reserves in the form of U.S. dollars will be $0.5–1.0 billion, rates which are presently being greatly exceeded and which are likely to be exceeded for the whole of the first basic period. If the figure +1.0 billion (the top of the range in the Managing Director's proposal) were replaced by -2.5 billion, the present allocation rate of $3.0 billion would have to be boosted to $6.5 billion to produce the same aggregate results in terms of world reserves. In the context of an agreed exchange rate policy aimed at producing a sustained U.S. official settlements surplus of $2–3 billion per year, other countries would necessarily be much more vulnerable to balance of payments difficulty, and might well be willing to support a higher rate of SDR allocation. Even at an allocation rate of $6.5 billion, the United States would receive around $1.6 billion per year, so that our net reserve position would be improving by around $4 billion per year.

4. Our willingness and wish to aim for such a surplus would represent, by comparison with the situation today, the provision of substantial additional real resources to the rest of the world—something in the neighborhood of 3/4 of one per cent of our GNP and around half that proportion of world GNP. For the rest of the world, that would represent some help in dealing with the inflation that nearly all of their Governors complained about at Copenhagen.[4] For us, it would involve

---

[4] The Annual Meetings of the IMF–IBRD were held September 21–25, 1970, in Copenhagen.

somewhat more of an export-led upturn, and the price changes involved (in the form of an exchange rate realignment) could assist materially in resisting protectionist pressures.

5. We could say that only after such a sustained period of official settlement surplus would we be willing to look seriously at a negotiation looking toward putting the world, including the United States, on a full reserve asset settlement basis. In other words, we would be willing to try to work ourselves out of the reserve currency business—always abstracting from reasonable working balances—but other countries would have to be prepared to accept the implications of this.

6. An indirect SDR–aid link, but one of substantial quantitative importance, would also be involved in this procedure. The LDC's would receive about one-fourth of any increase in SDR allocations resulting from the proposed shift in the U.S. position. If the assumption is made that their *absolute* reserve targets (whether implicit or explicit) would not change, the additional SDR allocations would—in effect—be the same as an equivalent amount of program aid. If the figures given above have some validity, the *additional* SDR allocations to the LDC's could be in the range of at least three-quarters of a billion dollars per year, an amount of no mean importance when compared with IDA plans.

151.   Editorial Note

On March 22, 1971, Charles A. Coombs at the Federal Reserve Bank of New York sent a memorandum to the President of the New York Bank, Alfred Hayes, entitled "The Outlook for the Dollar." In his memorandum Coombs noted that the United States could probably finance its balance-of-payments deficit in 1970 and early 1971, but reported the 1971 deficit seemed to be running well above the 1970 levels and thought the United States was "moving into the danger zone." Coombs discussed ways to obtain balance-of-payments equilibrium and defend the dollar, but then went on to consider options in the event the judgment was made that "the dollar was hopelessly overvalued." After reviewing the options, he concluded that suspending the dollar's convertibility to gold, "which could be made effective by executive decision from one minute to the next without prior consultations abroad," would be the preferred course over arduous and possibly confrontational negotiations for currency realignments that would be disruptive of foreign exchange markets. (Washington National Records Center, Department of the Treasury, Files of Under Secretary Volcker: FRC 56 79 15, 1971 Contingency Planning Papers) Federal Reserve Chairman Arthur Burns provided a copy of Coombs' memorandum to Treasury Under Secretary Paul Volcker on March 24. (Ibid.)

At this time many G-10 countries were faced with rising dollar inflows. These inflows were discussed by European Community Finance Ministers when they met in Hamburg on April 26 and 27. The Embassy in Bonn provided a summary of the meeting in telegram 5156 from Bonn, April 30. German Finance Minister Schiller reportedly suggested two approaches to dealing with the dollar inflows, a temporary joint float of EEC currencies or a multilateral parity adjustment, and personally preferred the former. Only the Netherlands supported Schiller's position, and France was opposed to any measures that would reduce the competitiveness of French export industries "and when pressed declared that if the choice were between inflation and a parity adjustment, they would prefer inflation." (National Archives, RG 59, Central Files 1970–73, FN 10)

The dollar inflows continued, and on May 5 Henry Kissinger sent a memorandum to President Nixon advising him that "Germany, Switzerland, The Netherlands, Belgium and Austria today suspended dollar operations of their central banks. They did so because of the tremendous inflow of dollars which reached $1 billion in Germany yesterday. It now appears that the dollar operation will continue suspended at least through this weekend." Kissinger informed the President that the capital inflows were due to speculation that the Mark, and perhaps other European currencies, would be appreciated against the dollar. He posited possible approaches by France and Germany and suggested that France might use its veto power over British entry into the European Community "to get German acquiescence on French monetary views." In the end, however, Kissinger concluded no U.S. action was required at that time and "we need only watch the situation carefully and await word on what the Europeans plan to do." (Ibid., Nixon Presidential Materials, NSC Files, Subject Files, Box 309, Balance of Payments)

When foreign exchange markets reopened on May 10, the Mark was allowed to float (see Document 155). The Embassy in Bonn on June 15 reported one responsible German official's view that the Mark would float for an extended period, possibly beyond the end of the year, and that German industry was becoming reconciled to the float as preferable to exchange controls or a large revaluation. (Telegram 7249 from Bonn, June 15; National Archives, RG 59, Central Files 1970–73, FN 10)

Continuing throughout the summer of 1971 until the New Economic Policy was announced on August 15 and beyond, the visible thrust of U.S. activity on international monetary policy continued to be the initiative for greater exchange rate flexibility. The Volcker Group discussed the subject on June 29, and draft position papers reflecting that discussion and proposed amendments to the Articles of Agreement on wider margins and floating rates were circulated to members of the Group as VG/LIM/71-21 on July 2. (Washington National Records Center, Department of the Treasury, Volcker Group Masters: FRC 56 86 30, VG/LIM/71-1) See Documents 162 and 163 regarding the U.S. initiative at the IMF Board meeting on July 19.

---

152. Paper Prepared in the Department of the Treasury[1]

Washington, May 8, 1971.

CONTINGENCY

1. Our Basic Objective

To take advantage of the present crisis to achieve a (i) lasting improvement in the balance-of-payments position of the United States, (ii) a more equitable sharing of the responsibilities for world security and economic progress and (iii) a basic reform of the international monetary system.

2. Our Basic Premise

Given our defense and economic assistance burden, the underlying balance of payments of the United States is in basic disequilibrium and likely to get worse rather than better without substantial realignment of exchange rates of a number of countries. Even then a lasting equilibrium may depend on a reassessment of defense and other burdens. Furthermore, it is only in an atmosphere of crisis and disturbance that other important changes in the policies of European countries and Japan can be brought about.

---

[1] Source: Washington National Records Center, Department of the Treasury, Files of Under Secretary Volcker: FRC 56 79 15, 1971 Contingency Planning Papers. Confidential; Eyes Only.

3. Specific Objectives

To achieve:

a) A significant revaluation of the currencies of major European countries and Japan as a result of floating rates or other actions. (See Tab A for an analysis of U.S. balance-of-payments trends and the need for corrective action.)[2]

(b) A fairer sharing of the balance of payments and budgetary costs of the military burden. (See Tab B.)[3]

(c) An improvement in the trade policies of the European countries and Japan. (See Tab C.)[4]

(d) A sharing of foreign aid, which takes into account U.S. defense burdens. (See Tab D.)[5]

(e) Monetary improvements, including greater rate flexibility and phasing out of gold and avoidance of excessive use of controls. (See Tab E.)

The U.S. should prepare for intensive negotiations with other industrial countries in each of these areas.

4. Basic Approach

Accept and use the opportunity provided by the monetary crisis to undertake negotiations on these major issues. While it is hoped that the disturbances will not be great, one must be prepared for such a contingency.

5. Foreign Objectives

Generally speaking, the other major industrial countries can be expected to pursue the following objectives:

(a) to maintain their competitive positions in international trade;

(b) to minimize adverse effects of international trade and payments on their domestic economies; and

(c) to minimize the assumption of financial burdens for military purposes, and to keep their economic aid burdens relative and modest.

The Common Market countries will attach great importance to the preservation of EC objectives, particularly the common agricultural policy and their hopes for establishing monetary unity. In the effort to preserve internal harmony, they may seek solutions through common, discriminatory controls on transactions with non-member countries. France,

---

[2] Not printed.

[3] Not printed. Tab B, entitled "Sharing the Cost and Defense of the Free World," discussed issues similar to those raised in the offset and burdensharing negotiations with the Federal Republic of Germany and the NATO allies. See Documents 18 and 22.

[4] Not printed. Tab C, entitled "Trade Portion of a General Negotiation," discussed the essential improvement in the U.S. trade balance and trading rules vis-à-vis the major U.S. trading partners.

[5] Tabs D and E were not found.

in particular, is likely to attempt to take advantage of the opportunity, for political reasons, to reduce U.S. hegemony in the international economic and financial area and to restrict U.S. freedom of action. These countries also wish to restore gold to the central role in the monetary system. They can be expected to seek to capitalize on any frictions which may develop to weaken U.S. ties with other European nations and to urge the use of restrictions on capital transactions as a device for restricting the operations of U.S. firms in Europe and reducing European dependence on U.S. high technology equipment (e.g., aircraft).

6. U.S. Tactics

(a) Permit foreign exchange crisis to develop without action or strong intervention by the U.S.

(b) At an appropriate time when there is growing realization that substantial changes will need to be made, the U.S. should indicate its own preferred solution.

(c) At that time, the U.S. should be prepared to indicate and, if necessary, use the following measures as negotiating leverage:

(i) suspension of gold convertibility;[6]
(ii) imposition of trade restrictions;
(iii) diplomatic and financial intervention to frustrate foreign activities which interfere with the attainment of our objectives; and
(iv) reduction of the U.S. military presence in Europe and Japan.

(d) In the monetary area the "fall back" position would be simply to remain on the system of "floating rates" already largely in place under this scenario. It would be necessary in order to maintain our bargaining position taken through inconvertibility under (i) above, that the U.S. make clear from the start that the U.S. would be prepared to live with the floating rate systems indefinitely.

7. Procedure

(a) The Secretary of the Treasury will be prepared, on short order, to begin negotiations on the monetary issues should the timing for such

---

[6] On June 3 Congressman Henry Reuss introduced a "Sense of Congress Resolution" that said that if an international monetary conference was not promptly convened, the United States should terminate the convertibility of the dollar to gold; permit the dollar to float until any disequilibrium had been removed; and entertain claims for compensation by foreign official dollar holders only for those who cooperate on proper exchange rates and adhere to the March 1969 two-tier gold agreement (see Document 145). A copy of Reuss' resolution was circulated to members of the Volcker Group and its Working Groups as VG/Uncl. INFO/71-30 on June 4. (Washington National Records Center, Department of the Treasury, Volcker Group Masters: FRC 56 86 30, VG/Uncl. INFO/70-1–) See also *The New York Times,* June 4, 1971, p. 45. No record of a vote on the resolution was found.

negotiations appear appropriate. While it seems likely that the Group of Ten (the EEC, the U.K., Canada, Japan, Sweden, Switzerland and the U.S.) would be the best forum in which to begin the negotiations, the Secretary of the Treasury should give consideration to the negotiating forum as well as strategy. Negotiations on the monetary issues should take into account the progress being made in the separate negotiations on the other issues.

(b) To prepare for negotiations on the related issues the President should direct:

(1) The Council on International Economic Policy to develop positions with respect to trade relationships with the European Common Market and Japan;
(2) The National Security Council to develop positions designed to achieve objectives with respect to the sharing of the defense burden;
(3) The Secretaries of State and Treasury to develop positions with respect to the redistribution of the burden of foreign aid for review by the Council on International Economic Policy.

Positions on these issues should be developed and approved by June 30 in order that international negotiations may begin shortly thereafter.

8. Probable Foreign Response

Other countries, led by the EC, would be likely to respond by:

(a) Public attempts to place all responsibility for the monetary crisis on the U.S. as the deficit country and to argue that corrective action is a U.S. responsibility. The French would offer a change in the price of gold as the required action;

(b) Introduction of common EC exchange controls on capital flows or a dual exchange rate market with a penalty rate for inward capital transactions (though the effectiveness would be uncertain);

(c) Possible drive to exclude and isolate U.S. from the bulk of the trading world through enlargement of and association with the EC on a preferential basis;

(d) Seeking to discuss the issues of trade policy, military expenditures and aid burdens in separate channels, wholly divorced from the monetary problems. They would hold that—

(1) the U.S. has more restrictions on trade than the EC and any reduction of barriers must be matched by reductions in U.S. barriers of equal value;
(2) they are already contributing larger shares of GNP to foreign aid than does the U.S. and military expenditures are not relevant.

Increases in defense budgets beyond those contemplated are not politically feasible in the present world climate and in any event increased expenditures designed to ease the financial burden on the U.S. are out of the question in part because of the appearance of paying "occupation" costs and in part because of public antipathy toward support of the U.S. while it continues to be involved in Viet Nam.

---

153.   Paper Prepared in the Department of the Treasury[1]

Washington, May 9, 1971.

U.S. NEGOTIATING POSITION ON GOLD

The official dollar gold price would not change

The United States would make clear at the outset of negotiations that it does not regard any change in the official price of gold as part of the negotiations. This posture will be necessary because the French, with varying degrees of support from countries such as Belgium, Switzerland and certain elements in the United Kingdom, may seek a devaluation of the United States dollar in terms of gold. French private citizens hold large amounts of gold on which they would like to make a profit, and Swiss bankers have substantial holdings for their clients and have been managing South African gold sales and on occasion, trying to stimulate gold speculation by their actions and speeches. Both French and British financial interests hold large blocks of South African gold mining stocks. A rise in the official gold price would help the private holders by raising the private market price and enlarging the scope of that market, in the judgment of the French and Swiss.

Fortunately the Germans and Italians do not favor an increase in the gold price, so that the French are unlikely to achieve a unified position in the European Community. The Germans and Italians hold very large reserves in dollars, on which they would gain no profit if the official gold price rose. Their officials might even incur criticism because other countries had profited by holding a larger share of their reserves in gold. The Japanese and even the Canadians could also be embarrassed.

---

[1] Source: Washington National Records Center, Department of the Treasury, Deputy to the Assistant Secretary for International Affairs: FRC 56 83 26, Contingency Planning 1971. Confidential. A typed note at the top of the page reads: "2nd Draft 5:00 p.m."

The French argument

The main argument that the French may make is that the United States as the deficit country should devalue, because we have sinned and should expiate. Other countries (France) have devalued and the United States should behave like other countries and do so. Surplus countries should not have to revalue because the United States does not wish to change the price of gold, particularly since these surplus countries have followed virtuous anti-inflation policies and kept their balances of payments in order.

The French suggest a moderate increase in the official dollar price, while other countries maintain their existing gold prices or raise them to a lesser degree than the United States thus effecting a change in IMF parities (which are stated in gold) that would depreciate the dollar exchange rate in terms of their currencies.

In effect, the French attitude boils down to the suggestion that if the United States does penance and helps the private gold holders to make a bigger capital gain, this would ease the discomfort of appreciating their exchange rate and becoming less competitive with the U.S. in the U.S. market and world markets.

U.S. counter arguments

Against this point of view, the United States would make the following counter arguments:

1) *The deficit is only partly due to U.S. economic policies.* While the United States at some periods has augmented its balance of payments deficits by inflationary policies, our record of price stability was much better than all major countries except Belgium and Germany in 1950–65; and slightly better than these two. U.S. deficits have also been forcefully affected by (a) our heavy external costs for military expenditures to protect Europe and Japan, (b) by trade practices abroad that have cut back the growth trend in our agricultural and other exports, and (c) especially by the undervalued exchange rates which were fixed in the forties and fifties, at a time when foreign productive capacity was abnormally low relative to foreign demand, and which have been jealously preserved for trading advantage. Moreover, the recent large short-term flows have been due to divergent monetary policies in the U.S. and Germany—both needed for their domestic situations.

2) *Other countries decided to peg to the dollar long ago.* Other countries decided long ago to use the dollar as a reserve currency and to peg their currencies to the dollar. By doing so, they took to themselves the responsibility for fixing exchange rates, leaving the U.S. in a passive position, and have prevented their currencies from rising in response to natural market pressures that would have caused these currencies to

appreciate. Some have devalued whenever their competitive position was weakened, and this fact raises questions as to whether they could be counted on to maintain their initial appreciation vis-à-vis the dollar under the French scheme.

3) *A moderate gold price increase would be unstable.* A moderate increase in the official gold price would be analogous to the "Munich settlement"; it could quite likely last only a short time—perhaps less than a year. It would establish a strong presumption that the prescription would be repeated if speculative pressures again became strong, and dollar reserves built up abroad again. Because central banks holding gold would have gained a gold profit, while holders of dollars would not, many central bankers would face public criticism for holding dollars. This would be likely to induce substantial requests for conversion of dollars into gold, especially by smaller central banks. U.S. gold reserves could shrink fairly quickly, offsetting or more than offsetting the devaluation gold profit (which itself would be about matched by a write-up in our gold guaranteed liabilities to the IMF and other international agencies). This factor of additional drain on U.S. reserves for conversion *arises from the re-emphasis on gold inherent in the change in the U.S. official gold price.* It would *not be present* if exchange rates are adjusted without a change in the dollar price of gold.

4) *SDRs are better reserves for the future than gold.* It is highly desirable to continue the trend toward greater reliance on SDRs than gold for international reserves. The fact that there has been a private commodity market for gold, in competition with monetary use of gold, subjected the monetary system before the two-tier system to speculative drains of gold to private hands, which weakened all currencies. The SDR and the two-tier gold system recognized that gold was no longer satisfactory as a source of reserve growth, and, if so, there is no logic to increasing the official gold price. It would be turning back the clock.

5) *A gold price increase would be hard on those who have held dollars.* An increase in the gold price is discriminatory and inequitable. It enlarges the reserves of those countries that hold gold, while leaving unchanged reserves held in the form of dollars. This is unfair to some of our closest cooperators, and benefits a few large gold holders who do not need reserve writeups.

6) *It could weaken the two-tier gold system and benefit gold producers and speculators.* The psychological reaction of raising the commodity price of gold would benefit Russia, South Africa and other producers as well as private hoarders and speculators. The spread between the official and private price might well widen, and this could make it harder to maintain the two-tier system. The system was regarded as favoring

the United States rather than the French gold philosophy, and a gold price rise would sow new doubts.

7) *Differential rather than a uniform exchange rate adjustment is needed.* The Japanese adjustment, for example, might need to be steeper than the European, and all the Europeans might not be the same. To cover this spread the U.S. change in gold price could be undesirably large.

8) *The U.S. would convert dollars into SDRs instead of gold.* With major modifications in exchange rates and other improvements that should make the future drain on U.S. reserves manageable, the U.S. is prepared to resume responsibility for conversion of dollars into international reserve assets, which it alone has carried since 1945. But it would convert official dollars into SDRs or other claims on the Fund, rather than gold. We would use gold as needed to acquire these assets from the IMF. This procedure would continue the gradual evolution of the monetary system toward SDRs as the basic reserve asset, with gold gradually declining as a portion of world reserves. This process has already gone a long way, since gold reserves represented only 40 percent of global reserves at the end of 1970, as compared with 70 percent in 1948. Turning back the clock would be a very serious decision, and would be resisted in many quarters of the academic, banking and Congressional world.

9) *Congressional opposition could be strong.* A number of influential members of Congress (Patman, Widnall, Senator Long, Reuss, Senator Bennett) seem likely to be doubtful or critical. Some don't like to pay out gold to foreigners. Some want to de-emphasize gold. Many are likely to feel that the Executive should have specific Congressional authority, and a Congressional debate could lead to very serious market uncertainty and speculation. The attached correspondence with Congressman Reuss has been accepted by Congressman Reuss as indicating that action would not be taken without Congressional approval. If this were not the Treasury view, he had indicated that he would submit legislation making this quite specific. (See attached correspondence.)[2]

10) *A massive gold price increase would be generally rejected in a worldwide inflationary period.* A doubling of the price of gold at one swoop, as recommended by Rueff of France for many years, is probably not likely to be put forward now. We understand Rueff himself no longer puts it forward, as it is too unrealistic. It would be resisted very widely as it

---

[2] Not printed. Attached were a February 6, 1969, letter from Secretary Kennedy to Congressman Reuss reaffirming the position taken in a January 23, 1968, letter from Under Secretary Barr to Reuss, and a copy of Barr's letter. It was Barr's view that the $35 per ounce price of gold notified to the IMF could only be changed by Congressional action.

would enlarge world reserves by about $40 billion all at once. The 1970 addition to world reserves was $14 billion. Such a large increment to world reserves, even though initially immobilized in central bank reserves, would have a marked inflationary potential. It would probably be resisted by most members of the Fund, and by U.S. public opinion. One danger of a moderate change in the gold price is that by a series of crises, the same result might be approached.

154.   Information Memorandum From Ernest Johnston of the National Security Council Staff to the President's Assistant for National Security Affairs (Kissinger)[1]

Washington, May 10, 1971.

SUBJECT

Political Repercussions of the European Monetary Crisis

Though somewhat bypassed by events, attached at Tab A is a memorandum to the Acting Secretary of State by the Bureau of European Affairs on possible political repercussions of the European monetary crisis.[2] The situation will take time to become clear, but after the joint Community decisions over the weekend, State's memorandum seems a bit alarmist. Nevertheless, it raises fundamental problems which will persist.

The memorandum lists four political trouble points:

—European resentment against the United States for our balance of payments policy, which contributed to the crisis.
—U.S. Congressional hostility toward a German revaluation, which will increase costs of troop support in Europe.
—Internal strains within the Common Market over delay in EC monetary unity and particularly over inevitable adjustments in the Common Agricultural Policy.
—Spill over effects on British entry negotiations.

---

[1] Source: National Archives, Nixon Presidential Materials, NSC Files, Subject Files, Box 32, European Common Market, Volume II 1971–1972. Confidential. Concurred in by Sonnenfeldt.

[2] Not printed. A copy of the undated memorandum for the Acting Secretary of State was forwarded to Kissinger without comment under cover of a May 8 memorandum that Robert Brewster signed on behalf of Executive Secretary Theodore L. Eliot, Jr. (Ibid.)

The markets today have been relatively quiet with a comparatively small transfer of money. Though the Germans got pretty much what they wanted—Community agreement to their float—the agreement was dressed up in such a way that the Community appeared to reach a collective decision. The Germans did promise to put into effect some of the controls the other members wanted and to aim at restoration of the previous exchange parities. Consequently, since there is no public admission that the other members were faced down, some of the bitterness mentioned in State's memorandum may be avoided.

Most of the European central bankers do blame the United States for the underlying circumstances that brought on the revaluation, but generally the governments have avoided pointing too much in our direction.

We should be able to counter any Congressional reaction on higher troop costs with the solid economic argument that the German revaluation will contribute to improved U.S. balance of payments. We shall, however, definitely feel this pressure in regard to German offset arrangements.

Community disputes over the Common Agricultural Policy would be dampened by a reasonable German position at Tuesday's meeting of the Agricultural Ministers although much will depend here on how much the Germans insist upon avoiding any lowering of their farmers' high agricultural prices. However, France will resent the delay in implementation of EC monetary unity. The weekend's events made it obvious that such unity would at best be tenuous until closer agreement is reached on common monetary and fiscal policies, as the Germans had clearly prophesied.

Reports from France so far do not indicate that the French will seize the revaluation as an excuse to fight the Germans on UK entry, but this issue will not be clear for some time. The final result may even favor French support for British entry, since the German power play will alert the French that they may need help in controlling a stubborn and strong Germany.

Though the German/Dutch float and the Austrian/Swiss 5 to 7 percent revaluations have undoubtedly caused great turmoil in financial circles, we have definitely gained on the economic front because of the impetus that these moves will give toward greater exchange flexibility, which is an essential element for continued liberal trade policies. In addition, German and French persistence in appearing to reach accord within the framework of the Community policy apparatus will have a positive effect despite the fact that the currency crisis has shaken some of the substance of agreed Community policies.

155. Editorial Note

On May 12, 1971, German Chancellor Brandt wrote President Nixon to inform him that the monetary crisis had "created great difficulties for the Federal Government" and several other European governments. He noted the importance his government attached to "the development of a European economic and monetary union" and thought the fact that President Pompidou and Prime Minister Heath had agreed to meet boded well for British entry into the Community. He looked forward to discussing these and other matters with the President during a mid-June visit to the United States. (National Archives, RG 59, S/S Files: Lot 73 D 288, Box 836, NSC Misc. Memos)

On May 28 Secretary Connally gave a major speech at the International Banking Conference of the American Bankers Association in Munich, Germany. Connally reviewed the evolution of economic power centers in the postwar era, noted U.S. concerns on burdensharing and trade issues, and said there "is a clear and present danger to our monetary system . . . . Flexibility is essential . . . . We are not going to devalue. We are not going to change the price of gold . . . . No longer can considerations of friendship, or need, or capacity justify the United States carrying so heavy a share of the common burdens . . . no longer will the American people permit their government to engage in international actions in which the true long-run interests of the U.S. are not just as clearly recognized as those of the nations with which we deal . . . increased cooperation among us all must play a key role in maintaining a stable monetary system." The full text of Connally's speech, circulated to the Volcker Group as VG/Uncl. INFO/71-28, is in the Washington National Records Center, Department of the Treasury, Volcker Group Masters: FRC 56 86 30. The text is also printed in Department of State *Bulletin,* July 12, 1971, pages 42–46.

Chancellor Brandt made a private visit to the United States in mid-June to receive an honorary degree from Yale. He continued on to Washington for an unofficial visit on June 15 and 16. He met with President Nixon at the White House on June 15 from 11:02 a.m. to 12:34 p.m., and was the guest of honor at a White House dinner that evening. (National Archives, Nixon Presidential Materials, White House Central Files, President's Daily Diary) A taped recording of his meeting with President Nixon, which included discussion of monetary matters, is ibid., White House Tapes, Recording of Conversation between President Nixon and Chancellor Brandt, June 15, 1971, 11:02 a.m.–12:34 p.m., Oval Office, Conversation No. 520–6.

156.   Memorandum of Conversation[1]

Washington, May 20, 1971, 11:30 a.m.

PARTICIPANTS

France
Giscard d'Estaing, Minister of Economy and Finance
Marc Vienot, IMF Executive Director

United States
Secretary of the Treasury Connally
Under Secretary for Monetary Affairs Volcker
Assistant Secretary Petty
Deputy Assistant Secretary Cates

M. Giscard explained that he was here to promote a French export drive in the United States, adding that France is one of the U.S.'s best trading partners. The U.S. has a surplus of $800 million in trade. Secretary Connally asked if this included tourism and remarked that tourism was a sizable offset to the trade surplus. M. Giscard remarked that the U.S. main bilateral deficit was with Japan and Canada. He added that France is not bilateral minded, but he believes that exports are a good test of competitiveness. He is promoting sales of electrical and other machinery and also steel. Secretary Connally remarked that the Japanese will run both the U.S. and France out of business in steel if we are not careful. There was a discussion of Japanese wage levels and competitive ability.

M. Giscard turned to the subject of the recent monetary turmoil saying that this had been felt much more acutely in Europe than in the U.S., insofar as he gathered from reading the U.S. press. In Europe there was a feeling of real crisis. France, however, had remained calm as she was not directly concerned, having been insulated from the monetary flows. While France agreed with her Common Market partners not to let her views be openly known, Giscard felt that some parts of the German Government want the float to end up in a revaluation while other parts do not. This ambiguity on the part of the Germans is likely to impair the European monetary union.

M. Giscard felt there was a new feeling in the (Saturday night) Ministerial meeting.[2] Hitherto the French had been the "bad boys," by

---

[1] Source: Washington National Records Center, Department of the Treasury, Files of Under Secretary Volcker: FRC 56 79 15, France. Confidential. The meeting was held in Secretary Connally's office. Drafted on May 21 by Cates and approved, as amended, by Volcker.

[2] Presumably a reference to a May 8 European Community Ministerial meeting; see Document 154.

being relatively inflexible in their views while the Germans were in part more flexible. In the recent crisis the Germans spread rumors and declared that the real cause of inflation was the inflow of dollars. The American attitude for some time, said Giscard, had been to pursue discussions of exchange flexibility in the expectation that other countries could be induced to revalue their currencies from time to time as necessary, but for the first time Giscard detects a willingness in Europe *not* to revalue. Notably, the Italians were very firm on this point and some of the Germans as well. Therefore, said Giscard, the route of revaluation is closed.

At the same time the attitude of central banks will change. They will not want to accumulate any more dollars. This will lead us to a multiplication of restrictions and regulations in the Western world, a very unpleasant development in Giscard's view. While France has maintained currency restrictions, Giscard does not feel they are a good thing in the long run and if they proliferate it would be very damaging.

Mr. Volcker objected to the idea that the U.S. had engaged in discussions of exchange flexibility in an effort to induce expected revaluations. He could understand confusion on this point because some individuals have made statements to this effect, but it is not the view of the government. Indeed, it was difficult for him to visualize effective arrangements if other currencies were repeatedly revalued against the dollar. Secretary Connally expressed his agreement with Mr. Volcker's statement emphasizing that he could name individuals who believe in a high degree of exchange rate flexibility and that revaluation by other countries are the basic answer to our problems. These statements are misleading because they do not represent government policy. Government policy, the Secretary added, was made in the Treasury, the White House and the Federal Reserve Board. He had had many discussions with Dr. Burns and the two were in agreement in opposing floating rates.

The Secretary added that it is, in his opinion, impossible to expect monetary arrangements to deal with all of the economic conflicts among nations. For example, the Germans have their problems with inflation. We have ours, which are the reverse. Many of the problems are political in nature. The Secretary pointed out that the U.S. Government had taken very tough political decisions in 1969 and 1970. In order to cure inflation we have a 6 percent unemployment rate, which is a politically difficult situation.

The Secretary emphasized that we have not been practicing benign neglect for the past 25 years. He reiterated that monetary means alone are not enough to solve the problem. He added that we do not like to see $50 billion in the Eurodollar market with no controls. The steps we have taken during the crisis were designed to calm the waters, but it might be that greater flexibility around parities would serve to counter the enormous capital flows of the type we have been seeing. The U.S. does not want to see exchange controls if they can be avoided.

The Secretary pointed out that the monetary system is tied to the dollar not because we wanted it that way, but because it grew up that way. What good would it do, he asked rhetorically, if we should devalue? He pointed out for example that yen revaluation would in itself not much help the U.S. because of the many Japanese restrictions on imports.

The Secretary emphasized that this government does not want go back to isolationism and that the Mansfield Amendment[3] defeat was a reflection of that. However, basic trade adjustments are needed and the U.S. spends too much abroad. As an example of the needed adjustments in trade, he cited the fact that five years ago Canada was in trouble while we had a $640 million surplus with Canada. As a result we signed the Auto Agreement and now that surplus has been turned into a substantial deficit. This Agreement was unfair and has to be restructured.

Turning to the subject of inflation, the Secretary complimented the Minister on his recent analysis of his internal inflation problem, pointing out that the U.S. and France had the same problems—built in wage demands by labor. He cited in the U.S. the construction industry, the railroads and steel. He added that with regard to incomes policies, President Nixon does not want to take half-way measures. But if the President decides to have an incomes policy, he will go all the way to some kind of mandatory system rather than take half-way measures such as some wage price advisory board where he could not enforce the recommendation. This is the reason for the President's hesitation.

The Secretary said that we are trying to expand the economy gradually. The inflation rate is down to 3 percent in the first quarter but will go up somewhat for the year. We will stabilize, but we cannot expect to cure the balance of payments problem this year. That situation should be a lot better in 1972 and 1973. In the meantime, we must get back to stability with perhaps a little more flexibility by way perhaps of wider bands or otherwise.

M. Giscard said that he does not oppose wider bands per se. However, the problem lies in whether international public opinion will believe that a currency going to one margin of a wider band will return to its parity again. Otherwise flexibility may lead to further speculation. For example, if the DM after the present float returns to its former par-

---

[3] Not further identified. Mansfield and a number of other members of Congress had proposed amendments restricting U.S. activities overseas to curtail U.S. involvement in Southeast Asia.

ity, this will be a good lesson and a good argument for greater flexibility. If however the DM does not, the speculators will remember and will not believe that the next currency which floats or moves will return to its parity.

M. Giscard pointed out that over the past ten years there has been a U.S. balance of payments deficit. This gives rise to skepticism about the U.S. desire not to have others revalue. It also has given rise to saturation of the rest of the world with dollars. Now, said M. Giscard, we need proposals for the use of the dollars thus accumulated. Others do not want to hold more dollars. The recent problems are likely to recommence and therefore we must think about this in advance.

Secretary Connally pointed out that in 1969 we had sopped up dollars from the Eurodollar market and in 1970–71 we paid them back again. Now we will have to prove to the skeptics about our balance of payments. To do this we must cut back foreign spending and that means other countries, in particular Japan, Canada and Germany, must contribute more to defense and aid. Twenty years ago, said the Secretary, we were relatively rich in productive capacity and reserves but this is no longer the case. The Mansfield Amendment is in part a reflection of the reality that we have been spending too much.

M. Giscard warned that if there are no joint actions to stabilize the international monetary system he foresaw increasing exchange controls on the European side.

(N.B. During his press conference[4] M. Giscard said it was regrettable that the European monetary union had been damaged, *the more so because of* (interesting phrase, spoken in French and not translated) Britain's imminent entry into the Common Market.)

William C. Cates

---

[4] Not further identified.

157. Memorandum From the Chairman of the Council of Economic Advisers (McCracken) to President Nixon[1]

Washington, June 2, 1971.

SUBJECT

International Monetary Reform

We have just muddled through another international monetary crisis. We can congratulate ourselves that we have so far escaped the worst of outcomes—which would have been commitment to restriction of the domestic economy and widespread controls both at home and abroad. However, we cannot be sure of having escaped entirely or permanently. Several countries, notably Japan, have introduced new controls. Protectionists in Congress and elsewhere interpret the event as additional evidence that the U.S. cannot hold its own in an open world economy. On the other hand the experience of the last few months, allowing a "crisis" to develop and then floating outside the rules of the system, is too uncertain and risky to be repeated.

A system that combines rigidly fixed exchange rates with free trade and capital movements appears to be unworkable. But the recent practice of unregulated exchange rate changes and floating disrupts the monetary order that has generally prevailed so far. There seem to be two alternatives—either more extensive use of direct controls to support a system of fixed exchange rates or an internationally-agreed upon system of greater flexibility. You recognized this two years ago and opted for the second alternative when you decided (in June 1969)[2] that the U.S. would propose and support a study of greater flexibility in the IMF. This study was made but it has not so far led to concrete results because some countries do not like its conclusions while the attitude of some of our own representatives has been lukewarm at best.

If we allow things to drift further we may well wind up with more extensive use of direct controls, which would be highly burdensome to our trade and investment interests. Our businessmen and bankers also appear to be generally opposed to wider use of floating rates.[3] However, the prospects of going back to the existing rules are dim.

---

[1] Source: National Archives, Nixon Presidential Materials, NSC Files, Agency Files, Box 218, Council on International Economic Policy. No classification marking. A stamped notation reads: "The President has seen." He wrote extensive marginal notes which were covered over and cannot be read on the source text, but see Document 159.

[2] Presumably a reference to the international monetary policy meeting on June 26, 1969; see Documents 131 and 140.

[3] A handwritten note in the margin reads: "not so clear."

Unless timely reforms are made the IMF could easily go the way of the United Nations.

I believe a decision has to be made urgently on the direction in which we would like the international monetary system to develop. In my opinion our best course would be to support implementation of the IMF's flexibility study, published last year.[4] This requires prompt action since the IMF annual report is now being written. Unless recommendations can be brought before the IMF meeting this coming September the public is likely to assume that the flexibility study is dead.

I recommend that you convene the Council on International Economic Policy to reassert our position in favor of an updating of the IMF rules. Most of the preparatory work has already been done so there is no need for another lengthy in-house study. The immediate result of the CIEP meeting could be a public statement reaffirming our attachment to the basic principles of the Bretton Woods System, our opposition to extensive controls, and our interest in working with other nations to adapt the international monetary system to contemporary needs.[5]

Paul W. McCracken[6]

P.S. Read to Paul McCracken, who is currently in Europe, and approved by him.

---

[4] Presumably a reference to the paper for the Annual Meeting in Copenhagen; see footnote 4, Document 148.

[5] A handwritten note in the margin reads: "I doubt usefulness of CIEP but such a statement would be good."

[6] The memorandum bears McCracken's handwritten signature despite the typed postscript.

158. Memorandum From Secretary of the Treasury Connally to President Nixon[1]

Washington, June 8, 1971.

A memorandum addressed to you by Paul McCracken on June 2 on international monetary reform has just come to my attention.[2] I must take vigorous personal exception to its premises and conclusions.

The simple fact is that, given our present international economic and financial position, some monetary disturbances—which the press will label "crises"—are virtually inevitable. The test is whether these can be met without impairing our basic domestic (or international) objectives.

Far from "muddling through" the recent disturbance, I believe these essential objectives were maintained:

(1) Quite deliberately, we avoided a strong reaction. By maintaining, insofar as possible, the focus in Europe, we helped deflate concern over a "dollar crisis." Pressures for strong domestic action, either with respect to higher interest rates or strongly intensified controls (or both) never built up.

(2) International sentiment was calmed fairly quickly and effectively in the circumstances.

(3) By making the point that the "crisis" grew most immediately out of domestic German political and economic concerns, we helped limit the repercussions on the dollar and set the stage for maintaining the IMF's role in exercising surveillance over exchange rate practices. The latter seems to be Mr. McCracken's principal objective.

(4) Finally, and not least important, a basic spirit of cooperation has been maintained. Thus we retain a base for dealing promptly with two major problems:

---

[1] Source: Washington National Records Center, Department of the Treasury, Records of Secretary Shultz: FRC 56 80 1, JBC–Memoranda From the White House 71. Attached to a June 8 note from Peterson to Connally regarding McCracken's June 2 memorandum to the President (Document 157). Peterson reminded Connally that "a couple of weeks ago" they had discussed the Council's role in international monetary reform. Peterson noted that he and Connally "agreed that I would prepare a study memo in draft form that would suggest a *broader* frame of reference than just monetary—to include discussion of the causes of the persistent problem and a *projection* of the future balance of payments situation—including defense, trade balances, etc. The monetary approaches would also have to be included as one part of this but I see it in this broader context and something that you approve in advance. I hope to have a draft in your hands next week." No such paper was found. Also attached to Peterson's June 8 note to Connally is Connally's June 9 memorandum to Huntsman (see footnote 4, Document 159), Huntsman's June 8 memorandum to Connally (Document 159), and McCracken's June 2 memorandum to the President (Document 157).

[2] Document 157.

(a) Achieving more influence over the Eurodollar market and short-term capital flows generally.

(b) Reaching a consensus on methods of attaining some needed flexibility in the exchange rate structure, without simply falling into the trap of "everyone for himself."

Changes in our present international economic and financial position must be achieved without—and this is the key—undermining confidence in the dollar and the general stability of the monetary system. Should we fail, forces of economic nationalism and isolation in one country after the other—including the United States—could become unmanageable.

I do not underestimate the extent to which the problems are complicated by differing views among economists and businessmen, and among countries. In particular, I believe we must realize there is a strong element of thinking within Europe that would take advantage of weakness or clumsiness on our part to promote the Common Market not as a partner but as a rival economic bloc, competing vigorously with the dollar and reducing or shutting out, as best it can, U.S. economic influence from a considerable portion of the world.

These threats to monetary and economic order will require action in a wide variety of areas. Most important is success in dealing with inflation and growth at home. In the vital areas of trade, aid, and a better sharing of defense costs, where a clear focus for Government policy-making has been absent, the Council on International Economic Policy obviously has a lead role.

But one distinction should be clear. As I have understood it, the genesis of CIEP did not lie in an idea it could or should take over the role of responsible operating agencies. In the international monetary area, that role, by law and tradition, lies under your direction with the Treasury, which, in turn, must operate in close coordination with the Federal Reserve.

Specifically, I fail to see the merit in convening CIEP to "reassert" in general terms a position with respect to exchange rate flexibility that only a few days ago I reiterated in Munich.[3] In view of recent developments, it is hard for me to see how informed observers could think the flexibility issue is dead. But its specifics do involve difficult tactical as well as substantive questions upon which important countries are not agreed. These questions are under active review within the Treasury and in the Volcker Group.

Obviously, relevant CIEP agencies and Peter Peterson are being and will be kept informed—they are, indeed, participating. But I do not think it useful or productive to convene a CIEP meeting for the purpose of issuing a broad public statement reaffirming what everyone already

---

[3] Reference is to Connally's address to the Annual Meeting of the American Bankers Association in Munich on May 28; see Document 155.

knows but leaving unanswered all those difficult questions of substance and tactics that are the heart of the matter at present.

My understanding has been that you believe it is appropriate and desirable to continue to proceed in this area in the manner I have outlined. If this understanding is not correct, I assume you will so advise me.

John B. Connally[4]

---

[4] Printed from a copy that indicates Connally signed the original.

---

159.   Memorandum From Jon Huntsman of the White House Staff to Secretary of the Treasury Connally[1]

Washington, June 8, 1971.

SUBJECT

International Monetary Reform Memorandum submitted to the President June 2, 1971 by Paul W. McCracken

Memoranda from both the President[2] and you[3] crossed my office desk today relative to the above subject. In order to make you fully aware of the President's views on the subject I am noting below the comments he made after reading the McCracken paper. You may, after reviewing them, want to alter your memorandum. Then again, you may not. I will hold it here in my confidential file until I hear from you regarding disposition.[4]

---

[1] Source: National Archives, Nixon Presidential Materials, NSC Files, Agency Files, Box 218, Council on International Economic Policy. Confidential; Eyes Only. A copy was sent to Peter Peterson.

[2] Reference is to the President's marginal comments on McCracken's June 2 memorandum; see Document 157 and footnote 1 thereto.

[3] Document 158.

[4] In a June 9 memorandum to Huntsman, Connally expressed his appreciation for being informed of the President's reactions to McCracken's memorandum and requested that Huntsman forward his June 8 memorandum to the President. (National Archives, Nixon Presidential Materials, NSC Files, Agency Files, Box 218, Council on International Economic Policy) Huntsman forwarded Connally's memorandum to the President under cover of a June 10 memorandum, which reminded the President of his handwritten "notations and directives" on McCracken's memorandum and informed him that Connally was "well aware of your reaction to the McCracken memorandum" and had requested that his memorandum go forward. (Ibid.)

Specifically, the President requested that you consult with Paul McCracken, Arthur Burns, George Shultz, Peter Peterson and your own experts. . . . then give him a "recommendation for action." The President further suggested that we "move on the problem, " not "just wait for it to hit us again—e.g. in the fall of '72."

He noted particularly the last paragraph of page 2—the part which recommends that he convene the Council on International Economic Policy to reassert our position in favor of an updating of IMF rules. His (the President's) comments were: "*No*—this is too large a group with too many people who talk a lot about subjects they know little about".

The President went on to say, in writing, "The Connally 1-man responsibility route is the best. This is an area in which he should be the lead man. Peterson, of course, should be consulted."

I am taking the liberty of sending Mr. Peterson a copy of this memorandum and would suggest that you contact him directly regarding the matter.

Thank you.

Jon M. Huntsman

---

160. **Memorandum From Ernest Johnston of the National Security Council Staff to the President's Assistant for National Security Affairs (Kissinger)**[1]

Washington, June 23, 1971.

SUBJECT

International Monetary Reform

Attached at Tab III is an exchange of correspondence involving Paul McCracken, Secretary Connally, Jon Huntsman and the President on the question of international monetary reform.[2]

Paul McCracken wrote to the President on June 2 (Tab A) that we have just "muddled through" another international monetary crisis.[3]

---

[1] Source: National Archives, Nixon Presidential Materials, NSC Files, Agency Files, Box 218, Council on International Economic Policy. Confidential.

[2] Tab III, not printed, is a June 10 memorandum from Huntsman to President Nixon with Tabs A–D; see footnotes 3–5 below.

[3] Document 157.

He recommended that we move immediately in the IMF toward exchange rate flexibility and suggested that we work out a position in the CIEP. On June 8 Connally commented to the President on McCracken's memorandum (Tab D).[4] Connally defended U.S. reactions to the crisis, stated that we had come out quite well, and argued that there should be no such review in the CIEP.

(The two memoranda bear out the usual positions on this issue: CEA using all occasions to press flexibility, Connally defending the status quo.)

The President (Tab B) rejected McCracken's proposal that action be given to the CIEP, but suggesting that we "move on the problem", not "just wait for it to hit us again, e.g. in the fall of '72."[5] He requested that Connally consult with McCracken, Burns, Shultz and Peterson, and give him a recommendation for action. Responsibility is to lie with Connally. Unfortunately the President did not recommend that Connally confer with you or Secretary Rogers, so that the foreign policy community has been omitted from the exercise.[6] This raises a major problem, since any new U. S. action in this field—including no action—will have major consequences for overall U.S. foreign policy.

If we are to change the current system or respond to crises in new fashions, there are several paths we could follow:

1. An *economic* solution could lie in "benign neglect" of our balance of payments problems, as George Shultz maintained.[7] This, however, would thoroughly anger the Europeans and might be the cause of a general run on our gold stock, forcing us to close the gold window and initiate a U.S. float in the midst of serious international ill-will. It would clearly spill over into our political relations.

2. We could institute even tighter capital controls and perhaps institute trade controls, which I suspect might be Secretary Connally' s preference—it was the preference of the last Administration. Tough capital controls might be welcomed in at least some quarters abroad, but not in most, and trade controls would cause serious international repercussions—in the current political climate, they could decisively tip the scales in favor of protectionist pressures and trigger major trade war.

3. A doubling or tripling of the dollar price of gold, toward which Arthur Burns has in the past inclined, is one response to a crisis, though it would be ineffective over any length of time and would be very damaging

---

[4] Document 158.

[5] See Document 159.

[6] Kissinger's handwritten note at the top of the page reads: "All of this (illegible word) be handled informally. State, Peterson and I should be involved."

[7] Not further identified.

to those countries (such as Germany) which at our urging have held large quantities of dollars. Their governments would suffer sharp criticism from a U.S. policy that doubled or tripled the dollar value of the reserves of the gold countries, while the value of their own reserves remained stable.

4. The best solution from the foreign policy standpoint is continued slow progress toward greater exchange rate flexibility, as pushed by McCracken. This is the most probable outcome and one we could expect if the more eccentric positions of the advisers cancel each other out, but the consequences are too serious to neglect should this not prove the result.

Fred Bergsten feels strongly that you, and perhaps the Secretary of State, should be involved in any recommendations on this issue so that the foreign policy consequences are given due weight. I agree with Fred. My own time here is very short; but Fred's replacement should have the opportunity to comment to you, and you to the President, on any Connally recommendation.[8]

You may wish to raise this with the President verbally; if not, I have included a memorandum plus a notification to Connally, if you wish to handle it that way, though it is of course delicate bureaucratically.

The memorandum for the President requests that Connally seek your comments before presenting his recommendations. This is an awkward procedure for it means that you would be one of a number of persons whose views would be included in Connally's memorandum. However, since Secretary Connally seems to have made arrangements to send his memoranda to the President without internal White House staffing, this seems the only way to make sure you are involved.[9]

Recommendations:[10]

1. That you seek the President's concurrence in requesting that Connally seek your views before presenting recommendations to the President on international monetary reform. (You may wish to use the memorandum at Tab I.)

2. That, subsequently, you inform Secretary Connally of the President's decision. (You may wish to use the memorandum at Tab II.)

---

[8] Johnston, a career Foreign Service officer, was completing a tour at the NSC and was about to be reassigned. Bergsten moved to the Brookings Institution during this time, and Hormats, who had joined the NSC Staff in 1969, assumed his responsibilities.

[9] Johnston's memorandum and its attachments were attached to an August 2 memorandum from Jon Howe to General Haig that reads: "Per your instructions, I talked to Jon Huntsman who assured me that he would provide to both Peterson and HAK staffs any memoranda received from Secretary Connally concerning international monetary reform or related subjects."

[10] There is no indication of Kissinger's approval or disapproval of the recommendations and the memoranda at Tabs I and II, not printed, are unsigned.

161. Memorandum From the Assistant Director of the Office of Management and Budget (Schlesinger) to the President's Assistant for International Economic Affairs (Peterson)[1]

Washington, July 20, 1971.

Hidden in the minds of economists are certain presuppositions from the theory of international trade—inclusive of obsolescent elements—which many of us carry about as relics of our graduate student days. The basic premise is the existence of self-equilibrating mechanisms bringing appropriate adjustments of trade and payments—and operating without fail on all nations. (There should be no exception, at least among nations that adhere to the rules of the game.) Flowing from this premise are entrancing visions of adjustments achieved through smoothly-functioning monetary and price mechanisms. The vision is commendable; the departure from reality is substantial; so that the overall impression approaches "the dreamland of equilibrium" as Arthur Burns phrased it in another connection.[2]

The processes of adjustment, whether price-level or exchange rate, are based on the presumed willingness of all major trading nations to adhere to the rules of the game. Earlier theorists did not envision the range of measures available to put off the required day of adjustment. No nation, guilty of deviant behavior, would have a major share of trade or of capital flows. If necessary, enlightened self interest would elicit the appropriate degree of game-plan behavior. A situation such as the present in which one nation, the United States, serves as international banker and upholds a system of relatively fixed exchange rates on which it has virtually no direct influence was not envisaged.

In one sense, the older attitude was enshrined in the Bretton Woods agreement. The notion of "fundamental disequilibrium" was more than a technical concept; it was a moral concept in that it distinguished between proper and improper behavior and pointed directly to those nations which were failing to adhere to the rules of the game. In the Bretton Woods concept no nation was to be permit-

---

[1] Source: Washington National Records Center, Department of the Treasury, Files of Under Secretary Volcker: FRC 56 79 15, CIEP. No classification marking.

[2] Not further identified.

ted to follow beggar-my-neighbor policies. In this concept, use of an undervalued exchange rate to enhance domestic employment and production at the expense of others was clearly proscribed.[3]

How different is our world today in which undervalued exchange rates are employed by major states engrossing a considerable share of international trade. These are clearly beggar-my-neighbor policies in the older conception and (you should try to make it so) in the new. Undervaluing the yen, for example, by a full 20 percent is a beggar-my-neighbor policy. There is no reason that the United States should be willing graciously to tolerate such a condition. While the methods of adjustment today, self-equilibrating or otherwise, are much weaker than hitherto, the case for moral and political force grows so much stronger. I would take it to be primarily your job to harness such moral and political forces.

The impact of undervalued currencies, perennially in a state of "fundamental disequilibrium" without adequate adjustment, underlies many of our trading problems. The undervaluing of foreign currencies works a particular hardship on producers of goods as opposed to producers of services. The existence of palliatives and patch-up mechanisms means that such producers of goods are subject year after year to these hardships, which might as well be described as an unfair degree of competition.

The fundamental point, however, is the following: these hardships ought not to be dealt with and cannot be cured by patch-up adjustments on the trade side. This would lead only to a jerry-built structure of controls and to inefficiencies. One must go to the heart of the matter—i.e., the monetary machinery and adjustments of the structure of exchange rate. This is the kernel of truth in the observation of your economist critics, that too much stress is being given to the decline of American competitiveness and that monetary adjustments should substantially alleviate the problem. By and large this is true. But such adjustments do not come about automatically; there are no self-equilibrating mechanisms. That is what is wrong with their arguments. What is required is a code of behavior or a new set of rules to which the major nations will adhere either voluntarily or per force. To develop such a code and provide vitality for it is your principal task.

---

[3] Although he did not use these terms, Bank of Italy Governor Carli seemed to agree with this approach during a meeting in Rome with an Embassy officer on October 16: "According to Carli, basic cause of current monetary and other economic problems is mercantilist approach adopted by most countries over past decade or more. Other countries have allowed exports lead their economic growth and have enjoyed U.S. deficit while complaining about it. President Nixon's program has exposed this contradiction and has engendered process of adjustment in thinking and policies which not yet completed." (Telegram 6622 from Rome, October 18; National Archives, RG 59, S/S Files: Lot 73 D 153, Box 124, Morning Summaries)

It is a truism that comparative advantage varies with and depends upon the exchange rate. An adequate set of exchange rates would eliminate many of the problems of the producer groups—in autos certainly and in steel to a lesser degree. It would also lead us very close to a balance of payments equilibrium that would be maintainable in the long run.

Under such conditions many problems associated with the so-called "U.S. loss of competitiveness" would disappear. Of course, the standard of living in the United States would grow in ratio to increased efficiency in production, but the pace of efficiency in the U.S. vis-à-vis the other countries would no longer be the type of problem that it is today. From the standpoint of self-esteem and perhaps national power, the problem would remain, but it would not spill over into crippling of the performance of the economic machinery.

This also bears immediately and directly on the structure of U.S. trade. The undervaluing of foreign currencies has fostered an undue dependence upon high-technology products. Rather than cure the disease, we seem ready to embrace the effects of the disease. Since we have steadily in the years after World War II, in effect, subsidized high technology products, it should come as no surprise that these products make a major contribution in the sale of U.S. goods abroad.

However, a goal of achieving balance by the subsidization of high technology products to compensate for the discrimination practiced against our products in general seems less than ideal. Once again, the moral seems clear: elimination of the discrimination practiced through undervalued currencies or quantitative restrictions against U.S. products is the way to proceed. This is economically more efficient and politically more reasonable than reliance upon and subsidy of high-technology products. High-technology products, which others cannot produce and are inclined to accept, are a desirable part of our trade pattern; they should not be viewed as a means of deliverance from undesirable conditions created by persistent exploitation of the U.S. international position as banker and world leader.

What should be done about these matters? It is inefficient and unjust to use tariffs, or general trade barriers, or general adjustments of the exchange rate to deal with the problems created by the violation of the rules of the game by a few of the major trading states who in the present era are consciously exploiting the absence of self-equilibrating mechanisms. To deal with beggar-my-neighbor policies and the maintenance of fundamental disequilibria for exploitational purposes requires a sense of discrimination in the better meaning of that word. Given the structure of the international economy at the present time, the most favored nation clause provides unintended protection for the very nations which are indulging in exploitative practices. We should recognize the problem and deal with it on that basis. A Tariff Commission finding, for example, which hurts all nations is not the most desirable way to proceed—when the fault lies with a single nation which has a drastically undervalued currency. To proceed in that manner is inefficient and unfair. We should deal with the real problem without hurting bystanders. If this requires reexamination of the traditional bromides, so be it. This will require careful examination of the arsenal of tools which can deal specifically with the offenders. And these tools should be employed in such a manner that they deal with the fundamental problems—of monetary and price maladjustments—so that they contribute directly or indirectly to a closer achievement of equilibrium. The importance of avoiding further expanding of a jerry-built structure of trade and capital restraints should be kept in mind.

Jim

---

162.   Telegram From the Department of State to the Embassy in France[1]

Washington, July 26, 1971, 2156Z.

135133. Ref: Paris 12595.[2] Subject: Limited Exchange Rate Flexibility.

Deliver McGrew 9:00 A.M. Tuesday, July 27.

Following is message from Under Secretary Volcker to Giscard d'Estaing in response to his message to U.S. financial authorities on limited flexibility exercise:

"We appreciate your concern and the difficulties to which you alluded. We recognize that pressing for a decision on limited exchange rate flexibility can create problem not only for you, but possibly also for others because of more general speculative pressure that could be induced by discussion of this matter. For that reason, our initiative in

---

[1] Source: National Archives, RG 59, Central Files 1970–73, FN 10. Confidential; Priority; Limdis; Greenback. Drafted in Treasury by Cross and cleared in draft by Volcker; cleared in State by Beigel (EUR/FBX) and approved by L. Kennon (E/IFD/OMA).

[2] Telegram 12595 from Paris transmitted a message from Giscard. (Ibid.)

the Fund Board[3] has not been paralleled by public discussion. Nevertheless, we felt several factors made it desirable to present to the IMF Board more concrete proposals on the flexibility question at this time.

"From past discussion, we were particularly aware of the problems which the French authorities have raised with respect to flexibility, and we felt important elements in our proposal would be more acceptable to French view than other flexibility proposals which have been discussed. Speaking frankly, we hoped we could identify some areas of common ground.

"In particular, wider bands would under our approach not be generalized but would be adopted at the option of an individual IMF member (or group of members) where, for example, that member felt the wider margins would be useful in dealing with disequilibrating movements of mobile capital.

"In the case of the transitional float, our approach envisages the float essentially as a method of changing exchange rates. Thus a finding of fundamental disequilibrium would be required (as with any exchange rate change). A Fund review process is envisaged, and the Fund would be empowered to set conditions on the float or to withdraw authority for a continuation of the float. This should provide protection against too frequent or too long floats.

"These conditions are designed to recognize and encourage fixed parities as the norm, with an explicit international code of good behavior with respect to the use of 'flexible' options.

"On the other hand, we recognize that the width of the band mentioned in our approach—up to 2-1/2 or 3 percent on either side of parity—goes beyond French thinking. Our view is that the short-term capital flow problem is of serious concern and that an option for margins of this size may be needed as one of the tools for dealing with it. We understand, of course, that the EC faces problems in dealing with the question of wider margins which do not confront individual countries. However, the framework we have proposed was designed to avoid any special difficulty for the EC beyond those posed by other proposals for wider margins.

"Throughout the discussions in the Fund and G-10, the U.S. had, as you know, refrained from presenting its views with any precision, in part to see whether a broader consensus might emerge among the G-10 members. However, if progress is to be achieved in September, we felt that this was the last opportunity to table a clear statement of U.S. thinking, prior to the August vacation period, in order to give foreign offi-

---

[3] Reference is to the initiative of July 19; see Document 163.

cials time to reflect on a specific proposal. We have no intention of pressing for agreement within the IMF Board during the present discussions; now that our suggested approach is on the table, we do not intend to take further initiative in the matter until we can see whether there is a possibility of reconciling present differences among the G-10 members in the G-10 meetings to be held in September. Meanwhile, the EC can shape its own views with some clearer indications of the views of its trading partners.

"I would not pretend that the approach we have outlined necessarily represents our final thinking on the subject. Nevertheless, we have been concerned that in the absence of some consensus on appropriate rules of conduct, individual countries, in response to speculative pressures or otherwise, may revert excessively to use of exchange rates as a supplementary tool of domestic policy, as recent events have demonstrated. We have tried to set forth an approach consistent with the general thrust and spirit of the Bretton Woods objectives. We are interested in hearing the reactions of others in the hope that a broad consensus can be reached in September. Certainly, an early resolution of this matter would be in the interest of all."[4]

Rogers

---

[4] In Giscard's absence, the Embassy passed Volcker's message to Deputy Director of Treasury for International Affairs Larosiere on July 27, who said he would bring it to Giscard's urgent attention when he returned to Paris the next day. (Telegram 12952 from Paris, July 28; National Archives, RG 59, Central Files 1970–73, FN 10) Telegram 13154 from Paris, July 30, reported a discussion of Volcker's reply with Giscard on July 30. Giscard seemed to have a more open mind on limited exchange rate flexibility than his advisers. (Ibid.) In a July 22 letter to Sam Cross in the Office of the Assistant Secretary for International Affairs, Treasury Attaché McGrew reported that a key member of Giscard's staff was as rigid as ever on limited exchange rate flexibility and speculated that at decision time Giscard had been unable to convince Pompidou on a compromise. (Washington National Records Center, Department of the Treasury, Files of Under Secretary Volcker: FRC 56 79 15, France)

163.   Telegram From the Department of State to Certain Posts[1]

Washington, July 26, 1971, 2331Z.

135453. Subject: U.S. Views on Limited Exchange Rate Flexibility.

1. There follows, FYI only, a brief summary of U.S. views on limited exchange rate flexibility as presented to IMF Executive Board July 19, 1971. Addressee posts should not take initiative to discuss subject, or to interpret U.S. position if questioned. We wish to maintain low profile, without public discussion.

2. *Wider Margins.* Margins should remain at present one percent under "normal" circumstances. A member of the Fund (or group of members) should have option to utilize margins up to 2-1/2 to 3 percent, temporarily or for longer period, by notifying the Fund and explaining its reasons for using wider margins, presumably in terms of actual or potential disequilibrating mobile capital flows facing the member. Fund would have residual right to challenge a member's use of wider margins.

3. *Transitional Floats.* Members of the Fund should be able to utilize floating rates as a transition between par values established in accordance with the IMF Articles of Agreement. Thus a member would be required to represent that it had an actual or emerging fundamental disequilibrium, and Fund concurrence with this representation would be necessary. During the period of a float, the Fund would review the country's situation and have authority to approve (or not object to) continuation of float or to prescribe conditions on float.

4. U.S. would be prepared to support an amendment of the IMF Articles which includes the points in paras (2) and (3) above. We believe that smaller and more frequent changes in par values than have generally occurred in the past are perfectly feasible under the existing Articles and that it is not necessary to envisage a specific provision in the Articles on this subject for countries that might want to make such changes.

5. In presenting these U.S. views, U.S. Executive Director made clear that he was mentioning number of details and elements of pre-

---

[1]   Source: National Archives, RG 59, Central Files 1970–73, FN 10. Confidential; Limdis; Greenback. Drafted in Treasury by Leddy and cleared by Cross and Volcker; cleared in State by Kennon (E/IFD) and A. Katz (EUR/RPE) and approved by Trezise (E). Sent to Bern, Bonn, Brussels, The Hague, London, Ottawa, Paris, Rome, Stockholm, Tokyo, USOECD, and USEC.

cision in order to give clear idea of main lines of U.S. approach, but in many instances these elements were tentative.[2]

6. Fund document containing text U.S. statement will be pouched when available.[3] Caveat in first paragraph applicable to this document also.

Rogers

---

[2] France was not alone in raising questions about the July 19 U.S. initiative in the IMF (see Document 162). Responding to a German query on U.S. motives for taking its proposals to the IMF Board at this time, transmitted in telegram 9012 from Bonn, Treasury prepared the following guidance to the Financial Attaché, transmitted in telegram 140323 to Bonn, August 3: "throughout the discussion of this subject in the IMF and the G-10, the U.S. had refrained from presenting its views with precision, in part to see whether a broader consensus might emerge among the G-10 members. However, if progress to be achieved in September, we felt that this was the last opportunity to table a clear statement of U.S. thinking, prior to the August vacation period, in order to give foreign officials time to reflect on a specific proposal." (Both in National Archives, RG 59, Central Files 1970–73, FN 10) The German response read in part: "the U.S. initiative, if anything, was proving helpful in pushing the EEC toward a common position since the EEC would not want to have only a U.S. proposal on the table." (Telegram 9516 from Bonn, August 4; ibid.)

[3] Executive Director Dale's July 19 statement was circulated to members of the Volcker Group as VG/WG/71-31 on July 26. (Washington National Records Center, Department of the Treasury, Volcker Group Masters: FRC 56 86 30, VG/WG/71-1–)

---

164.   Editorial Note

The distressed foreign exchange markets of May 1971 had calmed in June and July but as August began were roiled again. President Nixon, on August 2, 1971, met several times with Secretary of the Treasury Connally and Office of Management and Budget Director Shultz. (National Archives, Nixon Presidential Materials, White House Central Files, President's Daily Diary) Haldeman concluded that the result of these meetings was a "huge economic breakthrough," which on the international side would provide for closing the gold window, floating the dollar, and imposing a 10 percent import tax. (*The Haldeman Diaries: Inside the Nixon White House,* pages 335–336) At Treasury, these measures had been anticipated in a contingency paper in May, Document 152.

Tapes of the President's conversations with Connally and Shultz on August 2 corroborate Haldeman's conclusion and portray Connally as the primary architect. The President met with Shultz and Connally at

9:58 a.m. on August 2. The discussion opened on domestic issues, specifically rail and steel strikes. During that discussion Congressional and private sector support for an incomes policy was raised, and the President was sympathetic, saying it was necessary to convince the public the administration was doing something. Shortly before his departure at 10:28 a.m., Shultz turned the discussion to international monetary policy and told Connally they needed, in the next few days, to discuss Connally's proposals, which needed careful consideration. Shultz thought that whether or not to do the "big steps" should be "examined carefully."

Following Shultz' departure Connally stayed on until 11:53 a.m. Haldeman entered late in this segment but was generally silent. Connally outlined forcefully for the President, with great specificity, virtually all the essential elements of the New Economic Policy the President would announce on August 15. On the domestic side Connally set out the wage/price freeze, reinstitution of the investment tax credit, and various expenditure reductions and/or deferrals, with numbers to illustrate exactly what would be the impact on the budget. On the international side he set out suspending convertibility and floating the dollar and the 10 percent import surcharge, which at one point he even portrayed as part of the domestic program, bringing $4 billion annually to the budget. On the international side the only missing element was the 10 percent reduction in foreign assistance expenditures. Connally insisted the domestic and international aspects of the program were linked, with the domestic measures indicating U.S. willingness to take difficult measures to defend the dollar. Connally thought convertibility could not be maintained through the 1972 election and probably would have to be suspended before the end of the year. He urged the President to act soon, to show that he was in charge of events rather than responding to them, and to show that he had the courage to take a position before being forced into it.

As Connally pressed his program, the President warmed to it, despite his reservations about a wage/price freeze and closing the gold window. They discussed alternatives: acting that week, before Congress adjourned on August 4, during the coming week, or during the week after Congress reconvened in September or in November, which would still allow time to lift the wage/price freeze before the election in November 1972. The President was inclined to favor a November/December timeframe, but Connally warned of the increasing danger of leaks if the program were delayed. As Connally prepared to leave, President Nixon was leaning toward acting during August if necessary, possibly as early as Friday of that week. The President said that if consultations abroad were required, Connally should take it up with Kissinger who had channels to Pompidou, Heath, and Brandt.

Under no circumstances was the State Department to be consulted as that agency represented foreign governments. Within the administration, Connally thought Peterson and McCracken were on board for the program, but that Shultz and Burns would have to be convinced.

Following Connally's departure the President reviewed what would become the New Economic Policy with Haldeman. The latter viewed Shultz as a free trader. Nixon said Shultz would oppose the wage/price freeze and thought he was also concerned that during the 1972 Presidential campaign the President would be portrayed as the one who had devalued the dollar.

The tape log reports Connally's return to the Oval Office at 1:24 p.m. (which was not recorded in the Daily Diary), and when the discussion turned to the New Economic Policy, the President was hesitant to go with the international part of the program. He thought closing the gold window could be held in reserve, but the administration could go ahead with the domestic measures to strengthen the dollar. Connally pressed for a linked domestic and international program. He said that gold would have to be done within 3–4 months and that former Federal Reserve Chairman Martin agreed, but if that measure were undertaken alone it would have no concurrent domestic measures for cover. The President agreed, sent Connally off to bring Shultz along, and asked him to report back after 4 p.m. that day. (National Archives, Nixon Presidential Materials, White House Tapes, Recording of Conversation Among President Nixon, Secretary Connally, and others, August 2, 1971, 9:58 a.m.–2:05 p.m., Oval Office, Conversation No. 553–6)

The President met again with Connally on August 4 from 2:19 to 2:55 p.m. in the Oval Office. The two discussed several aspects of the program and the President seemed to be on board. Connally, thumping the desk, advised the President not to defend or explain what was happening, but instead simply to acknowledge there were problems that the administration will solve. He advised the President to create the perception that he was as interested in domestic as foreign affairs, where he already enjoyed high marks, and said that when they returned in September and the President took the strong actions, that perception would change overnight. Connally advised against attempting to change the perception during August, but told the President he would have no choice but to do something before bilateral meetings with the Japanese scheduled for September 9 (see Document 75) and before the Bank/Fund meetings in Washington at the end of September. The President said they needed to run against the tide; they needed to turn the tide. Connally used a stampede analogy: do not run in front of the cattle but alongside the cattle and gradually turn them. He said this "dramatic action" would do it.

Midway through that meeting they were joined by Shultz. The three then discussed several unrelated domestic issues before Nixon outlined for Shultz his discussion with Connally on the new program. The President thought the positives outweighed the negatives and that the day after Congress returned in September would be the best time to announce the program, which would give delegates to the Japanese bilateral meetings and the Bank/Fund meetings time to get instructions. Connally was to work it out. Shultz stated, somewhat in the form of a question, "You have decided to go with this big program, including the gold window and all that? Our task between now and September 8 is to think it through." The President said he needed to have it by August 23 to have time to reflect on it. He was concerned with leaks and said it was to be just between the three of them; Peterson was not to be told. (National Archives, Nixon Presidential Materials, White House Tapes, Recording of Conversation Among President Nixon, Secretary Connally, and Budget Director Shultz, August 4, 1971, 2:19–2:55 p.m., Oval Office, Conversation 554–7)

On Monday, August 9, Council of Economic Advisers Chairman McCracken sent a memorandum to President Nixon summarizing the weakening of the dollar against other currencies and the amounts of dollars that had been taken that day. (Ibid., NSC Files, Agency Files, Box 218, Council on International Economic Policy) McCracken thought the August 6 report of the Reuss Subcommittee on International Exchange and Payments of the Joint Economic Committee, which concluded that the dollar was overvalued and that unless exchange rates were realigned the United States would unilaterally have to suspend the dollar's convertibility to gold and establish new parities, contributed to the flurry of activity that day. The Reuss report is *Action Now To Strengthen the U.S. Dollar: Report of the Subcommittee on International Exchange and Payments of the Joint Economic Committee, Congress of the United States, Together with Minority Views* (Washington, U.S. Government Printing Office, 1971).

An August 7 Treasury press release regarding the Reuss report stated it did not reflect a "wide body of Congressional opinion" and there were no plans for discussions on exchange rate realignments at the IMF or elsewhere. The press release then noted that the U.S. approach to these matters had recently been discussed by Secretary Connally in Munich (on May 28; see Document 155) and claimed that the administration was constantly reviewing measures to strengthen the balance of payments and encourage a healthy, non-inflationary domestic economy. The press release (and the Subcommittee report) is with paper VG/Uncl. INFO/71-40 in the Washington National Records Center, Department of the Treasury, Volcker Group Masters: FRC 56 86 30, VG/Uncl. INFO/71-1-71-.

165.   Editorial Note

Foreign central banks continued to take large dollar inflows during the week of August 9, 1971. In that atmosphere Office of Management and Budget Director George Shultz met with the President from 4:45 to 6:31 p.m. on Wednesday, August 11, in the President's office in the Executive Office Building. The tape of that conversation is of poor quality and many parts of the conversation are inaudible, but it is clear that the focus of the discussion was on the implementation of what the President would announce on August 15 as the New Economic Policy. The President acknowledged that "Arthur [Burns] is very nervous about this." Shultz said that if the United States took this aggressive act against its trading partners, it was to stabilize a situation all agreed needing correction, and that the United States would have to follow up with constructive proposals.

Shultz counseled the President that if he were to close the gold window and took no other action, he might not get the needed change in the exchange rate if others intervened to maintain the value of their currencies. Shultz told the President his instinct to equate a 10 percent border tax with a devaluation was exactly right, that other nations did the same thing. Shultz advised that it was better to get the desired change through a devaluation than through an import tax and suggested an immediate closing of the gold window and a temporary import tax, i.e., a devaluation, followed by negotiations. As the conversation concluded, the President seemed to lean toward undertaking some of the program as early as Friday, August 13, but also thought the program might be timed to coincide with the return of Congress in September. (National Archives, Nixon Presidential Materials, White House Tapes, Recording of Conversation Between President Nixon and Budget Director Shultz, August 11, 1971, 4:45–6:31 p.m., Executive Office Building, Conversation 272–17)

At noon on August 12 the President phoned Secretary Connally in San Antonio. Connally reported he would be leaving Texas by plane at noon to return to Washington. He informed the President that Volcker had all the information and they could expect a bad day on Friday. He thought "we are losing the initiative." The President and Connally exchanged views on doing the program piecemeal, perhaps as early as that evening or Friday morning, or doing the entire program at one time, the approach Connally preferred. Connally did not want to leave the impression they had acted "in haste" and "were unprepared." The President invited Connally to come directly to his office upon his arrival in Washington. (Ibid., Recording of Telephone Conversation Between

President Nixon and Secretary Connally, August 12, 1971, 12:01–12:12 p.m., Conversation 7–112)

The President met with Shultz in his office at the Executive Office Building during the afternoon of August 12 and requested that Haldeman join them. Shultz reviewed the scale of dollar conversions since August 2 and thought the U.S. reserve and negotiating position were weakening. The President thought they should not panic. He said they were not ready to go ahead with the entire package, but that if all the key players went to Camp David they could be prepared to act by Monday. He thought September 7 was the right day to do the whole package, including the budget provisions, but that Connally could announce in a low-key way now that the gold window was closed due to speculation. He thought the wage/price freeze could also be done immediately and then on September 7 he could announce the remainder of the program. Haldeman recapped: close the window and slap on the freeze now and come back in 3 weeks with the rest of the package. The President thought most of his advisers would concur in the program but that Burns and Volcker, who was "obsessed" with international things, would have difficulty with its international aspects and would have to be brought along. Shultz should try to sell the program to Burns, who had to understand that there were only two or three choices, and the President wanted to know which one Burns would go along with. (Ibid., Recording of Conversation Among President Nixon, Budget Director Shultz, and Haldeman, August 12, 1971, 3:11–4:20 p.m., Executive Office Building, Conversation 273–7)

Connally and Shultz met with the President from 5:30 to 7 p.m. on August 12 in the Executive Office Building. The President set out three policy options. First, to prevent speculation Connally could make a low key, non-prime-time announcement that the gold window was temporarily closed and that the administration was prepared to discuss with other nations now a "new, better, more stable system." Connally could also say the administration would take action on the budget front when Congress returned, but remain silent on the wage/price freeze. The second option was to announce now the wage/price freeze and intentions to present a legislative package when Congress returned. International aspects could be negotiated as needed, in lieu of a unilateral closing of the gold window. The third option was to close the gold window and announce the wage/price freeze, which were the only actions required to deal with the current crisis, and the legislative package could be prepared for September 7. The downside of that approach, the President said to Connally, was that it missed his "big, bold" approach, but, he mused, could we do the whole program now, tonight? Tomorrow night? Let's go to Camp David tomorrow and announce the whole program on Monday, he continued.

Connally thought the President needed to convince the American people that he had thought through the entire program. If it were done piecemeal, the public would speculate on "what comes next." Ideally the entire package would be announced on September 7, he said, but due to international developments they could not wait that long. If they just did the gold window at that time, it would give the impression the President was "forced to do it" because of what had happened in Europe during the last 2 weeks, that he did not know what to do, and that it took until September 7 to figure it out. To date, Connally went on, there was no public speculation on a comprehensive package, and if the President did it all now it would give the impression he knew what was happening and was on top of it; "you picked the time."

Shultz said Burns thought they should do the domestic program now, including the border tax, and see if that would stabilize the dollar. Connally argued that if they were to do the domestic program now, they should go ahead and close the gold window as well, rather than wait until the following week, a point the President thought was well taken. The President proposed, and Shultz and Connally concurred, that they meet at Camp David over the weekend "to set the whole thing up." The only participants were to be the three of them, plus "Arthur and McCracken and Peterson," and as for staff "the fewer the better." Connally suggested that at Camp David all should be encouraged to participate in the discussion, without their letting on that the decisions had already been made. Shultz said that at Camp David it would be necessary to set up sub-meetings to develop the specifics of various parts of the program. The President agreed and said he had pretty much decided what he wanted to do; following perhaps a 3-hour meeting beginning at 3 p.m. on Friday to develop an agreement, they would break into groups and reconvene Saturday at 3 p.m., which would give him time to prepare his speech. Shultz suggested giving the speech on Sunday night to prevent speculation on Monday, a point the President took, provided they could get it ready. The conversation concluded with the three discussing the essential modalities for secrecy surrounding the Camp David meeting. (Ibid., Recording of Conversation Among President Nixon, Secretary Connally, and Budget Director Shultz, August 12, 1971, 5:30–7 p.m., Executive Office Building, Conversation 273–20)

Shortly after the conversation the President phoned Connally and reported on his discussions with Shultz on the border tax and how it would give them negotiating leverage, which the President character-ized as the program's best element politically. He said he wanted to be sure Connally understood the President's signal that Connally should take the lead in the general discussion Friday afternoon. A clearly elat-ed President told Connally the economic program would be like the

"China thing," totally unexpected coming at that particular time. (Ibid., Recording of Telephone Conversation Between President Nixon and Secretary Connally, August 12, 1971, 7:22–7:26 p.m., Executive Office Building, Conversation 273–24)

---

166.   Memorandum From the Acting Assistant Secretary of State for Economic Affairs (Katz) to Secretary of State Rogers[1]

Washington, August 13, 1971.

FINANCIAL UNEASE

The Setting

The dollar is under severe pressure in major financial markets in Europe and Japan. By pressure I refer to the fact that the dollar is worth less in terms of such currencies as the German mark, Dutch guilder and Canadian dollar, which are floating, and that enormous amounts of dollars are being purchased by central banks in other financial centers in order to comply with the IMF rules of maintaining parity relationships between their currencies and the dollar.

In this atmosphere impressive sums are moving speculatively, betting that the dollar will be devalued. Large companies are hedging in order not to lose money should this occur. Countries like Japan, which hold large amounts of dollars as a proportion of total foreign reserves, are uncertain as to what to do since a devaluation of the dollar could be costly to them by reducing the real value of these reserves.

This uncertainty in Japan and elsewhere makes countries reluctant to reach agreements with us on other economic and political issues until they can see the overall situation more clearly.

There are many reasons for the weakness of the dollar. These include our persistent and growing balance-of-payments deficits; the fact that our trade account has moved into deficit, with every indication that this deficit will grow; our gold stock is diminishing; respectable voices in the financial community and in academia are asserting with

---

[1] Source: National Archives, RG 59, Central Files 1970–73, FN 10. Confidential; Nodis. Drafted by Deputy Assistant Secretary Weintraub.

some vehemence that the dollar is overvalued and that this situation should be corrected; there was a report last week by a subcommittee of the Joint Economic Committee, chaired by Congressman Henry Reuss, which advocated the devaluation of the dollar.[2] That our economy is sluggish and our inflation continuing does not help.

Most observers expect us to do something, and foreign governments and private traders are now behaving under the assumption that we will do something; this heightens the speculative fever.

What Can We Do?

The classic remedies for persistent balance-of-payments deficits are either devaluation of one's currency and/or slowing down internal economic activity. A devaluation makes imports more expensive and exports more lucrative, thus helping to shift output from internal to external markets. Deflation, by reducing demand pressure, works in much the same way. Because of the central role of the dollar as the currency to which most other currencies are pegged, we have always felt that devaluation of the dollar was not a proper course. We have tried deflation over the past several years but it has not worked. We have had the worst of all worlds, a sluggish economy with more inflation than desirable, and a growing balance-of-payments deficit. It is this demonstration that past policy has not accomplished its balance-of-payments function that heightens the present unease.

The President, for political as well as technical reasons, may be reluctant to devalue the dollar, despite the fact that we are getting such advice from many in Europe and at home. The dollar could be devalued by raising the price of gold (which would require Congressional approval) only if other countries consented not to similarly raise the price of gold in relation to their currencies; that is, the relationships among currencies would thus be altered. We also could devalue by closing the facility which permits foreign central banks to convert their dollar holdings into gold at $35 an ounce, if other countries then permitted the dollar to float vis-à-vis their currencies until it found a new devalued level, or if we then devalued outright. This is essentially what Congressman Reuss advocated. Since other countries would have to consent to letting the dollar depreciate with respect to their currencies, a dollar devaluation would require some advance negotiation among the major countries.

If other major currencies revalued upwards in relation to the dollar, such as Switzerland and Austria recently did, and which Germany and Canada and the Netherlands are in fact doing through their present

---

[2] See Document 164.

floats, this in effect means devaluation of the dollar. The one important currency that all agree is now undervalued is the Japanese yen. One major problem with revaluations by others is that we leave the initiative to them, and in the case of the Japanese are put in the position of demandeur.

In addition, changes in currency relationships operate effectively only with time lags so that the impact on our balance of payments might take some time, perhaps even a year or so, to work itself out.

Another set of possible correctives would be to change only the prices of imports and exports, which in effect would be a devaluation of the dollar only on trade account, rather than across-the-board, to include as well such things as tourism and capital transfers, in which our accounts also are in deficit. Under the GATT, countries in balance-of-payments difficulties are authorized to impose quotas on their imports. However, this requires complicated administrative machinery to institute. Quotas also operate through controls rather than through the marketplace. For these reasons, in recent years countries which have taken trade actions have preferred not to use quotas.

One trade technique now under intensive examination, and which Wilbur Mills and the Williams Commission have advocated, is to impose a surcharge on all imports of an amount sufficient to have a significant effect in diminishing imports. The surcharge would raise the price of imports, and thus operate here the way a devaluation would. The trade impact could be even more powerful if we were also to give a subsidy to exports as an initiative to encourage these. I use the word "could" since other countries could take action to offset the effect of an export subsidy. The combination of import surcharges/export subsidies could have a powerful trade effect if it were large enough, say of about 15 percent. The budgetary cost of the export subsidies (say 15% of about $40 billion of exports, or $6 billion a year) could be met mostly by the extra revenue raised from the import surcharges. The two need not go together, and indeed there is much more international experience with import surcharges, but the two in tandem on all imports and exports are more powerful than either alone. We expect that were the United States to impose a surcharge this would be understood by most important foreign countries despite its lack of explicit GATT sanction; an export subsidy would be more controversial. A subsidy/surcharge system also could have a stimulative domestic psychological impact.

I will not go into the complex detail here on how surcharges or subsidies might work administratively. We would have to make clear that these trade actions were intended to be temporary until the situation was corrected, and that the rate of surcharge/subsidy would decline over time. These assurances would not be easy to accomplish legislatively. The initial rate would have to be sufficiently large to convince the world that it would work. We think such trade action on our part would be credible only if it were accompanied by further domestic measures to cope with inflation; these might include some policy on prices and wages.

Action only on trade account would maintain what others would consider to be an overvalued dollar for capital movements, and this certainly would lead to criticism by others that it permits U.S. investors to buy up foreign enterprises cheaply.

Conclusion

The choices open to the U.S. at present thus fall into one or a combination of three overall categories.

The first is that we do nothing and ride out the present storm. I doubt that this is feasible since everybody now anticipates that we must do something; and if the Executive does not act, it is probable that the Congress will act, such as by imposing import quotas on a haphazard basis. Much more significant than this, however, is the danger that the speculation against the dollar will continue and perhaps accelerate, and the Europeans and Japan could force us to take action by demanding that we exchange the dollars they are getting for other reserve assets, such as our declining gold stock.

The second choice is to alter exchange rate relationships, either by devaluation of the dollar, or upward revaluation by others (particularly the yen), or most likely a combination of these. Any effective U.S. devaluation would require consent of others.

The third choice is some partial action, such as dealing primarily with the trade account. (In the past we have taken partial actions to limit capital outflow, such as our foreign direct investment controls, and theoretically capital controls could be further tightened. We doubt that the President would wish to do this.) Many would interpret trade measures as a precursor to dollar devaluation.

We are urgently proceeding with analysis of these options and we know that other agencies are doing the same. We are in touch with them.[3]

---

[3] On August 13 Volcker sent the following note to Connally: "I just got a call from Jack Irwin urgently requesting that State be involved in any decision-making in the international monetary area. He had been talking with Rogers, who is at home. I simply told him I would not be making this decision but would pass it on to you but also said I understood his concern." (Washington National Records Center, Department of the Treasury, Records of Secretary Shultz: FRC 56 80 1, Economic Game Plan Background, Camp David 8/13–15/71)

Recommendation

If you have not already done so, you should speak with George Shultz about this subject (a) to reflect our great interest in making an input as the choices are examined; and (b) to make certain that our expertise on how one would implement any scheme internationally is brought into play sufficiently early no matter what choice is made.[4]

---

[4] Although there is no indication if Rogers approved or disapproved the recommendation, he wrote in the margin, "This was done," and initialed. The date of August 17 is stamped below the Secretary's initials.

---

167. Information Memorandum From Robert Hormats of the National Security Council Staff to the President's Assistant for National Security Affairs (Kissinger)[1]

Washington, August 13, 1971.

SUBJECT

International Monetary Crisis

Although I recognize that the subject of this memorandum is far from your major areas of interest, you might wish to be kept abreast of the current international monetary crisis, since it does have major foreign policy implications for the U.S.

The Problem

Throughout 1971 there has been an erosion of European confidence in the stability of the dollar. This has worsened since May, as it became apparent that the U.S. inflation was not being contained, that wage settlements in this country were extremely high, and that the U.S. balance of payments deficit was worsening. The latter is extremely important. Under the present system central banks of other governments purchase dollars when an over-supply of dollars causes the value of the dollar to drop below a given point, i.e. Britain will, if the value of the dollar falls below a specified point, buy up excess dollars and thereby raise the price of the dollar to within one percent of its established parity vis-à-vis the Pound. Thus European central banks have been taking in large

---

[1] Source: National Archives, Nixon Presidential Materials, NSC Files, Subject Files, Box 376, President's Economic Program. Confidential. Initialed by Kissinger. A copy was sent to Sonnenfeldt.

amounts of dollars in order to keep the value of the dollar from falling vis-à-vis their own currencies. However, because Pounds, Marks, etc. must be spent by the central banks in order to purchase these dollars, the money supply of the major European countries has increased significantly, and severe inflationary pressures have resulted.

The crisis of this spring came when on May 3 and 4 alone, about $1 billion flowed into Germany and greater amounts were expected to follow. The Germans were thus forced to close their foreign exchange market and, on May 10 they floated the D-Mark., i.e. the Bundesbank did *not* purchase dollars when the price of the dollar fell and thereby allowed the value of the dollar to fall still further vis-à-vis the value of the Mark. Thus, because individuals wished to rid themselves of dollars and purchase Marks, the value of the Mark increased vis-à-vis the dollar and is now approximately seven percent above its value at the close of April. Other European countries have been forced to hold large amounts of unwanted dollars which they are legally entitled to demand that the U.S. redeem in gold.

The Present Crisis

Last week, with no end to the U.S. inflationary and balance of payments problem in sight, there was another rush by speculators to sell dollars for European currencies. Then, on Saturday, Henry Reuss, Chairman of the Joint Economic Committee on Exchange and Payments, released a report which:

—suggested that the dollar was overvalued and should be allowed to "float" downward in value;
—criticized the Treasury for doing too little to correct the balance of payments deficit (which could amount to $7 or $8 billion this year as compared to $3 billion last year).

On Monday, August 9—with confidence in the stability of the dollar further eroded by this publication—the sale of dollars increased and the value of dollars decreased (i. e., holders of dollars used them to purchase Pounds, D-Marks, Swiss francs, etc. because they felt these currencies would either be revalued or the dollar would be devalued in the near future). The dollar fell to its lowest point vis-à-vis D-Marks since World War II. On the same day the Treasury stated that the Reuss report did not represent Congressional views on the subject and pointed out that the reduction in the balance of payments deficit depends not on modified exchange rates but on a healthy and non-inflationary domestic economy.

On Wednesday, August 11, speculation against the dollar abated somewhat—one reason being that the central banks of France and Switzerland instituted measures to prevent domestic banks from purchasing speculative dollars. However, on Thursday over $1 billion were again forced on European central banks.

There is little likelihood that the situation will work itself out without either a revaluation of European currencies (which is the most probable course of action for the Europeans, given the present crisis); a devaluation of the dollar; or U.S. measures to restrict the imports of foreign goods to this country and encourage U. S. exports (which will take legislation). There will also probably be strong efforts on the part of the Europeans to restrict the amounts of dollars held by their central banks and to apply other stringent measures against the dollar.

168.   Editorial Note

From 3:15 to 7 p.m. on August 13, 1971, President Nixon met with a number of his economic advisers and three members of his White House staff at Camp David to detail the New Economic Policy the President had agreed to in his meetings with Shultz and Connally on August 2 and August 12 (see Documents 164 and 165) and would announce during a 9 p.m. television address on Sunday, August 15. According to the President's Daily Diary for August 13, Connally, McCracken, Burns, Volcker, Stein, Peter Peterson, Haldeman, Ehrlichman, Shultz, and Safire attended the Camp David meeting. (National Archives, Nixon Presidential Materials, White House Central Files, President's Daily Diary) William Safire recalled that the President directed all participants in the meetings to sign a guest book, according to which Caspar Weinberger, Arnold Weber (OMB), Kenneth Dam, Michael Bradfield (Treasury), and Larry Higby (Haldeman's assistant) also attended the August 13 meeting. (Safire, *Before the Fall: An Inside View of the Pre-Watergate White House,* page 511) The meeting continued intermittently, with a few changes in attendees, until 11:30 a.m. on August 15.

No comprehensive options papers for this meeting were found, although some materials were assembled at the Treasury Department for Connally's use. (Washington National Records Center, Department of the Treasury, Records of Secretary Shultz: FRC 56 80 1, Economic Game Plan Background, Camp David 8/13–15/71). During an April 8, 1998, interview with the editor, Stein confirmed that there were no options papers for the Camp David meeting, but added that some aspects of the program had been worked on earlier in the year. Stein said that in response to Congressional interest in a wage price freeze, some thinking on modalities had been done at the Council of Economic Advisers, and he thought the

Office of Management and Budget had worked on the issue as well. At Treasury, considerable thought had also been given to the international dimensions. See, for example, Documents 152 and 153.

The Department of State and the National Security Council were not represented at the Camp David meeting and, according to memoranda to Rogers and Kissinger (Documents 166 and 167), they were unaware the meeting was taking place when it began. Kissinger's memoir corroborates this: "a decision of major foreign policy importance had been taken about which neither the Secretary of State nor the national security adviser had been consulted." (*White House Years*, page 954)

Haldeman reported that the President decided to go ahead with the NEP the following week after meeting with Connally late in the afternoon on August 12. The Camp David meeting was then set up, in the greatest secrecy, around the Economic Troika, to begin on the afternoon of August 13. (*The Haldeman Diaries: Inside the Nixon White House*, page 340) Haldeman took detailed handwritten notes of the key NEP planning meeting which lasted for nearly 4 hours that afternoon, as well as more limited notes later in the weekend. (National Archives, Nixon Presidential Materials, White House Special Files, Haldeman Notes) Haldeman also prepared full diary entries for the weekend, which were later included as part of a compact disc publication, *The Haldeman Diaries: Inside the Nixon White House, the Complete Multimedia Edition*, pages 340–346. The President's leadership in formulating the execution of the NEP, Connally's role, especially on the NEP's international aspects, and Burns' lonely and unsuccessful attempt to keep the gold window open are among the highlights in Haldeman's notes. Haldeman's handwritten notes and diary also reveal that on August 14 President Nixon said Secretary Rogers should be informed and asked whether he agreed with a 10 percent reduction in foreign aid. Apparently Deputy Under Secretary of State Samuels was away from Washington, as Haldeman's subsequent notes indicate Rogers should call him back.

The President's August 15 address to the nation announcing the NEP is in *Public Papers of the Presidents of the United States: Richard M. Nixon, 1971*, pages 886–891. On the domestic side the NEP imposed a regime of wage and price controls and established the administrative machinery for their monitoring and enforcement; on the international side the NEP imposed a 10 percent import surtax on all dutiable imports from most-favored-nation countries, suspended the dollar's convertibility to gold, and reduced foreign assistance expenditures by 10 percent. During the April 8, 1998, interview, Stein indicated he thought it was unclear to attendees at the Camp David meeting if closing the gold window implied a floating of the dollar. He said that at Camp David there was no discussion of what outcome was sought in the international economic policy arena and that in the absence of representatives from the State Department and the National Security Council there was little consideration of international political implications.

169.   Telegram From the Department of State to the Embassy in Germany[1]

Washington, August 16, 1971, 0245Z.

149439. Please deliver soonest following personal message from the President to His Excellency Willy Brandt:

"Dear Mr. Chancellor:

I am tonight announcing a comprehensive program to curb inflation, increase employment, restore strength and confidence in the United States dollar, and improve the international monetary system. This major action is necessary to preserve confidence in the dollar and to maintain an international monetary system which will serve the world's needs. It was our responsibility to act and we have done so.

I am imposing a 90-day freeze on wages and prices in the United States. I am cutting certain taxes to stimulate consumption and employment and I am sharply curtailing US Government expenditures. I am also levying temporary surcharge on all dutiable imports not already subject to quantitative limitations by the United States, and I have directed that the convertibility of the dollar into gold or other reserve assets be suspended.

I recognize that these actions will be of concern to Germany as they are vital to us.

What we need now is an early agreement on improvements in the international monetary and trading system. I have asked Treasury Secretary Connally immediately to get in touch with your Finance Minister to consult on how we can bring about these improvements.

I am sure you will find that what we have done will contribute to economic expansion in a world at peace.

I look forward to continuing to work with you on these matters of such concern to both of our countries as well as to the rest of the world. Sincerely, Richard Nixon."

FYI. Under Secretary of Treasury Volcker is proceeding immediately tonight to London and hopes to have a meeting tomorrow at 1500

---

[1] Source: National Archives, Nixon Presidential Materials, NSC Files, Country Files–Europe, Box 685, Germany, Volume IX 4-8/71. Confidential; Exdis. Drafted and approved by U. Alexis Johnson. Identical cables with this message from President Nixon to certain other heads of government were also sent on the evening of August 15. (Ibid.) The originals of the typed messages sent to the Department of State for transmission are in the National Archives, RG 59, Central Files 1970–73, E 1 US. Circular telegram 149446 to all diplomatic and consular posts, August 16, transmitted a summary of Under Secretary Volcker's briefing of the Washington diplomatic corps at 10 p.m. on August 15. (Ibid.) The full transcript of Volcker's briefing was sent to all posts in telegram 156086, August 25. (Ibid.)

London time with financial authorities of France, Italy, Germany, Canada, and Japan.[2] Arrangements are being made through Treasury–Ministry of Finance channels.

Rogers

---

[2] See Document 170.

---

170. **Memorandum of Conversation**[1]

London, August 16, 1971, 4 p.m.

PARTICIPANTS

U.S.:

Under Secretary Volcker
Governor Daane
Sam Y. Cross

France:

Mr. Pierre-Brossolette, Ministry of Finance
Mr. Clappier, Bank of France

Germany:

Dr. Schoellhorn, Ministry of Economics
Dr. Emminger, Bundesbank
Dr. Hankel, Ministry of Economics
Dr. Neubert, German Embassy

Italy:

Dr. Ossola, Bank of Italy

Japan:

Mr. Hara, Embassy of Japan
Mr. Iyami, Bank of Japan

U. K.:

Mr. Neale, HMTreasury
Mr. Morse, Bank of England
Mr. Kirbyshire, Bank of England

---

[1] Source: Washington National Records Center, Department of the Treasury, Files of Under Secretary Volcker: FRC 56 79 15, France. Confidential. Drafted on August 23 by Cross and approved by Volcker. The meeting was held at Wychwood House.

SUBJECT

President Nixon's New Economic Program

Mr. Volcker said he had suggested the meeting because he thought it would be a good idea to get together promptly, to explain the reasoning behind the President's new economic program and hear any initial reactions of other participants. He had not come for the purpose of negotiations and one question to be considered was what kind of negotiating group would be appropriate when it was time for negotiations. The U.S. did not presently have a fixed view on that question.

Mr. Volcker explained the reasoning behind the President's program. Everyone was familiar with the domestic background in the U.S. of excessive unemployment and an expansion which was proceeding but not with great speed. There was considerable pessimism about the strength of the expansion and bad psychology had developed about the inflation problem. Our progress on both the inflation and unemployment problems had been disappointing, and some measures which seemed to help on one of those problems hurt on the other. On top of this domestic situation, there was a difficult external problem. There had been a persistent erosion in the U.S. external position since the mid-1960's and this had been aggravated by two factors. First, our trade position had moved into considerable deficit in the second quarter, and even if the second quarter figures exaggerated the difficulty, the trade position was far from satisfactory. Secondly, protectionist pressures had increased in the past two years, and some had pointed to the difficult external situation as an excuse and justification for protectionist moves. We had been conscious of all these problems for some time but our concern had intensified in recent months. Thought had been given to various measures, particularly on the domestic side, for some time. The situation over the past couple of weeks had brought several of these problems into a single focus. The President had decided not to act in a piecemeal fashion dealing with each of these various problems but to adopt a comprehensive and integrated program. The most controversial measure was the convertibility decision. That decision was taken with the full knowledge of the President that one could not fully predict all the results and implications for the future. The President came to the conviction that now was the time to face the convertibility problem since if it were not faced now, it would have to be faced at another and perhaps more difficult time.

Mr. Volcker said he was impressed by the headlines in two adjoining articles which he had seen in this morning's *Times*, which expressed very clearly the U.S. situation as he saw it. The first was that "it was time for the U.S. to face facts," and the second was that "the U.S. needs growth and competitiveness." He could not improve on those two headlines as a theme for his view of the present situation.

Discussing the components of the program, Mr. Volcker said that the President had decided to go all the way on wage-price policy and establish a freeze. Even though the freeze was only for ninety days, it would have a psychological shock effect while the follow-on program was set up. The President had taken a few selective revenue measures which would spur the economy both now and in the long run. All three of the proposed tax cuts required legislative action, but the prospects for that action were good. On the expenditure side, the President had taken some measures which were politically very difficult in deferring his revenue sharing and welfare programs. These were his two prize domestic programs. While the tax and expenditure actions balanced in amount, the stimulation from the tax cuts would be greater than the drag from the expenditure changes.

On the external side, the Administration had felt that the strong domestic measures included in the new program alone would have stopped the speculation of the past couple of weeks. But the President had looked beyond the next few weeks or months and had decided to go ahead with the convertibility decision, which he felt would release some of the inhibitions and free the world's hands to deal with matters of exchange rates and the monetary system, without such concern about speculation. It had been very difficult even to consider possible measures for reform of the monetary system when the possibilities of speculation were so great, and our move should remove some of these inhibitions.

On the surcharge, the Trade Expansion Act had been used for the authority since the President wanted to act by executive action rather than legislation. While it would not be difficult to get Congress to authorize a surcharge, it would be very difficult to get authority to end the surcharge when the time came.

On the international monetary system, all were conscious of the desire to restore a sustainable stable system. The U.S. had not spelled out any program in the President's message or elsewhere. The U.S., at this stage, had no program which it was going to spring on anyone. The background material explaining our new program said that some changes in exchange rates might take place and might be helpful to stable functioning of the system. From the U.S. point of view, after years of erosion, we wanted a fundamental strengthening of our position. We had balance-of-payments deficits for a number of years and a declining trade position for a number of years, and we would not be satisfied without a reform that could repair the erosion which had taken place in the U.S. position over the years. We did not want a short-run solution that would deal with the immediate market situation but not lead to long-term improvement. We want to restore stability to the system for a period of years. If we did not get a lasting solution, the problems would simply reappear in a month or six months or a year.

The President had instructed us to put clearly in our explanatory documents that there would be no change in the price of gold. We were aware that in the very immediate market sense, a change in the price of gold might temporarily restore exchange market equilibrium. But we were firmly opposed to that solution for three reasons, any one of which was sufficient to assure our opposition to the move: first, there was a political inhibition to such action in that some legislative action would be required. Second, even if there were no political problem we were opposed because what might look like a quick and easy solution would leave one vulnerable to the same problems in three months or six months or a year. Third, the world had been on a course of evolution which had gradually reduced the importance of gold in the system over the years and we were not going to move in the opposite direction of moving toward rebuilding a system based on gold. Although some argue that changing the price of gold is a clean and quick solution which would stabilize the system over night, that view did not prevail with us.

Mr. Volcker said investment restraints would remain in effect but their future disposition would be under review. Certain of the programs were crumbling. They were adopted as emergency measures and not expected to be sustained for a long period. Bills recently passed in Congress would decimate certain parts of the program. We don't like such restraints philosophically, and we would be reviewing this whole question.

Dr. Schoellhorn asked whether there had been any decisions on monetary policy.

Mr. Volcker said the discount rate had not even been discussed at Camp David. Since the President was announcing a freeze, he would not want to flaunt this by raising interest rates.

Governor Daane said that Chairman Burns fully supported the new program. On monetary policy the money supply had been growing more rapidly than we would like but the latest figures indicated progress in getting it under better control.

Dr. Emminger said he was impressed at the comprehensiveness of the program. He was concerned about reopening foreign exchange markets on a credible basis. The markets could not be reopened at present parities without large movements of dollars and the credibility of the fixed parity system would be in doubt. Also markets could not be kept closed for a long time. Although Germany was not tied to a parity at this time, the Japanese had apparently taken in $700 million today and the Swiss had taken in a large amount last week. How could those countries reopen on the old parity system without floods of dollars? Would it be possible to reopen the markets without changes in parities? Could we envisage these parity changes would come about in the next few days?

Mr. Neale asked what sort of changes were going to be required if the U.S. was to be free of its deficits? He agreed with the importance of building a lasting system but said this was a big agenda which went beyond the three or four days which markets could be kept closed.

Mr. Volcker said he had not come for the purpose of trying to negotiate changes in parities. We had worded our statement as mildly as possible to avoid prejudicing any more than necessary the position of other countries. It would not be credible for the U.S. to say there would be no changes in parity. In the end our view is that after years of deficits, the U.S. is entitled to run surpluses.[2] Our aim is to establish the conditions to run such surpluses. Apart from that basic proposition we were not going to say that one parity should change by this amount and another parity by that amount. The basic dilemma was with the entire system. We must repair the erosion that had taken place over a period of years in the U.S. position. Beyond that we did not want to prejudice what changes must be made. This quickly got into the question of what was the proper negotiating forum. He had talked to Schweitzer before leaving Washington. We made clear we did not want a new Bretton Woods conference. One potential group for negotiation was the Group of Ten. This had some defect in that there was no LDC participation and it was a little bit large but it certainly was a possible forum. He did not think the IMF Board was a possible forum since the Executive Directors in many cases did not have sufficient authority of their governments and there was probably too much LDC representation for this kind of negotiation. We would like to keep the IMF in the center as much as possible and perhaps one possibility would be a special committee of governors. The U.S. had no fixed view at this time on the question of the negotiating forum, but would like to know what others thought. Perhaps some ad hoc arrangements would be best.

Mr. Volcker said that if the others present thought it was a good idea Secretary Connally would be receptive to inviting their Ministers to go to the U.S. and to talk these matters over during the coming weekend (August 21–22). Certainly we did not say that the problem could necessarily be resolved by the half dozen main countries in brief informal discussions but if there was a strong consensus that such a meeting would be useful, Secretary Connally would be prepared to host it.

Dr. Schoellhorn thanked Mr. Volcker for the elaboration of the U.S. views. He could give only a personal reaction since there had been only a few hours to think about the U.S. moves. On the wage price freeze, he thought the U.S. might find that 90 days may not be sufficient. The experience in Europe had been that it takes a longer time. He noted that

---

[2] See Document 76, which sets out the U.S. balance-of-payments objectives adopted in September.

monetary policy had apparently not been revised in a way which would increase U.S. interest rates and impede the flow of funds. Perhaps the most serious measure announced was the 10 percent surcharge. Germany had had a revaluation in excess of 7 percent and now an additional 10 percent resulting from the U.S. surcharge added up to a large amount. Germany already had strong pressures from German exporters for some form of export program, and these pressures would now become irresistible. Also it would be most difficult to find any willingness of countries to revalue their currencies as long as the U.S. 10 percent surcharge existed. And there might not be any positive proposal about what to do with the monetary system as long as there was the surcharge. The position of the dollar as a key currency was now unclear. When markets were reopened, the U.S. program might stop speculation but there were many dollars floating around and there could be many unquiet weeks. He wondered what would be decided in Washington at the September IMF meeting.

Mr. Volcker asked whether any markets were open at the present time.

Mr. Emminger said no markets were open in Europe. However, it would not be possible to keep the German markets closed for more than about three days unless there were going to be some major changes to announce.

Dr. Ossola said that it might be possible to keep the Italian market closed for about four days.

Mr. Volcker said there was no intention to keep the New York market closed for any extended period, but if one of the governments represented at the meeting felt that a day or two closing of the New York market would be essential to their decision making, we would ask that trading in New York cease for a day or two.

Dr. Ossola said that the urgent problem in Italy was tourism. Italy had a free market for bank notes and banks were buying dollars at 600 lire to $1. He asked whether Mr. Volcker was content to let the market set that bank note rate. Mr. Volcker indicated that he did not see the Italian bank note rate as a particular problem.

Mr. Morse said he was surprised at the timetable. Mr. Volcker seemed to envisage a period of weeks or months before a return to fixed parity. He thought the danger was that if there was no agreement within a week or so there would be a situation of general floating of all currencies, from which it would be very difficult to get back to a fixed parity system.

Mr. Volcker said there was a credibility problem which began with the devaluation of sterling and other currency changes. Markets could no longer be convinced that exchange rates would not be changed. In some cases letting the markets tell us what would be a credible rate might not be entirely bad. If all the questions could be resolved soon that was fine, but we did not want to be jumping from one financial crisis to another. We should not come out with an announcement that we had created a system as follows, and then six months later have it collapse.

Mr. Kirbyshire said it would be difficult for the markets to show what the proper rates were since there were many dollars floating around.

Mr. Volcker said there were tremendous problems of the monetary system and these questions were not going to be decided in a short-run time. A sustainable system implied a sizable change in the U.S. position. The U.S. position had been both weak and eroding.

Mr. Morse asked whether there was a pattern of exchange rate changes which would be sufficient in Volcker's mind to make the system a credible one within a short period of time so that the U.S. would reopen the gold window, or was there no such pattern.

Mr. Volcker said he had no little piece of paper in his pocket about what rate changes were needed. He recognized that it was conceivable that credibility in the immediate market might be temporarily restored by small revaluations by certain countries and by the U.S. domestic program, but would it make sense to restore convertibility in the same way we had it. The U.S. needed to reverse the long-term erosion in its position. Other countries might have other issues which they felt should also be considered, and these also should be on the table.

Dr. Emminger said this resolution of all these problems might take a year or two.

Mr. Volcker said that the basic condition was the system would have to be sustainable.

Dr. Emminger asked what the U.S. would do to maintain the parity of the dollar. Would we maintain parity in the same way as most other countries, e.g., market intervention.

Mr. Volcker said we would not do so immediately. We would be in the same position as Germany or Canada already was in.

Dr. Emminger reiterated the importance of the 10 percent surcharge. He asked how long was "temporary" and whether there was a connection between the surtax and the restoration of a credible system.

Mr. Volcker said the elimination of the surcharge did not depend on the restoration of the system. We needed to restore a strong U.S. position and the surcharge would go off as soon as we made the judgment that our position was the one we were seeking.

Dr. Schoellhorn said every government would be reluctant to revalue because of the surcharge. Even though the overall percentage of total

German exports covered might not be so large, the surcharge would be very important in particular industries and regions in Germany.

Mr. Volcker said the problem of particular industries and regions was precisely the one the U.S. had had in its problems with protectionist pressures and had to be resisted aggressively. The surcharge was one action the U.S. could take unilaterally toward getting a strong position.

Dr. Emminger said there was a danger that we would be building the surcharge permanently into the system.

Mr. Volcker agreed that was a danger if the surcharge lasted too long. The President wanted to utilize his present authority to apply the surtax rather than seek new legislative authority in order to reduce the danger that the surcharge would be kept on too long.

Dr. Ossola said he shared Dr. Schoellhorn's views about the surcharge. He could understand the closing of the gold window as a measure, and he could understand the application of the surcharge as a measure, but he could not understand both since they seemed contradictory and countries might not move on the exchange rate.

Mr. Volcker said it was a sort of simultaneous equation. It was not clear that some countries would want to move on the exchange rate.

Mr. Morse said Mr. Volcker said the surcharge would be removed when the U.S. got a strong position and asked what that meant.

Mr. Volcker said the U.S. should have a period of surplus. We have had an extended period of basic deficits and we needed a period of surpluses. In addition there were questions of financing the defense shield and some trading arrangements and obstacles around the world which must be dealt with as well. One example was the agricultural arrangements in Europe which caused problems for the U.S. Agriculture was not the only problem. There were many outstanding issues of that sort on which we would like to work and see progress in developing the framework within which the U.S. could develop a strong balance of payments.

Dr. Schoellhorn said our governments did not know what was required to get rid of the surcharge. He asked whether there was any relationship to the non-tariff barrier discussions which were going on.

Mr. Volcker said it would not depend on those discussions.

Governor Daane said we were not looking at adjustment just for the short run but one that was sustainable for a long period of time.

Dr. Schoellhorn asked what we would do if others introduced surcharges.

Mr. Volcker said that we had been told for many years that the U.S. had a balance-of-payments emergency. We had a long period of deficits. No other country was in that position.

Dr. Emminger said all countries were interested in the restoration of strength of the dollar. They had found out that difficulty for the dollar meant difficulty for their own currencies and they understood that the monetary system could only be based on a common position. He was concerned about the immediate problem of how to reopen exchange markets on a credible basis that would not require first one country and then another to take measures to protect itself. We were all in a position of interdependence. The dollar position must be credible and the position of other currencies must be credible.

Mr. Neale referred to Mr. Volcker's discussion of a possible meeting of ministers in Washington. He said there should not be a meeting until we knew where we were going. There had to be preparations. It would be tragic if a meeting were held and nothing happened.

Mr. Volcker said the meeting he had suggested would not be designed to settle all problems necessarily though if problems could be solved that would be fine. He did not agree with Mr. Neale that we could not have a small and informal meeting of the kind he had envisaged. If we couldn't even meet on these problems because we think the problems are too difficult, we may never get them resolved. We in the U.S. have thought that one advantage of biting the bullet and suspending convertibility was that it would eliminate some of the inhibition and we would be freer to talk about the problems and try to solve them.

Mr. Morse said from the technical viewpoint he would expect to open the market on Thursday unless there was clearly something to expect very soon. If markets were reopened now, there was no chance that the old parity would be credible. He thought there was a grand prize in getting quick agreement to avoid that situation. He hoped the U.S. would want a quick solution.

Mr. Volcker said we would want a quick solution consistent with the premise within which we operate of needing a world-wide framework within which a sufficient strengthening of the U.S. position can take place.

Mr. Morse said the U.S. needed an effective and sizable devaluation relative to other currencies.

Mr. Volcker said he should make clear he had no authority to negotiate exchange rate changes and no intention of trying to do so.

Dr. Schoellhorn said he was in the same position.

Mr. Neale said the representatives other than the U.S. may want to talk among themselves about these matters.

Mr. Volcker said they were welcome to remain in the meeting room as long as they wished for any further discussion.

Mr. Iyami said the Tokyo market had been the only one open on Monday and the banks had bought $700 million. However, there was no inflow from abroad and the $700 million was purchased from local people and banks.

Mr. Morse said no answer could be given to Mr. Volcker's offer of a meeting in Washington until after the Monetary Committee meeting on Tuesday.

Mr. Volcker said he did not have in mind a grand and formal ministerial meeting with fixed agenda and large staff. It might be helpful in permitting Secretary Connally to express his views directly and get the views of others directly. If this would help resolve the issue that would be excellent, but we should not make any promise that such a meeting would resolve the issues.

(The U.S. representatives left and the others remained for further discussion.)

S.Y. Cross

171.   Memorandum of Conversation[1]

Paris, August 17, 1971.

PARTICIPANTS

U.S.:

Under Secretary Volcker
Governor Daane
Mr. C. Petrow

France:

Valery Giscard d'Estaing, Minister of Economics and Finance

SUBJECT

President Nixon's New Economic Program

Minister Giscard d'Estaing wondered whether the U.S. would completely refrain from intervention in the exchange markets. Mr. Volcker said normally we would not intervene, although there might be exceptional circumstances which he could not anticipate which might require intervention. Giscard asked what the difference was between the present dollar float and the Canadian float. Mr. Volcker said that in the legal sense our position was the same as the Canadian and the German, but the legal similarity did not mean very much. Basically, the U.S. had not changed the parity of the dollar. Others would make that decision; we could not. We did not assume that there would be no changes in parities. We simply didn't know in which direction the dollar would move. Giscard asked whether we would request an exception from our obli-

---

[1] Source: Washington National Records Center, Department of the Treasury, Files of Under Secretary Volcker 1969–1974: FRC 56 79 15, France. Confidential. Drafted by Petrow on August 26 and approved by Volcker. A similar, telegraphic version of the memorandum of conversation was transmitted to the Department of State in telegram 14016 from Paris, August 18. (National Archives, RG 59, Central Files 1970–73, E 1 US) Paris was Volcker's only stop after the meeting in London (see Document 170). Italian Treasury Minister Ferrari Aggradi found his bypassing of Rome "not acceptable" in view of Italy's "friendly" approach to U.S. monetary issues and the facts that Italy at that time chaired the EC Council and Aggradi would preside over the EC meeting in Brussels on August 19 to decide the EC's stance on the New Economic Program. (Telegram 5208 from Rome, August 18; ibid., POL 7 US/VOLCKER) Perhaps in response to these concerns, following the WP-3 and G-10 Deputies meetings in Paris September 2–4 (see footnote 3, Document 173 and Document 174), Volcker continued on to Rome for a "friendly, frank exchange" with Italian officials who "emphasized the feeling that size of adjustment U.S. wants of other countries so large and issues (including political ones of burden sharing, etc.) so complex that reasonable time-span must be allowed for process to work out." (Telegram 5601 from Rome, September 6; ibid., FN 10 9/1/71) Daane briefed Netherlands official Zijlstra by phone from Paris, and Zijlstra told Ambassador Middendorf he was quite satisfied with the briefing he received. (Ibid., FN 17 US 1/1/71)

gation under the IMF to limit changes in parity to 1 percent. Mr. Volcker replied that the legal situation was difficult. The question is, who would be failing to fulfill his obligations—the U.S. or the other countries? To repeat, we don't intend to intervene in the exchange market and, in that sense, our position is the same as the Canadians' and the Germans'.

Giscard said that Canadians and the Germans had said that they were floating for a limited time and that the U.S. had not said this. Mr. Volcker on the contrary replied that, we had said that our action was for a limited time. Mr. Volcker then briefly reviewed the philosophy outlined in the President's three-part program. He noted that the decision on suspending convertibility of the dollar was not in the original scenario but had been added because of the way the exchange markets were behaving in August. He said the U.S. appreciated what the French had been trying to do during that period. They had been very helpful in their efforts to deal with the problem of speculation. Other countries had been more nervous, however, so we had had to go ahead. In fact, if the Germans hadn't begun selling dollars this summer, he wouldn't be here now. As for how long it would last, the U.S. first must move decisively toward a strong external position after years of weakness and reestablish confidence in the dollar in some lasting form. Before we could terminate our measures, we had to be satisfied that the adjustment in the position of the dollar (i.e., the restoration of balance-of-payments surpluses) was assured. The burden of adjustment would lie less on Europe than on Canada and Japan.

Giscard referred to our decisions to suspend convertibility of the dollar into gold. Mr. Volcker reminded him that this included other assets as well, including SDR's. Giscard asked why SDR's were included. Mr. Volcker replied that we had to protect ourselves against total obligations against our gold stock. Giscard said we would not be able to adhere to this position very long. We would soon have to be discussing further SDR allocation. Mr. Volcker repeated that the question of how long the dollar would continue floating depended on the actions of the other countries.

Giscard asked whether we still adhered to the basic principle of the Bretton Woods system, namely, fixed parities. Mr. Volcker said, broadly speaking, "yes," but the United States must reestablish a strong external position. Moreover, the system itself needed improvement. It had been subject to recurrent crises. We should take advantage of our present opportunity to reshape the system so that it could serve for the next twenty-five years. He was not advocating an international monetary conference at this time and not saying that we would continue the suspension of convertibility until the system had been reshaped. The ending of the suspension of convertibility would depend instead on the recovery of the dollar's strength. Mr. Volcker said we had no plans to propose for reshaping the system. We wanted to hear the views of the other countries so that we could reach a consensus.

Giscard said that, because of our measures, daily life in the monetary system would be different now. Sixty to sixty-five percent of the world's currency transactions would now be floating. He feared that we were in effect moving from a system of fixed parities to one of floating parities. What made the U.S. think that we could go back to a system of parities? Nations would accept the new situation and take whatever measures, such as border taxes, as were necessary to protect themselves. France was concerned that everything that the U.S. had achieved over the past twenty-five years in terms of monetary stability and free convertibility would be lost. Mr. Volcker replied that we equally recognized this danger, but there was an even greater danger of growing protectionism in the United States if we had not acted to prevent further erosion of our external position. The President felt that this latter danger was great enough to justify the risks inherent in the measures he had taken.

Giscard said that this was not the vein in which Mr. Volcker had spoken to the group in London yesterday. Yesterday he had said "we've made our move, now it is your turn", and had shown no awareness of the dangers involved. Mr. Volcker replied that, if that was what Giscard had been told, then he had obviously failed to make himself clear. We were certainly aware of the dangers but we didn't want to patch up another temporary settlement with a 4–5 percent change in parities. We wanted a long-term solution.

Giscard asked what would happen at next month's IMF meeting. Mr. Volcker replied that we were ready at the appropriate time to go back to a system of fixed rates but with some changes, perhaps along the lines of our proposals on wider bands and temporary floats. He considered our proposal on floats more conservative than the Belgian proposal and more in line with French thinking. We had proposed that there be no float unless there was a fundamental disequilibrium, but our proposals were based on a strong presumption of fixed parities. We obviously could not settle everything at next month's IMF meeting, but we ought to be thinking hard at that meeting about the direction in which we wanted to go.

Giscard said the French would have to consider what position they should take. It was a real problem. They didn't like to let the market fix exchange rates. The German experience was an example of how bad this could be. The mark had floated much higher than the Germans had expected. Appreciation had not been 3, 4 or 5 percent but 8 to 10 percent. Now the Germans were unhappy. Mr. Volcker replied that they should have thought of that before they acted. If we are to return to fixed parities, we must convince the market that they are sustainable.

Giscard said France had warned the Germans they were headed down a dangerous path. He said France feared the current trend toward floating rates would lead to protectionism. If there were no clear determination that the U.S. was prepared, not necessarily to restore the old system in every detail, but at least to retain the principle of fixed parities, then there was a danger that we would go back to the chaos of the 1930's. Mr. Volcker said the President was aware of the unpredictable elements in this program. Before going back to fixed parities, however, we have a sizable adjustment to make in our external position. We can't solve the problem by little adjustments.

Giscard said that one consequence of our measure would be a reluctance by central banks to hold dollars in the future. This was how the U.S. had financed its deficit during the last ten years. It would have to find a new way of doing this now. Mr. Volcker replied that we didn't want to finance our deficits, we wanted to eliminate them. Giscard said that would take 10 to 18 months and we had to find a way to finance them in the meantime. Mr. Volcker said we wouldn't have to wait that long. Once people were sure that the tide had turned there would be a reflux of short-term dollars. Giscard said the market was likely to push the dollar down farther than we wanted. Mr. Volcker said it might well go down, and maybe it needed to go down. No one could say now how much it would go down. However, the U.S. must have an adjustment. He did not think this adjustment would have a major effect on Europe.

Giscard said jokingly that France had anticipated our program and was selling only luxury goods to the United States. Mr. Volcker said the major effect would be on Japan and Canada. Giscard added "and the Germans." Mr. Volcker replied that German exports did not loom so large in the total picture except for automobiles.

Returning to the U.S. proposals to the IMF Directors,[2] Giscard said we had spoken of temporary floats to prepare a change of parity. In the case of the dollar float, were we preparing to move to a new parity or to return to the old one? Mr. Volcker replied that the parity of the dollar was normally expressed in terms of gold. We did not intend changing that parity but that wasn't the parity that counted. The one that counts is the parity between the dollar and the other currencies. As for the dollar-gold ratio, we believe that small changes in that parity would be destabilizing. They brought about temporary solutions but they created the expectation of further changes the next time the dollar came under pressure and thus provoked speculation. Moreover, the monetary system had been gradually moving off gold. The U.S. wanted this evolution to continue. Possibly the present dependence on the reserve currencies also needed to change.

[2] Reference is to the July 19 proposals on wider margins and transitional floats; see Documents 162 and 163.

This was something the U.S. was prepared to look at. Perhaps SDR's provided a possible future base for the system. For these reasons there was no prospect of a change in the gold-dollar ratio.

Giscard replied that, be that as it may, we could not escape questions. He also asked about the IMF obligation of other countries to support the dollar. As a result of our measures, they would be faced by a need to buy immense quantities of dollars to meet this obligation. Mr. Volcker replied that the quantities might not be immense. We were aware of the problem and it had not been easy for us to make the decisions that we had. What other countries would now do he could not say.

Giscard replied that nonetheless, we must think of the problems of people who have believed for years that they must respect the rules and who now realize that, if they continue to respect the rules, they will be creating enormous problems for themselves. Something will have to be done. Mr. Volcker said we understood this, but Giscard should remember that our action in suspending convertibility was tied to a domestic program. That program was our contribution to restoring the international stability of the dollar. It was the instability of the dollar that had been causing the influx problem that France had been fighting for the past month or so.

Giscard observed that, in the present circumstances, a Group of Ten meeting would probably be useless since there was no possibility of taking common decisions at the present moment. Mr. Volcker said we were looking ahead to an extended period of negotiations on possible changes in the system. He asked what Giscard thought of trying to form a new group, perhaps under IMF auspices, possibly with some LDC representation, though not too much to make it unmanageable, rather than sticking to the Group of Ten.

Secondly, he asked whether Giscard thought it would be useful for him and some of the other Finance Ministers to go to Washington to meet with Secretary Connally. Obviously it was impossible to settle everything in an afternoon, but would such a meeting be useful?

Giscard replied that it was too early to decide either of these questions. The dust had to settle first. The European governments had to devote themselves to practical decisions in the days immediately ahead. He thought it better to let things take their natural shape. Mr. Volcker said this was all right so long as the shape did not turn out to be a bad one. Giscard said he thought there was no danger of this, at least not right away. Another reason for not convening the Group of Ten was that the Europeans were particularly concerned about the import surcharge, which was not a matter for the Group of Ten.

Giscard also mentioned that in the last few weeks the French had been concerned about the mounting pressures on the dollar and had taken measures to prevent the situation from being aggravated. Mr. Volcker replied that the U.S. was very conscious of this. Giscard promised that France would continue to cooperate in the coming days and would refrain from comments which might aggravate the situation.

S.Y. Cross

---

172.   Editorial Note

During the week following announcement of the New Economic Policy on August 15, 1971, most foreign exchange markets were closed. Beginning on August 17, over the signature of Executive Secretary Theodore L. Eliot, Jr., the Department of State sent daily memoranda to Henry Kissinger summarizing foreign reactions to the President's program, and Hormats, in turn, summarized developments as he transmitted the memoranda to Kissinger. In general, media reaction was highly critical but official reaction centered more on how to cope with the new situation; criticism was directed more at the 10 percent import surcharge than at suspension of the dollar's convertibility to gold. The European Community, at its Ministerial meeting on August 19, was unable to agree on a common approach, but decided that when foreign exchange markets reopened on Monday, August 23, each member would adopt its own approach. (National Archives, Nixon Presidential Materials, NSC Files, Subject Files, Box 376, President's Economic Program)

On August 18 Canadian Acting Prime Minister Mitchell Sharp, following consultations with Prime Minister Trudeau, wrote a letter to President Nixon endorsing the U.S. program's objectives for improving the international monetary system, but expressing grave concern over the import surcharge, which he thought would be very damaging to the Canadian economy and the American economy in turn. A Canadian Ministerial delegation, headed by Minister of Finance Benson, was coming to Washington to discuss the program with Secretary Connally. (Ibid.) Mexican President Echeverria also wrote President Nixon that he was sending a delegation to Washington to seek exemption from the surcharge. Echeverria's letter has not been found but is summarized in an August 18 memorandum from Executive Secretary Eliot to Kissinger regarding foreign reactions to the President's program. (Ibid.)

On Friday, August 20, Ambassador to Luxembourg Kingdon Gould, Jr., cabled that he would be seeing the Prime Minister on Saturday and thought that in view of the inconclusive and uncoordinated EC reaction to the U.S. program the United States had an opportunity to make an input to the "eventual nature and direction" of the Community's response. Ambassador Gould asked for guidance on how the administration would like the Community to respond in both the short and long run. (Telegram 467 from Luxembourg, August 20; ibid., RG 59, Central Files 1970–73, FN 10 8/18/71) Telegram 153872 to Luxembourg, August 21, informed Gould the United States was not yet ready to put forward specific ideas on how the international monetary system might develop, and repeated the theme that in view of the "years of erosion" in the U.S. international position, substantial modifications in the international monetary and trading systems, which were interrelated, were required. Citing Connally's response to a question on the August 19 *Today Show*, the cable noted that "other countries are going to have to recognize that so long as we bear the burden of providing the defense shield for the free world that one way or another they're going to have to help pay for it." (Ibid., FN 10 8/21/71)

In an August 21 memorandum to Kissinger summarizing foreign reactions to the NEP, Hormats reported on an August 19 request by the Canadian delegation for an exemption for Canada from the surcharge. Connally reportedly told the Canadians the United States thought it important to have no exemptions, but "for diplomatic reasons did not flatly turn down the request and assured the Canadians that we would consider their problem and that further discussions could take place." Hormats concluded his memorandum by raising the danger of unleashing protectionist forces abroad if others chose to defend themselves against the U.S. actions. He noted that IMF Managing Director Schweitzer had proposed drawing up an integrated plan on exchange rates, the surcharge, temporary widening of margins, gold prices, and restoration of convertibility. Hormats agreed with the Treasury Department "that a large meeting at this time would probably not be productive" but continued that "if Treasury argues that an IMF paper would be unacceptable, since it might lean toward the European position, Treasury should come up with a similar document which lays out in broad terms what we expect of others and where we hope to come out of this exercise." In sum, Hormats concluded, the United States needed to give its trading partners "a clear picture of what we expect from them" and develop an integrated negotiating scenario lest "protectionist forces get out of hand with the serious foreign policy and economic costs which will result." (Ibid., Nixon Presidential Materials, NSC Files, Subject Files, Box 376, President's Economic Program)

173.   Memorandum From Deane R. Hinton of the Council on
        International Economic Policy Staff to the President's
        Assistant for International Economic Affairs (Peterson)[1]

Washington, September 1, 1971.

SUBJECT

   Volcker Group

Pete:

   The Volcker Group met for three hours August 31 for a lively, but
as usual, quite inconclusive exchange of views. Paul obviously enjoyed
himself playing games with the rest of us.

   We began by discussing the August 28 paper on balance of payments equilibrium.[2] The main issue seemed to be whether this paper, or
something like it, should be given to the Deputies of the Group of 10. It
was agreed that there was a case for quantifying what we were after—
apparently, Paul has previously only said "substantial improvement"—
but it was also agreed that this paper would have to be rewritten before
it could be passed out. As usual, Paul was left with a free hand to do
what he thinks best, but it is possible that he will use the OECD
Working Party 3 paper (attachment 1), and comment orally to the effect
that the OECD estimates are very conservative.[3]

   There was some discussion of the agenda (attachment 2)[4] and what
kind of answers Paul would give. If you have questions I could, perhaps, answer. He stressed that they would not discuss exchange rates
leaving that for the Ministers at the September 15–16 meeting.[5] Paul
agreed that the issue of exchange rate realignments, *at the best*, would
not be resolved before the IMF meetings at the end of September.

---

   [1] Source: National Archives, Nixon Presidential Materials, White House Central
Files, FG Federal Government Organizations, Treasury 1/1/71–2/29/72, Box 2.
Confidential. A copy was sent to Richard Allen (without attachments).
   [2] Not found, but see Document 76 which is presumably the successor of the August
28 paper.
   [3] Not printed. The August 30 WP-3 paper is entitled "Brief Résumé of Material
Relevant to Assessment of Present International Payments Situation." The OECD WP-3
and the G-10 Deputies met in Paris September 2–4. According to a September 12 memorandum from Eliot to Kissinger on "Foreign Reactions to the President's Economic
Program—Afternoon September 10," during the previous week's G-10 Deputies meeting
Volcker estimated the United States needed a $13 billion balance-of-payments adjustment,
primarily in the trade account. (National Archives, RG 59, Central Files 1970–73, E 1 US
9/1/71)
   [4] Not printed.
   [5] See Document 175.

Paul noted that both the OECD and U.S. ideas of equilibrium call for the LDC's to bear a significant part of the adjustment burden!

At one point, he introduced into the discussion some estimates of what we are after in "non-monetary areas" recognizing, however, that a large enough monetary adjustment would reduce the pressure to deal with these problems. His list, as I understood it, follows:

Multilateral defense offset in Europe—$1–1.5 billion;
Canadian trade practices, including auto agreement—$100 million;
Japanese QR's—$250 million;
Dismantling the Common Agricultural Policy—$250 million;
Eliminating European agricultural subsidies in third markets—$150 million.

There were some pointed remarks about the unlikelihood of accomplishing much on these in negotiations with the Europeans, at least in the short run.

The discussion then turned to the August 30 options paper[6] and we went round and round with almost everyone but Paul arguing that these were not the kinds of options that should be put to the President. At the very minimum, we urged that Option 1 be developed to spell out the main elements of a possible new international monetary system, that is, to examine such questions as:

Should the dollar remain a reserve currency and, if not, what should take its place?—i.e., how consolidate a new reserve unit?
What is the future role of gold?
What kind of convertibility for the dollar should be envisaged?
Should there not be presumptive rules for exchange rate changes, particularly on the up side?
How else to get more rate flexibility?
How to provide sufficient liquidity, assuming the U.S. runs a large Current Account surplus?

Ezra Solomon, Nat Samuels, and Governor Daane also talked about the danger of the surcharge being frozen in the system. Paul just smiled.

Finally, you might find of interest two papers done in the Fed on reserve asset consolidation (attached),[7] as well as the attached IMF paper on the future position of the U.S. dollar.[8]

---

[6] Not found.

[7] Not printed. A paper entitled "Consolidation of Outstanding Official Dollar Balances," forwarded to Under Secretary Volcker by Ralph Bryant on January 2, 1973, and circulated to the Volcker Group Alternates as VGA/73-1 on January 4 appears to be a successor to these papers. (Washington National Records Center, Department of the Treasury, Volcker Group Masters: FRC 56 86 30, VGA/73-1–VGA/73-25)

[8] Not printed. The IMF paper, EBS/71/232, August 27, entitled "Some Thoughts on the Future Position of the U.S. Dollar in the International Monetary System," was circulated to members of the Volcker Group as VG/LIM/71-28 on August 31. (Ibid., VG/LIM/71-1–)

174. Memorandum From Robert Hormats of the National Security Council Staff to the President's Assistant for National Security Affairs (Kissinger)[1]

Washington, September 6, 1971.

SUBJECT

Talking Points for CIEP Meeting—Tuesday, September 7, at 8.30 a.m. in the Cabinet Room

There are several issues which might be raised at the meeting on which you may wish to comment. *On the first three issues your comments are particularly vital, since those primarily responsible for future plans regarding the New Economic Policy may have lost sight of, or given insufficient attention to, important foreign policy considerations.*[2]

Foreign Response to New Economic Policy

Recent Events: The Deputy Finance Ministers of the Group of Ten agreed on Friday[3] in Paris that their Finance Ministers should consider a general realignment of current parities at the forthcoming Ministerial Meeting in London on September 15 and 16. However, no agreement was reached on what sort of realignments are necessary. There was strong Japanese and European pressure for the United States to devalue the dollar outright—by raising the price of gold—in exchange for revaluation of the yen and major European currencies. Paul Volcker, the U.S. Representative, opposed this and indicated that the Administration is still planning to return to the $35 an ounce gold price, which was suspended on August 15. Volcker also added that the United States "did not have any particular plan" for solving the present crisis and believed the current phase was one of "consultation, not negotiation".

The Common Market is locked in a stalemate between France—which opposes any revaluation of the franc because it feels its weak competitive position cannot stand it, and which continues to demand

---

[1] Source: National Archives, Nixon Presidential Materials, NSC Files, Agency Files, Box 218, Council on International Economic Policy. Confidential. Some of the points in this memorandum were summarized in a multi-topic, September 7 memorandum from Jeanne Davis to Kissinger suggesting topics to discuss at a luncheon with Secretary Connally that day. (Ibid., Agency Files, Box 289, Treasury, Volume II, 1971) Hormats prepared another memorandum for Kissinger, September 11, containing many of the same points for Kissinger's September 14 breakfast meeting with Peterson. (Ibid., Box 218, Council on International Economic Policy)

[2] The President met with the Council from 8:33 to 10:35 a.m. (Ibid., White House Central Files, President's Daily Diary) For Peterson's report on the meeting, see Document 79.

[3] September 3.

that the dollar be devalued vis-à-vis gold (thereby increasing the value of French gold reserves)—and Germany, which wants the Common Market to float against the dollar. The Europeans also claim that the large amounts of U. S. capital outflow, not improper currency values, are the primary reason for the dollar crisis, and cite the fact that the U.S. had a $1.7 billion surplus with Europe last year.

The present problems, as indicated in previous memos,[4] are:

—Our major trading partners have not been able to agree on coordinated measures to meet the present crisis. This raises the possibility that one country or trade group such as the EEC might take actions which we consider acceptable, but we would be unable to remove the surcharge if another country such as Japan failed to take appropriate measures, thus making the EEC draw back and strengthening the hands of its domestic protectionist forces in Europe.

The longer the surcharge is in effect, the greater the possibility that our trading partners will institute export subsidies, capital controls on the inflow of dollars, or restrictions on the imports of U.S. products. In doing so they would strengthen their bargaining position in future negotiations and improve their economic positions vis-à-vis the U.S.; however, once instituted, such measures are politically difficult to remove, and will lead to a more restrictive trading world rather than the freer trading world which the President desires and which is most certainly in our interest. By the same token, the longer the U.S. surcharge remains in effect the stronger will be the vested interests in this country in retaining it, and the more difficult politically it will be for the President to remove.

With this in mind, it is important that you raise the following questions:

—*By not providing our major trading partners with a clear picture of what we expect from them (which the Europeans see as lack of leadership and evidence that the U.S. does not know what it wants), do we not run a major risk of their not being able to agree to reforms which are acceptable to us, and thereby prolonging imposition of the surcharge and raising the risk that our trading partners will institute measures which restrict trade and capital, or subsidize their own exports?*

—*Is there at present a scenario for an integrating set of negotiations with our major trading partners should the forthcoming Group of Ten meeting in London and the IMF meetings in Washington at the end of September in Washington produce no results?* If September passes without an agreement as to how to proceed, isn't it possible that the situation will deteriorate into chaos?

---

[4] See Document 172.

Leverage Value of the Surcharge

Since the President's speech, a number of USG spokesmen have indicated that we would remove the surcharge only after a major exchange revaluation by our trading partners *plus* a removal of trade barriers and a more "equitable" arrangement for sharing the burden of U.S. troops stationed abroad. It is, however, doubtful that the surcharge is a strong enough or appropriate lever for securing all of these goals. Moreover, as Vice Chairman Emminger of the Bundesbank has recently indicated, this may prove to be an "indigestible negotiating fare", at least within the time span within which one would wish to move from the present provisional state of affairs. And continued use of the surcharge runs the risks discussed above.

One way of using the surcharge would be to regard it as a lever *only* for securing appropriate currency revaluations; subsequently, we would use the lack of gold convertibility as a lever for developing a new international monetary system, and negotiate away restrictions on U.S. exports by our trading partners by holding out the possibility of the removal of our own restrictions on imports as a carrot.

Should this issue be raised, you should *question whether or not we are over-estimating the power of the surcharge to secure our major trade and monetary objectives.*

New International Monetary System

There is considerable danger that the President will not be given a full range of choice in making the decisions on what sort of monetary system we wish for the future. There has been a "conventional wisdom" that a system of relatively fixed exchange rates allows for greater exchange rate predictability for traders and investors. Floating rates have been regarded purely as a transitional device for use in emergency situations in order to determine the "market rate of exchange" for currencies, and have been relatively unused.

Recently, however, we have learned more about floating rates:

—Germany and Canada have been floating their currencies for the last several months. They have neither fluctuated irradically nor spiraled upward in value as some had predicted. In addition, they have posed no major problems for traders, who, with the help of banks which insure traders against changes in currency value, have shown little sign of discontent with the system.

—We have become painfully aware of the costs of maintaining fixed exchange rates which are out of line with the market values of currencies:

(a) An overvalued dollar has meant that the U.S. exports have fallen far below imports, which has had serious effects on U.S. employment, and has caused an increase in U.S. investment abroad—which also has a serious effect on jobs in this country.

(b) Speculators, including large U.S. corporations, predicting large changes in the price of major currencies, have sold dollars and purchased such currencies as the franc, the yen and the mark, thereby causing the number of dollars held by foreign countries to expand absolutely and relative to the small ($13.5 billion) amount of reserves held by the U.S.

(c) There has been increased pressure from at home and abroad to curtail military spending abroad, reduce troop levels, and decrease foreign assistance and security assistance because of the "dollar drain".

—The American public has become increasingly aware of the fact that floating exchange rates, by decreasing the value of the dollar vis-à-vis other currencies, can be used to increase U.S. exports and cut down the flow of foreign imports into the U.S.

—The present fixed rate system, which had been praised for its ability to insure stability—so that foreign investment and industrial decisions can be made with a minimum of risk—has, by the inherent instability and inviability of fixed rates—actually caused more instability and greater risk in the monetary system than has floating rates—which when they change do so more gradually than "fixed" rates.

—Monetary crises have aggravated political relationships between Europe, Japan, and the U.S. and have caused major domestic political crisis in our trading partners. Floating exchange rates would, by making exchange rate changes smaller and more frequent, eliminate most major political crises relating to monetary problems (i.e., in many Latin American countries a devaluation causes a major Governmental crisis; in Brazil, which devalues by small amounts monthly, it is regarded as routine. Britain suffers a Government crisis when it devalues. Germany, before the float, suffered similar crises when it revalued.).

Although you may not wish to advocate floating rates, *you should indicate that there are strong arguments for a floating exchange rate and greater flexibility which you believe the President wants to hear before making any decision. And that you would like to have a look at whatever paper goes forward to the President, since there are important foreign policy implications to whatever we do.*

[Omitted here is the concluding section concerning the forthcoming report of the Williams Commission on International Trade and Investment.]

175. Telegram From the Embassy in the United Kingdom to the Department of State[1]

London, September 17, 1971, 1124Z.

8639. From Under Secretary Volcker to Treasury for Petty. Subject: Meeting of Ministers and Governors of the Group of Ten.

1. Other G-10 Ministers generally followed lines foreshadowed by Deputies meeting and EC Finance Ministers meeting.[2] With varying emphasis, they suggested that (A) United States adjustment goal too ambitious particularly in short time, (B) realignment should include U.S. action to change dollar parity in terms of gold, (C) U.S. import surcharge should be eliminated as part of multilateral realignment, (D) effort should be made to return to fixed parities as soon as possible, to avoid tendencies to build in restrictions on trade and investments if present situation continues long time. Some countries, notably Italy (speaking as Chairman of Six Finance Ministers) and Japan, sought improvements in monetary system by greater reliance on Special Drawing Rights.

2. Secretary Connally, speaking from notes, stated U.S. position in statement covered in full in separate message.[3]

3. On procedural problems, Schweitzer listed number of main issues and proposed division of issues into three groups—immediate, intermediate, and longer run. First group concerned realignment, price of currencies in gold, wider margins and abolition of U.S. surcharge. Intermediate group included B/P adjustment measures other than

---

[1] Source: National Archives, RG 59, Central Files 1970–73, FN 10. Confidential; Limdis; Greenback. Repeated to Bern, Bonn, The Hague, Ottawa, Paris, Rome, Stockholm, Tokyo, USEC, and USOECD.

[2] The G-10 Ministers met in London September 15–16. The G-10 Deputies met in Paris on September 3; see footnote 3, Document 173, and Document 174. According to a September 11 memorandum from Hormats to Kissinger, on September 10 the Executive Commission of the European Community proposed a U.S. devaluation of the dollar as part of an international currency realignment in the context of a system of fixed parities, albeit with wider margins. The Commission also recommended prompt lifting of the U.S. 10 percent import surcharge, an expanded role for SDRs, and the phasing out of national currencies as sources of international liquidity. Hormats noted that the EC Finance Ministers would consider the Commission's recommendations on September 13 prior to the G-10 Ministerial meeting. (National Archives, Nixon Presidential Materials, NSC Files, Agency Files, Box 218, Council on International Economic Policy)

[3] Not found. The full text of Secretary Connally's statement, along with those of other Ministers, Chairman of the G-10 Deputies Ossola, and IMF Managing Director Schweitzer were circulated to the Volcker Group as VG/LIM/71-35 on September 20. (Washington National Records Center, Department of the Treasury, Volcker Group Masters: FRC 56 86 30, VG/LIM/71-1–) See Document 78 for a summary of Connally's remarks on the balance of payments.

exchange rates (presumably including defense burden-sharing), the future type of convertibility, and methods of handling flows of capital. Long-range group was future role of reserve currencies and other basic reform of international monetary system. Barber (U.K.) and Schiller (Germany) pushed for prompt action on first group of issues, and France and others gave milder support.

4. Secretary Connally felt division of issues into separate groupings was premature, prejudiced substantive judgments and priorities, and concentrated too much attention on further U.S. contributions to equilibrium through change in dollar price of gold and abolition of surcharge. Such proposed work programs did not give adequate effective and prompt attention to issues of special interest to U.S., such as sharing of defense burden and elimination of unfair trade practices on part of other countries. Secretary Connally also stated President's position in opposition to change in dollar price of gold was absolutely clear. He suggested that Working Party Three examine statistics on size of correction needed and Deputies meet to prepare a work program that might meet with general acceptance. This was agreed and stated in communiqué (see separate text).

5. Deputies meeting scheduled for 3:30 p.m. September 25, Ministerial September 26.

Annenberg

176. **Action Memorandum From the President's Assistant for National Security Affairs (Kissinger) and the President's Assistant for International Economic Affairs (Peterson) to President Nixon**[1]

Washington, September 20, 1971.

SUBJECT

Negotiating the New Economic Policy Abroad

As the shock effect of August 15 wears off and other countries develop their negotiating strategy, defining where we want to go becomes increasingly essential. We need to:

1. Refine our objectives: what exactly do we want others to do?
2. Define our priorities: which objectives should we push hardest, and in what time frame?
3. Determine our own negotiating strategy: how do we achieve our bilateral aims vis-à-vis countries in a variety of different areas (monetary, trade, and defense) in the same time frame we are negotiating multilateral understandings?

We propose making a hard-hitting analysis of the leverage we have gained by making the dollar inconvertible and by imposing the surcharge. Relations with our allies and friends could deteriorate if we have an inadequate understanding of what we can reasonably expect to achieve by our actions.

Recommendation

That you approve establishment of a small coordinating committee, chaired by Peter Peterson and including high-level representatives from Treasury (Volcker and Petty), State (Samuels and Trezise), CEA (Solomon), OMB (Dam), and the Federal Reserve Board and NSC Staff. This group will develop and refine the options available to us in the near term, with a view to presenting them to the Quadriad augmented by Secretary Rogers, Henry Kissinger and Peter Peterson. Secretary Connally has agreed that in view of the broad range of issues involved,

---

[1] Source: National Archives, Nixon Presidential Materials, NSC Files, Agency Files, Box 218, Council on International Economic Policy. Confidential. Attached to a memorandum from Peterson to Kissinger that indicated Peterson had discussed the joint memorandum with Secretary Connally, who found it acceptable. Peterson noted that Connally thought it urgent to decide what to say to the Japanese on Saturday (September 25) and at the IMF, and Peterson wanted to call a meeting on September 22 if the President approved. (Presumably Connally was referring to bilateral meetings with Japanese officials who would be in Washington for the Annual Meeting of the IMF the following week.) Peterson asked Kissinger, if he approved the joint memorandum, to "please sign it now and I will have somebody waiting outside to get it into the President's office." Peterson wrote at the bottom: "Sorry to bother you."

this kind of White House-chaired coordinating committee is necessary and desirable. Secretary Rogers, deeply concerned about the foreign policy aspects, concurs in the need for such a committee. George Shultz and Paul McCracken also agree.[2]

---

[2] There is no indication if the President approved or disapproved the recommendation, but a Coordinating Committee was soon established; see Document 179.

---

177. Memorandum From the President's Assistant for International Economic Affairs (Peterson) to President Nixon[1]

Washington, September 20, 1971.

SUBJECT

  Coordinating Group—Planning the Negotiations for the New Economic Policy Abroad

It is agreed by all of us that we do not want a patchwork settlement that would only lead to another financial crisis in a few years. However, it is increasingly apparent that it is not enough to say that we need a $13 billion swing in our balance of payments, exchange rate realignment, reform of the monetary system, and more equitable deals on trade and

---

[1] Source: National Archives, Nixon Presidential Materials, NSC Files, Agency Files, Box 216, Council of Economic Advisers. Confidential. An accompanying September 22 handwritten note to Kissinger initialed by Kennedy reads: "This is of interest in view of your discussions in the 'Breakfast Group'." Also attached are a September 22 note from Jon Huntsman to General Haig indicating Peterson's memorandum went to the President that day along with a September 22 memorandum from Kissinger to Connally, Shultz, and McCracken transmitting some slightly redrafted proposed remarks for the President that Kissinger thought they should discuss "at our meeting in the morning." The draft Presidential remarks were intended for President Nixon's use at a question-and-answer session at the Economic Club of Detroit on September 23; see *Public Papers of the Presidents of the United States: Richard M. Nixon, 1971*, pp. 965–980. On September 21 Federal Reserve Chairman Burns had also provided the President proposed remarks for Detroit, and underlining by the President indicates that he read them. (National Archives, Nixon Presidential Materials, NSC Files, Agency Files, Box 289, Treasury, Volume II) Burns' proposed remarks for Detroit were attached to a September 23 memorandum from Kissinger to Connally suggesting he "work some of these thoughts into the speech that is being prepared and which will be discussed at the meeting tomorrow." Presumably Kissinger was referring to the President's remarks during his September 29 reception for principals attending the IMF and IBRD Annual Meeting; see *Public Papers of the Presidents of the United States: Richard M. Nixon, 1971*, pp. 1014–1016.

defense sharing. So far, we have left it to others to adjust to the situation we have created. But soon we will have to clarify what we want multi-laterally and what we want bilaterally from key countries. Most feel that having taken the essential but shock-producing moves of August 15, we should be prepared to propose some positive initiatives in the reasonably near future.

We need to define more precisely four areas: our objectives, our priorities among them, our negotiating leverage, and our negotiating strategy.

1. *Refining Our Objectives (including the magnitude and timing of the balance of payments swing)*

a. In the *exchange rate area*, we first need to determine whether our interests are best served by a prolonged float or an early return to a realigned, fixed rate system. If the latter, we need precise ideas about how far each major country is prepared to go in revaluing now, and how far later. What combinations of revaluations are the minimum acceptable to us at this point in time?

Is some exchange rate action by us needed to assure achievement of our parity realignment objectives? (Most feel this should *only* be considered as part of a long-term basic reform of the system.)

Related to these exchange rate questions is the position we take on investment controls.

b. On *monetary reform* there are many tough interrelated questions. For example, do we or don't we want to return to fixed parities? In what circumstances? Should the dollar as a major reserve component be gradually phased out, along with gold, in favor of SDRs? A composite reserve unit? What precise actions by ourselves and others are needed to accomplish this objective? Over what time frame?

c. *Defense* is a major drain on our balance of payments. With a big trade surplus it is manageable. But that surplus is at least 18 months off. What do we mean by increased defense burden sharing? This might take the form of larger purchases of U.S. equipment by those countries where our expenditures are high (e.g., Germany, Japan). Offset negotiations with Germany are well along. Alternatively, we could try to get direct contributions from NATO as a whole. Do we now want to place greater emphasis on budget contributions as opposed to balance of payments offset purchases? Essentially, we must be more precise about what we want and can get in relation to action on the surcharge and dollar convertibility, what is not feasible in that context, and what may be negotiable over a longer period.

d. What are our specific *trade* objectives, and with which countries? For example, a change in the Common Agricultural Policy of the

European Community is one of our high priority objectives. Yet, this is likely to be a long-term negotiation. On the other hand, could we get agreement on stopping any further agricultural price increases? and/or on a longer-term target of moving toward direct European budget support of agricultural subsidies? Others include a reduction or complete removal of the discriminatory aspects of European Community preferential arrangements; a reduction in trade restrictions, including non-tariff barriers by Japan, revising the Canadian automobile agreement, etc. Which of these actions, if any, do we expect to achieve now in exchange for removing the surcharge or otherwise, and which must we carry over for later negotiation? Also, what, if anything, are we willing to put on the negotiating table? Finally, we cannot ignore the less developed countries where there are some special problems.

e. Longer term, what kind of future economic/political model of the U.S. in relation to other major trading blocs (in particular the EC) should guide us? How do we want the whole international economic system to evolve? A new U.S. centered bloc? A much larger free trading area including the EC, Japan, U.S.?

2. Defining Priorities Among These Objectives

For example, agreeing to major revaluations now may in practice preclude certain reforms of the monetary system.

Should we push hard for the reforms, recognizing that they will take time to negotiate, in the meantime encouraging other countries to float their currencies upward, without declaring a formal revaluation? What emphasis should be put on trade barriers, as opposed to financial issues?

If our negotiating strength is insufficient to achieve all our objectives in the near term, where should we put the emphasis?

3. Negotiating Leverage

What negotiating instruments are at our disposal, and how much leverage do they give us? Negotiating concessions we can make include: (a) removal of surcharge; (b) reduction of surcharge in stages; (c) restoration of "limited" dollar convertibility into gold, or other reserve assets; (d) restoration of "full" convertibility into gold, or other reserve assets; (e) removal of the "buy American" aspect of the Job Development credit; (f) differential (i. e., for some countries but not others) removal of surcharge, action on job development credit, restoration of convertibility; (g) devaluation of the dollar vis-à-vis gold.

We need to be clear about the risks and advantages, domestic and foreign, economic and political, involved in the use or rejection of each option, and the timing involved in each. We need to explore the legality of undertaking each. We also need a clearer idea of how much leverage each gives us, and what combinations add most to that leverage in general and with which particular countries. With time other countries may learn to live with the surcharge and their resentment may lead to stubborn refusal to give up anything for its removal, or even to retaliation. Domestically, it may become addictive and encourage protectionism, raise costs, weaken our competitiveness, and worsen our problem of inflation.

4. What is our negotiating strategy?

Up to this point, we have been imprecise about both what we want from others and within what time frames we want it. In addition, if the assessments resulting from the answers to the questions posed above lead us to conclude that we should ask for different actions from different countries, we will have to develop a strategy for making our specific bilateral demands clear—e.g., from Canada, from Japan, from Germany, from Britain—and for the kinds of actions we will take if particular countries either meet or refuse to meet these demands. At some point, we must know when and how to compromise without prejudicing the achievement of those fundamental objectives which are more clearly longer-term than others. Any negotiating strategy must weigh carefully the effect of what we are doing and how we do it on our foreign relations and security policies. For example, it should include the possibility of forthcoming Presidential initiatives at appropriate times.

We also need to know the strong points of resistance by others, e.g., the EC has stated publicly that it will not agree to a major realignment of parities unless the U.S. participates by devaluing. Some other countries may also insist on additional action by us (e.g. eligibility for their exports to qualify under the full Job Development credit) before they will agree either to adequate revaluations, negotiations about monetary reform, defense burden sharing, etc. We need an assessment of how serious these demands are, and the risks and advantages to us involved in acceding or not acceding to them.

Finally, we need to decide on a mechanism for carrying out the diverse and multi-faceted negotiations. Most of the issues are Treasury's main line of responsibility, but our objectives range also into the areas of trade and defense. This will create problems for other governments, whose internal division of responsibility is often quite strict, and will require a suitable mechanism on our part.

178.   **Memorandum From the Executive Secretary of the Department of State (Eliot) to the President's Assistant for National Security Affairs (Kissinger)[1]**

Washington, September 24, 1971.

SUBJECT

Foreign Reactions to the President's Economic Program—Afternoon September 24

Foreign official views (probably in part substantive and in part tactical on their part) about the international monetary situation as reflected at last week's meeting of the Group of Ten Finance Ministers[2] are: (1) the US adjustment goal of a $13 billion turnaround, largely on trade, is too ambitious, particularly in the relatively short time frame of a year or two; (2) the general realignment of exchange rates should include US action to devalue the dollar; (3) the US import surcharge should be eliminated; (4) fixed rates should be quickly reestablished. Some countries, notably Italy and Japan, urged improvement in the international monetary system through greater reliance on Special Drawing Rights (SDR's). The Group of Ten will meet again in Washington on September 25 at the Deputy level and September 26 at the Ministerial level, in preparation for next week's IMF meeting.

At the G-10 meeting, the Managing Director of the IMF, Schweitzer, suggested a procedural approach consisting of dividing the issues into three groups to be dealt with in stages: (1) realignment of exchange rates, relationship of currencies to gold, wider margins of fluctuation around par rates, and abolition of the US surcharge; (2) balance of payments adjustment measures other than exchange rates, such as defense burden sharing arrangements, future type of convertibility, and methods for handling flows of capital; (3) the future role of reserve currencies and other questions relating to basic reforms of the international monetary system. Secretary Connally noted that the United States did not agree with this approach and the placing of issues into separate groups.

Governor Wormser of the Bank of France believes that an early settlement of the monetary crisis is essential to avert a worldwide recession and that there are only five or six months to negotiate a long term solution. Otherwise, he believes, the world economic situation will

---

[1] Source: National Archives, RG 59, Central Files 1970–73, E 1 US. Confidential. Drafted by R.J. Smith and L.J. Kennon (E/IFD/OMA) and cleared by S. Weintraub (E/IFD) and Katz (E).

[2] The G-10 Ministers met in London September 15–16; see Document 175.

deteriorate markedly, with increasing national restrictions on trade and payments coming into being, partly in response to the US surcharge.

This week's meeting of the EC Council of Ministers (September 20–21) concluded that there was no need at this time to revise positions on the US economic measures. The French and Germans stressed the dangers of retaliation and no active consideration was given to retaliatory or compensatory measures at this time. The Community intends, however, to watch the evolution of the situation closely in order to adopt "any new decisions which may appear necessary".

Our Embassy reports that large segments of Japan's business community, especially the trading companies, favor unilateral Japanese action to revalue the yen. The Bank of Japan and the Ministry of Finance are reported as resisting this pressure on the grounds that Japan should wait for further multilateral movement. Government officials believe any unilateral action to revalue the yen now would be treated by others merely as an opening bid.

The dollar weakened further today and the major trading currencies reached their highest levels since the floats began. The Deutschemark rose to nearly 10 percent above par following reported purchases yesterday by the German Central Bank of more than $100 million in the spot and forward markets.

Further memoranda in this series will be submitted as warranted by developments.

Parker W. Borg[3]

---

[3] Borg signed for Eliot above Eliot's typed signature.

179.	Memorandum From the President's Assistant for
	International Economic Affairs (Peterson) to the President's
	Assistant for National Security Affairs (Kissinger)[1]

Washington, September 24, 1971.

This is about as hurriedly thrown together as anything can be since the Coordinating Group has only been in operation since yesterday morning.[2] It is so much a first draft that the rest of the Group are getting copies the same time you are.[3]

However, given your Alaskan trip[4] and the forthcoming IMF meetings, I felt that your looking at this might at least give you a preliminary glance of where we stand.

P

Attachment

SUMMARY[5]

We can, perhaps summarize the present status of discussion within the Government as follows:

A. Areas of Agreement

1. We agree on a two-phased Negotiation. Phase I, to be completed, hopefully, in 6 to 8 weeks and no later than Christmas would involve negotiations on monetary, trade, and defense issues that would provide clearly identifiable results of our negotiating efforts and a basis for removing the surtax and the discriminatory aspects of the investment tax credit. Phase II would involve long-range negotiations on key monetary, trade, and defense issues—the outline of which would hopefully be agreed to.

2. The surcharge—a domestic economic liability, although politically very popular—as an international asset will soon begin to deteriorate,

---

[1] Source: National Archives, Nixon Presidential Materials, NSC Files, Agency Files, Box 218, Council on International Economic Policy. Confidential.

[2] Presumably the group Kissinger and Peterson proposed in their September 20 memorandum to President Nixon, Document 176.

[3] A September 24 memorandum with similar wording directed the attached paper to Volcker and Petty at Treasury. (Washington National Records Center, Department of the Treasury, Files of Under Secretary Volcker: FRC 56 79 15, CIEP)

[4] Kissinger accompanied President Nixon to Anchorage for his September 26 meeting with Japanese Emperor Hirohito.

[5] This is the summary of a 23-page paper, which is not printed.

unless constructive negotiations are underway promptly. Therefore, if we are to avoid serious complications, both internationally and domestically, we must promptly remove it in return for achievement of Phase I objectives.

Promptly means at the latest before Christmas. More desirable would be to end international Phase I simultaneously with the end of the 90-day domestic Phase I (November 15).

3. The highest priority Phase I objective is an exchange rate structure that promises to redress the United States balance of payments.

4. We need tangible trade and defense achievements in Phase I, as well as significant exchange rate realignment (in fact or through a credible process).

5. In no circumstances will we agree to more than "limited convertibility" in Phase I, since this is our major negotiating leverage for Phase II reform of the monetary system.

6. In Phase II highest priority attaches to reform of the monetary system so that we will not find ourselves in a few years back in the same situation which led to our August 15 actions.

7. In addition, in Phase II we want far-reaching trade liberalization and a significant shifting of defense responsibilities to our allies.

8. Finally, we want the President at the earliest possible date to put before the world a vision of our international goals for this country which would add to the Phase II elements mentioned above (trade liberalization, defense burden sharing, basic monetary reform), the prospect of the developed world more fully sharing its wealth with the less developed countries.

B. Issues

1. We have done considerable work but are not entirely agreed on specific trade and defense concessions we would want and expect as minimum consideration for removal of the surtax.

2. We have not defined precisely the minimum levels at which we would agree to return to fixed parities with limited dollar convertibility although the Deutsche Mark and the Yen both somewhere over 10%, agreement might be desirable . . . particularly if the outlines of an improved monetary system had been agreed to that would presumably correct any imbalances in the future.

3. Others argue that a continuing honest or bona fide float, particularly if it were agreed that reserve accumulation and any significant intervention would be ruled out for key countries, would, for now, be preferable to fixed parities at almost any level.

4. Although we have a clearly preferred view of not changing the price of gold in Phase I, there is an issue over what we would actually do if others insist, and this is a route to getting a substantial adequate realignment.

Why have others asked for devaluation of the dollar vis-à-vis gold? Politically, because such a move would appear to make the necessary exchange rate adjustments in other countries more easily tolerable. Also, the bookkeeping effects are certainly not negligible to some countries. Strategically, because some, i.e., the French, want to force us back to convertibility at a higher fixed gold price. The wealth redistribution effects of a price change are tolerable for us and others, although not desirable. Politically, devaluation is difficult for the President, but perhaps not impossible, and the atmosphere is clearly changing. There is a practical difficulty due to legislative requirements which argues for action only in the context of system changes which also would require Congressional approval but which would come near the end of the Phase II negotiation rather than Phase I.

5. What we mean by "limited convertibility" and how far we would go in what circumstances is also an issue.

6. While there are issues concerning our minimum trade terms, with respect to Japan, Canada, and the U.K., and some disagreement as to how much we originally ask for, the major trade issue concerns the European Community.

We know what we want from the Community *but* we recognize that the chances of obtaining much, if anything, on agriculture, preferences, and industrial policy in Phase I may be small.

A specific central issue here is whether or not to try to use the situation to seek a standstill on the European Community negotiations with the EFTA non-applicants. Success would be valuable, but the cost of trying and failing could be high, both on the monetary and political fronts.

7. Are there circumstances in which we would differentially lift the surcharge for some countries who had cooperated with us in making meaningful adjustments but not doing so for remaining countries ? This raises major policy and legal questions, including heightened dangers of retaliation and probable incompatibility with our international obligations. Fortunately, the decision is not needed now, but there are quite different legal and policy views on this within the government and we have much to do here.

8. While we prefer not to discuss our investment control programs and let the liberalization take place at a quiet but accelerating pace, others will probably make an issue of this. Eventually, we seek elimination of our controls and, indeed, action now would put more pressure on the rate structure, but it would also stimulate others to go even further in applying exchange controls.

9. We recognize that the existing situation inequitably places a large adjustment burden on developing countries, but until our Phase I objectives are achieved, most would agree that we cannot make major con-

cessions through the less developed countries. However, if progress is not made promptly, further consideration of surcharge exemption for the less developed countries collectively or on products of major interest to them should be explored.

10. Last, but not least, there are issues concerning the negotiating scenario. How do we coordinate bilateral trade, defense, and monetary negotiations with the general multilateral discussions of questions involving the payments and trading systems? What is the proper role of various departments and individuals in Phase I? Phase II?

---

180.   Memorandum From Lawrence H. Berlin of the Program and Policy Coordination Staff, Agency for International Development, to the Assistant Administrator for Program and Policy Coordination (Stern)[1]

Washington, September 24, 1971.

SUBJECT

IBRD/IMF Annual meetings: Briefing of U.S. Delegation

The meeting of the U.S. delegation was chaired by Mr. Volcker, whose principal concern was with the questions likely to come up in corridor conversations among delegates concerning the new U.S. economic policies. He particularly stressed the danger that the press might be expecting some dramatic solution to the current world monetary crisis to come out of the Bank/Fund meetings, and will report failure when such a solution does not materialize. There is in fact no intention to seek answers to the monetary, trade, and defense burden-sharing issues next week; as always, the Bank/Fund meetings will be largely routine.

There will, of course, be side meetings of the Group of Ten, but this is purely incidental to the Bank/Fund meetings. Members of the U.S. delegation were specifically urged to express ignorance if any questions are asked by foreign delegates about the prospects for a resolution to be passed by the IMF Governors dealing with the international monetary

---

[1] Source: Washington National Records Center, Agency for International Development, Office of the Administrator: FRC 286 75 13, Box 10, PRM 7-2 July 1971–October 1971 FY72. Confidential.

system. (FYI: Such a resolution is expected, but the subject is highly sensitive; the resolution will in any case merely call for studies. End FYI)

Mr. Volcker stressed the official U.S. view that the balance of payments problem reflects not merely the need for changes in the international monetary system, but also foreign trade practices which are biased against the United States, and the U.S. defense burden. Fundamental rethinking of these issues is necessary, and while the U.S. Government has views, it is not deemed good tactics to propose a "U.S. solution" at this time, resistance to which might well kill off meritorious ideas prematurely. We seek solutions arrived at mutually, which accept the fact that the relative economic position of the United States in the world has changed even though we remain in a position of strength and leadership. We also wish to avoid a patchwork solution to the monetary problem alone which would leave other basic issues unresolved and could therefore prove unequal to the task of restoring basic equilibrium in our balance of payments. The result of such a failure could be demoralizing.

The following specific questions, which could come up at the meetings, were noted:

1—*Were the recent European conferences of the Group of Ten[2] a failure? Answer:* No; there was no expectation that broad solutions would be reached so soon. There *was* agreement for the first time that a fundamental realignment of currency values is necessary, and it *was* agreed that the OECD, the Group of Ten, and the IMF would initiate needed studies.

2—*Does the United States have solutions to propose? Answer:* No; we believe the problems are difficult and require solutions which are carefully evolved and not rushed. Our minds are open.

3—*Why won't the United States agree to increase the dollar price of gold? Answer:* Our concern at this time, insofar as the monetary system is concerned, is with determining the magnitude of the changes in relative exchange rates which are required to re-establish monetary equilibrium, and with the basic direction of the international monetary system. We are also concerned about trade and about greater sharing of the defense burden. (FYI: Treasury, while recognizing that U.S. agreement to a token devaluation of the dollar at this time would ease the political problems of other countries in up-valuing their currencies, nevertheless believes such U.S devaluation could set a precedent and lead to demands for *further* devaluation of the dollar, if efforts to re-establish equilibrium are not successful. End FYI)

4—*Why won't the United States exempt LDCs from the 10 per cent surcharge? Answer:* There has been no change in the basic U.S. position on

---

[2] The G-10 Ministers met September 15–16; see Document 175.

trade policy, but we believe surcharge is required until the underlying issues are resolved in their totality and the prospects for the U.S. balance of payments have definitely improved. In the long run, the LDCs will be better off, since if satisfactory solutions are arrived at, the chances of a return to protectionism in world trade will be fewer. (FYI: Exempting LDCs from the surcharge would be interpreted by OECD as an indication that we intend to keep the surcharge indefinitely. End FYI)

Note: The U.S. delegation will have its offices in Room C-253 in the C Wing of the Sheraton Park. Delegates are asked to register there, on Monday morning, and AID officials who are not delegates can pick up badges at Room C-253 to permit them to attend sessions.

---

181.   **Memorandum of Conversation**[1]

Washington, September 25, 1971.

PARTICIPANTS

Germany

Karl Schiller, Economics and Finance Minister
Karl Klasen, Bundesbank President
Johann Schoellhorn, State Secretary in the Ministry of Economics and Finance

U.S. Treasury

Secretary Connally
Under Secretary Walker[2]
Under Secretary Volcker[2]
Assistant Secretary Petty
Mr. Hermberg (Recording officer)

---

[1] Source: Washington National Records Center, Department of the Treasury, Files of Under Secretary Volcker: FRC 56 79 15, Germany General. Confidential. Drafted on October 6 by Edward S. Hermberg, Financial Attaché at the Embassy in Bonn. The meeting was held at the Department of the Treasury. A September 24 briefing memorandum for the meeting is ibid. The German officials were in Washington for the Annual Meetings of the IMF and the IBRD the following week. On the fringes of those meetings other bilaterals were held, including Connally's meetings with Chancellor of the Exchequer Anthony Barber on September 25, with Japanese Minister of Finance Mikio Mizuta on September 27, and with Governor of the Bank of England Leslie O'Brien on September 29. Memoranda of these and other conversations are ibid., Secretary's Memos: FRC 56 74 17, Memcons 1971.

[2] Under Secretaries Walker and Volcker had to leave before the end of the meeting. [Footnote in the source text. The G-10 Deputies were meeting on the afternoon of September 25; presumably Volcker left to attend.]

SUBJECT

International Financial Situation

After welcoming Minister Schiller to Washington, Secretary Connally briefly reviewed the international monetary problems. The Secretary said that in talking to the Italians in London[3] he had outlined these problems as including the U.S. import surcharge and the question of a U.S. "contribution" to a settlement by a devaluation of the dollar in terms of the price of gold. Both of the above-mentioned problems were tied in with the question of an international realignment of parities and the problem of how much each country would change in such a realignment. This was a most difficult question. Since Germany, Canada, Japan and the U.S. were already floating, the Secretary continued, he had therefore suggested in his conversation with the Italians that it might be worthwhile to explore whether everyone should take off all controls and freely float for a while.

President Klasen interjected that such a proposition would be most difficult for most countries. Jokingly he continued that it would be more difficult for them than even a 20 percent devaluation would be for the U.S. Minister Schiller referred to the fact that some countries were even now floating "dirtily" and that what was needed was a "code of good behavior" for floating. In the present circumstances Germany was practically the only country which was floating freely and as a result the DM was appreciating at levels which everyone in Germany considered to be too high. As someone had said, everyone was cheating except Germany. State Secretary Schoellhorn interjected that as a result Germany might have to start cheating too. He said that the public mentioning of various suggested percentage figures for a DM appreciation by Reuss, the IMF, etc., was causing much trouble in the markets and driving the DM up. Schoellhorn observed that as a result of the DM appreciation during the last few days Japan in effect had devalued by 3 percent against the DM.

Secretary Connally said that the U.S. had talked with Japan and Canada, but that everyone wanted to proceed in a bloc and that we therefore had no one to talk to. President Klasen interjected that in the currency realignment it was necessary for everyone to know what everyone else was going to do. For Germany, thus for example, it was essential to know what France would do. Secretary Connally continued that we realized the difficulties involved for everyone. What was important was not to let these difficulties impair the excellent personal, political and military relationships between Germany and the U.S. We were flexible on how to get to a better alignment of parities and willing

---

[3] This meeting was presumably held on the fringes of the September 15–16 G-10 Ministerial meeting.

to do whatever would be helpful. We had talked bilaterally to the Canadians, Italians, and Japanese. We were prepared to talk and work with anyone bilaterally, multilaterally or both at the same time. But we could not go back to the old system and would have to work toward a new system which would satisfy us. Secretary Connally continued that he personally couldn't care less about the price of gold—which Klasen had raised previously—but this was a political matter. To change the price of gold the U.S. Government would have to go to the U.S. Congress and one could not know what would come out of the Congress if we did this. The import surcharge was a most popular measure in the U.S. There was much Congressional pressure to bring the troops home. While the price of gold in his view was not a big substantive issue, this was a touchy political question. Decisions on it could be made only on the political level. Minister Schiller said that he agreed that the price of gold was mainly a mythological matter, but it could help facilitate things.

Secretary Connally continued that as far as the import surcharge was concerned, before we could remove it, we would have some expression from others what they will do (in addition to the currency realignment). There were some special problems with Canada, Japan and Germany, but beyond that everyone was in the same boat. As far as Europe in general was concerned, there was not a great deal that we had to complain about aside from some specific cases. Thus, for example, France recently had told a major U.S. manufacturer that he could not sell in France unless he built a plant there. At the same time France constantly complains about U.S. foreign investments. We will have to work out such bilateral problems. Offset is one such problem which we have to work out with Germany. But beyond this what role do you want us to play? We are willing to talk with France, to negotiate, to do whatever is wanted. But it must be clear that we cannot go back to the old system.

Schiller responded by asking what would be the next step. The DM had now floated upward by 11 percent. This was too much. What would be the U.S. reaction if Germany would be forced to introduce capital controls? While he personally was opposed to using capital controls, the time might come when he would have to do so. The float of others was not an honest one. The continued deadlock was hurting Germany. Klasen interjected that through this deadlock the U.S. was punishing its best friend. Schiller said that in this situation it was essential to negotiate.

Secretary Connally replied that we were prepared to negotiate immediately. Schiller said that Germany could not negotiate unilaterally. What Germany could do depended, for example, very much on what Japan and France would do. It was necessary to talk about a deal in the

Group of Ten. Klasen interjected that Secretary Connally had mentioned a G-10 meeting in November. Germany could not afford to wait that long. Schiller said that the combination of the current rate of revaluation of the DM, the import surcharge and the discriminatory aspects of the tax credit amounted to an embargo of German machinery exports to the U.S. Klasen again stressed the unacceptability of the current 11 percent rate of revaluation of the DM and said that Germany could not continue to take the burdens of currency readjustments alone.

Secretary Connally responded that the November date for the next G-10 meeting was an Italian proposal. He stressed the current health and strength of the German economy and our readiness to do whatever the Germans wanted us to do to help. Schoellhorn suggested that the U.S. could express a willingness to participate in a realignment through an increase in the price of gold. The Secretary remarked that that was a political, not an economic, problem and asked if the German problem was a political one. Schiller responded that Germany's problem was that it could not move without its partners. If he knew that the U.S. was prepared to move for such and such a price, then he, Schiller, might be able to make progress with his partners. In response to a question by Secretary Connally what he wanted us to do, Schiller responded "what is your price for the surcharge?" Secretary Connally replied that we must be assured that we can get our balance of payments into equilibrium within a reasonably short period of time. We must have a better burden sharing in defense, through arrangements arrived at with certain countries either in concert or individually. We must get certain trade restrictions removed, particularly by Japan and Canada. In the trade field we were not asking too much from the EC. We felt that their preferential trade arrangements with Morocco and Israel, for example, violated the GATT and there should be no increase in agricultural protection. Mr. Petty said it would be most desirable that the EC limit the product coverage of the common agricultural policy to those products now covered. Secretary Connally said he realized that we cannot turn the U.S. balance of payments around over night, but by 1973 we certainly must see some change. We must be sure of a formula which gives us a real assurance that in a reasonably short period of time we can look for equilibrium in our balance of payments.

Schiller said that it seemed as though there might not be a solution for some period of time. But in the meantime the economic situation in Germany would change. What would be the U.S. reaction if after its economy had broken down, Germany would return to its old parity. Mr. Petty asked how effective the French system of controls was. Schoellhorn answered that it was very effective. France actually had sold dollars last week. Klasen said that France and Italy could afford to wait. Germany could not. Now the country which had helped the U.S.

the most was being hurt the most. Secretary Connally interjected that he appreciated the problems Germany was facing, but one should not lose sight of the fact that our relationship has been good to both of us and has made both of us pretty prosperous. Schoellhorn, while generally agreeing with the Secretary, mentioned German political sensitivity to inflation and the problems caused prior to the float by the inflow of liquidity. Schoellhorn continued that the Secretary had said that aside from the currency realignment we should look at problems of trade and burden sharing. Schoellhorn felt that it would not be possible to handle all three problems at once. He felt that we should start with the problem of the realignment of parities. If such a realignment could not be accomplished quickly, we would get a world of capital controls. There was very little time left.

Secretary Connally said that he felt we could do all three (trade, burden sharing and realignment) at the same time. It was not really as difficult as Schoellhorn implied. He, Connally, understood, for example, that we were very close on the offset problem—only $85 million apart. Schiller agreed that the offset was close to agreement. The Germans had adjourned the talks until just after the IMF meetings but then expected to conclude an agreement quickly. Nevertheless, Schiller felt that the conditions Connally had mentioned for the removal of the surcharge were very vague and hard.

Secretary Connally reiterated that in order to remove the surcharge the U.S. had to have a formula which gave real assurance that in a relatively short period of time we can look for equilibrium in our balance of payments. If others did not want to include trade restrictions and defense in the formula, then the currency realignment would have to be that much larger. Thus, for example, we could not get certain of our products—such as computers—into Japan at all. The Japanese tariff on our beef was over 100 percent. Exchange rate change alone could accomplish little in these situations. This was different in the case of Germany. With Germany we would not insist on including the question of burden sharing, but Germany should be interested in joining us to put pressure on Japan for the removal of trade restrictions. Schiller and Klasen agreed that pressure on Japan would be desirable.

Klasen asked the Secretary what ideas the U.S. had concerning the general realignment of parities, assuming that it received satisfaction on the trade and burden-sharing question. He felt that it was necessary to know a figure in order to have a framework. What average realignment of the dollar against the rest of world did the U.S. think to be necessary? Secretary Connally replied that we have not yet made such a calculation because we felt it would be presumptuous for us to tell others what to do. But we would now make such a calculation and tell our partners what we think they should do, what Germany should do, France, the

U.K., Japan should do. One figure will indicate what we think it will take. Secretary Connally stressed that while our partners can, of course, question our figure, he hoped that they would not question the honesty of our intentions. We did not want to take advantage of anyone and our figure would be a reasonable one. We would get to work on the figures this afternoon and provide them before the Germans left Washington.

Schiller, in discussing the interdependence of various national parity changes, stressed the key position of France. Germany, for example, could not revalue by 10–11 percent vis-à-vis the dollar if France did not move at all. Germany had already substantially revalued against France in the last few years and a further move of such magnitude vis-à-vis the franc could not be sold to the German public—20 percent of German exports went to France, only 10 percent to the U.S.

Secretary Connally asked whether the Germans thought that in the hypothetical case of a U.S. devaluation, the French would stay put or also devalue. Klasen replied positively that France would stay put, while Schiller was not so sure. Both agreed that in such a case the U.S. should insist on a price agreement by France not to follow suit. Schiller indicated the German position on the increase in the price of gold was "cool" but they felt it could facilitate a realignment. Mr. Petty pointed out that an increase in the price of gold would be a step backward by also increasing its role in the monetary system. Klasen said that the Germans do not think that after an increase in the price of gold, the U.S. should restore the full gold convertibility of the dollar. The Secretary said he had hoped Klasen would say that, because we could not do it.

Schiller said that in the last few days he had become very pessimistic. He was afraid there would not be any movement forward and Klasen stressed that the rest of the world had become accustomed to America taking the lead in a crisis. He felt the U.S. must make some proposal. Secretary Connally said that we will do this, even though the minute we do, everyone will accuse us of trying to dictate to the rest of the world.

Schoellhorn asked if it might be possible not to apply the discriminatory aspects of the investment trade credit. He said that $600 million of German exports are involved. In addition, there is the danger that others will copy this type of tax credit.

Secretary Connally indicated that he hoped to have some further discussions with Schiller during the week.[4]

Sy Cross[5]

---

[4] No record of additional discussions was found.

[5] Cross signed for Hermberg above Hermberg's typed signature.

182.   Information Memorandum From Robert Hormats of the
         National Security Council Staff to the President's Assistant
         for National Security Affairs (Kissinger)[1]

Washington, September 28, 1971.

SUBJECT

   Progress in Developing USG Position on International Aspects of NEP

Events since Thursday

On Thursday,[2] Ken Dam, Ezra Solomon (CEA), John Petty, Ed Cohen (Assistant Secretary of the Treasury for Tax Policy) and I met for approximately two hours to discuss our next moves on the international aspects of the New Economic Policy. Cohen relayed to Connally the conclusions of the meeting:

   —The surcharge is a wasting negotiating asset since it is not as detrimental to most foreign economies as many felt at the outset, and other governments will institute measures to compensate for it.
   —Our highest priority is an exchange rate realignment which redresses, or moves toward redressing, the U. S. balance of payments deficit.
   —There are major economic advantages in other nations floating their currencies, rather than repegging in the very near future.
   —The foreign policy costs of maintaining the surcharge without providing clear indicators of what we expect as quid pro quos for its removal are a decrease in the willingness of Europeans to cooperate with us and increasing foreign hostility to the U.S.

Since that meeting Connally has agreed in the Group of 10 meeting this weekend to negotiate removal of the surcharge.[3] However, it is unclear how forthcoming he will be in these negotiations. It is clear, however, that he will probably not accept the proposals contained in the Shultz/Dam memorandum which you, Connally and McCracken considered last Thursday.[4] For domestic reasons, it will be difficult for the

---

[1] Source: National Archives, Nixon Presidential Materials, NSC Files, Subject Files, Box 376, President's Economic Program. Confidential. A stamped notation on the memorandum reads: "HAK has seen."

[2] September 23.

[3] The G-10 Deputies met Saturday afternoon, September 25, to develop an agenda for a G-10 Ministerial meeting on September 26.

[4] The meeting has not been further identified. The reference may be to an untitled paper transmitted under cover of a September 23 routing slip from OMB Director Shultz to Secretary Connally. The paper begins with the following proposal: "The United States declares that it stands ready to abolish its import surcharge and capital controls immediately with respect to imports from any country that permits its currency to float freely." The paper then explores a number of issues relating to the proposal, such as the operational definition of a free float, how to deal with developing countries that traditionally had pegged their par values to the dollar or another key currency, and the legality under GATT rules of lifting the surcharge for some but not all countries. (Washington National Records Center, Department of the Treasury, Connally Correspondence: FRC 56 74 4, OMB)

President to remove the surcharge in exchange for other nations floating their currencies, as the OMB memorandum suggested. Nor do I believe that a free float would be accepted by the key trading nations, except perhaps Germany.

Also since Thursday, Pete Peterson's group has come up with suggestions on trade and defense burden sharing problems which can be negotiated with our major trading partners (Tab A).[5]

The Present Problem

Following the Bank/Fund meetings we should have a better feel for how far the Europeans and Japanese are willing to go in meeting our demands. However, we will still be far from an internal USG position. Forces within the USG which wish to squeeze every ounce of blood out of Europe and Japan regardless of the political costs will vie with those who wish to lift the surcharge without the quid pro quos which the hardliners would regard as acceptable. The logic of the former group would lead to no removal of the surcharge for a long period—i. e. until major trade and monetary concessions are realized—and will exacerbate political and economic relations with our trading partners, as well as running the risk of a trade war. The position of the latter, although commendable for its economic logic, is destined to be rejected on domestic political grounds.

Specific problems to be reconciled are:

—How long can the surcharge remain in effect before other governments are forced to take offsetting economic actions or retaliate. (The answer probably depends on how sincere and reasonable they believe we are in working out a solution which will enable us to remove the surcharge, but in any event the risk becomes greater if no significant progress has been made by the end of November.)

—Whether we can get a satisfactory *repegging* of other currencies without devaluing the dollar vis-à-vis gold. (The answer is probably negative, in which case a repegging exercise would be a long ordeal—with significant domestic political implications—during which the surcharge would probably remain in effect.)

—Whether we can negotiate within a reasonably short period of time significant trade and defense burden sharing arrangements which the President can point to as justification for removal of the surcharge. (On trade the answer is probably yes, although the hardliners might not be completely satisfied; on defense burden sharing we may have to settle for much less.)

---

[5] Document 179.

Suggested Scenario

I have drawn up a brief scenario which provides the relative hard-liners some quid pro quos, but enables the President to remove the surcharge by the middle of November, when the domestic Phase I is completed. Under this scenario we would:

—Begin immediately to negotiate trade and defense issues which would provide us with tangible results within a period of 6–8 weeks. (Peterson has a list of such issues.)

—Indicate *privately* and at the highest levels to Canada, Japan, Germany, and perhaps one or two other of our trading partners, minimum acceptable levels to which we would expect their currencies to *float* within the next two months; and, that while we would have no objection to their maintaining their rates at these levels temporarily, through central bank intervention, we would expect that once the surcharge was removed they would float upwards by an agreed number of percentage points. (Floating is preferable to repegging in that repegging negotiations would be prolonged, raise sensitive questions about the gold value of the dollar, *and* might limit the President's future options should he decide in Stage II to press for a floating or very flexible exchange rate system.)

—Seek *public assurances* at the highest levels from the key members of the Group of 10 that negotiations would begin immediately on *new* international monetary system (which would have greater flexibility and greater liquidity than the present system) and on our major trade and burden sharing problems.

—We would *not negotiate either convertibility or devaluation of the dollar vis-à-vis gold in the first round.* The former is our major lever for securing the desired international monetary reforms in the second stage. The latter would raise issues which could not be resolved within a two or three-month period (thus prolonging the surcharge) and could cause adverse domestic criticism by those who regard the value of the dollar as a sacred and inviolable concept. Moreover, it is *unnecessary* to devalue in Stage I since the level of the float is a transitional "half-way house".

—When the trade and burden sharing negotiations had borne sufficient fruit and major currencies had floated above the minimum levels (by early November), the President could announce removal of the surcharge, point to its success on the monetary, trade and defense burden sharing front, and to public assurances by other nations that there would be future negotiations on an improved monetary system and on additional trade and burden sharing arrangements favorable to the U.S. He would not at that time announce the agreement that other currencies would continue to float upward to the agreed levels (because speculation would force them up too rapidly), but could point to the increases subsequently in order to justify, ex post removal of the surcharge should he be attacked domestically for doing so. We would not resume gold convertibility nor, under this scheme, devalue the dollar vis-à-vis gold (although this would be a conceivable fallback if necessary).

If you agree in principle with this approach, you might encourage Peterson to work up his 6–8 week time-frame trade and defense burden sharing options as soon as possible, and encourage Connally, McCracken and Shultz to consider this scenario—which I can sketch out in greater detail if you so desire.[6]

---

[6] No record of Kissinger's action on Hormats' suggestions has been found, but see Document 186.

---

183. Letter From the Chairman of the Board of Governors of the Federal Reserve System (Burns) to President Nixon[1]

Washington, October 14, 1971.

Dear Mr. President:

I have been so busy of late that I have not found the time until now to give you a few quick impressions of the IMF meetings.

In general the atmosphere improved during that week in comparison with the period following the Group of Ten meeting in London. This improvement showed up in the agreement by the Group of Ten Ministers and Governors on the agenda of immediate issues that require resolution: the magnitude and method of a realignment of currencies, the adoption of somewhat wider exchange rate margins around par, the discontinuance of the import surcharge, and measures in the field of trade and defense burden sharing. At the same time the Ministers instructed their Deputies to explore the problems of longer-term reform of the international monetary system. The improvement also showed up in the tone of the comments, both public and private, of numerous officials. Certainly, Secretary Connally's speech contributed to the better atmosphere by its indication of a readiness to negotiate on the part of the United States.

---

[1] Source: National Archives, Nixon Presidential Materials, NSC Files, Name Files, Box 810, Arthur Burns. Personal and Confidential. A copy was sent to Secretary Connally. A handwritten note by Haig reads: "Hormats—*Went to Pres.*"

I turn now to a summary report on my private discussions with foreign officials.

Many Europeans stressed that Europe is on the edge of a distinct slowdown in economic activity, if not a recession. The relevance of this observation is that, as time goes on, it will become increasingly difficult for European governments to agree on a significant upvaluation of their currencies in relation to the dollar, since such a change in exchange rates will aggravate recessionary correlations. The same is true of Japan. This consideration reinforces what is already a good case for getting ahead with serious negotiations as quickly as possible.

In a lengthy discussion with the French (Finance Minister Giscard d'Estaing and central bank Governor Wormser), I was told that the price of gold in terms of francs is an important political issue in France, given the widespread and long-standing custom of the French population to hold gold as a hedge against inflation and political uncertainty. This makes it difficult, if not impossible, for a French political leader to agree to a revaluation of the franc against an unchanged dollar, since the franc price of gold would then fall. On the other hand, I came away from this candid conversation with the definite impression that the French Government would stand still for a 5 or 6 per cent increase in the dollar price of gold, leaving the franc price where it is. The British and the Italians are likely to follow the French lead.

The Japanese (Finance Minister Mizuta and Governor Sasaki) were not ready to talk seriously but stressed to me the uncertain durability of Japan's large trade surplus. It is notable, however, that the Japanese authorities have been permitting the market rate of the yen to creep upward day by day, so that it is now 9 per cent above the old parity. Moreover, I received indications from some dependable (I think) emissaries that the Japanese will be willing to settle for a 15 per cent appreciation, provided other countries move at the same time.

The Germans (Bundesbank President Klasen) have permitted their currency to float up about 10 per cent since May and are coming under severe pressure from businessmen, who are feeling the effects not only of the exchange rate change but also the surcharge and the job development credit (which, as you know, does not apply to imported equipment). The Germans are particularly sensitive about the movement of their exchange rate against the French franc. For these reasons, as well as the prospective slowdown in the economy, their officials indicated that they are anxious for an early settlement.

Secretary Connally and I met with the assembled Finance Ministers and central bank Governors of Latin America. We explained the rationale for the U.S. program and, after the Secretary left, I took their questions. The main concerns they expressed were: Why should the surcharge apply to them and other developing countries when we do not expect them to appreciate their exchange rates or take other actions to improve the U.S. balance of payments? How can the LDC's participate in the negotiations about both the immediate problems and reform of the international monetary system? I reassured them on the last point, and some overt moves in this direction are now being considered.

There is one highly important matter—regarding the arrangements for negotiations—on which I need to report to you in person. It is a matter which I arranged with foreign representatives and of which Secretary Connally has full knowledge.[2]

Sincerely yours,

Arthur

---

[2] Not further identified.

---

184.   **Letter From the President's Assistant for International Economic Affairs (Peterson) to the Under Secretary of the Treasury for Monetary Affairs (Volcker)[1]**

Washington, October 25, 1971.

Dear Paul:

As you know from our various discussions, I would think it very desirable if you would use the Volcker Group to start some intense dialogue and work soon on what kind of reformed monetary system we want.

This seems awfully important in two different contexts: First, as we move ahead in our Phase I negotiations, it may well be that where we want to end up in Phase II will affect what we should be willing to do or not do in Phase I. Second, the President and John Connally have repeatedly emphasized their commitment to basic monetary reform and I think it is incumbent upon us to define what we want that system to be. I know that men like Ken Dam and Ezra Solomon have strong views about what the shape of such a system might be. There are cer-

---

[1] Source: National Archives, Nixon Presidential Materials, White House Central Files, Federal Government Organizations, Treasury 1/1/71–2/29/72, Box 2. No classification marking. Copies were sent to Shultz, Ezra Solomon, and Dam.

tain key issues—like whether it is in the long-term U.S. interests to have any convertibility at all and the related issue of whether a reserve currency status is or is not in the interests of the U.S.—that I hear very different views on, as I listen to various experts.

I asked Dick Cooper, who works with us, if he couldn't summarize for me what some of the key issues are on this whole area. I've attached a copy and sent one to Ken Dam and Ezra Solomon.[2]

I know how unbelievably busy you are, Paul, but I hope you can get the Volcker Group going on this whole issue of what kind of monetary system we want.[3]

Sincerely yours,

Pete

---

[2] Not found.

[3] The dominant topic in the Volcker Group papers for 1971, both before and after August 15, was the limited exchange rate flexibility initiative. None of the policy papers on negotiating the international aspects of the New Economic Policy prior to the Smithsonian Agreement on December 18 is part of this record. The dominant topic of the Volcker Group papers in 1972 was developing the terms of reference for the C-20 and drafting the IMF Report on International Monetary Reform paper for the 1972 Annual Meeting. None of the 1972 Contingency Planning papers for the currency crisis should the Smithsonian rates fail is included in the Volcker Group papers. (Washington National Records Center, Department of the Treasury, Volcker Group Masters: FRC 56 86 30)

---

185.   Memorandum From the President's Assistant for International Economic Affairs (Peterson) to Secretary of the Treasury Connally[1]

Washington, October 26, 1971.

SUBJECT

Negotiating the New Economic Policy Abroad—Work Group

You will remember our meeting in your apartment prior to the IMF meetings when I gave you a brief progress report on the staff work on this project.[2] The work is now much further along and ready for your review. I have talked to Rose about seeing you very briefly on a couple of delicate personal items relating to the planning for these negotiations.

---

[1] Source: Washington National Records Center, Department of the Treasury, Records of Secretary Shultz: FRC 56 80 1, CIEP–Peterson. Confidential; Eyes Only.

[2] This meeting has not been further identified.

I know the tremendous pressure you are under prior to leaving for Japan and think we can limit our time to several issues that are now out-standing.[3]

On the trade and defense side, there seems to be a large measure of agreement on the specific concessions and objectives we are after. State may still have a couple of reservations. But I'm not sure.

There are, however, several issues where there are differences of view, or at least questions:

1. *Lifting the surcharge reasonably soon* (next few months) vs. waiting. A particular question is the LDC's and Latin America where the President has some specific concerns.[4]

2. *Changing the Price of Gold as part of an exchange rate realignment.* If we get an average realignment of say 10–11% with a gold price change and 5–6% without it, are the benefits of the larger exchange rate realign-ment worth the costs of a gold price change? Can we devise ways of affecting a gold price change that minimize the costs and risks (politi-cal, implied movement toward gold and convertibility?)

3. *Convertibility during the interim period? How much or little? How do you limit it? What are its implications?* (Most agree there should be very little or none but some disagreement about how little and how.)

4. *Capital controls?* Take off very soon, i.e. now or with surcharge removal, or, take off as a goal in Phase II or, cut them back administra-tively and in a low profile way? What about interest equalization tax? What should we do about this?

I would propose getting the Quadriad together tomorrow (with Paul Volcker and anyone else you want, of course) but without the President. I see no point to bother him unless there are major differences of view. The meeting could be held at Treasury.

At that meeting, we would summarize briefly the outstanding issues and various approaches that have been discussed.

Then, depending upon the outcome, we could arrive at a set of marching orders on who does what while you are in Japan, vis-à-vis Canada, Europe, etc.

---

[3] Secretary Connally traveled to Asia October 28–November 14.

[4] As soon as the New Economic Policy was announced on August 15 there were calls for special treatment for Latin America and/or developing countries. The September 12 State Department report to Kissinger on "Foreign Reactions to the President's Economic Program" contains the following: "The Latin American countries protested US economic measures in a Manifesto issued following a meeting of the Special Commission for Latin American Coordination (CECLA) on September 3 and 4 in Buenos Aires. The Manifesto called on the United States to exempt developing coun-tries from the 10 percent import surcharge and reverse its decision to reduce the level of foreign economic aid. The meeting was called at the request of the Argentines, who along with the Mexicans and Chileans, were the most outspoken critics of the new eco-nomic measures, particularly the import surcharge." (National Archives, RG 59, Central Files 1970–73, E 1 US)

The attached paper has been given to Quadriad members only and has been read by them.[5] Obviously, Paul Volcker and John Petty have been deeply involved in all this and very helpful.

---

[5] Not printed; see Document 186. The Quadriad comprised Connally, Burns, McCracken, and Shultz. No record of a Quadriad meeting on October 27 has been found, but President Nixon met with the Economic Quadriad the next day; see Document 187.

---

186.   Editorial Note

The 36-page draft paper attached to the October 26, 1971, memorandum from Peterson to Secretary Connally (Document 185) is dated October 25 and entitled "Negotiating the New Economic Policy Abroad." Classified Secret, it is divided into nine sections: Introduction—Some Backdrop, Objectives and Their Priority, Negotiating Levers and Issues, Overall Negotiating Scenario, Decision Points and Coordination, The Official Price of Gold, U.S. Convertibility in the Interim Period, Fundamental Monetary Reform, and Negotiating Strategies—Surcharge and Capital Controls. The scope of the paper is broad and deals with monetary issues, trade issues, defense burden-sharing issues, and the free flow of investment. There are sections specifically directed at objectives with Japan, Canada, and the European Community. The paper contains a number of specific negotiating strategies and objectives, including the following:

"The surcharge provides little leverage against France, and France does not abhor the trade wars and bloc formation which could develop. We can therefore achieve an effective French revaluation only by devaluing the dollar. . . . The United States should agree to devalue the dollar against gold by 5% to 8% if the following monetary conditions are met: 1. Simultaneous revaluations of *at least* 10% by Japan and 5% by Germany, leading to effective exchange rate changes of *at least* 15%–18% for Japan; 10%–13% for Germany; and 5%–8% for France, Italy, Britain (hopefully)." (pages 21–22)

These are, in effect, the measures agreed to by Presidents Nixon and Pompidou in the Azores (see Document 220) and by the G–10 in the Smithsonian Agreement on December 18 (see Document 221).

The draft paper received only limited distribution; another copy is marked "#2 of 5." On the cover sheet of that copy Kissinger wrote: "For meeting with Peterson," and Haig wrote: "HAK wants staffed (Bob—this came 'eyes only' from Peterson)" when he routed the paper to

Hormats. (National Archives, Nixon Presidential Materials, NSC Files, Subject Files, Box 376, President's Economic Program)

In his October 26 covering memorandum, Peterson noted that the attached draft paper had been given only to Quadriad members, but an October 29 memorandum from Deputy Under Secretary of State Samuels to Peterson entitled "Your Memorandum on the New Economic Policy," is presumably a State Department response to the paper. Generally, the State Department agreed with the basic conclusions and priorities set out in the draft paper. (National Archives, RG 59, Central Files 1970–73, E 1 US)

---

187.   Editorial Note

OMB Director George Shultz discussed currency matters with President Nixon on October 25, 1971. He opened the meeting with the suggestion that they be prepared to lift the surcharge for any country that would conduct a clean float of its currency. The President thought that would be illegal under GATT rules, but Shultz reported that staff work at OMB suggested it could be done. He said it would not be discriminatory against any country and it would be a "way to get the ball rolling." Although not in agreement on this issue, the President nonetheless clearly wanted Shultz to take a more aggressive role in bringing the international monetary crisis to resolution. He said Shultz understood the subject and could better "broker" a solution than the others. He did not want to find himself in a situation where Peterson or Connally dictated what they were going to do. The President said "we have to get Connally on board" for finding a solution.

A major topic Shultz and the President discussed on October 25 was restoration of convertibility. Shultz was concerned that policymakers were "drifting back to the old system of parities, but with different exchange rates," the solution he thought was preferred by the "axis" of European bankers, Daane at the Federal Reserve, and Volcker at Treasury. Shultz was not sure where Burns stood on the issue and thought he was more concerned with maintenance of the wage/price freeze; he thought Connally would agree with the President there should be no return to convertibility and that Volcker would have to be instructed to work on a plan with that approach. Shultz carefully explained, and the President agreed, that if there were a return to fixed parities and convertibility, the only way to address a balance-of-payments deficit would be to deflate the domestic economy to lower prices, creating "unemployment to satisfy international pressure." The President said he did not want domestic policies to be affected by the outmoded system and "we can build a system without convertibility." Although he did not press the point, Shultz clearly favored a floating rate system.

Shultz and the President also discussed the price of gold. Shultz expressed the opinion that with all the gold in French "mattresses," gold was a big political problem in France, and it might be necessary to change the relationship of the dollar to gold in order to devalue the dollar. The President agreed that "damn gold has a mystique" but said "I'll be damned if we will raise the price of gold like Arthur wants." (National Archives, Nixon Presidential Materials, White House Tapes, Recording of Conversation Between President Nixon and Budget Director Shultz, October 25, 1971, 4:35–6:01 p.m., Executive Office Building, Conversation 304-17)

During this October 25 meeting with Shultz, the President made it clear he wanted to meet with Connally before the latter's trip to Asia October 28–November 14 (which would include stops in Vietnam for President Thieu's inauguration, Thailand, Indonesia, the Philippines, and Japan), and that a Quadriad meeting could be scheduled if necessary. Under cover of an undated, handwritten letter to the President, Connally provided "Suggested Talking Position for Meeting with Chairman Arthur Burns and Secretary Connally" that could "serve as a basis for your remarks to the Cabinet." Connally added that his points had not been seen by "Paul and Geo." (presumably McCracken and Shultz, the other two members of the Quadriad), and recommended the President get their judgment on them. Butterfield stamped "The President has seen" on Connally's talking paper. (Ibid., White House Central Files, Federal Government Organizations, Treasury 1/1/71–2/29/72, Box 2)

The Economic Quadriad met on the afternoon of October 28, prior to Connally's departure that evening. Those present were the President, Connally, Burns, McCracken, Shultz, Flanigan, and Peterson. Flanigan left at 4:24 p.m. and Peterson at 4:42 p.m. Kissinger joined the meeting at 5:02 p.m., and he and Connally remained with the President until 5:54 p.m. following Burns', McCracken's, and Shultz's departure at 5:20 p.m. (Ibid., President's Daily Diary) The President set the agenda for the meeting, announcing they would first take up international issues, followed by domestic issues. There would also be a short break for a photo opportunity of Connally with the President to bolster Connally's image, primarily for his visit to Japan.

The tape of the Quadriad conversation evinces a wide-ranging discussion of international economic policy issues. Connally was praised for bringing the issues forward from where they were in August, and Shultz said that now that "we have their attention" it was time to move vigorously on negotiations. While Connally was traveling, Shultz would work with Kissinger to see what leverage the United States had with France, which he said would not revalue (by changing the franc price of gold). Burns returned to that point later in the conversation and in a lengthy discourse explained how gold was a "huge political problem" for the French. He said his discussions with French officials convinced him France would settle for a stable price of gold in terms of French francs, and indicated that if the United States could otherwise get a good settlement, the United States should not be stuck on "gold theology." Burns said the French would let the franc appreciate in terms of dollars, thought the other Europeans and the Japanese would support France on this position, and said domestically France had less of a political problem than in 1968 when the market price of gold equaled the official price. Under the two-tier system, with the market price above the official price, Burns said Congressman Reuss and Senator Proxmire would support a small increase in the official price of gold. Shultz terminated that subject, noting that the President had said they would not increase the price of gold. He then posed the question of whether they were going to return to fixed parities or try to operate with floating rates. He said the price of gold was incidental to this more fundamental question and the complementary issues of trade and burdensharing agreements. He said the administration needed to have a clear picture of where it wanted to come out.

Connally set out a five-point program that he thought could be negotiated during the next few months: first, a significant realignment in currency parities; second, no return to convertibility for at least 2 years, other than small transactions in SDRs as required for technical purposes; third, an agreement on trade principles and the removal of trade barriers, with the details to be worked out later; fourth, an agreement on a substantial, if not complete, reduction in the role of gold in the international monetary system; and fifth, agreement that the dollar would no longer be the sole vehicle currency.

Connally said the average U.S. citizen neither understood nor cared about monetary policy, but did care about trade and the fact that the administration was looking out for U.S. interests. Politically, it was thus necessary to discuss trade and burdensharing even if that were to delay his negotiating strategy for another year. Currency realignment, he said, was much less important than not giving the impression the United States was losing ground. Connally noted that it would be a "mistake of major political importance" for the President to get just a currency realignment without also obtaining the other objectives.

The President concluded this segment of the discussion suggesting that in Connally's absence the others work on the process on a very confidential basis, and they not have a further discussion "at this level" until Connally returned. The official line would be that there would be no action in Connally's absence, the President was still examining the options, and would await a report from Connally when he returned from Japan.

Following a brief photo opportunity for Connally with the President, the Quadriad then discussed domestic economic issues. Connally and Kissinger stayed on after the meeting concluded. Connally reported on his conversation with Shultz the previous day, and explained their recommendation that the President should say there should be no discussion of the price of gold or convertibility. See Document 189.

The President, Kissinger, and Connally then commented briefly on aspects of international economic policy before turning to Connally's forthcoming trip. Japan was central, and the President expressed the opinion that Burns was incorrect in his view that Japan would not deal on the international economic issues unless Europe also made a deal. Connally agreed. The President suggested that Connally take the approach that "this President intends to keep the United States in the Pacific and the Pacific should receive more attention." In that context, what sort of deal could Japan make. Connally requested the President's authority to tell the Japanese that with European consolidation European nations were increasingly speaking with one voice and should have only one vote in the G-10. The President agreed the G-10 should be changed. He also requested that Connally raise the SST with the Japanese (see footnote 1, Document 194) and instructed him to meet with Sato privately without the Ambassador being present. (National Archives, Nixon Presidential Materials, White House Tapes, Recording of Conversation Among President Nixon, Secretary Connally, and others, October 28, 1971, 3:03–5:54 p.m., Oval Office, Conversation 606-2)

188.   Information Memorandum From Robert Hormats of the National Security Council Staff to the President's Assistant for National Security Affairs (Kissinger)[1]

Washington, November 1, 1971.

SUBJECT

Talking Points for Your Meeting with George Shultz, Tuesday, November 2, at 8:45 a.m.

Shultz apparently wants to inform you of the results of the Quadriad Meeting which took place last Thursday,[2] and get your views on the present international economic situation. With regard to the latter, there are two points which you might stress.

—The longer the surcharge is retained, the less of a bargaining asset it is and the greater the risk that it will harm our overall economic, foreign policy and security interests.

—Recognizing this, the surcharge should be removed in return for small amounts of additional depreciation of the yen, mark, and Canadian dollar, plus a minimum list of additional desiderata in the area of trade and defense burden sharing which can be negotiated within four to eight weeks.

Background

Secretary Connally seems to have departed from what many had perceived to be a more "cooperative" line. Last week in San Francisco he told the American Bankers Association that the surcharge "is going to stay on for a while because it frankly is to our advantage to keep it on for a while."[3] The Europeans, Canadians, and Japanese, as the result of this and other such statements, increasingly believe that the U.S. is unwilling to cooperate with them to bring about conditions for removal of the surcharge. And there are indications that they feel that even if they are forthcoming, the U.S. will maintain an unreasonable posture and retain the surcharge indefinitely.

---

[1] Source: National Archives, Nixon Presidential Materials, NSC Files, Agency Files, Box 268, Office of Management and Budget. Confidential. Initialed by Haig. A stamped notation on the memorandum reads: "HAK has seen."

[2] October 28; see Document 187.

[3] No text of Connally's remarks has been found. According to *The New York Times,* October 21, Connally delivered some extemporaneous remarks at the closing session of the American Bankers Association Annual Meeting on October 20. The focus of the article is on changes in the prime lending rate, but the language Hormats quotes in his memorandum is in a brief section on international economic policy, followed by: "It is going to come off when this nation has some assurance that our balance-of-payments deficit will indeed be rectified or until we can be assured that the mechanism is established by which it can be rectified."

526 Foreign Relations, 1969–1976, Volume III

Disadvantages of retaining the surcharge

—Many of our key trading partners (including Italy and Germany) are faced with economic recessions and growing unemployment. While the U.S. surcharge is obviously not the *main* cause of these problems, it may be a *partial* cause. At any rate, because of it the U.S. will be used as a scapegoat, thus making it increasingly difficult for other nations—no matter how well disposed they or their leaders have been toward us—to cooperate with us on economic, political, or security matters.

—Canada and others are taking, or are considering taking, countermeasures such as instituting restrictions on monetary or trade flows. Vested interests in those countries will seek to maintain these controls thus making future negotiations more difficult. And such negotiations could become primarily efforts to eliminate countermeasures rather than the trade barriers and exchange rate inequities which were our original targets. [State (Tab A) indicates that Germany, as well as other European nations, may soon be forced to take such measures.][4]

—As other nations institute countermeasures, and become less disposed and less able to cooperate with us to bring about the changes we desire, the surcharge becomes a wasting asset. In addition it becomes increasingly detrimental to our overall economic and political interests. By contributing, even at the margin, to a deterioration in international trade and in the economies of our major trading partners, which will decrease U.S. exports, it runs the risk of harming our overall economic interests and, rightly or wrongly, increasing the intensity of domestic and foreign criticism of the President. And to the extent that the international political system is harmed by the spillover effect, the same reaction will occur. *Far from being in our interest, long-term retention of the surcharge can be extremely detrimental to our interests.*

You might, therefore, indicate to Shultz that our economic, foreign policy, and security interests will best be served if we move promptly to negotiate conditions which will allow us to remove the surcharge *by the end of the year.*

---

[4] Brackets in the source text. Tab A, not printed, is another of the end-of-the-week Department of State reports from Executive Secretary Eliot to Kissinger entitled "Foreign Reactions to the President's Economic Program" for October 29. The report indicated that about 20 diplomatic notes had been received protesting one or more U.S. actions and most of the U.S. major trading partners had threatened "appropriate compensatory measures should the DISC proposal be enacted." The report noted that a senior German official told the Embassy in Bonn that the European Community had turned its attention to internal solutions, was hardening its position toward the United States, and that "Germany's ability to urge a flexible EC position toward the U.S. was weakened by confusing reports of a possible deal between the U.S. and the FRG for selective removal of the surcharge."

Conditions for surcharge removal

There are several conditions for surcharge removal which would a) be acceptable on domestic political grounds, b) allow us to realize some significant gains in terms of international economic policy, and c) we could reasonably expect to obtain by the end of the year:

—A small increase in the parities of the yen, mark, and Canadian dollar.[5]

—Additional trade measures with Japan as a follow-up to the ECONCOM.

—An understanding with the Common Market about future negotiations on the reduction of tariff barriers, plus a reduction in their export subsidies on agriculture.

—An agreement with Canada relating to the Canadian-U.S. Auto Agreement.

—A favorable offset agreement with Germany.

—A commitment from Japan (already made in principle) to purchase additional military equipment in the United States.

You might wish to determine what conditions Shultz would attach to surcharge removal, whether he would agree with the above, and, if you agree with one another, the best method of getting Secretary Connally to act on the basis of your views.[6]

---

[5] All three had already floated to new parities since May.

[6] No record of a meeting between Kissinger and Shultz was found.

189. Memorandum From President Nixon[1]

Washington, November 2, 1971.

MEMORANDUM FOR

> Honorable John Connally
> Honorable Arthur Burns
> Honorable George Shultz
> Honorable Paul McCracken
> Honorable Peter Peterson
> Honorable Peter Flanigan

After our discussion in the Quadriad meeting October 29, 1971,[2] I believe it is essential that there be no further speculation within the Administration which might get into the press or into foreign circles with regard to changing the price of gold or a return to some form of convertibility. Our planning at this time should proceed on the assumption that we are not going to move in that direction.[3]

Richard Nixon

---

[1] Source: National Archives, Nixon Presidential Materials, NSC Files, Agency Files, Box 268, Office of Management and Budget. Secret. Attached to a November 3 note from Shultz to Kissinger that reads, "I know you will be interested in the attached."

[2] The Quadriad meeting was on October 28; see Document 187. President Nixon met again with Arthur Burns from 11:01 to 11:30 a.m. on October 29 and with George Shultz from 4:15 to 5:16 p.m., but there was no meeting of the Quadriad. (National Archives, Nixon Presidential Materials, White House Central Files, President's Daily Diary) Connally was out of Washington on his Asian trip.

[3] In a November 1 memorandum from Shultz to President Nixon, Shultz suggested four points he and Connally thought the President should make at the Quadriad: "you have thought and read a great deal recently about international monetary matters; you continue to feel that it is a mistake to make a change in the price of gold and do not want discussions going on that would lead people to think the President might recommend a change; you also will not entertain suggestions for even limited forms of convertibility; you want work to proceed on the assumption of these two conditions: no convertibility, no change in the price of gold." (Ibid., Federal Government Organizations, Treasury 11/1/71–2/29/72, Box 2) Shultz' memorandum is stamped "The President has seen."

190.   Telegram From the Embassy in Germany to the Department of State[1]

Bonn, November 5, 1971, 1716Z.

13810. Department pass Treasury for Under Secretary Volcker and State for Deputy Under Secretary Samuels. Ref: Bonn 13633.[2]

1. *Summary:* During the EEC Finance Ministers' meeting[3] Giscard gave an indication of the degree of a dollar devaluation France would be willing to accept on the basis of which Schiller believes a package can be put together at the November 22 G-10 meeting involving a 10 percent improvement in the US competitive position which he hopes the US can accept as a quid pro quo for the removal of the import surcharge.

2. Economics Ministry Deputy Assistant Secretary Tietmeyer gave the Financial Attaché today the following information concerning the EEC Finance Ministers meeting in Paris. Tietmeyer said that he had discussed with State Secretary Schoellhorn the question of informing the Financial Attaché and that Schoellhorn had agreed provided the information would be held very closely and "not reported through normal diplomatic channels."

3. At the outset of the meeting Giscard reported on the Pompidou letter to Brandt.[4] The Dutch, Belgian, Italian and Luxembourg Finance Ministers thereupon suggested that the EEC countries should suggest to Secretary Connally to cancel the November 22 G-10 meeting if no decision can be made until after the Brandt–Pompidou meeting.[5] Giscard and Schiller felt the G-10 meeting should proceed as scheduled and this was agreed at the end of the Finance Ministers' meeting. The Germans feel this correctly reflects the progress made by the Finance Ministers which now brings an agreement at the G-10 meeting into the realm of the possible.

4. At the restricted session of the Finance Ministers, Schiller took the position that in calling for a US contribution (i.e., devaluation) to the currency realignment, the EEC must be able to tell the US for how large a devaluation of the dollar in terms of gold its members would be willing to stand still (i.e., not also devalue their own currencies). In the

---

[1] Source: National Archives, RG 59, S/S Files: Lot 73 D 153, Morning Summaries. Secret; Immediate; Exdis.

[2] Not printed.

[3] The meeting was held in Paris on November 4.

[4] Not further identified.

[5] Brandt and Pompidou met in Paris on December 4. The G-10 Ministerial was held in Rome November 30–December 1.

ensuing discussion Giscard gave the other Ministers a clear idea how large a US devaluation France could accept. While Tietmeyer was not willing to give the Financial Attaché the exact figure, the Financial Attaché gained the impression that it is more than 5 percent (a change of the dollar parity to 37 or possible 37-1/2 ounces of gold). Giscard also indicated that France could accept a devaluation of this magnitude only if the following other conditions are met: (A) France's competitive position vis-à-vis Italy and the UK is not impaired, i.e., Italy and the UK also do not devalue their currencies in terms of gold; (B) France's competitive position vis-à-vis the Benelux countries is slightly improved, i.e., these countries revalue by at least 2 percent; (C) France's competitive position vis-à-vis Germany is improved substantially—Tietmeyer did not specifically indicate by how much, but the Financial Attaché gained the impression that the figure is in the 5–6 percent range.

5. Schiller feels that with a French position as outlined by Giscard an agreement might be possible at the November 22 meeting of the Group-of-Ten provided that (A) Giscard's position at the EEC Finance Ministers meeting has or will receive the blessing of Pompidou and (B) the US would be willing to make the "contribution" of dollar devaluation of this magnitude and would be willing to remove the import surcharge in return for a package of revaluation and "standing still" by the other industrial countries which together with the US devaluation would improve the competitive position of the dollar by roughly 10 percent vis-à-vis the other major industrial countries as a group. On the basis of his conversations in Washington Schiller apparently has gained the impression that while the US would like to gain more, such a package or something close to it might be a minimum acceptable to the US.[6]

6. Schiller will be going to London on Monday in the hope of selling this position to the UK. There also is still some difficulty whether Italy would be able to "stand still" for a US devaluation of this magnitude. Finally, Germany could make its contribution only if Japan is willing to at the very least match the German revaluation and Canada revalues substantially. But Schiller is relatively hopeful that it will be possible to put together a package leading to agreement at the G-10 meeting. The EEC Finance Ministers are scheduled to meet in Rome at 11:00 a.m. on November 22 to review the situation just prior to the G-10 meeting.

Rush

---

[6] Presumably a reference to Schiller's meeting with Secretary Connally on September 25; see Document 181.

191.   Editorial Note

A meeting of the G-10 Ministers, chaired by Secretary Connally, was scheduled for November 22–23, 1971, in Rome. In view of an anticipated, but still unscheduled meeting between Chancellor Brandt and President Pompidou and general uncertainty on whether the Ministers would be able to close on a solution, some thought the Rome Ministerial should be postponed. Secretary Connally concurred and informed Prime Minister Sato during their November 12 meeting he had just taken that decision (see footnote 3, Document 194). Alternative dates were considered and the Rome Ministerial was rescheduled and held November 30–December 1.

On November 12 Peterson sent Kissinger a memorandum informing him the November 22 G-10 Ministerial had been postponed and speculated it would not take place until after the Brandt–Pompidou meeting. He considered the need for sending them some high-level communication" before their meeting, a communication that proved unnecessary when the G-10 meeting took place before the Brandt–Pompidou summit in Paris December 3–4. Peterson concluded his memorandum to Kissinger with the following: "What I would appreciate from you, Henry, is your sense of the politics and your reaction to the idea since this issue has become so highly political. Frankly, I am worried that the channels between Treasury and European Finance Ministry people and between Arthur Burns and Central Bank Governors, good as they are, may not be giving full weight to the political dimension of the situation in Europe." (National Archives, Nixon Presidential Materials, NSC Files, Agency Files, Box 289, Treasury Volume II)

President Pompidou also had some views on scheduling the G-10 Ministerial. On November 2 Kissinger had sent a back channel telegraphic message to Ambassador Watson in Paris informing him that President Nixon was considering initiating a series of bilateral discussions with principal European leaders prior to his visits to China and the Soviet Union in February and May 1972 and wanted the first bilateral to be with President Pompidou. Kissinger suggested the meeting take place in French Guyana December 3–4 or during a 2-day period between December 10 and 14. (Ibid., President's Trip Files, Box 473, Azores–Pompidou Dec 13/14, 1971)

After 10 days of discussions about a venue outside France and the United States, including a quick trip by Watson to Washington to consult on the matter, Watson sent a back channel message to Kissinger on November 12 informing him Pompidou had agreed to meet President Nixon in the Azores (in a hotel, not on the U.S. base) between December

11 and 15. Watson added, however, that Pompidou had a problem with the timing of the G-10 Ministerial and wanted the Rome meeting to be held on November 30, not December 7–8, because the monetary meeting had to take place before he met with Chancellor Brandt in early December. (Telegram 1853 from Paris, November 12, 2005Z; ibid.)

Another copy of Ambassador Watson's November 12 message is attached to a November 13 memorandum from Kennedy to Kissinger regarding "Your Meeting with Secretary Connally." Kennedy noted that Connally had been delaying the G-10 meeting and that Sonnenfeldt thought Kissinger should take it up with Connally in view of the message from Paris. Kennedy added, parenthetically, that Watson probably had not used the State Department communication channel to avoid disclosing he had been talking with Pompidou. Kennedy told Kissinger the issue was whether U.S. interests were best served by having the monetary meeting before or after the Brandt–Pompidou summit. (National Archives, Nixon Presidential Materials, NSC Files, Agency Files, Box 289, Treasury Volume II 1971)

On November 17 Kissinger sent a back channel message for delivery to Watson at the opening of business on November 18 informing him that he, Kissinger, hoped to have a decision on the timing of the G-10 Ministerial early the following week. Kissinger noted that he would be meeting with Connally on November 19, with the intention of obtaining an early decision on the G-10 meeting and a position on related economic problems. (White House telegram 11024, November 18, 0300Z; ibid., President's Trip Files, Box 473, Azores–Pompidou Dec 13–14 1971)

On November 18 Kissinger sent another back channel message to Watson informing him that he had "succeeded in having the President direct Secretary Connally to proceed with the G-10 meeting in Rome on November 30th." Kissinger asked Watson to confirm the December 13–14 dates with the French and to work with them (and keep secret until then) on a joint announcement for November 24 that, on the U.S. side, would also include announcements of meetings with Prime Minister Heath in Bermuda December 20–21 and with Chancellor Brandt at Key Biscayne December 28–29. (White House telegram 11026, November 18, 2051Z; ibid.)

The President met with Kissinger from 10:13 to 10:50 a.m. and again from 11:40 to noon on November 18. (Ibid., White House Central Files, President's Daily Diary) Haldeman was present at both meetings, and his handwritten notes indicate that one of the points Kissinger raised in the first session was Pompidou's insistence that the G-10 Ministerial be held on November 30. Later in the morning Haldeman's notes indicate Pompidou should be scheduled for December 13–14. (Ibid., White

House Special Files, Box 44, Haldeman Notes, Oct–Dec 1971) The President phoned Secretary Connally and talked with him from 4:17 to 4:24 p.m. that day. (Ibid., White House Central Files, President's Daily Diary)

Prior to Kissinger's arrival for his first meeting with the President on November 18, the President discussed with Haldeman having Connally, Shultz, and Kissinger come to Key Biscayne Friday night (where the President went on the afternoon of Thursday, November 18, returning on Sunday, November 21) for a meeting on either Saturday or Sunday. The President then considered having that meeting on Monday, November 22. See Document 203 regarding the President's meetings with his economic advisers on November 23 and 24.

192. Letter From the Vice President of the Deutsche Bundesbank (Emminger) to the Under Secretary of the Treasury for Monetary Affairs (Volcker)[1]

Frankfurt, November 12, 1971.

Dear Paul:

Attached please find my understanding of the present situation as concerns exchange rate re-alignment. You will understand that I could not put in any more concrete figures; but the attainable magnitudes have now become fairly clear.

This is, of course, only for your personal information.

With best regards,

sincerely

Otmar Emminger

[1] Source: Washington National Records Center, Department of the Treasury, Files of Under Secretary Volcker: FRC 56 79 15, Germany General. Personal. An attached note, dated November 16, reads: "Informed by Mr. Bennett that he has been instructed by Mr. Volcker to give Dr. Emminger an oral answer in Paris this week." No record of Volcker's answer was found.

Attachment[2]

November 11, 1971.

The strategic situation on re-alignment

After the meeting of the Finance Ministers of the Six in Versailles on November 4, the situation regarding further progress has become much clearer. It can be summed up as follows:

1. No move can be expected in the *gold* parity of the French Franc. This has to be taken—and has been accepted (willy-nilly) by the Six—as an *immovable corner stone* of any future arrangement. However, in the case of a downward adjustment of the dollar parity, the French are prepared to maintain their present gold parity, or in other words, to tolerate a de-facto appreciation in relation to the dollar (this has been told by Giscard d'Estaing, although indirectly, even to the press).

2. The French Franc will serve as a "leading indicator" (or example) for the exchange rate policies of Italy and Britain. Neither of the two is prepared to move its parity up in relation to the Franc (which they, rightly, consider to be inherently stronger than their own currencies). Both these other countries seem, however, to be prepared to maintain, in case of a downward adjustment of the dollar, their previous parity, provided the French do the same. Some other European countries are likely to take their cue, too, from the French Franc (plus the Lira and the Pound).

3. The readiness of the French to stay put as concerns their gold parity depends, of course, on the amount of the downward adjustment in the dollar parity. No one could at present say whether the "threshold of tolerance" is 5 or 6. There are, however, enough signs to the effect that the tolerance level would be high enough to permit an average shift between the dollar and the other G 10 currencies (incl. the Swiss franc) of 9 to 10%. The exact magnitude of the French "tolerance level" can only be found out once it is assured that the dollar itself moves.

4. A de-facto appreciation of the French Franc in the foreseeable magnitude would in all probability allow the German DMark to be raised sufficiently high vis-à-vis the dollar, while attaining a more reasonable relationship vis-à-vis the Franc and other important European currencies. This would then also permit to bring the Japanese Yen into the proper line, viz. a fairly high appreciation in

---

[2] No classification marking.

relation to the dollar, a more moderate upvaluation in relation to the main European currencies.

5. If on the American side there were no readiness to reduce the dollar parity, then the whole negotiating process would get stuck. It is *simply erroneous* to believe, that a German-French tête à tête could in any way break the deadlock. Even if it were to lead to an agreement on the future relationship between the DMark and the Franc (which would certainly be on a lesser disparity than at present), there would be no way from there to a satisfactory collective agreement on the re-alignment question.

6. It is, therefore, a misjudgment to believe that a German-French summit, if it preceded the G 10 meeting, could do much good for the latter. Ideally, the time sequence should be reversed: If the G 10 meeting should end in visible failure, then a subsequent German-French meeting might perhaps lay the foundation for a regional (European) monetary set-up.

---

193.   Telegram From the Embassy in the United Kingdom to the Department of State[1]

London, November 12, 1971, 1744Z.

10453. Dept pass Treasury and FRB. Subject: UK reaction to Secretary Connally's Tokyo press conference.[2]

1. A.D. Neale, Second Permanent Secretary, HMTreasury, called in Treasury Attaché to express their concern over today's *Times* report on Secretary Connally's remarks at press conference in Tokyo. Derek Mitchell, HMT Rep in Washington, was also present. *Times* reports Secretary Connally saying that settlement of monetary crisis depends entirely on other nations and that European countries were having difficulty in finding common position. Hence, he would not be surprised if the present unsettled situation dragged on beyond the end of the year. On G-10 postponement, *Times* says Secretary said reports from Europe

---

[1] Source: National Archives, RG 59, Central Files 1970–73, FN 17 UK. Confidential; Limdis; Greenback. Repeated to Bern, Bonn, Brussels, The Hague, Ottawa, Paris, Rome, Stockholm, Tokyo, USEC, and USOECD.

[2] Tokyo was the last stop on Secretary Connally's Asian tour.

had indicated that substantive progress would not be possible (septel gives full report on press coverage of G-10 meeting).[3]

2. Neale said Chancellor Barber had found this report most disturbing. He realized that Secretary had been in Far East and was not sure how much he had been able to keep in touch with most recent developments but felt that the French willingness to hold the present gold parity of the franc in face of increase in dollar price of gold was very significant concession on their part. He was thus puzzled by press report that Connally was attributing the delay to difficulties within Europe. He said that the G-10 participants had been quite willing and prepared for November 22 meeting and that the postponement was attributable to the US.

3. In response to questions to what extent Europeans had agreed on actual numbers among themselves, Neale said his feeling was agreement between French and Germans on franc–DM differential was in the offing and could be realized fairly quickly. He said that on dollar–franc differential, thinking centered around figure of 5 percent but he did not have figure for franc–DM differential. The other European exchange rates, he felt, would come along and fall into line without much difficulty. He pointed out that all this, of course, depends on how far the Japanese are prepared to move since the thinking is there must be some differential between European rates and the yen. Hence, in his view, the key rates were the franc–DM rate and the DM–yen rate. But the European settlement was dependent on the US being prepared to raise the price of gold (implicitly 5 percent).

4. We pointed out that US continues to feel that it is incumbent on the other countries to take initiatives and make constructive proposals. We were aware that French reportedly prepared to maintain the gold parity of franc but this did not seem to us a move so significant as to put the ball back into our court. Apart from the substantive issues, there was some feeling in Washington that the Europeans were approaching the problem entirely in terms of individual national interests whereas we felt a more constructive multilateral approach to a common world problem was in order. We also noted that trade and burdensharing were factors in the overall settlement and we had seen no disposition on the part of the Community to even consider what they might do in the trade area. Neale said he was not familiar with precisely what the US was pressing the Community for on trade and said he understood that we were not gunning for the UK in this area. Mitchell said that his discussions in Washington had revealed a good deal of naïveté about what could be done on trade matters in the Common Market. He said they

---

[3] Not found. No G-10 meeting in London during this time has been identified. The reference is probably to press coverage of Connally's postponement of the G-10 meeting. See Document 191.

don't seem to realize that the obverse of their various demands on the CAP were very difficult political problems for the EC countries.

5. Neale summed up by saying that if Secretary Connally is reported accurately and continues to take such a viewpoint, it would be very discouraging to all the participants and makes for a bleak outlook for a settlement.[4] He felt that continuation of uncertainty on the international monetary front was affecting domestic economic situations, that businessmen in Europe, and he understood in the US, were holding back because of this uncertainty. He was most anxious, therefore, for some indication from the US that some progress could be made fairly quickly.

6. *Comment:*

British had read into US postponement of G-10 meeting possibility, or at least hope, that US reassessing its position and/or some behind the scenes discussions going on that required more time for fruition. Secretary Connally's press conference remarks, if made in knowledge that French willing to hold franc–gold parity in face of dollar devaluation, appears to them to preclude both these possibilities. Neale today did not emphasize necessity of US declaring itself first on gold price increase, as he has before. Their immediate concern now appears to be that the US not preclude the possibility ahead of time.

In UK view, there are no real difficulties within Europe, rather the basic obstacle is the US and possibly Japan. If the US is prepared to move on the dollar gold price and the Japanese revalue enough to leave a sufficient DM–yen differential, the intra-European exchange rate realignment could be agreed among the Europeans fairly quickly. While Neale did not say how much differential between the DM and yen was required, he gave as illustrative figures 15 percent for the yen and 10 percent for the DM.[5]

Annenberg

---

[4] In a November 12 memorandum to Kissinger regarding the surcharge, Huntsman wrote: "The President noted in the November 12 News Summary that Paul Samuelson, Henry Wallich, and Milton Friedman said the surcharge must soon be ended or the nation will face a trade war that could hurt the world. Samuelson denounced as 'a bad way to negotiate,' Connally's statement in Japan that the surcharge will continue until the US wipes out its payments deficit. The President suggested that you note the above remarks in your talks with Secretary Connally." (National Archives, Nixon Presidential Materials, NSC Files, Agency Files, Box 289, Treasury Volume II, 1971)

[5] On November 12 President Nixon sent Kissinger a memorandum that reads: "Before Connally returns it might be well for you to go over and have a talk with Volcker if he is in town and if not with Walker, and if both are here with both of them, to get them programmed for some of the problems we will have to discuss with Connally when he returns. It is important that Volcker and Walker not set up a cabal against the White House as we make these very important decisions." (Ibid., Subject Files, Box 341, HAK/RN Memos 1971)

194.   Memorandum of Conversation[1]

Tokyo, November 12, 1971, 6:05 p.m.

PARTICIPANTS

Prime Minister Eisaku Sato
Ambassador Hideki Mazaki (Interpreter)
Terou Kosugi—Private Secretary to the Prime Minister (Excused himself after
   opening remarks)

Secretary of the Treasury John S. Connally
Ambassador Armin H. Meyer (Excused himself after opening remarks)
James J. Wickel—American Embassy, Tokyo (Interpreter)

SUBJECTS

(1) Opening Remarks
(2) China
(3) Vietnam and Korea
(4) Second Kissinger Visit to Peking
(5) President's Moscow Visit
(6) Economic Matters
(7) Okinawa: Nukes and Bases
(8) Closing Remarks

[Omitted here is discussion of the first five subjects.]

(6) Economic Matters

The Secretary explained that the President had to take the steps he did on August 15 to prevent any decline in our ability to maintain adequate military strength to ensure security, and to avoid the destruction of our ability to maintain an economic assistance program. Only by maintaining a strong economy, he reasoned, could we support our economic assistance efforts and even some increase in our defense establishment. The President is now able to move to reduce tensions with the

---

[1] Source: Washington National Records Center, Department of the Treasury, Records of Secretary Shultz: FRC 56 80 1, Subject Files 1971–74. Secret; Nodis. Drafted by Wickel; a typed note indicates the memorandum, which is marked "Draft," was not cleared by Secretary Connally. The meeting was held at Prime Minister Sato's residence. Another memorandum records the section of the conversation on economic matters in which Connally, at President Nixon's behest, asked if Japan would like to join the United States in a joint venture to develop and produce an SST. Connally explained that Boeing had developed a better prototype than either the Concorde or the Soviet TU-14 but Congress had refused to appropriate additional funds for tests and manufacturing and the project had been set aside. The United States would contribute the $1 billion in research data already in hand if Japan was prepared to finance the next stage. Connally noted that the President had discussed this with very few persons and asked the Prime Minister to keep it in strictest confidence. Sato agreed to keep the proposal in confidence, expressed some interest, but said he would have to study the proposal and would respond later. (Ibid.)

USSR and the PRC because he is dealing from strength, but he cautioned the American economy must be kept strong.

The Prime Minister said that the Secretary bears a heavy responsibility on his shoulders. He appreciated that the President's peace diplomacy depended on the continued maintenance of a strong deterrent posture in the interest of peace, and agreed that the American economy must be kept strong to ensure that purpose.

The Prime Minister said that Finance Minister Mizuta had informed him of his earlier discussions with the Secretary.[2] He speculated that the present monetary situation would not be easily resolved, since the EEC tends to move as a bloc, but one of its members, France, does not understand why it should move at all. He recalled meeting General DeGaulle, who threw out his chest and proclaimed that France would develop nuclear weapons to ensure its own defense; even though he admitted that France was too poor to afford a nuclear parity with the United States, DeGaulle wanted a force d'frappe to free France from its dependence on NATO. He commented that France is incapable of cooperating with anyone, even in economic matters. Japan is cooperating, he noted, but there is a need to persuade France to do so, much more than Germany.

The Secretary agreed completely, and said that it is easier to persuade all the other European countries than France, which seems to have a fixation about nuclear weapons as well as gold.

The Prime Minister said that the United States had been generous with many countries, and that Canada and Japan, and the NATO countries, including Germany, would cooperate in an effort to rebuild the United States economy, but he feared that this objective could not be easily achieved in the G-10. He asked for the Secretary's frank and confidential appraisal of the prospects and of the role he expected Japan to play.

The Secretary replied that he had just postponed the G-10 meeting supposed to be held November 22–23, because discussions with the representatives of its members gave clear signs of a direct collision with

---

[2] No record of this conversation was found, but a memorandum of Connally's 6:30 p.m. November 11 conversation with Foreign Minister Takeo Fukuda indicates that Connally met with the Finance Minister prior to his meeting with Fukuda. The memorandum records that Connally told Fukuda "there is a strong feeling in the United States that the United States has given freely of its natural resources and its people these past 25 years and that frankly this is being abused by some of our friends around the world. For example, he said, in 1971 Japan's growth included a 25% increase in exports, and the accumulation of foreign exchange assets at the rate of $1 billion per month, to the point that Japan's foreign exchange totals $13.5 billion, more than any other country except Germany, and greater than the United States. The American people don't understand Japan's restrictions against computers, aircraft and agricultural products." (Ibid.)

France over the gold and monetary problem.[3] The other nations feared that no good would come of a meeting at this time, he said, and presently consideration is being given to a meeting December 7–8, although a new date has not been fixed.

The Prime Minister agreed that it would be best not to meet until adequate preparations had been made. He apologized for not catching the news story about the postponement by explaining that he rarely reads newspapers because he finds their excessive hostility to his government distasteful.

The Secretary, by way of clarification, said that a meeting for the G-10 was not planned for November 22–23; the members were merely being sounded out, but the French leaked a report that it would be canceled.

The Prime Minister said little good would be served by speaking ill of France, but he noted that General DeGaulle, indebted as he was for the help of the Allied Powers, never thought of returning any favors.

The Secretary said that France had its problems, and that the UK would probably follow the French lead, at least until it obtained full membership in the EEC.

The Prime Minister said that the UK could probably play a useful role in the EEC vis-à-vis France in view of its special relationship with the United States.

The Secretary replied that one would think so, but these days, with its membership in the EEC pending, the UK could hardly be called helpful.

Still the Prime Minister thought that UK membership in the EEC would be beneficial in the long run since its presence would make it easier for the United States to present its views to the EEC.

Changing the subject, the Prime Minister said that he is deeply concerned that Japan and many other countries are feeling a sharp recession, which could, if unchecked, slip into a world depression. The United States economy is fundamental to this situation, he observed, but it could not be called bankrupt. Nevertheless mounting waves of recession could be seen on all sides and a reliable world system had to be rebuilt quickly. He did not believe that a breakdown in the system would lead to war at this late date in history.

The Secretary agreed that the United States had to correct its imbalance. Had it not acted August 15 to suspend gold convertibility it would

---

[3] During Connally's conversation with Foreign Minister Fukuda the previous evening (see footnote 2 above), the Secretary said he had been discussing postponing the G-10 meeting with Under Secretary Volcker, and Fukuda, also referring to France, had agreed there was no point to a G-10 meeting without some prospect for success.

have been exporting its depression to the world, he said, and the President felt that he had to act to bolster our own economy which was weakening to the danger point.

The Prime Minister said that he fully understood the need to suspend gold convertibility, but felt that the time had come to consider replacing it with a new system, based perhaps on SDRs.

The Secretary agreed.

The Prime Minister felt that it might get easier to deal with floating rates, and as more experience is accumulated exchange rates might be decided more naturally on that basis. He suggested considering a new system because there could be no return to gold convertibility, and perhaps floating exchange rates would provide a self-adjusting basis for realignment. He had not given up hope of a return to fixed rates (but not gold convertibility) although he conceded that the day of fixed rates might also end at some point.

The Prime Minister added that monetary adjustments are also of vital concern to the one million Okinawans who live on a dollar economy. Fortunately he worked out an arrangement with Finance Minister Mizuta to provide for the Okinawans to exchange their dollar holdings for yen upon reversion at the old rate, 360–1.

The Secretary then told the Prime Minister that he had made no specific suggestions about currency adjustment, burden sharing or trade liberalization in his discussion of United States economic problems with the GOJ Cabinet Ministers he had met; he had only outlined the nature of the United States problem and expressed the hope that they would consider how best Japan could help. He said that he informed all the Ministers that the United States seeks only to balance its payments, not to gain advantage over any other country, and looked forward to receiving suggestions on how Japan would help in whatever manner is politically acceptable and least offensive and economically feasible.

The Prime Minister asked whether all the Ministers passed this examination.

The Secretary said that all were interested in the amount expected of Japan. Our own study, he explained, disclosed that the Yen would have to be revalued 24%, the Mark 18% and the Franc 13% to yield the $13 billion swing the United States needed in its payments, but he conceded that this much might not be politically feasible for Japan, in one bite. Although the OECD and other international agencies disagreed with our own $13 billion figure, nevertheless he noted they did agree that the United States needed a swing ranging from $8–$10 billion to balance its payments. Of all the Ministers he met, he said he only informed Minister Mizuta of this 24% figure; he listened without comment.

The Prime Minister asked whether Minister Mizuta fainted, and whether the Secretary is serious about the 24% figure.

The Secretary replied that Minister Mizuta might have been shocked, but he didn't faint. He is quite serious about his figures, the Secretary said, because a Federal Reserve Board computer study showed that the United States needed a $13 billion swing to balance its payments. Even after deducting the $1 billion allowed for errors and omissions, and $1 billion for safety, the figures showed, to be objective, a need for an $11 billion swing, which is not too far out of line with the $8–$10 billion swing the IMF and OECD admit the United States needs. Calculations based on the $13 billion figure showed that the Yen had to be revalued 24%, the Mark 18% and the Franc 13%, but he admitted that 24% might be unrealistic to expect of Japan in one step.

The Prime Minister noted the September improvement in the United States balance, and asked whether this trend is expected to continue, or whether it resulted from special circumstances.

The Secretary did not know the cause, but did not believe that the September improvement was that great. Our Balance of Trade for the first six months was in deficit, he said, and this year for the first time since 1893 it was expected that the United States would run a trade deficit. In a sense there had been some revaluation, with the Yen floating upward some 9-1/2% and the Mark upward some 9%, all of which helped, he said, toward balancing our payments, but these floats amounted to less than what should be made. Politically and economically he supposed that 24% would be difficult for Japan.

The Prime Minister asked whether the United States would leave the surcharge.

The Secretary said that we would remove it, with adequate revaluation.

The Prime Minister, almost thinking aloud, said that the 10% surcharge, plus the float, almost equaled the Secretary's figure.

The Secretary observed that the situation might correct itself if the Yen floated freely for a number of months, without government intervention; realignment might thus become unnecessary.

The Prime Minister hoped that Minister of International Trade and Industry Tanaka had explained what a great effect the surcharge is having on Japan's trade and economy; he also hoped the Secretary understood the impact of the Yen float on Japan's export contracts, which had declined some 40%.

The Secretary observed that Japan's export customs clearance figures for September and October didn't show any appreciable decline.

The Prime Minister said that September was too early to show a decline, which only began to show up in October.

To be fair, the Secretary wondered whether both nations could agree to a relatively short bilateral arrangement, say for two years, with a trigger point for reappraisal if the agreement turned out to be bad for either side. He emphasized that he was thinking of a short term arrangement, which would not lock either side into a precise long-term position, because situations do change.

The Prime Minister said that he would have more to say about Yen parity later, but now wished to ask whether the United States is considering any more voluntary restraint requests, similar to the one presented through Ambassador-at-large David Kennedy.

The Secretary said that he hoped that it would not take three years to negotiate trade liberalization, since the GOJ is on record with its own trade liberalization program. There are a number of ways to correct the United States balance of payments situation, he said, but at the moment there are no product lines as urgent as textiles. However, he hoped that Japan would accelerate its tariff reductions and relax its administrative restraints as soon as possible. He then expressed appreciation for the Prime Minister's efforts to successfully conclude the textile agreement.

[Omitted here is discussion of the last two subjects.]

195. Information Memorandum From the President's Assistant for International Economic Affairs (Peterson) to President Nixon[1]

Washington, November 15, 1971.

SUBJECT

Status of International Economic Negotiations—Your Meeting This Morning with John Connally[2]

1. At the informal news conference upon his arrival, John Connally is reported to have said that the current monetary uncertainty could continue for "an almost indefinite period", that the U.S. would not suffer if it did and that the U.S. "is doing very well".[3]

This precipitated telephone calls to me from a variety of sources expressing concern that we did not understand the "precarious" stock market situation and the other effects on U.S. companies of this continued uncertainty and impending European recession.

Also, Treasury has indicated that Connally's speech before the Economic Club of New York tomorrow evening is a "major policy" statement. Apparently, the draft will not be ready until sometime today.[4]

In some of these calls to me, I am asked to do what I can with yourself and John Connally to "cool it", quit the "saber rattling", and stop the "don't give a damn attitude".

You might want to give John Connally some overall guidance on what you want our overall stance to be on the international negotiations.

---

[1] Source: Washington National Records Center, Department of the Treasury, Records of Secretary Shultz: FRC 56 80 1, Council on International Economic Policy–Peterson. Confidential. A stamped note on the memorandum reads: "The President Has Seen." It is attached to a November 24 memorandum from Huntsman to Secretary Connally informing him that the President suggested Connally receive a copy but that "the President does not endorse any of the views expressed herein."

[2] According to the President's Daily Diary, there was no meeting between the President and Connally on November 15. Connally had talked with the President twice by phone following his return from his Asian trip on November 14 and he and Mrs. Connally had dined with President and Mrs. Nixon that evening, probably obviating the need for a November 15 meeting. (National Archives, Nixon Presidential Materials, White House Central Files, President's Daily Diary)

[3] See The New York Times, November 14, 1971, p. 1.

[4] Connally addressed the Economic Club of New York on November 16. The press reported that "the Treasury Secretary's address had been billed in advance, perhaps mistakenly, as a major policy statement." See ibid., November 17, 1971, p. 65. The text of Connally's remarks is printed in Annual Report of the Secretary of the Treasury on the State of the Finances for the Fiscal Year Ended June 30, 1972, pp. 232–236.

2. Assuming that you decide that we should begin negotiations reasonably soon, I believe we should convene a small group in a setting that you think appropriate to resolve where we go from here.

There are a couple of open items.

I am having some intensive work done on the problems of *selective* lifting of the surcharge on a country-by-country basis, or hemispheric basis.[5] State feels it cannot be done because it abrogates some of our international treaties and obligations. I have two other sets of lawyers trying to figure out how we *can* do it.

On trade negotiations, I thought the agencies were virtually in total agreement on what we wanted and how to go about it. This weekend, Treasury submitted a paper saying we should expand significantly our requirements from the European Community.[6] Since a top Treasury man chaired the trade task force, it is of course possible that this rather surprising reversal is simply a signal that we may not really want to proceed with negotiations.

If you decide the time has come to get serious about some forward movement in these negotiations, we could be ready as early as next week to present you with negotiating options.

3. At Arthur Burns' request, I met with the ex-Prime Minister of the Netherlands (now President of the Netherlands Bank and the Bank of International Settlements) who has been operating behind-the-scenes to see if he can suggest the elements of a deal with the Europeans that would have a reasonable chance of meeting both our requirements and their economic and political situation.[7]

He brought up the gold price question and I told him of your strong views on this. On the question of zero or very limited convertibility, he was reasonably confident that this would not be a serious problem. On the gold price question itself, he said he hoped you understood that, with impending recessions and significant political (labor) problems in some of the key countries, it would be extraordinarily difficult for them to *initiate* a revaluation. He is, at the same time, aware of your political problem here and is working on a way of doing this through an IMF

---

[5] On December 1 Peterson sent President Nixon a paper on "Selective Lifting of the Surcharge." Peterson referred to the President's concern over relations with Latin America (see also footnote 4, Document 185), but noted that selective lifting of the surcharge would be contrary to GATT MFN obligations and similar provisions in many Friendship, Commerce and Navigation treaties. One option would be to lift the surcharge for all developing countries, which he thought would encounter little opposition from developed countries. (Washington National Records Center, Department of the Treasury, Records of Secretary Shultz: FRC 56 80 1, CIEP–Peterson)

[6] Not found.

[7] See footnote 2, Document 215, regarding the Working Paper Jelle Zijlstra sent Secretary Connally on November 23.

action which *might* put off any requirement for U.S. legislative action until after next year's election. A very similar approach was worked on by my coordinating group and shows some promise.

While I agree completely that we have very little to gain at this time by indicating flexibility on this gold question, I think it's going to end up being a "crunch" issue. Each percentage point of exchange rate realignment vis-à-vis the dollar improves our balance of payments (trade) by about 800 million dollars. If, indeed, the difference between some or no gold price change, or its equivalent, is 4% to 5% in overall exchange rate realignment, this issue could mean as much as *3 to 4 billion dollars* difference in our trade account.

To sum up, I think you will soon have to decide whether you want the U.S. to adopt a more positive stance on the international economic negotiations. To repeat what I've said elsewhere in more detail, beginning a serious negotiating process does not mean, in my view, "caving in" and certainly does not mean accepting a "bad deal". It does mean, however, conveying to the U.S. public and foreign countries that it is in our mutual interests to take positive steps to *try* to resolve this situation constructively.

---

196. Telegram From the Embassy in the Netherlands to the Department of State[1]

The Hague, November 15, 1971, 1010Z.

4157. Subject: SYG Luns concern about economic split in Alliance.

1. *Summary:* During his official visit to Netherlands SecGen Luns called at Embassy Nov 12 on informal and confidential basis to convey his mounting concern re effects of commercial and monetary rift developing between U.S. and NATO partners and to propose that matters be addressed at NATO Ministerial December. *End summary.*

2. Luns told me that he had discussed with PermReps in Brussels and in Bonn with FonMin, DefMin and Chancellor Brandt his mounting concern over effects on Alliance of monetary and economic crisis and

---

[1] Source: National Archives, RG 59, S/S Files: Lot 73 D 153, Morning Summaries. Secret. Repeated to Ankara, Athens, Bonn, Brussels, Copenhagen, Lisbon, London, Luxembourg, Oslo, Ottawa, Paris, Reykjavik, Rome, USEC, and USNATO.

differences with U.S. He said that while MBFR, CESC and Berlin were important he thought top priority belonged to economic crisis which affected all these other issues. He fears that if differences go unsettled for four or five months, they will get wound up in internal politics, especially U.S. elections, and will get out of control. There will then be retaliatory measures on both sides, recession with further diminution of defense budgets, and general dissipation of confidence in Atlantic Community.

3. Luns said under such circumstances exchanges of paper formulae with Soviets on balanced force reductions would become complicated and meaningless. Soviets will simply sit back to see what happens, while Western Europeans make own trade and monetary arrangements and relations with U.S. deteriorate. Luns said he thought necessary precondition to progress on this issue was that France and FRG should compose their present differences. He also felt this matter was too crucial to be left to financial technicians such as Schiller and Giscard, and that political leaders of governments should get involved.

4. Luns has therefore proposed to Germans in Bonn and to other PermReps in Brussels that matter should be introduced on agenda for NATO Ministerial Dec 8 to 10. He had at first envisaged (1) item entitled implications of current monetary and financial problems for Alliance, and (2) participation of MinFins in NATO meeting. But in view of modus operandi of MinFins and danger of their getting separated from context of main meeting, as well as personal problems (Schiller–Giscard), Luns thought it better not to push for their participation. He also found it better to water down terminology of item so it could be treated under heading "state of Alliance" and thus avoid implication NATO was horning in on OECD, EEC, GATT, etc. Luns plans therefore include strong pitch in his opening remarks as SYG which he would circulate to PermReps in advance.

5. Luns said he had discussed matter fully in Bonn and Brussels. He had found Schmidt, Scheel and Brandt very positive. Brandt was greatly concerned with problem and reacted favorably to Luns proposal. (Chancellor also confirmed he would meet with Pompidou before end November but was not very optimistic.) In Brussels Luns said his approach had been generally well received with some reservations; French were unhappy over NATO injection into financial matters but he detected some signs of anxiety on their part over continued crisis and consequences of rift with Germany. In any event Luns concluded that he thought it imperative for SYG and NATO to register strong concern so that by osmosis, urgency of situation as it affected Alliance should get quickly to national govts even though NATO could take no formal action itself.

6. I told Luns I quite agreed regarding urgency of situation both for domestic and general economic reasons but I stressed need for European action. I said I had spoken with officials in Washington including Under Secy Volcker and had impression that some real European movement (even if not total solution) on currency values, CAP problems and on burden sharing was essential if present deadlock were to be broken. Luns agreed but said that press and specially U.S. reporters were unduly playing up EDIP shortfalls and failing give any credit for European contributions, for example, from Germans and British. On other hand he was dismayed by Danish decisions to cut Navy and reduce troops to seven thousand and he anticipates rough session with Krag when he makes official visit to Copenhagen.

7. After above was drafted Luns telephoned to say that FonMin Schmelzer had also reacted favorably to his proposal. Schmelzer had added, however, that time was too short to solve all aspects of transatlantic economic problems within next few months. For positive NATO impact, rather than waiting to take all issues in one bite, Schmelzer thought one should try to register some progress soonest on European revaluation and gold price with perhaps some start on trade barriers, reserving other trade and monetary issues for later negotiation.

8. Dept may wish pass Treasury.

Middendorf

---

197. **Telegram From the Embassy in France to the Department of State[1]**

Paris, November 15, 1971, 1555Z.

19279. Subj: Growing French concern about delay in settling monetary crisis.

1. I am increasingly concerned about the effect that prolonged delay in resolving the international monetary crisis is likely to have on our interests in France and in Europe, in the weeks immediately following Aug. 15. The GOF behaved with restraint and in fact went out of its way

---

[1] Source: National Archives, RG 59, S/S Files: Lot 73 D 153, Morning Summaries. Confidential. Repeated to Bonn, Brussels, The Hague, London, Rome, and USEC.

to assure us that it was seeking to minimize the damage the NEP might cause to Franco-American relations.

1. In the last few weeks, however, I have detected a disturbing change in the French attitude. Key French officials have begun to warn us that, if we do not soon indicate clearly what our terms for a settlement are, opinion will turn decisively against us, with incalculable consequences for our political interests in Europe (Paris 18571).[2] Our British colleagues have told us they are convinced that, if the next G-10 Ministers' meeting is unproductive, the French will lose hope of reaching an agreement in that forum and will start considering alternative possibilities (Paris 19092).[2] Leading financial journalists like Alain Vernay of *Le Figaro* are increasingly critical in their conversations with Embassy officers of what they describe as US intransigence, and increasingly pessimistic about the future. There have been disturbing signs recently that measures aimed at the multinational corporations are being considered more and more seriously by the French authorities.

3. The underlying cause of the French malaise is a growing feeling that, by failing to indicate more concretely what our terms for a settlement are, we are blocking a negotiated solution of the crisis. Continued delay in settling the crisis has led to growing uncertainty among French businessmen and is beginning to cause them to defer important investment decisions. The effect the crisis is having on Franco-German relations and on Germany's economic prospects is also a matter of growing concern to the GOF. Behind these immediate concerns lies the deeper fear that if the crisis is not ended soon nations will be increasingly inclined to take defensive measures, with the resulting contraction of world trade leading to a world recession.

4. The result of all this is a growing conviction among government and business circles in France that a solution of the international monetary crisis in any acceptable time frame (i.e., before US and France are swept up in their respective elections campaigns), is no longer possible. If this view becomes established GOF policy, serious damage to important US interests seems inevitable. Initially, this might take the form of action, presumably in concert with France's EC partners, to protect the French trade position through the adoption of special export incentives and a more restricted policy toward US imports.

5. But as the atmosphere deteriorates, the French are likely to move from protective measures to outright retaliation. The most obvious area in which they could retaliate is foreign investment (about 10 percent of the $24 billion of US direct investment in Europe is in France), since here

---

[2] Not printed.

they can act independently of their EC partners. They could adopt a much more restrictive policy on approval of new investment requests (although this is unlikely so long as they are not assured American investors turned down in France could not go elsewhere in the EC). More likely forms of retaliation would be (1) restrictions against borrowing by US firms in overseas markets and withholding of government-owned credit facilities in France and (2) imposition of exchange controls to block multinational firms from repatriating earnings. (In 1970, US firms repatriated $6.2 billion in profits; about $100 million of them came from France.)

6. Another consequence of failure to get an early settlement of the monetary crisis, as pointed out in Paris 19092, would probably be an effort by the GOF to get a purely European agreement on a return to fixed parities. This would not be in our interests, since one feature of such an agreement would undoubtedly be some lowering of the present level of the Mark relative to the dollar.

7. Admittedly, the French position has not been helpful. The French have adamantly refused to consider the revaluation of the franc, and this has made it difficult for the Germans to agree to a higher revaluation of the Mark. Their allegation that we have failed to lay our cards on the table overlooks the fact that we have tried unsuccessfully in WP-3 and the G-10 to [gain?] acceptance of our estimate that we need a $13 billion swing in our balance of payments to get us out of our chronic deficit. French (and European) insistence on a small increase in the price of gold injects a large element of inflexibility into their position. The fact remains that today we are perilously near a stalemate, and the longer this persists, the greater becomes the danger that the French and the other Europeans will take measures which will seriously damage important US interests on this continent.

8. This makes it essential, I believe, that the field play a far more active role than it has been able to play so far in combating the increasing pessimism and negativism of the French. To do this, we will need more informative and timely guidance on our objectives in the monetary crisis than we have been getting. In particular, we must be better prepared to deal with the charge that the US has not stated its objectives precisely enough to permit meaningful negotiations. While this charge is unfair as applied to the realignment of parities, it has considerably more substance as applied to the trade side.

9. What all this adds up to is a conviction that time is not necessarily on our side and that, therefore, a major effort on our part to break the present stalemate is needed.

Watson

198. Letter From the Chairman of the Board of Governors of the Federal Reserve System (Burns) to President Nixon[1]

Washington, November 16, 1971.

Dear Mr. President:

I think you ought to know this: Unemployment in recent months has risen in every foreign country belonging to the so-called "Group of Ten"; namely, Belgium, France, Germany, Holland, Sweden, Switzerland, the United Kingdom, Canada, and Japan. For some reason that eludes me, the Italian figures on unemployment are ambiguous; but it seems clear from other data, particularly on industrial production, that Italy is in trouble.

I am by no means ready to conclude that an international recession has begun. But the evidence at hand does seem to support the view that the rate of growth of the outside economy is definitely slowing down. This may have far-reaching implications for the kind of monetary and trade settlement that we can work out with the outside world.

Sincerely yours,

Arthur

---

[1] Source: National Archives, Nixon Presidential Materials, NSC Files, Name Files, Box 810, Arthur Burns. No classification marking. Attached to a November 18 memorandum from Hormats to Kissinger recommending Kissinger sign a transmittal memorandum to the President that summarized Burns' memorandum. On Hormats' memorandum Kissinger wrote "OBE."

---

199. Telegram From the Embassy in Germany to the Department of State[1]

Bonn, November 17, 1971, 1450Z.

14309. Subj: Emminger on international monetary question.

1. *Summary:* In a conversation with the Financial Attaché, Bundesbank Vice President Emminger outlined the type of agreement

---

[1] Source: National Archives, RG 59, Central Files 1970–73, FN 10. Confidential; Limdis; Greenback. Repeated to London, Paris, Rome, Brussels, The Hague, USEC, and USOECD.

on international monetary problems which the EEC thought possible now along lines similar to those previously reported and stressed that in his view the deteriorating economic situation in Germany and pressure for an interim EEC solution would make it impossible to arrive at even this type of agreement by the spring of 1972. If an agreement along the lines outlined is not acceptable to the US, everyone, therefore, would have to make his arrangements for a long period of non-agreement. The Bundesbank would have to start to drive the appreciation of the Mark down to lower level. *End summary.*

2. Emminger said he felt that the postponement of the G-10 meeting had been due to a great misunderstanding by those (he specifically mentioned the Dutch) who had suggested it to us. Actually, Europe was now as prepared as it would ever be and it was in everyone's interest to meet quickly and if at all possible to settle the currency issue within the next six weeks or so. With recessionary tendencies coming more and more to the fore in Germany and elsewhere in Europe, it would be politically impossible next spring for the European governments to settle on as high a parity change vis-à-vis the dollar as they would be willing to do now.

3. Emminger confirmed what we had previously heard in Bonn and what has also been reported from London and Paris concerning the outcome of the last EEC Finance Ministers' meeting. Giscard for the first time clearly indicated that France would "hold still" for a modest dollar devaluation provided that the UK and Italy also would "hold still" and the DM would appreciate by 5–6 percent vis-à-vis the French franc (always compared to the pre-float parities). While Emminger did not specify the degree of dollar devaluation in such a package, he mentioned 6 percent "as an example." Emminger said that he had calculated that—assuming a 12–14 percent Japanese appreciation (vis-à-vis the dollar, less vis-à-vis gold)—the kind of package envisaged at the EEC Finance Ministers' private meeting would involve an average 9 percent "devaluation" of the dollar. It would take some hard negotiations to persuade the UK that the pound should "hold still" in such a situation. Hard bargaining might also succeed in adding another percentage point, or at the very most 2 percentage points, to the average dollar "devaluation" versus other currencies. Finally, it might be possible to get "something", but not very much, on trade policy and burden sharing (mainly in the form of promises to try to work something out) as part of such a package and some agreement on wider bands, continued dollar non-convertibility into gold, and on the general direction of the reform of the international monetary system (which, however, would take two years or so to work out and agree in detail).

4. It was important for the Europeans to know if such a package was acceptable to the US as a basis for the quick return to fixed parities and

including the dollar devaluation involved (and presumably also the removal of the surcharge). Emminger stressed that in his opinion such a package was possible only if agreed quickly. The business cycle situation would make it politically unsaleable in Europe next spring. Germany, for one, could not wait that long. While Germany was willing to see a 10 percent appreciation of DM vis-à-vis the dollar, it could not continue to accept such an appreciation vis-à-vis other currencies, and particularly vis-à-vis the franc. French steel imports were already causing serious difficulties and automobile imports were next. Schiller would not be in a position to resist pressure for help from these two important industries. In the absence of an agreement now, Germany, therefore, would have to start to drive the DM rate of appreciation down from its current level. Emminger professed great confidence that this would be done relatively easily through monetary policy. He pointed to the present DM 19 billion short term indebtedness of German industry abroad. By lowering the German interest rate below those abroad, the Bundesbank could induce the outflow of these funds and a consequent easing of the DM rate of appreciation. The Bundesbank was reluctant to do this now because it foresaw a 10 percent revaluation of the DM against the dollar in a general settlement and this would be psychologically difficult if the rate now dropped significantly below this. But in the absence of a quick general settlement, the Bundesbank would have to proceed.

5. In the absence of a general settlement, Emminger felt it would also be impossible to resist a "European solution" now. Such a solution most likely would involve an appreciation against the dollar considerably less than that in the type of international solution outlined in para 3 above, with some more controls and some very sticky and relatively small outside flexibility. While Emminger felt that Germany could live with such a solution, it would be definitely a second best from everyone's point of view.

6. In this connection Emminger warned that one should not overestimate the strength of Minister Schiller to insure that whatever would be done would not be too nonsensical. Schiller's position in the Cabinet now was weaker than Emminger had ever seen it. He was under vicious attack by the SPD left (Economics Ministry Parliamentary Under Secretary Rosenthal's resignation and criticism of Schiller had been announced just prior to the conversation). He was under constant attack by the "Europeans." Industry and the right were attacking him for a float. Schiller, according to Emminger, simply was not in a position to continue the float. He had to return quickly to a fixed rate or the Cabinet would disavow him. Emminger almost visibly shuddered at the thought of what might happen in the economic policy field if Schiller, with his constant liberal and outward (beyond the EEC) looking influence, should be forced from office.

7. Emminger reiterated that for all of these reasons, the US would not be able to get a better deal by next spring than it could now. If the US now indicated that the type of deal outlined in para 3 was not acceptable (with minor improvements), then everyone would have to settle down for a long period with no worldwide agreement and make his arrangement accordingly. Emminger urged that in looking at the deal, the US bear in mind that: (A) wide margins would in effect make it possible to increase the "dollar devaluation" 2–3 percent beyond the parity changes agreed, and (B) the US "concession" of a dollar devaluation in fact would work out to an advantage since it would increase the value of our gold reserves. Emminger said that all their reports and conversations with visiting American bankers indicated that a gold price increase had become much less of a political issue in the US, and he hoped this would not be a stumbling block. It was the only way by which Germany could upvalue 10 percent against the US without also doing so against France, the UK and the rest of the EEC. Emminger (protect) mentioned that while he realized Congressman Reuss was not the US Congress, it was interesting that Reuss had told him that he, Reuss, could "guarantee" that Congress would pass a dollar devaluation bill within two days, provided it was vigorously supported by the administration and it was part of a sensible package of international parity realignments and at least some elements of international monetary reform. The Financial Attaché asked Emminger whether he had the impression that Reuss would consider the kind of realignment outlined in para 3 above as sufficient and whether Reuss would also "guarantee" no Congressional amendments to an "insufficient" package. Emminger replied that, of course, Reuss wanted a larger realignment, but with strong administration support and the further flexibility provided by wide margins, he, Emminger, hoped that the type of realignment now negotiable could be made acceptable to the Congress.

8. Emminger asked that he should not be quoted to any German or foreign official. Please protect.

Rush

200.   **Editorial Note**

On or about November 18, 1971, the Office of Management and Budget and the Department of the Treasury circulated papers proposing negotiating strategies to resolve the international monetary impasse. A copy of the 8-page OMB paper, dated November 16 and entitled "Tactics for an Early Conclusion of the Surcharge Round," was sent to Kissinger on November 18 at the request of Director Shultz. The OMB paper has three attachments. Haig forwarded the paper to Kissinger under cover of a handwritten note that reads: "Shultz cut at surcharge round." (National Archives, Nixon Presidential Materials, NSC Files, Subject Files, Box 356, Monetary Matters) In a November 20 note from Coleman to Kissinger regarding the paper's disposition, Coleman offered four options: "Send to Staff, File, Hold, Other." Kissinger checked the Hold option and wrote "This is HIGHLY sensitive—as are *all* monetary matters. Please put in separate file." (Ibid.) Hormats summarized the OMB paper for Kissinger in a November 22 memorandum. (Ibid., Box 376, President's Economic Program)

The undated, 21-page Treasury paper is entitled "Proposed Approach Toward Monetary-Trade-Burden Sharing Negotiations Over the Next Month." It is accompanied by a "Scenario" paper and Attachments A–I. A handwritten note on the paper reads: "From Secretary Connally. Copy sent to HAK in NY 11/20/71." (Ibid.) Another copy of the Treasury paper is accompanied by a November 22 memorandum from Hormats to Kissinger entitled "Monetary–Trade–Burden Sharing Negotiations," which expressed the opinion that the paper was a reasonable attempt at a position to remove the surcharge. Hormats recommended that "the main elements to stress are that the surcharge is a wasting asset and that the longer it is on the greater the likelihood that other countries will compensate economically, that retaliatory measures will take place, and negotiations for its removal will be more difficult." (Ibid., Box 356, Monetary Matters)

Both papers look to significant exchange rate realignments and trade and burdensharing agreements. Neither considers restoring convertibility. OMB adheres to the President's directive that there be no increase in the price of gold (see Document 189), but Treasury, with a view to France as the greatest obstacle to a successful negotiation, reluctantly leaves open the door for a possible accommodation.

In his November 22 commentary on the OMB paper, Hormats noted that if the United States remained firm in its intention not to devalue the dollar vis-à-vis gold, one outcome could be the U.S. purchase of francs with dollars to push up the value of the franc relative to the dollar, a unilateral declaration by the United States that the franc was revalued. If the United States bought francs to increase the franc's value and if France attempted to maintain the original parity by using francs to buy dollars, the result would be politically disastrous.

Tab C of the OMB paper, "An Outline of a Possible Statement on International Monetary Negotiations," contains the following:

"A. If our principal trading partners (Japan, Canada and the EC) will meet our minimum trade and burden-sharing requirements and if they are prepared to revalue as follows:

Japan—15%
Canada—Maintain float
Germany—10%
France—5%
etc.,

"then we will immediately lift the surcharge as to all countries.
"B. For the present we will only consider lifting the surcharge on an MFN basis. But we recognize that this policy permits one country to hold up surcharge lifting as to all countries (including LDCs). Hence: 1. We may be forced to consider whether selective lifting may not be the only way to reach final elimination of the surcharge. 2. We will entertain proposals from any country as to how recalcitrant countries can be induced to take part in the global settlement."

The Treasury paper contains the following: "An average exchange rate depreciation of the dollar vis-à-vis G-10 countries of 10% (11% in terms of G-10 appreciation), *as compared to May 1, 1971,* would be consistent with a depreciation of 17% against Japan, 13% against Germany, and 8% against France, the U.K. and Italy, assuming a Canadian commitment to revalue (which is unlikely). These figures are not consistent with a $13 billion adjustment . . . they are somewhat above a realistic appraisal of settlement terms for most countries, and the Canadians will presumably only agree to a float. Such a proposal thus appears to leave ample room for realistic negotiation in comparison to a probable counter offer of 15% Japan, 10% Germany, and 5% France, U.K., and Italy."

The G-10 Communiqué from the November 30–December 1 Ministerial in Rome; a transcript of Connally's remarks at the end of the Ministerial, pages with Connally's handwritten notes and doodles during the Ministerial; Volcker's handwritten notes/comments that were presumably passed to Connally who chaired the meeting (e.g., "If the Group of 10 cannot discuss trade, why are they discussing the surcharge, etc.?"); and a typescript that highlights the interventions in the November 29 G-10 Deputies meeting (see Document 210), along with additional documentation, is in the Washington National Records Center, Department of the Treasury, Records of Secretary Shultz: FRC 56 80 1, Rome G-10 Meeting 11/30–12/1/71.

Background material is also ibid., including a November 22 paper entitled "Scenario for G-10 Meeting and Aftermath," which suggests actions in late November, at the Ministerial, and follow-up in December at NATO, and undated papers including "Summary of Proposed Approach Toward Monetary–Trade–Burden Sharing Negotiations Within the Next Several Weeks" (a summary of Document 201), "Selective Lifting of the Surcharge," and papers on bilateral issues with the European Community, Canada, and Japan. This material, along with other background papers, is in a Briefing Book in the Washington National Records Center, Department of the Treasury, Office of the Assistant Secretary for International Affairs Central Files: FRC 56 86 24, World/1/544, Monetary–Trade–Burden Sharing Negotiations. A November 9 CIEP paper requesting interagency defense burdensharing studies and the Treasury Department's proposed strategy, which was thought to be different from the State Department position, is also ibid.

There is no indication that these papers came to the President's attention but they provided the context for his advisers during their meetings with the President on November 23 and 24 (see Document 203). The essential elements of Volcker's proposals at the November 29 G-10 Deputies Meeting in Rome (see Document 211) are also contained in these papers.

---

201.   Paper Prepared in the Department of the Treasury[1]

Washington, undated.

SUMMARY OF PROPOSED APPROACH TOWARD MONETARY–TRADE–BURDEN SHARING NEGOTIATIONS WITHIN THE NEXT SEVERAL WEEKS

This memorandum outlines briefly proposed initiatives in the immediate future for a resolution of the pending issues in monetary, trade and burden-sharing matters. It is hoped that these proposals would be negotiable; they do involve a limited movement on the gold issue. The basic objectives would be:

---

[1] Source: Washington National Records Center, Department of the Treasury, Records of Secretary Shultz: FRC 56 80 1, Rome G-10 Meeting 11/30–12/1/71. No classification marking. Prepared as background for the G-10 Ministerial meeting; see Document 200.

If the negotiations are successful: Substantial improvement in our external position; removal of the surcharge, retention of leverage for subsequent negotiations; avoidance of extended uncertainty; and forestalling of political tension that could accompany a prolonged impasse.

If the negotiations are unsuccessful: More favorable U.S. position to the public; better base for continuation of the present situation, or for alternative strategies, including interim settlements with particular countries or areas entailing selective removal or reduction of the surcharge.

I. The Present Setting

Since August 15, the yen has appreciated about 9-1/2%, but the overall exchange rate change (in terms of our weighted OECD trade) has been only about 3%; since May 1, 1971, it has been about 4-1/2%. This is well below the needed adjustment.

France has managed to avoid revaluation, at least on trade transactions, and has enjoyed some depreciation relative to Germany and some other competitors. Thus France, with some other countries, can bring pressure on their trading partners. France, Japan, and some other countries have instituted new controls. These conditions, together with the existing uncertainty and fears of recession, limit the maneuvering room for Germany and some other countries and increase the pressures for settlement.

The principal negotiating obstacle is the inflexible position of France, its pressure on its immediate trading partners, particularly Germany, and its emphasis on the gold price.

Despite a strong urge for an interim settlement evidenced by our leading trading partners, especially Canada and Japan, and the general awareness of a firmer U.S. position than we have taken in the past, there is still an unwillingness or inability to recognize the size of the needed adjustment, as we perceive it.

A continuing impasse, without an American initiative based upon a proposal that can be publicly defended as "reasonable," courts the risk of increasing criticism of the U.S. for blocking agreement. If other matters (i.e., the exchange rate realignment and trade and burden-sharing issues) could be resolved, a strong effort is warranted to unblock the opposing positions of the U.S. and France for an interim settlement regarding gold.

II. Our Judgment of Present Negotiating Positions

Canada. Will continue to float and perhaps make some commitments to keep float "clean," but adamantly opposed to overt revaluation. Will likely make some trade concessions of high symbolic importance, but it is doubtful we can attain our full objectives.

Japan. Willing to appreciate by some 15% and, under pressure, slightly higher (perhaps to 300 yen to the dollar), provided they are within 4 or

5 points of Germany. Extent of trade action uncertain, but some movement likely.

Germany. Flexible on exchange rates, provided mark revaluation not more than 4 or 5 points above the French franc. Cannot long tolerate present differential of some 9% revaluation above the French franc; continued impasse would probably trigger controls and lower exchange rate.

France. Will accept exchange rate revaluation of 5%, or perhaps slightly higher, if achieved entirely through U.S. devaluation relative to gold, and franc maintains present relationship to sterling and lire.

United Kingdom. Likely to adhere to the French line and maintain present exchange rate with French franc.

Common Market. Intransigent on short-term trade adjustments, apart from the marketing of current surplus crops. We seek a commitment regarding any change in the support price under EC Common Agricultural Policy (CAP). Agreement upon framework for subsequent negotiations on CAP appears very difficult. No "give" apparent on preferences for remaining EFTA countries, African affiliates, etc.

III. Proposals

A. *Trade.* Trade negotiations must proceed bilaterally and intensively in coming weeks. While we are flexible, some "tangible progress" must result with Japan, Canada, EC, and LDC's, and a framework established for longer range negotiations. Key issues:

Canada—

Auto Agreement
Used Cars
Defense Production Sharing
Industrial Policy
Tourist Allowances

EC—

Disposal of Current Surplus
CAP Price and Unit of Account
Preferences (pursue GATT remedies and seek compensation)
Steel Accord

Japan—

Agricultural Quotas and Tariffs
Numerous High Technology Industrial Items
Commitment to Bilateral Trade Balance

LDC's—

U.S. Car Discrimination
Mexico Tourist Allowance
Longer Term Review of LDC Commercial Policy

B. *Defense-Burden Sharing.* We must decide promptly if U.S. wants to press beyond the European Defense Improvement Program. If so, we should so state in the G-10, laying the basis for subsequent NATO discussion. Most promising, but still difficult approach: NATO assumption of bases (and related costs) where manned by troops in a foreign country (e.g., U.S. bases in Germany).[2] Maximum savings from this approach would run above $600 million annually.

C. *Exchange Rates.* An average exchange rate depreciation of the dollar vis-à-vis G-10 countries of 10%, as compared to *May 1, 1971.* This would indicate 17% against Japan, 13% against Germany, and 8% against France, U.K., and Italy, if Canada revalued (which is unlikely). These figures are consistent with $9.6 billion adjustment on IMF calculations, which we consider optimistic. Probably counter-offer will be 15% Japan, 10% Germany, and 5% France, U.K., and Italy, and Canada will presumably only agree to float.

All rates agreed upon would be provisional, subject to review before long-term reform.

D. *Wider Bands.* We should propose 3% bands, although the French and others will resist 3%. Persistent one-way intervention within the band should be avoided, with IMF surveillance. Two-tier markets of the French variety should be forbidden.

E. *Convertibility.* We should insist on absence of convertibility, stressing probable inadequacy of the exchange rate adjustment. We should have support from Japan, Canada, and (apart from a probable common EC position) Germany; but the issue is extremely sensitive for others, because of the connotation of a full "dollar standard."

F. *Gold.* An immovable U.S. position on the gold issue may well prevent any monetary solution for some time, or at least prevent an adjustment of a size adequate to justify removal of the surcharge. Some U.S. flexibility on this issue may substantially improve our bargaining strength on other matters and permit satisfactory interim solution.

To reach some accommodation with the French (and the French-dominated EC position), the U.S. could offer to put to a vote of the IMF Governors a proposal to declare a modest de facto devaluation of the dollar. The amount of the devaluation to be voted on would be determined either (a) on a "horse-trading" basis by agreeing upon an arbitrary figure, perhaps arrived at by "splitting the difference" with the lowest revaluer (the French), or (b) a formula approach aimed at keeping the price of gold unchanged in terms of a weighted average of all relevant currencies. With such a vote free of entanglements with other

---

[2] See Document 84.

elements of the bargain, the LDC's might join with us to keep the dollar price of gold unchanged.

An alternative possibility would be to put to an IMF vote an increase in the dollar price and the gold price of the SDR, and thus to "devalue" the dollar against the SDR instead of against gold. This would be accomplished by raising the gold content of the SDR. Such a change would boost the role of SDR's without boosting gold. Procedurally, relying on emergency provisions of the IMF Articles, it would require unanimous approval by the IMF Executive Board and by 80% of the IMF Governors.

In any event, we should insist upon establishing a framework for negotiation of long-term monetary reform, including perhaps an enlargement of the G-10 membership.

Attached is a possible scenario for the proposed initiatives.[3]

---

[3] "Scenario for G-10 Meeting and Aftermath"; not printed, but see Document 200.

---

202.   Information Memorandum From Robert Hormats of the National Security Council Staff to the President's Assistant for National Security Affairs (Kissinger)[1]

Washington, November 22, 1971.

SUBJECT

Talking Points for your Meeting with the President and Secretary Connally, Tuesday, November 23, at 10:00 a.m.[2]

The meeting will focus on negotiations on the international aspects of the New Economic Policy—specifically, conditions for removal of the surcharge. There are several points which you might wish to make:

---

[1] Source: National Archives, Nixon Presidential Materials, NSC Files, Agency Files, Box 289, Treasury Volume II, 1971. Secret.

[2] On November 22 Kissinger and Shultz sent a joint memorandum to President Nixon with talking points for his meeting with Connally. Their talking points were similar to those that Hormats suggested. (Ibid.) President Nixon met with Secretary Connally from 10:04 to 11:40 a.m. on November 23. Kissinger joined the meeting from 11:11 to 11:39 a.m. For a summary of the discussion, see Document 203. Shultz did not attend, but met with the President later in the day from 5:38 to 6:07 p.m. The President also talked with Connally by phone from 5:44 to 5:47 p.m. and again from 5:58 to 5:59 p.m. (National Archives, Nixon Presidential Materials, White House Central Files, President's Daily Diary)

—It would be useful to *view the international negotiations connected with the New Economic Policy in terms of two "rounds"*—a surcharge round (in which we achieved conditions which would allow us to remove the surcharge), and a gold-convertibility round in which we achieved reform of the international monetary system and negotiated trade concessions. We should not expect in round one to achieve all we want in terms of exchange rate adjustments, trade, or defense burden sharing. Our objective should be to arrive at an interim solution which enables us to get a significant appreciation of exchange rates and some trade measures while remaining firm in our intention not to restore convertibility. With regard to gold we should be in a position to discuss raising the dollar price of gold and perhaps reach tentative agreement to do so but not, in any case, resume gold convertibility. *Convertibility* will be our major *point of leverage* in bringing about the exchange rates we want in the *second round* and in achieving major reforms of the international monetary system.

—*When we remove the surcharge,* there is still *significant pressure on Europe to resolve the monetary situation* in a way which is favorable to our interests. The EC has five basic options:

—Each country could continue to do as it is doing (i.e., no European "solution").
—The EC countries could return to fixed parities vis-à-vis one another, but float together against the dollar.
—The EC countries could return to fixed parities against one another and float together against the dollar with capital controls, and perhaps trade controls, to decrease the appreciation of their currencies.
—The EC countries could return to fixed parities vis-à-vis one another and the U.S. without trade and capital controls (which would mean that Europe would again take in large amounts of dollars, unless the new parities were fixed above present levels).
—The EC countries could fix parities vis-à-vis themselves and the U.S., with capital and trade controls to limit the intake of dollars.

In the long run, Europe will probably be unwilling to take in large amounts of dollars and probably unable to maintain capital controls. It is thus likely that there will be pressure on it to float collectively against the dollar or to appreciate their currency values so that capital controls are unnecessary and they do not accumulate larger amounts of dollars. The one thing we should guard against is an EC-wide dual rate system (which means one exchange rate for trade transactions—a commercial rate—and another presumably higher rate—a financial rate—to reduce the inflow of capital). Such a system would reduce the pressure on Europe to float their trade (commercial) rate upward, and thereby be counterproductive in our efforts to realize a trade surplus.

—If we do not make any moves at all to accommodate the Europeans on the gold question, we must recognize that we will not get the amount of dollar devaluation vis-à-vis the other currencies which we believe is necessary. France has stated that it does not intend to revalue the franc vis-à-vis the dollar, but instead wants the dollar to be revalued with respect to gold. If France will not revalue, Germany will probably reestablish the value of the mark at no more than 6 percent higher than the value of the franc (it is presently about 9 percent above the franc and dollar), and Japan will permit the value of the yen to rise no higher than 5 percent above the value of the mark. These appreciations will be far less than will be adequate to bring about the improvement we seek in our balance of payments. (The value of the dollar is now approximately 3.5–4 percent below the overall value of the other major currencies as of April.) Treasury estimates that for every 1 percent devaluation in the value of the dollar, our balance of payments improves by $800 million dollars. Thus, we should seriously consider measures to devalue the dollar, if possible, without having Congress involve itself in our negotiations, and *without going back to convertibility.*

—The negotiations should be handled in such a way that we do not attempt to play one European country off against another. Any scheme to deal harshly with one European will lead all Europeans to believe that we are attempting to split the Common Market countries, and is likely to lead to a severe reaction in Europe. Throughout these negotiations we should consider the EC as one entity and, while we may wish to use Brandt as an instrument for influencing Pompidou and the others, we should not attempt to split Germany and France.

—We can get maximum economic advantage out of the surcharge within the next month or so. If we go beyond that, countermeasures will increase, there may be an increasing number of retaliatory actions, and the U.S. will be increasingly viewed as a "scapegoat" for Europe's economic woes. This will certainly make negotiations difficult, and it will be less easy for us to accomplish our economic objectives.

—On the political side, the longer we go without a reasonable U.S. position, the more confused our friends become, the more skeptical they are that we want to cooperate to solve the present problem, and the more vulnerable they are to the importunements of those who wish to develop a European position counter to our interests on economic issues, and political/security issues as well.

—We should be careful not to demand too much in the area of trade. Other nations feel that we have as many restrictions on imports of their products into this country as they do on our products. And, they view trade as an area in which reciprocal quota and tariff reductions should be negotiated, not as an area in which countries should make unilateral concessions. (The Common Market feels especially strongly about this, while Japan seems somewhat less reluctant to move unilaterally on specific issues.) While we may be able to get some concessions, and the promise of negotiations on a number of issues, we should not make removal of the surcharge contingent upon a long list of major concessions from other nations.

203. Editorial Note

On November 23 and 24, 1971, the President had several meetings with his economic advisers. He was scheduled to travel to San Clemente on the evening of November 24, and this was his last opportunity to take up international economic policy with his advisers before Connally and Volcker traveled to Rome for the G-10 Deputies and Ministerial meetings November 29–December 1.

According to a tape recording of their meeting on November 23, Connally told the President he would have a bilateral meeting with the Italians before the G-10 Ministerial and would seek bilaterals with the Japanese and Canadians as well. Connally said the international matter could be settled and it was only a question of how much to give. He repeated what he had told the President on October 28 (see Document 187), that currency realignment alone would not be too meaningful to the average American. Connally wanted agreement on trade issues as well, which would be politically important to the President. He nonetheless agreed with the President's recap of his position that a monetary deal would have to be concluded before a trade deal, which would take a long time, particularly because of European difficulties in negotiating on agriculture, which Connally had discussed with Ossola earlier that morning.

The President asked for Connally's views on gold before Shultz and Burns came in (they never arrived at this meeting). Connally said, "gold is a crucial point. The French have a phobia on gold." Connally gave the President a lengthy explanation of issues and possible magnitudes of changes in exchange rates between the dollar and other currencies, and among the other major currencies, and summarized Ossola's presentation that morning that if the United States changed the price of gold and removed the surcharge, the Community would be willing to discuss trade. Connally said, and the President agreed, "the real money is in the realignment, but the politics are in the trade issue." Connally thought the United States was in an excellent negotiating position and said he would hate to bargain away both gold and the surcharge for an inadequate realignment package. He considered the possibility of having Volcker, prior to the G-10 Ministerial, perhaps in a press conference or during a Deputies meeting, indicate that the United States was prepared to submit to Congress a bill to increase the price of gold in return for a 17 percent revaluation of the yen, etc., and would remove half the surcharge now and the remainder once a package of trade concessions had been agreed upon. Connally did not believe gold was important domestically, but advised the President against giving in to Pompidou without getting something in return. The President agreed, and thought the gold issue might be held in reserve for the Summits.

Following Kissinger's arrival at 11:12 a.m., Connally, Kissinger, and the President agreed that a forthcoming Peterson trip should be scrubbed, that there was no reason for him to be meeting with European Prime Ministers or even Economic Ministers at that time. The President did not want any of his economic advisers, Peterson, McCracken, Stein, or Stans, traveling at this stage in the negotiations. The three agreed that they, along with Shultz and Burns, should meet the next day; that Peterson should not be included; and that Connally's proposal should not go beyond their limited group. The President was inclined to reserve on gold at the G-10 Ministerial, and instead take it up with Pompidou. Kissinger expressed the opinion that Connally should stand fast on gold and work it out with Pompidou who would need something from the Summit. Connally outlined his approach to the Rome meetings: "All we have to do is make progress. We can both make proposals the others cannot accept. The fact of the meetings will maintain the momentum." (National Archives, Nixon Presidential Materials, White House Tapes, Recording of a Conversation Among President Nixon, Connally, and Kissinger, November 23, 1971, 10:01–11:40 a.m., Oval Office, Conversation 623-3)

On November 24 the President met with Connally and Burns on international monetary and trade matters from 11:45 a.m. to 12:27 p.m., and, after a meeting with Secretary Rogers, lunched with Connally, Burns, Shultz, and Kissinger in the Executive Office Building from 1:13 to 2:35 p.m. The tape of the luncheon conversation is almost inaudible, and no reliable policy conclusions can be extracted from it. (Ibid., Recording of a Conversation Among President Nixon, Connally, and others, November 24, 1971, 1:13–2:35 p.m., Old Executive Office Building, Conversation 305-1) The tape of the earlier conversation with Connally and Burns, however, is good, and the President was clearly told there would have to be some change in the price of gold. All three also agreed there had to be some progress in Rome.

During the conversation the President reported on the announcement that morning of the schedule of Summits, including the Azores
Summit with President Pompidou "to wrap up this whole thing."
Concerning the gold price and convertibility, the President told Burns,
"you, John and I should get the tactic together for the luncheon."

Connally told the President that he and Burns had discussed the
international economic issues at breakfast that morning. Connally said
he suggested trading the surcharge for a 17 percent revaluation of the
yen, etc., but that Burns had "wisely" advised against giving specific
percentages for particular currencies, which would reveal the U.S. bargaining position. Instead, once the others in the G-10 make an inadequate offer Connally would counter with a proposal for an average
realignment of perhaps 11 or 12 percent. Pursuant to the President's
sentiments, they agreed that at that stage they could not touch gold, but
in view of the French position on gold they eventually would have to
give something on the gold price. Burns said he was "convinced" they
could not get a settlement without giving something on the gold price.

The President returned to the question of convertibility. Burns and
Connally, at some length, explained why, for technical reasons, the
United States would have to agree to provide limited amounts of
reserve assets from time to time—gold, SDRs, or something else—but
that would not be restoring convertibility in the traditional sense.
During their explanation of the technical reasons, Connally revisited the
gold price question and said that if the United States were to increase
the price of gold, it should be "our deliberate decision," unrelated to
procedures in the IMF, and the administration should submit it to
Congress for its action. Connally said convertibility would come up in
the G-10 meeting, but the important issue was the realignment and,
politically, all that could be achieved on trade. He dismissed the other
matters as "nickels and dimes stuff." The President said he would like
to get something on offset as well, but in the end would rather get something from Germany on trade. If press questions about their luncheon
arose later that day, the agreed line was that the President thought it
important to have progress in Rome. Principles would be agreed on
there for consideration by higher authorities. (Ibid., Recording of
Conversation Among President Nixon, Connally, and Burns, November
24, 1971, 11:46 a.m.–12:27 p.m., Oval Office, Conversation 624-20)

The November 25 edition of The New York Times carried an article
entitled "Nixon Is Hopeful on Money Talks" (page 61). The Times
reported that in a brief statement following a meeting with the
President, Burns said that "President Nixon 'expects definite progress'
to be made at the meeting in Rome next week of the Group of 10." The
same Times story reported that during an informal news conference
Volcker said the world should not expect a "settlement" but that he

hoped for "real progress." Volcker also reportedly said the U.S. delegation in Rome would have "expertise" in the fields of trade and agriculture despite the fact that the G-10 normally dealt only with monetary matters.

---

204. Memorandum From the Chairman of the Council of Economic Advisers (McCracken) to President Nixon[1]

Washington, November 24, 1971.

At the Economic Policy Committee meeting of the OECD in Paris last week two matters emerged that are worth calling to your attention.

First there is growing concern among the major industrial nations about their own domestic economic conditions, and this does have implications for the exchange rate appreciation, relative to the dollar, that we can expect from them. As they become more worried about rising unemployment, they will tend to become less generous about the appreciation they will accept—with its adverse effect on their international competitive position relative to the United States.

Because of these growing domestic economic concerns, these countries will tend to pursue more expansionist monetary policies. This is particularly true in Germany, where not too long after the turn of the year, easier monetary policies can be expected. In private conversations they made this clear to me. As these occur, international monetary flows will be induced that will tend to move the exchange rate of the D-mark downward. It is not reasonable to expect the Germans to agree to any change in the exchange rate pattern which would require their moving the D-mark exchange rate up above its then present level. Their exporters are already bringing heavy pressure to bear on the German government because the D-mark appreciation is giving their exports an increasingly hard time in world markets.

---

[1] Source: National Archives, Nixon Presidential Materials, NSC Files, Agency Files, Box 216, Council of Economic Advisers. No classification marking. The memorandum is Tab A to a December 1 memorandum from Hormats to Kissinger that summarized three reports on foreign reactions to the international aspects of the New Economic Policy. McCracken's November 24 note sending Kissinger a copy of this memorandum noted that he was sending it to Kissinger "because my major impressions from this meeting seem to center more in the political than in the economic domain." Tabs B and C were papers from the Department of State.

The clear implication of these developments is that the exchange rate adjustments we can expect from other industrial nations are apt to be smaller as we move beyond the turn of the year.

Second, a pro-American French line[2] was evident at the meeting. Traditionally in these Economic Policy Committee meetings the French delegation could be expected to flay the American position at some point in the deliberations. This time any intimation of any anti-American comment from the French spokesman was conspicuous for its complete absence.

Moreover, at his initiative, I had dinner (at Laserre) with M. Jean Rene Bernard, Economic Adviser to President Pompidou. This dinner was at M. Bernard's initiative, and he came to the dinner from having been in bed with the flu. I know him well enough for a serious conversation, but not well enough for him to have arranged a purely social evening. The dinner was, therefore, presumably arranged for him to communicate a basic message.

M. Bernard also took the same intensely pro-American line. While this might be dismissed as tactical, I believe it was more than that. The French do seem genuinely worried about the political implications of a continued international monetary problem. For one thing, he considered it quite important that the G-10 meetings November 30 and December 1 should at least start the process for an orderly solution in order that the Pompidou–Brandt meeting on December 3 would not take place against the backdrop of a continued international monetary impasse. He also expressed the view that if this could be resolved, the United States could then resume its overall international leadership without which, in his judgment, it might be difficult for European unity to survive.

He was cool to "regional" solutions (including a European regional system), and not optimistic about their workability. And he seemed concerned about longer-run relationships between France and Germany.

I pass these observations along because they may be pieces of a larger jigsaw puzzle that carry implications beyond economic policy in the narrow sense.

Paul W. McCracken

---

[2] On another copy of the memorandum the President circled this phrase and in the margin wrote: "K-note." (Ibid.)

205.   Telegram From the Embassy in Belgium to the Department of State[1]

Brussels, November 24, 1971, 1810Z.

3910. Dept pass Treasury and FRB. Subj: G-10 meeting in Rome.

1. *Summary.* During discussion of forthcoming G-10 meeting on November 24, Belgian FinMin Snoy told Chargé he saw a possibility of substantial progress at G-10 meeting in Rome if U.S. were agreeable to modest devaluation of dollar. Otherwise he foresees a deadlock which would force the Europeans to seek their own solution, beginning with the Pompidou–Brandt meeting. Snoy expressed concern that the deteriorating economic situation in many countries including Belgium would make it increasingly difficult for governments to meet U.S. desires. It was, therefore, urgent to reach agreement soon. Snoy believed that settlement of exchange rate question would still leave the problem of dealing with the convertibility of the dollar. He also recognized existing problems in the trade field which needed to be discussed. In response to Snoy's defense of Community proposal for EFTA non-applicant members, the Chargé said that efforts to avoid new restrictions between former EFTA members should not be used to raise impediments on trade between Europe and the U.S. *End summary.*

2. Chargé accompanied by Economic Counselor called on FinMin Snoy Nov 24 to seek Belgian thoughts on forthcoming G-10 meeting.

3. Snoy said he thought it best public posture to approach this meeting without too much expectation. He was nevertheless deeply concerned by the dangers of the present situation. He referred to the deterioration of the economies of Germany, Belgium and elsewhere. This deterioration increases protectionist pressure on governments and makes it more difficult to make adjustments desired by the US. He mentioned that increasing unemployment in Belgium and a sharp drop in investments were reflected in the success of recent Belgian state loan.

4. Snoy, therefore, sees urgency of early agreement. He was confident that such an early agreement would be possible if it could include a modest devaluation of the dollar by perhaps 5 percent. If that were impossible there would be a deadlock in Rome. He said that some progress on the European position had been made in Versailles, but this had more to do with the procedure than with the substance. Further steps would depend on the G-10 meeting. Regardless of what happens

---

[1] Source: National Archives, RG 59, S/S Files: Lot 73 D 153, Box 124, Morning Summaries. Confidential. Repeated to Bonn, Bern, London, Luxembourg, Paris, Rome, The Hague, Tokyo, USOECD, and USEC.

Snoy thought that some progress on the first stage of the Werner Plan would have to come out of the French-German meeting. Futhermore, if there were no success in Rome, the urgency of the European situation might well make essential an ad hoc European solution in the monetary area and the Pompidou–Brandt meeting would just be the beginning of this process.

5. Snoy thought that even if agreement were reached on exchange rates there would still be the question of convertibility of the dollar. He foresaw that the need would continue for foreigners to accept dollars even if agreement were reached. He did not see how a solution of this problem would be possible without discipline of the IMF. For example, central banks would not hold dollars without some assurance through IMF on their value and usability. He asserted that US Treasury had so far resisted IMF discipline such as had been accepted by the British.

6. On the degree of flexibility that would be required he thought it depended on the degree of realignment. The closer the realignment to US desires the less flexibility that would be required.

7. Chargé referred to the question of trade. He stressed that an outward looking attitude by the Community on a number of questions such as grain stocks, agricultural prices, and citrus fruits, would be useful over the short run. Snoy was sympathetic, but noncommittal. He suggested that if the dollar were devalued it would be helpful to the Community on agricultural prices. This would make it possible to retain the unit of account and make it easier to resist protectionist pressures that would otherwise emerge in establishing a new unit.

8. While he recognized that EFTA non-applicants were a problem, Snoy pointed out that Community could not increase "boundaries" on trade between former EFTA members. The Chargé responded that the US is not interested in creating such new "boundaries" but at the same time does not believe that the EC reconciliation with the EFTA should result in new hurdles for US trade. He stressed that US ability and willingness to accept new elements of discrimination had greatly changed over the last 10 or 15 years, and more active attention by Europe to third-country interests would be in order.

Boochever

206.   Telegram From the Embassy in Germany to the Department of State[1]

Bonn, November 24, 1971, 2045Z.

14641. Department pass Treasury and Federal Reserve. Subject: German views on the G-10 Ministerial and the Brandt–Pompidou summit.

1. Our discussions with German officials on their preparations for the G-10 Ministerial and the following Brandt–Pompidou Summit meeting have essentially only confirmed information reported by a number of posts regarding the parameters of the European position. The Germans continue to seek a quick, world-wide solution. The Foreign Office has stressed, in this regard, that a quick solution will avoid a confrontation with the US which might otherwise develop, and will prevent a long delay in resolving issues which, if left open much longer, could turn US/European economic/commercial and political relations in the wrong direction. The Foreign Office insists that the EC is ready to play its part in attaining a world-wide solution which would include at least something on the trade side. We are told that the Germans are optimistic the French would go along. From our side, the Europeans need an indication that the US also wishes a quick world-wide solution and that the US is prepared to make a contribution itself to this end.[2]

2. In order to maximize the results of the subsequent Brandt–Pompidou discussions, the Foreign Office has urged that the US be as specific as possible at the G-10 Ministerial as to its wishes on trade. The Foreign Office has held out to us a hope that the Germans could make a contribution to the problem of what to do about the value of the unit of account of the CAP by limiting its revaluation in the general upward realignment of EC currencies. The Foreign Office has also reflected a positive attitude toward the limitation of price increases in the agricultural sector; towards helpful agricultural storage policies; and towards a reciprocal trade package in industry. We are told that what is needed, however, is concrete US trade proposals which would "thereby put the ball clearly in the European court."

3. The alternative to an early world-wide solution is, according to the Germans, an interim European solution which would be less desirable from everyone's point of view.

Rush

---

[1] Source: National Archives, RG 59, S/S Files: Lot 73 D 153, Box 124, Morning Summaries. Confidential. Repeated to Brussels, The Hague, London, Luxembourg, Paris, Rome, USEC, and USOECD.

[2] Earlier in the day the Embassy had reported on a meeting of the Bundesbank's Central Bank Council and President Klasen's comment that there was a real chance for a successful G-10 meeting in Rome, but no chance without a dollar devaluation (i.e., an increase in the official price of gold). (Telegram 14625 from Bonn, November 24; ibid.)

207. Telegram From the Department of State to Certain Posts[1]

Washington, November 25, 1971, 0021Z.

213813. For Ambassador. Subject: G-10 Ministers' meeting.

No specific action suggested now at your initiative, but following is for your use as appropriate.

On August 15 the President launched his New Economic Policy designed to restore vitality to our economy at home and competitiveness to our goods abroad. Our international financial position had deteriorated to the point where we were not able to sustain our policy of redeeming dollars for gold, necessitating the painful decision to suspend gold convertibility. In addition, the President's announcement provided an opportunity to intensify our efforts to foster trading practices which would improve market access to U.S. goods as well as to the goods of other countries.

Immediately following the President's August 15 statement, we commenced intensive negotiations with our trading partners to achieve the exchange rate realignment necessary to restore equilibrium to the U.S. international financial position. At the same time contacts regarding outstanding trading issues were intensified. Many of these trade issues such as those with Canada and Japan are best pursued bilaterally, and that is what has happened. With respect to the Economic Communities, we have proceeded with discussions in Brussels and Washington.

There is a close interrelationship between the exchange rate realignment and trading practices if the latter tend to vitiate the increased competitiveness which exchange rate adjustments are designed to achieve. Most importantly, the Common Agricultural Policy could well operate to deny to our agricultural exports any benefit which an exchange rate adjustment would otherwise provide. Likewise, the extension of the preference system to a broader area of trade further compromises the most favored nation principle. Already a major portion of world trade is conducted at preferential duty rates, and the portion is increasing. We believe at this critical turning point in financial and trading relationships, we must press for reconsideration of the trends in these areas.

---

[1] Source: National Archives, RG 59, Central Files 1970–73, FN 10. Confidential; Priority. Drafted in Treasury by Assistant Secretary Petty on November 24, cleared in State in E/OT and by Kempe and Katz, and approved by Deputy Assistant Secretary Weintraub (E/IFD). Sent to Bern, Brussels, Ottawa, Paris, Bonn, Rome, Tokyo, The Hague, London, Stockholm (G-10 capitals) and to USOECD, USEC, and the Mission in Geneva for Eberle. Repeated to Canberra, Copenhagen, Dublin, Helsinki, Madrid, Oslo, and Vienna.

We recognize that these are difficult and contentious issues involving practices which have developed over the years and that they are not given to easy solutions. But we must impress upon other governments that the time has come to reverse trends which prejudice our trading position, not only because of economic importance but because political support for liberal, outward looking policies in U.S. is dependent on visible evidence of improved treatment. The United States believes that with the exchange rate realignments and monetary questions now under negotiation, opportunity must not be lost to make progress on trade front as well.

European governments strongly wish to separate monetary and trade issues. The United States recognizes that the compartmentalization of financial responsibilities and trade responsibilities in the organization of governments, including the U.S. Government, and international institutions have impeded joint negotiations in the past. Thus, we are concerned that lack of progress on trade matters, particularly with EC, could block acceptable general settlement. However, desire for monetary settlement should encourage willingness to examine trade issues if European governments understand movement in trade area (particularly greater recognition of interests of other countries in CAP) is necessary part of settlement.

Our position is consistent with communiqué of G-10 Finance Ministers, meeting in Washington on September 26, which referred to "some other measures outside the exchange rate field designed to improve the U.S. balance of payments."

Specifically, the U.S. Delegation to the G-10 Ministers' meeting in Rome on November 30 will be seeking to advance the negotiations on trade matters, with particular emphasis on agricultural matters in the EC. (Bilateral discussions with Japan and Canada are reasonably well advanced.)

We believe EC Finance Ministers will be generally more sympathetic with our concern over CAP than other elements in EC governments. However, because these matters are not normally in the jurisdiction of Finance Ministries, it is important the weight we attach to these matters be kept in mind in your contacts with host governments.

For London: Our trade complaints with the EC regarding the Common Agricultural Policy are consistent with the U.K. concern.

For Tokyo and Ottawa: This is not intended to indicate any dissatisfaction with pursuing our bilateral trade issues through the channels now being employed.

Irwin

208. Telegram From the Embassy in France to the Department of State[1]

Paris, November 26, 1971, 1815Z.

20133. Subject: Bank of France Governor on international monetary situation.

1. *Summary:* Governor Wormser of Bank of France professes not to have any hard-or-fast views about outcome of next week's G-10 Ministerial. He thinks that if U.S. were prepared to undertake small devaluation of dollar against gold, general rate realignment would fall into place fairly easily. He is more concerned about several questions that would arise once new rate structure decided: width of support margins; responsibility for defense of new parities as between U.S. and other countries; appropriateness of U.S economic policies as means of consolidating new dollar parity. Embassy officers stressed to Wormser that any settlement satisfactory to U.S. would of necessity have to have sufficient weight to trade aspects of B/P problem. *End summary.*

2. Economic Minister and Financial Attaché called on Governor Wormser of Bank of France today for reading of his views on international monetary situation on eve of Rome G-10 Ministerial next week. Wormser professed not to have any hard-or-fast feelings about what might happen at Rome. He commented that even if U.S. were prepared make "contribution" to parity realignment by small devaluation of dollar against gold, it was by no means clear to him that Secretary Connally would be willing to play this "trump card" next week. If it was true—as alleged this morning in private newsletter published in Paris—that the Secretary was making plans for new meetings of Group of Ten in January, it would appear that in U.S. thinking, settlement of monetary problem was still some distance away.

3. Wormser remarked that assuming small U.S. "contribution," general rate realignment should fall into place fairly easily. In his opinion, of far greater importance, and far more difficult to answer, were several questions as to what would follow decision on new rate structure.

(A) What would be width of margins around which new parities would be defended? This seemed to Wormser a question on which views diverged widely from country to country. In particular, Six did not see eye to eye, and certainly U.S. and French positions were quite far apart.

---

[1] Source: National Archives, RG 59, Central Files 1970–73, FN 10. Confidential. Repeated to Bern, Bonn, Brussels, The Hague, London, Rome, Tokyo, and USEC.

(B) Who would be responsible for defending new parities? If U.S. continued to take position it had no responsibility therefor, this problem would be pushed back on other central banks, which would face possibility of having to accumulate additional unwanted, inconvertible dollars, since it was clear that massive U.S. deficit would not go away overnight. In other words, when exchange markets started operations under new rate structure, what, if anything, would Federal Reserve be prepared to do to defend parity of dollar in New York exchange market, as Bank of France and other central banks did in their markets?

(C) For how long would new dollar parity remain valid unless U.S. could create firm basis for new parity by following "orthodox" economic and financial policies? When we asked Wormser what he meant by "orthodox policies," he referred to reports that U.S. FY 1972 budget deficit would be $28 or $29 billion, and said this was an example of what was not "orthodox." No currency devaluation had ever been successfully consolidated where fiscal and monetary policy was loose.

4. Drawing on State 213813,[2] we emphasized U.S. view of close interrelationship between exchange rate alignment and trading practices. We said U.S. delegation to Rome meeting would specifically be seeking to advance negotiations on trade matters, and that only a settlement which gave sufficient weight to this aspect of balance-of-payments problem would be satisfactory to U.S. Wormser took note, but made no comment.

Watson

---

[2] Document 207.

209. Information Memorandum From the President's Assistant for International Economic Affairs (Peterson) to President Nixon[1]

Washington, November 27, 1971.

SUBJECT

IMF Views on NEP Abroad—Messages for You

Pierre-Paul Schweitzer of the IMF was particularly anxious that I convey some messages to you. Earlier, this same group met with Paul Volcker with the same messages for John Connally.[2]

First, there were the deep concerns about world recession, trade and investment retaliation, blocs, etc., but you've heard these more than once.

On the gold price issue, they were particularly persistent that you have their views. Schweitzer has just seen some of the European prime ministers and he wanted you to know why *their* revaluing was "politically impossible".

(1) Italy—IMF claims Italy is already in a recession, with serious political problems with labor unions. A revaluation by Italy that makes their exports less competitive and generally deflates their economy and costs jobs would be "politically impossible".

(2) France—Pompidou devalued in August 1969 and at "great political risk"—given de Gaulle's adamant stand against devaluation. It is now argued that for him to reverse himself and revalue this soon would be "politically impossible". The other reasons related to the "Gaullist gold mentality" you've heard before.

(3) England—Heath is in a major battle with the Labor Party over entry into the E.C. Unemployment is up significantly and any initiative on revaluation would make Heath look insensitive to the critical jobs problem.

You asked exactly what we would get out of a willingness to devalue. The IMF's answer is as follows: the U.S. will get a substantially larger total exchange rate alignment since certain countries which agree to hold their exchange rates at present levels if the U.S. devalues by 5% or so, would *not* take the initiative and the political heat of revaluing on their own—even if the economic effects are the same. Also, certain countries (like Germany) are deeply concerned about their relative posi-

---

[1] Source: National Archives, Nixon Presidential Materials, NSC Files, Agency Files, Box 218, Council on International Economic Policy. Secret. Attached to a December 8 memorandum from Hormats to Haig recommending the NSC not object to Peterson's memorandum going to the President.

[2] No records of Schweitzer's meetings with Volcker or Peterson have been found.

tion vis-à-vis other countries (like France). Thus, the less the franc/dollar rate changes, the less Germany will do vis-à-vis the dollar.

Here are the kind of numbers they suggest:

Exchange Rate Realignment vis-à-vis the Dollar	With a U.S. Change in Price of SDRs or Gold	Without a Change in Price of SDRs or Gold
Japan	15%–16%	10%–11%
Germany	10%–12%	6%–7%
France, Italy, Britain	5%–6%	—

Various experts estimate that each additional percentage point of exchange rate realignment gets the U.S. an additional $800 million of positive trade effect. Thus, since a change in the dollar price of SDRs or gold reportedly buys us an extra 5% total realignment, it means about a $4 billion improvement in the U.S. trade picture. When you recall that our total 1971 basic balance of payments deficit is something over $8 billion, the gold price issue could be *decisive.*

In view of all this, the entire IMF group said they are at a loss to understand why we are being so difficult on the gold price issue, particularly since it is "no longer much of a political problem to the U.S." They claim that Reuss, Proxmire et al now make it much easier, as does changing the price of SDRs (rather than the price of gold).[3] I responded by saying (1) they were greatly underestimating the potential for U.S. political demagoguery, particularly in an election year; (2) they did not understand yours and John Connally's resolve to reform the monetary system and to maintain non-convertibility during the interim period while the new system was being worked out. (They acknowledged that the climate for negotiation on *non-convertibility* was much better than it had been.)

Where do I come out? We should *not* yield on the gold/SDR price issue now since it will be taken for granted and we could get less in other areas, such as trade and defense.

However, *if* and *when* John Connally has clear evidence that the total deal is a good one that can be presented to the U.S. as a great Nixon Administration success, and *if* it can be orchestrated politically (by

---

[3] On November 18 Congressman Reuss and Senator Javits introduced legislation to permit the United States to change the price of gold in the context of an international realignment of currencies. A Treasury release that day said the administration did not support the legislation. (Volcker Group paper VG/Uncl. INFO/71-47; Washington National Records Center, Department of the Treasury, Volcker Group Masters: FRC 56 86 30, VG/Uncl. INFO/71-1–)

changing the price of SDRs, getting bipartisan support, etc.), then, but only then, would I recommend that you consider the gold/SDR price change.

In the meantime, unless you tell me differently, I tell anyone who asks that the U.S. position on a gold price change is negative and firm.

---

210.   Editorial Note

The G-10 Deputies met in Rome on November 29, 1971, at 3:30 p.m. A paper entitled "Highlights of Meeting of Deputies of the Group of Ten," which summarizes the Deputies' discussion, is in the Washington National Records Center, Department of the Treasury, Records of Secretary Shultz: FRC 56 80 1, Rome G-10 Meeting 11/30–12/1/1971. Section I of the paper was drafted in Secretariat format and may be Chairman Ossola's draft of his prepared remarks for the opening of the G-10 Ministerial on November 30. Section II is presumably a U.S. draft of Volcker's response to Ossola and remarks of other Deputies following Volcker's intervention.

Section III of the paper, entitled "Comments on Volcker Statement of U.S. Substantive Position," is the U.S. record of the Deputies' debate about releasing the U.S. position. "After the Volcker statement, including his intention to make the statement public, all of the other nine delegations expressed the view that publication of a formal U.S. statement before the Ministers met would inject an element of inflexibility into the U.S. position that would change the whole atmosphere of the discussions. The French, in particular objected to the last sentence of paragraph 5 dealing with no dual markets, mentioning this passage as not appropriate in light of the forthcoming Nixon–Pompidou meeting. . . . Mr. Volcker argued that the U.S. statement was an attempt to put forward a reasonable, realistic position that met the desires of others for the U.S. to be more specific. The U.S. was concerned that parts of the U.S. position would be leaked in an unfavorable light. The position had to be seen as a package."

The paper that Volcker presumably gave the G-10 Deputies was transmitted to the White House on November 30; see Document 211. No other paper that might have been the text of that proposal was found in White House, Treasury Department, or State Department records. In his memoirs Volcker reports giving the Deputies a paper with the U.S. proposal. (Paul A. Volcker and Toyoo Gyohten, *Changing Fortunes: The World's Money and the Threat to American Leadership,* Times Books, 1992, page 85)

On November 30 Secretary Connally met with Prime Minister Colombo and Treasury Minister Aggradi at 9 a.m., prior to the G-10 Ministerial that would convene later that day. Colombo said that he understood the United States had distributed a document to the G-10 Deputies the previous day. Subsequently, Aggradi returned to that point and said "the document distributed by the U.S. yesterday has caused concern to all the Europeans. The document seems to broaden the debate back to general principles rather than focusing it on specific problems. He was afraid that when the Ministers of the Six would meet at 11:00 A.M. that morning they would be very reticent to go forward with the idea of presenting their common proposals to the G-10 meeting."

Connally replied that "he could not agree that the United States' document was broadening the issues. We have been consistent from the very beginning in holding that the areas for discussion were three: currency realignment, trade issues and burden sharing. It is true that up to now we have not been very specific on trade and burden sharing because we were afraid of being put in the position of seeking to dictate to others. However, the United States has been taken to task as being overly silent, and thereby of obstructing negotiations, because it did not put forward specific proposals. Now that we have been more specific there are objections because we have done so. What is the European position then? Do you want us to be specific or don't you?"

As the discussion concluded Connally made two points: "First of all, he recognized that the G-10 was not the ideal forum for tackling questions of trade and burden sharing. Yet it was after all true that the ultimate decision on these matters rests with heads of government and not with individual ministers and the decisions could therefore be expressed in this forum. Secondly, in a philosophical vein, he wanted it understood that in these times of fast change the United States is deeply committed to continuing and to strengthening free trade policies. We are strongly concerned that the existence of various international entities such as the IMF, the OECD, the EEC and the GATT are not always coordinated and tend to impede the solution of problems. In a fast moving age, when problems arise we cannot afford to be bogged down by hide-bound institutional arrangements or by considerations of pride and prestige of nations or heads of State." The memorandum of the conversation is in the Washington National Records Center, Department of the Treasury, Records of Secretary Shultz: FRC 56 80 1, Rome G-10 Meeting 11/30–12/1/71.

211. Telegram From Secretary of the Treasury Connally to the White House[1]

Rome, November 30, 1971, 1243Z.

456. To White House for Henry Kissinger and George Shultz.

U.S. Proposals for Settlement of Monetary and Related Issues[2]

Analysis of recent developments and statistics confirm, in the judgment of U.S. authorities, the basic validity of the analysis that a massive swing will be required in the underlying balance of payments position of the U.S. over the period ahead to assure a strong dollar, a firm basis for liberal trading policies and the continued discharge of the U.S. responsibilities for aid and defense, and international financial stability.

Over the first nine months of 1971, the U.S. basic deficit has run at an estimated annual rate of $10 billion or more.

The most recent forecasts suggest that, in the absence of exchange rate changes and the surcharge the deficit would remain in that magnitude in 1972.

For seven months, our trade position has been in deficit by some $3 billion at an annual rate, calculated FOB. (Calculated CIF on imports as is the practice of many other countries, the deficit rate would approximate $7 billion.)

Based upon earlier discussions and information available to us at this time, the principal trading partners of the U.S. apparently do not contemplate exchange rate and other actions that would permit adjustment commensurate to the forecasted need. At the same time, there is a widespread desire to achieve a prompt settlement of outstanding issues in a manner that will permit elimination of the U.S. surcharge and more fundamentally provide an environment in which trade and payments can proceed with reduced controls and greater certainty.

In the interest of expediting such an early settlement, the U.S. is making an integrated set of proposals to the Ministers of the Group of Ten countries.

The U.S. proposals must be considered an integrated package. They are based on the presumption of no change in the official dollar price of

---

[1] Source: National Archives, Nixon Presidential Materials, NSC Files, Back Channel Files, Box 423, Europe–Mid East–Latin America 1971. Secret. [text not declassified] According to a handwritten notation, the telegram was distributed to Kissinger, Haig, and Shultz, and an attached November 30 note indicates that Haig directed that a copy be given to Hormats.

[2] This is presumably the text of the U.S. proposal that Volcker gave to the G–10 Deputies on November 29; see Document 210.

gold; in the present position of the U.S., there can be no presumption of convertibility of the dollar into reserve assets, nor is the U.S. in a position to offer exchange guarantees. United States policy also continues to be based on a presumption that its present restrictions on capital outflows will also be eliminated over time, and that some liberalization steps are anticipated shortly.

Proposals

1. The U.S. will eliminate its ten percent surcharge and the related provision of the proposed investment tax credit.

2. To assure better a successful adjustment process consistent with freer and fairer trade, tangible progress is required in dealing with artificial restraints on the competitive opportunities of U.S. exporters. Early decisions on some matters of immediate consequence should be made, particularly with respect to agriculture, and commitments are necessary with regard to ensuing negotiations. These matters have been under intensive bilateral review with Canada and Japan. We have sought a similar review with the EC and its members. The U.S. is prepared to continue to negotiate intensively in coming weeks.

3. Progress is needed toward achieving a better sharing of mutual defense expenditures. To this end, certain bilateral matters are near decision, and multilateral efforts should be intensified at the forthcoming NATO meeting.[3]

4. A pattern of exchange rates should be established providing, at the minimum, a weighted average appreciation of currencies of all other OECD countries of eleven percent, measured in U.S. cents per unit of foreign currencies, with a base point of May 1, 1971. (The appreciation is calculated on the basis of weighted share of U.S. trade with these countries.) Based on an appraisal of individual country positions, depreciation of foreign currencies in terms of its own trading partners should not be contemplated.

5. The new exchange rates should be accompanied by margins of three percent, plus and minus. IMF surveillance should be directed to assure that there be no heavy market intervention in exchange markets within the band for the purpose of keeping market rates artificially low. There should be no manipulation or arrangements of exchange markets designed to maintain undervaluation of exchange rates for current account or trade purposes.

---

[3] The NATO Ministerial was held in Brussels December 9–10. In the final communiqué, the Ministers "noted with satisfaction the further, specific and important efforts announced on 7th December by those European member countries which participated in the European Defence Improvement Program, and recognized the emphasis which the European member countries are placing on modernizing the equipment of their forces, land, sea and air." (*NATO Final Communiqués 1949–1974* (Brussels: NATO Information Service))

212. Editorial Note

When the G-10 Ministers met in Rome November 30–December 1, 1971, Secretary Connally was under some pressure about the issue of the gold price. At a December 2 White House Staff Meeting, which was not attended by the President, Shultz spoke as follows:

"Problem. Connally offered devaluation of the dollar and it now appears Arthur is winning on convertibility. These are both firmly opposite to the President's directions [see Document 189]. We now have changed the price of gold and the problem is how we get this through Congress. The price of gold doesn't matter if it is not convertible, but the real problem of devaluing is in the Senate and now everything hangs on this and we have to have Congressional authority.

"Question. Is Connally doing this under pressure of the meeting?

"Now back to a procedural problem. What are we doing? What is our policy? Change in the price of gold is now irretrievable. How do we make it an asset and market it through the Senate?" (Haldeman's handwritten notes; National Archives, Nixon Presidential Materials, White House Special Files, Haldeman Notes, October–December 1971)

On December 8 Hormats sent a memorandum to Haig regarding Peterson's November 27 memorandum to the President on the NEP, Document 209. Concerning the gold price issue, Hormats wrote: "given events in Rome, I have sent Peterson a 'line' on gold which I have cleared through Treasury" and which "should bring Peterson's views on gold up to date." He attached the following two Questions and Answers:

"*Question:* What is the U.S. position on the price of gold?

"*Answer:* The U. S. delegation to the Rome meeting of the Group of Ten made no offer or commitment regarding a change in the official dollar price of gold. However, in discussion of various hypothetical changes in exchange rates, moderate increase in the official gold price was mentioned by the delegation. We have made clear that we don't want to see an emphasis on gold in the monetary system, and have been opposed to a change in the price of gold for that reason. Several other countries do want a change. The question is whether such a change would contribute to a better all-around solution—and we haven't seen the evidence on that.

"Certainly it should be clear we do not intend to resume convertibility into gold.

"*Question:* Has the U.S. offered to devalue the dollar by raising the price of gold, in order to help solve the monetary crisis?

"Answer: No. At the Rome Meeting, the U.S. took the position that we could accept an average exchange rate adjustment of 11 percent provided it was accompanied by progress on trade and burden sharing. To facilitate discussion, alternative methods of achieving adjustment of that magnitude were discussed in a purely hypothetical way. Neither the U.S. nor any other country made any offers or any commitments." (Ibid., NSC Files, Agency Files, Box 218, Council on International Economic Policy)

---

213.   Telegram From the Department of State to Certain Posts[1]

Washington, December 3, 1971.

To the Ambassador.

1. Please deliver the following message:

2. "You should be aware of the following which transpired during an executive session of the recent Rome meeting with myself, Chairman Burns, and Under Secretary Volcker in attendance. After prolonged and difficult discussion, the G-10 Ministers of the Six on Wednesday[2] unmistakably understood and accepted trade issues to be part of the current negotiation. Italian Minster Ferrari-Aggradi, speaking formally on behalf of the Six during an executive session of the G-10 Ministers, solemnly assured the USG that the EC Ministers were directing the Commission to begin immediate repeat immediate trade negotiations looking toward constructive resolution of problems. This commitment followed prolonged EC caucus suspected to include consultation with capitals by some Ministers. 'Immediate' was defined as beginning that afternoon. EC Commissioner Barre, who was present, was asked directly if he understood the instructions. After he indicated concern that EC members were not acting in formal Council meeting, it was accepted on all sides that such formal action should be taken to ratify action but that negotiation would indeed begin immediately.

---

[1]   Source: Washington National Records Center, Department of the Treasury, Secretary's Memos: FRC 56 74 17, Classified Miscellaneous 1971. Confidential; Immediate. Drafted in Treasury by Assistant Secretary Petty on December 3 and sent to the State Department for transmission to Bonn, Brussels, The Hague, London, Luxembourg, Paris, Rome, USEC, and USOECD. According to telegrams from the addressees (see Document 215), it was transmitted as telegram 219288.

[2]   December 1.

You should be advised of this considered commitment which was critical part of the Rome meeting. It was an ingredient essential to the progress that was made there. It is an ingredient essential to future progress.

It is of the utmost importance that no USG official reflect any doubt whatsoever on this commitment. Since commitment made in executive session without written record we want to be alert to any possibility of EC bureaucracy dragging its heels on trade through procedural delays and otherwise, particularly in view of public view recently expressed by the Commission representatives that trade negotiations would have to await interim monetary settlement. We have been assured by the FinMins of the Six that any such statements by the Commission have been totally unauthorized.

For your background, extensive discussions in executive session identified the following trade areas of prime interest to the U.S. in the short run: most-favored-nation treatment of citrus; tax harmonization scheme on tobacco; 10% grain stock piling for 2 crop years; and the common support prices for grain, including both the unit of account and the inflation factor. We also look for framework for negotiation on other areas, such as preferences and farm price policy, during 1972. Mr. Barre was not present during most of this discussion which identified these areas of prime interest but EC Finance Ministers took exception to none of these as legitimate areas of negotiation.

Ambassador Eberle will be returning to Europe next week to pursue with the Commission the negotiation of these matters.

Ambassador Eberle, as Special Trade Representative, has been authorized by the President to conduct these negotiations on behalf of the USG, with the assistance of State, Agriculture, and Treasury officials as necessary.[3] John B. Connally."[4]

---

[3] In a December 6 memorandum to President Nixon, Connally noted that he had sent a message to the U.S. Ambassadors in the Common Market countries and the United Kingdom. He also suggested that when the President asked Secretary Rogers to convey Presidential greetings at a Chiefs of Mission meeting in Paris December 6–8, he ask Rogers to remind the Ambassadors to give every possible support to Ambassador Eberle. (National Archives, Nixon Presidential Materials, NSC Files, Agency Files, Box 289, Treasury Volume II, 1971)

[4] Printed from a copy that bears no signature.

214. Telegram From the Mission to the European Community to the Department of State[1]

Brussels, December 3, 1971, 1523Z.

4012. For Julius Katz, E; for Eberle (STR) from Schaetzel. Subj: EC trade aspects of monetary settlement.

1. In response to your telephone message,[2] I have talked with Barre, Dahrendorf and Ruggiero. We have also been in touch with Hijzen. The EC Commission is still sorting out its understanding of what happened. But they are aware that Ferrari-Aggradi said, in effect, that the Community could negotiate with us on a trade component if a mutually satisfactory monetary deal is near at hand. The Commission understands that the EC side would have the right to raise trade problems that the Community has with the US.

2. Under these circumstances, a Commission delegation which will probably consist of Dahrendorf, Mansholt, Hijzen, and Ruggiero, is ready to meet with a Washington delegation led by Eberle on Wednesday, December 8.

3. The Commission wishes to be clear about the basis on which this meeting will take place. They emphasize this in order (A) to take into account the political and constitutional imperatives inherent in the Community's internal procedures and (B) to avoid misunderstandings that could detract from the improved atmosphere developed at Rome.

4. In essence the Commission cannot "negotiate" with us until it receives a mandate from the EC Council of Ministers. The Commission would have to make a proposal, have it vetted at the official level with the member states (Perm Reps and Article 113 Committee), and have it formally approved by the Council. A Council of Ministers meeting was already scheduled for next Saturday, December 11. Provided that the member governments give the necessary political directives, the normal Community procedure can be speeded up and telescoped at least in part. We are of course urging the Commission to move quickly.

5. In light of the considerations outlined above, the Commission advises us that they have no choice but to view the December 8 bilateral US–EC meeting as an exploration with us of the agenda of trade items advanced by the American side in Rome.

---

[1] Source: National Archives, RG 59, S/S Files: Lot 73 D 153, Box 124, Morning Summaries. Secret; Exdis. Repeated to Paris for Deputy Under Secretary Samuels. Similar messages were received from the Embassies in Bonn (telegram 15042, December 3) and Rome (telegram 7658, December 4). (Both ibid., Central Files 1970–73, FN 10)

[2] Not further identified.

6. Please advise us urgently as to (A) whether we should confirm the December 8 meeting with the Commission and (B) the composition and travel plans of the US team.[3]

7. I personally believe it important, at this juncture, that the team come from Washington and lay out the US position. For one thing, the Commission needs to have as clear an understanding as possible during the next critical week or so when it must take the initiative in putting together a Community position

Schaetzel

---

[3] No record of the details of arrangements for trade talks have been found, but Hormats, in a December 9 memorandum entitled "Economic Policy at the Summit," informed Kissinger that Eberle would begin trade negotiations with the Community during the coming week. (National Archives, Nixon Presidential Materials, NSC Files, Subject Files, Box 356, Monetary Matters) In telegram 23063, December 23, the Department of State informed various European posts that Eberle had undertaken a series of negotiations with the Commission, based on understandings reached in Rome and Washington. (Ibid., RG 59, Central Files 1970–73, E 1 US) See Document 221.

---

215. Telegram From the Embassy in the Netherlands to the Department of State[1]

The Hague, December 6, 1971, 1315Z.

4366. Pass Treasury for Connally and Federal Reserve for Burns. Subject: Dutch views on monetary and trade settlement.

Summary: Zijlstra and Oort, chief architects of Dutch monetary policy, are convinced from outcome of Rome G-10 meeting that all parties now have political will for early solution. Main imponderables now are how far dollar can devalue without pulling sterling, franc, lire, and krona down too, how far US is willing to pare down 11 percent revaluation demand, and how much further revaluation Canada can stand. Dutch feel issues of margins and IMF convertibility of dollar must also be addressed at next G-10. For their part, Dutch are ready to accept revaluation of 9–11 percent if necessary to early settlement. *End summary.*

---

[1] Source: National Archives, RG 59, Central Files 1970–73, FN 10. Secret; Exdis. Repeated to Bern, Bonn, Brussels, London, Luxembourg, Ottawa, Paris for Deputy Under Secretary Samuels and Ambassador Middendorf, Rome, Stockholm, Tokyo, USEC, and USOECD.

1. Ambassador Middendorf, accompanied by Econ Counselor, met Dec 3 with Treasurer General Oort and Dec 4 with Central Bank Governor Zijlstra and received following impressions on what transpired at Rome G-10 meeting and what is likely to happen next. In single instance where their accounts differed Oort's version is shown in parentheses but we consider Zijlstra's version more reliable as he was present in executive sessions.

2. Both paid high tribute to Connally's chairmanship. Zijlstra called it "masterful display of leadership." Both felt that high degree of secrecy maintained and discussion of key issues in executive session were vital preconditions for success achieved.

3. Meeting got off to unpromising start because of tough US proposal unofficially surfaced at Deputies' meeting, but things went smoother at Ministerial meeting where discussion focused on Zijlstra's package proposal.[2] On monetary side this called in essence for 5-1/2 percent devaluation of dollar and weighted average revaluation of major currencies against dollar of 11 percent over 1970 parities. This formula modified during discussion to permit possibility of deeper dollar devaluation and use of May 1, 1971 as base date for 11 percent revaluation (i.e. require that 11 percent be over and above Canadian revaluation of 8 percent accomplished prior that date). Since this would have effect of raising US BOP swing from $8.9 billion under Zijlstra formula to $10.5 billion, most members thought it excessive (Oort said, on other hand, that no one seemed "shocked" at figure).

4. Discussion then centered on Zijlstra formula for splitting bill among other nine. This formula, which Zijlstra said he developed after extensive discussions with all Governors and Ministers involved, would call for dirty float currencies (UK, France, Italy and Sweden) to maintain gold parity (i.e. revalue by 5-1/2 percent against dollar), Germany, with weight of 10 percent in US imports, to revalue by 12–15 percent against dollar, Japanese, with weight of 19 percent, to revalue by 15–20 percent against dollar, and Benelux to revalue halfway between "dirty four" and D-Mark, i.e. 8–10 percent. No one flinched audibly at this formula, including Dutch, but it was soon obvious that unless Canada, with weight in US imports of 25–36 percent (depending on definition) is in position to contribute additional 4 percent more in revaluation, other countries would have to push their revaluation to

---

[2] Presumably Zijlstra's undated paper entitled "Working Paper," a copy of which he sent Secretary Connally under cover of a November 23 letter. Zijlstra noted that he had prepared the paper in compliance with a request made at the Annual Meeting of the IMF in Washington in September. (Washington National Records Center, Department of the Treasury, Records of Secretary Shultz: FRC 56 80 1, Rome G-10 Meeting 11/30–12/1/71) For the U.S. proposal at the G-10 Deputies meeting, see Document 211.

unacceptable levels to reach US 11 percent target. Monetary discussion terminated at this point and discussion on trade ensued along lines of State 219288 (Exdis).[3] Elements of Zijlstra package covering burden sharing, agriculture, margins, and convertibility were not seriously addressed.

5. Zijlstra considers there are three variables in monetary formula to be resolved between now and Dec. 17. He is uncertain what his role can or should be in bringing his considerable influence to bear on these issues in interim period but Ambassador expressed hope he would leave no stone unturned to promote their satisfactory resolution. Zijlstra commented that happy coincidence of BIS meeting next week will provide good opportunity for further missionary work. Three variables are:

A. How much less than 11 percent average revaluation ($10.5 billion BOP swing) is US prepared to accept?

B. How much more revaluation can Canada stand and how can floating Canadian dollar be strengthened even if this is intent?

C. How far can dollar be devalued in terms of gold without triggering pursuit by "dirty four"?

6. Zijlstra anticipates that Dec 17–18 G-10 will concentrate on four issues: monetary variables, progress on trade negotiations, margins, and restoration of limited dollar convertibility in IMF.

7. On margins, Dutch favor 2–2-1/2 percent maximum and maintenance of 1/2 percent in EEC.

8. On convertibility, Dutch see no reason why dollar could not become convertible for minor IMF debt repayments. Zijlstra feels US should have enough assets to absorb this in view of (1) additional SDRs forthcoming Jan 1, (2) availability of gold tranche and (3) likelihood of early repatriation of up to $10 billion in speculative dollars invested abroad as soon as new fixed parities are established. Zijlstra considers fixed parities without convertibility unworkable and over longer haul favors his own proposal to let IMF decide what mix of assets Central Banks must accept in conversions through Fund, although he recognized some ad hoc arrangements will have to be made to accommodate British debt to IMF and to pare down $59 billion (as of Aug 18) in hands of non-residents. (According to Zijlstra, $45 billion in hands of Central Banks, $14 billion in individual hands.)

9. Perhaps most significant observation Zijlstra made about Rome meeting was that he is convinced that all ten major currency countries now have political will and strong desire to achieve immediate settlement of monetary and trade issues. Dutch, who have so much to lose from international trade war, clearly share this will and desire.

---

[3] Document 213.

Although Dutch are deeply concerned about present downward trend in their business cycle, which up to now has been due to excessive wage settlements, they are even more fearful of growing atmosphere of corporate uncertainty engendered by floating exchange rates. Their improving BOP outlook for 1970 gives them little comfort because it is due more to declining imports of investment goods than to rising exports (except to Germany). Thus we are inclined to believe that they would now settle for guilder revaluation in terms of dollar of as much as 11 percent, provided this is essential to agreement and provided D-Mark revaluation is at least 3 points higher.

Bovey

216. **Telegram From the Department of State to Certain Posts**[1]

Washington, December 7, 1971, 0050Z.

220210. Please deliver at opening of business December 7. Subject: Summary of G-10 Rome Meeting. From Secretary Connally.

1. In view of the importance of the negotiations and the prominent treatment in the press I wanted to provide you with my assessment of the Rome meeting and give some guidance on what I see lying ahead.

2. Multilateral negotiations between a sizable number of Finance Ministers and Central Bank Governors involving precise—even if hypothetical—exchange rates are a matter of highest sensitivity on the markets around the world. By restricting discussion to only the principals, a very lively and free give and take was achieved. This procedure is likely to continue in Washington.[2]

3. On Monday afternoon, Under Secretary Volcker at the Deputies meeting made a specific proposal incorporating a substantial concession by the United States.[3] Our analysis has determined that a roughly

---

[1] Source: National Archives, RG 59, Central Files 1970–73, FN 10. Confidential. Drafted in Treasury by Petty on December 6 and cleared by Volcker in draft; cleared in State by D.B. Timmins (E/IFD/OMA) and approved by Weintraub (E/IFD). Sent to G-10, OECD, and NATO capitals and to USEC and USOECD.

[2] The G-10 Ministers were scheduled to meet again at the Smithsonian Institution in Washington December 17–18.

[3] See Document 211.

$13 billion swing is needed if we are to return to approximate equilibrium in our basic position. This would involve, in the absence of other measures, an exchange rate adjustment on the order of 15–20 percent. Mr. Volcker said the U.S. could accept an 11 percent adjustment (figured from May 1, 1971), provided it was accompanied by progress on trade (particularly agriculture) and burden sharing. However, because the adjustment proposed was below what is likely to be necessary for a secure external position, Mr. Volcker emphasized the offer was based on a presumption of no convertibility into reserve assets and no change in the dollar price of gold. It was pointed out the U.S. could not assume responsibility for maintaining exchange rates when other countries would agree to substantially less change than what we felt was necessary to achieve equilibrium.

4. The U.S. was prepared to publish this offer, but withheld at the unanimous request of other Deputies.

5. On Tuesday the Common Market Ministers and the U.K. sought a common position and, as previously, they were able to agree mainly that the U.S. should offer to change the gold price.

6. To facilitate discussions on various formulas for achieving the exchange rate realignment the U.S. proposed discussion proceed in a hypothetical manner by asking what exchange rate changes might ensue with the U.S. changing the gold price in various ways. The ensuing discussion (and silences) made it apparent that despite the strong politically motivated desire in Europe for a gold price change, most European countries desired only small and inadequate exchange rate adjustments. It was apparent to all in the discussion that the U.S. could not unilaterally determine its exchange rate by any mechanism.

7. No country made a specific offer. Each nation has maintained its full prerogatives and future negotiations will proceed with all options open. However, each of us is now more intimately aware of not only the range of possibilities but also of likely magnitudes of adjustment.

8. As reported to you earlier, much time was spent in firmly establishing the point that trade measures must be part of the solution. We left Rome having created a strong momentum for a monetary settlement. However, large differences of substance remain. I cannot predict that settlement will be found in Washington. Too much depends on the trade negotiations, the prospect of which is difficult to assess at this time. Moreover, it is clear that exchange rate realignment which many countries are prepared to allow us is substantially below the minimum requirement which Mr. Volcker announced Monday of 11 percent and also below what the OECD and IMF studies have considered necessary. So in Washington I hope to find that the other countries have raised their sights a bit. In sum, the sense of progress which the press has

reported and which the markets have reflected are justified. I hope it will be possible to have agreement by early in the New Year. However, to achieve that result, the time has come in which our trading partners must be more forthcoming than has been apparent so far.

Rogers

217. **Telegram From the Embassy in Germany to the Department of State**[1]

Bonn, December 10, 1971, 1152Z.

15341. Subject: Nixon/Pompidou meeting: EC trade negotiations. Ref: Bonn 15229; Paris 2977 (exdis).[2]

1. *Summary:* I am concerned that the GOF might hold up approval of the EC trade negotiating mandate until the Nixon/Pompidou meeting. Department should be alert to the possibility that Pompidou might also concede on grain prices in full recognition of the fact that it would be politically difficult for the Germans to move on this issue.[3] I believe the GOF should not be allowed to shift the entire burden for seeking a grain CAP modification to the USG but should share the responsibility with other EEC members of working out an overall acceptable trade response. *End summary.*

2. I have noted reports suggesting that GOF might seek to hold up the EC mandate on trade negotiations so that Pompidou can gain political mileage by reaching agreement with President Nixon. It is also conceivable that Pompidou will offer us some satisfaction on grain during the Azores meeting while at the same time expecting that this would be

---

[1] Source: National Archives, Nixon Presidential Materials, NSC Files, Subject Files, Box 356, Monetary Matters. Secret; Exdis. Repeated to The Hague, Luxembourg, London, Paris, Rome, Brussels, and USEC. Attached to a December 9 memorandum from Hormats to Kissinger regarding economic policy at the Summit.

[2] Neither printed.

[3] In his December 9 memorandum to Kissinger (see footnote 1 above), Hormats noted that Connally believed that he received a commitment from the Europeans at the G-10 meeting in Rome to empower the Commission immediately to begin trade negotiations. Hormats then referred to reporting from Paris that at the EC Ministers' meeting on December 11 France might oppose giving an immediate mandate. Hormats concluded it was far from certain that the international economic situation had been resolved.

politically impossible for the Germans as stated in para 3 reftel B. Such a development would admittedly put the Germans in an extremely difficult position. However, in my view this would not necessarily be detrimental to our interests; such a move by Pompidou might thus bring additional pressure on the Germans to offer some satisfaction on grain prices; perhaps also the reverse system could be used with Brandt to put pressure on the French on other "impossible" issues.

3. For some time now the Embassy has urged the FRG to reduce grain prices. We have made it clear that present CAP prices are a serious burden to American agriculture and undermining support for liberal trade in the U.S. In recent weeks we have strongly re-emphasized the necessity for a reduction of EC farm prices and the use of production neutral income payments to compensate German farmers for the effects of revaluation and requested price reductions.

4. Admittedly grain price reductions will be extremely difficult for the Germans. Brandt and the SPD are dependent on the Free Democratic Party to continue in power. The FDP has important strength in agricultural constituencies making Brandt particularly dependent on Minister of Agriculture Ertl who is a conservative member of the FDP and a Bavarian farmer. Alienation of Ertl could bring down the Brandt government thus explaining the difficulty of obtaining any price movement on grain prices in the short-run.

5. However, as is clearly evident from ref B, all difficult agricultural decisions are politically impossible in the EEC in view of the unanimity rule involving significant policy issues. Therefore we must keep pressure on to bring about economically essential solutions to trade issues and their possible adjustments. This should of course be done in a manner as not to jeopardize our relations with the FRG or our broader European policy interests.

6. I believe the Department should be alert to all the various political and economic infighting now going on in the EEC such as is clearly evident in ref B. This applies especially to responsibilities for trade policy in agriculture, making it essential that the US place emphasis and responsibility on the total EEC for its trade actions rather than in any way supporting one country against another.

Rush

218.   Telegram From the Mission to the European Community to the Department of State[1]

Brussels, December 12, 1971, 0114Z.

4124. Pass Treasury for Secretary Connally/White House. Pass Eberle. Subject: EC–US trade negotiations.

1. Due to French opposition, the EC Council was unable at its meeting on December 11 to adopt a formal mandate to the Commission to begin trade negotiations with the United States. Instead, the Council adopted a "declaration of intent" (text not available) which stated that the Community should open negotiations with the US "as soon as possible." The Counsel instructed the EC PermReps to prepare a formal mandate, and said that the Commission should report to the council on the results of the negotiations at the end of January.

2. According to Commission Secretary General Noel, the mandate which the PermReps will prepare will require formal Council approval before negotiations can actually begin. This could be accomplished, however, by "written procedure," which would not require a meeting of the Council. Noel, Commission Vice President Mansholt and other Community officials expressed doubt, however, that a mandate will be approved in time for negotiations to begin next week.

3. The "declaration of intent" adopted by the Council also states that a realignment of parities should lead the Community to make a significant contribution to the solution of trade problems and the balance of payments problems of the United States. It says that the special characteristics of agricultural trade and the growing importance of non-tariff barriers open up opportunities for new initiatives, which could include adjustments in the GATT. It says that the Community is prepared to negotiate on the basis of mutual advantage and reciprocity.

4. During the Council discussion, the EC Commission and all the member states except France strongly advocated immediate adoption of a formal negotiating mandate, on the basis of the commitment made by Italy's Treasury Minister Ferrari-Aggradi at the Rome meeting of the Group of Ten. French Foreign Minister Schumann maintained that Ferrari-Aggradi's statement had not been a Community commitment. He pointed out that the member states had only received proposals

---

[1] Source: National Archives, Nixon Presidential Materials, NSC Files, Subject Files, Box 356, Monetary Matters. Confidential. The copy of the telegram printed here does not have the list of posts to which the telegram may have been repeated. It is attached to a December 11 memorandum from Peterson to Kissinger entitled "Trade Negotiations Status—To Take With You to Azores Meeting."

from the Commission on the day before the Council meeting, and said that serious matters of this kind required careful consideration. Schumann stressed that the Community should not put into effect any trade concessions in the United States before it was certain that the US could participate in a general realignment of parities (i.e., before Congress approved a change in the price of gold).

5. While the other member states sought approval of a mandate at this meeting, most of them expressed the view that the US has been pressing too hard and that the belief that trade negotiations could produce results in the course of next week was beyond the realm of the possible.

Schaetzel

---

219.   **Editorial Note**

President Nixon and French President Pompidou met in the Azores December 13–14, 1971. Memoranda of the Presidents' conversations, plus memoranda of Kissinger's breakfast meetings with Pompidou on both days regarding international monetary and related issues, are in the National Archives, Nixon Presidential Materials, White House Special Files, President's Office Files Beginning 12/12/71. The joint statement issued at the end of the Summit dealt only with international economic issues. For text, see *Public Papers of the Presidents of the United States: Richard M. Nixon, 1971*, pages 1190–1191.

Among the briefing materials for the economic dimension of the Azores Summit is a December 10 paper entitled "Framework for Monetary and Trade Settlement." A number of the elements in the draft agreement Kissinger marked up during his December 14 breakfast meeting with President Pompidou are in this paper; see footnote 1, Document 220. Also included in the briefing papers is a 17-page, December 10 memorandum from Connally to the President entitled "Monetary and Trade Issues Aiming at the Azores Meeting." In it Connally reviewed the role of France in the European Community, touched on its NATO role, and highlighted its economic differences with the United States. He included a number of specific recommendations for items Nixon should concentrate on with Pompidou, including, in the hope of a final agreement that would include trade and burden-sharing, U.S. consideration of a change in the dollar-gold price, despite the fact that it was not clear if "a negotiable package serves our *economic* interests as well as a long period of floating exchange rates." All the briefing materials are in the National Archives, Nixon Presidential Materials, NSC Files, Subject Files, Box 356, Monetary Matters.

Ambassador Watson reported in telegram 20627 from Paris, December 3, that President Pompidou's agenda at the Azores Summit would include, in addition to the international economic, financial, and monetary situation, other items such as the changing global power alignments as China emerged more fully on the world stage and bilateral narcotics issues. (Ibid., RG 59, S/S Files: Lot 73 D 153, Box 124, Morning Summaries)

A set of materials that includes papers on non-economic issues at the Summit, problems involved in its scheduling, and how the meetings would be conducted is ibid., Nixon Presidential Materials, NSC Files, President's Trip Files, Box 473, Azores–Pompidou. These records indicate the broad scope of the Summit and President Pompidou's desire to meet privately with President Nixon, avoiding as much as possible expanded meetings.

Based on the President's Trip Files, the memoranda of conversation, and the President's Daily Diary, the course of the Summit went as follows: On December 13 Kissinger breakfasted with Pompidou (accompanied only by interpreters) to discuss a framework for monetary negotiations. Pompidou agreed that Kissinger might join the two Presidents for discussion of monetary issues. Presidents Nixon and Pompidou then met privately from 10:05 a.m. to 12:45 p.m. to review non-economic issues, accompanied only by their interpreters (Walters on the U.S. side). Simultaneously, Secretary Rogers and Foreign Minister Schumann met on "political issues" (accompanied by Kissinger, Ambassadors Watson and Kennedy, Assistant Secretary Hillenbrand, and Sonnenfeldt on the U.S. side) and Connally and Volcker met with Finance Minister Giscard d'Estaing on economic issues. Following the morning session, President Nixon lunched alone with Kissinger (according to the President's Daily Diary), but Kissinger reports that Connally was also present (according to *White House Years*, page 961), and Nixon agreed to provide Kissinger with a proposal for Kissinger's breakfast meeting with Pompidou the next day.

On the afternoon of December 13 Presidents Nixon and Pompidou met from 3:35 to 6:13 p.m. (accompanied by interpreters and Kissinger on the U.S. side). The majority of the discussion entailed an exchange of views on international monetary and related matters. President Pompidou emphasized the importance of fixed parities, a devaluation of the dollar in relation to the price of gold, and the eventual restoration of convertibility. The Presidents touched on acceptable exchange rate margins and target parities for a number of currencies, subjects they took up in greater detail on December 14. Simultaneously, the Rogers–Schumann political meeting and the Connally–Volcker–Giscard economic meeting continued. That evening both Presidential parties attended a dinner given by Portuguese Prime Minister Caetano.

On December 14 Kissinger again breakfasted with Pompidou to discuss monetary reform and related matters. Kissinger worked from a draft set of undertakings drawn up in consultation with Connally, which he marked up during the breakfast meeting. See footnote 1, Document 220. Presidents Nixon and Pompidou then met from 9:35 a.m. to 1:35 p.m. (accompanied by interpreters and Kissinger on the U.S. side) for detailed discussion of monetary and related matters. At 11:05 a.m. Connally, Volcker, and Giscard (according to the President's Daily Diary) plus Rogers and Schumann (according to the memorandum of conversation) joined the Summit and remained with their principals until the conclusion of the meeting. Following exchanges on a number of specific issues, President Nixon asked Pompidou if he could agree with the general terms of the U.S. draft. Pompidou equivocated, suggesting there was room for give and take. The memorandum of conversation does not further elaborate on an agreement, but the Presidents did sign a confidential agreement on a framework for a monetary and trade settlement. See Document 220.

In their brief statements at the end of the Summit both Presidents referred, without any specifics, to wide-ranging discussions, but the joint statement released at that time referred only to the economic issues. The December 13 remarks of Secretary Rogers and Foreign Minister Schumann on trade and foreign policy matters and Connally's December 13 press briefing on economic and monetary affairs are printed in *Weekly Compilation of Presidential Documents: Week Ending Saturday, December 18, 1971*, pages 1656–1660.

220. Paper Agreed by President Nixon and President Pompidou[1]

Angra, The Azores, undated.

FRAMEWORK FOR MONETARY AND TRADE SETTLEMENT

The following proposals providing a framework for an early settlement of monetary and trade issues should be considered as an integrated whole:

1. The U.S. will remove the ten percent surcharge and the related provisions of the Job Development credit.

2. The U.S. will propose to the Congress a suitable means for devaluing the dollar in terms of gold to $38.00 per ounce[2] as soon as the entire set of related measures (including short-term trade measures) is available for Congressional scrutiny.

3. The French Government will reaffirm its intention, under these conditions, to maintain the present gold parity of the French franc. Consistent with this decision, it is anticipated the German mark will be revalued by 5–6% and the Japanese yen by 9–11%.[3] It is anticipated also that sterling and the lire will remain in line with the French franc.

4. Pending resolution of longer-term means of monetary reform, provisions will be made for 2-1/4 % margins[4] of exchange rate fluctuation above and below the new exchange rates.

---

[1] Source: National Archives, Nixon Presidential Materials, NSC Files, Subject Files, Box 356, Monetary Matters, Envelope marked Bermuda. No classification marking. Initialed by Presidents Nixon and Pompidou at the bottom of the first page and signed by both at the end. An earlier version of the paper that Kissinger marked up, apparently during his breakfast meeting with Pompidou on December 14, is ibid. According to the memorandum of conversation of that meeting (see Document 219), Kissinger read Pompidou the proposed text of item 6 as formulated by Connally. Pompidou said he could not agree to the statement as read; he could not accept the absence of any mention of fixed parities. Kissinger wrote in the left margin of the draft: *"Fixed Parity* must be in." In the expanded meeting at the conclusion of the Summit, Connally noted that the item 5 language had been modified. See also footnote 4, Document 223. The text of the earlier version of the paper is indicated in footnotes 2–9 below.

[2] Instead of "to $38.00 per ounce" the earlier paper read "by ten percent." In the margin Kissinger calculated this to be an 8.6 percent change, but when Pompidou held out for $38, Kissinger said "we would not raise our voices on that."

[3] The two percentages were "4–5%" and "8–10%," respectively, in the earlier paper.

[4] The earlier paper read "three percent margins." During breakfast Pompidou said France could accept 2 percent margins. Kissinger told Pompidou he would prefer to wait on this and would be prepared to discuss it if there were agreement on other matters. He said the President was prepared to split the difference between 2 and 2-1/2 percent. In the closed Summit meeting Kissinger noted the U.S. preference for 3 percent margins and the French willingness to accept 2 percent margins. Connally reportedly was prepared to accept 2-1/2 percent and left it to the principals to work out the difference. President Nixon said he would "bow" on 2-1/2 percent and would give 75 percent.

5. The United States intends to assist in the stability of the system and the defense of the newly fixed[5] structure of exchange rates in particular[6] by vigorous implementation of its efforts to restore price stability and productivity.

6. Discussions will be promptly undertaken in appropriate forums to resolve longer term issues of international monetary reform. Attention should be directed to the appropriate monetary means and division of responsibilities for defending stable exchange rates and for insuring a proper degree of convertibility of the system;[7] the proper role of gold, reserve currencies, and Special Drawing Rights in the operation of the system; the volume of liquidity; reexamination of the permissible margin of fluctuation around established exchange rates and other means of establishing a suitable degree of flexibility; and other measures dealing with movements of liquid capital. It is recognized that decisions in each of these areas are closely linked.[8]

7. Questions of trade arrangements are recognized as a relevant factor in assuring a new and lasting equilibrium in the international economy. The French Government therefore will support an appropriate mandate for the Commission of the European Community to enter into negotiations immediately with the U.S. to resolve pending short-term issues[9] at the earliest possible date and to establish an appropriate agenda for considering more basic issues in a framework of mutual cooperation in the course of 1972 and beyond.

8. The United States believes commitments undertaken at the recent NATO meeting represent a constructive approach toward dealing more adequately with a proper sharing of defense burden.[10]

---

[5] The earlier paper had "established" instead of "fixed."

[6] The words "in particular" were added to the final text.

[7] This phrase ended with "defending established exchange rates" in the earlier paper.

[8] The earlier paper read: "suitable flexibility in exchange rates. It is recognized that decisions in each of these areas will be interdependent."

[9] The parenthetical phrase "(particularly affecting agricultural products)" was included at this point in the earlier version. The memoranda of conversation do not indicate when it was deleted. At the end of the earlier version of the paper, Kissinger wrote: "World organization of grains." During the initial, limited Summit meeting on December 14 Pompidou said the EC had adopted a draft statement that once monetary measures had been taken France was ready for general trade discussions. He said citrus was not a problem for France but would be for others. Tobacco could be on the table, but for the time being cereals production, except for soft wheat could not. "If the leaders were to give the European farmers the impression that they were tampering with European agriculture, it would create an impossible political problem." Pompidou later returned to the point and said "frankly (and this was very favorable to the U.S.)" that as French and Europeans they were ready to discuss world grain market organization with the United States and Canada, a point on which President Nixon expressed satisfaction.

[10] See footnote 3, Document 211.

9. The United States and France will join with other nations to consider promptly means of appropriately facilitating the operation of the International Monetary Fund.

G. Pompidou

Richard Nixon

---

221.   Editorial Note

The G-10 Ministers met at the Smithsonian Institution in Washington on December 17 and 18, 1971, and agreed on a realignment of exchange rates similar to that agreed to by Presidents Nixon and Pompidou in the Azores. See Document 220. Addressing the Ministers at the conclusion of the meeting, President Nixon called their agreement "the most significant monetary agreement in the history of the world," even in comparison with the 1944 Bretton Woods agreement that had established the postwar regime of fixed exchange rates and the International Monetary Fund. For text of the President's address, see *Public Papers of the Presidents of the United States: Richard M. Nixon, 1971,* pages 1195–1196.

At his press conference with Federal Reserve Chairman Burns, Under Secretary Volcker, and Governor Daane following the G-10 meeting, Secretary Connally said the dollar would depreciate by an average 12 percent against other OECD currencies, but declined to disclose what the new exchange rates would be. Connally said the Ministers had agreed that each country would announce its parities at the time and in the manner it saw fit. Connally also said the administration would approach the Congress for authority to increase the gold price to $38 per ounce, and that the 10 percent import surcharge would be lifted, probably during the coming week. A transcript of the press conference and a copy of the G-10 Communiqué are in the Washington National Records Center, Department of the Treasury, Volcker Group Masters: FRC 56 86 30, 1971, VG/Uncl. INFO/71. The President's statement and the G-10 Communiqué are also printed in Department of State *Bulletin,* January 10, 1972, pages 32–34. President Nixon announced the removal of the surcharge on December 20, during his meeting with British Prime Minister Heath in Bermuda. See *Public Papers of the Presidents of the United States: Richard M. Nixon, 1971,* page 1197. The G-10 Communiqué and the President's statement lifting the surcharge are also in *Annual Report of the Secretary of the Treasury on the State of the Finances for the Fiscal Year Ended June 30, 1972*, pages 369–371.

Reports from the Embassy in France indicated that Finance Minister Giscard d'Estaing on December 21 announced the new franc parity for current account transactions, but said the financial franc would not be bound by the 2.25 percent margins agreed to in Rome and Washington. The Embassy reported that on December 21 the commercial franc was trading at 5.22–5.23 per dollar, within the new 5.23 ceiling, but that the financial franc was as high as 5.28. (Telegram 21746 from Paris, December 21; National Archives, RG 59, Central Files 1970–73, FN 10 FR)

In response to President Pompidou's remarks during a TV interview on the international economic situation, during which Pompidou reportedly said there could be no damage to the Community's Common Agricultural Policy in the trade negotiations (see also footnote 9, Document 220), the Department of State provided certain European Missions with Departmental press guidance for their use as appropriate. The guidance indicated that Ambassador Eberle had undertaken a series of trade negotiations with the Community's Commission based on understandings reached in Rome and Washington and that the administration intended to submit the trade package "for Congressional scrutiny at the same time we submit our legislation on a change in the price of gold." (Telegram 230632, December 23; ibid., E 1 US)

Reporting from Bonn [*text not declassified*] indicated that Chancellor Brandt thought that the fact that the G-10 reached agreement was evidence of "cohesion in the Western Alliance" despite the "fact that in reaching an economic agreement 'some nations' had 'ganged up' on the FRG and placed before the Germans some already-agreed-upon decisions" (understood to be the Azores Agreement). Brandt reportedly hoped it would be possible to reach agreement with France on agricultural policies, but Minister of Agriculture Josef Ertl highlighted difficult obstacles to an agreement with the United States as U.S. proposals would depress the prices received by German farmers. Minister of Economics and Finance Schiller was concerned with reaching agreement with France on the Mark–franc exchange rate and "complained that the French were insisting on fixed parities and were not agreeing to the general guidelines laid down by the Ten, particularly as far as parity bands were concerned." (Telegram [*document number not declassified*] from Bonn, December 23; ibid., Nixon Presidential Materials, NSC Files, Country Files–Europe, Box 686, Germany, Volume X 9/71–12/71)

Background information provided to Congress in February 1972, when the administration sent forward the proposed legislation on modification of the par value of the dollar included the following tabulation on new parities:

"Country	Percent appreciation against U.S. dollar vis-à-vis par values on April 30, 1971	Old exchange rate per dollar	New exchange rate per dollar
Belgium	11.57	50.00BF	44.8BF
Canada	float	float	float
France	8.57	5.55FF	5.12FF
Germany	13.57	3.66DM	3.22DM
Italy	7.48	625 lira	581.5 lira
Japan	16.88	360 yen	308 yen
Netherlands	11.57	3.62G	3.24G
Sweden	7.48	5.17K	4.81K
Switzerland	13.88	4.37SF	3.84SF
U.K.	8.57	.42 pounds	.38 pounds"

(Ibid., Subject Files, Box 376, President's Economic Program)

---

222.   Urgent Information Memorandum From Robert Hormats and Helmut Sonnenfeldt of the National Security Council Staff to the President's Assistant for National Security Affairs (Kissinger)[1]

Washington, January 24, 1972.

SUBJECT

French Concern about Strength of the Dollar

We want to be sure that you focus urgently on a growing problem between us and the French arising from the decline of the dollar since the Azores and Smithsonian agreements. The precise issues are

---

[1] Source: National Archives, Nixon Presidential Materials, NSC Files, Country Files–Europe, Box 678, France Volume 9 Jan–July 72. Secret.

explained below but the political point is that spirit of U.S./French and President/President relations achieved in December runs grave risk of being undermined. Indeed the process is well underway. We think you need to get together urgently with John Connally, and also Arthur Burns, on this matter.

A number of high-level French officials, including President Pompidou, have expressed concern about continued decline in value of the dollar.[2] They have indicated that while it was clear to them at the Azores that the U.S. could not return to convertibility at this time, it was expected that the U. S. would act to maintain the strength of the dollar at the new parity. In their view, low U.S. interest rates are forcing dollars abroad in order to push up the value of other currencies and push down the dollar's value. (Between January 7 and 21 the Swiss franc appreciated by 1.1 percent, the Belgian franc by 1.5 percent, the French franc by 0.8 percent, and the guilder by 1.7 percent.) If the outflow of dollars continues, and our low interest rates, and the expectation of continued inflation resulting from the large budget deficit announced by the President have led some to believe that it will, pressure will increase on France and other European countries to purchase dollars in order to keep the value of the dollar from depreciating further within the "band" set as the result of the Smithsonian Agreement.[3]

France may see a sinister plot behind our actions. A number of the officials fear that they are the work of Secretary Connally, and others who believe that the realignment agreed upon in Washington was not large enough. If this distrust of our moves is not rectified, it is bound to cause political friction. Moreover, if the dollar outflow continues, thereby widening the difference between the value of the franc and the dollar, Pompidou could be prompted to reconsider whether to devalue the franc. This would completely destroy the Group of Ten agreement.

The problem is complicated by several additional factors:

—There is some talk in the Congress that the dollar was not devalued enough and that whatever legislation is submitted to formalize the devaluation should be amended to devalue the dollar by an amount greater than that decided on at the Smithsonian, which the French and other G-10 countries could not tolerate.

---

[2] In a brief telegraphic message Ambassador Watson advised the Department of State that President Pompidou had taken him aside at a dinner Pompidou hosted for Chiefs of Mission on January 15 to express concern over the international monetary situation and his hope that the understandings reached with President Nixon in the Azores with respect to the dollar could be fully carried out. (Telegram 1250 from Paris, January 20; ibid.)

[3] Nearly a month later, on February 22, Hormats and Sonnenfeldt sent a similar memorandum to Kissinger informing him of Ambassador Rush's February 18 farewell call on Economics and Finance Minister Schiller during which the latter expressed concern about the inflow of dollars to Germany. (Ibid., Agency Files, Box 290, Treasury Volume III)

—We still have not reached the desired trade agreements with Japan, Canada and the European Community.[4] The longer we wait, the greater the pressure on the dollar and the greater the possibility of an increase in speculation.

Given the fact that the low interest rates are primarily the result of large increases in the monetary supply necessary to boost our domestic economy, it is highly unlikely that Arthur Burns or any other official in this Government would attempt to raise interest rates at this time merely to satisfy the Europeans. However, it *is necessary to restore European confidence that we intend to carry out the Smithsonian Agreement by requesting of the Congress in the very near future* (pending the desired trade concessions) *the precise amount of dollar devaluation we are committed to seek* and that we will press the Congress to pass this legislation without any deviations from that Agreement. There must also be a show of confidence in this country that the realignment agreed upon by the Smithsonian was completely satisfactory and that we expect it to result in an improvement in the U.S. balance of trade and payments. Without a display of commitment and confidence, the Europeans will continue to distrust our motives. Speculation against the dollar may again grow to significant proportions, and the entire Smithsonian Agreement may come apart.

---

[4] On December 15, 1971, following the Azores Agreement (of which he had not been apprised) and prior to concluding the Smithsonian Agreement, Hormats sent an information memorandum to Kissinger with his view that convertibility of the dollar to gold was the major U.S. lever "in Round II for securing the type of new international monetary system we want for the future." He cautioned against pressing too hard on broad trade issues. (Ibid., Subject Files, Box 402, Trade, Volume IV 7–12/71)

223.   Letter From President Pompidou to President Nixon[1]

Paris, February 4, 1972.

My dear President,

At the time of our meeting at the Azores, we reached agreement on two texts, namely an official communiqué and a document intended, in principle, to remain confidential.[2]

But the essential fact in my opinion is that our conversations of December 13 and 14, 1971, were characterized by a frankness and mutual understanding that were particularly useful on account of the very general character of most of the problems which were raised.

It is notably within this framework that the international monetary problems were touched upon in a more technical and precise fashion. Without doubt, it was impossible in our brief conversations to discuss these questions in detail. Nonetheless, very important accords were concluded on numerous points.

For these reasons, I feel obliged to describe to you more than six weeks after our conversations my uneasiness with regard to the evolution of the international monetary situation. I should like to call your attention to certain shortcomings which risk weakening the correct implementation of our agreements as well as to my preoccupation over steps taken or of positions envisaged by your administration and which, at first glance, do not seem to me to be consistent with what we agreed.

First, however, I would of course not permit myself to pass a judgment on your internal economic policy. I know that you have obtained remarkable results insofar as the movement of prices and salaries are concerned. Nevertheless, I am not confident that the combination of a large budgetary deficit and of a policy of systematically low interest rates can strengthen the confidence of the international financial com-

---

[1] Source: National Archives, Nixon Presidential Materials, NSC Files, Agency Files, Box 290, Treasury, Volume III. No classification marking. The French text of Pompidou's letter was sent telegraphically. (Ibid., Subject Files, Box 356, Monetary Matters) This translation is attached to an undated memorandum from Haig to Kissinger, which indicates that the translation, made by Sonnenfeldt, is a "slightly sanitized" version of Pompidou's message, which Kissinger could give to Secretary Connally. Haig reminded Kissinger that an interim response had been sent to Pompidou indicating his message would be given "careful and serious consideration" when Connally returned from Texas. The interim response was not found. Additional documentation concerning this letter, including a memorandum from Kissinger transmitting this "hot line" letter to Connally, drafts of President Nixon's response, and Sonnenfeldt's comments on the drafts are ibid.

[2] Document 220.

munity, always very sensitive. Nor do I believe such a course affords in the best of circumstances for the defense of the new parity of the dollar which you yourself have fixed.

At the time of our Azores conversations, I well understood that there was no question of the complete convertibility of your currency. But I did indicate to you that if you agreed to control the movements of capital, initiate a system which would permit the consolidation of dollar balances and also the defense of your currency, the dollar balances notwithstanding, this would in effect mean a convertibility from currency to currency.

I also told you that I understood very well that you insisted on refraining from an official and immediate declaration but that all these things were understood. [I also said] that failing these steps there would be no real defense of the dollar and it would become necessary for the Federal Reserve Board to defend your currency by exchanging it, if need be, against other currencies.[3]

It was my understanding that you understood well[4] that in the new monetary system the dollar would be defended pursuant to the methods that I had described; that it appeared evident that there was no

---

[3] Brackets in the source text. In addition to some "editorial" changes that were made in translating President Pompidou's letter from French to English, at this point a phrase in the French text was omitted to the effect that Kissinger had also made this point. According to the memorandum of the Presidents' conversation on the afternoon of December 13, during his review of the current international economic problems Pompidou said he understood that during a discussion that morning (presumably the meeting with Giscard), "Secretary Connally had said that we would defend the dollar." At the conclusion of Pompidou's intervention, "Dr. Kissinger said that we would have to buy dollars with other currencies in order to defend it. President Pompidou replied that this was correct. There was no other defense." See Document 219.

[4] The language in the French text for this phrase indicates that after he discussed this matter with President Nixon and Secretary Connally, Kissinger had assured Pompidou the next morning that these were President Nixon's understandings. According to the memorandum of Kissinger's December 14 breakfast conversation with Pompidou, Pompidou opened the discussion noting that he had talked with Connally and thought Connally had then talked with Kissinger. Pompidou said "he had found someone who had firm ideas. He had said that the U.S. would defend the dollar after devaluation." Kissinger replied that "he understood what President Pompidou was saying. After talking to him he had spoken to the President and the President's view is that when we speak of defending the dollar, as he understood it, we are talking about what happens in the new monetary system. The President believes that as long as there is the expression on our part that is what President Pompidou described as defending the dollar, but President Pompidou seemed to feel that there were others. Leaving aside the present balances, the way to defend is to buy when it falls." In the ensuing discussion President Pompidou said "he understood that the present dollar balances would not be included as they were too big. The President apparently felt we were thinking of something else. " Kissinger replied "that his impression after talking to Secretary Connally is that the Secretary feels if the exchange alignment is correct then we will be prepared to operate the system." Kissinger then read Pompidou item 6 of the draft Framework Agreement, with Connally's formulation on "what we were prepared to do as part of a general package on margins and rates." See Document 219. For the Framework Agreement, see Document 220.

other method and, not counting the existing dollar balances, the new methods on which agreement had been reached represented in a way a form of convertibility.

In any event, these intentions have not for the moment come into play since, on the money markets, the dollar is not at its support level and the problem therefore has not posed itself for the United States to defend its currency as any other country would, by intervening to preserve the dollar rate within the margins defined by the Washington accords.

Nevertheless, the reversion of floating capital towards the United States which you and I expected has not yet occurred, perhaps for psychological reasons but also because of the interest rates that prevail, in practice, in your country. Moreover, the widening of the dollar margins, which was decided in Washington following our meetings, gives speculators the possibility to realize more substantial gains in capital without a new modification of the parity of your currency.

You yourself proposed setting the enlargement of these margins of fluctuation at 2.25 percent on either side of parity which represented on your part, as on mine, an important sacrifice in relation to our initial positions of principle. Therefore, I could not fail but note that in the report of your advisors which accompanied the message you addressed to Congress on January 27 on budgetary and economic problems,[5] note was made of a growing consensus in favor of greater flexibility in exchange rates. This does not seem to conform to the undertakings that were reached between you and me. I would add that the experience of the last six weeks gives me reason to believe that, setting aside these formal considerations, the above mentioned remark (by the President's advisors) does not correspond to a clear analysis of the present situation.

You must no doubt be impressed to see the extent to which we Europeans are directly interested in the strength of your currency. This is true because it is evident that it would be disastrous for the international monetary system and thus for the entire free world should the accords of December, whose historic character you yourself noted, become only a precarious pause along the path towards a new crisis.

The central problem of course remains that of your balance of payments, which, all things being equal, one cannot expect with certainty to correct in a short period of time. For that reason I suggested to you that you increase your controls on the movement of capital. You indi-

---

[5] The President's "Annual Message to Congress: The Economic Report of the President," dated January 27, is printed in *Public Papers of the Presidents of the United States: Richard M. Nixon, 1972*, pp. 111–114.

cated to me that you were initiating certain measures in this regard which were not substantial, but that you were ready to go further. This course would have clearly improved the situation of your balance of payments, and therefore the level of the dollar on the exchange markets. It was for this reason that I was surprised to see not only that nothing has started in this direction, but that the Treasury of the United States has—at a moment where for psychological and technical reasons, it would seem necessary to improve confidence in the dollar—postponed from December 31, 1971 to February 29, 1972 the date at which the subsidiaries of American corporations established abroad must repatriate their profits. Such a measure taken at such a moment does not appear to me consistent with the objectives we set.

Lastly, I would add that you provided me with certain details about the procedure, which you obviously are alone competent to judge, that you intended to pursue with respect to Congress regarding the legal devaluation of the dollar. You also indicated to me in this connection that you would convene the Committee Chairmen with a view to speeding consideration of a bill which, according to you, was desirable since the Congress was adjourning immediately after the conclusion of our conversations. Thus have I welcomed with all the more pleasure the February 3 notification from Mr. Connally to Mr. Giscard d'Estaing, of the transmission in the very near future of this text to the Congress.

I wish in closing to emphasize the point that my concerns are those of a friend, that the prosperity of the United States and the maintenance of the value of the dollar are of fundamental importance for the entire Western world, and I would thus be happy if you could dispel these concerns which I have very freely brought to your attention in the spirit of our good conversations of 13 and 14 December, 1971.

Please, my dear Mr. President, accept my highest regards.

Georges Pompidou[6]

---

[6] Printed from a copy that bears this typed signature.

224. Letter From President Nixon to President Pompidou[1]

Washington, February 16, 1972.

Dear Mr. President:

My intensive preparations for my trip to China have somewhat delayed a response to your message of February 4.[2] I have wanted to consider that important communication with care and now, just before my departure, I should like to reply in the same spirit of candor and friendship which you displayed in your message. I assure you that I remain convinced that maximum mutual understanding between us on these difficult issues is essential.

I recognize the force of the concern you express that the prosperity of the United States and the stability of the dollar are important to the entire Western world. I also can well appreciate that, viewed from abroad, the high level of our prospective budgetary deficits in the United States could raise questions. Yet, viewed in the perspective of economic conditions in the United States and in the framework of our total economic policies, I am convinced these deficits are appropriate. To a considerable extent, the new forecast of a higher deficit in the current fiscal year is merely the reflection of reports received since our meeting in the Azores, indicating slower growth than had been estimated earlier for the second and third quarters of 1971. The slower growth in those quarters leads automatically to an expectation of lower tax receipts in the first half of 1972. In part, however, the new forecast of a higher deficit this year is the result of a purposeful acceleration of Government expenditures to provide some needed impetus to nudge the economy on to a more satisfactory recovery path. Under the circumstances, I believe the deficit is of an appropriate size not just in the context of our domestic needs but in terms of a broader view of the evolution of the monetary system and the world economy.

You have emphasized that the prosperity of the United States and the value of the dollar are of fundamental importance to the Western world. I agree, and I believe the force of the point is redoubled at a time of sluggishness and even fear of recession in some important countries.

---

[1] Source: National Archives, Nixon Presidential Materials, NSC Files, Subject Files, Box 356, Monetary Matters. Secret. "HOT LINE" is typed at the top of the page. Earlier drafts of this letter and Sonnenfeldt's comments on the drafts, which express concern that they did not adequately address measures to defend the dollar and the U.S. position on convertibility, are ibid. Sonnenfeldt thought Pompidou would view those inadequacies as evasive and unresponsive to his concerns.

[2] Document 223.

Steadily rising levels of business in the United States will help assure growth in markets for our trading partners—and confidence in that growth—even as the effects of the currency alignment are absorbed.

As our joint press statement at the Azores (as well as our private communication)[3] emphasized, the most important contribution the United States Government can make to the stability of the monetary system and the defense of the newly fixed structure of exchange rates is through vigorous efforts to restore price stability and productivity to the United States economy. Without reviewing all the details of our present programs, I assure you that these fundamental objectives remain the basis of our domestic policies. We shall break the back of inflation in the United States. We shall seek new breakthroughs in productivity growth. These steps seem to me the indispensable backbone for any realistic defense of the dollar.

This defense will have many facets. New tax measures and new regulatory approaches have been adopted to spur productivity. To assure that the economic expansion is accompanied by further progress toward price stability, we are maintaining our price and wage controls, and I have requested of the Congress a firm expenditure ceiling for fiscal year 1973 at a level only 4 percent above this year's expenditures. This will assure that revenues come into line with spending as the slack in the economy dissipates.

In view of the objectives of our total economic program, I have been pleased to receive reports that the Organization for Economic Cooperation and Development, in the meeting in Paris of its Economic Policy Committee a few days ago, found general accord with its forecasts that, in 1972, the United States will succeed both in having the most satisfactory recovery of economic growth and in having the lowest level of price inflation of any of the major member countries.

As we see the coming months, our forecast budgetary deficit will insure that we do not have to place undue reliance on monetary policy for promotion of economic expansion. Indeed, the financing of the deficit is likely to force some increase in short-term interest rates, to which international exchange markets are sensitive. I frankly hope this adjustment can be made without disturbing our long-term rates, which remain high. But my advisers tell me that conditions in a number of countries abroad are likely to lead to a reduction in their interest rates, a development which will reduce present disparities in interest rates among major countries.

In view of the major disturbances which were experienced during 1971, we have recognized that the foreign exchange markets could not be expected to return immediately to entirely settled and normal attitudes.

---

[3] Document 220.

For this reason, since December 18, we have refrained from any steps to relax our controls on capital, despite the doubts I expressed to you as to their effectiveness and usefulness and despite my strong wish to move away from these controls as promptly as possible. The small technical change in our regulations which you mention in your letter had actually been announced some days before our meeting in the Azores. Our general objective remains, however, the gradual relaxation of these controls, and we must, within the coming weeks, announce the details of our direct investment control program for the calendar year 1972.

In the light of conditions in the exchange markets in recent weeks, I believe we are fortunate that our compromise has permitted a wider band of fluctuation to absorb and diffuse movements of funds without requiring large scale central bank intervention. I confess that your concern over the comments on flexibility in the recent report of my Council of Economic Advisers surprises me in the light of our conversation, since I believe we both recognized this question would need to remain an open issue for the planned discussions of the future of the international monetary system. Similarly, I believe that I made clear in our conversation that it is our view that questions of convertibility of the dollar should be discussed in the context of broad consideration of the many inter-related aspects of future reform of the monetary system. Now, however, that the period of intensive short-term trade discussions is behind us, we are intensifying our deliberations and preparations within the United States Government for these important international deliberations on monetary reform, including various proposals for the consolidation of dollar balances, the desirability and feasibility of various measures to deal with short-term capital movements, and the appropriate exchange rate regime.

To assure the maximum accomplishment in these discussions, and to help deal with current issues of monetary cooperation as they arise, I have asked Secretary Connally and his staff to remain in close consultation with your advisers in the months to come.

Mr. President, you played a crucial role in preparing the ground for the Smithsonian Agreement. With transmittal of the formal request for dollar devaluation to the U.S. Congress, this should be a time of personal satisfaction to you.[4] I hope for speedy action on that request,

---

[4] Legislation to increase the dollar price of gold was sent to Congress on February 9, under cover of a letter from Secretary Connally to Vice President Agnew in Agnew's capacity as President of the Senate. Connally's letter, the draft legislation, and background material were circulated to the Volcker Group as VG/Uncl. INFO/72-1 on February 10. (Washington National Records Center, Department of the Treasury, Volcker Group Masters: FRC 56 86 30, 1972) Congress completed action on the legislation on March 31, and President Nixon signed it into law on April 3. See *Public Papers of the Presidents of the United States: Richard M. Nixon, 1972*, pp. 513–514.

although I must in frankness confess my own disappointment that the European Community has apparently taken the decision that, in the important area of agriculture, the normal competitive benefits of a devaluation will be denied to us.

Plainly, we have many fundamental issues before us, both in the monetary and trade areas—issues, indeed, that cannot be disassociated from each other. We have no choice but to attack them openly and frankly.

We have, I believe, made good progress in recent months. I hope we can continue to convert old issues into new agreements.

I look forward to staying in close communication with you on the entire range of issues that concern both our countries and would, of course, welcome your further views on the subject matter of this message. I expect to communicate with you concerning my impressions in China as soon as I have returned from there.

With warm personal regard,

Richard M. Nixon[5]

---

[5] Printed from a copy that bears this typed signature.

---

225.   Editorial Note

On February 22, 1972, Treasury Under Secretary Volcker sent a memorandum to Dewey Daane, William Dale, Kenneth Dam, Peter Flanigan, Nathaniel Samuels, and Marina Whitman regarding "Development of Proposals for U.S. Positions in Further Discussions of International Monetary Reforms." Volcker proposed they constitute a group known as "Volcker Group Alternates" (VGAs) to meet three times a week for several hours to draft papers for consideration by the Volcker Group on various aspects of the long-range reform of the international monetary system. Volcker proposed that Deputy Under Secretary for Monetary Affairs Jack Bennett would represent Treasury on the VGAs, and asked each addressee to designate a representative who could devote considerable time to the endeavor in the coming months. Volcker's February 22 memorandum is attached to a March 7 memorandum from Willis to the Volcker Group Alternates. (VGA/72-1; Washington National Records Center, Department of the Treasury, Volcker Group Masters: RG 56 86 30, 1972, VGA/72-1–VGA/72-50) As the VGAs came into being, the four Volcker Group WGs established in 1969 and 1970, which had not met for some time, were terminated.

In his February 22 memorandum, Volcker proposed a series of papers for the VGAs and an early meeting of the Alternates to discuss the proposed papers as well as a recent Treasury paper on "a desirable organizational framework for international negotiations on international monetary reform." The Treasury paper was revised several times in March. Its final version, a 14-page March 20 memorandum from the Volcker Group Alternates to the Volcker Group, entitled "Organization for Negotiations on Monetary Reform," considers options and provides ample scope for U.S. support for creation of the C-20 at the IMF annual meeting in September 1972. (VGA/7-19 Rev.; ibid.)

On February 22 Deputy Under Secretary of State for Economic Affairs Samuels also sent a memorandum to Under Secretary Volcker regarding "A Start Toward Negotiating International Monetary Reform." Samuels thought an early start could help stabilize current short-term capital flows and address European concerns. He proposed a series of topics for discussion in the Volcker Group (many of them similar to those proposed by Volcker for the VGAs in his February 22 memorandum) and discussed at length the "forum" question with a sympathetic leaning to "the idea advanced by the IMF management and others of using a so-called Governors Committee (G-20) within the IMF." On February 24 Samuels sent a memorandum to Volcker welcoming "the convergence of thought" in their respective February 22 memoranda and suggested an early meeting of the Volcker Group to discuss the suggested topics for the VGAs. On February 29 Samuels sent a letter to Volcker proposing a restructured list of Volcker's suggested papers for the VGAs, and designated Deputy Assistant Secretary Weintraub as the State representative on the VGAs. Samuels' two memoranda and letter are in the National Archives, RG 59, Central Files 1970–73, FN 17 US.

On February 24 Dean Hinton sent a memorandum to the President's Assistant for International Economic Affairs, Peter Flanigan, in response to Volcker's February 22 memorandum. Hinton wrote that "Treasury seems to be pulling itself together" for the international monetary reform negotiations and recommended that Flanigan inform Volcker that Richard Erb would represent the CIEP on the VGAs, but that Hinton might also attend from time to time. Hinton said he would like to continue as the CIEP member of the Volcker Group, but recognized that Flanigan would wish to participate occasionally. (Ibid., Nixon Presidential Materials, White House Central Files, Federal Government Organizations, Treasury, 11/1/71–2/29/72, Box 2)

The forum for negotiation of long-term international monetary reform was as important an issue in early 1972 as the shape of reform itself. On January 12 Bundesbank President Carl Klasen, thinking in the G-10 context, told the Financial Attaché at the Embassy in Bonn that "he could see adding a country like Australia, but he could not see adding Brazil or other LDCs. The G-10 as the body of the major industrial and monetary powers was sure to be needed in future crises and its usefulness would be destroyed by opening it to LDCs." (Telegram 474 from Bonn, January 12; ibid., RG 59, Central Files 1970–73, FN 10)

By contrast, in the United States there was some concern that European interests were disproportionately reflected in the G-10 and on balance might be inimical to U.S. reform interests. The OECD was another possible forum, but monetary reform was not obviously part of its mandate and taking it up in that also-Eurocentric organization could raise hackles in the IMF. With an eye to forthcoming positions toward the LDCs at the UNCTAD III Ministerial scheduled to convene in Santiago in April, and in the hope of lessening the chance the United States might be isolated in more Eurocentric fora, there was some sentiment, clearly reflected in Samuels, February 22 memorandum to Volcker and the March 20 memorandum to the Volcker Group, for finding scope for LDC participation in the forthcoming international monetary reform negotiations.

On March 8 the Volcker Group Alternates met with British officials at the Treasury Department to discuss a U.K. paper on international monetary reform. The paper and the discussion were wide-ranging and included liquidity creation and distribution, an aid link, convertibility, and gold. Regarding the forum for discussions, the paper noted that the "discussion cannot be restricted to a small group of developed countries. Arrangements must be made for the developing countries and others outside the Group of Ten to make their voices heard." The U.K. paper and a record of the discussion are Volcker Group paper VGA/72-14. (Washington National Records Center, Department of the Treasury, Volcker Group Masters: FRC 56 86 30, 1972, VGA/72-1–VGA/72-50)

---

226.   Editorial Note

On March 11, 1972, Ambassador Watson sent a telegram to the Department of State on the subject of "French Reaction to International Monetary Developments Causing Growing Strain on Franco-American Relations." Following a summary the opening paragraph read: "With increasing frequency and virulence, media here have been criticizing US for A) 'benign neglect' re international position of dollar; B) failure support dollar devaluation with appropriate monetary and fiscal policies, as evidenced by our large budget deficits and low interest rates; C) unwillingness to commit ourselves to even partial return to convertibility; and D) indifference to problems caused for Europeans by their role in defending new exchange rate structure." Ambassador Watson thought none of these criticisms well-founded but emphasized they were not limited to the press and had been made by a number of official and non-official contacts in Paris. He recounted steps the Embassy had taken to counter the arguments, but concluded with the recommendation that the time had come "for more intensive high-level US effort to counter European charges that US is indifferent to fate of dollar." He also recommended making clear that the United States was "fully committed to continued cooperation with them in interest of restoring stability to the system and indeed improving it." (Telegram 4718 from Paris; National Archives, RG 59, Central Files 1970–73, FN 10)

In a March 14 memorandum Sonnenfeldt and Hormats summarized Ambassador Watson's message for Kissinger and called his attention to the general weakening of the dollar abroad and the interventions required by European and Japanese authorities to keep exchange rates within the agreed Smithsonian margins. Sonnenfeldt and Hormats noted that "the public atmosphere in Europe to which the Ambassador refers has become unpleasant enough to warrant your talking with Secretary Connally about it as soon as possible, if you have not already done so." They recommended that Kissinger speak to Connally prior to his Council on Foreign Relations speech on March 15 and suggest Connally make positive remarks on "our dedication to cooperative restoration of stability to the international monetary system." A typed notation on a note attached to the memorandum reads: "Action Requested Is *Phone Call Today.*" Kissinger wrote on the note: "Time is not yet ripe." (Ibid., Nixon Presidential Materials, NSC Files, Subject Files, Box 356, Monetary)

On March 24 Hormats sent an information memorandum to Kissinger informing him of a marked improvement in the international monetary situation, with the dollar having strengthened against all major currencies except the yen. Hormats attributed the improvement to Burns' assurances at the Bank for International Settlements on March 11–12 that the United States was not "neglecting" the situation, Connally's "more cooperative posture" in his March 15 speech, and President Pompidou's "more optimistic" stance in a March 16 speech. (Ibid.) Burns' intervention at the BIS has not been identified. Connally addressed the Council on Foreign Relations on March 15; the text of his remarks is in *Annual Report of the Secretary of the Treasury on the State of the Finances for the Fiscal Year Ended June 30, 1972*, pages 411–416.

227.   Telegram From the Embassy in Italy to the Department of State[1]

Rome, April 26, 1972, 1857Z.

2398. Pass Treasury and Federal Reserve; also IMF for Dale, Santiago for Zagorin. Subject: EC Finance Ministers meeting April 24–25.

1. *Summary:* Informal EC FinMins meeting April 24–25 touched virtually all current topics of interest this group. No definite actions taken. Ministerial views expressed on international monetary matters coincided with those expressed to Volcker over weekend at margins Ditchley Conference,[2] i.e., large agreement to creation G-20 as "emanation of IMF," to discuss monetary questions (taking into account commercial and others matters) but with Secretariat that would draw on other institutions and agencies. No definitive views on SDR creation, but France in favor and Italy revived Colombo's link proposal. Ministers approved continuation by Benelux of narrower 1.5 percent currency margins. Most EC countries in favor declaration new parities to IMF, soon as US has done so. EC FinMins will hold special informal meeting in London mid-July to discuss international monetary questions. *End summary.*

2. FinMins and Central Bank Governors of EC held periodic quarterly meeting in Rome April 24–25, under chairmanship Treasury Min Colombo. Reps from four applicant members attended for first time. According Italian sources (including Ossola) following were highlights of this "interesting meeting" at which, however, no definitive decisions taken:

Forum for discussing international monetary reform

3. Views expressed by Mins and Governors fully in keeping with those indicated to UnSec Volcker at margins of Ditchley Conference last weekend. All countries of present EC, plus four applicants, pronounced themselves favorable to creation of Group of 20 as principal forum for

[1] Source: National Archives, RG 59, Central Files 1970–73, FN 10 EEC. Confidential; Limdis; Greenback. Repeated to Bern, Bonn, Brussels, Copenhagen, Dublin, The Hague, London, Luxembourg, Ottawa, Oslo, Paris, Santiago (where the UNCTAD III Ministerial was getting underway), Stockholm, Tokyo, Vienna, USEC, and USOECD.

[2] On the margins of the Ditchley monetary conference in London, held April 22–23, G-10 Deputies met and agreed to a new group in the IMF as a forum for negotiating international monetary reform. That agreement was further refined in informal discussion by Deputies on the margins of the American Bankers Association conference in Montreal in May. See Document 229 for the record of these discussions. See also Margaret de Vries, *The International Monetary Fund 1972–1978*, Volume I: *Narrative and Analysis*, pp. 153–155.

discussing international monetary reform. (In view Paris 7864[3] we specifically asked whether Giscard d'Estaing was in accord with this view and our sources replied that Giscard clearly associated himself with those in favor of G-20.) Reasoning adduced by many spokesmen was that G-20 logical and necessary not simply because US had proposed it but in recognition that in such important discussions LDC's should have appropriate participation.[4]

4. Meeting reemphasized European view that G-20 should be "emanation of IMF," that chairman of G-20 should choose Secretariat which could call on institutions other than IMF (e.g., OECD) for necessary support and ideas and that mandate of group should be mainly focused on monetary system, although taking into account commercial and other relevant questions.

5. Mins did not discuss whether Deputies of G-20 group should be IMF Exec Directors or other competent persons nor did Mins delve into substance of international monetary reform. Not much emphasis given to question of what might be continuing functions of G-10. At invitation Chancellor Barber, Mins and Governors planning to hold special informal meeting in London in mid-July devoted to international monetary reform and progress of institutionalizing G-20. In addition EC Mins are meeting in Luxembourg in mid-Sept, prior to IMF annual meeting.

SDR's

6. Considerable time devoted to whether or not opportune have new activation SDR's. On negative side, Germany (Schoellhorn) argued there was plenty of world liquidity and advisable have two year pause in SDR creation. Dutch advocated one year hiatus. UK, Belgium, Netherlands, Denmark, and Ireland supported SDR creation of token amount, particularly in order meet liquidity needs of LDC's. French (Wormser, representing Giscard who had left meeting at that point) in surprise move, reversing French position in EC Monetary Committee, advocated SDR duration of two billion dollars for two years, to complete first five year basic period. French indicated they hoped that (A) LDC's would in one way or another become beneficiaries such SDR activation and (B) those countries receiving allocations which have

---

[3] Not printed.

[4] Telegram 1595 from The Hague, May 3, reported on a discussion with Netherlands Treasurer General Oort, who indicated that the Netherlands, along with other EC partners, was generally sympathetic to an IMF-based G-20, at least as a forum for working out a new international monetary system. The Netherlands representatives thought it might be "irritating" to continue to make use of the G-10 forum and hence were displeased with Ossola's proposal for a G-10 Deputies meeting in June. Regarding global liquidity, the Netherlands saw no need for additional SDR creation for 1973 but was willing to go along with a "token creation to keep the system alive." (National Archives, RG 59, Central Files 1970–73, FN 10 EEC)

excess amounts of their currency held by other countries should utilize new SDR's to absorb such excess currency (finger obviously pointed to US). Colombo recalled his 1968 SDR–aid link proposal and suggested link question be studied again before decision is made on new SDR creation.

7. Thus SDR discussion inconclusive. However, Ossola noted he is planning to hold G-10 Deputies meeting on the subject June 13 in Paris.

Declaration of New Parities

8. Majority view in favor of formal declaration of new parities to IMF, as soon as US has done so.[5] Germany somewhat cautious and Italy indicated it would prefer to keep "central rate" for time being. However, all EC countries agreed they would act in common.

Other Topics

9. Belgium and Netherlands proposed to continue narrower margins of 1.5 percent between Belgian franc and Dutch guilder. Other EC members saw no difficulty in accepting "Benelux worm, within EC snake, within Smithsonian tunnel."

10. Mins agreed work should continue on drafting scheme for creating EC central reserve fund, which would gradually be given progressively wider functions.

11. On other aspects of EC economic and monetary union, Mins focused on nature of directive on economic development and stabilization which EC Commission working on. Widely recognized that in order to be able to act promptly and in concert would be useful for EC member countries to have anti-cyclical instruments akin to those which govts possess in UK (e.g., regulator) and Germany. It was, however, emphasized that institutional framework varies from country to country and that specific recommendations to be made by Commission should take account of these divergencies while at same time being as simple and concrete as possible.

Martin

---

[5] Circular telegram 79216 to all posts, May 5, informed the posts that that day Secretary Connally had informed the Managing Director of the IMF that effective May 8, 1972, the United States would change the par value of the dollar from 1/35 to 1/38 of a fine troy ounce of gold. The telegram noted that this was the final step in implementing the Smithsonian Agreement to devalue the dollar and was made possible by the completion that day of necessary appropriation legislation in the Congress. (Ibid., FN 17 US)

228. Volcker Group Paper[1]

VGA/72–40   Washington, April 27, 1972.

Recommendations

The United States should recommend that the reformed international monetary system include:

1. A ministerial committee on adjustment. This committee should monitor balance of payments developments and government policies in light of their contributions to adjustment, question member governments with respect to their policy objectives and policy measures, issue periodic reports regarding the adjustment policies of members, make recommendations regarding the appropriate adjustment measures to be taken by members, and make decisions regarding the application of sanctions.

2. A set of discretionary sanctions that encompass both capital and current account transactions. The adjustment committee should be free to decide whether the sanctions should be permissive, recommended or mandatory, depending on the degree of support in the committee for the imposition of such sanctions. One sanction would be the imposition of a tax on all purchases of a currency, and a subsidy on all sales of such a currency. Alternatively, restrictions could be imposed on all foreign exchange transactions along the lines of the scarce currency provisions of the IMF Articles of Agreement. In specific cases, where a country was attempting to prevent adjustment in the current account, or in the capital account, the committee should be able to recommend specific restrictions on current accounts or capital account transactions.

3. A set of presumptive criteria to guide the committee in making judgments regarding the adjustment required in the balance of payments positions of individual members. Ideally, such criteria would also provide the basis for a scale of reference that could indicate the degree of disruptiveness of a given country's failure to adjust. One possibility would be to establish a set of bands based on reserve holdings of members. There is some disagreement among members of the Volcker Group Alternates, however, over the suitability of reserve holdings as a measuring rod for the adjustment required.

---

[1] Source: Washington National Records Center, Department of the Treasury, Volcker Group Masters: FRC 56 86 30, 1972, VGA/72-1–VGA/72-50. Confidential. The April 28 cover memorandum from George H. Willis to the Volcker Group Alternates indicates these are revised recommendations for the VGA/72-34 paper on this subject prepared in OMB by Geza Feketekuty. VGA/72-34, dated April 12, was circulated to the VGAs on April 13. An earlier version of Feketekuty's paper, entitled "Methods of Inducing Surplus Countries To Adjust," was circulated as VGA/72-26 on April 5. (Both ibid.)

229.   Volcker Group Paper[1]

VGA/72-50 Rev.   Washington, May 10, 1972.

MINUTES OF THE DISCUSSION IN LONDON CONCERNING
PROCEDURES FOR PREPARING MONETARY REFORM
(April 23, 1972)

I. Scope of future work on reforms

1. While the main task would no doubt be the reform of the international monetary system, there was a consensus that the future equilibrium of the world economy was also dependent on adequate trade rules, on rules for the responsibilities of surplus and deficit countries respectively ("burden-sharing" in the widest sense, as well as burden-sharing in the narrower sense of sharing aid and military burdens), rules on capital flows, etc. The U.S. representative mentioned also the relationship between the GATT and the IMF as a possible subject of review and reform. The close linkage of reform of the monetary system with other problems was generally acknowledged. However, there was a prevalent opinion to the effect that the preparatory work for solving the totality of these problems could not be entrusted to one single group but had to be delegated to several bodies.

II. Group of Twenty

2. There was general agreement that a new "Group of Twenty" (G 20) should be the main forum for discussing the reform of the monetary system. This Group should be set up by a decision of the Board of Governors of the Fund as a special committee of Governors of the IMF. Its composition should correspond to the regional composition (the "constituencies") of the Executive Board of the Fund. The Managing Director of the IMF would be an ex-officio member. Switzerland could participate as an observer.

3. There would be one chief representative for each constituency (and possibly one or two alternates). The Group would elect its own Chairman. As the Governor's Committee would hardly be able to assemble frequently and undertake the detailed work, a committee of deputies would have to be established which would prepare the work

---

[1] Source: Washington National Records Center, Department of the Treasury, Volcker Group Masters: FRC 56 86 30, VGA/72-1–VGA/72-50. Confidential. Willis' May 31 cover note circulating the paper to the Volcker Group Alternates indicates the minutes are a revised version of the April 23 discussion in London. See footnote 2, Document 227.

of the Governor's Committee. The idea was mentioned that the Chairman of the deputies should perhaps work on a full-time or nearly full-time basis and he should be assisted by adequate staff.

4. The terms of reference would request the G 20 to prepare proposals for reform of the monetary system. This could also include rules for balance-of-payments adjustment, for capital movements, etc. Adequate reference should also be made in the mandate to the close linkage with some non-monetary problems. The G 20 should be authorized to draw not only on the work and staff of the IMF but also on other international organizations and on work done outside such organizations. The Group would submit its proposals to the Board of Governors of the Fund who would decide upon them.

III. Other international organizations

5. It was emphasized that trade negotiations would fall within the competence of GATT, and that any proposal for changes in trade rules would also have to be acted upon by GATT.

6. It was recognized that the so-called "non-monetary problems" could not be thoroughly dealt with by the Group of Twenty which would mainly be occupied with problems of the international monetary system. There were suggestions that these "non-monetary problems"— and also rules for the respective responsibilities of surplus and deficit countries and for capital movements—could be discussed, and proposals could be worked out, by appropriate committees of the OECD. To this end, existing OECD groups could be re-structured, or a new OECD group could be established. The OECD would enter the picture only as a forum for preparatory discussion and it would submit its proposals to the appropriate organizations.

7. The Group of Ten should have no specific mandate for participating in the preparation of monetary reform. It should continue within its narrower mandates in the framework of the GAB and in the consultation procedure for SDR allocations. It was left open whether it should be used also for other tasks of coordination among the major industrial countries.

8. Several participants in the discussion in London emphasized that the work to be done in G 20 or in other groups should in no way impinge on the competence and work of other international organizations.

IV. Further procedure

9. Draft minutes of the discussion in London should be sent to the participants and, if possible, agreed upon in the course of May. A draft of possible terms of reference for the Group of Twenty should be pre-

pared by one of the participants. Mr. van Lennep said that he will prepare a paper for the Council of OECD on how the OECD could contribute to the discussions on monetary and non-monetary issues and in particular their inter-relationship. As concerns the establishment of G 20 the aim was to have a decision by the Board of Governors of the Fund somewhere in June or July.

O. Emminger[2]

---

[2] Printed from a copy that bears this typed signature.

---

230. Volcker Group Paper[1]

VGA/72-64   Washington, June 5, 1972.

RECOMMENDED PREMISES AND OBJECTIVES OF THE U.S.
IN FORTHCOMING REFORM NEGOTIATIONS

Premises

In formulating recommendations on the objectives which the U.S. Government should seek in the forthcoming economic reform negotiations the Alternates have proceeded on the basis of a number of important premises:

A. that these objectives must seek to serve the U.S. national interest both in terms of the health of the U.S. economy and in terms of U.S. political relations with foreign nations;

B. that the U.S. national interest would be served by an international economic system providing an environment which

i. facilitated international trade and capital flows among nations;

---

[1] Source: Washington National Records Center, Department of the Treasury, Volcker Group Masters: FRC 56 86 30, 1972, VGA/72-51–VGA/72-107. Limited Official Use. Drafted by Jack F. Bennett. "Draft" is typed above the date. Willis' June 7 cover memorandum that circulated the paper to members of the VGAs indicated it was the latest version of the paper. Earlier drafts are ibid., and the text printed here seems to be the final revision. After the drafting exercise began in March, members of the VGAs contributed papers on U.S. objectives: Geza Feketekuty at OMB on March 6 (VGA/72-4); Robert Solomon at the Federal Reserve on March 6 (VGA/72-5); Jack Bennett at Treasury on March 13 (VGA/72-12); and Ralph Bryant at the Federal Reserve on April 5 (VGA/72-27). (All ibid., VGA/72-1–VGA/72-50)

ii. involved a minimum of governmental restraints and subsidies on international economic transactions;

iii. preserved the habit of cooperations which has become established in international economic fields; and

iv. did not contain features likely to lead to periodic political confrontations among governments; and

C. that, in the complex task of reshaping the world's economic system, a balanced "package" approach must necessarily be employed in judging proposals on specific aspects of the system; the full implications of no part of a proposed system can be judged fully until the broad outlines of the whole package are in view; in order ultimately to reach an agreement embracing all major trading nations, the U.S. may be faced with the necessity of accepting less than full achievement of some objectives.

Objectives

With the premises in mind the Alternates have agreed that the objectives they recommend for the U.S. Government in the coming negotiations may usefully be summarized as follows:

1. reform of the international monetary system in a manner which will increase the probability that changes in exchange rates among major currencies, including the dollar, will in future more promptly reflect changing circumstances, such for example as differential rates of inflation and productivity among nations;

(*Comment:* the Alternates are of the opinion that increased flexibility for exchange rates will:

a) enhance economic growth and stability through more efficient allocation of resources and avoidance of the disruptive effects on resource use and capital flows of delays in exchange rate changes followed by large discrete adjustments of exchange rates;

b) impose fewer restraints on governments in attempting to choose the mix of domestic fiscal and monetary policies best suited to the goals of price stability, high employment, and improving standards of life; and

c) create an environment more resistant to special interest efforts to promote controls, subsidies, and other forms of governmental interference in international trade and investment transactions.

The Alternates have not included a recommendation with respect to the extent to which multilateral agreement will be needed on the creation of additional international monetary reserves since it has been recognized that the extent of the need will depend upon the extent and nature of the additional rate flexibility provided in the reformed international monetary system. And the Alternates did not feel that either retention or phasing-out of the reserve currency role of the dollar should be regarded as a U.S. objective in the negotiations.)

2. a new international commitment to a set of basic guidelines and procedures:

a) which will both enhance economic standards of living and promote international payments equilibrium through reduction in governmental barriers and subsidies which distort international trade; (*Comment:* the Department of State recommends against inclusion of the reference to payments equilibrium in this paragraph.)[2]
b) which will avoid discrimination against or among investors from abroad while providing host governments with adequate control over business activities within their territories;
c) which will limit distortion of international transactions by tax and other forms of governmental incentives affecting location of economic activities and selection of markets for production.

3. agreement on procedures and guidelines for multilateral consultations and actions designed to stimulate corrective steps by governments pursuing seriously disruptive behavior in the international economic area; possible actions should include withholding of access to international assistance funds and placing burdens on the international transactions of the offending nations; and

4. provisions for continuing high level consultation with respect to the operations of and interrelations among the international monetary system and national laws and regulations affecting international trade and investment.

Continuing Work of the Alternates

In submitting these recommended general objectives the Alternates would like to make clear that they have not yet been able to reach agreement on:

—how the objective of flexibility can best be achieved in practice;
—how "presumptive," i.e. how near to automatic, should the actions be to induce corrective steps by disruptive governments;
—how detailed would be the guidelines for governmental trade measures, investment controls, and domestic incentive programs; and
—by what means the role of gold can best be diminished in the international monetary system.

Work has begun and is continuing on these subjects.

---

[2] No further record of this dissent has been found.

231. Telegram From the Embassy in France to the Department of State[1]

Paris, June 15, 1972, 1011Z.

11472. Treasury pass Under Secretary Volcker from Bennett. Subject: Highlights of G-10 Deputies meeting, June 13, 1972.

1. *Summary:* G-10 Deputies held half-day meeting June 13 under chairmanship Ossola (Italy). Bennett and Daane represented U.S. Principal subject for discussion was allocation SDRs in second basic period. Chairman emphasized this was first exchange of views without commitment. Deputies generally favored short allocation period, two years being most frequently cited. Views on amount varied rather widely from zero through "token" and "modest" to normal (i.e., approximately 3 billion SDR rate of first allocation period). U.S. leaned toward normal and indicated that if there were a zero allocation in 1973, it should be followed by 3 billion SDR creation in 1974. Little support for attaching to this transitional activation either SDR–aid link or proposal that industrial countries agree use at least portion their allocations to redeem foreign official balances in their own currencies. Chairman suggested another session at time IMF annual meeting in Washington, but timing and place left open. *End summary.*

2. Group first exchanged views on IMF projections re future reserve needs. IMF had calculated that global reserves at end March 1972, totaling 125 billion SDR, were about 15 or 20 billion SDR in excess of needed reserves. Extrapolating from three historical data series (global reserve growth, ratios of reserves to imports, and ratios of reserves to money), IMF estimated global reserve needs in 1977 in range of 150–185 billion SDR, meaning needed reserve creation in range of 6–12 billion SDR annually over next five years. IMF representative pointed out decisions on amount SDR allocations required to meet these needs would have to take account of expected changes in other forms of reserves, which IMF staff did not attempt to project.

3. In discussion on IMF projections, several Deputies emphasized that creation of reserves in other forms was very important element. There was, however, general recognition of difficulties in estimating this factor. Chairman suggested that perhaps SDR creation could be corrected year by year as function of reserve creation in other forms. Several speakers also expressed doubts about whether or not future

---

[1] Source: National Archives, RG 59, Central Files 1970–73, FN 10. Confidential; Limdis; Greenback. Repeated to Bern, Bonn, Brussels, The Hague, London, Ottawa, Rome, Stockholm, Tokyo, and USEC.

needs could be extrapolated from past experience, citing possibility that reformed monetary system might be one that could be operated with lower level of global reserves than in past. Brossolette (France) and Emminger (Germany) both questioned whether or not any past period could be assumed to be one in which there was equilibrium between need for, and supply of, reserves. While questioning assumptions in this particular exercise, Oort (Netherlands) said methodology was sound.

4. Discussion then turned to exchange of views on length of next allocation period, amounts, criteria for distribution (whether on basis of existing quotas, as provided in Fund articles, or whether there should be some SDR-aid link favoring LDCs), and possible conditions, such as gentlemen's agreement among industrial countries to devote part of their allocations to redemption or balances of their currencies held by other central banks or IMF. Chairman emphasized this was first exchange of views without commitment.

5. In view of Chairman, principal conclusions of this phase of discussion were:

(A) Generally agreed that this was worst possible period in which to try to evaluate long-term reserve needs, given transitional phase through which monetary system passing and many uncertainties about its future shape.

(B) Probably not desirable that G-10 Deputies should reach unanimous conclusion on all questions re second SDR allocation period. In particular, G-10 must keep in mind sensitivities of LDCs. Aim should be to make G-10 views available to IMF managing director, so that he can take them into account, along with views of other IMF member countries, in formulating his proposals re next activation.

(C) Widely held feeling monetary system should be based on SDRs, and that SDRs should be strengthened. (In subsequent comment on Chairman's summary, Bennett cautioned against overstating, during this transitional period, desirability of strengthening SDRs, lest we prejudge shape of future monetary system; in U.S. view best way to avoid prejudging would be to continue allocations in previous range.)

(D) Gilbert (BIS) and Handfield-Jones (Canada) felt composition of reserves was important consideration bearing on decision re further allocations. If objective was system which relied less on reserve currencies, it was important to continue creation SDRs in significant quantities, regardless of additional reserves that might be created through U.S. deficits.

(E) Most Deputies favored short allocation period. Two years was length most frequently cited. Reasons advanced were transitional phase through which monetary system now moving and coincidence of this time period with next review of IMF quotas and GAB renewal.

(F) Views on amount were varied. Germany, Netherlands and Belgium favored zero. France said 2 billion SDR over two years could be considered for essentially political rather than economic reasons, but that an alternative would be simply to defer decision until economic need clearly emerged. U.K. favored "modest" amount (2 billion over two years). Italy suggested "disguised token" creation, which would consist of zero allocation for first year and 2 or 3 billion in second. Canada, Japan and Sweden favored "normal" amount, described as rate of creation during three-year period now ending. While preferring normal creation, U.S. said it could understand reasons why some countries advocated zero creation for one year; in that case, however, would want to see creation at normal rate of around 3 billion in second year.

(G) Italy, with support from France, argued merits SDR-aid link, at least on voluntary or indirect basis. However, prevailing feeling in group was that no attempt should be made to establish such a link for upcoming allocation period, and that link question was properly for agenda of long-term monetary reform.

(H) Suggestion that industrial countries agree utilize some portion of their allocation to redeem foreign official holdings of their own currencies received little support. Hosomi (Japan) said he had no objection if others agreed.

6. In presenting U.S. position, Bennett made following points:

(A) In present period of negotiation and discussion re future trading and payments system, we should avoid decisions on future SDR allocations that would prejudge long-term reform issues. Thus, next allocation period should not extend beyond two years, and U.S. could see merit in one year.

(B) U.S. recognized that SDR-aid link and "redemption" or "consolidation" were issues to be considered under heading of long-term reform, but they would not be suitable for inclusion in any decision on allocations during this transitional period.

(C) Re amounts for 1973 and 1974, strong economic case for activation at present is absent. However, positive decision would indicate continued interest in SDR as reserve asset and lessening dependence on gold, as well as underlining continued monetary cooperation.

(D) Taking all these factors into account, U.S. could support positive decision for next year or next two years. But we can understand why others may feel no allocation warranted in present circumstances. Since we believe choice would not have important economic impact, we could also join in decision to take no action for 1973, although we have slight preference for activation. Pure "token" allocation does not appeal to us, either psychologically or logically. Not clear whether "token" would be regarded as act of faith or lack of faith.

(E) In any case, we would want to review this year's decision again next year in light of both reform discussions and new developments.

7. Strongest plea for substantial allocations in next basic period came from Sjonander (Sweden), who based his argument on premise that SDRs were designed meet long-term reserve needs, and that dollar reserves, even if now excess, did not meet that need, especially considering possible extinction through reversal of capital flows. However, he also favored period of not more than two or three years, while labeling this issue as "minor." Handfield-Jones (Canada) also strongly advocated continuing at least allocation rate of first period.

8. Chairman raised briefly question of future role for G-10, both at Ministerial and Deputy level. He pointed out Deputies would presumably continue function as representatives of GAB participants if IMF had need for new call on GAB resources and would also be concerned with GAB renewal. He asked Deputies to reflect on what other tasks group might perform in connection with monetary reform process.

9. Chairman asked IMF representatives to report substance of discussion on SDR activation to Managing Director. Chairman suggested group might meet again for further exchange of views in Washington at time of IMF annual meeting. Was agreed date and place would be left open in light of further developments.

Watson

---

232. **Memorandum From the President's Assistant for International Economic Affairs (Flanigan) to President Nixon**[1]

Washington, June 23, 1972.

RE

Floating the English Pound

The British government announced early this morning (June 23rd) that the English Pound would be permitted to float. This action was

---

[1] Source: National Archives, Nixon Presidential Materials, NSC Files, Country Files–Europe, Box 729, UK Volume VII 9/71–9/72. No classification marking.

taken after the Bank of England had bought $1 billion of pounds on Thursday, half that amount on Wednesday, with total Bank support during the week estimated by the Fed at $3 billion.[2]

The cause of the speculative run on the pound has been the decline during the past several months of Britain's visible trade balance from a healthy surplus to no surplus, the competitive prospect associated with entering the European Community, and the recent threat of a dock strike. The action is taken, however, when Britain's current technical position in terms of reserves and balance of payments had been considered relatively strong.

The British action shows the wisdom of U.S. refusal to consider convertibility until a new and stable monetary system is in place. The European community announced two months ago narrower bands for exchange rate parities between currencies of the ten members. These good intentions did not prevail against the massive movement of short-term funds, as the community had devised no mechanisms to give economic validity to the new parities. The central banks of the members did attempt to support the pound, with the Germans having bought $500 million worth on Thursday. It will be interesting to see to what extent the other central banks continue to support the pound.

The British action will have some negative effect on the U.S. balance of payments, undoing to some extent the effect of the December actions.[3] Arthur Burns expects the pound to devalue 5% to 8% against the dollar. The Smithsonian Agreement resulted in a revaluation of the pound by 8.6%.

Among other results of the pound float, the Irish pound will undoubtedly follow the English pound, as may some Scandinavian countries, Portugal, and some others. The Community will clearly have to rethink its monetary arrangements. Arthur Burns is concerned that speculation against the lira could come shortly. George

---

[2] In a June 24 telegram to President Nixon (dispatched at 1430Z and sent directly to the White House), Prime Minister Heath told the President that the Secretary of the Treasury and Federal Reserve Chairman had been informed of the decision to float late Thursday (June 22) night. The Prime Minister said that during 5 working days the outflow from sterling had reached $2.5 billion and the rate of outflow was accelerating. The Prime Minister concluded that this episode showed how urgent it was to achieve radical reform of the international monetary system. (Ibid.) Prime Minister Heath sent a follow-up telegram directly to President Nixon at the White House on June 26 (1620Z) emphasizing the need "to think in terms of much more radical changes than we have as yet envisaged" and the need to shorten the time frame for such reform from "that to which we are at present working." Prime Minister Heath indicated he would be interested in hearing President Nixon's thinking on substance and timing. (Ibid.)

[3] Reference is to the Smithsonian Agreement reached on December 18, 1971; see Document 221.

Shultz will head a small group considering what actions by this government are appropriate.[4]

---

[4] George Shultz was sworn in as Secretary of the Treasury on June 12, replacing John Connally whose resignation had been announced May 16. The Shultz group, in effect chaired by Volcker, included Secretary of State Rogers, Federal Reserve Chairman Burns, CEA Chairman Stein, CIEP Chairman Flanigan, and the President's Assistant for National Security Affairs Kissinger or his designee. Secretary Shultz and the Shultz group increasingly became the forum for decisions on international monetary reform.

233.　Letter From President Nixon to Prime Minister Heath[1]

Washington, July 10, 1972.

Dear Mr. Prime Minister:

Thank you very much for your personal messages with respect to your decision on the pound.

I share your conclusion that this latest episode in a series of monetary crises over recent years illustrates the need for fundamental changes in the monetary framework. To the extent this point is generally grasped, the cause of practical reform will have been reinforced—and, I hope, speeded. This can be a highly constructive by-product of otherwise unfortunate turbulence. I particularly welcome your reaction because so much of my own concern in the period since last August 15 has been directed toward establishing the point that we need to go beyond a simple patching up of the Bretton Woods system.

---

[1] Source: Washington National Records Center, Department of the Treasury, Files of Under Secretary Volcker: FRC 56 79 15, UK British Float. Confidential. There is no indication of when or how the letter was sent. It is attached to a July 10 note from Hormats to Volcker indicating that the text had been cleared by Flanigan, Kissinger, and the White House speechwriters but that Kissinger wanted Volcker to have "a final crack at it" before it was transmitted to London. The President was responding to June 24 and 26 messages from Prime Minister Heath; see footnote 2, Document 232. On June 30 Hormats had sent Volcker copies of Heath's messages and stated his assumption, "as in the case of similar missives in the past," that Volcker would want to draft the reply. (Washington National Records Center, Department of the Treasury, Files of Under Secretary Volcker: FRC 56 79 15, UK British Float) An earlier draft was transmitted to the President in San Clemente under cover of a July 6 memorandum that proposed an equally forthcoming tone to Heath's acceptance of the need for radical reform. This draft includes language looking to the IMF Autumn 1973 meeting as a useful target date for an agreement, which was dropped in the final text. The final paragraph of the cover memorandum reads: "In general, the British have been one of our major substantive antagonists, while maintaining a facade of wishing to cooperate closely as a mediator between the Common Market and the U.S." (Ibid.)

Frankly, we have felt the point has not been generally accepted in the past, even though certain underlying problems—such as the large mass and volatility of short-term money that you mentioned—have become increasingly evident.

I recognize that our effort to focus thinking on underlying problems could be, and has been, interpreted in some public discussion as an attempt to block or delay progress on specific reform proposals, or to promote purely national goals. Yet, I have accepted that risk in the firm belief that the cause of *lasting* reform—serving the needs of all—will be advanced only by a willingness to face up to the fundamental issues, political as well as economic. Any other course invites failure. It is often said that a crisis is required to focus our minds and energies. I am confident we have within our power the ability to grasp this opportunity.

I am the last to underestimate the difficulties ahead. In a situation permitting different avenues of approach and with success totally dependent upon a sense of shared responsibilities and benefits, we have not felt it useful to press for a specific single "American plan". Similarly, I trust that European thinking will not become frozen prematurely.

Against the background of recent events I do feel the time is ripe for engaging in open-minded and candid exploration of certain basic alternatives with our close partners. We should no longer be inhibited by the fear that certain approaches can be unthinkingly damned by some as too "radical" a departure from the past.

I know that Secretary Shultz looks forward to discussing these matters with the Chancellor at an early date and hope that our thinking can be tested against yours at all stages.

Sincerely,

Richard Nixon[2]

---

[2] Printed from a copy that bears this typed signature.

234. Memorandum From Secretary of the Treasury Shultz to President Nixon[1]

Washington, undated.

Since the British decision on June 24 to float the pound, strong speculative pressures have again developed in the foreign exchange markets. In two days at the end of last week,[2] $2-1/2 billion flowed into foreign central banks. The total flow of dollars into the central bank reserves in the past three weeks has amounted to almost $5 billion.

In terms of the direct and short-term impact on the U.S. economy and trade position, this turmoil is of limited significance. It is quite possible that, without further action by us, the foreign central banks will continue to support the dollar until the present speculative pressures pass. They have a strong interest in not allowing the dollar to decline.

However, this outcome is not certain and the situation poses important *potential* difficulties for the United States and for the future evolution of the monetary system.

1) A breakdown of the pattern of exchange rates embodied in the Smithsonian Agreement could lead to some repetition of the general uncertainties evident last Fall. A tendency for countries to act unilaterally to protect their own interests, and for the Common Market to withdraw behind a defensive wall of controls, would be aggravated. Rightly or wrongly, fears accompanying a breakdown of the Agreement could affect domestic business sentiment and, more directly, the stock market.

2) This sense of failure of the Smithsonian Agreement, in circumstances in which the United States is widely felt abroad (and in some quarters at home) to be playing an entirely passive role, would be a poor launching pad for a constructive trans-Atlantic dialogue on longer-term reform.[3]

---

[1] Source: Washington National Records Center, Department of the Treasury, Files of Under Secretary Volcker: FRC 56 79 15, UK British Float. Confidential. There is no indication that the memorandum was sent to President Nixon. Its probable date is July 18; see footnote 2 below.

[2] July 13 and 14. Addendum A, not printed, is a tabulation by day of central bank interventions to buy dollars following the reopening of foreign exchange markets on June 28 after Britain floated the pound. The totals for the seven banks listed on July 13 and 14 were $1,090 million and $1,450 million, respectively. The seven central banks also took $217 million on July 17, suggesting that this memorandum was prepared on July 18. From June 28 through July 17 the banks' total purchases were $4,925 million.

[3] On July 6 the Embassy in Bonn reported that President Pompidou reportedly had told Chancellor Brandt (during their Summit meeting in Bonn) "that he considered it an anomaly that the Europeans were now 'defending the dollar' while the US sat by and did nothing." The Embassy reported that Chancellor Brandt was considering a high-level approach to seek a U.S. "contribution" to the "defense of the dollar" and that the Embassy had been asked very informally how such an approach would be received in Washington. (Telegram 9346 from Bonn, July 6; National Archives, RG 59, Central Files 1970–73, FN 10)

Certainly, some antagonism in political terms could add to the economic uncertainty.

We face an inherent dilemma in dealing with this situation. Our trade and balance of payments position is still very weak, and the prognosis is still not assured. Thus, we cannot assume present exchange rates are satisfactory—and, in the case of Japan, the rate probably sooner or later will need to change. Should a crisis result in further exchange rate revaluations abroad, these decisions would ultimately benefit our trade and balance of payments position. The dilemma is such benefits are improbable without a period of turmoil and tension, with the risks cited above.

In this situation, three general courses of action can be distinguished:

1) *A relatively passive approach,* leaving present crisis decisions virtually entirely to the Europeans. Within this general posture, we can, of course, try to convey an interested, if inevitably somewhat detached, attitude.

This approach would recognize the realities that, in present circumstances, our ability to assist in calming speculative fears is limited. In contrast, actions interpreted as acknowledging a responsibility for maintenance of present exchange rates could stimulate hopes and demands by others for limited forms of U.S. convertibility or for more generalized guarantees of foreign dollar holdings against exchange risks. In addition to the need to guard against unsustainable financial commitments, we do not want to take actions that might tend to prejudice some aspects of monetary reform in a direction against our long-term interests.

On the other hand a passive approach also means we lose an opportunity to resolve the short-run crisis and runs a large risk of encouraging already widespread beliefs that "we don't care."

2) *Limited initiatives to intervene directly in foreign exchange markets to support the dollar.* This would entail borrowing foreign currencies (either by the Federal Reserve or by the Treasury) and use of those currencies to buy dollars in selected exchange markets. The objective would be to obtain a favorable psychological impact both from a visible strengthening of the dollar exchange rate and from the mere knowledge in the market that the United States is prepared to take some financial risks in supporting the Smithsonian exchange rate structure.

The direct financial risks are limited to the potential loss on foreign currency borrowings if exchange rates do change. To have a reasonable chance of success, it is believed we should be willing to borrow at least $1 billion if this course is chosen. However, we would have serious reservations about extending this type of operation beyond, say $2 billion. The potential loss could range as high as 10 percent of the amount borrowed but would be expected to be much less. There is a good chance of no loss or small gain.

This approach is outlined in detail in Addendum B.[4]

In favor of this approach, our attitude would be visibly "cooperative" and "constructive." We should, therefore, have some greater chance of influencing European decision-making. If the operation is successful, we could obtain our immediate objectives with very little cost. If the operation is unsuccessful, in the sense that the Smithsonian rates break down anyway, the attempt to help salvage the Agreement could provide a more favorable atmosphere for the longer-term negotiations.

Against this approach, limited intervention by the United States could easily lead to demands for "doing more." The action proposed is technically neither convertibility nor a general guarantee of foreign dollar purchases. However, public pressures to move in those directions could well be heard again, on the argument the market needs still further reassurance. Moreover, chances of failure are appreciable, and our activity could possibly highlight any domestic political fallout from a breakdown of the Smithsonian arrangements.

3) *A series of broader initiatives* beyond that discussed above, or in lieu thereof. Possible actions, ranging from the small measures of largely psychological impact to more substantial action, fall into several categories:

A. More forceful U.S. and multilateral statements, following a special meeting of Finance Ministers. (However, a meeting, itself, would be dangerous and potentially counterproductive unless accompanied by more concrete actions.)

B. Borrowing of U.S. dollars abroad from foreign central banks or privately, at somewhat more favorable terms than we pay at home. Actions of this type would have numerous precedents and would not raise awkward questions of convertibility or guarantees of dollar holdings. However, while a useful supplementary action, such borrowings by themselves would probably not have a major impact on the current situation.

C. Some modification of domestic monetary and debt management policies, ranging from modest efforts to increase slightly short-term interest rates while depressing long-term rates to some visible tightening of monetary policy generally. Such actions, if important enough to have a significant impact, raise a question about consistency with domestic objectives.

---

[4] Not printed. Addendum B, "Proposed U.S. Foreign Currency Operation," outlined use of a swap network to acquire foreign currencies, which in turn could be used by U.S. authorities to buy dollars, supporting the dollar's value.

D. Tightening of controls on banks or corporations in an attempt to reduce outflows of short-term funds. Foreign governments would particularly welcome this action. However, it would be difficult to implement and would not be consistent with our longer-range objectives.

On balance, the practical option in present circumstances is to engage in limited exchange market intervention, as described in Addendum A [B]. I would want to keep this operation under daily review, and would not want to borrow more than $2 billion without full review with you.

---

235. Information Memorandum for the Record[1]

Washington, July 20, 1972.

SUBJECT

> Meeting between Helmut Schmidt, Minister of Economics and Finance, Federal Republic of Germany and Dr. Kissinger, July 20, 1972, 2:40–3:30 p.m., Dr. Kissinger's Office (Also present were Rolf Pauls, Ambassador to the United States, Federal Republic of Germany, and R. G. Livingston, NSC Staff (note-taker))

Minister Schmidt: I want to discuss international monetary affairs. We are facing a very bad situation.

Dr. Kissinger: The Minister now has an opportunity to talk with one of the leading experts in this field. But you probably don't know much more yet than I. Whenever you come through Washington you should come in for a talk. I value your opinion on the German and US political situation. If the monetary situation was indeed becoming very bad, I could help perhaps.

---

[1] Source: National Archives, Nixon Presidential Materials, NSC Files, Country Files–Europe, Box 687, Germany Volume XII 5/72–12/72. Secret; Sensitive. Drafted by Robert G. Livingston on July 22. Attached to a July 22 memorandum from Livingston to Kissinger that indicates Kissinger's approval. As background for Schmidt's visit to Washington Ambassador Hillenbrand, on July 18, sent a telegram [text not declassified] to the White House that noted that on the economic side Schmidt was keeping his Washington appointments but had missed an EC Finance Ministers' meeting until he knew his new portfolio better. This gave the United States an opportunity to get across U.S. monetary and trade views before Schmidt was "subject within the EC to French conceptions." Ambassador Hillenbrand reported that Schmidt "told his Economics Ministry staff that his Washington discussions would be get-acquainted visits in which he himself would not raise specific issues." (Telegram [document number not declassified] from Bonn; ibid.)

Minister Schmidt: It is bad and could become worse. I thought that even ten days ago before I took on this portfolio. Last year I tried to make you understand the political effects in Europe of Secretary Connally's actions. The United States cannot embark on international monetary reform before its elections. Nor is this necessary.

[Omitted here is discussion of the political situation in Germany.]

Minister Schmidt: I have a personal rule never to mind what others make of comments of mine which leak to the press. I want to turn the conversation back to international monetary issues, however. Billions of dollars are floating about the world and Germany is taking in too many of them.

Dr. Kissinger: What is the cause of this?

Minister Schmidt: The US economic situation is improving. Within two years or so this may have an impact on the US trade balances. Meanwhile, there are too many dollars circulating in the world. New York bankers are selling dollars and the German Federal Reserve System is having to buy them up at a fixed rate to prevent the dollar from falling below 3.15 against the DM. The German Federal Bank is handing out far too many DMark, billions in a week. This has a very bad internal effect. The German price level is rising far too fast. The inflation rate is 5.4 percent at present. This will be the number one campaign issue. If I am to survive politically, I will have to do something about this as Minister of Finance and Economics.

Dr. Kissinger: We want you to survive, which is not to say, necessarily that we want your government to do so. We appreciate how much you have done as Defense Minister.

Minister Schmidt: My main objective is to have US-German cooperation survive. The dollar problem remains and the German inflation rate may reach 6 percent. To prevent this I may have to cut off the purchase of the dollars "immediately." This will be done by means of regulations on capital inflows and corresponding regulations on trade.

Dr. Kissinger: Like the French.

Minister Schmidt: There is no other way. Schiller was against that but the whole cabinet was for it. That is why Schiller had to go. Last year there had been a DM float and DM revaluation. There can be no revaluation this year. I want you to understand the situation and the background to the action I may have to take.

Yesterday, however, Chairman Burns has done what I came to the United States to ask him to do. By intervening in the international monetary market to sell DM he took an action which serves as a token of US determination to defend the Smithsonian Agreement.[2] That is essential: to defend the Smithsonian Agreement and not let the situation get out of control.

There has as yet been no German cabinet decision to stop buying dollars. I am not going to ask for one, if the United States government continues actions such as the Federal Reserve Bank's of yesterday. The difficulties may be ironed out in that case. The problem is the rumor mill among international bankers. The meeting of the EEC finance ministers July 17–18, and the rumors coming out of it has made the July 19 intervention of the Federal Reserve Bank necessary

Ambassador Pauls: The Fed's action has raised the dollar by a point and a half.

Dr. Kissinger: Last year the situation had to get very bad before I was able to intervene within the government. Then the crisis was brought under control. You should know that Secretary of the Treasury Schultz thinks that floating is the right policy. However, I understand that a US float will make it impossible for the German government to control inflationary pressures. The Germans are saying to the US that either you defend the Smithsonian Agreement by intervention of your own to strengthen the dollar or we will defend it by means of controls.

Minister Schmidt: That is the choice. An important aspect is the psychological impact of US action on bankers in New York and in Frankfurt, whose psychology I do not understand very well.

Dr. Kissinger: I cannot give you an answer right now. What is required is day-to-day actions, a series of them. This is not an issue which you can bring up to the President in the form of a single paper to be signed. Secretary Shultz and Chairman Burns will have to take actions daily. It is the totality of these, no single action, which is impor-

---

[2] In a July 20 memorandum to Kissinger with "Additional Information" for his meeting with Finance Minister Schmidt, Hormats reported that on July 19 the U.S. Government for the first time, through the Federal Reserve Bank of New York, sold German Marks to buy dollars to help sustain the Smithsonian exchange rates. Hormats noted that this was "a departure from the Connally position, which had been that the Europeans should continue to bear sole responsibility for maintaining the Smithsonian rates." (Ibid.) On July 29 the Embassy in Paris reported that the Governor of the Bank of France thought the current calm in foreign exchange markets was due both to the strong support of European monetary authorities for the Smithsonian rates and U.S. moves to support the dollar and reopen the U.S.-German swap line. The Embassy also reported the irritable and disgruntled Governor had "no sympathy" with France's passively and unconditionally buying "inconvertible" dollars, which put him on a different course from Finance Minister Giscard d'Estaing and probably President Pompidou as well. (Telegram 14554 from Paris, July 29; National Archives, RG 59, Central Files 1970–73, FN 10)

tant. This is different than the situation last year. Then there was a concrete set of decisions to be taken.

I will talk with Secretary Shultz and Chairman Burns. I need two weeks time for this.

Minister Schmidt: I want the White House to understand that even a strong supporter of cooperation with the United States such as I am may have to act suddenly in the international monetary field.

Dr. Kissinger: Our situation with the Europeans is precarious. I know that. A unilateral European move in the monetary field could trigger an unexpected reaction in the United States. Strangely, the old internationalists in the United States have now become isolationists. And the old isolationists, who have become internationalists now, are good on defense but remain isolationists at heart in economic affairs. I hope you will hold off any restrictive move for at least ten days.

Minister Schmidt: I am not going to act within the next ten days.

Dr. Kissinger: I know that you are meeting with Shultz and Burns today. I will call Shultz and explain to him that you are no anti-American economic nationalist. Mr. Burns needs no convincing. The problem with him is the way he presents his views. He is a difficult personality to orchestrate in a coordinated policy. However, Burns favors the Smithsonian Agreement and the need to defend it.

Minister Schmidt: The Agreement must be defended until the elections.

Dr. Kissinger: After I have been in touch with Burns and Shultz I will inform you confidentially of the outcome through Rolf Pauls. That way the communication will remain completely private.

What do you think about European-American relations?

Minister Schmidt: The greatest present uncertainty is how soon the European Community will clarify its views on relations with third countries, particularly the United States, on European economic and monetary union, and on European political consultations. None of this depends on the United States; it depends on Pompidou's interpretation of France's interests and on the strength of the British Pound. I don't understand the significance of the French Cabinet reshuffle.

Dr. Kissinger: It may be a move in the Gaullist direction.

Minister Schmidt: The central problem is whether the European Community would be outward-looking, as Germany wants, or inward-looking, as the French want. Germany does not want the European Community to become a currency bloc against the dollar. Schiller's problem was his inability to deal with the French tactfully on this issue. As Economics and Finance Minister I will try to establish cooperation with Giscard as I did with Debre.

Dr. Kissinger: I want you to know that we will miss you in the Defense Ministry. As far as you personally are concerned, I am happy you can leave this suicidal post.

What do you think of US policy?

Minister Schmidt: You made two mistakes in 1971, the first in handling of Japan and the second in handling the Europeans until Secretary Connally was called home.

Dr. Kissinger: To some degree the Japanese are making a profession out of being hurt. What could we have done to handle them better?

Minister Schmidt: When I was in Japan I got the impression that the Japanese are somehow stirred up, intrigued with the potentiality of relations with mainland China. They couldn't seem to see that mainland China can't buy any more from Japan, that it is no bigger a market than Taiwan. Somehow the Japanese have lost direction and feel dropped by the United States.

This year the United States has done well—with the Moscow Summit and the Berlin Agreement, on which the Germans and the Americans had cooperated. You helped Brandt to carry out his Eastern policy while strengthening the security foundation in the West.

Dr. Kissinger: We helped the Eastern policy as much as we could without going public about it.

Minister Schmidt: We have nothing to complain about.

Dr. Kissinger: As far as our handling of the Europeans last year is concerned, you should understand that Texans like Secretary Connally are used to dealing with problems in a forceful way. The Secretary is a strong, able, and attractive man.

Minister Schmidt: Yes, he is. I advised the Chancellor last year that financial and economic matters should be taken out of the hands of men like Connally, Giscard and Schiller and put into the hands of statesmen. With billions of dollars floating around, the monetary crisis of 1971 can easily repeat itself.

Dr. Kissinger: Give me two weeks time to determine attitudes in the United States on international monetary policy. I will let you know candidly about these attitudes.

[Omitted here is discussion of the U.S. presidential campaign and Vietnam.]

236.   Memorandum of Conversation[1]

Washington, July 25, 1972, 4:30 p.m.

PARTICIPANTS

Henry A. Kissinger
Arthur F. Burns, Chairman, Federal Reserve System
Robert D. Hormats, NSC Staff Member

B: I wanted to see you to bring you up-to-date on the international monetary situation. You and I talked about that last before the Smithsonian agreement.

K: Yes, I recall. We settled on your scheme, but Connally got the credit.

B: I am not concerned about credit.

K: As I recall, I convinced Pompidou to agree to your scheme.[2]

B: The fact that you have not been involved in the last several months has made it difficult for me.

K: The reason I could become involved last time was that we were moving toward the Summits, and that imposed a need for a solution to the monetary problem. Also, I could tell the President that unless we did something we were clearly headed for a crisis. Now these conditions do not exist.

B. But there was a blow up. The system was in disarray. I had to put it together again last week. I went to Basel in March.[3] The thing nearly exploded then, but I talked frankly to the central bankers and we were able to hold it together.

K: What made it explode?

B: The situation was delicate. Once there was speculation against the dollar, it shook the entire financial community. People did not have confidence in the Smithsonian rates. I told the central bankers what the Fed was doing about the interest rate, and of the President's plans to get hold of the budget. I also told them that they had made a few mistakes of their own. They respect me and know that I deal frankly with them. That was good for a few weeks. But we had to do something more tan-

---

[1] Source: National Archives, Nixon Presidential Materials, NSC Files, Country Files–Europe, Box 687, Germany Volume XII 5/72–12/72. Secret. No drafting information appears on the memorandum.

[2] Presumably a reference to Pompidou's statement in his February 4 letter to President Nixon that Kissinger had told him "the following morning" that President Nixon's understanding was that the United States would intervene to support the dollar at the new exchange rates. See footnote 4, Document 223.

[3] See Document 226.

gible. I got Connally to make a good speech at the Council on Foreign Relations to indicate that we would help Britain repay its obligations to the IMF and get monetary reform talks underway.[4]

K: I have never understood Connally.

B: I understand him. There are numerous problems. He wants these problems to go away. He resents people fooling around with these issues and just hopes that they can go away.

K: Has the system been patched up now? Will we have a crisis the next time there is a run on the dollar? I spoke with Finance Minister Schmidt recently. He said we should go back to convertibility.[5]

B: That is impossible. We can't go back to convertibility at this time.

K: Or some other means of defending the dollar.

B: We are defending the dollar. It was under attack. Foreign central banks had to take in over $6 billion since December. The system just won't work if this sort of thing keeps up. On Thursday, two weeks ago, they took in $1 billion–$1.5 billion.[6] This couldn't go much further. I went over the map of possibilities and decided that the best way to deal with this was to have the Fed borrow currencies from foreign governments to intervene in the currency market. This was done without committing our reserve assets. The response around the world was one of jubilation.

K: Did you do this on your own discretion?

B: No, I needed the consent of the Treasury. I previously had had endless conversations with Paul Volcker, who is negative about everything. I experienced some difficulty with Shultz, but won him over. We took this to the President and he agreed.[7]

K: Will this keep things in balance?

B: It should, but we can't be sure. We committed a negligible sum—less than $50 million—but got remarkable results. We are ready to commit a sizable sum. But we can't categorically say it will be successful. However, the chances of success are very good. Also, there is some movement on reform of the Treasury. Before I couldn't get Connally or Volcker to move on a plan for reform or to determine the US position.

---

[4] Secretary Connally addressed the Council on Foreign Relations on March 15; see Document 226.

[5] See Document 235. There is no record that Schmidt recommended restoration of convertibility.

[6] July 13; see footnote 2, Document 234.

[7] On July 18 the President was in San Clemente and called Shultz in Washington and talked with him from 8:45 to 9:24 a.m. PDT. (National Archives, Nixon Presidential Materials, White House Central Files, President's Daily Diary) This is the only recorded contact the President had with Shultz or Burns before the United States intervened in foreign exchange markets to support the dollar on July 19.

K: Why?

B: They thought it would be leaked. However, they had no position of their own. I gave a talk in Montreal which I wanted Treasury to give.[8] They had no objection to what I was saying. Later they began fussing about it, but there was nothing that they really objected to.

K: What is the schedule for proceeding now?

B: There will be a meeting of the Group of 20 in September. But I want to add that although the President approved my plan to do what I did, I need continuous support from the President. If I lose it, Shultz will back off at once. The Fed in the international area can't move without the Treasury. Shultz and I have worked well together and will continue as long as I have the President's support.

K: I can be helpful there.

B: I have held this together since December.

K: After December there were people trying to break the thing up. I have never understood Connally. Connally was attempting to use Canada as a key element in breaking up European policy. But at the same time he was attacking Canada.

B: Connally uses brutal techniques. He did well on his trip to Brazil but in Peru, shortly after he left, the President made a violently anti-American speech.[9] When I was there, the speech was repeated three times over the air. I was told numerous times that this speech was an answer to the Connally visit. In Argentina Lanusse, after I was in his office two or three minutes, told me that he had found out where I spent my first day in Argentina and where I will spend my remaining days. He was very pleased that I was talking to Argentine officials and businessmen. He said to me, "Do you know what Connally did? He went to see a ranch—a ranch!" The President said he was very angry. When

---

[8] Burns addressed the 1972 American Bankers Association International Monetary Conference in Montreal on May 12. In his prepared remarks Burns set out ten elements he "would expect to find in a new monetary system that met the test of both practicality and viability." Under Secretary Volcker also addressed the Conference on May 12 and made similar remarks. Volcker was questioned closely on Burns' ten elements during a press conference later in the day. Volcker said he would share some of Burns' principles but distanced himself from endorsing the ten elements. The texts of Burns' and Volcker's prepared remarks and a transcript of Volcker's press conference are in the Volcker Group Papers (VG/Uncl. INFO/72-26 and VG/Uncl. INFO/72-27); they were circulated to members of the Group on May 15 and May 22, respectively. (Washington National Records Center, Department of the Treasury, Volcker Group Masters: FRC 56 86 30, 1972, VG/Uncl. INFO series) Volcker's remarks are printed in *Annual Report of the Secretary of the Treasury on the State of the Finances for the Fiscal Year Ended June 30, 1972*, pp. 436–440.

[9] After he stepped down as Treasury Secretary, Connally was sent by President Nixon as his personal emissary to 14 countries in Latin America, Oceania, and South and Southeast Asia.

Connally gets into foreign relations, God help us. When Shultz got in, I was quite negative. He did not know much about this. Before he was very difficult to deal with, very theoretical. Now he thinks more pragmatically.

K: I was concerned he might be too doctrinaire. What is the schedule of meetings?

B: There will be nothing substantive until next year.

K: This is after the German, US elections, and a Canadian election. Are the Canadians having an election?

H: I recall that Trudeau said recently there would not be an election this winter, at least not in the fall.

K: They have to give two months notice so that means there probably won't be one.

B: We have an opportunity now to rebuild the world.

K: Which direction should we move?

B: The IMF is the only thing which stands for international law in the monetary area. There should be established the principle of symmetry between deficit and surplus nations. Right now, when a country has a deficit, it is an international sin. With a surplus, it is practicing an international virtue. We should do away with morality in our thinking. Apply rules that surplus countries have the obligation to reduce and eliminate surpluses and deficit countries have a similar obligation to reduce their deficits. We should establish rules to achieve this.

K: Like what?

B: In the first year, a warning. In the second year, if it continues, then withdraw convertibility. Previously convertibility has been taken for granted. It was felt there was a right to convertibility. No longer should it be an automatic right. The country would have to accumulate foreign currencies and could not necessarily convert them.

K: This wouldn't stop the Japanese-type of accumulation, would it?

B: No, but convertibility would be a privilege in some circumstances. We must also recognize that this is a delicate problem since it means sanctions against surplus countries and some loss of sovereignty. But there was some loss of sovereignty in the SALT Treaty in Moscow.

K: Any treaty limits a nation's scope of action. You give up something you otherwise would have the right to do.

B: But we should be careful. While the degree of sovereignty would have to be limited, we should be careful in the way we present this to Congress. It is a delicate matter.

K: This is the way I see it. We can't afford a blow up in the monetary area since it affects relationships in the non-Communist world.

Without reform there will be a blow up. I respect your judgment and expertise. I can't get involved all the time, but I will if need be.

B: I will get you involved only when necessary. It has been a lonely battle for me.

K: When you want to see me, we will fix a time within twenty-four hours. We will meet within twenty-four hours whenever you request a meeting.

237.　Editorial Note

Pursuant to preparatory work by the G-10 Deputies (see Documents 227 and 229), the Executive Directors of the International Monetary Fund, at their meeting on June 23, 1972, decided to submit a resolution on the establishment of a committee of the Board of Governors (which became known as the C-20) to the Board of Governors for a written vote to be received on or before July 28. IMF Document SM/72/122, Supplement 3, dated June 26, was sent to members of the Executive Board explaining the voting procedure, with the draft resolution attached. This document, which was circulated to the Volcker Group Alternates as VG/INFO/72-36 Supp. 3 on June 27, is in the Washington National Records Center, Department of the Treasury, Volcker Group Masters: FRC 56 86 30, VG/INFO/72-1–VG/INFO/72-39. A number of earlier drafts of the resolution and commentary by members of the VGAs are ibid.

On July 27 IMF Document SM/72/122, Supplement 4, was sent to all members of the Executive Board informing them that 308,766 votes had been cast in favor of the resolution, far more than the 2/3 majority required for its approval. There were no negative votes and 1 abstention, and 11 members had not voted. The votes of three members were not counted for technical reasons. The IMF document was distributed to members of the Volcker Group Alternates as VG/INFO/72-36 Supp. 4 on July 28. (Ibid.) France cast its 15,250 votes in favor of the resolution.

The resolution was adopted by the Governors of the International Monetary Fund during the Fund's Annual Meeting in Washington in September. The resolution established an ad hoc Committee of the Board of Governors on reform of the international monetary system. The Committee was to "advise and report to the Board of Governors with respect to all aspects of reform of the international monetary system, including those that involve international trade, the flow of capital, investment, or development assistance." The resolution provided for a Chairman and a Deputies Committee to prepare the work of the Committee. At its first meeting on September 28 Mohammed Ali Wardhana, Finance Minister of Indonesia, was elected Chairman of the C-20. Jeremy Morse of the Bank of England was selected to chair the C-20 Deputies. Draft minutes of the first C-20 meeting and the Deputies meeting on September 29 were circulated to members of the Volcker Group Alternates on October 10 and October 11 as VGA/72-90 and VGA/72-91. (Ibid., VGA/72-51–VGA/72-107)

---

238.   Telegram From the Embassy in France to the Department of State[1]

Paris, July 31, 1972, 1716Z.

14620. Subject: IMF Report on International Monetary Reform. Pass Treasury for Secretary Shultz.

1. The Director of the French Treasury has asked us to transmit a personal letter from Finance Minister Giscard d'Estaing to Secretary Shultz regarding the report of the IMF Executive Board on International Monetary Reform. An Embassy translation of letter follows. French text being forwarded by air pouch to Treasury/OASIA.[2]

2. "Dear Mr. Secretary. The Executive Board of the International Monetary Fund is now completing the report it was asked to prepare on reform of the international monetary system. This is the culmination of a lengthy project begun last spring on the basis of a text which, in accordance with normal procedures, the Fund staff prepared. The initial text has been substantially modified during numerous discussions of the Executive Board, in which the Directors designated by the United States and France played an active part.

3. No one considers the result of this work completely satisfactory. It could not be otherwise considering the difficulty of the subject and the varying conceptions of the member countries. Moreover, we are still

---

[1] Source: National Archives, RG 59, Central Files 1970–73, FN 10. Confidential; Immediate; Limdis; Greenback.

[2] Not found.

beginning the process of study and reconciliation of ideas to be undertaken by the Group of Twenty, the organ we have created specifically for this purpose.

4. I note, however, that the imperfections of the report, particularly the fact that it poses numerous problems without resolving them and does not exclude a priori and feasible reform of the international monetary system, make it nearly acceptable to everyone. In certain respects, this preserves the possibility of a subsequent agreement on the modalities of reform.

5. I am informed that, at the end of last week, the Executive Director nominated by the United States proposed to introduce numerous additions to each of the five chapters of the report, on which the Board had virtually reached agreement. These belated proposals, which very naturally reflected the views of your government, jeopardized the equilibrium which until then had been preserved among conflicting views. For this reason, they threatened the whole project. In any case, the French Executive Director could not approve a report which included both the present text and the numerous paragraphs proposed by your Executive Director.

6. I understand, of course, that it is completely normal for the United States to take a position on international monetary reform. In fact, I would say it is desirable for your colleagues to be better informed on this point than they have been until now. But, insertions in the document being discussed at the Fund are not the appropriate means to do so and, in my view, these insertions have been introduced at a time when they cannot validly be considered.

7. In addition, I fear that difficulties at this stage would be badly interpreted by the general public and thus would risk compromising recent efforts undertaken on various sides to bring more order to exchange markets. Neither would they represent an encouraging introduction to the work of the Group of Twenty.

8. I strongly hope that you will give the present message all the importance it merits and that you will reconsider the means at your disposal to make your positions on international monetary problems known. Let me add that I am looking forward to meeting you in Washington at the end of September under circumstances which will allow us to lay out and discuss these problems at a suitable level within reasonable bounds. Sincerely yours, Valery Giscard d'Estaing."

Watson

239. Paper Prepared in the Department of the Treasury[1]

Washington, July 31, 1972.

MAJOR ELEMENTS OF PLAN X

A. Exchange Rate Regime

1. General rule: Countries will declare central values for their exchange rates expressed in SDR's, with permissible margins of 3–4 percent on each side.

2. Floating rule: With permission a country can float:

a) transitionally to new central value
b) indefinitely if it declares willingness to avoid "balance of payments" controls on capital and trade and obeys more restrictive reserve management criteria—both subject to special surveillance.

3. Unit rule: A group of countries wishing to maintain narrower margins and declaring intention to move toward reserve pooling, can be declared "monetary and trading unit" and treated as single country.

4. Intervention: Countries with central values will be expected to intervene in their domestic markets to avoid depreciation beyond lower margin of currencies of leading trading partners with central values.

B. Reserve Regime

1. "Primary reserves" would consist of gold, SDR's and IMF gold tranches.

2. Each country would have a "normal level" of primary reserves related to IMF quotas (e.g., 4 times each country's quota).

3. Total world "normal" reserve *must* equal total world primary reserves. Dollars and other foreign exchange can be converted into SDR's during a limited "open season." SDR allocations will make up any shortfall of primary reserves below world "normal reserves."

4. Countries acquiring foreign exchange can present it to the issuing country for primary reserves, so long as both countries are maintaining central rates.

5. Negotiated official credits permitted.

6. Foreign exchange holdings are neither encouraged nor prohibited. Countries would need to respect any limits established by the issu-

---

[1] Source: Washington National Records Center, Department of the Treasury, Deputy to the Assistant Secretary for International Affairs: FRC 56 83 26, Contingency Planning, 1965–1973. Confidential. The paper bears no drafting information.

ing country, and U.S. would negotiate limits on foreign official holdings of dollars. Foreign exchange holdings include all commitments and forward controls.

7. Adjustments would be called for at certain thresholds:

a) *total* reserves (primary plus forex of a country at *50* percent of "normal level": devaluation required—3–4 percent per year without approval, more (subject to approval) if underlying conditions so justify.

b) *primary* reserves at *75* percent of "normal level": devaluation permitted—3–4 percent per year without approval, more (subject to approval) if justified.

c) __reserves at (unspecified) level *and* after drawing of say 50 percent of IMF and capital controls in effect: surcharge permitted.

d) *primary* reserves at *150* percent of "normal level": revaluation required—at least 3 percent per year.

e) *primary* reserves at *175* percent of "normal level": no right to convertibility.

f) *primary* reserves (primary plus forex) at *200* percent of normal level and maintained for period (e.g., *6* months) would indicate persistent surplus country, which would be expected, e.g., to increase aid, liberalize imports and unless corrected, subject to discriminatory restrictions (e.g., surcharge).

8. Gold would be sold by official holders only at official price to IMF, which would be free to sell in private market with profits going to IDA.

9. SDR's created for "open season" conversion of foreign exchange should be extinguished, up to a fixed amount per year, as the country with the currency liability obtains primary reserves above its "normal level." Total SDR volume would be maintained by equivalent new allocation distributed by the usual formula.

10. Holding limits and restrictions on use of SDR's by official institutions would be abolished.

11. An SDR-aid link could be grafted onto the system, but would not be proposed.

a) No country expected or compelled to maintain restrictions on ·*outward* flow of capital (though permitted to do so) *except* that countries applying surcharges (in addition to IMF borrowing) should be willing to apply internationally sanctioned capital controls.

b) Countries with below normal reserve holdings over a period should not be permitted restrictions on *inward* flow of capital imposed for balance-of-payments purposes. (Restrictions defined to include special interest incentives or penalties.)

c) In other circumstances, presumption (but not prohibition) against use of controls on *inward* flows. Presumption expressed by international review and surveillance when controls enforced for more than six months, and maintenance justified only by showing exchange rate not fundamentally undervalued. Sanctions, including elimination of right to hold foreign currencies before other countries could discriminate on trade, should be included.

d) Two-tier exchange markets would be treated as form of capital control and treated as above.

e) Nations should apply consistent set of regulatory standards on "foreign banks" to assure equitable treatment of Euro-currency markets.

C. Constitutional Regime

1. Completely new international monetary agreement needed covering monetary and related broad trade principles.

2. Parallel restructuring of GATT required.

3. Articles of two institutions should interact; joint meetings and working parties should be sought.

4. Monetary organization should be "politicized"

—maintain Executive Directors at Deputy Minister level
—Keep C-20 in being.

---

240.   Telegram From the Embassy in Germany to the Department of State[1]

Bonn, August 1, 1972, 0935Z.

10466. Subject: Conversation with Economics and Finance Minister Schmidt.

---

[1] Source: National Archives, Nixon Presidential Materials, NSC Files, Subject Files, Box 356, Monetary. Secret; Exdis. Attached to an August 2 memorandum from Hormats to Kissinger apprising Kissinger of the increase in the free market price of gold to $70 per ounce and reminding him of the need to contact Schmidt, pursuant to his July 25 conversation with Arthur Burns, regarding U.S. willingness to defend the dollar lest the Europeans come "to believe that we are returning to Connally's policy of letting them bear the *sole* burden of defending the Smithsonian rates." See Documents 235 and 236. Kissinger wrote on Hormats' memorandum: "Hormats—Let's do it. Draft something." No record of a written reply has been found. On August 9 Hormats sent Kissinger a briefing memorandum for his August 10 breakfast with Shultz, which inter alia, suggested he sound out the Secretary on his agreement with Burns to commit a "sizable amount" to support the dollar. (National Archives, Nixon Presidential Materials, NSC Files, Agency Files, Box 299, Treasury Volume III) No record of the August 10 meeting was found, but on September 1 Hormats sent Kissinger talking points for his meeting with Ambassador Pauls, indicating that Kissinger had discussed the international monetary system with Burns and Shultz and the United States would cooperate in the effort to defend the dollar rate, including, when appropriate, selling currencies drawn under swap agreements. The talking points continued: "However, the major responsibility for defending present rates should continue to lie with nations whose currencies might be under upward pressure in the market." (Ibid., Country Files–Europe, Box 687, Germany Volume XII 5/72–12/72)

1. The new FRG Economics and Finance Minister Helmut Schmidt used the occasion of my first call on him on July 31 to press home his views on the international monetary situation. He began by saying that, although he had had good and full conversations with Secretary of the Treasury Shultz, Federal Reserve Board Chairman Burns, Peter Flanigan, Henry Kissinger, and others, during his recent visit to Washington, there had since been a further evolution in his thinking which he wanted to bring to our attention. Since we had known each other personally for nearly 20 years,[2] he felt he could be absolutely frank.

2. He could not understand the passivity of the US in the international monetary field during recent months. This had made it extremely difficult for our European friends to believe that the US really wanted to adhere to the Smithsonian Agreement. The recent intervention of the Federal Reserve on behalf of the dollar had been a good thing psychologically, even if it had but only a symbolic effect quantitatively considered, but even that would be lost quickly if it were not repeated from time to time. One point on which he wanted to be absolutely frank was that, if a heavy flow of dollars into Germany should resume for whatever reason, he would not hesitate to impose controls even though these would inevitably also have some trade impact. The former Minister of Economics and Finance had fallen on precisely this issue. He had been opposed by the majority of the Cabinet and the German banking community.

As far as Schmidt was concerned, he approached this whole question from the viewpoint of a politician who had not asked for his present post but had accepted it out of a sense of obligation to his party. The political stakes were simply too high to leave the subject to the technicians or even to a conventional Minister of Finance. This was the position he had taken with Brandt before the Schiller showdown and was one he would maintain in his present office. There were two major reasons why he could not accept the possibility of a further German float and would have to resort to exchange controls if necessary: (A) the "already not so good prospects" for Brandt in the forthcoming elections would be completely ruined if the European Summit were not to take place, and it could not take place unless the German position on dollar inflow were to come closer to the French, and (B) the long-range requirements of the German economy and its export potential likewise were not compatible with a further float.

3. He was aware of course, Schmidt continued, that no fundamental action could be expected in the monetary field before the American

---

[2] A career member of the Foreign Service, Ambassador Hillenbrand had been assigned several times to posts in the Federal Republic of Germany, including Deputy Chief of Mission at the Embassy in Bonn in the mid-1960s.

and German elections, but he was concerned about the possibility that pre-electoral rumors, perhaps in October, would set off another wave of speculation against the dollar. This would trigger the kind of German reaction which he had indicated he would be forced to take. If it were possible to get through the fall period without such a development, then 1973 would be a year in which there would be real need for an inconspicuous but real American leadership in the international monetary field. Without it, any hope of basic reform would be illusory. He was not certain, after his visit to Washington, which line of thinking would prevail, but it was clear that it was in our common interest to change a situation which, from the European point of view, had become untenable.

4. I observed that since he had had an opportunity, during his recent trip to the US to receive at first hand the views of the senior American officials whom he had met, there was little I could add at this time to what they had told him. We are not indifferent. We too consider international monetary reform and trade negotiations a matter of urgency and want to get on with them as expeditiously as possible. I would report his views and hoped that he would feel free in the future to convey any information or thoughts which he might have through me to my government. He said he would not hesitate whenever he felt it necessary to get in touch with me immediately. *Comment:* It is clear that Schmidt is not particularly happy in his new role as Minister of Economics and Finance. I believe he is sincere in saying that he took this position mainly out of loyalty to his party and to the Chancellor. He would be the first to acknowledge that his understanding of the complexities of international finance is still elementary, but he is a quick learner as well as one of the most articulate politicians on the current German scene. His influence with the Chancellor will be very great in the months to come, and the views he expressed will carry much weight in cabinet deliberations. In talking about his health, Schmidt could only say that while he felt better than he had in many months, he had come to appreciate that he is no longer a young man. He intended to go off on a month's leave immediately after his appointment with me, but added, somewhat apologetically, that he would be in constant touch with his Ministry and prepared to return to Bonn at any time if necessary.

Hillenbrand

241.   Telegram From the Department of State to the Embassy in France[1]

Washington, August 4, 1972, 1933Z.

142290. Subject: IMF Report on International Monetary Reform. Ref: Paris 14620.[2] For FinAtt.

1. Please transmit following letter dated August 4 (and attachments) from Secretary Shultz to Finance Minister Giscard d'Estaing.

2. "Dear Mr. Minister: Thank you for your letter of July 31 concerning the work of the Executive Board of the Fund on its report concerning international monetary reform. I appreciate the frank and direct expression of your view.

You have certainly been correctly informed that the U.S. Executive Director has recently put forward in the Fund certain views of the U.S. Government concerning the questions which are at issue in the projected international economic and monetary reform.[3]

In this effort, I fully share your wish that the report, however imperfect, pose relevant problems, explore feasible alternatives and, especially, 'preserve the possibility of subsequent agreement on the modalities of reform.' This is our entire purpose in the drafting proposals we have made. The apparent question in your mind as to our purpose can perhaps be answered most clearly by reviewing the background of this matter, and the manner in which our own concern with this objective has been expressed.

To that end, I asked that a short memorandum be prepared reviewing our approach. I attach it for your interest.

---

[1]   Source: National Archives, RG 59, Central Files 1970–73, FN 10. Confidential; Priority; Limdis; Greenback. Drafted in Treasury by Under Secretary Volcker on August 4, and cleared in State by Armstrong (E), Weintraub (E/IFD), Springsteen (EUR), and Curran (S/S) and approved by Acting Secretary Irwin.

[2]   Document 238.

[3]   On August 11 the Embassy in Paris reported on an article in that day's issue of *Le Monde*, based on "rumors from Washington," that the U.S. Executive Director at the IMF had proposed about 20 changes in the Board's report on international monetary reform, and that the French Executive Director had objected that these reflected the U.S. viewpoint but would not be so identified in the report. (Telegram 15401 from Paris, August 11; ibid.) The Department of State responded, informing the Embassy that following Giscard's July 31 letter to Shultz the French Executive Director had proposed two inserts to the IMF report to make it clear the French did not believe "exchange rates in the past had been sticky and that the U.S. should not expect to correct its balance of payments problems only by current account improvements." The French statement also made it clear France wanted to increase the role and price of gold in the international monetary system. (Telegram 146942 to Paris, August 12; ibid.)

I should note that the substantive views put forward in writing by the U.S. Director are entirely consistent with those which have been articulated for many months by high U.S. officials in public and private statements.

In the light of our experience, I believe you will agree that, since the staff draft failed to take adequate account of our views, we had no alternative to proposing such additions as we felt essential. Indeed, we have found others welcomed this direct expression of views on matters of such direct concern to us.

If the draft Fund report had, in fact, left open an adequate range of realistic options for an appropriate reform of the international economic and monetary systems, we would have been satisfied. That is all we seek. But we are convinced the drafts at hand did not accomplish that purpose. We are frankly very disappointed at this.[4]

I look forward to the opportunity to discuss these questions with you directly, and you may be assured we will bend every effort to speed the process of reconciling views and achieving fundamental reform. In that process, all my experience in other areas of public policy and negotiation suggests the wisdom of openly addressing the basic issues involved, and patiently seeking a sound solution, rather than accepting at the start a formula for discussion that obscures important dimensions of the problem. Sincerely yours, George P. Shultz".

Begin text first attachment.

Memorandum (dated August 2, 1972) for Secretary Shultz. Subject: IMF Board of Executive Directors Consideration of Report on International Monetary Reform.

From the very first suggestions that a report on this subject be completed by the Executive Board prior to this year's Governors' meeting and before the agreed negotiating forum was established, I have expressed serious doubts that the Executive Board should try to reach definite conclusions in a report at this early stage. These views were repeated in the Executive Board in May, when I suggested "only a report providing a genuinely neutral description of various policy options would have any chance of being adopted."

We were therefore disappointed, when the original staff draft of the report was issued in early June, that instead of developing underlying issues and basic options the draft adopted a narrow focus pointing almost exclusively toward a particular form of an asset settlements sys-

---

[4] Draft chapters of the IMF Report on International Monetary Reform and Commentary of U.S. Officials are in the Volcker Group Alternates papers from the summer of 1972. (Washington National Records Center, Department of the Treasury, Volcker Group Masters: FRC 56 86 30, 1972, VGA and VG/INFO series)

tem and a confined range of technical possibilities relevant thereto. With this in mind, on June 19, I distributed a written statement (copy attached) expressing our views on the report, emphasizing our belief that the most useful contribution of a report would be to identify and reach a consensus on the essential nature of the problems, without fore-closing policy options. I urged a "less technical" but "more fundamental" approach concentrating on achieving an agreed description of the kind of world to which the reforms must be addressed and developing the key policy issues which the Governors would wish to address.

In addition to my written and oral comments in the Fund Board, our concern over the direction of the draft report was also strongly stressed in direct discussions with the Managing Director and top Staff of the Fund, and with a number of Executive Directors, by the Under Secretary for Monetary Affairs.

We were aware that the approach adopted in the draft, if pressed, would inevitably place the primary burden on the U.S. to inject other and broader viewpoints by a process of addition and amendment. While we were willing to accept that responsibility, we also recognized some misunderstanding or question of our motives could arise. We, therefore, greatly preferred to work with staff drafts that more fully developed the problems and basic options.

These strongly stated views were not adequately reflected in the revised draft distributed in the first part of July. Accordingly, to achieve the analysis and balance we felt necessary, we had no alternative to sub-mitting written material reflecting U.S. views, attempting to focus more attention on what we consider to be the real issues and appropriate pol-icy options. In this process, I have, in important areas, taken care to emphasize the United States, itself, had reached no conclusion and final judgment. William B. Dale. *End Text First Attachment.*

Begin Text Second Attachment

Mr. Dale's Overall Comments on Report to Governors—June 19, 1972

With the opening of discussion based on four draft chapters for a report to assist in the reform discussions, it is important to consider what kind of product we can realistically hope to agree on that would also be helpful—not only to the Governors in general, but in particular to the prospective Governors' Committee as it begins its work. At this early stage of work on reform, the critical task is to insure a fully ade-quate—a wide enough—variety of approaches to the problem so as not to preclude options at too early a stage.

We are not satisfied that the draft as it stands does that adequately. While it leaves some options open, it basically narrows down the dis-cussion quite rapidly—prematurely in our view—to only one set of basic options, a somewhat improved par value system coupled with a reserve asset settlement mechanism with the SDR at its center. We do not deny that such a system has certain attractions, but so may other combinations that have not been considered in the draft, and in any event it is by no means evident to us—from reading the draft and from other thoughts and sources—that such a system could in fact be made to work realistically even assuming it were generally considered desirable after examination of the alternatives.

There seem to me to be four main possibilities for a report:

1. One which puts forward a full and really open-minded discussion of a range of technical and policy options adequately broad for the depth and scope of the reform negotiation which lies ahead;

2. One which would be a mish-mash of undigested and inconsistent ideas, which might be the result if everyone simply tossed his favorite idea into the hopper;

3. A less technical and perhaps shorter report, but quite possibly a more fundamental one, concentrating on:

a. a description of the world which the trading and monetary systems must be addressed to; and

b. discussing in reasonably brief and non-technical manner the key policy issues to which the Governors' Committee will wish to direct its attention.

4. No report, because in the end we found ourselves unable to reach sufficient agreement.

The first outcome, while ideal, may as a practical matter be out of reach. The second or fourth outcomes constitute very real possibilities, neither of which would be particularly useful from any point of view.

The third option may well be the most realistically useful, and could provide very helpful material indeed for the work that lies ahead. *End Text Second Attachment.*

Irwin

242. Editorial Note

The float of the British pound in June 1972 and German Economics and Finance Minister Schmidt's remarks to Henry Kissinger and

Ambassador Hillenbrand (see Documents 232, 235, and 240) were two examples during the summer of 1972 of the fragility of the foreign exchange parities in the Smithsonian Agreement of December 1971. In the exchange of messages between President Nixon and Prime Minister Heath following the float of the pound, the two leaders agreed that "radical reform" going "beyond a simple patching up of the Bretton Woods system" was required. See footnote 2, Document 232.

Under Secretary of the Treasury Shultz' oversight, planning got underway during the summer of 1972 on how to respond to a breakdown of the Smithsonian Agreement and move ahead on a specific international monetary reform agenda. Central to the latter was building significantly greater exchange rate flexibility into a reformed international monetary system than had been envisaged and provided for in the Bretton Woods system. Providing scope for greater flexibility had been one of the major drafting objectives behind U.S. proposals for revisions in the IMF's Report on Reform of the International Monetary System, which was released in Washington on September 6. See Document 241. Secretary Shultz addressed this, the use of changes in reserves as a presumptive indicator of the need to make exchange rate adjustments, and other reform issues in a speech to the Governors on September 26. Shultz' address, entitled "Needed: A New Balance in International Economic Affairs," was printed in *The New York Times* on September 27. It is also printed in *Annual Report of the Secretary of the Treasury on the State of the Finances for the Fiscal Year Ended June 30, 1973,* pages 400–404.

Treasury Department records from this time period relating to international monetary reform are in the Washington National Records Center, Department of the Treasury, Deputy to the Assistant Secretary for International Affairs: FRC 56 83 26, Contingency Planning, 1965–1973. These include the following three sets of papers:

"Papers Related to Plan X (July 1972 through May 1973)." These 34 papers dating from July 20, 1972 to May 11, 1973, were to be prepared in Treasury at the staff level. Paper #3, "Major Elements of Plan X," is printed as Document 239.

"Briefing Book—Special Working Group–August 1972." The Briefing Book is divided into two parts: first are "Papers Prepared for Top Level" consisting of four "International Monetary Reform Issue Papers" as follows: "Discussion Outline of Proposed Monetary Plan," "Outline of Proposed Plan," "Questions of Negotiating Strategy," and "Broad Policy Issues Raised by U.S. Participation in a New International Monetary Agreement." (These four papers are also in the Washington National Records Center, Deparment of the Treasury, Files of Under Secretary Volcker: FRC 56 79 15, PAV–International Monetary Reform 1972.) The second section of the Briefing Book contains Selected Papers

and Documents, generally prepared at the staff level in Treasury, OMB, the Federal Reserve, STR, and CIEP.

"*Briefing Book*—Papers Relating to International Monetary Reform Prepared by Special Working Group—August, September, October 1972." This set of papers was compiled against an August 30, 1972, list of 13 papers that was revised and expanded on September 20 to include 19 papers. They were generally drafted at the staff level in the agencies listed above. The Special Working Group has not been identified with any precision. Among the persons to whom specific drafting assignments were made are Bennett, Willis, Cross, Nelson and Bradfield at Treasury, Dale at the IMF, Erb at CIEP, Bryant at the Federal Reserve, Dam at OMB, Whitman at the CEA, and Malmgren at STR. These may have been the staff for the small group headed by Shultz; see footnote 4, Document 232.

---

243. Information Memorandum From Robert Hormats of the National Security Council Staff to the President's Assistant for National Security Affairs (Kissinger)[1]

Washington, October 3, 1972.

SUBJECT

World Press Reaction to the President's and Shultz' IMF Speeches

World press reactions to President Nixon's speech and the proposals for monetary reform outlined by Secretary Shultz at the annual IMF/IBRD meeting have been mixed but generally positive.[2] (State and USIA summaries are attached at Tab A.)[3] European comment was generally favorable while a more negative tone came from Japan, Australia, and the developing countries. The Japanese felt that there was an anti-Japanese

---

[1] Source: National Archives, Nixon Presidential Materials, NSC Files, Agency Files, Box 306, IBRD/IMF. Limited Official Use.

[2] President Nixon addressed the opening session of the Annual Meeting of the Fund and Bank Boards on September 25. See *Public Papers of the Presidents of the United States: Richard M. Nixon, 1972*, pp. 907–911. The President made a strong linkage between trade negotiations and monetary reform and said Secretary Shultz would outline proposals on the latter, "which represent the best thinking of my top economic advisers," during his speech later in the meeting. Secretary Shultz addressed the Annual Meeting on September 26; see Document 242.

[3] Not printed.

tone to the emphasis on the need for adjustment by surplus countries, enforced by sanctions if necessary, while the developing countries have stressed the lack of attention to their problems in the two speeches.

There was a widespread feeling of relief that the United States had decided to resume a position of leadership in monetary affairs. Most commentators felt that the United States' proposals provided a basis upon which serious negotiations could begin, even if they disagreed with specific portions of the proposals. Several reports credited the American initiatives with giving the IMF meeting a sense of direction which had previously been missing. A recurring theme was that the President's and Secretary Shultz' speeches reflected increased American confidence based on improvements in American economic performance and our diplomatic initiatives with the USSR and the PRC. Some reports noted that the speeches had firmly defended American interests, while abandoning the extremes of the "Texas approach".

European commentators generally felt that the Shultz proposals were basically constructive and welcomed the evidence that the U.S. is willing to move forward in monetary reform. The initial French reaction was negative or neutral, but after the speech of Minister of Finance Giscard d'Estaing, French commentary became more optimistic. The French felt that the generally conciliatory Giscard speech had sidetracked the gold price issue, while Shultz had opened the door toward dollar convertibility. There was speculation in the press that the atmosphere of cooperation is the result of a recent Kissinger–Pompidou agreement.[4]

The Canadian press generally felt that the American proposals provided a framework for negotiating monetary reform, while reacting with concern to Shultz's call for "more stringent" standards for countries that float their currencies (as Canada is now doing).

The Japanese appear to view the Shultz proposals as threatening. Several press comments referred to the anti-Japanese tone of the speech and worried that it was an effort to set the stage for unilateral imposition of import surcharges on Japanese products or for increased pressure for yen revaluation. There was some worry that the Europeans may now support these efforts (a *Newsweek* story quoting a top U.S. official at the meetings "as saying the U.S., Britain, and West Germany planned to force a revaluation of the Japanese yen" will fuel these fears). The Japanese press felt that the Shultz proposals represented an effort to make the surplus

---

[4] Not further identified. The point was made in a September 30 "Foreign Reactions" report from the Executive Secretary of the Department of State to Kissinger: "There is speculation in the press that the 'atmosphere of cooperation' is the result of a recent Kissinger–Pompidou agreement. The newspaper *France-Soir* stated that the success of U.S. diplomacy and economic policy in the last year allowed the U.S. to be conciliatory while guarding the essential elements of U.S. demands." The report is included in Tab A.

nations bear the adjustment burden, although many Japanese commentators called for increased Japanese government action to reduce that nation's trade surplus. The Australian press echoed the Japanese press in worrying about being the target of rules against surplus countries, while calling the Shultz speech "demanding but reasonable".

The developing countries, while generally welcoming the U.S. decision to move forward on monetary reform, were disappointed by the lack of attention to development problems in either speech. This omission, coupled with Chilean attacks on the U.S. for blocking IBRD lending to Chile and the general lack of progress on the question of a link between Special Drawing Rights and development, seemed to some LDC's to confirm their fears that the U.S. is not greatly interested in the problems of the developing countries.

---

244. Editorial Note

On October 3, 1972, Hormats sent a memorandum to Kissinger apprising him that, in contrast to the roiled foreign exchange environment during the summer, the dollar had recently strengthened in European foreign exchange markets. During the previous week it had strengthened against all major European currencies and none of the European central banks had been required to purchase dollars to support their exchange rates. Hormats attributed this to an improving trade position and President Nixon's and Shultz' positive approaches at the IMF–IBRD meetings. (National Archives, Nixon Presidential Materials, NSC Files, Agency Files, Box 306, IBRD/IMF)

As 1972 ended, the newly established C-20 and its Deputies Committee began its work on international monetary reform, but the pace was slow. The first Ministerial on September 28 (see Document 237) was the only Ministerial during 1972. A second Deputies meeting was held November 27–29. The Embassy in London reported that during an EC Monetary Committee meeting on November 21 there was a constructive exchange of views on monetary reform. The Embassy noted there was scope for fruitful analysis of reserve gains and losses at the forthcoming Deputies meeting, but U.S. insistence on rigid, automatic criteria (for exchange rate adjustments) would not be acceptable. (Telegram 11273 from London, November 22; National Archives, RG 59, Central Files 1970–73, FN 10)

Index

ISBN 0-16-050884-3

90000